797,885 Books
are available to read at

Forgotten Books

www.ForgottenBooks.com

Forgotten Books' App
Available for mobile, tablet & eReader

ISBN 978-1-332-00421-8
PIBN 10266809

This book is a reproduction of an important historical work. Forgotten Books uses state-of-the-art technology to digitally reconstruct the work, preserving the original format whilst repairing imperfections present in the aged copy. In rare cases, an imperfection in the original, such as a blemish or missing page, may be replicated in our edition. We do, however, repair the vast majority of imperfections successfully; any imperfections that remain are intentionally left to preserve the state of such historical works.

Forgotten Books is a registered trademark of FB &c Ltd.
Copyright © 2015 FB &c Ltd.
FB &c Ltd, Dalton House, 60 Windsor Avenue, London, SW19 2RR.
Company number 08720141. Registered in England and Wales.

For support please visit www.forgottenbooks.com

1 MONTH OF FREE READING

at
www.ForgottenBooks.com

By purchasing this book you are eligible for one month membership to ForgottenBooks.com, giving you unlimited access to our entire collection of over 700,000 titles via our web site and mobile apps.

To claim your free month visit:
www.forgottenbooks.com/free266809

* Offer is valid for 45 days from date of purchase. Terms and conditions apply.

Similar Books Are Available from
www.forgottenbooks.com

Across Unknown South America, Vol. 1 of 2
by A. Henry Savage-Laondor

Industrial and Commercial South America
by Annie S. Peck

Military Notes on Cuba
November, 1898, by Unknown Author

Brazil
Its Condition and Prospects, by C. C. Andrews

Venezuela
by Leonard V. Dalton

Penetrating South America's Darkest Part
by Alexander Rattray Hay

The True History of the Conquest of Mexico
Written in the Year 1568, by Díaz Del Castillo

In Jesuit Land, the Jesuit Missions of Paraguay
by W. H. Koebel

South America
by Hezekiah Butterworth

The Andes and the Amazon
Or Across the Continent of South America, by James Orton

Paraguay
by William Henry Koebel

A New Era in Old Mexico
by G. B. Winton

The History of Cuba, Vol. 1
by Willis Fletcher Johnson

History of the New World Called America, Vol. 1
by Edward John Payne

Argentina and Uruguay
by Gordon Ross

The History of Peru
by Henry S. Beebe

A History of Latin America
by William Warren Sweet

A History of Chile
by Anson Uriel Hancock

South America on the Eve of Emancipation
The Southern Spanish Colonies in the Last, Half-Century of Their Dependence, by Bernard Moses

The History of the Discovery and Settlement of America
by William Robertson

AND THE

CANARY ISLANDS

WITH THE

AZORES

A PRACTICAL AND COMPLETE GUIDE

FOR THE USE OF

INVALIDS AND TOURISTS

WITH

TWENTY COLOURED MAPS AND PLANS

AND NUMEROUS

SECTIONAL AND OTHER DIAGRAMS

BY

A. SAMLER BROWN

SIXTH AND REVISED EDITION

(All rights reserved)

London:

SAMPSON LOW, MARSTON & CO., LIMITED
ST. DUNSTAN'S HOUSE, FETTER LANE, FLEET ST., E.C.

J. C. JUTA & CO., CAPE TOWN, PORT ELIZABETH
AND JOHANNESBURG

1901

copy Envelope

[Return address
in upper left hand
corner envelope]
"Expédié par
Monsieur Joseph Silva,
Cortland, New-York, U.S.A.
(Les États-Unis d'Amérique du Nord.)

Senhora Luiza da Silva,
39, Rua da Praia,
Funchal, Madeira (Madère,)
Portugal (Le Portugal.)

WATERLOW AND SONS LIMITED,
PRINTERS,
DUNSTABLE AND LONDON.

COPIES OF THIS BOOK MAY BE PROCURED

IN LONDON and SOUTH AFRICA—from any Bookseller, from most of the Shipping Companies, or at the Publishers' Offices.

Depôts
- IN MADEIRA—Messrs. Blandy Brothers & Co.
- IN SANTA CRUZ, TENERIFFE—Messrs. Hamilton & Co.
- IN PUERTO OROTAVA, TENERIFFE—Mr. Peter S. Reid.
- IN GRAND CANARY—Messrs. Miller & Co.

The book is also stocked by several shops and hotels in the different Islands.

The price in the Canary Islands is the same as in England, namely, 2s. 6d. In Madeira it is 3s., an addition being made on account of the duty. The price in the local currency depends upon the rate of exchange at the time.

Opinions of the Press.

"**THE SATURDAY REVIEW**" *says:—*

(*FIRST EDITION*).—For the increasing number of tourists and invalids Mr. A. Samler Brown has written a handy guide, *Madeira and the Canary Islands*, which is as useful as it is timely. Mr. Brown's excellent little book comprises all the information that travellers need, with a series of legible maps, a useful bibliography, and tables of steamship routes, fares, hotels, and other indispensable matters. The descriptive and historical sections of the book are carefully compiled, and thoroughly readable.

(*SECOND EDITION*).—Mr. Samler Brown's compact and useful guide to Madeira and the Fortunate Islands has reached a second edition, and has been equipped with much new and useful information about these popular resorts. In some respects Mr. Samler Brown is the very model of a guide. We hardly know another writer of his class who writes so little "about it and about it," and comes so directly to the point. Of talkee-talkee, even about Guanches, there is hardly any; the very dragon-tree does not beguile Mr. Brown from the austerity of a model examination answer. But for distances, paths, prices, the number of beds to be expected at this and that Fonda, the places where you should not drink water, and all such things, he is a pearl of commentators, and all in scarcely a hundred pages, with good, though uncoloured maps. His name, if we may jest on names, really ought to be Sampler and not Samler.

(*THIRD EDITION*).—We have twice before praised Mr. Samler Brown's *Madeira and the Canary Islands*; but this fact shall not prevent our doing it a third time. Like a good man and author Mr. Brown has not contented himself with merely reprinting his second edition and putting third on its title-page, but has revised his text, redrawn his maps, and added a good deal of miscellaneous information, all of which is to the point. He draws, and is right in drawing, special attention to his advertisements, which, as he justly boasts, are all but invariably concerned with the subject of the book itself, and tell you something that you may get, or somewhere whither you may go in Madeira or the Canaries.

"**THE FIELD**" *says:—*

(*FIFTH EDITION*).—This handbook has now reached its fifth edition, which has been revised and brought up to date. It is a thoroughly practical work, and great pains must have been taken by the author to collect so much information, and give it in the comparatively small space of this volume. Tourists and invalids may, with advantage to themselves, consult its pages on all subjects connected with these islands. We recommend it to our readers, etc., etc.

"One of the most scientific and accurate guide-books ever written, full of facts and free from embroidery."—"Climatic Treatment in Grand Canary," by Dr. Brian Melland, M. Sc. (Vict.), M.B. (Lond.)

PRICE 2s. 6d.

THE GUIDE TO SOUTH AFRICA

(*FORMERLY BROWN'S SOUTH AFRICA*),

FOR THE USE OF

TOURISTS, SPORTSMEN, INVALIDS AND SETTLERS,

With Coloured Maps, Plans and Diagrams.

Edited annually by A. SAMLER BROWN and G. GORDON BROWN for the Union-Castle Mail Steamship Co., Ltd. Ninth Edition, 1901-2. Crown 8vo, 470 pages.

Publishers: In London, Messrs. Sampson Low, Marston & Co., Ltd., St. Dunstan's House, Fetter Lane, Fleet Street, E.C., and the Union-Castle Mail Steamship Co., Ltd., 3, Fenchurch Street, London, E.C. In South Africa, Messrs. J. C. Juta & Co., Cape Town, Port Elizabeth and Johannesburg.

"Contains a great deal of information on all subjects that can interest travellers in South Africa."—*Times.*

"It may be heartily recommended to all who have ideas of visiting South Africa."—*Scotsman.*

"The amount of information furnished is simply marvellous, and the care taken in condensing the greatest quantity of valuable data into the smallest possible compass, consistent with lucidity, is most creditable."—*Port Elizabeth Telegraph.*

BY THE

Author of Brown's Madeira and the Canary Islands, and issued by the Union-Castle Mail Steamship Co., Ltd., 3, Fenchurch St., London, E.C.

"**The Illustrated Handbook of South Africa.**" (Third Edition.)

With Notes on the Agricultural and Industrial Capabilities of the Country, Mining Centres, State of Labour, and Principal Towns, with coloured map. 73 pages, price 3d., post free, 4d. *Fortieth Thousand.*

"The book is very well printed and illustrated, and is broken up into sections by boldly printed headlines, which enable the reader or searcher to see at a glance what subject is being treated of. We certainly advise all those interested in South Africa to get a copy as soon as possible."—*South Africa.*

"**Illustrated Handbook of the South African Gold Fields.**" (Third Edition.)

With Notes on their past, present and future; their methods of working; labour, wages, cost of living, and means of access, with five tables and coloured map. 76 pages. 3d., post free, 4d.

"**Illustrated Handbook on Health, the Voyage to South Africa and sojourn there.**"

With maps, meteorological tables, etc. 136 pages; pages 1 to 48, by A. Samler Brown, 3d., post free, 4d.

PREFACE TO THE SIXTH EDITION.

THE present issue has been brought up to date, both as regards the text and the maps. The portion devoted to the Azores has been remodelled and enlarged during a recent visit, and practical coloured maps of the Archipelago and of the principal Islands have been added.

The Historical Section is exact and sufficiently complete, and the Guide proper has been most carefully revised. All information obtainable has been embodied in the Commercial Appendix, no effort being spared to make this part of the work of use to actual or to prospective Residents.

The chapters on Geology and the pages devoted to a discussion of the Atmospheric Currents of the Mid-Atlantic, are of considerable interest to Invalids and Tourists. It is trusted that the drawings accompanying this part of the work will prove of service and that they will tend to render the text clear and readable.

The plan of the book remains unaltered, the proportion of the circulation to the number of visitors to the Islands showing that no other arrangement is likely to suit its purchasers better.

NOTE.—Steamship Companies, Proprietors of Hotels and others would be doing themselves a service by at once communicating any changes to the Editor, who will receive the same with thanks, and will do his best to bring them to the notice of visitors.

Letters should be addressed to
A. SAMLER BROWN,
3, FENCHURCH STREET,
LONDON, E.C.

CONTENTS.

	PAGE
PREFACE	vi
TABLE OF CONTENTS	vii
GENERAL INDEX	x
STEAMERS running to the Islands, with fares, etc. (*to face page*)	1
GENERAL INFORMATION	1 to 25

    Plan of the Guide (*p.* 1).—Order in which to visit the Islands (*p.* 3).—Hotels and Fondas (*p.* 4).—Population (*p.* 4).—Distances by measurement and by time (*p.* 4).—Expeditions and excursions (*p.* 5).—Animals (*p.* 5).—Clouds in the hills (*p.* 6).—Springs and waterfalls (*p.* 6).—Guides (*p.* 6).—Camping out (*p.* 7).—Picnics and country customs (*p.* 7).—The Euphorbia (*p.* 7).—Poisonous reptiles (*p.* 7).—Mosquitoes (*p.* 8).—Beggars (*p.* 8).—Outfit (*p.* 8).—Accommodation, etc. (*p.* 9).—Villas (*p.* 10).—Annual expenditure (*p.* 11).—Amusements (*p.* 12).—Native society (*p.* 12).—Shooting licenses (*p.* 13).—Coinage (*p.* 14).—Measures (*p.* 16).—Thermometrical degrees (*p.* 17).—Difference in time (*p.* 17).—Length of the solar day (*p.* 17).—Tides (*p.* 17).—Posts and telegraphs (*p.* 18).—Vocabulary (*p.* 20).

    (*A great deal of General Information is also given in the Commercial Section, for which see Index and Special Table of Contents.*)

METEOROLOGICAL STATISTICS AND RESUMÉ OF SAME	26 to 35
CLIMATIC CONDITIONS	36 „ 46

    In the winter (*p.* 36).—In the summer (*p.* 39).—Rainfall (*p.* 40).—Water-supply (*p.* 42).—Drainage (*p.* 43).—Winds (*p.* 43).—Storms (*p.* 44).—Tidal waves (*p.* 45).

Epidemics	45
Locusts	46
Mineral Springs	46
Submarine Springs	46
PERMANENT ATMOSPHERIC CURRENTS OF THE MID-ATLANTIC; THEIR CAUSES AND THEIR EFFECTS	48 to 54

CONTENTS.

	PAGE
Chapter for Invalids	55 to 58
Climatic Diarrhœa (*p* 57). Sea Sickness (*p*. 58).	
Article on Geology	59 ,, 75
The Sunken Continent of Atlantis	76 ,, 84
History of Madeira	85 ,, 91
,, ,, the Canary Islands	92 ,, 120
Guide to Madeira	121 ,, 146
,, ,, The Azores (*comprising* General Information and Notes on Geology, History, Agriculture, etc.)	147 ,, 149G
,, ,, La Palma	150 ,, 164
,, ,, Hierro	165 ,, 168
,, ,, Gomera	169 ,, 171
,, ,, Teneriffe	172 ,, 220
,, ,, Grand Canary	221 ,, 251
,, ,, Fuerteventura	252 ,, 253
,, ,, Lanzarote	254 ,, 257
Commercial Section (*for abstract of contents see special prefix*)	258 ,, 332
Forms of Animals and Vegetable Life	333 ,, 336
Bibliography	337 ,, 339

MAPS.

Climatic Map of the Atlantic Ocean, showing the Currents and Isothermals ... (*to face page*)	84
Map of the Canary Archipelago	84
,, ,, Madeira, with small map of the group and plan of Funchal	146
,, ,, The Azores (Archipelago), with separate maps of S. Miguel; of Terceira; and of Fayal, Fayal Channel, and part of the Islands of Pico and S. Jorge ,,	149G

Map of La Palma, with map of the Great Crater ... ... (*to face page*)	170
,, Hierro ... ... ,,	170
Gomera	170
,, Teneriffe, with plan of Santa Cruz and map of the Peak and its surroundings ... ... ,,	220
Grand Canary, with plan of Las Palmas and of the Puerto de la Luz ... ... ,,	250
,, ,, Fuerteventura	256
Lanzarote	256

DIAGRAMS.

Atmospheric Chart of the Mid-Atlantic... (*to face page*)	54
Profile Section of Teneriffe ...	54
Geological Sketch Map of Teneriffe ...	66
Ideal Group of Satellite Volcanoes	71
The Garganta de Güimar	73
Outline Sketches showing formation of Madeira, Porto Santo, The Desertas, Grand Canary, Teneriffe, Fuerteventura and Lanzarote	74

INDEX.

Figures in larger type denote principal references.

	PAGE
Abona	186
Abrigos	186
Accommodation	9, 147
Achada do Campanario	133, 141
Adeje	188, 215
Advice to Invalids	55
Afur	193
Agaete	234, 235, 240
Agriculture	148, 268, 302
,, ancient	119
,, for foreigners	311
Agua García	193, 97
Agua Manza	185, 206
Agüimes	241, 245
Agulo	171
Alagoa	148F
Alcohol	148, 268, 283
Aldea de S. Nicolas	235A, 240, 247
Alegranza (Island of)	254
Alegría	132
Almagrurin adventurers	88
Almonds	267
Aloe, The	290
Alta Vista	207
Altitude, Effects of	292, 298
Alum	148C
Amusements	12, 147A
Anæmia	40
Anaga	181, 193
Angra	149A
Aniline dyes	278
Animals, Engaging	5
Animal life	333
Anjos	148B
Anthropology, Native	106
Antigua, La	253
Antilla, Island of	87
Ants, The	148B
Arafo	188, 185, 206
Architects	315
Arco de S. Jorge	139
Area, Larga	149C
Areynaga	248
Argual	158
Arguayo	188A
Arguineguin	249
Arico	186
Armásiga	193
Arona	188
Arrecife	255

	PAGE
Artenara	232, 234, 235A, 240
Arucas	232
Atalaya	238, 242
Atlantis	76
Atmospheric Currents	48
Azores, The	147
Azulejos, Los	210
Bajamar	197
Bañadero	234
Bananas	285
Barley (see Cereals).	
Barlovento	157
Barranco de Aduares	160, 162
,, Añavingo	184
,, de las Angustias (La Palma)	158
,, Azuaje	232
,, de Badajoz	185
,, de las Cabezas	200, 204
,, de Castro	211, 217
,, de Chamorga	182, 193
,, del Dornajito	216
,, del Dragonal	236
,, de Fatarga	247A, 249
,, de Guayadeque	245, 247
,, de Guiniguada	236
,, de Herques	186
,, de las Higueras	195
,, Hondo (North)	198, 199
,, ,, (South)	183, 198
,, del Infierno	188
,, de Lechucilla	240
,, de Llarena	200, 206
,, de Martianez	203
,, del Patronato	204, 210
,, de Poleo	157
,, del Rio (La Palma)	155
,, ,, (Güimar)	185
,, de Ruiz	211, 217
,, de S. Isidro	240
,, de Tejeda	235, 239
,, de Tenoya	232
,, de Tirajana	240, 241, 246, 249
,, de Utiaca	236, 240
,, de la Vera	204
,, de la Virgen	233
Bathing	56

INDEX.

	PAGE
Beaches, Raised	61, 148B
Beans (see Cereals or Vegetables).	
Beckford's Fort	132
Beetles	334
Beggars	8, 326
Belgara	168
Belmaco (Cave of)	162
Bemfeitoria system, The	303
Bencomo of Taoro	101
Bethencourt	95
Bibliography	337
Birds	333
Blake, Sir Robert	103
Boa Ventura	137, 188
Boca de los Tauces	188, 210, 216
Bocca dos Corregos	140
,, das Voltas	138
Boots (native)	8
Botanical Gardens (Orotava)	203
Bread	329, 331
Breña, The	162
Bricks	315
Buena Vista (La-Palma)	155
,, (Teneriffe)	188A, 214
Buen Paso	212
Bugio	144
Bulbs, Culture of	290
Bull Fights	12
Building	314
Buildings (native)	235, 247, 255
Butterflies	334
Cabeza del Toro	198
Cables, Telegraphic	19, 147B, 149C, 310
Cabo Garajão	134
,, Girão	133, 143
Caes do Pico	149C
Caldeira do Inferno	149C
Caldera de Bandama, Gran.	237
,, de La Palma, Gran.	150, 161
,, de la Vega	239
,, de Valleseco	240
Caletas, Las	163
Calheta (Mad.)	141, 143
Camacha	131, 135
Camara de Lobos	133, 143
Camping out	7
Cañadas, Las	185, 207, 209, 216
Canaries, The—	
,, ,, Climate of	36
,, ,, History of	92
,, ,, Trade in	266
Canary, Grand	221
,, ,, Invasions of	96, 97

	PAGE
Canary, Grand. Shipping in	262
Candelaria (Ten.)	183, 185
,, (La Palma)	157
Caniçal	135
Caniço	131, 134
Capellas	149
Carob bean	288
Carpenters	315
Carriages, Charges for (See end of each island.)	
Carrisal (Ten.)	188A, 214
,, (Can.)	248
Carthaginians, The	93
Castor oil	290
Cattle	301
Caves (Azores)	147D, 149C
,, (Grand Canary)	184, 234, 235, 238, 240, 243, 245, 248, 249
,, (Lanzarote)	257
,, (Lava)	73
,, (La Palma)	161, 162
,, (Teneriffe)	116, 195, 203, 213
Cédulas	324
Cement	314
Cemeteries, Native	117, 230, 235, 248
Cereals	295
Chahorra	208, 216
Chão, Ilheo de	144
Charco Verde	163
Charges — Landing, 3 (and locally); Horses, etc., 5 (and at the end of each island).	
Charity	326
Chasna (see Vilaflor).	
Cheese (Canary)	223
Chio	188
Cholera	91
Cigars	174
Cinder Beds	147D
Cinder Heaps	69
Cipango	87
Cisma de Gallego, La	242
Citrons	287
Cleavages, Volcanic	61, 76
Climate	26 to 58, 147C, and locally
Climatic Zones	292
Clothing required	8
Clouds	6, 37, 49, 147D, 202
Coaches, Public (Ten.)	220
,, ,, (Can.)	251
,, ,, (Mad.)	146
Coaling	148A, 261, 263
Cochineal	278
Cock-fighting	12
Coinage	14, 147A
Columbus	100, 148B, 170
Commercial Section	258

INDEX

	PAGE
Communication, Marine, and table of Shipping	147, 307
Confital Bay	230A
Contracts, Government	325
Co-operation	330
Corona, La	208, 211, 216
Corvo	149G
Cova da Cevada	140
Craters	69, 147D
Crime	326
Cruz de Afur	193
,, del Almorzadero	215
,, de S. Andres	193
,, de Lobrelar	239
,, de Taganana	181, 193
,, de Téa	215
,, de Tejeda	240
Cruzinhas (Sta Anna)	137
,, (Seizal)	141, 142
Cruz Santa, La (Ten.)	204, 206
Cuesta, La (Ten.)	183, 189
,, de Bacalao	206
,, de Silva	234
Cueva de los Verdes	257
Culata, La	214
Cultivation, Limit of	299
Cumbre Nueva (La Palma)	159
,, Vieja (,,)	159, 160, 162
Cumbrecita (La Palma)	160
Cumbres, Las (Canary)	232, 235A, 240, 247
Curral, Grand	138
,, do Mar	135
Curralinho	132
Currency	14, 147A, 312
,, payment in kind	334
Currents, Atmospheric	48
,, Oceanic	62
Custom duties	125, 147
Customs	7, 147B
,, ancient	108
Dacil	102, 117, 191
Daute	214
Deities, Native	114
Denudation	64, 121, 161, 221
Desertas, The	144
Diarrhœa	57
Diseases	45, 56
Doctors	56, 57
Dollabarets, The	148B
Domestics	327
Dragon-tree, The	117, 174
Drainage	43
Drake, Sir Francis	103
Drugs	8

	PAGE
Duties (see Customs)	
Earthquakes (see Volc. Activity)	
Education	322
Electoral Rights	322
Elevation of Land	65, 80, 148B
Elysian Fields, The	92
Emigration	322
Employers' Responsibility	327
Encumiada Alta	140
Entail	306
Epidemic Diseases	45
Eruptions (see Volc. Activity, also 72)	
Escobonal	186
Esperanza, La	193, 197
Estufas	273
Euphorbia Canariensis	7, 289
Exchange	14, 312
Expeditions, Arranging	5
Expense of Living	11, 147A
Explorers, Early	85, 87, 94, 147F, 148C
Exports	148, 264
Fajãa Escura	140
Fanal, The	140, 142
Fares by Steamers.—Table opp. xviii, 146, 147	
Farming, Profits on	293
Fasnia	186
Fatarga	247A, 249
Faults	78, 210
Fauna	333
Fayal—(Mad.)	134
,, (Azores)	149E
Ferns	336
Feteiras	148E
Fever, Malarial	57
Figs	287
Filters	42
Finca Corvo	233
Firgas	282, 238
Fish	319, 329, 331, 334
Fishing	147A, 315
Flamengos	149F
Flora, The	336
Flores	149G
Florida (Ten.)	206
Flowers	336
Fogs (see Clouds)	
Folk-lore	82, 85, 115
Fondas	4, 147
Food	313, 329, 331
Foreigners as Settlers	274, 311

INDEX.

	PAGE
Forests	147F, 299
Formigas, As	148B
Fortaleza, La	208, 216
Fossils	64, 147F
Fossil-beds	62, 135, 143
Franceses, Los	157
Franchise	322
Freight, Rate of	286
Fruit, Shipping	264, 267, 285, 298, 308
,, Packing	286
,, Tinned	290
Fuencaliente	163
Fuente de la Cruz	208
,, Fria	198
,, de la Grieta	209
,, de Guadalupe	232
,, de Ucanca	210
Fuerteventura	252
Funchal	26, 125
,, Shipping	261
Fungi	336
Furna do Enxofre	149C
Furnas	148E

Gáldar	235
Gallegos, Los (La Palma)	157
,, ,, (Canary)	246, 248
Gando, Punta de	245
Garachico	213, 214
Garafía	157
Garganta de Güimar	185
Garojonay	170
Garoe, El	165
Gaula	134
Geology	59, 147D
Glacial Epoch	81
Glas, George	315
Gloria, La	238
Gofio	119, 329
Golf	12, 192, 228
Golfo, El	167
Gomera	169
Government, Local	326
Graciosa, Id. of (Azores)	149C
,, ,, (Can.)	254
Granadilla	186, 187
Gran Caldera de Bandama	237
Gran Curral	138
Grand Canary (see Canary).	
Guajara	209, 216
Guamasa	194
Guancha, La	216
Guanche cave (Icod)	213
,, Kings	101, 173
Guanches, The	114

	PAGE
Guia (Ten.)	188, 215
,, (Can.)	284, 238
Guides	6, 208
Güimar	30, 184, 198, 206
,, Garganta de	184
Gulf Stream	63
Hæmorrhage	57
Harbours	148A, 309
Haria	257
Harimaguadas	115, 243
Harvests	295
Hawkins, Sir John	103
Heather, Giant	300
Hemp, Sisal	290
Hermigua	171
Hesperides, The	92
Hierro	165
Hills, Incline of	291
History 85 to 120, 147F, and locally	
,, Natural	333
Homem-em-Pé	138
Horizon, Distance of	17
Hornillas del Teide	215
Horses, Charges for (See end of each island).	
Horses, Hiring	5
Horta	149E
Hospitals	326
Hotel tariffs	4, 147
Houses on hire	10
,, building of	314
,, taxes on	297, 324, 325
Humiaya	114, 243
Ice cave	208
Ice Plant, The	277
Icod el Alto	208, 211, 217
,, de los Vinos	187, 211, 212
Icor	186
Idafe	116, 152
Idolatry	114
Igueste	181, 193
,, (de Candelaria)	183, 198
Implements, Agricultural	302
,, Native	118
Imports	264
,, Duties	125
Industries, How taxed	324, 325
,, Undeveloped	287
Ingenio	245
Inscriptions 93, 107, 162, 167, 246	
Insects	148A, 334
Invalids, Advice to	55

	PAGE
Irrigation, 294—Statistics of	303
Isleta	222, 230
Jams . . .	. 290
Jardim da Serra	. 140
Jinamar	236, 242
Juan Grande	246, 248
Juba, King	. 92
Justice	. 326
Krakatoa . . .	. 73
Labour .	327
,, Hours of	330
Lagoa de Fogo	. 149
Laguna, La .	181, 190
Lagunetas, Las	198
Lamaceiros Pass . .	134
Land, Area of Cultivated	321
,, Clearance of	280
,, Reclamation of	297
,, Rent of . .	297
,, Tax . .	297, 324, 325
,, Value of .	291, 295
,, Waste . .	297
Landing charges . .	3
(And under each island).	
Landlords .	11, 297
Language	. 3, 20
,, Ancient .	. 107
Lanzarote	254
Lava	. 71
Laws	. 326
,, Ancient .	. 108
Legends . 82, 85, 87, 115	
Leprosy . . .	. 122
Letreros, Los—Hierro .	167
,, Canary . .	246
Levada, Funchal .	132
,, do Furado .	136
,, dos Vinhaticos	. 137
Lichens . . .	. 336
Lighthouse—Anaga	181, 193
,, Isleta	. 230A
,, Maspalomas	. 249
Lime	. 314
Limestone 61, 141, 144, 148B, 241, 252	
Livestock . . .	. 301
Livramento Church	. 138
Llano de los Hermanos .	215
Llanos, Los, La Palma 158, 160, 163	
,, ,, Canary .	. 243

	PAGE
Lobos, Isla de .	254
Local Government .	326
Locusts	46
,, Bean	288
Lodging of Labourers	328
Lomba da Cruz .	148E
Lombadas . . .	. 149
Lugo, Alonso F. de	98
Lyonnese	83
Macary .	. 189
Machico	134, 135, 143
Machin .	89, 157
Madeira .	121
,, Climate of	36
,, History of	85
,, Shipping	261
,, Trade in	264
Magdalena (Pico)	. 149C
,, do Mar	141, 143
Maize, as a standard	293, 328
Malarial Fever	57
Manchas, Las	163
Manila . . .	. 290
Manure .	302
Market Prices	331
Marram Grass	288
Masca .	. 188A
Maspalomas . . 241, 247A, 248	
Matanza, La .	99, 198
Mazo .	. 162
Meals (Hotels) .	4, 147
Measurement of distances	4
Measures, Local	16
Meat . . .	. 331
Medano	186
Medianero System, The	302
Medical men . .	. 56, 57
Mercedes, Las . .	. 192
Mesa Mota . .	191, 192
Metade Valley .	. 136
Meteorology, Statistics .	26 to 35
Middlemen . . .	. 330
Midlen	. 276
Military duties .	. 325
Mina, La (Ten.	192
Mineral Springs, 46, 147D, 148F,	
151, 163, 166, 186, 204,	
222, 230, 232, 235A.	
Minerals . .	. 64, 260
Mining . . .	. 260
Miraflores . . .	. 155
Mists (see Clouds).	
Modorra, The . .	. 99
Mogan . 235A, 240, 241, 247, 249	
Monasteries . .	. 91, 105

INDEX.

	PAGE
Money	14, 147A, 312
Mña. de las Arenas	200, 203, 204
,, de la Atalaya	196
,, de Barracan	214
,, Blanca (above villa)	206
,, ,, (del Pico)	207
,, de Cabreja	239
,, de Cerro	197
,, de Chaves	200, 206
,, de Chipude	171
, de los Chupaderos	198
,, de Cifra	194
,, Clara, Isla de	254
,, de la Cruz Santa	240
,, de las Cuatro Puertas	114, 243
,, de Doramas	232, 233
,, de los Frailes	200
,, del Fuego, Lanzarote	254, 257
,, de Gáldar	235
,, de Guerra	196
,, de las Palmas	196
,, del Picon	196
,, del Pulpito	192, 194
,, de las Retamas	196
,, de Serrogordo	215
,, de Tagóje	156, 158
,, de Tigaiga	211
,, de Tirma	114, 235A
Monte, El	232, 233, 236
,, Verde, The	299
Moors, Attacks by	103
Mortgages	297
Mosquitoes	8
Mosses	336
Mosteiros	149
Moths	334
Mountain Climate	48
Mount Church	131
Moya	232, 233
Mules, Hiring	5
Mummies	116, 243
Museums	127, 148D, 154, 178, 226
Music, Public	12
Mutual Benefit Societies	326
Natives, Origin of	81, 106
Natural History	333
Negroes	268
Nelson, Admiral	103
New Road, Funchal	132
Nunneries	91, 105
Obsidian	118, 209
Ocean, Depth of	60

	PAGE
Oïdium Tuckeri	271
Oil, Castor	290
Oliva, La	253
Oranges	148, 286
Orotava, Puerto de	29, 201
,, Valley of	200
,, Villa de	185, 204, 211
Osiers	287
Osorios, Los	231, 233
Outfit	8
Oxen	301
Pack animals	5
Packing of Fruit	286
Pagador	234
Pájara	253
Palheiro	131
Palma, La	150
,, ,, Invasions of	96, 98
Palmar	188A, 214
Palmas, Las	27, 226
,, ,, Shipping	262
Parcels	18
Partidos, Los	215
Paso, El (La Palma)	160, 163
,, de la Plata	241, 247
Passports	4, 125
Pasture	301
Paul do Mar	142, 143
,, da Serra	140, 141, 142
Paz, La	112, 203
Peak of Teneriffe (see Pico de Teide).	
Peasant proprietorship	306
Peasants, Labour of	311
Pedro Gil	185, 198, 206
Penha d'Aguia	134, 137
Peñones de Garcia	210
Perdoma, La	206, 208
Perfumes	290
Petroleum	331
Phœnicians	93, 246
Phylloxera	272
Physicians	56, 57
Pickles	290
Pico, Island of	149C
,, d'Aboboras	134
,, Arrebentão	136
,, Arrieiro	132
,, de Bandama	238
,, de Barracan	214
,, dos Bodes	143
,, Canario	138
,, del Cedro	158
,, do Cidrão	138
,, do Fogo	149

	PAGE		PAGE
Pico, Grande .	138	Puerto de S. Marco	212
,, de Moranha	139	Puestelagua .	171
,, de los Osorios .	231, 232	Pumice Stone	260
,, ,, Pozos (Canary) .	241	Pumpkins .	330
,, Ruivo . .	137, 139	Punta Gando	243
,, ,, do Paul	140, 141	,, Gorda	. 157
,, de Salamão .	. 148E	,, de Teno	214
,, da Silva	. 131	,, Llana .	. 156
,, da Suna .	134	Purpuriæ, The	85, 93
as Torres .	. 139		
,, de Teide (Ten.)	113, 172, 207		
,, ,, Exc. to the	. 207		
,, ,, Hints to climbers	208	Rabaçal	. 142
,, Viejo .	. 208	Railways . .	146, 180, 310
Pileta, La .	. 245	Rainfall (*see* also Climate)	. 40
Pilgrims' Pass .	184, 199, 206	Rambleta, La . .	. 207
Pine Apples .	. 148	Realejo 204, 206,	210, 216
Pines .	299, 300	Rejon, Juan . .	. 97
Pintaderas . .	. 118	Religion . . .	. 322
Pipe, Capacity of the	16, 276	,, Ancient	113
Plants, Native, etc.	148, 209, 342	Rent .	10, 328
Plough, The . .	302	Reptiles	333
Poizo, The . .	131, 134, 136	,, Venomous .	7
Ponta Delgada (Mad.) .	. 139	Requirements, Clothing, etc. .	8
,, ,, (Azores)	. 148C	Retama, La .	209
,, do Pargo . .	. 142	Reyes, Los	167
,, ,, Sol . .	141, 143	Ribeira Brava .	140, 141, 143
Poor, Wants of . .	. 326	,, da Janella	140, 141' 142
Population 4, 147B, 320 and locally		,, Grande	. 148F, 149
,, Ancient	106, 321	,, Quente	. 148E
,, Statistics of	320, 321	Ribeirinha	. 149F
Pork .	331	Ribeiro Frio	136
Portella Pass .	134	Rigomaz	. 215
Portillo, El (Ten.).	207, 209	Rio (Ten.) .	186
Porto da Cruz	. 134	Rio, El (Lanz.)	. 257
,, Pargo . .	. 143	Risco, El (Lanz.)	. 257
,, Moniz . .	140, 142, 143	Roads, 122, 148A, 152, 175, 185, 201,	
,, Novo . .	. 134	212, 223, 254, 309	
,, Santo, 144 ; History of	85	Rocks, Order of	. 69
Porto, Villa do . .	. 148B	Romeiro, Ilheu de	. 148B
Postal Arrangements .	18, 147B	Roofs .	. 315
Potatoes .	. 284	,, of Churches	127, 211
,, Sweet .	148, 289	Roque de Bentaguaya	. 240
Povoação . . .	. 148E	,, del Moro .	. 234
Praia (Fayal) 149F; (Graciosa) 149C ;		,, de los Muchachos	157, 158
(Terceira) 149B.		,, Nublo . .	240, 241
Prayer, Forms of Native	. 115	,, de los Saucillos	. 240
Prazeres .	. 143	Rosario (Mad.)	. 140
Prices in Markets .	. 331	Rubber .	289
Priests, Native .	. 114		
Progress of Trade .	264		
Pronunciation .	. 25		
Ptolemy . . .	93, 106	Sabinosa	166, 167
Public Coaches, Ten.	220	Saddle horses, etc.	5 and locally
,, ,, Can. .	. 251	Salamanca . .	. 189
,, ,, Mad.	146	Salvages, The .	. 144
Puerto Cabras .	. 253	S. Amaro . .	. 132
,, de la Luz	. 225	S. Andres—La Palma .	. 157

	PAGE		PAGE
S. Andres—Hierro	167	Seeds, Culture of	291
,, Ten.	181	Seizal	140
S. Antonio—Mad.	132	Serra d'Agoa	140
,, Azores	149	Serrado, The	138
,, Ten.	199	Servants, Domestic	327
,, da Serra	131, 134	Sete Cidades	148E
S. Bartolomé (Tirajana)	241, 248, 249	Settlers	274, 311
S. Brendan or Borondon	86	Shells	334
S. Carlos	149B	Shipping Movements	261, 307
S. Fernando	233	,, of fruit	264, 266, 285,
S. Isidro—(Ten.)183; (Can.)	239, 240		298, 308
S. Jorge—Mad.	137	Shooting	12, 147A
,, Azores	149C	,, Licenses	13
S. José	162	Shops	8, 314
S. Juan de la Rambla	212	Silk	290
S. Lorenzo	231, 236	Silos, Los	214
S. Martinho	132	Slaves	268
S. Mateo	239, 247A	Sledges, Charges for	145
S. Miguel—Azores	148C	Snow	41, 147D
,, Ten.	187	Society	12
,, Lanzarote	256	Socorro	185
S. Pedro—Mad.	134	Soda, Manufacture of	278
,, La Palma	155, 162	Solar Day	17
S. Roque	132	Sombrerito, El	187
S. Sebastian	170	Sortija, La	12
S. Vicente	139, 140, 141	Spirits	148, 268, 283
Sand, Shifting	61	Sport	12, 147A
Santa Anna	137	Springs (see Mineral Springs).	
,, Brigida	237, 239	Spring-water, on sea surface	46
,, Catalina	230	Steamers, Fares. See table	
,, Cristina	234	opp. xviii.	146, 147
Santa Cruz—Florès.	149G	Stone—Building	315
,, ,, Graciosa	149C	Storms	44
,, ,, Mad.	134, 143	Strata, Commonly found	64, 147D
,, ,, La Palma	33, 154	Strata (at Guïmar)	184
,, ,, Ten.	28, 177	Stream, Gulf	63
,, ,, ,, Attack by Nelson.	103	Strikes	330
		Subsidence	76
,, ,, ,, Shipping	262	Sugar	268, 331
., Lucia	241, 247, 248	Sulphur	260
,, Magdalena	142		
,, Maria	148B		
,, ,, de Betancuria	253		
,, Ursula	199	Tacoronte	31, 183, 192, 194
Santiago—Ten.	188A, 214, 215	Tafira	231, 232, 236, 242
,, Can.	247	Taganana	181, 198
Santo Domingo (Garafía)	157	Tagasaste, The	289
Sardina	248	Tagoror	109
Sauces, Los	156	Taidía	241, 247
Sauzal	197, 198	Tamaraceite	231, 236
Scenery, 4, 6, 52, 59, 147D; also see locally and under introduction to each Island.		Tanks, Cost of	304
		Tanque, El	215
		Tanquinhas	141, 142
Schools	322	Tariffs, Hotel	4, 147 and locally
Sea, Depth of	60	Taxation	297, 323
Sea-sickness	58	Tazacorte	160
Seasons	38, 148A, 295	Tea	148
Seaweed	336	Tedesma	188

h

INDEX.

	PAGE
Tegueste	191, 194
Tejeda	235A, 240
Tejina (South) 188; (North) 191,	194, 197
Tejita	187
Telde	236, 237, 242
Telegrams (*see* also Cables)	19, 147B, 310
Temperature	26 to 56, 147D
Temples, Native	114, 235A, 238, 243
Tenants	11, 297
Teneriffe, 172; Invasions of, 96, 98, 99; Shipping, 262.	
Tenoya	232
Terceira	149A
Teror	231, 232, 233, 236, 238
Terraces on hills	280
Threshing, Method of	302
Thrift	326
Tidal Waves	45
Tides	17
Tigadaye	168
Tigalate	163
Tijarafe	157
Tijore	188
Tiles	315
Tilos, Los	232, 233, 234
Timber Imported, 315; Native, 299	
Time, El (La Palma)	158
,, Local	17
Times of Journeys	2, 4, 308
Tinerfe the Great	101, 173
Tinor	167
Tirajana	240, 241, 247, 249
Tobacco	148, 281
,, Duty on	125
Tomatoes	283
Torrinhas	138
Trade—Condition of	258
,, Progress of	264
,, Winds	48
Traditions	82, 85, 87, 115
Tramways	310 and locally
Trapiche	132
Trees	299, 336
Tronqueras, Las	215
Tunte	240, 241, 247, 249
Undeveloped Industries	287
Valleseco	232, 240
Valle del Bufadero	181, 193
,, de Guerra	192, 197
,, Hermoso	171

	PAGE
Valle de los Hijaderos	188
,, de Jimenez	189
,, de Tabarez	189
Valsequillo	238, 240, 243
Value of Land (*see* Land).	
Valverde	167
Vasco Gil	132
Vega, La (Icod)	215
,, de Abajo (Can.)	232, 236
,, de Arriba ,,	232, 239
,, del Centro ,,	231, 239
Vegetables	287, 298, 331
Vegetation, Effects of Altitude on	298
Vellas, Villa das	149C
Venomous Reptiles	7
Victoria, La	100, 199
Vilaflor	32, 187, 209
Villa Franca	148F
Villas	10
Vine, The	148, 271, 296
Virgen de Candelaria	183
Vocabulary, 20; Native	108
Volcanic Activity, 65, 122, 147E, 148C, 149A, 152, 172, 185, 215, 248	
Volcanoes, Formation of	60, 147D
Voyages, Duration of	2, 308
Wages	327
Walnuts	287
Waste Land	297
Water, Cost of	304
,, Courses	304
,, Rights	306
,, Supply	42
Wattle, The	287
Waves, Action of	63
Weapons, Native	118
Wells	304, 306
Whales	148A
Wheat (*see* Cereals).	
Whistling	20, 119, 169
Winds	43, 48
Wine	271, 331
Yaiza	257
Zargo	89
Zones, Climatic	292
,, of Cultivation	298

Name of Line.	Central Office.	When B
English. British and African S N. Co. (1900), Limited* African S. S. Co.*	African House, Liverpool Morocco House.	Fortnightl and six t to Tener Palmas.

OO LATE FOR INSERTION. (Opp. page xviii).

The Société Générale de Transports Maritimes à Vapeur has slightly altered its itinerary as given in the list of Passenger Steamers. The Mail Steamers of this Company now sail on the 24th of each month to Madeira, the intermediate ports being Valencia, Malaga and Gibraltar. On the return voyage, steamers sail twice a month from Teneriffe and once a month from Grand Canary.

Communications to be addressed to:

Paris: 8, rue Menars (rue du 4 Septembre). *Tel. Add.*, Transports, Paris.

Marseilles: 3, rue des Templiers. *Tel. Add.*, Transports, Marseilles.

Booth S. S. Co., Limited ...	Liverpool ...	Four time
Italian. La Veloce Nav. Italiana* ...	Genoa ...	Four time
La Ligure Brasiliana	Ditto ...	Monthly

NOTE.—There is a Tax on all passengers leaving the Can
THE INTERINSULAR POSTAL SERVICE OF
Canary twice a week. The round trip can be made for £4,
trade, fitted for passengers and offering similar facilities for
Blandy Bros. & Co.'s coas

INDEX.

	PAGE		PAGE
Tegueste	191, 194	Valle de los Hijaderos	188
Tejeda	235A, 240	,, de Jimenez	189
Tejina (South) 188; (North) 191, 194, 197		,, de Tabarez	189
		Valsequillo	238, 240, 243
Tejita	187	Value of Land (see Land).	
Telde	236, 237, 242	Valverde	167
Telegrams (see also Cables)	19, 147B, 310	Vasco Gil	132
		Vega, La (Icod)	215
Temperature	26 to 56, 147D	,, de Abajo (Can.)	232, 236
Temples, Native	114, 235A, 238, 243	,, de Arriba ,,	232, 239

Tradit...
Tramways
Trapiche
Trees . . . 299, 330
Tronqueras, Las . . 215
Tunte . 240, 241, 247, 249

Whistling . 20, 119, 169
Winds . . 43, 48
Wine . . 271, 331

Undeveloped Industries . 287

Yaiza . 257

Valleseco . . 232, 240
Valle del Bufadero 181, 193
,, de Guerra . 192, 197
,, Hermoso . 171

Zargo . . 89
Zones, Climatic . 292
,, of Cultivation . 298

NAME OF LINE.	CENTRAL OFFICE.	WHEN B
English. British and African S N. Co. (1900), Limited* African S. S. Co.*	African House, Liverpool	Fortnightl and six t to Tener Palmas.
Forwood Bros. & Co.*	Morocco House, St. Mary Axe, London, E.C.	Weekly
Union-Castle Line Mail S.S. Co.*	3, Fenchurch St., London, E.C.	Every wee
Aberdeen Direct (J. T. Rennie, Son & Co.*)	4, East India Avenue, London, E.C.	Fortnightl
Geo. Thompson & Co.*	7, Billiter Square, London, E.C.	Every thre
Natal Direct (Bullard, King & Co.)	14, St. Mary Axe, London, E.C.	Every ten
Shaw, Savill & Albion S.S.Co. New Zealand S. Co.	34, Leadenhall St., London, E.C. 138, Leadenhall St., London, E.C.	Two each
Royal Mail S. P. Co.	18, Moorgate St., London, E.C.	Fortnightl
Booth S. S. Co., Limited	Liverpool	Four time
Italian. La Veloce Nav. Italiana*	Genoa	Four time
La Ligure Brasiliana	Ditto	Monthly

NOTE.—There is a Tax on all passengers leaving the Can.
THE INTERINSULAR POSTAL SERVICE OF
Canary twice a week. The round trip can be made for £4,
trade, fitted for passengers and offering similar facilities for
Blandy Bros. & Co.'s coas

NAME OF LINE
French.
Fraissinet & Cie*
Soc. Gle. de Transpor times. (Itinerary vised.)
Chargeurs Reunis
Cie des Messageries M
N. Paquet & Cie
Belgian.
Cie Belge Maritime d
German.
Hamb. Sud amerik. Da Gesellschaft *
Woermann Linie m. b
Deutsche Ost Afrika l
Nord Deutscher Lloyd
Portuguese.
Empreza Insulana *
Do. Nacional
Spanish.
Hijo de J. Jover Serra
Cia. Trasatlantica
Pinillos Isquierdo & C
A. Folch & Cia
Soc. de Nav. é Indust

touche
twelve

GUIDE
TO
Madeira and the Canary Islands,
WITH THE AZORES.

PLAN OF THE BOOK.

THE object of the writer of this Guide has been to provide a hand-book by means of which the reader can ascertain how to reach the places described; how to visit the points best worth seeing after arrival, and how to calculate beforehand the approximate outlay whilst on the journey. It has been borne in mind that Madeira and the Canaries are well-established sanatoria, and that the wants of the invalid must receive as careful attention as those of the tourist.

In adding a mass of information for the use of residents and others, or in dealing with subjects which, if not actually of service, are at least of considerable interest to the traveller, care has been taken that such additional pages should be kept separate and that they should not be allowed to interfere with the "Guide" proper.

Steamboat fares are given in the large folding-sheet; landing and hotel charges under the town or village to which they appertain; the prices of carriages, horses, mules, guides, boats, omnibuses, etc., etc., at the end of the description of each island.

Those wishing to know the rent of houses, price of food, value of land, return from crops, cost of building, state of trade, etc., or to inform themselves on matters beyond those usually enquired into by the tourist, should turn to the Index. In such matters allowances must always be made. Each and all are affected by passing circumstances, and, in spite of every effort to be correct, accuracy cannot be guaranteed.

The system followed is to take the tourist along from the base to the end of some particular road, the side excursions being printed in smaller type. By the aid of the maps more extensive journeys may be planned.

To each island is affixed a general description, which will be found of use to those thinking of visiting it. The tables of coinage, the postal arrangements, etc., are correct and up to date, and the times of the coaches, prices of same and of private carriages are altered in each edition when necessary.

The facilities of communication with Europe and between the islands themselves, allow of a visit being made both to Madeira and to the Canaries within the short limits of an ordinary holiday.

It is trusted that the following pages will cause many to come to these charming Archipelagos, who might otherwise have remained at home.

To the invalid they are a haven of rest and of recuperation; to the tourist they are a play-ground open all the year round.

When the Alpine valleys are deep in snow and ice, the wooded precipices of Madeira, the forests of La Palma, the mountainous slopes of Teneriffe, and the irrigated valleys of Grand Canary, lie bathed in sunshine.

When the snows of Switzerland have gone to swell the waters of the Rhine and of the Rhone, and the mantle of white has melted from the Peak of Teneriffe, the mountain summits of Madeira and of the Canaries are at their best. In the summer they stand for months together above the clouds, in a world of their own, where the pure and exhilarating atmosphere allows of constant exercise under the most favourable conditions, and amidst the most lovely and interesting surroundings.

Time of Sea Journeys.—These vary, and those given below are only approximate.

Between Europe and the Islands, see page 308.

Madeira.—Between Madeira and Porto Santo, about 4 hours; Madeira and the Azores, about 44 hours.

Canary Islands.—Between Teneriffe and Grand Canary, about 8 hours; Teneriffe and La Palma, about 10 hours; La Palma and Hierro, about 7 hours; Hierro and Gomera, about 7 hours; Teneriffe and Gomera, about 4 hours.

Between Grand Canary and Fuerteventura, about 10 hours; Fuerteventura and Lanzarote, about 6 hours; Grand Canary and Rio de Oro, about 34 hours.

Azores.—Between Santa Maria and S. Miguel, about 5 hours; S. Miguel and Terceira, about 10 hours; Terceira to Graciosa, about 4½ hours; Graciosa to S. Jorge, about 3½ hours; S. Jorge to Pico, about 1 hour; Pico to Fayal, about 1½ hours.

GENERAL INFORMATION.*

The best order in which to visit the Islands, with hints to Tourists.

(NOTE.—Portuguese is spoken in Madeira and the Azores, and Spanish in the Canaries.)

Order in which to visit the Islands.—Leaving Northern Europe, those wishing to see both Madeira and the Canaries are recommended to stop first at Madeira, and to go from thence to Teneriffe. The latter island can at once be explored or the inter-insular boat taken to La Palma before the traveller has lost his sea-legs.

He can then either alight in La Palma, or, by taking a round ticket, pay a flying visit of three days to La Palma, Gomera and Hierro. Should he wish to spend a few days in one of these islands, he can return to Teneriffe by the following boat, the journey then occupying ten days.

If, on his arrival at Madeira, the weather happens to be bad, or there is no steamer going on shortly to the Canaries, he can omit that island and take it on his way home.

Whether the interior of Teneriffe or the Western Islands of the Canary Archipelago be taken first, the visitor must return to Santa Cruz (Teneriffe) on his progress eastwards, unless special arrangements are made with the inter-insular service of steamers, for which consult agents. Here it may be parenthetically remarked that one great advantage of the said steamers is that passengers and their luggage are taken on board and landed free in the ship's boat, a matter of some importance in small harbours where an extortionate charge might otherwise be made. The circular ticket gives the right of being put on shore at each port touched at and of breaking the journey at will.

Presuming that the Western Group of the Islands has been seen, passage may be taken to Grand Canary, where the arrival of the homeward-bound steamer may be awaited and the time passed either in the town, the mountains, or in visiting Fuerteventura and Lanzarote. Those coming from the South of Europe will probably find it best to make the trip in the reverse direction.

The shortest time in which Madeira, La Palma, Teneriffe and Grand Canary can be visited, and the return journey to Europe be

---

* NOTE.—General Information, the Commercial Appendix, etc., deal more especially with Madeira and the Canary Islands, and not with the Azores. The incorporation of a mass of extraneous details concerning the Western Islands does not appear necessary to the author. The special pages devoted to the Azores, however, are complete and correct, and are confidently recommended as being all that is required by the ordinary tourist and as the only publication dealing with the whole archipelago in a concise and practical manner.

completed, is about three weeks. This allows of time to see little more than the ports stopped at, and must be regarded as a yachting cruise. The time necessary for seeing each island will be found under the description of the island.

It only remains to be stated that the most beautiful scenery is to be found in La Palma, Teneriffe, Madeira, Gomera and Grand Canary. Fuerteventura and Lanzarote are not attractive.

Those visiting the Azores will probably do so from Madeira or from Lisbon, and are referred to the detailed description of the islands, page 147 onwards.

Passports.—Passports are not required in the Canaries, and all ports are free except for certain articles of consumption. Luggage is rarely examined. In Madeira and the Azores passports are also unnecessary. Extracts from the customs affecting visitors will be found under Madeira.

Hotels and Fondas.—These and the prices they charge are given under the description of each town or village, to find which refer to the Index.

The charges are calculated from experience on a fair basis. Though more than a native would pay, they are probably less than will be asked from strangers in the first instance.

A difference is always made between native and English people in the native hotels. English wishing to live at local prices must adopt the native style: Coffee early; a full breakfast at from 9.30 to 11 a.m., and dinner from 5 to 7 p.m. Wine is always placed upon the table. The English service means tea or milk if required when called, a meat breakfast at 9, a meat lunch at 1, afternoon tea, and dinner at 7. Coffee is served after dinner in both cases. Many of the native hotels are very good, and by accommodating one's self the expense is much lessened. The native sanitary arrangements are indifferent, but the linen may be reckoned on as being clean and the proprietors as being invariably willing to oblige in every way.

All hotels will reduce their prices to those staying for a long period, if arrangements are made beforehand. A married couple are sometimes considered as one and a half when occupying the same room.

Parties of more than three should send a telegram or letter on ahead when visiting small towns with limited accommodation. Letters of recommendation are of advantage in very out-of-the-way places.

Population.—The populations given in this work are those of the district, not that of the village itself, which is often a most insignificant centre to a widely-distributed parish. In all the islands the figures given are those of the census of 1900. The population statistics are given in the Commercial section, page 321.

Distances by measurement and by time.—All land measurements have been carefully worked out into English statute miles and French kilometres. Geographical miles are only used for long sea journeys.

Unless otherwise stated, times given on bridle roads are those necessary for mules or horses and no allowance is made for stoppages. On carriages roads distances are given.

The time is usually given from the writer's own experience. As, however, the footpaths and bridle roads cover a distance of many thousands of miles, it has been impossible to visit them all personally. Information procured at second hand has often been found most erroneous, even when given by Englishmen. Where recourse has been had to the peasants, whose ideas upon the subject of time are vague in the extreme, accuracy has been impossible. Those leaving the beaten tracks cannot, therefore, place implicit reliance upon the times given, though these are constantly being amended as opportunity allows.

This general carelessness about time also causes the public coaches to start sometimes a little before, sometimes a little after, the hour fixed. Those using them must, therefore, take 'the necessary precautions against being left behind.

Expeditions and Excursions.

Animals.—It is advisable, when engaging men and animals for expeditions, to fix a price before setting out and to stipulate that the drivers and the guides must find everything for beasts and selves. A little relaxation from this rule at lunch-time, and a moderate tip at the end of the journey, is likely to satisfy all parties thoroughly.

A good deal of bargaining is necessary. When a beast is engaged it is understood that the man goes with it. In the Canaries the "arrieros" are exceedingly clever in loading horses, especially if the rider will use a native saddle, "albarda." In Madeira, however, nothing will persuade them to put anything on to the horse which is to be ridden.

In hiring horses the visitor must remember that, owing to the many scandalous cases of over-riding, for which our countrymen and women are chiefly responsible, low prices will only be accepted when the hirer is known as a moderate rider. Again, it is only natural that the hire of the animal should vary with its appearance and condition, and with the state of the saddlery.

Pack animals, which have brought cargo from the other side of any of the islands, can be engaged to take back passengers at considerably lower prices than those usually current. Animals of this sort are accustomed to the roads and are rarely very much overworked. Those who know how to bargain may often economise a good deal by remembering this. The "arrieros" from the country are also less contaminated by the influence of the town, and are better acquainted with the district traversed.

Before starting it is as well to see that horses, if they are shod at all, are well roughed, some of the roads being very slippery in wet weather. If they have never been shod so much the better.

Those relying on native saddlery should never omit to put a good length of stout string in their pockets.

Clouds in the hills.—Travellers leaving for the mountains will please note that the start should always be made at an early hour, in order to avoid the fogs and mists which frequently gather later on. Such mists are encountered at all altitudes in accordance with the weather. In the Canaries they are, however, most clearly defined, gathering, as a rule, at an altitude of from 3,500 to 5,500 feet and forming a floor some 1,000 to 1,500 feet in thickness. When such clouds assemble during normal weather it is quite safe to climb through them, as the sky is sure to be clear above, and the heat of the sun rapidly dries the tourist's clothes. Well-defined clouds like these are caused by the warm trade wind, which is thrown up by the land, meeting a colder region. They rarely form before sunrise nor last for long after sunset.

In the Canaries, where the altitude is less than 6,000 feet, one cannot be sure of getting above them. In Madeira, which is too far north for the full effect of the trade wind to be felt, and where the influence of the gulf stream is more noticeable, the risk of getting no view when clouds are about is still greater. In the Azores cloudy days are more common than in either Madeira or the Canaries.

At times all of the islands are clear for days or weeks together, and this is the best time for excursions. When the clouds are very low and threatening, or the hills are visible with the sky above them obscured at a great altitude, it is best to stay near home. Even two or three streamers, pointing away from the island as a centre, should be taken as a warning. Invalids should not remain out after sunset, especially when up in the hills.

Springs and Waterfalls.—Care must be taken not to pay too much attention to local descriptions of scenery. The scarcity of water on some of the southern slopes causes the natives, who have never been elsewhere, to regard a spring or stream of the smallest dimensions as an object of beauty, and bepraise it in a manner quite incomprehensible to Englishmen. By following their advice many an hour is wasted in fruitless wanderings.

Guides.—Under ordinary circumstances the reader will find the information in this book sufficient, but in the mountains, where clouds or fog may occur, it is as well to be accompanied. For any of the passes the "arriero" who drives the horses or mules is all that is required. A practised guide is, however, necessary in the case of the Peak of Teneriffe, especially in the winter. When the snow and ice lay thick upon the slopes of this mountain, even the native guides are of little use, and none of them can be relied upon in case of exceptional difficulty or danger.

Best way to cross an island.—In many cases it is impossible, and in others unadvisable, to go round by the coast, unless, of course, a *carretera* has been made. The *Camino Real* (King's highway) often goes up and down into the *barrancos* in the most amazing manner. By shirking what seems an unnecessary climb of some 5,000 or 6,000 feet, the traveller may find at the end of the day that the sum total of his ascents has doubled this figure; that he has not gone so far as he hoped, and that, by choosing the lower road, he has missed much of the best scenery.

Camping out.—When preparing for camping out, regard must be had to the fact that all baggage will have to be carried by mules or horses, and that these should not be required to take more than from twelve to fourteen stone when on a journey. Tent pegs should be made of iron or hard wood, owing to the nature of the ground. Petroleum can generally be bought in the villages. Those wishing to remain for the summer months will do wisely to remove to the hills. Tents may not be pitched without permission from the Department of Forests.

Picnics and Country Customs.—Parties picnicking or lunching in the open should always offer something to those who pass. Unless offered more than twice and pressed, this will be refused, but it is as well that at least one member of the party should offer it. This is the custom of the country which should never be omitted. The same rule applies in small country inns when strangers enter and find others at meals.

There are other local customs and prejudices which English people would do well to acknowledge. For instance, it is usual for strangers meeting in an inn to recognise one another's existence, and for a lady to bow to a gentleman who leaves the footpath on her account.

The Euphorbia.—Tourists unlucky enough to get any of the juice of the *Euphorbia canariensis* (*cardon*) into the eye, can neutralise the burning of the caustic by squeezing some of the juice of a fleshy-leaved species of house-leek into the same place. The two plants are usually found in the same neighbourhood, if not actually intermingled.

Poisonous Reptiles.—Pedestrians walking through woods need have no fear of venomous reptiles. Snakes are unknown. Poisonous spiders exist, but are rare. Scorpions are only found in a few places, where they have been introduced with timber, etc., from abroad.

Mosquitoes.—These are most abundant on the eastern and southern sides of the Canary Islands, especially those nearest Africa. When present, the night must be passed under curtains, which should be high and airy, allowing a single bed not less than 120 cubic feet. Ammonia should be applied to the bites as soon as possible.

Beggars.—These are sometimes very importunate. It must, however, be remembered that there are no poorhouses and that a very little is made to go a very long way. Alms should be given on Saturday, and it is best to act under local advice.

Outfit.

Those things absolutely necessary, and not likely to be found in the islands, must be taken. Invalids using drugs which are little known, had better carry these with them.

There are some good shops in Funchal, Las Palmas, Santa Cruz (Teneriffe), Santa Cruz (La Palma), Orotava, Ponta Delgada, Angra, and Fayal.

In the Canaries, clothing is cheap. Good flannels are to be had in Las Palmas and Teneriffe, and capital shoes and boots in most of the islands. The latter are made from the native tanned goat-skin. These, with the rough side out, are to be preferred to any other footgear for the bad lava roads in the mountains. If hobnails, as used in Switzerland, are desired, they must be brought from England.

Intending climbers should take light alpine stocks with them; axes are not required. As regards clothing, both warm and light suits must be taken, but, for ordinary purposes, light woollen dresses for the ladies, and flannels or tweeds for the men, are to be preferred during the daytime. Mackintoshes are indispensable in the mountains, but are apt to rot if kept over six or eight months. The native washing is very bad, and linen is quickly frayed and torn to pieces, partly owing to the habit of drying it upon the tops of the prickly aloes.

The best hat is a broad, light felt.

Accommodation, etc.

As the recovery of an Invalid and the comfort of a Tourist depend fully as much on the accommodation obtainable as on the conditions of the climate, a few words on this subject are necessary.

Madeira has been so long a health resort that the requirements of visitors have become one of the staple productions of the country. Hotels are consequently able to provide themselves with luxuries more easily than in the Canaries. In the latter the immediate effect of the concourse of visitors and of the increase in the number of ships calling has been to overtax the existing resources, which have not yet had time to accustom themselves to circumstances.

Fowls, for instance, a few years ago were much cheaper in the Canaries than in Madeira; now they cost considerably more.

This difference in price will disappear when the Canary peasant at last realises that a constant market has been provided which will not vanish as quickly as it grew. Then again there is more water and consequently more verdure in Madeira, which means better cream, cheaper butter, and should mean cheaper vegetables, though, curiously enough, this is not the case.

As regards luxury of surroundings, furniture, etc., there is nothing to choose between the best hotels in Madeira, Teneriffe, or Grand Canary. All strive to do their best. Madeira certainly is favoured by possessing a number of trained servants accustomed to the work for years, but this is an advantage which every season tends to make less apparent.

To a certain extent the officials in **Madeira** recognise the fact that it is worth while to make the town attractive, the gardens being well kept and out-door life generally fairly well organised. The new railway and tram-line are also of great benefit in a place where locomotion, in spite of hammocks, "carros" and horses, was formerly somewhat tedious.

There is only one carriage road. Those too weak to walk can get about easily in the town, or even penetrate a short distance into the country by means of the local sleigh drawn by oxen, whilst the hammocks afford a luxurious means of visiting districts along paths where even mules cannot pass. Horses are fairly good and usually carefully shod. There are a multitude of pretty industries to be bought as mementoes, from basket-chairs to jewellery, many of which are highly attractive. The Custom duties are vexatious and cause everything to be dearer. (No duties are paid on ordinary luggage.) The peasant classes here, as well as in the Canaries, are obliging and honest.

Passing on from Madeira to **Teneriffe** the attention is first directed to the valley of Orotava, where there are a number of hotels at different levels, capable of accommodating some five hundred people, a most remarkable advance since 1885, when there was barely room for a dozen guests. At Santa Cruz, Tacoronte, La Laguna, Güimar and Icod there are more hotels, some of which are very good indeed. At Güimar there is a properly regulated sanatorium.

Communication by carriage is easy, and agreeable drives can be taken, but the bridle paths are indifferent. There are no Custom duties on travellers' luggage, a great advantage common to all the Canaries. The lower classes are uninventive, and the only trivialities worth purchasing are embroidery and some curious flowers made from fishes' scales.

The largest hotels in **Grand Canary** are in or near Las Palmas and up in the Monte district. The country fondas are fair in one or two instances.

Carriage roads lead to several parts of the island and bridle paths to the rest. The customs are the same in all the islands, but the Canarians show little taste in adorning the outside of their houses, which are sadly tame as compared to those in Teneriffe and La Palma. Embroidery and knives are worth buying, the handles of the latter being particularly handsome.

At Santa Cruz, **La Palma,** there is a fairly comfortable fonda. Out of Santa Cruz there are inns at El Paso and at Los Llanos.

A good road is being constructed, an immense improvement. Those in need of fresh air are able to drive in an open carriage by an easy gradient at a height of 1,000 feet above the sea. A fair bridle path crosses the island. The customs of the country have altered less by contact with the outside world than is the case in the other larger islands, and cock-fighting is indulged in more than in any part of the Canaries, a large permanent building being erected on purpose. Many knick-knacks may be bought, as well as strongly-made silks of various colours.

There is practically no accommodation for invalids in the remaining four islands, and but little in the Azores. What there is will be found to be sufficiently described in its proper place.

Villas and Houses.—If spending a winter or two away it will often be found more economical to hire a villa. A good deal of information is given on this subject in the Appendix, where the cost of food, servants, etc., can easily be found by means of the Index.

Villas are plentiful in Madeira, but a good deal wanted in the Canaries. Houses in Madeira are generally very well furnished, and let at from £60 to £300 for the season or the year. For houses in the Canaries, from £4 to £12 per month is asked. The tenant may leave in the latter place without giving notice and can only be forced to pay up to the day of leaving. The landlord can turn a tenant out at the end of the month by giving eight days' notice.

Those wishing to take houses, either in Madeira or elsewhere, must be prepared for long negotiations. Prices asked of the English in the Canaries are several times as much as were paid a few years ago. Above all, strict enquiries must be made regarding the supply of water and what chance there is of its being pure.

Visitors should avoid sleeping in ground floor rooms, unless they are quite sure that the moisture cannot be drawn up into the walls. In native houses this part of the building is, as a rule, only intended for cellars : the walls are built with earth instead of mortar, and damp is generally to be feared.

Annual Expenditure.

The vital question to many, of how much per annum it is necessary to spend is rather difficult to answer. Those who care to do so can, be extravagant here as they can elsewhere, but, as every extra luxury means extra labour and worry to the master or mistress, it is better for them to indulge themselves in another part of the world, unless they bring an entire staff of European servants with them.

Generally speaking, there is but little entertaining amongst the English and less amongst the Portuguese and Spaniards. The greatest dissipation is to go to a dance, or to be five deep for afternoon tea. As those who go out for their health should avoid so much excitement, it may be roughly calculated that a husband and wife and one or two young children can live very nicely, have friends to lunch two or three times a week, and keep a pony and trap, two maid servants and a man, and barring rent and education of the children, spend from £300 to £400 a year. That is to say, while it is possible to live on less than half these sums, one can spend as much as £500 or £600. Above this all is vanity and vexation of spirit. The chief economy of the place lies in the fact that drink, tobacco and such amusements as can be found are cheap. Added to this it is not easy to throw away an occasional fiver.

Some of the first necessaries of life, such as bread, are dear, but the producer and the consumer come more readily together than is the case in larger communities, and the iron hand of the middle-man is only noticeable in the price of imported articles.

Amusements.

Visitors for long periods should bring something to employ their time. There is little to do and riding constantly along the same roads becomes monotonous. If saddlery is bought, it should not be new, as the men are extremely careless.

The chief amusements are excursions, picnics, sketching, taking photographs, or making collections of objects of natural history, etc. Sport can scarcely be said to exist, though there are partridges, woodcock, and rabbits to be found in all the islands. An exception may perhaps be made in the case of quail shooting which is sometimes very good, especially during the first half of August. The deep-sea fishing often gives very good sport, but ordinary visitors find it too hot upon the water.

In the large towns, such as Funchal, Santa Cruz, Las Palmas, Ponta Delgada, and sometimes Orotava, open-air musical promenades are given. Cock fights take place in most of the towns during the springtime, and occasionally there are bull fights in Santa Cruz, Teneriffe, and in Angra, Terceira (*see* description).

The "*corridas de sortija*", which take place more frequently in Orotava than elsewhere, are a species of tournament where ladies and gentlemen gallop on horseback under a bar and endeavour to put a diminutive lance through a ring. The ring is attached to a ribbon, wound round a reel, which the successful rider carries away as a prize.

Paper chases sometimes take place, more particularly at Orotava. At Las Palmas and near Orotava (Teneriffe) there are golf links. At Las Palmas there is also a cricket club, and, once a year, a battle of flowers. In all the chief resorts there are lawn tennis grounds.

Of an evening many of the hotels get up dances or other entertainments, and there are the usual games at whist, billards, etc.

Native Society.—The people in all the islands are friendly and courteous, with somewhat stately and old-fashioned manners. Education is much neglected, and but little interest is usually displayed in matters other than local, or which take place outside of Portugal or Spain.

This is owing to the domestic habits of the gentlemen, many of whom do not care to go far out of sight of home. The duenna still reigns supreme, but the young ladies are sighing for the liberty enjoyed by their English sisters. Though the lover still stands and gazes from the street at his fair one in the balcony, or at most converses with her occasionally through the "postigo," there are signs of a desire for proceedings a little more Britannic. The "postigo," as it is called in the Canaries, is a small wooden shutter, hanging on hinges, which is slightly pushed open from inside when the occupant of the window seat wishes to look out at a passer-by. It was once common in Andalusia, but is now seldom met with in Europe.

It is incumbent upon every visitor, whether he wishes to associate with the islanders or not, to respect their customs and prejudices, and endeavour to conform a little to views which may occasionally clash with his own. Instances could be given of such outrageous behaviour on the part of English and other visitors, who should have known better, that too much emphasis cannot be given to this remark.

Shooting Licenses.—To carry arms of any sort in the Canaries, from 7 to 30 pesetas; to shoot game, 15 to 40 pesetas, which includes the right to carry arms. The amount is regulated by the class of Cedula Personal held by the applicant. Season, August 1st to February 15th. In Madeira to carry arms, 2,600 reis. To shoot game a license must be obtained in each Camara (district) at a cost of from 1,500 to 4,000 reis. Season, September 1st to January 31st.

Coinage.

{ Note.—Owing to the extraordinary fluctuation in the exchanges between Portugal and Spain and the rest of Europe since the Spanish-American war of 1898, the reader will bear in mind that currency prices given in this book, though as correct as possible at the time of issue, cannot be absolutely relied upon.

Portuguese Money used in Madeira.

(Taken at the official rate of exchange of 4$500 to the £ sterling. With the exchange at 5$000 the dollar is worth only 4s., and with exchange at 6$000 only 3s. 4d. and so on. It is impossible to state all these amounts, which the visitor must work out for himself in the column provided for that purpose.)

With exchange at.............. the equivalent is

Copper.
- 3 Reis = $\frac{4}{5}$d. ...
- 5 „ = 1$\frac{1}{5}$d. ...
- 10 „ = 1$\frac{8}{5}$d. ...
- 20 „ = 11$\frac{1}{5}$d. ...
- 40 „ = 21$\frac{2}{5}$d. ...

Silver.
- 50 Reis = 2$\frac{3}{8}$d. ...
- 100 „ = 5$\frac{6}{18}$d. (called a bit or testaō)
- 200 „ = 10$\frac{2}{3}$d. ...
- 500 „ = 2s. 2$\frac{2}{3}$d. ...

Gold.
- 1 Dollar = 4s. 5$\frac{1}{3}$d. (also called a pataca)
- 2 „ = 8s. 10$\frac{2}{3}$d. ...
- 5 „ = £1 2s. 2$\frac{2}{3}$d. ...
- 10 „ = £2 4s. 5$\frac{1}{3}$d. ...

English sovereigns and half-sovereigns used to pass current in ordinary transactions as 4$500 and 2$250 respectively. Portuguese gold coins were always rare and are now never seen, all gold being snapped up at once at a premium, either for hoarding or for export to Lisbon. Even silver has been very largely replaced by paper money.

Spanish Money used in the Canary Islands.

(Taken at the rate of exchange of 25 pesetas to the £ sterling. With the exchange at 10 % premium = 27½ peseta; at 20 % premium, 30 pesetas, and so on for all component parts.)

GENERAL INFORMATION. 15

		With exchange at. .... the equivalent is
Copper.	One centimo = 100 to a peseta ...	
	Half a cuarto = about 1½ centimos	
	Two centimos = 50 to a peseta	...
	One centimo de escudo = 2¼ centimos, 100 to an escudo	...
	One cuarto = about 3 centimos ...	
	Five centimos = the "perra chica," 20 to a peseta	...
	Two cuartos = about 6 centimos	
	Ten centimos = the "perra grande," 10 to a peseta = about 1 penny ...	
Silver.	One real de vellon = 25 centimos	...
	One fisca = about 31 centimos, or 10½ cuartos	...
	One real de plata = about 47 centimos, or 16 cuartos	...
	One half peseta = 50 centimos	...
	Two fiscas = 62½ centimos...	...
	One peseta = 100 centimos, or nominally tenpence	
	One toston = 125 centimos	...
	Two pesetas = 68 cuartos	...
	One escudo = 2½ pesetas, or half-a-dollar	
	One dollar = 5 pesetas, or four tostones	
Gold.	One gold dollar = 5 pesetas	...
	Two gold dollars = 10 pesetas	...
	Four „ = 20 „	...
	Five „ = 25 „ or one sovereign nominal	...
	Eight „ = 40 pesetas or one pound twelve nominal	...
	Sixteen „ = one "onza," 80 pesetas or three pounds four nominal	...

The coinage is in a state of transition and is rather difficult to understand. The rates at which pesetas, reales de plata, cuartos, and tostones are exchanged against one another cannot be made to tally exactly. The peseta and the centimo are fast replacing the old forms of money. Several of these are already obsolete, but are still used by the peasantry as a basis for estimating values.

Gold has disappeared from the Canaries for the same reasons as in Madeira, high premiums being paid on behalf of Madrid.

Measures.

PORTUGUESE.

A few weights and measures are: One polegada = 1·102 inches; one covada = 26¼ inches; one vara = about 43 inches; one league = 6,760 yards; one acre = 5·16 alqueires; one alqueire = 0·1938 of an acre, or 0·04789 of a hectare; one arrotel or libra = 1·0011 pounds avoirdupois; one arroba = 32·035 pounds; one almude = 3·88784 Imperial gallons; one barril = 7⅔ gallons; one pipe of wine = 92 Imperial gallons, or 418 litres; one alqueire = 1·55 pecks; one moio = 23¼ bushels.

Since the adoption of the metric system by Portugal, the above measures, though often used, are not legal.

SPANISH.

Twelve pulgadas = 11·128 inches; one vara = 33·141 inches, or 83½ centimetres; one hundred Spanish libras (a quintal) = 101·442 English pounds, or 46 kilos; one arroba = 25 lbs. Span; one fanega (of wheat) = 106 to 110 lbs.; (of slaked lime) = about 80 lbs.; (of maize) = about 130 lbs; (of barley) = 84 to 90 lbs.; (of liquid) = 62·66 litros. One cuartillo = 0·984 of a litro, or 1·73184 of a pint. 132,920 varas = one degree; one degree = 20 leguas.

One fanegada in Teneriffe	...	— 52 ares	·4829	= 1·2969	acres.
„	Grand Canary.	= 55 „	·365	= 1·36	„
„	La Palma ...	= 52 „	·5763	= 1·292	„
„	Lanzarote and Fuerteventura	= 136 „	·9591	= 3·3844	„

A fanegada in Teneriffe is approximately a square of 79 English yards or 86 Spanish varas.

The measure known as the alqueire and the fanegada mean, or once meant, a space of land on which an alqueire or a fanega of wheat might be sown broadcast, and are in themselves a species of valuation of the capability of the soil.

In Spain as in Portugal the metric system is officially recognised.

METRIC SYSTEM.

The *French Metric* system used in all the islands is here compared with the English as regards a few of the units: one metre = 39·371 inches. Eight kilometres, roughly speaking, equal 5 miles. One litre = 1·76 pints. One gramme = 15·4323 grains Troy. One hectare = 2·471 acres. One are = 119·6033

GENERAL INFORMATION.

sq. yards or 1/100 of a hectare. One kilogramme = 2·20462 lbs. avoirdupois; 70 kilos = (approximately) 154 lbs. or 11 stone.

For the convenience of those wishing to reduce altitudes from metres to feet or *vice versâ* the following table is appended:—

1 metre	=	3·2809 feet.		6 metres	=	19·6854 feet.
2 „	=	6·5618 „		7 „	=	22·9663 „
3 „	=	9·8426 „		8 „	=	26·2472 „
4 „	=	13·1235 „		9 „	=	29·5281 „
5 „	=	16·4042 „				

Thermometrical Degrees.

To reduce Fahrenheit to Reaumur, deduct 32°, multiply the remainder by 4, and divide by 9, Fahrenheit to Centigrade, deduct 32°, multiply by 5, and divide by 9.

Difference in Time.

The time in Funchal is 1 hr. 7 m. 40 sec. later than in London; in Valverde, Hierro, 1 hr. 11 m. 20 sec.; in Santa Cruz, La Palma, 1 hr. 10 m.; in S. Sebastian, Gomera, 1 hr. 8 m. 40 sec.; in Santa Cruz of Teneriffe, 1 hr. 5 m. 12 sec.; in Orotava, 1 hr. 6 m. 20 sec.; in Las Palmas, Grand Canary, 1 hr. 1 m.; in Puerto Cabras, Fuerteventura, 55 m. 12 sec.; in Arrecife, Lanzarote, 54 m. 20 sec.; and in Ponta Delgada, Azores, 1 hr. 42 m. 44 sec.

Length of the Solar Day.

In the Canaries the shortest solar day is 10 hrs. 11 m. 12 sec., and the longest, 13 hrs. 48 m. 48 sec.

Tides.

The usual rise and fall of the tide in Madeira is about 7 feet; in the Canaries it is about 9 feet; in the Azores from 4 to 6 feet.

Distance of the Visible Horizon.

To ascertain at a given altitude above sea-level the distance in English miles from the observer to the *visible* horizon—take the square root of the altitude in English feet and multiply the same by 1·32.

Example: Required the distance of horizon at 2,500 feet. Square root of 2,500 = 50. Multiply by 1·32. Result 66 English miles. (*Note.*—The visible horizon is about 7 per cent. further than the actual horizon, the increase being due to refraction of the light rays by the atmosphere.)

Post and Telegraph.

Madeira, Teneriffe, Grand Canary, Lanzarote, La Palma, and the Azores are all connected by telegraph with Europe, and are also part of the Postal Union. Letters, ½ oz., 2½d.; Post Cards, 1d., Newspapers, ½d. per 2 oz.; Samples, ½d. per 2 oz., with a minimum charge of 1d.; Commercial Papers, the same, with a minimum of 2½d.

Samples to Madeira or the Azores must not weigh more than 250 grammes (about ½ lb.), or they will be opened in the Custom House. They must be marked "*Amostras.*"

Parcel Post to Madeira.—Not over 3 lbs., 2s.; not over 7 lbs., 2s. 6d.; not over 11 lbs., 3s. Limit of weight, 11 lbs. Parcels can be insured up to £20. Charges up to £12, 5d.; up to £20, 7½d.

To the Azores.—The same limits, etc., but the prices are 2s. 5d.; 2s. 10d.; and 3s. 3d.

To the Canaries.—There is no parcel post.

Madeira.—*Inland Postage* (15 grammes), 25 reis. Post Cards, 10 reis. Newspapers, each 50 grammes, 2½ reis. The same rates apply to Portugal, the Azores, Spain and the Canaries (*viâ* Lisbon).

Postal Union.—Letters, 50 reis per 15 grammes (½ oz.); Post Cards, 20 reis; Newspapers, per 50 grammes, 10 reis; Commercial Papers, the same, with a minimum of 50 reis. To this tariff a variable percentage is added. In June, 1901, 30%, making a ½ oz. letter 65 reis.

To India, West Coast of Africa, West Indies, Australia, Ascension, St. Helena, Cape Colony and Natal. Letters, 100 reis; Cards, 30 reis; Newspapers, 20 reis (50 gs.), to which add the variable 30%.

Letters insufficiently stamped are not delivered to countries outside of the Postal Union.

Inland Parcel Post (limit of weight 5 kilos; of size 20 decimetres cubic and 60 centimetres largest measurement). Rates to be ascertained at the Post Office.

Foreign Parcel Post (limit of measurement the same). Weights and charges to be ascertained at the Post Office.

Telegrams.—Inland, 65 reis the first word, and 10 reis per word afterwards; to Portugal, 0·675 francs per word; to Spain, 0·865 francs per word; to the Canaries, 1·765 francs; to England, 0·89 francs; France, 1·065 francs; Germany, 1·265 francs; Italy,

GENERAL INFORMATION.   19

1·265 francs; New York, 2·325 francs; Cape Colony or Natal, 6·765 francs; Delagoa Bay, the Transvaal, etc., 6·965 francs. By direct cables the prices are rather higher, and can be ascertained at the Post Office. Francs are converted into reis at a rate of exchange fixed in Lisbon (in June, 1901, 30% premium.)

Canary Islands.—*Inland or Inter-insular Postage.* Letters (15 grammes), 15 centimos; Post Cards, 10 c.; Newspapers, ¼ c. each; Commercial Papers and Samples (each 20 grammes), 5 c., with a minimum of 10 c. The same rates apply to Spain.

Postal Union, which includes nearly the whole world. Letters, 25 centimos; Post Cards, 10 c.; Newspapers (each 50 grammes), 5 centimos; Commercial Papers and Samples the same, with a minimum of 25 centimos.

Those wishing to send parcels will find Messrs. Forwood Bros. and Co., of London, or Messrs. Elder, Dempster & Co., of Liverpool and London, both reasonable and obliging.

Telegrams.—Inland, 50 centimos for 15 words and additional words, 5 c. each.—Inter-insular, 2 pesetas for 15 words and additional words 15 c. each; to Spain, 4 pes. for 15 words and additional words 30 c. each. Besides this there is a tax of 5 c. on all telegrams.

England, 0·95 francs a word; France, 0·80; Germany, 0·85; Italy, 0·88; Belgium, 0·85; Madeira, 1·53; Gibraltar, 0·75; Tangiers, 0·80; Senegal, 0·95; Bathurst, 4·04; Sierra Leone, 5·25; New York, 2·20; Argentina, 4·40; South Africa, 5·25. All the above are payable in francs, but Portugal is 0·70 pesetas a word.

The francs are payable in pesetas at a rate of exchange fixed by the Spanish Government each three months (in June, 1901, it was 36% premium). By the cables of the Eastern Telegraph Co., except in the case of England, Gibraltar and Tangiers, the rates are higher than those quoted.

Vocabulary

of a few words which will be found constantly used in this book in preference to their English equivalents.

Portuguese.—Ribeira, a large ravine or stream.—Ribeiro, the same but smaller.—Arco, Lombo, a mountain spur.—Levada, an aqueduct.—Encumiada, the summit of a range of hills or mountains.—Lagôa, a crater with water in it.—Quinta, a farm or villa.—Achada, a small plain.—Bocca, a gap or mouth.—Caminho, a road.—Capella, Ermida, a chapel.—Igreja, a church.—Ponta, a cape.—Porto, a port.—Praça, a square.—Rua, a street.—Pinheiral, a pine forest.—Curral, a cattle fold.—Vereda, a mountain track.—Cidade, a city.—Villa, a town.—Freguezia, a parish.—Furado, a tunnel through rock.

Spanish.—Patio, a courtyard.—Azotea, a flat roof.—Calle, a street.—Barranco, a ravine.—Carretera, a carriage road.—Caldera, a crater.—Monte, uncultivated mountain land.—Monte Verde, the same, covered with heather or shrubs.—Pinar, a pine forest.—Cumbre, the summit of a range of hills or mountains.—Finca, â farm or villa.—Albarda, a pack saddle.—Arriero, a mule boy.—Venta, a wine shop.—Atarjéa, acéquia, an aqueduct.—Algibe, a covered-in tank or cistern.—Ciudad, a city.—Villa, a town.—Pueblo, a village.—Camino real, the king's high bridle road.—Malpais, country covered with lava, etc.—Fielato, an octroi or municipal custom-house.—Mina, a tunnelled spring of water.—Carro, a waggon, cart.—Iglesia, a church.—Capilla, Ermita, a chapel.

In Spanish, among the guides, *volcan* does not mean a volcano, but the lava which flows from it. The volcano itself is called Caldera, Montañeta, etc., etc.

For the whistling language of Gomera turn to Gomera itself.

A VOCABULARY OF WORDS NECESSARY IN SPEAKING TO SERVANTS, ETC.

English.	*Portuguese.*	*Spanish.*
Bacon	o toucinho	el tocino
Basin	a bacia	la palangana
Bed	a cama	la cama
Beef	a carne de vacca	la carne de vaca
Blanket	o cobertor	la manta
Bread	o pão	el pan
Butter	a manteiga	la manteca
Candle	a vela	la vela

English.	Portuguese.	Spanish.
Chair	a cadeira	la silla
Chamber pot	o bacio	la escupidera
Chicken	a gallinha	la gallina
Coffee	o café	el café
Counterpane	a colcha	la colcha
Cup	a chicara	la taza
Dirty	sujo	sucio
Drink	beber	beber
Eat	comer	comer
Egg	o ovo	el huevo
Envelope	o sobrescripto	el sobre
Fish	o peixe	el pescado
Fork	o garfo	el tenedor
Fruit	a fructa	la fruta
Glass	o copo	el vaso, la copa
Hour	a hora	la hora
Jam	a jelêa	el dulce
Jug	o jarro	el jarro
Knife	a faca	el cuchillo
Lamp	o lampeão	el quinqué
Matches	os phosphoros	los fosforos
Mattress	o colchão	el colchon
Meat	a carne	la carne
Milk	o leite	la leche
Mirror	a espelho	el espejo
Mosquito curtain	o mosquiteiro	el mosquitero
Mutton	o carneiro	la carne de carnero
No	não	no
Paper	o papel	el papel
Pillow	a almofada	la almohada
Plate	o prato	el plato
Postage stamps	sellos do correio	sellos
Sheet	o lençol	la sábana
Sleep	dormir	dormir
Soap	o sabão	el jabon
Soup	a sopa	la sopa
Spoon	a colher	la cuchara
Sugar	o açucar	el azucar
Table	a mesa	la mesa
Tea	o chá	el té
Veal	a vitella	la ternera
Wake	accordar	despertar
Wine	o vinho	el vino
Yes	sim	si
One	um, uma	uno, una

English	Portuguese.	Spanish.
Two	dois, duas	dos
Three	tres	tres
Four	quatro	cuatro
Five	cinco	cinco
Six	seis	seis
Seven	sete	siete
Eight	oito	ocho
Nine	nove	nueve
Ten	dez	diez

A FEW PHRASES NECESSARY TO THOSE MOVING ABOUT.

English.	Portuguese.	Spanish.
On the Steamboat.	A bordo do vapor.	En el vapor.
I want a boat to go on shore; how much?	Preciso d'um barco para ir a terra; quanto é?	Quiero un bote para ir á tierra ¿ cuanto cuesta?
How much to go and return?	Quanto é para ir e voltar?	¿Cuanto cuesta para ir y volver?
This is my luggage, how much will it cost?	Esta é a minha bagagem, quanto quer para leval-a?	Este es mi equipage, ¿ cuanto cuesta llevarlo?
That is too much and more than I will give.	Isso é muito. é mais do que eu quero dar.	Es muy caro; no pago tanto.
All right, you can take it.	Bem, póde leval-a.	Esta bien, llévelo.

On Shore.	Em terra.	En tierra.
Take my luggage to—	Leve a minha bagagem para—	Lleve mi equipage á—
Which is the way to—	Por onde se vai para—	¿Por donde se va á—
I want a carriage to go to	Quero uma carruagem para ir a ...	Quiero un coche para ir á ...
I want a horse to go to—	Quero um cavallo para ir a—	Quiero un caballo para ir á—
I want a donkey to go to—	Quero um burro para ir a—	Quiero un burro para ir á—
I want a mule to go to—	Quero uma mula para ir a—	Quiero un mulo para ir á—
I want a camel to go to—	Quero um camêlo para ir a—	Quiero un camello para ir á—

GENERAL INFORMATION.

To take a drive (or ride)	Dar um passeio	Dar un paseo
We are two [three] [four] [five] persons	Nós somos dois, (or duas), [trez] [quatro] pessoas	Somos dos [tres] [cuatro] [cinco] personas
We want two ladies' saddles	Queremos duas sellas para Senhora	Queremos dos sillas para Señora
We want pack animals	Queremos animaes de carga	Queremos bestias de carga
We want a guide to take us round the town	Queremos uma pessoa que nos mostre a cidade	Queremos un guia para que nos enseñe la ciudad

(The custom house is best left to the proprietors of the hotels.)

In the Hotel.   *No Hotel.*   *En la Fonda.*

Have you a bedroom for me (for us)?	Tem um quarto para mim (nós)?	¿Hay una habitacion para mi (para nosotros)?
We want single ⎱ beds double ⎰	Queremos camas pequenas — camas de casal	Queremos camas de una persona — de dos personas
On the first second ⎱floor third ⎰	No primeiro ⎱ segundo ⎰ andar terceiro	En el primer ⎱ segundo ⎰ piso tercer
The room is too small [too expensive]	O quarto é muito pequeno [muito caro]	La habitacion es muy pequeña [muy cara]
I want some hot water	Quero agua quente	Quiero agua caliente
I want some cold water	Quero agua fria	Quiero agua fria
I want a hot bath	Quero banho d'agua quente	Quiero un baño caliente
I want a cold bath	Quero banho d'agua fria	Quiero un baño frio
Are the sheets dry?	Estão seccos os lençoes?	¿Son secas las sábanas?
I want drinking water	Quero agua de beber	Quiero agua para beber
I want clean towels	Quero toalhas limpas	Quiero tohallas limpias
I want bath towels	Quero toalhas de banho	Quiero tohallas de baño
At what time is breakfast?	A que horas é o almoço?	¿A que hora se almuerza?

At what time is lunch?	A que horas é o lunch?	¿A que hora se toma lunch?
At what time is dinner?	A que horas é o jantar?	¿A que hora se come?
Call me at four [five] [six] [seven] [eight]	Chame me ás quatro [ás cinco] [ás seis] [ás sete] [ás oito]	Despiérteme á las cuatro [cinco] [seis] [siete] [ocho]
Where is the lavatory?	Onde é a casinha?	¿Donde está el excusado?

Walks and Expeditions.	*Passeios e Expedicoes.*	*Paseos y Expediciones.*
How far is it to the spring?	Qual é a distancia d'aqui á nascente?	¿Que distancia hay de aqui á la fuente?
How far is it to the path leading to...?	Qual é a distancia ao caminho que dá para...?	¿Que distancia hay al camino que va á...?
How far is it to the mountain of...?	Qual é a distancia ao monte de...?	¿Que distancia hay á la montaña de...?
How far is it to the top?	Qual é a distancia ao Pico?	¿Que distancia hay á la cumbre?
How far is it to the bottom?	Qual é a distancia ao fundo?	¿Que distancia hay hasto abajo?
How far is it to the crater?	Qual é a distancia á cratera?	¿Que distancia hay á la caldera?
How far is it to the stream of lava?	Qual é a distancia á corrente de lava?	¿Que distancia hay 'al volcan?
How far is it to the church?	Qual é a distancia á egreja?	¿Que distancia hay á la Iglesia?
How far is it to the valley?	Qual é a distancia ao valle?	¿Que distancia hay al valle?
How far is it to the view of...?	Qual é a distancia á vista de...?	¿Que distancia hay á la vista de...?
How far is it to the ascent of...?	Qual é a distancia á subida de...?	¿Que distancia hay á la subida de...?
How far is it to the descent to...?	Qual é a distancia á descida de...?	¿Que distancia hay á la bajada de...?
How far is it to the (mountain) spur?	Qual é a distancia ao lombo de?	¿Que distancia hay al lomo de?
How far is it to the sea?	Qual é a distancia ao mar?	¿Que distancia hay al mar?
How far is it to the inn?	Qual é a distancia á hospedaria?	¿Que distancia hay á la fonda?
How far is it to the drinking shop?	Qual é a distancia á taberna?	¿Que distancia hay á la venta?

How far is it to the village of...?	Qual é a distancia á aldeia de...?	¿Que distancia hay al pueblo de...?
How far is it to the town of...?	Qual é a distancia á villa de...?	¿Que distancia hay á la villa de...?
How far is it to the city?	Qual é a distancia á cidade?	¿Que distancia hay a la ciudad?
Tie the blanket on to the pack saddle.	Amarre o cobertor á sella.	Sujete la manta en la albarda
Do you think it will be clear at the top?	Julga estar claro lá em cima?	¿Cree V^d que estará claro por encima?
Do you think it will rain to-day?	Julga que choverá hoje?	¿Cree V^d que llovera hoy?
Is the road bad?	O caminho é máo?	¿Es malo el camino?
Is the road very bad?	O caminho é muito máo?	¿Es muy malo el camino?
Can animals pass?	Os animaes podem passar?	¿Pueden pasar bestias?
Are you sure you know the way?	V^{cê} tem a certeza que conhece o caminho?	¿Esta V^d seguro que conoce el camino?
I shall not pay you if you don't.	Não lhe pagarei se V^{cê} não souber	No le pagaré á V^d si no sabe.
Where is the market?	Onde é o mercado?	¿Donde está la recoba?
Where is the post office?	Onde é o correio?	¿Donde está el correo?
Where is the chemist?	Onde é a botica?	¿Donde está la botica?
Where is the club?	Onde é o club?	¿Donde está el casino?

Pronunciation.

Portuguese.—*lh* is pronounced like the *ll* in million; *nh* like the *n* in renew; *ç* like *s*; ão (with a til) like *an*; *ch* like *sh* in English; *j* soft as in French; *qu* is soft as in quilt before *a*, *o* and *u*, but hard before *e* and *i*; vowels are broad and the *u* is like *oo* in moon. The people in Madeira drop the ends of words more than is the case in Lisbon. An *accent over a vowel* indicates that that vowel forms the principal syllable of a word.

Spanish.—*ll* is pronounced like the *ll* in million; *ñ* (with til) like the *n* in renew; *ch* soft as in English; *j* like *h*; *g* like *h* before *i* and *e* but hard before *a*, *o*, and *u*; *h* is not sounded; *qu* is hard like *k*; *cu* is soft like *qu* in quilt; vowels are broad and the *u* is like *oo* in moon. All letters are sounded, including the *final r*. An *accent over a vowel* means the same as in Portuguese.

METEOROLOGICAL OBSERVATIONS.

The greatest care has been taken to make the following statistics as accurate as possible. Many of them have been averaged by the author, the monthly tables not always being added up by the recorders. This gave a large amount of work, and accounts for some of them spreading over so few years.

This opportunity is taken of thanking the gentlemen who were so very kind as to supply them and to allow of their publication.

FUNCHAL, MADEIRA.

		October	November	December	January	February	March	April	May	No. of years of observations
Temperature. Shade.	Mean of Mean Daily Fo	68.6	65.0	61.8	60.3	60.3	60.8	62.4	64.4	25
"	Minimum "	63.9	60.5	57.3	55.7	55.1	55.2	57.6	59.6	19
"	Range "	9.9	9.8	9.3	9.5	10.0	9.9	9.4	9.2	—
Moisture of Atmosph.	Rel. Humidity " Sat. 100	66.0	68.3	68.2	69.0	66.0	63.4	65.9	65.5	=
Rain. Amt. of	Mean Monthly Inches.	2.30	4.78	4.10	4.58	2.64	2.83	1.75	1.07	=
No. of days on which rain fell ('01" of an inch or more)		—	10.0	10.7	12.0	6.7	8.4	7.0	5.7	11
" during day time "		8.7	—	—	—	—	—	—	—	—

Sunshine 1 axis are not been taken in Madeira. Absolute Maximum, July, 88, 90.5. Absolute Minimum, March, 88, 43. Temperature of Sea at Funchal, Maximum, 75°, M, 63.

Total annual rainfall, 26.71 inches (17 years' observations). During 1895-6 no less than 58.28 inches of rain was measured at 250 feet above the sea. Of this 18.43" fell in October and 9.12" in February, 1895. This abnormal fall was followed by a long drought both in Madeira and in the Canaries.

Observations were taken at an altitude of 82-89 feet, at 9 a.m. and 9 p.m., in the years 1826 to 1831, and 1865 to 1883, by the late Fortaleza, F M, and by Drs. Men and Renton. Piazzi Smyth, working from observations made in 1834-35 by Dr. Mn, estimated the mean difference between the wet and dry webs as 4.6° F. His Relative H ... for that year average about 8 per cent. more than these given above. It will be ... that none of these ... 70 per cent., an incomprehensibly low figure for a warm mic climate.

NOTE.—When required the mean maximum can always be found by adding the mean daily range to the mean minimum. The absolute maximums and minimums only include those brought to the notice of the writer, and may therefore be incorrect.

GENERAL INFORMATION.

LAS PALMAS, GRAND CANARY.

			October	November	December	January	February	March	April	May	No. of years of observations
Temperature.	Shade.	Mean of Mean Daily	Fo 71·4	67·6	64·7	62·3	62·9	63·0	64·6	66·5	5
,,	,,	Minimum ,,	" 66·8	63·2	59·7	57·8	57·9	58·8	60·0	61·9	,
,,	,,	Range ,,	- 9·2	8·9	9·0	9·1	10·1	9·5	9·2	9·2	,
,,	Sea.	Surface. ,,	" 72·4	70·1	67·5	65·7	65·1	65·4	65·9	67·3	"
Moisture of Atmosph.		Rel. Humidity { Day ... Night...	Sat. 100 " 68 76	66 73	65 75	68 73	66 75	66 74	65 74	65 74	"
Rain.	Amt. of	Mean Monthly	Inches 1·06	1·75	1·57	1·68	0·57	0·79	0·40	0·35	"
,,		No. of days on which rain fell ("·01" or more) ,,	— 6	11	12	10	5	7	4	2	,
,,		during day time ,,	— 3·2	5·4	7·4	5·6	2·2	3·2	2·0	0·6	,
Sunshine		Total amount ...	Hours 189	165	161	168	183	189	190	18	"

Absolute Maximum, 95°, Sept. 15, 1897. Absolute Minimum, 47°, February, 1884.
Total annual rainfall, 8·348 inches. At San Mateo, 2,680 feet above the sea, the annual rainfall is estimated at 25 inches.
Observations were taken at 9 a.m., noon, 3 p.m., and 9 p.m., by Dr. J. Cleasby Taylor, M.B., C.M. Edin. Univ., M.R.C.S., Eng., by whom the above figures were kindly supplied, and the absolute minimum by A. H. Bechervaise, Esq. Observations taken during two winters by Dr. Brian Melland will be found in his work, "Climatic Treatment in Grand Canary." Tables of comparative statistics, for which there is no space in this volume, will be found in the book named and in "The Health Resorts of the Canary Islands" by Dr. J. Ceasby Taylor.

SANTA CRUZ, TENERIFFE.

		October	November	December	January	February	March	April	May	No. of years of observations
Temperature. Shade.	Mean of Mean Daily °F	71.0	69.0	66.0	64.0	63.0	64.0	65.0	68.0	8
,, ,,	Minimum ,,	*74.2*	*68.7*			*60.8*	*61.9*	*64.3*	*67.0*	,,
,, ,,	Range ,,	63.0	59.0	56.0	56.0	53.0	55.0	57.0	59.0	,
		66.0	*62.2*			*53.7*	*53.3*	*57.3*	*59.4*	
		15.0	15.0	15.0	13.0	15.0	15.0	14.0	15.0	
		16.4	*13.1*			*14.3*	*17.2*	*14.0*	*15.3*	
Moisture of Atmosph.	Rel. Humidity ,, Sat. 100	67	64	67	73	66	66	62	60	9
Rain. Amt. of	Mean Monthly Inches	0.98	1.59	2.48	1.97	1.64	1.53	0.58	0.31	22
,, No. of days on which rain fell ('01" or more) ,,		7	6	9	11	9	8	7	2	
,, ,, during day time		5	4	5	7	7	5	5	1	,
State of Sky (0 clear, 10 fully covered)		4	4	5	5	4	4	4	3	
Sunshine. Mean Daily Hours		5.4	4.4			6.7	6.0	6.7	7.9	5

Absolute Maximum, 30th July, 1893, 101°. Absolute Min, 17th January, 1889, 46.8°.
Total annual rainfall, 11·72 inches (17 years).

Observations were taken at an altitude of 118 feet at 11 a.m. and 5 p.m., in the years 1880 to 1889 incl. Min, 1865 to 1889, by Sr. D. Francisco de Aguilar y Fuentes, Ayudante de Obras Publicas, Santa Cruz de Tenerife, by whom the above figures were kindly supplied.
The figures in Italics were taken in Salamanca, on the upper outskirts of Santa Cruz, 250 feet above the sea, in 1893 only, by Captain E. H. Baines, who was good enough to allow the writer to use them.

GENERAL INFORMATION.

PUERTO DE OROTAVA, TENERIFFE.
(70 feet.)

		January	February	March	April	May	June	July	August	September	October	November	December	No. of years of observations
Temperature. Shade.	Mean of Mean Daily	F°	61·2	61·6	62·6	64·0	68·3	69·8	72·5	73·3	72·7	71·2	67·1	63·7	8
,, ,,	Minimum	,,	54·4	54·5	55·6	57·1	58·6	62·6	65·9	66·7	65·6	64·4	60·0	56·7	,,
,, ,,	Range	,,	13·6	13·7	13·9	13·9	14·5	14·3	13·2	13·6	14·0	13·7	13·9	13·6	,,
Moisture of Atmosph.	Rel. Humidity 9 a.m.	Sat. 100	71·3	67·7	70·3	69·5	69·1	69·2	72·9	73·0	72·1	73·4	73·0	72·2	,,
	,, 9 p.m.		79·4	77·1	79·1	80·9	77·9	79·7	83·6	86·4	83·9	83·1	81·0	78·9	
	,, Average		75·4	72·4	74·7	75·2	73·5	74·4	78·3	79·7	78·0	78·2	77·0	75·5	,,
Rain. Am of	Mean Monthly	Inches.	3·10	1·83	2·31	1·34	0·49	0·05	0·02	0·05	0·27	2·64	2·09	2·50	,,
,,	No. of days on which rain fell ('01' or more)	—	8·5	6·8	8·5	5·3	2·2	0·3	0·5	0·5	1·8	6·8	9·5	8·7	,,
,,	during day time	—	5·5	4·0	3·1	2·9	0·5	0·1	0·0	0·1	0·7	3·4	5·5	4·7	,,
Sunshine	Total amount	Hours	147	167	170	174	200	192	165	165	180	166	153	145	,,

Absolute Maximum, Sept. 26th, 1896, 90·1° Ft. Absolute Minimum, Feb. 8th, 189 48·4° F
Total annual rainfall 16·69 inches.

Observations were taken at an altitude 0·70 feet, at 9 a.m. and 9 p.m., from 1890 to 1897 inclusive, by Mr. Alfred F. Perry, of the Sitio de Cullen, with instruments furnished by the Meteorological Society of London. The above averages have been kindly furnished to the author by Messrs. Alfred F. Perry and Frederick Lishman, M.D., of Puerto Orotava.

GÜIMAR, TENERIFFE.
1,200 feet.

Temperature.				October	November	December	January	February	March	April	May	Annual Mean.	No. of years of observations
	Mn of Mn Daily		F°	—	—	58·6	57·8	59·9	57·4	—	—	66·6	1
	Minimum			—	—	52·3	52·0	53·1	50·0	—	—	57·7	"
	Range			—	—	12·7	11·6	13·6	14·9	—	—	—	"
Moisture of Atmosph.	Rel. Humidity		Sat. 100	—	—	64·5	59·5	60·3	62·0	—	—	64·9	"
Rd. Am. of		Mn Mthly	Inches	3·70	0·25	0·08	4·34	1·04	2·26	1·45	0·18	13·7	"
"	No. of days on which rain fell (0·1" or more		"	—	—	2	1	1	10	—	—	—	"
"	" during day time		"	—	—	—	—	—	—	—	—	—	"
Sunshine	Total amoun.		Hours	—	—	106	222	174	195	—	—	—	—

Temperature:—Mean of six warmer months (October to March) at 9 a.m. 63·1 F°.; of six warmer months (April to September) 70·2 F°. Mn maximum: war, 69·0 F°.: summer, 76·7 F°. Anal max tmum : war, 89·0 F°. (war); summer, 95 F°. (August). Anual minimum : Inter, 47·0 F°. (January and, 190); war, 51·0 F°. (April). Mn maximum whole war, 72·9 F°. During 190 the sun shone for 8 hours or more on 268 days. There were very few days on which there was no sunshine.

Observations were taken at an altitude of 1200 feet, at 9 a.m. and 9 p.m.; from December 11 h, 1889, to March, 890 by Dr. A. J. Wharry, and hose ign in italics by Dr. Stanford Harris during the year 1900 (365 days).

TACORONTE, TENERIFFE.
(1,525 feet.)

				September	October	November	December	No. of years of observations.
Temperature.	Sde.	Mn of	Mn Daily	Fo 69·1	65·6	58·6	54·3	1
,,	,,	,,	Mm	, 56·1	58·3	53·8	50·3	1
,,	,,	Range	,,	, 16·9	14·6	9·7	7·9	1
More o Atmosph.		Rl. Humidity		Sat. 100 75·5 %	83 %	78 %	84 %	1
Rain. Am . or		Mn Mon thy		Inches —	—	—	—	
	No of days on wh ch rain fell			— 1	15	17	—	1
	,, during day time			— 1	11	12	—	1
State of Sky (o lar, 10 ully r od)				— 2·33	4·75	3·76	5·70	1
Barom-ter (not corrected)				Inches 28·44	28·44	28·39	28·52	1

Observations were taken in 1897, at 8 a.m., 2 p.m., and 8 p.m., by the ??. Only a part of September and only 10 days of December are ??. The ??ly ??al curve for the whole period and at the hours named, was 28·46—28·42—28·46. During the period of observation, a rising glass was ??ly ??d by rain.—The l ?? Rl ??e Humidity was generally ??n ?? ?se and the time of the arrival of the ??oisture-laden breeze from the sea, ??th happens at ??ut 8 a.m. For instance, on September ??g, between 8 a.m. and 6.10 a.m., the dry bulb temperature fell with the arrival of the sea breeze from 75·2° F. to 69·7° F. and the Rel. Humid. rose f?om 12½ per cent. to 78 per ??. During fine ??er there is a sudden jump in Relative Humidity immediately before or after sunset. Invalids should ??re ??ke ??ir exercise before breakfast and about the middle of the day, and should get in early in the afternoon.—Observations were taken ??h?ut a proper ??n ??d on a ??th wall. If errors a?e ben ??, the ?? sa-??um temperature is ??ly rather too low, and the humidity r?her too high. It is ??ted that these observations will some day be ???d by others spreading over a more extended period. It ??ld be mentioned that the l ?? tel ??ris some 150 feet hig ?r than the ?? in ??h the ??ns were ??. The situat oh ? occupies enjoys a ??r ??ir and ??re bracing climate ??n the less exposed portions of the village ??.

VILAFLOR (CHASNA), TENERIFFE. (4,335 feet.)

		January	February	March	April	May	August	September	October	November	December	No. of years of observations
Temperature. Shade.	Mean of Mean Daily F°	44·9	47·6	52·5	57·8	56·8	76·7	66·8	58·0	56·2	45·2	1
,, ,,	Minimum ,,	34·3	37·9	40·8	44·7	44·5	68·4	54·7	48·3	41·4	35·8	,,
,, ,,	Range ,,	16·8	16·3	19·4	21·9	20·3	13·6	18·2	17·7	21·5	16·7	,,
Moisture of Atmosph.	Rel. Humidity ,, Sat.100	71·3	62·7	61·9	56·7	63·3	35·7	53·6	70·8	66·6	86·7	
Rain. Amt. of	Mean Monthly Inches	1·75	2·07	1·59	0·17	1·78	0·00	0·03	3·85	0·11	6·61	
,, No. of days on which rain fell ('01' or more) ,,	—	9	5	6	1	4	0	1	8	1	15	
,, ,, during day time ,,	—	5	1	5	0	1	0	0	6	1	8	
S shine	Total amount ... Hours	156	169	164	206	256	138	275	189	224	123	

Absolute Maximum, September, 89, 89° F°. Absolute Minimum, January, 1891, 28° F°

Total rainfall, 11 months, 18·01 inches, and series five entries a day, between 8 a.m. and 11 p.m. from the 20 h August, 1890, to 15th June, 1891, by Mr. P. R. Bedlington, Asoc. M. Inst., C.E., by whom the above figures were duly supplied. In July to September, 1882, a few observations were made by Mr. Herman Honegger, with have also been used.

GENERAL INFORMATION.

SANTA CRUZ, LA PALMA.
(131 feet.)

		October	November	December	January	February	March	April	May	No of years of observations
Tempera ure. Shade Mean of M an Dail)	F°	70·2	65·9	61·9	60·2	60·8	63·6	64·9	68·1	8
,, ,, Minimum		65·7	60·4	56·7	55·7	56·2	58 4	57 8	61·1	,,
,, ,, Range		11·1	11·9	12·9	11·8	14·1	13·7	14·9	14·5	,
Moisture of Atmosph. Rel. Humidit	Sat. 100	71	69	75	74	71	68	66	67	7
Rain, Amt. of Mean Monthly Inches		4·91	5·82	3·17	5·41	2·86	3·10	0·68	0·61	,,
,, No. of days on which rain fell ('·01" or h ore ,,		11	14	14	15	8	11	6	4	,
,, ,, during day time ,		—	—	—	—	—	—	—	—	
State of Sky (0 clear, 10 fully covered)		5·2	5·8	5·5	6 3	4·9	4·3	3·8	4·3	3

Absolute Maximum, 91·4°, August, 1892. Absolute Minimum, 51·8°, January and February, 1891.

Rainfall, for eight months, 26·56 inches, as compared with 24·05 inches in Funchal, Madeira. Observations were taken at 131 feet above the sea at 7 a.m., 2 p.m., and 11 p.m., from 1858-60 and 1889-98. The last were the most complete, and were made by Sr. D. Sebastian C. Arozena, catedrático de Física y Química del Instituto de Santa Cruz de la Palma, by whom the above figures were kindly supplied.

Anybody who will correct or augment the above tables at any future period will greatly oblige the author, who will be glad to receive and incorporate the records of *bonâ fide* observations.

Meteorological observations extending over a very short period are often misleading. However, where these only could be obtained, it appeared the proper course to insert them, in the hope of improving them later on.

The plan adopted, which has been approved of by several medical men as giving all that is absolutely necessary in as short a space as possible, may, perhaps, serve as a basis to those who find a pleasure in working for the furtherance of scientific knowledge, or who wish to be of service to their fellow-creatures.

Barometrical Readings are not given, but they show, allowing for compensation for temperature, an annual average at the sea level of 30 inches (29·99 to 30·02) in Madeira, and 30·09 (30·08 to 30·10) in the Canaries.

The fall is about one inch per thousand feet, and the daily curve, both on the coast and in the hills, is lowest at midday or a little later.

The result of the tables given shows that the mean of the *mean monthly temperature* over the eight months from October to May inclusive is—for Santa Cruz (Teneriffe), 67·5°; Las Palmas, 65·4°; Orotava, 65°; Santa Cruz (La Palma), 64·4°; Funchal, 62·7°; La Laguna, 58·5°; Vilaflor, 52·3°.

The mean of the *mean daily range* for the eight months is as follows:—Las Palmas, 9·3°; Funchal, 9·6°; Santa Cruz (La Palma), 13·1°; Orotava, 13·8°; Santa Cruz (Teneriffe), 14·6°; La Laguna, 16·6°; Vilaflor, 18·8°.

The mean temperature for the eight months given above shows that, at least up to 4,500 feet, the rule of a fall of one degree in temperature per 300 feet of altitude applies fairly well even in the Canaries. That this should be so is rather surprising, as the disturbances due to local topography are a recognised and prominent feature both in the Canaries and in Madeira.

In order to make a comparison with European resorts to which patients are sent for the sake of warmth, one may quote the averages for the five coldest months in Torquay and Mentone, these being 43·4° and 50·8° respectively. The average for the same five months in Funchal is 61·0°; in Las Palmas, 63·5°; in Santa Cruz (Teneriffe), 64·4°; and in Puerto Orotava, 62·6°.

The mean percentages of *relative humidity* for eight months, are:—In Santa Cruz (Teneriffe), 65·6; Funchal, 66·5; Vilaflor, 67·5; Santa Cruz (La Palma), 70·1; Las Palmas, 70·2; Orotava, 75·2; La Laguna, 80·0.

GENERAL INFORMATION (METEOROLOGY). 35

Future observations will confirm or correct the above, the results of the figures having been given as they were obtained. It has, however, already been remarked that the humidity recorded for Funchal is mainly calculated from the figures supplied by the Government Observatory, which are generally believed to be too low.

It must also be remembered that the humidity of the day time and of the night time vary very greatly, and that the average result depends upon the hours at which the records are taken. For instance, in Las Palmas the saturation during day averages 66 per cent. and during the night 74 per cent., giving a mean of 70 per cent., which might be made to show a very much smaller percentage of moisture if the 9 p.m. reading were omitted.

MADEIRA AND THE CANARY ISLANDS.

Climatic Conditions, etc.

However accurate the figures may be, machine-made records can never hope to give more than a comparative idea of a climate. The thermometer, for instance, may stand at 51° Fahrenheit on a dry day in England and the human body feel warm. The same number of degrees on the sea level in Madeira or in the Canaries will sometimes be attended by rain or great humidity; by a warm upper current, heavy evaporation, reeking damp, and general discomfort. So low a temperature, however, cannot well occur except at night or in the evening, when an invalid can light a fire or an oil stove, or go to bed. The higher the general temperature of the resort chosen, the rarer are such spells of cold weather.

It does not follow that a low temperature is invariably accompanied by damp, even at the sea level. Such extreme instances as those cited may not occur six times in the course of a winter, even in positions where they are most to be expected.

When living in the hills cold and damp are less and less associated according to the altitude chosen and to the special nature of the surroundings.

Climate of Madeira in the Winter.

Figures of temperature, humidity and rainfall are given elsewhere, and a comparison has been made between Madeira, Torquay and Mentone. From the statistical tables and from the subsequent remarks the reader can gather as much precise information as is usually required.

Though situated some two hundred and fifty miles to the N. of Teneriffe, the temperature of Madeira is but little lower than that of the Canaries, being maintained nearly constantly at a high degree by the Gulf Stream, which, dividing at the Azores, sweeps southward and envelopes the island in its warm embrace, skirting the Canary Archipelago on its way back towards Central America.

Reference to the general climatic map will make this matter clear at a glance.

Speaking in a general way, Madeira, in spite of its reputation for cloud and damp, is a warm and sunny place even in the winter. As far as most invalids are concerned, the island begins and ends at Funchal, the capital and the site of all the principal hotels.

Note.—The Azores are treated separately, *see* description.

Invalids and others may visit the hills during fine weather, but the winter is not the best season to explore the recesses either of Madeira or of the Canaries. Still a man in ordinary health may go where he likes at any time of year.

In the upper parts of Madeira rain may fall from morning to night, or snow may even lie thick upon the ground. On the South and near the sea, the wettest days have fine intervals. Showery weather, though it may force one to keep within reach of home, is sometimes most charming. The banks of clouds are usually followed by a bright blue sky, through which the sunshine pours as through a burning glass. Before the eye has turned from gazing at the rainbow hanging over the other side of the town, there is fresh pattering on the leaves, a dark shadow sweeps along the street, and every one runs for shelter. As quickly as it comes the storm passes away, the sun breaks through again; the streets dry as though by magic, and the crowd of chattering men and women hurry backwards and forwards as before.

Madeira is certainly somewhat relaxing and tends to keep invalids in a state of repose, which is exactly what most of them want. When rest has allowed them to achieve the necessary repairs, it is easy enough to go somewhere else, if the physician considers it necessary.

There are, however, positions in Funchal itself which differ widely in this particular. The climate near the beach, that at the top of the town, that above the *levada*, and that on the East or West Cliffs can scarcely be compared.

At the top of the railway, barely 1,900 feet above the sea, the air begins to have some of the exhilarating properties of a mountain atmosphere. Yet the vine can be grown and will bear fruit, and the vegetation is a further proof that cold in our sense of the word is unknown.

Between the Monte Church, which is just beyond the terminus of the railway, and the Mole there is a wide choice where a man may find an agreeable and sufficiently bracing climate amidst most lovely surroundings. Above this level the climate is certainly unsuitable for invalids during the winter.

The particular feature of Madeira is the conjunction of a very warm, equable, somewhat moist climate, with an almost absolute freedom from dust. The last point is not due to calm, the air being generally in motion, but to the paving of the streets and to the absence of wheeled vehicles.

Dense, stationary clouds, such as those commonly formed against the mountain slopes of Madeira and of the Canaries, accumulate foul or partially exhausted air immediately beneath them. For this reason it is well to reside in some place outside of their influence, that is to say, near enough to the coast to be beyond the fringe to which their shadow reaches in normal weather. The climate is also much drier low down than it is along the neighbouring slopes.

It must not be supposed that the greatest degree of dryness must necessarily afford the greatest amount of benefit in all cases of illness. On the contrary, a moderate amount of moisture is often far preferable. Where the dryness entails exposure to a great amount of dust, it may be actually harmful.

Quite close to the beach the air is much cooler and more invigorating than it is fifty or a hundred yards inland. Those of an irritable temperament, however, generally find it preferable to live beyond the belt to which the salt spray of the sea is thrown, and to avoid the excess of ozone common near the beach. Experience, or the advice of a medical man, should decide the choice.

The coldest and rainiest months are generally January and February. The winter season proper extends from the middle of October to the end of April or well into May, the earliest date on which invalids should return to Europe.

Generally speaking, those wishing to explore the islands and to visit remote parts should endeavour to give Madeira the most favourable chance, as there is more rainy weather there during the winter than is the case in the Canaries.

The tables of figures are of course the best means of ascertaining which month or fortnight is the most likely one to be fine, though it is only occasionally that any one year is likely to agree with the average of a decade.

The tourist will do well to make such arrangements that, when passing Madeira, he can go ashore if the weather happens to be favourable, or, if otherwise, that he can proceed at once to the Canaries, taking Madeira on his return. There are such lovely walks and excursions in all the islands, that it is worth while to take some little forethought on the subject.

Climate of the Canaries in the Winter.

The difference between Madeira and the Canaries is not very great. Many of the remarks made in describing the former must be held to apply equally well to the latter.

The two do, however, vary in many important particulars.

Firstly, the Canaries are windier. Were it not so the temperature of the two would differ more widely. As it is, the freer movement of the atmosphere causes the North Coast of the Canaries to be only slightly warmer than the South Coast of Madeira.

Invalids and others visiting the Canaries have a very much wider choice of residence, and are able to get about more freely than in Madeira, where the North Coast is too cold and damp during the winter, even for the average tourist.

This freedom of movement, and the more exciting nature of the Canary climate, are too often an inducement to undue exertion. When the weather is at its best, doctors do not always find that their patients make the most progress.

Then again the wind causes more dust. In this particular the islands must not be compared with health resorts on the African main-land, be they in the North or in the South. They are, however, dustier than Madeira, which, as previously said, is peculiarly favoured in this respect.

The difference between Madeira and the Canaries is very well indicated by the date palm, which, when grown in sheltered positions, bears fruit in both places, although it is only in the Canaries that the fruit will ripen.

The writer believes that those to whom absolute rest is necessary will do best by taking Madeira first on the list, Orotava second, and Santa Cruz (Teneriffe), Güimar, Gáldar or Las Palmas third.

Those requiring a warm atmosphere with bracing conditions on the sea level will find them at their best in Grand Canary. In Teneriffe the most bracing coast climate is to be found in the environs of Santa Cruz, and in Madeira on the West Cliff.

Those desiring to live at a considerable altitude during the winter should go to the Monte in Grand Canary, 1,300 feet; La Laguna, Teneriffe, 1,800 feet; Güimar, Teneriffe, 1,200 feet; or Tacoronte, Teneriffe, 1,700 feet.

Gáldar in Grand Canary and Icod in Teneriffe are intermediate resorts, which may perhaps be compared with the West Cliff in Madeira, allowances being made for variations due to latitude, surroundings and aspect. Gáldar is a very dry place, with a large amount of sunshine. Icod, lying on the shoulder of the island, catches a good deal of the Trade Wind, and is inclined to be cloudy.

The Summer Climate.

This subject is more fully discussed in the article headed "Permanent Atmospheric Currents of the Mid-Atlantic," to which the reader is referred.

A few remarks, however, seem to be called for in this place.

Tourists and others will find the summer the best time for expeditions, the climate in the hills being superb. On the coast it is sometimes oppressive but never excessively hot during normal weather. For instance, 88° F. is very high, even in Santa Cruz, Teneriffe, which is notoriously a warm place. In Madeira the residents usually retreat to the upper part of the Valley of Funchal, to which access by means of the railway is now rendered easy. Camacha is also a favourite resort.

In the Canaries, La Laguna and Tacoronte, Teneriffe, and the Monte, Grand Canary, are the most fashionable resorts.

In none of the islands is there any accommodation at the true summer level, that is to say, at an altitude above that at which the clouds are formed. The highest available is Vilaflor in Teneriffe, but the place is not easy of access.

As, however, rain very rarely falls during the summer months, even invalids may camp out in the hills. The writer, in fact, though suffering from chest complaint, has slept in the open by a fire at an altitude of over 7,000 feet. The expense of purchasing proper tents must be balanced against that incurred by hiring a villa or by making a trip to England.

Those who have been living by the sea all the winter require a change of some sort. Both in Madeira and in the Canaries, the hills are usually chosen, but in the latter there is an alternative, namely, to move to some place on the South Coast and to live actually on the beach or close to it. Why this is so, is explained in the article on "Atmospheric Currents."

To remain all the year round in those positions which in the winter are most agreeable and most conducive to the recovery of an invalid, is to run the risk of suffering from anæmia and from an impaired liver. A wider daily range of temperature is necessary. A complete change of surroundings is also beneficial, whilst the attenuated atmosphere and comparative freedom from excess of ozone, from dust and from bacterial life for a few weeks, may have the most important results on the health.

The recuperating effects of the mountain air on a constitution requiring a change is considerable, but a short visit to Europe in the summer is a more certain tonic than six months in a semi-mountainous resort. However, the latter is a most delightful way of spending the time. Fine as the climate of Madeira and of the Canaries may be in the winter, it is infinitely finer and more enjoyable in the summer.

Rainfall.

The statistics show that the amount of rain falling in Madeira is greater than is the case in the Canary Islands. It is also certain that, commencing with Fuerteventura on the E., which is the driest, and where the annual rainfall does not average more than five or six inches, the Canary Islands themselves become gradually damper as the distance from the African desert increases.

At Cape Juby, on the Morocco coast, the rainfall is said to be only about three inches per annum.

The N. and W. sides of Teneriffe and the Islands of Gomera, Hierro, and La Palma are much on a par with one another, the altitude of the mountains being an equivalent in the first to the greater influence of the Gulf Stream in the others.

In estimating the probable amount of rainfall in any particular island where no figures are obtainable, regard must be had to the vegetation found, not only as an indication of what the climate is like and of what the island can produce, but as being in itself at times a direct incentive to the accumulation of vapour.

Taking Madeira as the first on the list, we find an elevation of rather over 6,000 feet, and a group of mountains, many of which are densely wooded. Next in order comes the western portion of the Canary group, La Palma (7,760 feet) being also well provided with much the same forest trees, though the pine is of a different species (*Pinus canariensis*). We then pass to Gomera (4,400 feet) and Hierro (4,990 feet), both with a considerable rainfall. In the former, water is especially abundant and the forest vegetation most luxuriant.

The west and north of Teneriffe have a few forests. In places a great quantity of moisture is derived from the Peak (12,192 feet), which is covered with snow for the greater part of the year. This mountain, with its surroundings, naturally serves as a constant attraction to clouds or vapour, whether caused by a general disturbance, of which the Peak may be the centre, or by the deflection of the trade wind, of which mention is made in the hints given to those thinking of starting on expeditions and in the article on "Atmospheric Currents."

In Grand Canary (6,400 feet) a greater extent of forest land would probably be an advantage and lead to a more equable distribution of moisture. The mountains are, however, sufficiently high to gather clouds around them, though the number of tanks shows that water in the summer is more precious than further west.

In Fuerteventura and Lanzarote there are no forests. Both are very dry. Except in the northern part of the latter island, which is sparsely provided with moisture, both are entirely dependent upon rain water and tanks. The indigenous plants are puny or even microscopic. Large crops of cereals, however, are grown in favourable years. The cochineal cactus and the vine can be cultivated over a very large area. Lanzarote of late years has also become a place from which large quantities of tomatoes are shipped.

Snow line.—It should here be remarked that the supposed line of perpetual snow is—for Madeira about 11,500 feet, and for the Canaries about 12,500, an elevation very nearly attained in the latter instance.

During the winter the lowest limit where snow may fall and lie for a few hours in the very worst weather is approximately as follows :—Madeira, north side, 2,500 feet; south side, 3,000 feet. Teneriffe, north side, 3,000 feet; south side, 3,500 feet. Grand Canary, 4,000 feet. For snow to fall at so low a level is most exceptional, and it is very rare for it to lie even during the night.

Water Supply.

Passing to the water supplies, we find in Madeira a soft water, almost without lime, running in open channels and with roads specially engineered to avoid damage by heavy rainfalls. The ravines are, however, dry on the south side, except in the wet months. Complaints recently made regarding the drinking water of Funchal have led to improvements.

In La Palma the water is very soft, the channels are almost invariably covered in, and the barrancos are generally dry, with the exception of that leading out of the Caldera to Tazacorte. The same remarks apply to Gomera, but here, the island being smaller, barrancos are shorter. In Hierro the rainfall is plentiful, but there are practically no springs, and water during summer can only be obtained from tanks or *algibes* (cisterns).

On the western slopes of Teneriffe the water is harder and there are fewer tanks. On the south side, especially near Santa Cruz, water is preserved at all costs, and pollution between the source and the town is carefully guarded against.

In Grand Canary tanks are to be seen everywhere, the channels are open, and, being very lengthy, are liable to much vegetable pollution.

For this reason the drinking water coming to Las Palmas is caught up at a spring issuing in a ravine above the town, and brought down in covered aqueducts and pipes. The previous remarks about Fuerteventura and Lanzarote are sufficient to indicate the nature of the supply in those islands.

The filter in general use is the dripstone, well known in the West Indies, but probably inefficient in bad cases of pollution.

Intending residents should provide themselves with a really reliable filter, preferably one where the medium can be changed or cleansed.

To reassure intending visitors it may be stated that the source of the water supply is in most instances greatly superior to that of London, and that considerable care is taken that water carried to the drinking fountains should not be contaminated whilst *en route*. It is usual to fetch water from these in barrels. In Orotava there is a particularly good spring known as the Fuente de Martianez.

In all the large towns it is contemplated to gradually replace the aqueducts by iron pipes. In Funchal and in Las Palmas this has practically been accomplished, and the little town of Icod is supplied by an iron pipe several miles long.

Drainage.

The drainage of the towns themselves is in every way deficient, but it must not be forgotten that the porous nature of the soil, which readily absorbs all moisture, and the constant movement of air consequent upon the proximity of mountains and open sea, greatly tend to prevent any epidemic diseases, from which, indeed, all the islands are singularly free. There are bad smells to be found, but nearly all Continental towns are decidedly worse off in this respect. The large hotels have naturally availed themselves of every opportunity to ensure safety in this particular, many having spent very large sums of money upon their sanitary arrangements. The first-class hotels leave nothing to be desired, and compare favourably with those of London.

However energetic the hotels may be, the municipalities themselves require to be reminded that they are far behind the times, and that they show no haste in making the advances legitimately to be expected.

It is to be hoped that the inevitable competition between Madeira and the Canaries will eventually force the authorities in both, and especially in the latter, to recognise the fact that it is their duty to provide proper promenades and amusements for their guests, as well as an adequate and complete system of water supply and drainage. The necessary expenditure could scarcely fail to yield a handsome return by reason of the increased popularity such measures would ensure.

Winds.

Another important item to be considered is the prevalent wind. In all cases this blows from the N.E., but, in Madeira, is less felt than further south. In Madeira it is said to prevail during about 200, and in the Canaries during about 240 days out of the 365. In La Palma there is nearly always a soft healthy breeze. In Gomera and Hierro strong puffs and currents spring up rapidly and, after blowing with considerable force for a time, die away again. On the N.W. side of Teneriffe there is a certain amount of breeze consequent upon the varying temperature of the mountain sides, but the trade wind is only noticeable in exposed positions. Except in unusual disturbances, the movement of air is less than in La Palma, though greater than in Madeira. In Grand Canary there is an almost constant dry wind from the N.E., which is a great advantage to certain classes of invalids. In Fuerteventura and Lanzarote there is the same or even a drier wind, which does not blow quite so hard.

The S.E. side of Teneriffe (Santa Cruz), divided from the Orotava side by a high ridge of mountains, has an entirely different climate. The breezes of Grand Canary are present in a modified form, and the aspect of the hills, facing the sun, causes a high temperature during the daytime. The climate is dry, and this district has many advocates, particularly for those suffering from asthma. Further along the South Coast the breeze is a local one due to the influence of the sun.

The trade wind always blows most strongly and persistently in the summer.

South wind.—Excessive warmth may occur for three or four days during the prevalence of a south wind, when it is often hotter in the hills than on the coast.

Such winds, though distressing to many, are not always disliked, and in any case never last very long, nor do they occur very frequently, being more usual in the summer than in the winter.

The origin of the wind is believed to be some disturbance on the African mainland. The heated air from the desert is supposed to rise to a great height and to descend upon the place to which it is carried, which may happen to be the Canaries or elsewhere. During its prevalence clouds usually disappear, but the atmosphere is hazy and sight obstructed.

The supposed reason for this is excessive dryness, the quantity of moisture in the air being so exceedingly small that the space between the atoms is not filled, and the light is refracted.

At times dust falls, sometimes in large quantities, as was the case on February 16-20, 1898, when for more than two days the view was limited to some 200 yards, and everything was covered with a fine white powder. The area of the storm, measured from north to south, was about 1,800 miles. The dust, when collected in a mass, is of a sandy red colour, and, when magnified to say 75 diameters, is found to consist of small, clean crystals, closely resembling moist sugar, with foreign substances scattered here and there throughout the mass. During the storm of 1898, and during one which occurred in 1862, the air was full of moths, butterflies, and other insects carried over with the sand.

Storms.

These occur at intervals but are not frequent, the worst effect being usually the prevention of vessels from coaling in an open roadstead, such as that of Funchal, or of Santa Cruz, Teneriffe.

Sometimes, however, the weather is very violent. In 1842, and again in 1848, five vessels were driven on shore at Funchal. In

1724, 1803, 1842, and 1856, water swept down from the hills into Funchal and did great damage. On the first occasion a great part of the town of Machico was swept away. On the second, many houses in Funchal were destroyed, and 400 lives are said to have been lost. The beach was also extended for a considerable distance and the anchorage markedly improved.

The worst storm on record in the Canaries raged from Nov. 6th till Nov. 9th, 1826. Though felt throughout the archipelago and very violent in Grand Canary on the 6th and 7th, it was fiercest in Teneriffe, where it arrived on the 7th.

In the Puerto de la Orotava the sea was driven up into the Plaza de la Constitucion, and floods of water came from the mountains, carried away numbers of houses, men and cattle, and created a wide waste now known as the Barranco de las Cabezas. In the Valley of Orotava it is said that 225 houses were destroyed, and that 235 human beings and 804 head of cattle perished. In the neighbouring village of Icod el Alto, 51 lives were lost.

The damage was not confined to that part of the island. La Laguna and Santa Cruz suffered severely, and at Candelaria, on the south, part of the Dominican Monastery was destroyed, the famous image of the Virgen de Candelaria being swept into the sea and lost. Owing to a sudden change in the wind there were also numerous wrecks.

The storm was no doubt accompanied by a waterspout, which burst somewhere in the mountains and discharged itself both in Grand Canary and in Teneriffe.

Thunderstorms occur but rarely, and the lightning is not usually destructive. There are years, however, when they are fairly frequent (1897, for instance), and there have been cases where trees and houses have been struck.

Tidal Waves.—The last recorded instance of a tidal wave of any great magnitude is that of 1755, when the earthquake at Lisbon caused a body of water to break upon Madeira. The wave is said to have been 15 feet in height, to have advanced and receded three times, and to have done great damage to the lower part of Funchal. The writer has not been able to ascertain its volume at the time it reached the Canaries.

Epidemics.

At various times the islands have been attacked by contagious diseases, which, after raging for a time, were stamped out. Though not entirely free from malarial influences, neither Madeira nor the Canaries can be said to suffer from any chronic and ineradicable malady, unless, of course, one includes that universal scourge, tuberculosis.

Yellow fever, small-pox, cholera, and typhoid have been introduced at various dates during the present century, but, in spite of the backward state of sanitary appliances, have not usually led to great mortality. The disease claiming most victims during recent times has been the cholera, but the last attack, which happened in Teneriffe in 1893, was not severe.

In previous centuries bubonic plagues were much more deadly, and probably would be again if once introduced.

Locusts.

These have been brought over from Africa at various times, but never seem to have been able to establish themselves and to breed. Records state that they appeared in the Canaries in 1588, 1607, 1659 (badly), and 1754.

Mineral Springs.

Invalids, especially when suffering from cutaneous diseases, may derive benefit from some of the natural waters found in the islands. A more minute investigation of their value is wanted, but some are known to be efficacious, and several are commonly used by the islanders. Those best known are at Vilaflor and Agua García in Teneriffe; at Sta. Catalina, Agaete and Firgas in Grand Canary; at S. Antonio in Madeira; at Charco Verde in La Palma; and last, but not least, at Sabinosa in Hierro.

When possible, analyses are given in their proper places.

Submarine Springs.

All who have lived by the sea must have speculated as to the cause of the smooth oily streams sometimes to be seen meandering in different directions on the surface of the salt water. Those who have watched them constantly will have noticed that under the same conditions of tide and weather, the same patterns recur, and that, if any such stream be cut by a passing vessel, it regains its old shape in the course of half-an-hour or so.

In Madeira and the Canaries, owing to the great height of the cliffs and to the more languid current of the tides, this phenomenon can be observed at its best.

The reason is that fresh water is forced by hydraulic pressure to emerge from submarine outlets. Being lighter than the salt water, it comes to the top by force of gravity. If the surface be smooth, it does not mix at once with the salt water, but spreads out as oil would do. A mere thread of fresh water may thus cover an appreciable breadth.

As the surface of the sea is always moving and the thread continues to rise in the same place, the consequence is that the oily streak is carried away to the horizon. The set of the tide being affected by the nature of the bottom, the fantastic curves and eddies, ejected from scores of springs and covering the whole sea-scape, are, to a certain extent, and especially when the water is not too deep, a sort of drawing or aquagraph of the rocks beneath.

Fresh water may be seen thus in the very midst of the ocean, hundreds or even thousands of miles from land. The actual depth of such a stream being perhaps a mere fraction of an inch, the smallest amount of wind causes it to disappear.

In Madeira and the Canaries a number of similar streams rising near some particular part of the coast, clearly indicate that water is escaping by subterranean channels.

Permanent Atmospheric Currents of the Mid-Atlantic; their Causes and their Effects.

The climate of Madeira and the Canaries generally has already been dealt with. Meteorological tables are given, and the local peculiarities are described, as accurately as possible, in their proper places.

There are, however, great controlling forces, not yet considered, which are of the highest interest to the student, and of the utmost importance to the resident. In dealing with these the writer will endeavour to show that the islands offer resources for the alleviation or destruction of disease far beyond those usually recognised or as yet rendered available. When all parts of them have been fully developed, physicians may perhaps accept them as sanatoria, where the curative and antiseptic conditions are equal to those found in any other part of the world.

If it can be shown that the results sought in the Upper Valleys of the Alps or on the frozen plains of Colorado are obtainable in Madeira or in the Canaries under more genial conditions, and in places lying within an hour's journey of a healthy, semi-tropical climate, the facility of movement from one to the other would give the Atlantic archipelagos the preference over almost any other part of the globe.

At present a journey from the coast to the summit of any of the islands entails a ride of several hours on horseback or in a hammock along roads bad beyond all description. Until this is altered no comfort can be expected at the upper end.

How the change may be brought about, time will show. For the moment, however, it may be pointed out that a wire-rope railway from the Valley of Orotava to the summit of the Peak of Teneriffe would be scarcely ten miles long; it might be constructed for some £6,000, and would take passengers from the one point to the other in a few minutes. Although perhaps out of place in this article. it may be added that such lines, erected in any of the larger islands, would, if properly directed, immediately secure a heavy goods traffic.

Atmospheric Chart of the Mid-Atlantic.—*See* plate opposite p. 54.

In that part of the Atlantic swept by the "Trades," and especially during the summer when these winds blow with the greatest force, a stratum of cloud will often form about the altitude where the surface drift of the Trade Wind Current encounters the cool, upper atmosphere. Usually broken, the masses of cloud are sometimes continuous, and this most particularly when the wind blows strongly and meets with some centre of obstruction, such as an island. The moisture-laden current is then thrown suddenly upwards, and banks of visible vapour are formed around the mountains, extending at times to a considerable distance on either side. The prevalence of this cloud-layer is of great interest to those staying in Madeira or the Canaries, and the following description should be of service.

In drawing up the accompanying chart, a sectional view of the Island of Teneriffe has been chosen, because the greater height and more regular formation of the mountains, and the acuteness of the angle of ascent from the sea-level to the summit of the Peak, are all most favourable for the purpose of illustration. Were this not so, Madeira or any of the Canary Islands would serve equally well, though it would probably be more difficult to determine the limits of the atmospheric currents in the former than in the latter, as the trade wind, though prevalent in both archipelagos, blows with more force and constancy in the latitude of the Canaries.

Though the cloud-layers and currents depicted are those ordinarily to be observed during the greater part of the summer, they are by no means peculiar to that part of the year, the same conditions being frequently reproduced during a spell of fine weather in the winter. The trade wind, however, during the latter season blows more softly and less continuously, and there are periods when the sky is completely overcast at varying altitudes for days together, or when, on the contrary, the entire heaven is free from cloud.

Even in the summer similar interruptions occur, but such periods are abnormal, and seldom last for any length of time.

Clear weather during the summer may be due to more than one cause. For instance, the view is rarely impeded whilst the "Levante," or hot wind, is blowing from the African deserts, though the atmosphere at the time is always hazy, for the reason given under the heading "South Wind." At other times the trade wind cloud condenses at a greater altitude than usual, and the vapour driven over the lower parts of the islands, such as that to the north-east of La Laguna in Teneriffe (about 3,000 feet), does not, as is usually the case, become visible. A record of the connection between the readings of the barometer in the hills, and this phenomenon, which is evidently due to a change in the altitude of the lower stratum of the upper atmosphere, would be most interesting.

Occasionally the Peak is visible from the sea, but the sky above it is covered by a grey mass of vapour suspended at an immense altitude, perhaps at a distance of from 30,000 to 40,000 feet from the water. Such clouds do not commonly assume the form of cirrus, and appear to be due to an excess of electricity in the atmosphere. They are often followed by thunder and lightning, the storm being probably unaccompanied by rain, and wearing itself out without approaching much nearer to the earth.

Next to the Gulf Stream, which helps to regulate the temperature of this part of the world, the most important factor from a climatic point of view is the trade wind, which blows during the greater part of the year from the north-east.

It is merely an under-current, and, where there is no land to influence it, is probably confined between the surface of the ocean and an altitude of from 800 to 1,500 feet, its force increasing towards mid-day and moderating as night draws on.

The nearer the trades come to their destination, which is a little to the north of the Equator, the more steadily they blow, continuing to gather moisture from the ocean, whose surface catches and retains most of the dust or impurities the wind may carry with it.

On encountering the "doldrums" or "equatorial calms," the current of air is forced upward in a great curve, which gradually bends over to the north, in which direction it continues to move until it again sinks to the sea-level, somewhere about latitude 37° north, when it curves downwards to the south, and becomes once more an integral part of the trade wind, the circle of motion being thus complete.

The writer has done his best to make it perfectly clear that the trade wind is a body of air constantly revolving on a vertical plane. On the sea-level and for a few hundred feet above it, it blows strongly towards the Equator, reappearing at a greater altitude as a vast mass, many thousands of feet in depth, flowing gently onward in a reversed direction, with a tendency to descend as it progresses.

The transformation of the N.E. trade wind into the "great southerly return current" or "counter trade," is attended by a phenomenon of considerable importance to an invalid visiting the islands.

On rising from the sea-level, the air at once commences to suffer a loss of temperature, and is compelled, by reason of a well-known law, to part with most of its moisture, which falls in the shape of tropical rain, thoroughly cleansing the air from which it comes and that through which it passes. The upper return current, therefore, commences its return journey from the Equator in a state of singular purity.

Close to the line, the height to which it is carried must be immense, and the decrease in temperature must be proportionate. On its way back it gradually falls and regains some of its warmth, descending upon the summits of Madeira or of the Canaries in a very dry state, that is to say, with a capacity for taking up moisture.

To enjoy this aridity to the full, it is necessary to live above the clouds, or otherwise in places where there is no accommodation at present, and where no proper meteorological statistics have been made.

Immediately below the clouds, at Vilaflor, a village on the south side of Teneriffe, lying at a height of 4,335 feet above the sea, records show the low relative humidity of 35·7 per cent. for the month of August, a figure which is without doubt considerably reduced a thousand feet or so higher up.

What the actual degree of humidity on the Peak of Teneriffe or on the Cumbres of Grand Canary may be, the writer does not know, but that of Vilaflor, in August, compares very favourably with that of Aliwal North, in Cape Colony, during mid-winter (June), which is 31 per cent., the driest record for a warm climate with which the writer is acquainted. It is probable that the average summer humidity in the highlands of Grand Canary, Teneriffe, or even Madeira, would compare favourably with those of a South African winter. In any case, by living at a great elevation, the invalid is removing himself to an atmosphere where damp is present in very minute quantities.

Other advantages of height and of the downward flow mentioned, are that bacterial life is decreased, as in the Alps during the winter, and is probably present in very minute quantities, the air before rising having been filtered by a long journey over the sea, and finally washed by the tropical rains. The writer can give no figures on this subject, but Piazzi Smyth, who resided on and near the Peak of Teneriffe during July and August (1856), declared that there was a complete absence of dust above the level of 9,000 feet.

The reader must be careful not to confuse the southerly return current with the south or hot desert wind already alluded to. The latter is usually known in the Canaries by the name of the "Viento del Sur," or "Levante," and is an abnormal current of short duration, rarely blowing for more than three days at a stretch.

By turning to the chart it will be seen that the "trades," on encountering the north coast of the island, are forced, as by a wedge, to a considerable altitude. In rising, they gradually die away. the resistance of the upper atmosphere compelling them to find an outlet over or round the shoulders of the island.

Reference should here be made to the sectional outline of Teneriffe from east to west, given under the Atmospheric Chart.

In the meantime, that portion of the wind which directly meets the land and climbs the side of the mountain range is robbed of its vapour in the same way as the whole trade wind is robbed later on when it meets with the doldrums. The trade wind clouds and their position as regards the mountain slopes are clearly shown on the chart, and attention is called to the gradual diminution in their altitude towards the north, that is to say, before they are influenced by the inclination of the land.

It will also be noticed that the lower part of the cloud is composed of rounded cumuli, which, under the circumstances, might be expected to shed an almost continuous series of showers.

The capacity of absorption of the upper current, however, to which the superficial flatness is due, and that of the mountain side itself, with the foliage which covers it, supply the necessary outlets. The latter attracts the grosser particles of vapour, and together they allow the cloud to relieve itself without condensing into rain, falling rain from such clouds during the summer being a sign that the weather is not normal.

The trade wind cloud usually makes its appearance at about nine o'clock in the morning and fades away about sunset, at which time the sea-breeze also dies away. The latter is presently replaced by a gentle land-breeze, which itself disappears a little later, and is followed by a calm night.

The effect of the trade wind cloud is to hinder radiation from below, and to shade all that it covers from the sun. The inhabitants prefer to live beneath it; but this choice may be due to custom, as those parts under its influence are naturally the most fertile and best watered. The diminution in heat due to its shadow is more imaginary than real, for it is a well-known fact that any obstruction to free radiation, even though it be but a snow-covered mountain obtruding into the field of view, will at once cause a rise in the thermometer. The cloud also prevents the egress of the bad gases generated during the day, and the air, more especially immediately below it, generally lacks freshness.

Above it, on the other hand, though the heat in the sun is greater, that registered in the shade is far less, and every breath exhilarates. The atmosphere is so dry that perspiration rarely soils the clothes, and the glorious view, which extends to the furthest limit of the horizon, is most cheering and in itself beneficial to health. Here the invalid may live for months under a rainless blue sky and in a genial climate, wandering amongst gorgeous forests and magnificent precipices; below him a vast sea of billowy cloud, out of which the summits of the other islands rise, beckoning him to new explorations.

The fall of temperature at night is enough to make a fire agreeable and to act as a mild tonic, very necessary to those living for any length of time in the more equable climate of the sea-coast.

Practically the only shelter to be obtained at these levels is that of a cave or of a canvas tent; but, as the total cost of the latter is considerably less than the rent of a furnished villa in the hills, and as it will serve again or can be sold, a good tent or two cannot be regarded as an extravagance.

The flat-topped cloud to the south of the island is noticeably higher than those resembling it on the north, with which it has no connection whatever.
After passing round the shoulders of the island, the divided trade wind is unable to effect a junction until it has travelled several miles further towards the Equator. It follows that behind or to the south of the land, there is a space which is neither controlled by the trade wind nor by the upper return current.
The winds circulating inside this sheltered triangle are necessarily regulated by the local action of the sun.
As might be expected, the result is a land-breeze in the morning and the evening, and a sea-breeze during the middle of the day. From nine in the forenoon until sunset, the slopes directly opposed to the sun heat the air resting upon them, and cause it to flow upwards, the vacuum being re-filled by atmosphere drawn from out to sea. This blows strongly or freshly on the beach, gathers warmth as it rises, and is eventually forced to curve over by the pressure of the upper atmosphere, after which it travels out to sea again, losing heat on its progress, and finally returns to the shore re-converted into a cool sea-breeze. The circular movement here described is an exact miniature repetition of that adopted by the trade wind itself on its travels between the Temperate Zone and the Equator.
The cloud to the south of the island is therefore composed of the moisture gathered up within a short distance of the southern coast, or on the sun-baked slopes of that coast itself, and is consequently small in extent, often does not appear at all, and at other times is found as a thin film at the head of the broadest valleys, but is invisible elsewhere. Unlike the trade wind cloud on the north side, it is denser in the winter, when the ground is moist, than in the summer, when it is parched and dry.
The coolest resorts on the southern side must evidently be on the beach itself or above the eddy. Residents from half-way up the slope visit the beach during the hot season for the sake of the bathing and of the fresh air.

Whether on the south side or on the north, it is, however, above the clouds that the invalid, whose strength allows of his doing so, should spend the summer months; seeking the health-giving shade of the pine forest during the heat of the day, and sleeping under canvas at night. He is then breathing an ideal atmosphere, and, if he can obtain a proper food supply, is living a delightful life under most favourable conditions: conditions which may some day cause Madeira and the Canaries to be looked upon as one of the pleasantest resorts for the summer tourist, where he will find many of the advantages of the Alps, combined with the certainty of perpetual fine weather.

It is impossible to give any precise meteorological statistics for the mountains, and a great deal of what takes place can only be indicated. Neither have any exact experiments been made in these latitudes of the effects of a great altitude upon the blood and upon the various organs, though a properly conducted series of observations would be of immense service to the medical profession.

It is, however, obvious that the returning trade-wind, or rather upper-current, must be of a highly antiseptic nature, and that the treatment of disease must be aided by the possibility of letting a patient pass the day in a banana-garden, and the night in the Arctic regions, for both these climates, or any modifications of them, can be found in the few miles lying between the Port of Orotava and the Peak. In the other islands the extreme on the cold side is not so great; but so very drastic a measure as the construction of a sanatorium, 12,000 feet above the sea, need not enter into one's ordinary calculations. Sick people generally would probably be satisfied with half this height, which can be attained both in Madeira and in Grand Canary, and which, as far as the summer clouds are concerned, is a full thousand feet more than is absolutely necessary.

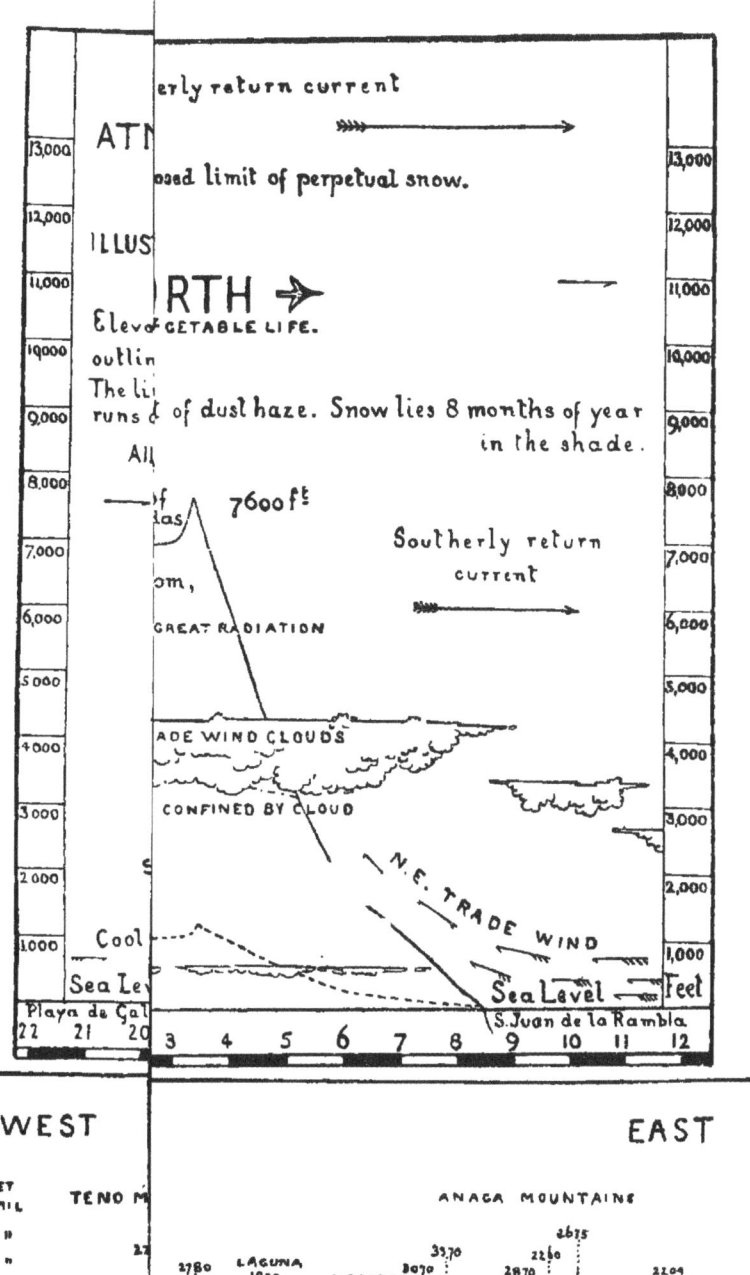

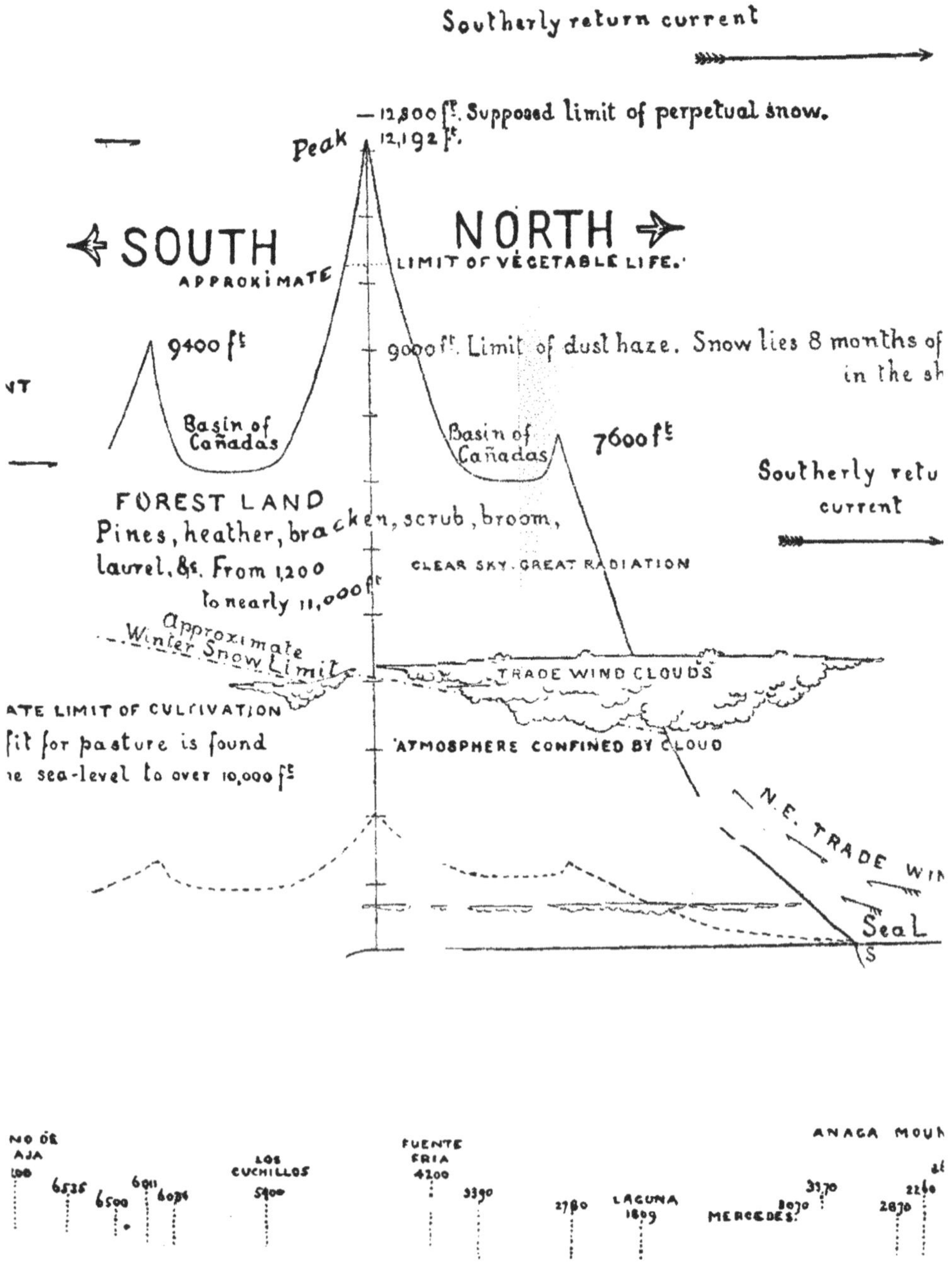

CHAPTER FOR INVALIDS.

INVALIDS in an advanced stage of illness are cautioned against visiting the islands alone, or are advised to place themselves under close medical supervision in some properly organised sanatorium such as that at Güimar, Teneriffe. So many distressing instances have occurred of deaths taking place with no one to help or understand the dying man, that the presence of a friend or nurse cannot be too much insisted on.

That, even amidst the somewhat prejudicial surroundings of a gay hotel, remarkable instances of prolongation of life and even of absolute recovery constantly occur cannot be disputed. For the latter a lengthened residence may be necessary, or it may be found advisable, after the health has been partially restored, to complete the cure by changing the mild climate of the islands for one that is more invigorating and antiseptic.

Madeira and the Canaries are an agreeable home for those suffering from bad health in a less temperate zone. To the sick man, hoping again to become robust, they are stepping stones on the way to health, where he may tarry and recuperate himself for a time before visiting other countries where the conditions are not so well adapted to an invalid.

It is urged that too much attention should not be paid to any one personal experience, which may have been prejudicially affected by individual carelessness or misfortune. Invalids are too apt to imagine that the mere change of climate permits them to take liberties with their strength and stomach such as they would never dream of in Europe. Elated and excited by the charm of a nearly constant sunshine and of a temperature which permits them to be out at almost any hour in the day, they fail to see the necessity of dieting and watching themselves carefully, presume on the increase of vigour common after a sea voyage, and, acting in an imprudent manner, frequently so accelerate the ravages of the disease from which they suffer, that they never recover, being subsequently cited as examples of the insalubrity or inefficiency of the climate. To these must be added those who, commencing cautiously, destroy all the good effects of months of care by some sudden freak of madness. Also those who are either sent away too late, or who, through want of knowledge on the part of their medical advisers, have been ordered off to a place entirely unsuited to them. It must be obvious that all degrees of climate being obtainable, all the islands and all elevations cannot be equally well adapted to all classes of disease, and that a careful study of the case by the consulting physician must be accompanied by an equally careful study of the nature of the district to which he is sending his patient.

This variety of choice is a great point in favour of the islands as a health resort, and one which is more fully dealt with in the chapter about the prevalent atmospheric currents.

Rapidly growing in popularity, they are attracting the attention of physicians of all nations. In addition to the Portuguese or Spanish doctors, there are a number of medical men from other countries, and patients have the advantage, when desired, of detailing their symptoms in their mother tongue. It is from the doctors to be found in the islands that the most exact information regarding the various necessary conditions are to be obtained. A letter from the physician who has been treating the case would enable one of these to send the patient to the most favourable locality, and afterwards, should the conditions require to be changed, to despatch him elsewhere to find in a situation, probably only a few miles away, a complete alteration in the climatic conditions, thereby administering a tonic or a sedative as may be required.

The author takes this opportunity of saying that medical men do not always insist as they might on the necessity of these occasional changes, and are too apt to allow listless patients to have their own way, and to lounge about in their accustomed surroundings when they ought to be elsewhere.

Many visitors come to the islands expecting nothing else but sunshine and fine weather, and forget that only a very small part of the world, and that by no means the most favoured, is absolutely rainless. Again, one season is naturally worse than another. An average of years must be taken into account, as well as the probability that many in an advanced stage of illness will live longer in these islands than anywhere else, and, if they can manage to occupy their minds, will probably enjoy life more.

The even temperature which can be enjoyed all the year round by moving such short distances and the extremely favourable conditions under which a variety of maladies can be specially treated, are matters worthy of the attention of medical men. Sufferers, for instance, who would have to wait until the summer months in other latitudes, may be taken in hand at once in a climate where the warmth and total absence of miasma guarantee, if a little foresight is used, a practical immunity from chills and damp. Where a doctor would hesitate to put a patient on "Banting" diet further north, he need have no fear so far south. Gout, rheumatism, diseases of the kidneys, etc., are more easily attacked, and a great advantage is gained by the constant supply of green vegetables, tomatoes, fresh fruit, etc. The Trauben Kur (grape cure), so much practised in Germany, can be commenced earlier and spread over a longer period. Sea bathing, when proper arrangements have been made, can be indulged in all the year round.

A contributor to the *Lancet* (January 27th, 1894) states that Madeira is suitable for some forms of bronchitis and laryngitis; for irritable nervous affections, diseases of the kidneys, scrofula, and anæmia, and for those convalescent and requiring rest after dangerous illnesses, malarial fever, etc. For cases of phthisis in its early stages, when attended by hæmoptysis, it is said to be extremely good, but in phthisis generally it is held to be rather palliative than curative. This agrees practically with the general opinion of those consulted by the writer, and bears out his remark that the islands should be used as a stepping-stone by consumptive patients on their way to a more vigorous atmosphere. In all probability there is no warm country in the world where the irritating influence of wind and dust is so completely absent as in Madeira.

In the Canaries bronchitis sometimes does well, but laryngitis or a tendency to severe hæmorrhage would generally do better in Madeira. Rheumatism, neuralgia, Bright's disease, gout, scrofula, venereal and other diseases find the climate most suitable, and are greatly helped by the constant supply of fresh fruit and vegetables common to all the islands.

The first and second stages of consumption often show material improvement. As in Madeira, the free and open-air life, which can be indulged in all the year round, sometimes almost leads to a cure, and generally allows the patient to gain sufficient strength to face the more trying period of a South African winter.

If strength permits, excursions should frequently be made to the hills or to the mountains, the change of air, even if only for a few hours, being of great advantage. All the hotels will provide luncheon in a basket. The ascent to the mountains from the south in all the islands is more gradual than is the case on the north.

Cases of hæmorrhage will do well to keep quiet when the barometer is exceptionally low.

Cases of *malarial fever* which do not improve in the Canaries will do well to try Madeira, a better half-way station for many constitutions enfeebled by residence in Africa.

This article might be indefinitely prolonged and extracts from one medical man after another given. Let it suffice, therefore, to quote a few words of the late Dr. Andrew Combe, who, in writing to a friend, says, "If I must forego the pleasures of home, it is better to resort at once to the *most* advantageous climate than to adopt the half-measure of going to Italy, Jersey or the south of England."

Doctors will be found practising in Madeira, Teneriffe and Grand Canary, who speak English, French and German.

Climatic Diarrhœa.—In all the islands, and indeed in all southern countries, foreigners, especially English people, occasionally suffer from diarrhœa, shortly after their arrival. The complaint is sometimes difficult to get rid of and may last for weeks, but can be avoided by care. Chlorodyne, bismuth and laudanum are among the best remedies, or a retreat to the mountains will generally effect a cure. All comers must be most cautious as regards fruit, native wine, excessive fatigue, or even undue exercise. Meat should only be eaten twice a day. These attacks of diarrhœa are due to the presence of unsympathetic matter in the stomach, and the cure should generally be commenced by a dose or two of castor oil, taken in the early stages.

Sea Sickness.

Now a few lines regarding sea-sickness. Let the medical adviser give an efficient aperient two or three days before the patient starts and another on arrival on board the steamer, and let the patient aid this treatment by eating sparingly of simple food for his last few days on shore.

When attacked by vomiting the greatest comfort is to be found in lying down. A belt drawn tightly round the stomach is at times a relief. As a remedy a solution containing bicarbonate of soda, chloroform, or bromide of potash and sal volatile is of great assistance. Efforts should be made to keep the digestive organs at work. For this purpose a few apples and dry biscuits are in every way most convenient. It is rarely that sickness gives much trouble after the second day.

A Sketch of the most prominent Geological Features of Madeira and of the Canary Islands,

WITH HINTS AS TO THEIR EFFECTS UPON TOPOGRAPHY, SCENERY, CLIMATE, VEGETATION AND HISTORY.

THE following article is not intended as a scientific discussion of geological problems, for which the student will turn to other works. Visitors generally are, however, interested in the formation of the country, whether they be tourists or invalids, and physicians are specially concerned with its effects upon climate, whether local and otherwise. The usual results of elevation are very much affected in Madeira and the Canaries by the immediate surroundings, a matter that does not always receive the recognition to which it is entitled, and regarding which it is felt that a few remarks will be useful.

The formation of the islands has again an important bearing upon their history, both ancient and modern, and must be considered when treating of ancient legends, of race problems, or of the methods of life adopted by the residents of to-day.

The investigations of Alexander von Humboldt, Leopold von Buch, James Dwight Dana, Sir Charles Lyell, Piazzi Smyth, Dr. G. Hartung, Karl von Fritsch, W. Reiss, Dr. A. Rothpletz, and others, though not agreeable in all their particulars, have provided a mass of literature upon the geological phenomena, from which the student may gather ample material to aid him in further researches. As regards Madeira the data have been most ably collected and edited by Mr. James Yate Johnston, in his "Handbook for Madeira." The intimate acquaintance of the author with the island in question has enabled him to add many valuable notes resulting from his personal observations.

More than thirty years ago the researches of Sir Charles Lyell showed the plutonic and volcanic formation of Madeira and of the Canaries to be more closely associated with the landscape of to-day than is the case in countries where denudation or submersion have played a more important part in the building up of the visible contour of the land.

The geological problems presented by the archipelagos of the Eastern Atlantic have much in common, and the groups of islands from the Azores on the north to the Bouvet Islands on the south resemble one another in that they are isolated mountains of igneous origin, in some of which the volcanic forces are still active, and in all of which there are indisputable evidences of recent energy.

NOTE.—The Azores are treated separately. *See* description.

The depth of the ocean immediately surrounding them is usually very great, and the density of the water, by which they are partially supported, has allowed the superstructure to rest upon a base so small, that, were the water drained away and the sides exposed to view, the islets would, in some instances, appear as slender cones, towering many thousands of feet into the air. Even the channels separating the component parts of the archipelagos are not always raised much above the general level of the ocean bed, though soundings have traced a number of submarine elevations lying above what is doubtless one of the principal fissures traversing the crust of the globe.

The greatest depth of the ocean between Madeira and the Canaries is 2,400 fathoms (13,200 feet). Long before the bottom is reached the pressure must be so enormous and the power of gravitation so reduced, that only very closely grained matter could sink to the bottom. Under such circumstances even sheets of basalt, of which the density as compared with water is about 2·6, might protrude far beyond the underlying stratum, immense caverns being created, in whose recesses living forms may exist of which we have no cognisance. It was possibly from such a ledge as this that the lead fell when the route of the cable from Cadiz to Teneriffe was being surveyed, and the sounding line suddenly ran out for 1,400 feet without a stoppage.

At a short distance below the surface of the sea the action of the waves ceases; temperature is maintained at a constant level (about 36° Faht.), and the "weathering" of the rock, which, under exposure to the atmosphere is constant and often very rapid, must be limited to tidal influences, and to the corroding action of marine growths or to that of matter held in solution by the ocean itself.

In our study of the nature of the submarine formation of mountains, we should, paradoxical as it may appear, turn to the moon.

On the side of the satellite turned towards us, the force of gravity, though greater than at the bottom of the Atlantic, is only one-sixth of that to be found on the surface of the earth. The absence of atmosphere and of water in the moon and of active disintegrating influences at the bed of a terrestrial ocean, may again be compared, for in both cases the surface of igneous rock would remain unchanged for an indefinite length of time. It is, therefore, probable that volcanoes extruded from the bottom of the sea do not stand upon wide-spread declivities of talus, but consist of acute peaks sometimes encircled by very precipitous walls, as is the case with the lunar group of Catharina, Cyrillus and Theophilus. The fact that volcanic islands which have appeared above the surface within historic times, as for instance in the Azores, have usually disappeared shortly after the cessation of

GEOLOGICAL FEATURES. 61

activity, would seem to indicate the absence of a long submarine fore-shore, and of any form of breakwater capable of hindering surface erosion.

Raised beaches, etc.—Traces of former coast lines and marine deposits are found in various parts of the islands, often far removed from the present level of the sea. The relative position of the land and of the water may have altered many times in both directions, and it is probable that, were the islands again to be raised, evidences of atmospheric weathering would be disclosed in places now lying far below the surface.

During the Helvetian stage of the Upper Miocene Epoch, limestone was deposited near São Vicente in Madeira, at a point now situated some 1,300 feet above the sea. On the islet of Baixo, to the S.W. of Porto Santo, an ancient coral reef, formed about the same time, has been lifted some 200 feet, and in Porto Santo itself a raised beach, about 40 feet above the sea, contains specimens of marine shells belonging to species now living.

In Teneriffe the evidences of wave action are a matter of deduction rather than of proof. It is believed that some of the inland cliffs of the valley of Orotava were formed by the sea, and Piazzi Smyth stated that part of the S.W. wall of the Cañadas, lying at a height of some 7,000 feet above the sea, showed signs of having been subjected to marine influences, an assertion of which some confirmation is desirable.

Grand Canary, whose geological conditions merit a closer study than has yet been accorded to them, has most undoubtedly been, at least, partially, subjected to submersion, perhaps more than once. Even the shallow cup-like formation of the extreme summit may be owing to other forces beyond those of mere denudation.

Limestone is quarried at Jinamar, on the east coast, some 260 feet above the sea, whilst to the S.W. of the island there are instances of cinder-heaps (fumaroles), planed down to an absolute level with the detritus by their side, in places where the existing conditions do not indicate their disappearance to be due to water running down from the hills.

There are also extensive deposits of limestone in Fuerteventura, though these are situated at no great height above the sea and call for no especial remark, beyond directing the reader's attention to the fact that both in Madeira and in the Canaries the lime used for building is taken from the eastern part of the archipelagos, and that the districts in which it is found are in each instance partially covered by drifted sand. Some of the calcareous deposits are said to be due to the decomposition of the basaltic rocks.

Blown sand and the line of cleavage.—A minute examination of the ocean bed and the set of the currents points to a connection between the presence of sand in the Eastern islands and the line of cleavage traversing the Eastern Atlantic from north to south, the position of which is indicated by the Azores, the Madeiras, the Salvages, the Canaries, the Cape de Verdes, St. Helena, etc. The series of vents marking this line of cleavage finds its nearest and best parallel in the long chain of volcanoes forming the backbone of the two Americas, a fact to which reference will subsequently be made when discussing the question of the sunken continent of Atlantis.

With one or two exceptions, the sand is cast up by the sea. The set of the tides and the direction of the trade wind are influenced in an increasing ratio by the proximity of the African coast; the course of the Gulf Stream being deflected by the same cause, and by irregularities in the bed of the ocean which further tend to turn it aside and in places to convert it into eddies of considerable magnitude.*

Porto Santo in the Madeiras, where a great part of the surface is covered by sand, lies about 380 miles west of the nearest point on the African coast. The channel separating Fuerteventura in the Canaries from the mainland is barely sixty miles in width. African sand is also cast up in Grand Canary in two places, both some 130 miles distant from Africa.

In Fuerteventura and Lanzarote, which lie close together, it is a matter of common occurrence for sand to form on the east coast in the shape of a demi-line, and to march straight across the island, moving probably in almost exactly the same manner as the sand-dunes to be found in certain parts of the desert of Sahara. The bed of calcareous sand in which the fossil remains are found at the north-western extremity of Madeira, has its counterpart in the Canaries and elsewhere. There is reason to suppose that in the case of Madeira the deposit was brought by the wind from a beach on the north coast which has now disappeared.

The presence of African sand is a matter of meteorological importance, for it is fair to assume that those parts in which it is most abundant must be affected by the agencies by which it is carried. The primary motive power is no doubt the sea itself. Should the set of the tide, and of the wind be allied, however, as is usually the case with oceanic currents, the air beating upon the land must give the climate a more continental character than in places where the atmosphere is renewed by a breeze subject to no other influence than that of an artificially warmed sea-surface such as that of the Gulf Stream.

Be this as it may, it is a fact that the islands of the Canary group nearest to the African coast are exceedingly dry; that moisture increases towards the west, and that the humidity in Madeira is greater than in any of the Canaries. Porto Santo is too distant from the mainland to be much affected by the causes con-

---

* NOTE,—The temperature of the surface water in the full flow of the Gulf Stream off Madeira, is about 8° higher than off. Mogador on the Moorish coast.

trolling the climate of Lanzarote and of Fuerteventura. The smaller rainfall on that island and on the eastern part of Madeira must be attributed to the lesser altitude of the mountains, above which the rain-clouds might often pass without meeting a surface on which to condense themselves.

Action of the waves.—It has been pointed out that the channels separating the various islands are usually of great depth; that the foreshores are narrow, and the sub-oceanic decline exceedingly steep.

We find, therefore, that the waves are driven on to the land with great force, and that on the north and north-west, where the coast is exposed to the full fury of the Atlantic, the cliffs are usually most precipitous, and the breakers, even in calm weather, roll in with a power and majesty of which the little wavelets of the North Sea are but a poor imitation.

The constant agitation of the water creates a fine cloud of spray, which is, of course, impelled against the coast when the breeze moves in that direction, and plays an important part in the climatic conditions of the districts in which it is common. The wind usually sets towards the shore during the hottest part of the day. The effect is so marked that observations of the humidity of the atmosphere taken within 100 to 150 feet of the sea level on the north side of any of the islands, are useless unless the incrustation of sea salt be washed from the wet-bulb every twenty-four hours. The same remark applies, though in a lesser degree, to the south coast. On the north a certain quantity of salt is probably carried to the same height as that to which the trade wind is driven. Telegraph wires crossing Teneriffe, *viâ* La Laguna, are corroded by salt at an altitude of over 2,000 feet.

The Gulf Stream.—The depth of the channels has the effect of allowing the Gulf Stream to flow very freely around and amidst the islands, which seem to afford little interruption to its passage. It progresses to the west at the rate of from 12 to 15 miles a day, but its power is mitigated in the Eastern Canaries by the neighbourhood of the African coast and by the eddies mentioned when referring to the sand drifts.

The general direction of the Gulf Stream and of the trade wind are the same. Both bear down upon the islands from the N.N.E. The moisture which the former yields to the latter has been and is still an important factor in the shaping of the hills and valleys, and is the main cause of the dissimilarity of the northern and of the southern slopes. As a result the angle of subaërial ascent on the north is usually the steeper; whilst the submarine coast line, to a depth of 50 fathoms or more, advances further from the land and is less irregular.

Formation of the Land.—The sections of strata exposed by the inroads of the sea or along the sides of the ravines almost invariably disclose a succession of beds of igneous rock, divided by layers of tuff or of volcanic detritus, sometimes metamorphosed by heat throughout their entire thickness. In the neighbourhood of a centre of volcanic energy these are frequently interlaced by numerous dykes, crossing and intersecting one another in every direction.

The soil of which the surface is composed is generally shallow, but, where the adjacent and most recent volcanoes are of friable material, decomposition has often led to deposits of considerable thickness, varying from a few feet to many yards. In such cases the earth nearest to the underlying stratum is generally much compressed, and, though not impervious to water, can only be broken by blows from a sharp, heavy pick.

In this, and in every instance where the rock is sufficiently pulverised to allow of the growth of plants, the land proves most fertile, and wherever there is enough moisture the vegetation is luxuriant.

Fossils.—Fossils are by no means frequent, but are found both in Madeira and the Canaries, both animal and vegetable forms having been preserved.

In an excavation made in Santa Cruz, Teneriffe, the strata were as follows :—Basaltic lava, 30 feet ; conglomerate, 6 feet ; volcanic tuff, 6 feet. Fossils of the common snail (*caracol de viña*), still found on the vine and on the prickly pear, were found in the conglomerate below the basalt.

Minerals.—Amongst minerals, specular iron, iron pyrites, olivine, augite and a few others occur both in Madeira and the Canaries. In the latter (Peak of Teneriffe) there are deposits of sulphur, and in La Palma globules of copper have been found. Obsidian is common in many parts of the archipelago, and in almost all the islands there are mineral springs, of which the analysis has been given wherever possible. (See *Index.*)

Denudation.—It has been previously stated that the effects of denudation are less apparent than is the case in most parts of the British Islands or of the Continent.

The weathering of the rock has, however, been a material factor in the modelling of the contours, and there are many instances where volcanic outflows have been precipitated into the channels of old water-courses, ravines having again been formed through the obstacles thus created, which in their turn have been filled up by the results of subsequent eruptions, through which the water has once more worn or is now wearing a passage.

The geological conditions are thus sufficiently complicated, but the steep incline of the mountains and the proximity of the sea to the centres where water is collected, have prevented the accumulation of alluvial deposits on that vast scale common in countries of greater extent.

The vegetable or animal refuse, by reason of its lesser weight, is usually the first to be carried into the sea, and is rarely to be found in any considerable quantity. The preservation of soil suitable for plant life is commonly due to local irregularities, which have hindered the rapid flow of the water, or to artificial obstructions raised for the purpose of creating arable land. The cultivated portions of the island are consequently lined with terraces, where the lava has often been removed to expose the former surface, or where soil has been carried and placed between restraining walls built of the same material.

Elevation of the land.—In those islands where the investigations have been most thorough, it has been shown that the rocks belong to distinct geological epochs, and that some of the islands at least were lifted to a considerable height above their former level, possibly after a period of prolonged if partial quiescence.

The position of the limestone bed at São Vicente shows Madeira to have been raised to the extent of at least 1,300 or 1,400 feet. In Teneriffe marks of wave action at a high level are based upon less positive evidence, but the limestone beds of Grand Canary and Fuerteventura prove that these islands have been elevated above their former position. In Porto Santo there are evidences of elevation at three distinct epochs, and it may be presumed that a series of seismic disturbances has agitated the bed of the ocean at irregular intervals.

Since the last upheaval or series of upheavals there is no evidence of further subsidence, if one excepts cases where portions of an island may have faulted away from the rest, as, for instance, in the Valley of Orotava.

The exposure of the islands may, of course, be due to shrinkage elsewhere and to the removal of the water to a lower level, but cannot well have been caused by any ordinary exhibition of force similar to that required for the mere raising of a volcano or for the ejection of a stream of lava.

If the rise of all the islands was simultaneous the movement now seems to have ceased, or if the land is still being lifted the motion must be exceedingly slow.

Volcanic activity.—The alteration in the levels was followed by a lengthened period of volcanic activity, during which the old islands were partially covered by the rocks thrown out, and their altitude thereby further increased.

Sir Charles Lyell came to the conclusion that Madeira was originally dome-shaped, the sides sloping at an angle of from 3° to 8° towards a flattened summit with an elevation of from 4,000 to 5,000 feet. Here, as elsewhere, denudation has already been actively at work, and had eaten deeply into the rock.

He thought that there were signs of two parallel systems of volcanoes, running from east to west, and that the southern chain was overwhelmed by the other to the depth of 2,000 feet or more.

The space between the two was filled up, and part of it is now an elevated marshy tract known as the Paul da Serra. A smaller elevated plain on the east is known as S. Antonio da Serra.

This building up of the island did not continue uninterruptedly, but was retarded by periods of repose, during which denudation did its best to carry away the volcanic deposits. It was in one of these intervals that the lignite and leaf beds of S. Jorge in Madeira were formed, some 1,200 feet of rock being afterwards piled upon the top of them. Eventually, however, the lava flows ceased, and the water was left to work its will on the accumulated masses of cinders, slag and detritus.

Exactly what the height of Madeira may have been at this time it is difficult to determine, though it probably did not much exceed that of the present day (Pico Ruivo, 6,059 feet). Even from the summit, however, much has been removed, and the fantastic walls and columns forming so characteristic a feature of the centre of the island, are the exposed remains of what were once necks of craters, or veins of intrusive rock (dykes).

These few scattered fragments are constantly being robbed of their foundations, and it is no longer disputed that the immense chasms of which the Curral and the Serra d'Agua are such conspicuous examples, are due to the wearing action of water. The first passes from the northern through the southern line of volcanoes, and was doubtless aided in its course by fissures in the rock, as was probably the case with ravines generally in all the archipelagos.

Both valleys are of immense size, even in Madeira, where the water-courses, taken in relation to the size of the island, are gigantic. Their only counterparts in the Canaries are the Barranco de Tejeda and the Barranco de Tirajana in Grand Canary, and the Great Crater (Caldera) in La Palma, the latter of which may have been partially shaped by other forces than those of erosion. In Teneriffe the hollows worn by the streams are comparatively small.

The original dome-like shape of Madeira has been described, and reference has been made to the northern chain of volcanoes, which, as it overwhelmed its southern neighbour, may well have entered into activity at a later date. It remains to be added that the latest exhibitions of volcanic force appear to have found their vent at a lower altitude, and the surfaces characteristic of recent eruptions of lava indicate that the latest eruptions broke through the crust of the earlier rocks and were of a parasitic nature.

In Teneriffe the surface before the last great upheaval seems to have been more irregular than was the case with Madeira. It has been traced in the west at Teno; in the south-west near and about Adeje, and in the north-east at Anaga and to the north of La Laguna. The last is the most extensive outcrop, and exhibits a large area but little affected by the latest disturbances. In each instance the surface has been deeply scored by denudation, and the summits have assumed a most bizarre and highly picturesque form.

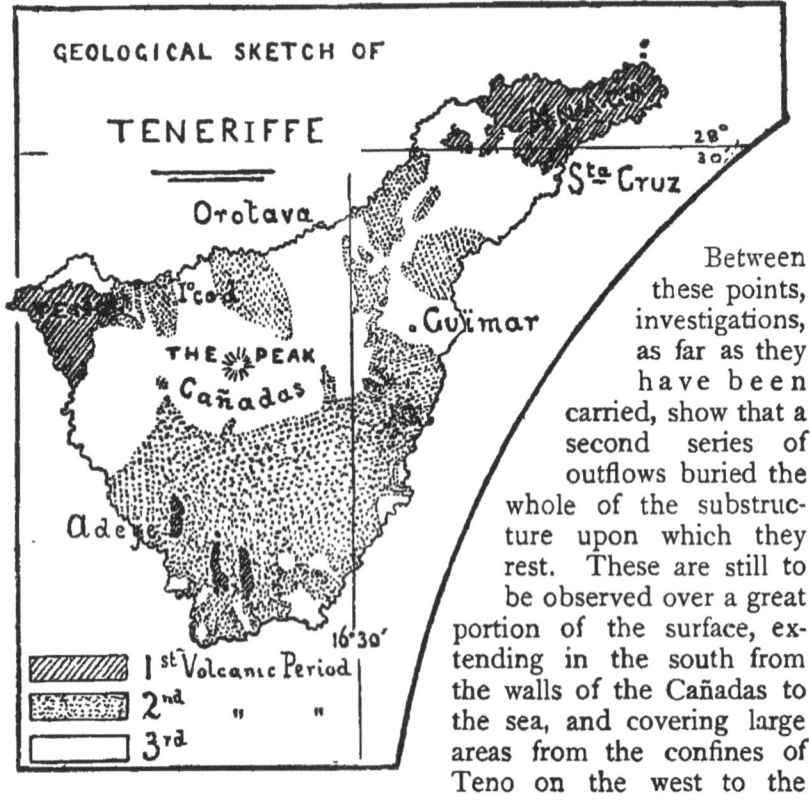

Between these points, investigations, as far as they have been carried, show that a second series of outflows buried the whole of the substructure upon which they rest. These are still to be observed over a great portion of the surface, extending in the south from the walls of the Cañadas to the sea, and covering large areas from the confines of Teno on the west to the neighbourhood of La Laguna on the east. The third and last series of strata includes the Peak and the plain upon which it stands, and in all probability once concealed nearly the whole of the northern slope from Teno on the west to Anaga on the east, the interruptions now existing in this formation being partly due to subsequent denudation. Volcanic rocks of the third period are also present in isolated patches near the south coast. The ravines by which the third series is intersected are rarely of great depth.

The elevated plains in Teneriffe are two in number. One of them, about the centre of which La Laguna stands, is due to lava and detritus having filled up the space between two chains of hills. The other is the floor of the great crater surrounding the Peak, the form of which is probably due to explosive forces.

In La Palma the newest formations lie to the south of the great crater, whose presence, since the time of Leopold von Buch, has justly caused La Palma to be regarded as one of the most interesting and wonderful of all oceanic islands. Recent outbreaks of lava stretch from near Fuencaliente on the south to Los Llanos on the north, and have generally flowed in a westerly direction. The irregular form of the basin of the crater itself, appears to be due to disturbances, which, though of ancient date, were posterior to those to which the major portion of the basaltic walls were built. The direction of the great ravine or Barranco de las Angustias leading to the south-west, was perhaps partly determined by seismic movements, occurring at a period after the crater had been formed and before the chain of mountains running to the south had assumed its present aspect.

Grand Canary seems to have reached a period of quiescence at a much earlier epoch, and, as is the case in Madeira, the latest volcanic outbreaks are usually situated at a comparatively low altitude.

In Lanzarote, the only one of the eastern islands now active, the volcanoes are distributed in lines with a general direction of from east to west. In Fuerteventura, from which it is divided by a narrow strait scarcely twenty fathoms in depth, and which has long been quiescent, the direction of the mountain ranges is from north to south.

Hierro and Gomera, which belong to the western group, have been at rest for many ages.

Those thinking of taking up their residence in the islands and who are afraid of eruptions or earthquakes, may possibly like to know what chances they have of being buried alive. During modern times the following eruptions have been recorded:—1585, La Palma (moderate); 1646, La Palma (violent); 1677, La Palma (extremely violent, accompanied by terrific noise and an enormous flow of lava); 1705, Teneriffe (moderate, preceded by earthquake); 1706, Teneriffe (locally violent); 1733, Lanzarote (violent); 1796 and 1798, Teneriffe (moderate); 1824, Lanzarote (insignificant). Madeira and the other islands have been undisturbed by eruptions, but shocks of earthquake are recorded in the former in 1748, 1755, and 1816, the first doing a certain amount of damage to the cathedral and to churches in other parts of the island. In no case do there appear to have been any dangerous showers of ashes during historical times, and, to judge from the position and apparent age of isolated pinnacles of rocks, earthquakes must generally have been local.

Order of the rocks.—It would be hazardous to make any definite statement as to the succession of rocks in the islands generally.

Basalt has been stated to be most common in the oldest formations, and trachytic lavas in the more recent. Basaltic rock has, however, been poured out during some of the very latest eruptions, and there are wide stretches of deposits of the third period in which trachyte is either absent or far from plentiful. In the valley of Orotava, for instance, the streams of lava flowing from the Cumbres towards the lower part of the valley, are chiefly composed of andesite, a rock forming a connecting link between the basic and the highly acid groups. In Teneriffe the walls of the Cañadas are of basalt, but the Peak itself is formed of trachyte, pumice, obsidian and ashes. The Montaña Blanca, as the rounded hump adjoining the Peak is called, is a shell of trachyte, probably forced up the vent of an old blow-hole, and resting upon the accumulation of ashes through which it issued. Similar dome-shaped craters are to be seen in the Puy de Dome district (Southern France).

Cinder heaps and craters.—Rounded heaps of cinders, or *fumaroles*, as they are called locally, are common enough throughout the islands and are of all colours and consistencies. Those composed of black ash and scoriæ usually resist the action of the weather best. A good example is the Montañeta, just above the Grand Hotel in Orotava, Teneriffe.

Some, and these generally of a lighter colour, disintegrate rapidly, covering the neighbourhood with a species of volcanic alluvial, and retaining their rounded form to the last. The group of *fumaroles* between La Laguna and Tacoronte are a case in point.

Others, of an earthy but more compact nature, weather to a point, and assume a peak-like shape. A conspicuous instance is that of the Pico de Gáldar in Grand Canary.

Some of the cinder heaps, after attaining a certain elevation, died away, leaving a circular rim at the summit enclosing a shallow depression. Such craters are to be seen in many places, notably at S. Antonio da Serra in Madeira, and between Tacoronte and La Laguna in Teneriffe. In Madeira, the cup at the top is sometimes converted into a small lake during the winter. Hence the local name of Lagão.

Blow-holes of this description are, however, usually broken down on one side by a flow of lava. The mass of igneous rock which overwhelmed Garachico, in Teneriffe, proceeds from a group of cinder heaps, and similar instances on a smaller scale exist in all the islands.

Such volcanoes are usually parasitic and are most common in the third series of eruptions, the earlier examples having been swept away or hidden by later deposits. Instances of hidden blow-holes have been found in the Socorridos ravine and near Boa Ventura in Madeira.

There are a few cases in which the rock has welled up to the brim of the crater, and then subsided without forcing an outlet.

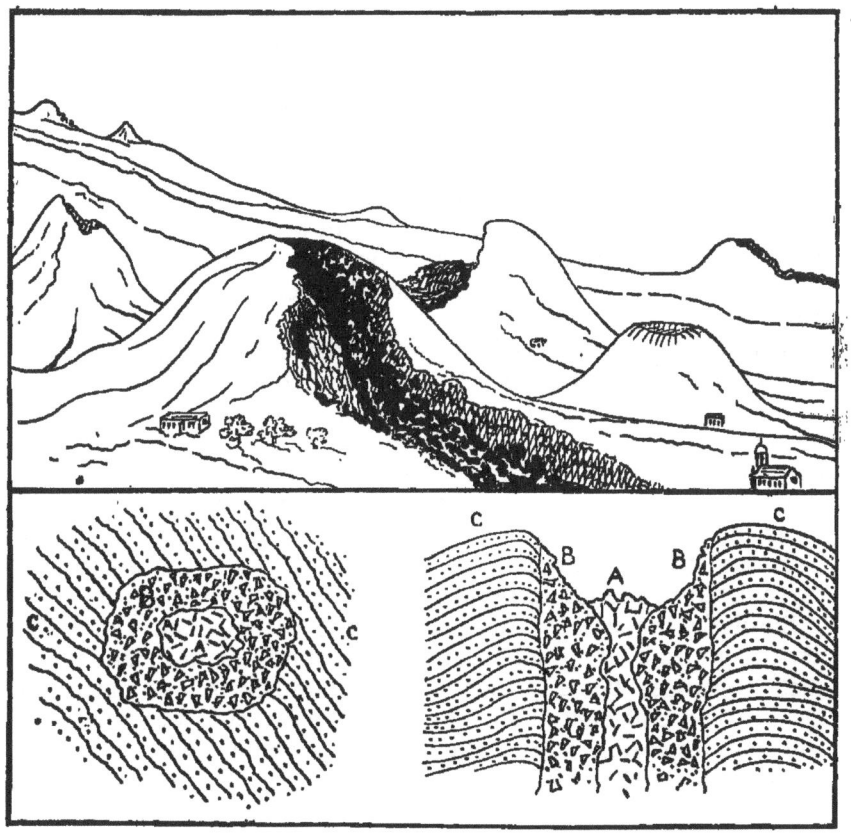

IDEAL GROUP OF SATELLITE VOLCANOES (FUMAROLES), WITH GROUND-PLAN AND SECTIONAL VIEW OF A CRATER NECK.

A—Lava.   *B*—Slag and Detritus.   *C*—Cinders, Pumice, etc.

In these the inside walls are usually steep, incrusted with rings of slag and cinders, and corroded by the heat and motion of the molten lava they contained. The difference between the inside of a cup from which the igneous rock has been suddenly discharged through a breach, and that of a flawless crater of this order, can be well observed by comparing any of the broken volcanoes with the Gran Caldera at Tafira in Grand Canary, where the sides are intact and the bowl is of colossal dimensions. (See *Index*.)

An excellent object lesson of the formation of a cinder heap is to be seen in South Kensington Museum.

Dr. Edward Hull, the author of "Volcanoes Past and Present," ascribes the force necessary for blowing out the materials of which the walls are formed, to the ascent of igneous rock by fissures torn through water-bearing strata. The result of the impact is the rapid generation of super-heated steam, by which "ashes, scoriæ, and blocks of rock torn from the sides of the "crater throat and hurled into the air, are piled around the vent "and accumulate into hills or mountains of conical form. After "the explosion has exhausted itself, the molten lava quietly "wells up and fills the crater." He therefore formulates the general principle that "where water in large quantities is "present, we shall have crater cones built up of ashes, scoriæ and "pumice; but, where absent, the lava will be extravasated in sheets "without the formation of such cones; or, if cones are formed, "they will be composed of solidified lava only, and will be easily "distinguishable."

These quotations explain many of the phenomena frequently seen in Madeira and in the Canaries, and show us that the crater cones may be regarded as a series of subterranean borings by means of which we are enabled to ascertain to a certain extent the nature of the sub-soil lying beneath them.

For instance, if the ash cone on the summit of the Peak of Teneriffe is caused by the explosion of vapour beneath the Cañadas, it may be argued that the nature of the lower strata is reproduced in the rapilli by which it is crowned.

Similarly the colours of many of the recent craters must be dependent upon their subterranean surroundings, and the fact of such volcanoes being present in any number in one particular locality, is a sufficient indication that the strata is water-bearing, and that it possibly merits attention in a country where water is so exceedingly valuable.

Lava.—The most remarkable example of the penetrative power of molten rock with which the writer is acquainted is to be seen on the western coast of La Palma, a little to the south of Las Manchas. The district is almost entirely covered by recent and furious discharges of lava, which falls in a succession of terraces towards the Atlantic. In one of the terraces or cliffs, a gully, some sixty feet or more in depth, has been created, the sides of which are almost absolutely precipitous, and which evidently owes its origin to a later stream of lava flowing over solidified rock. To one accustomed to the characteristic furrows of a lava stream, such as those to be seen above Garachico, the cleft mentioned in La Palma is most noticeable. The nature of the two rocks are somewhat different, that in La Palma having a greater tendency to weather concentrically than is the case near Garachico.

There are instances where the destruction of old volcanic walls or buttresses by later flows of rock has taken place on a gigantic scale.

A good illustration is afforded in Teneriffe, where about two-thirds of the walls encircling the Cañadas, which once were continuous and enclosed a lake of fire, from six to eight miles in width, have been carried away.

On the west the demolition was due to the flows of igneous matter from the gaping volcano of Chahorra and its parasites. On the north-east the chief agency was probably water.

Looking towards Chahorra from the west, the mountain side is seen to be composed of masses of rugged stone, of which certain streams have run into the sea, forming the jagged bulwarks now serving as a protection to this part of the coast

Viewed in this light the process of demolition cannot exactly be described as destructive, the material being merely removed from one site to another.

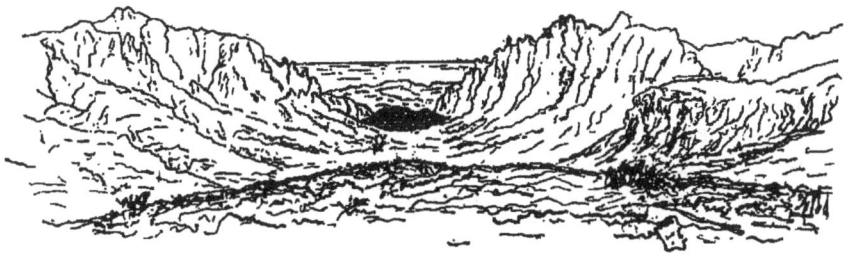

THE GARGANTA DE GÜIMAR SEEN FROM ABOVE.

Explosive eruptions.—There is, however, at least one instance where a portion of the island seems to have been removed by volcanic agency.

This occurs in what is known as the Garganta de Güimar or "el Valle," on the south side of Teneriffe, a narrow gorge through which the pass is carried from Güimar to Orotava.

The bed of the Barranco is covered by volcanic ash and by the detritus of the neighbouring rocks, but the sides, which are from 500 to 700 feet in height, have been but little affected by the action of water, and are interveined by an extraordinarily complicated system of dykes. The dip of the strata in the west has an angle of a little over 35°, and that on the east· of rather more than 32°, the rock exposed belonging to the second series of

GEOLOGICAL FEATURES.

eruptions, and the portion missing having entirely disappeared. The enormous force necessary to move so great a mass of rock may have been engendered by the contact of igneous rock with a subterranean deposit of water flowing from the Cañadas, the latter having some relation to the streams by which the valley of Güimar is now irrigated. The little volcano of Arafo, standing in the centre of the lower part of the cleft, was active in 1705, when it poured a stream of lava down the southern slope nearly as far as the coast.

Lava-caves.—This stream is one of the several instances to be found where the interior of the molten mass continued to flow after the crystallisation of the exterior crust, the result being the creation of a cave, sometimes of considerable length. That below Icod de los Vinos was used by the Guanches as a place of burial, and that beyond Haría in Lanzarote as a retreat during time of invasion.

Faults.—Among cases where denudation has been assisted by extensive faults, the valley of Orotava, which covers an area of some 45 square miles, may be mentioned. The faulting in the rocks is here most apparent to the west of Realejo. The gradual progression of the surface rock towards the coast forms a conspicuous feature in the landscape as viewed from the roof of the Grand Hotel when looking towards the Portillo and the Llano de Maja.

Chasms, or depressions, similar to those of the Cañadas, Orotava, Güimar, or Icod, may result from the matter supporting the solidified crust being extruded in a molten state from some neighbouring volcanic outlet.

It is also argued that they may have been created by explosive energy. If this were the case at Orotava and Güimar it must be presumed that the outer wall of each of these craters was afterwards destroyed by the action of the waves, the sea thus gaining an entry. The subsequent alteration in the landscape both at Güimar and at Orotava was largely dependent upon erosion.

The craters of the Cañadas and of Icod have been less subject to the action of water. Streams of lava, and, in the former case, showers of pumice, are mainly responsible for the nature of the surface now existing.

As examples of the energy required to achieve such stupendous results, the Val de Bove on Mount Etna, and the eruption of Krakatoa in 1883 may be cited. The latter is one of the most remarkable outbursts of modern times, and that of which the attendant phenomena were most accurately observed. A short description showing what may have occurred or might still take place in Madeira or the Canaries should prove of interest.

Krakatoa, which is situated in the Sunda Straits, between Sumatra and Java, appears to have been dormant till 1680, when there was an eruption, after which it remained in repose until 1883, the traces of the former outbreak being again covered with forests, and the volcano being regarded as extinct.

On May 20th, 1883, detonations, heard in Batavia, were followed by the ejection of flames and a great column of smoke, fissures being doubtless created about the same time, through which water gradually percolated. On August 26th, this must have come into contact with the igneous rock, for on that date faint explosions, first heard in Buitenzorg, increased in force as the night fell, and soon became so loud that sleep in the western part of Java was rendered almost impossible. This growth of energy was probably due to the creation of fresh fissures, through which large bodies of water were admitted.

At seven in the morning there was a fearful report, followed by shocks of earthquake; the sky became overcast, and by 10 a.m. the straits and the surrounding coast were in darkness, the wind rising to hurricane force.

Eye-witnesses state that the island was covered by a wall of black cloud, lit up by incessant shafts of lightning, and that the air was momentarily shaken by a series of frightful detonations. A column of watery vapour rose to a height, variously estimated as from twelve to twenty-three miles, at which altitude it spread into a huge canopy, from which atoms of dust slowly descended. Even pieces of pumice stone were carried to an enormous distance, and for some time navigation in the Straits of Sunda was hindered by the immense quantities left floating on the water. On August 29th, the day after the eruptions ceased, particles were collected from the deck of a steamer at a point 1,600 miles west of Krakatoa.

The dust itself was distributed over a far greater area, falling during September in British India, on the east and west coasts of Africa, in Trinidad, in Panama, in the Sandwich Islands, and elsewhere. During the latter part of 1883 and the earlier part of 1884, a corona, visible in Europe and the British Isles, surrounded both the sun and the moon, and the magnificent tints assumed by the sky at sunrise and sunset were a matter of common observation.

The atmospheric wave due to the explosion was recorded at numerous meteorological stations. After encircling the globe, it met at the antipodes of Krakatoa, whence it was returned to its source, the action being repeated seven times, after which it became too feeble to affect the most sensitive instruments.

The sound was carried to a distance of more than 2,000 miles, that is to say, a similar explosion in the Canaries would have been audible almost all over England.

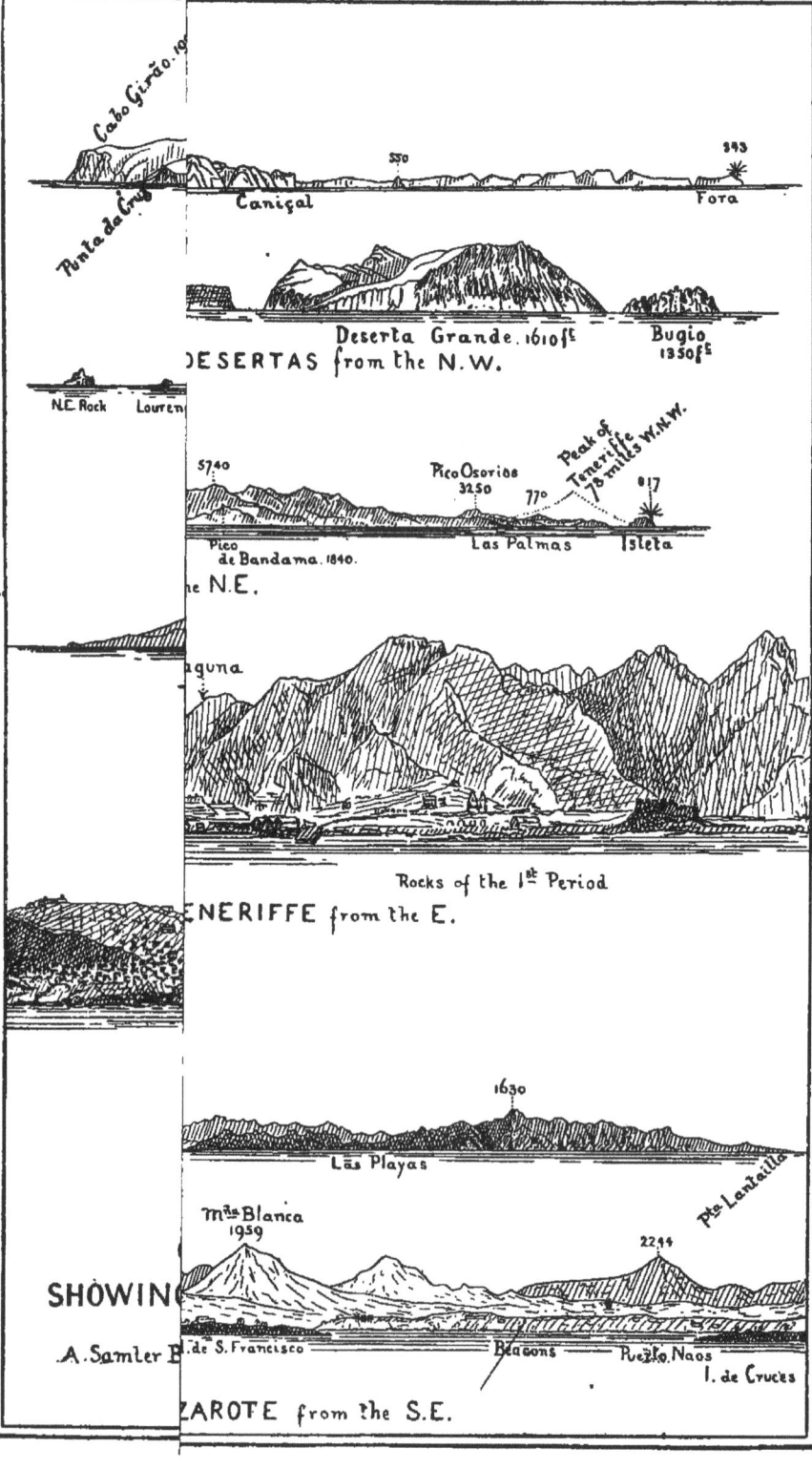

Lagōa
2478
S. Antonio da Serra
2310   2058
                                        550

n a ruz
from E.S.E.

Chão. 340 ft.   Deserta Grande
THE DESERTAS from the N.W.

Las Cumbres de los
6400 Roque Saucillos
                        5740   Pico Osorio
                                              3250

atarga   Aguimes   Telde Pico
                                de Bandama. 1840.
GRAND CANARY from the N.E.

Garganta de Guimar   The Peak   Laguna

the 2ⁿᵈ and 3ʳᵈ Period   Mole   Rocks of the
SANTA CRUZ. TENERIFFE from the E.

deta   phinx Head

                                                16

lancas   Morro de
                                Tarajal
FUERTEVENTURA from the S.E.

1860

P⁺⁹

GEOLOGICAL FEATURES. 75

At the point from which it originated, the tidal wave caused by the eruption is said to have attained a height of about fifty feet. Its effects were felt all over the globe in decreasing ratio, and, had it not been for the interruption caused by the two Americas, it would have reached the English coast from the westward as it did from the south *viâ* the Cape of Good Hope.

The shape of Krakatoa and the surrounding bed of the ocean were completely transformed. The cone of Rakata, 2,622 feet high, and the little island of Verlaten, which formed the outer rim of what, before the eruption of 1680, is believed to have been a volcanic peak of majestic dimensions, are all that is now left. The central groups of mountains known as Danan and Perboewatan, have sunk below the surface, and a portion of Rakata itself has accompanied them. The Sebesi channel was partially filled up by banks of volcanic rock, which rose in two places above the sea, but have since been swept away.

One hundred and sixty-three villages were entirely, and 132 partially, destroyed, and 36,380 human beings perished.

The most complete descriptions of this eruption are those published by the Royal Society, and by the Governor-General of the Netherland Indies (Chevalier R. D. M. Verbeck, 1886). The subject is also discussed at considerable length in " Volcanoes · Past and Present," by Dr. Edward Hull, to whom the writer is indebted for much of the above information.

It may be added that the distance between Verlaten Island and Rakata, the north and south walls of the crater as it now stands, is about five miles, or somewhat less than the breadth of the Valley of Orotava.

Those using this guide book will find that a great number of manifestations of volcanic and other forces have been dealt with locally.

The Sunken Continent of Atlantis.

THE legends and traditions which found a concrete form in Plato's "Timœus," invariably deal with the fabulous continent as an inhabited country. Perhaps it is for this reason that those believing in its existence are so often held up to ridicule, and that so few can approach the subject with an unbiassed mind.

Putting aside altogether the question of the presence of human beings, let us examine the matter simply from a geological point of view.

It has been stated on another page that there are two great parallel lines of volcanoes running from North to South, one in Western America and one in the Eastern Atlantic, and that these volcanoes are believed to stand above two of the great lines of cleavage traversing the crust of this Earth.

Such cleavages are probably due to the gradual shrinkage of the Earth through radiation of heat into space, and to the consequent falling in of the crust.

This falling in or subsidence could not affect the whole surface equally. Loss of heat would be more rapid in one place than in another, and, even were this not the case, the varying character of the supports upon which the different portions of the surface rested, would render uniformity of movement impossible.

It has been said that the loss of heat is continuous and gradual. It does not, however, follow that the contraction of the Earth must proceed uninterruptedly and at exactly the same rate.

We know that the crust is never entirely at rest, and we need not turn back many years to find cases where considerable areas have suddenly sunk far below their former level, as, for instance, when part of Kingston, in Jamaica, disappeared below the sea.

Where large tracts of country have been covered by the ocean and there is no historical record to which we can turn, it is difficult to obtain any positive evidence upon which to make a precise statement, the investigation of coral atolls affording, perhaps, the most exact data upon which calculations regarding the rate of subsidence can be based.

In the case of elevation, however, it is far different. The character of the fossils contained by the rocks enable geologists to give an approximate age to many of the great mountain chains, and to declare with a considerable amount of certainty the height at which they stood at various epochs.

Elevation is simply a comparative statement of the height of the land and the level of the sea surface. It is, therefore, possible for land to maintain the same position as regards the centre of the

Earth, but to gain in elevation as regards the sea, by reason of the water running away from it into some newly-created depression. Much of the so-called elevation of our mountains is probably derived from this cause.

On the other hand, there is actual, true elevation due to two causes. One of these is the building up by volcanic discharges, as is the case in the Canaries, in Madeira, and in the upper parts of the Andes, etc. The other is the crumpling of the dust of the Earth due to lateral pressure, which pressure, when exercised on a large scale, is probably brought about by shrinkage. Many of the extraordinary curves, folds and inversions of strata to be found, can scarcely be ascribed to any less potent influence.

Presuming that there is a line of cleavage intersecting Madeira and the Canaries and another parallel line on the western coast of America, these two great breaks in the Earth's crust may be complementary to one another, for, if elevation is dependent upon contraction and subsidence, it is obvious that a great mountain chain such as that of the Andes could not exist without an accompanying depression, which depression would necessarily form the bed of an ocean.

It will be noted that the distance between the cleavages in question, though great, is small in comparison to their length, and that the extreme elevation of the one does not differ very greatly from the extreme depth of the other.

Presuming that these changes in the position of the crust took place very gradually, it seems to follow that at one time America, Atlantis and Africa all stood at a general level, and that there must have been either an immense continent divided by great inland seas, or an almost boundless group of islands.

But if such a state of things as this can be imagined, then, by a slight further stretch of the imagination, Atlantis might be dry land with an ocean on either side of it. Such a species of see-saw motion, by which the ocean would be shifted alternately from one part of the surface to another, is consistent with the theory of contraction. Radiation of heat would be hindered by the interposition of a blanket of water covering an ocean bed, and the process of cooling, with its attendant shrinkage, might therefore be expected to proceed more rapidly in those parts where the surface was fully exposed to the sky.

The best proof of the former existence of dry land in the Atlantic is afforded by the traces of marine action in South America and in South Africa.

Darwin's investigations showed that specimens of living marine shells are to be found at considerable altitudes along the whole western coast of America for a distance of 2,000 or 3,000 miles south of the Equator. The same writer calls attention to the successive terraces or foreshores in that continent, whose cliffs are the evidence of the rate at which the land was raised above the level of the sea, or, which is the same thing, of the speed at which the ocean was drawn away.

The extreme height at which such terraces may have existed in South America can only be ascertained by an exact and extensive examination of the rocks upon which the later volcanic deposits rest, a matter of much labour even in an easily accessible and fully civilised country.

In South Africa, however, which is traversed by no such line of cleavage, and where the sedimentary strata has suffered less from violent seismic movements than is usually the case elsewhere, the same terraces are found in all parts of the continent, and there are abundant evidences that even the highest mountains of Basutoland did at one time form part of the ocean bed.

The forces generated by the sinking of so vast a portion of the Earth's surface in its close vicinity seem to have affected South Africa but little, the force generated finding its point of least resistance to the west. That this was so is to be argued from the fact that South Africa rose from the sea in the form of a great oval, encircled by a chain of mountains which remained unbroken, not only during the formation of the coal deposits in that country, but for a long time afterwards. Had the lateral pressure been exerted in an easterly direction, fissures must have been created in the surrounding wall, and the Orange and Zambesi Rivers must have drained the central plains of South Africa much sooner than is generally believed to be the case.

That the alteration in the disposition of the surface of the globe progressed very slowly cannot be doubted. Otherwise there could neither be a succession of terraces, nor a series of coal-fields, both of which extend in South Africa from the level of the sea or thereabouts (Santa Lucia Coal Beds in Zululand) to an altitude of 5,500 feet (Cyphergat, Cape Colony).

Gradual, however, as the changes no doubt were, the terraces seem to indicate that the shrinkage was occasionally accelerated, and that periods of comparative repose, such as those now existing, were followed by epochs of greater activity, when the bed of the ocean was rapidly or even suddenly depressed, and the continents were proportionately elevated.

Such an epoch would be most disastrous to all living things in those countries lying above the area of subsidence, and any inhabitants who might escape could be trusted to hand down traditions of the great deluge to the most remote generations.

After a period of rapid subsidence we might expect an outbreak of volcanic energy, partly due to the enormous heat engendered by the movement itself, and partly to the change in pressure from one part of the surface to another.

THE SUNKEN CONTINENT OF ATLANTIS.

The intensity of the heat that might be created may be imagined when it is stated that the warmth shed by the sun is supposed to be derived from a similar source.

The effect of the change in pressure may be demonstrated by comparing the weight of a column of sea water to that of a similar column of air, and by remembering that so very slight a change as a fall of an inch in the barometer is sufficient to cause seismic movements in certain very disturbed parts of the globe. More than this it has been stated that volcanic outbursts occur most frequently when the attractive force of the moon is at its greatest. In proportion, therefore, to the weight of the water as compared to the influence of the moon, would be the probability of an ejection of igneous rock.

In the Andes Mountains, that is to say, in the extreme west of the area affected, the line of least resistance would be by way of the crater necks lying above the line of cleavage. In the Eastern Atlantic the eruptions might be expected to occur exactly in the same sites.

At first the number of volcanoes along each of these lines might perhaps be about the same. Later on, as the weight of water above them increased, those craters in the bed of the Atlantic which remained passive for the greatest length of time, would also be those where a recurrence of activity would be most unlikely.

One by one they would be closed up and covered by a dense body of water. Eventually the vents for igneous rock or for superfluous force would be limited to those volcanoes most constantly in eruption.

The result would be that volcanic energy would make channels towards these vents as water does towards a well from which the accumulated liquid is constantly abstracted. As the general level of the ocean bed decreased, these few points would receive all the outpourings of Mother Earth, and would, in consequence, maintain their heads either very near to or far above the surface of the ocean.

The number of volcanic vents now remaining is identical with the list of islands in the Atlantic, and, were some further great subsidence to take place, all or any of these islands might at once be expected to burst into flame.

In the Azores the struggle between the ocean and the subterranean forces is still apparent. The Almagrurin adventurers spoke in the twelfth century of stinking water in this direction, and as lately as 1867, a crater, which has since disappeared, rose above the surface near Terceira.

The subaqueous character of the archipelagos has been treated of in the chapter on "Geology," and need not be repeated.

Many of the readers of this work may be inclined to dispute the possibility of such great seismic movements as those on which the author bases the above deductions. The following quotation is therefore given from the writings of the American naturalist, James Dwight Dana.

"After the Cretaceous period, and in the Pliocene Tertiary chiefly, or the Tertiary and Glacial period, the whole region of the Rocky Mountains was elevated; the elevation was 16,000 feet in part of Colorado; 10,000 feet, at least, in the region of Sierra Nevada; 10,000 feet in Mexico, and over 17,000 feet in British America, latitude 49° to 53°, and less to the north. The region of the Andes, at the same time, was raised to a maximum amount of 20,000 feet; the Alps, 12,000 feet; and the Himalayas, 20,000 feet. Moreover, at the close of the Champlain period there was another epoch of small elevation, introducing the recent period. These elevations, affecting a large part of the continental areas, could not have taken place without a counterpart subsidence of large areas over the oceanic basin; profound oceanic subsidence was hence in progress during the growth of coral-reefs. The subsidence cannot be questioned."

It will be noticed that Dana estimates the elevation of the Andes to have been perhaps 20,000 feet. The highest mountain in the Andes (Aconcagua) is said to have an elevation of 23,080 feet. A small allowance for volcanic deposits after emersion would, therefore, place the summit of the Andes *below the water* previous to the period of activity to which Dana refers.

Passing from the geological aspect of the question, which, if it does not absolutely prove anything, at least shows that such a country may have existed, let us consider for a moment why it may have had inhabitants.

Here again legends for the moment will be discarded, and the reader's attention will be directed to the extraordinary fact that, although no school of philosophy has ever presumed to maintain that mankind is descended from a number of separate human creations, the races as they now exist have drifted so widely apart that they almost belong to separate species.

Such a proposition is not based merely upon colour, upon anthropological proportions, or upon language, but upon the acknowledged truth that many of these races cannot be permanently mixed.

The result of the union of the horse with a donkey is a mule, which is never fertile. The result of the union of the Caucasian with the Asiatic or the Negro is the Eurasian or the Mulatto, which, if mated with its like, dies out in the second or the third generation.

It can only be imagined that the original human race was separated long ages ago, and remained apart for such an immense length of time, that its members, when they again met, were no longer blood relations. What drove them from one another and what prevented their reunion is a mere matter of guess-work, but it does not seem unreasonable to presume that the first movement was caused by great changes in the surface of the earth, and that the subsequent absence of communication was due to impassable barriers of ice, raised during the cold period of exhaustion which followed the wave of heat conjured up by the previous outburst of energy.

Dana says the elevation took place "after the Cretaceous, and in the Pliocene Tertiary, or the Tertiary and Glacial Period." It is by no means certain that man did not exist in the Cretaceous Period. Even if he were not born until long after this, there was still time for him to occupy the earth long before the Glacial Epoch commenced. If he had not established himself prior to this date, at what period could the immense distinctions between the different races have developed themselves? Presuming that he had come into existence, there seems no reason why he should not have lived in Atlantis, supposing, of course, that Atlantis was a country suitable for human beings.

One word more before passing to legends.

Allowing that a continent of Atlantis did exist; that it was inhabited; and that it was gradually overwhelmed, is it reasonable to suppose that some of the people escaped?

The country was, perhaps, large; civilisation, for all we know, may have reached a far more advanced state than it has to-day, and the authorities must have received warning after warning.

Such admonitions would, as a rule, be disregarded. The every-day man about town would have declared that each subsidence was the very last, and the evening papers would have proved that the world was now so well consolidated and so completely shaken together, that all alarm might be dismissed.

It would, however, be noticed that great movements of the earth were preceded by increased volcanic activity, and observatories would be constructed in some of the mountains, perhaps already islands, where the most active volcanoes were situated.

In such observatories there would be a professor or so, his wife and family perhaps, students, helpers, servants, etc., and, when the final catastrophe occurred and the whole of Atlantis was swallowed up, some of these men or their descendants may have remained on their chosen watch-tower, and from such as these the Guanches and Canarios might be descended.

Not purely, perhaps. Visitors from newly-arisen Africa, themselves the descendants of an Iberian folk and of common ancestry with the Guanches, may, centuries afterwards, have been driven on to the islands. Later on the Phœnicians came, and so on down to the Spanish invasion and the repulse of Nelson, but the old stock lived on.

Probably the mixed race, if left to itself, might have died out like the Eurasian or the Mulatto, but fresh blood has always come in.

The Spanish conquerors took many a Guanche maid to wife. From the marriage sprang a vigorous race in every way superior to the pure-blooded Spaniard of the Peninsula.

There were rovers and adventurers of all sorts who came to look for mummies or what not and found fair living creatures. Jack was ashore and went away again, and was followed by the Negro, imported to work the plantations in the early sugar-days. Then came the Catholic persecutions in England, and emigration to Madeira and the Canaries was fashionable for a time amongst the Irish gentry, who became owners of vineyards, intermarried with the race, and brought fresh stamina with them.

Be this as it may it is obvious that if the bed of the Atlantic once was dry, and dry at a time when there were living people on the earth, it is more than probable that some of these people occupied it, and that, when it was swallowed up, a portion of the inhabitants escaped.

If such an event was followed by the great ice age, the scattered units would exist as best they could, meeting in later ages when civilisation and commerce had once more brought them together, a hotch-potch of black, red, yellow and white; eyeing one another now strangely, now fiercely; each working out its destiny, and the strongest fated, perhaps, to eventually exterminate all the rest.

If geological and racial problems give some negative sort of support to the theory of Atlantis, it is in the realms of folk-lore that we must seek something more positive; in tales of deluges, in traditions of lands and peoples that have disappeared, and in well-worn beliefs common to those living on the shores of the country submerged.

For these we naturally turn to Cornwall and Brittany where subsidence has been most rapid during the last few centuries, and where it is still a feature by which the coast line is noticeably modified.

The old Brittany legend of St. Brendan is given under the "History of Madeira," and is a sort of compound of two beliefs, namely, that of a lost country and that of an Eliseum. The idea of a land of the blest was probably derived from the mythology of Greece and Rome, which gave heroes and gods a final abode in the kingdom of the setting sun, and consequently in some part to the west of wherever the believer might happen to be.

In Cornwall, however, matters are more precise. Anybody in St. Just will point out the place below the circular British tombs where there once stood a town, and where the water now swirls with a little additional malignity. During calm weather dwellers in Penzance or Marazion can show the remains of a forest now lying at the bottom of Mount Bay, and can tell the names of some of those swept ashore by the rising water, though evidence does not indicate that the occurrence took place within historical times.

Florence of Worcester, the Monkish writer, who died in 1118, says that the country of Lyonnesse, lying between the Land's End and the Scilly Isles, and containing many fields, villages, towns, and 140 churches, disappeared in A.D. 1099, *i.e.*, the same year in which the Goodwin Sands were flooded. The legend, as it reached him, was probably so precise and clear that he could not imagine the event to have taken place at a very remote date.

Yet we know that there was open sea between the Land's End and the Scillies at least two thousand years before his time, and that the legend he wrote about was a tradition in the days of King Solomon. Solomon, by-the-by, lived some six or seven hundred years before Plato, whose description of Atlantis in "Timœus" was written about 380 B.C. Though declared by the author to be a true story, and though based in all probability upon folk-lore collected by himself or by others, the description given by Plato is altogether too circumstantial to be admitted as evidence, unless, indeed, he may have written it when inspired, as the author of this book was once seriously assured by a spiritualist.

But in matters such as these vague oral tradition is worth more than a written document embellished with each fresh fancy conjured up by the busy author.

Scarcely a hundred years have passed since the sister of the Vicar of St. Erth actually poured a certain decoction of herbs into the sea at Land's End, believing, when she did so, that the Land of Lyonnesse would reappear with all its living inhabitants, its villages and its churches, as described by Florence of Worcester.

When the inmate of a clergyman's household, however rustic his curacy may be, is so firm a believer in a legend, what a hold the tale must have had upon the people generally! The student may read his Plato and admire the philosopher's arguments, but what are these to tradition which will take an educated woman to the rocks at midnight, and bid her, regardless of influenza and ridicule, stand shivering in her nightgown in a gale of wind, whilst she awaits the arrival of a troup of gibbering ghosts out of the vasty deep?

In Portugal and Spain the tale is much the same as that to be found in Brittany and Cornwall, and it is probable that a similar story, in a more or less modified form, exists in the folk-lore of all parts of the world. A theory that would explain the disappearance of Atlantis would also apply in the Pacific Ocean, and might, perhaps, account for the vanished race to whom or to whose descendants the ruined buildings in Easter Island are due. The writer believes that he is correct in saying that no race has yet been found whose legends do not contain some reference to a great and universal flood such as that described in the Old Testament.

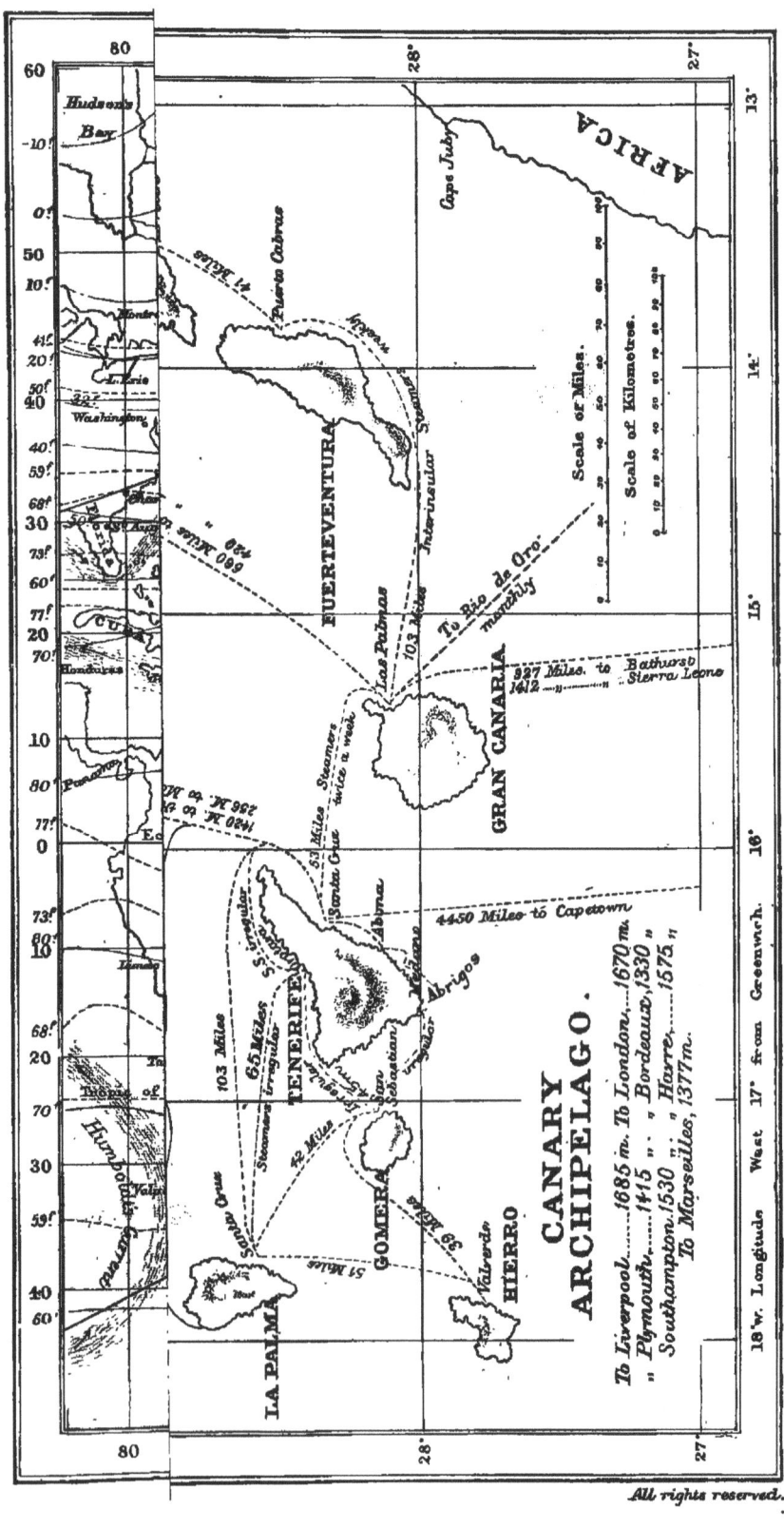

CLIMATIC MAP.
Specially prepared for
Brown's "Madeira and
the Canary Islands" 1901.

Antarctic Current

Mean Annu
dotted
Me

HISTORY OF MADEIRA.

THERE is no proof whatever that the Madeiras were visited by any of the early navigators. It has been suggested that they were the Carthaginian colony, known as the Cassarides, described about 250 B.C. as situated on an uninhabited island; but the description might apply to several places. The Portuguese on arrival found no traces of the former presence of man, and it is probable that the group was quite unknown until its discovery in A.D. 1418.

As will be seen later on, Pliny's "Purpuriæ" are much more likely to have been the Eastern Canaries. It is difficult to believe that the connection of this name with the Madeiras could have been long maintained, were it not that so great an authority as Humboldt, full of admiration of the violet and purple clouds and hazy mountains before him, lent new life to the theory by subscribing to it personally.

Both the French and the Spaniards claim to have touched at the islands about the middle of the 14th century, but no proof of the fact has been forthcoming.

Madeira and Porto Santo appear on the Medici Map (Florence) under the names of "Porto Sto," "I. de lo legname," and "I. deserte." If inserted at the date when the chart was drawn, A.D. 1351, the Genoese must have been the true discoverers. Unfortunately, another map, made in 1385, does not include the group; and there is strong reason to believe that they were drawn in on the earlier map after their present owners had taken possession of them, and that their names, as given in Italian, are simply a translation from the Portuguese.

The Norsemen may have sighted them during their plundering expeditions of the 8th and 9th centuries. Their ships are known to have visited the African coast, and to have called forth special defensive measures on the part of the Moors, both in Spain and in Morocco. Such forays, however, were usually made in galleys. The disposition of the sails did not allow of running at all close to the wind, and they rarely went far out of sight of land. The very name of "viking," king of the "wick" or inlet, implies that they were not navigators of the deep seas.

The Irish and the Arabs in their turn may have been more enterprising. Our own King Arthur, the stainless Knight (A.D. 500-530), whose kingdom, according to tradition, included Iceland, Norway, Ireland, Keltic-England, France as far as the banks of the Rhone, and perhaps Poland, maintained a numerous fleet commanded by three admirals; and some of his ships may have made what is, after all, only a small journey to the south.

The love of exploration was alive in his day, and finds its record in the legend of the seven years' voyage of St. Brendan the Elder, hero of the most popular romance of the middle ages, and Abbot of Clonfert on the River Shannon, a monastery founded by him in A.D. 558. His beautiful old cathedral, which has been burned, plundered or destroyed on no less than ten occasions, is now in course of restoration.

Kingsley, writing of the legend, calls it a "Monkish Odyssey," and says that it is manufactured out of dim reports of fairy islands to the West of the Canaries and of the Azores; out of tales of Arctic winters, of icebergs and of frozen seas; out of Edda stories of the Midgard snake which lies coiled round the world; out of scraps of Greek and Arab fables, and from myths of all sorts and of all ages, gathered by degrees and slowly woven together. As St. Brendan died in A.D. 578, aged 94, and the books which have to be consulted about him were written or printed as late as from the 11th to the 16th centuries, complete accuracy of detail is not to be expected.

After one of his return journeys from Brittany, St. Brendan received a visit from a hermit named Barintus of the royal house of Neill, who persuaded him to come away to an island in which he had lately been staying, and in which he had founded a monastery. This island was described as a most delicious resort. The sun always shone, the fruit was always ripe, and the birds, which wore golden crowns, sat on the trees and sang in harmonious concord, unless they were asked questions, when they left off at once, and answered both civilly and to the point. There were no harmful animals nor noxious insects in this earthly paradise, which did indeed so nearly resemble the heavenly one, that on his, Barintus', return to Ireland, every one believed him to have come from heaven because of the delightful fragrance which, for the space of forty days, clung to the garments he was wearing.

St. Brendan made up his mind to go; built a coracle of wattle covered with hides, tanned in oak bark and softened with butter; loaded it with forty days' provisions, and ordered his somewhat unwilling disciples to embark in the name of the Holy Trinity. Life in the beautiful island they eventually reached passed away like a dream. Though the absence from Ireland lasted seven years, the time seemed to be no more than a few months.

On his return St. Brendan built the monastery of Clonfert, in which there were at one time three thousand monks, all supporting themselves by the labour of their own hands. He then became a dispenser of miracles, and having visited Iona, the monastic metropolis of Western Scotland, which, a little later on, became the headquarters of Christianity, died and was buried at Clonfert.

Another legend states that he did not die, but made his appearance much later on off the coast of Portugal, whither he had come on the famous floating island of Antilla, or Cipango, or, as the Spaniards call it, St. Borondon. At the moment of his arrival the Christians were on the point of being driven into the sea by the conquering Moors, and were glad to avail themselves of the means of escape offered by S. Brandão, or Borondon, or Brandaines, as the French have it. They are still sailing about until the advent of the millennium, when they will reappear in perfect health, and will help to bring peace back to an afflicted world.

This is the island which is supposed to reappear from time to time (refer to Index), and whose mirage, fragile as all mirages are, has yet acquired the same circumstantiality that time and credulity have given to that of the "Flying Dutchman" or of the "Elysian Fields," of which latter the Island of Cipango is probably a better representative than any portion of *terra firma* yet discovered.

So strong was the belief in it at one time that Portugal, in the treaty of 1519, ceded it to Spain, calling it the "Ilha não truvota," or "Island not found." Viera y Clavijo publishes a picture of it in his history (1772), drawn by a Franciscan monk in Gomera in 1759, and it is from his book that part of the above is extracted.

Many expeditions have been sent with the object of finding it, and many a skipper, viewing it from the shores of La Palma or of Teneriffe, has set all sail in pursuit. Possibly the visitor may be fortunate enough to see it. Mirages are common enough in these latitudes at certain times; and the writer has often seen portions of the coast reproduced on the horizon with an absolutely startling fidelity.

Whether St. Brendan visited Madeira or the Canaries or not, independent testimony shows that the Irish monks were very great explorers. It is said that on the colonisation of Iceland by the Norse, in A.D. 870, Irish hermits were found there. The Icelanders first heard of the existence of America from the Irish, who stated that they knew of a land far away to the West over the ocean (possibly Greenland), where Christianity had been introduced, and where a small colony of Irish was established, of which the members had taught some of the natives to speak their own language.

The maritime history of the Moors must have commenced much later on, so that the Irish were able to explore any part of the Atlantic at this time without fear of interruption, and may well be credited as being the first to discover America, and as the most likely visitors to Madeira and the Canaries. It is even possible that the Moorish tradition that there was a land seven hundred leagues to the west, where the men and the women could not be distinguished apart because both of them had smooth faces; a tradition which is said to have become known to Columbus, and by which he is said to have regulated his sailing orders, may have had an Irish origin.

Be this as it may, traditions of some land to the west, commonly known as Brazil, Cipango or Cathay, were handed down in England and elsewhere. On July 15th, 1480, Captain Thylde, an Englishman, left Bristol in an eighty-ton vessel to find it, returning unsuccessful on September 18th. Five years afterwards Christopher Columbus laid the plans of his voyage of discovery before the Government of Genoa, the date when he actually discovered the West Indies (Guanahani in the Bahamas) being October 12th, 1492. John Cabota, a Venetian citizen, sailing from Bristol in an English ship, manned by English sailors, and despatched under letters patent of King Henry VII., discovered Newfoundland about June 24th, 1497. For his discovery of North America he was rewarded by the sum of £10, and afterwards by a pension of £20 a year.

In the spring of 1498, Cabota made his second expedition, during which he died. There were five ships, which, after his death, were commanded by the English captains, probably led by Lancelot Thirkill, by whom the whole of the Eastern coast of North America seems to have been discovered and marked out.

Though these facts do not precisely bear upon Madeira, they show that the archipelago may have been visited at a very early date; that the Irish believed in the existence of islands in the Atlantic with a warmer climate than that of England; and that our spirit of maritime adventure, though overshadowed for a time by that of Spain and Portugal, was never altogether dormant.

The possibility of discovery by the Arabs is rarely treated seriously. Belief depends upon the importance attached to a tale which may have some foundation, but which was certainly very "highly coloured" in the telling, namely, that of the Almagrurin adventurers, who are said to have sailed from Lisbon about the year A.D. 1100, or some century and a half prior to the expulsion of the Moors from Portugal.

These adventurers, whose name in Moorish meant the "finders of mares' nests," departed with the expressed intention of discovering something. The tale of their voyage, semi-fabulous as it no doubt was, yet agrees in time and distance very well with what might be expected from a badly built ship, driven across unknown seas, now in one direction and now in another. The district of the stinking and turbid waters which first frightened them back might well be the neighbourhood of the Azores, then probably in eruption. El Ghanam*, the island of the bitter sheep, where they went on shore, corresponds fairly well with Madeira, allowance being made for travellers' tales and for the vivid imaginations of a party of navigators, who half expected to meet dragons or monsters round every corner. The islands some few

---

* Note resemblance to Gannaria. *See* page 221.

days further south, where they were taken prisoners, and from which they were eventually conveyed blindfold to the African coast, might, with the same allowances, be an account of one of the Canaries. According to their own tale they were landed some six weeks distant from the Straits of Gibraltar, which they eventually reached on foot. Whatever deductions we may draw to-day, it is evident from the name given to them, and from the ridicule to which they were subjected, that neither they nor their story were very well received by their contemporaries.

Although legends which cannot be proved may be of little value, there remains one which can scarcely be left out. Portuguese historians state that, in 1344, an Englishman named Robert Machin, eloping with a certain Anna Arfet or Harford from Bristol, was driven to Madeira by a tempest. He found the island of surpassing beauty and without inhabitants, the latter fact proving that at least he could not have visited any of the Canary Islands. The tale goes on to say that he and his bride subsequently died there, and were both buried in the same grave near the little town of Machico, which is named after him, an altar and a cross being placed over them to perpetuate their memory. Another version, which seems more probable, taking into consideration the future importance of the island as a health resort, says that, a second storm arising, the ship, with all souls, was forced to put to sea, and was eventually wrecked on the coast of Morocco.

As was the case with St. Brendan, Machin, whose surname still exists in England, became the hero of a number of stories and poems. His name was changed according to the fancy of the author, as, for instance, in the old village play of Merry England, entitled, " *The true and ancient story of Maudlin, the merchant's daughter of Bristol, and of her lover Antonio. How they were cast away upon the shores of Barbary, where the mermaids are seen, etc., etc.*"

Whether Machin or Anna Arfet died, or, landing with the rest, were sold with them into slavery, does not affect subsequent events, as none of the actors re-appear. Many years afterwards a Spaniard named Juan Morales, being ransomed from the Moors, set sail for his native country, was taken prisoner by the Portuguese and carried to Lisbon, relating there, to the great admiration of the King, Dom John I., and his energetic son, Prince Henry the Navigator, the tale of the wonderful island which had been told him by his fellow-slaves.

Even then there was some delay. At last a ship, commanded by one Zargo, left Lisbon on the 1st of June, 1419, for Porto Santo, which had been discovered and colonised by the Portuguese for over a year. It speaks little for the enterprise of the time that Madeira should not have been discovered simultaneously.

Zargo found the people, who had come so far, terrified by strange noises, occasionally heard to issue from the great cloud looming in the horizon only twenty-three miles away. Although dissuaded from doing so, he resolved to investigate the cause, and, accompanied by the Spaniard, Juan Morales, landed in Madeira at the Ponta de S. Lourenço, afterwards visiting several parts of the coast. On July 2nd, another landing was made and a solemn service held, the island being formally taken possession of in the name of the King of Portugal.

Returning home Zargo was made governor of the part to the east of the Punta de Oliveira, and was granted permission to fire the forest in order to render the ground more suitable for cultivation. The result was a conflagration, said to have lasted for seven years, and to have done irreparable damage to the neighbourhood of Funchal.

Shortly afterwards the sugar-cane was introduced. In 1432, the first sugar-mill was erected. About 1460, the vine was brought to the island from Crete, by order of the indefatigable Prince Henry. In 1508, Funchal was created a city, and the cathedral was commenced. In 1514, the first bishop was appointed. From 1539 to 1547, when the authority was transferred to Goa, the city became the seat of an archbishopric.

In 1566, three French vessels, under De Montluc, ravaged and nearly destroyed Funchal. In 1582, Portugal, and with it Madeira, passed into the hands of Spain, their independence being once more recognised at the end of the protracted war in 1668. Madeira was, however, evacuated by the Spaniards in 1640.

After the marriage of Charles II. with Catharine of Braganza in 1660, special privileges were granted to English settlers; and, since that time, England and Madeira have always been closely connected.

The advent of the English, however, did not greatly influence the inherited customs of the inhabitants, nor did the presence of the foreigners banish the lawless manners conjured up by the disturbances of the times. At the end of the 17th century, paid assassination seems to have been the ordinary method of obtaining redress, and servants seem to have waited at table with swords by their sides.

In 1768, a frigate, aided by Captain Cook in the "Endeavour," which had just started on its voyage round the world, battered the fort on the Loo Rock in revenge for some insult to the British flag.

From 1801 till 1802, and from 1807 till 1814, the island was garrisoned by British troops, under the Treaty of Alliance.

Large exports of sugar and wine commenced early in the history of the island, the wine being in such request at the beginning of the present century, that in the year 1800 as much as 16,981 pipes were shipped. England took a large part of this, the taste having been implanted in the country by the officers returning from the American war of secession. This consumption, however, fell off greatly as people began to acquire a liking for French clarets. Though other markets were opened, the trade suffered considerably long before the oïdium in 1852 and the phylloxera in 1873 came to destroy the vineyards, and strike at the source of supply itself.

The commercial history of the vine will be found in greater detail elsewhere.

In 1834, monasteries and nunneries were placed under the control of the Government. Monks were ejected, but nuns were allowed to die out, though some of the nunneries are still occupied by novices. At the time of the suppression there were four monasteries and three nunneries.

In 1856, an outbreak of cholera carried off some 7,000 persons, the population at the time being 102,800.

Telegraphic connection with Europe was established in 1874, and, a few months later, with Brazil.

HISTORY OF THE CANARY ISLANDS.

Their position between 27° 4' and 29° 3' N. and 13° 3' and 18° 2' W. (med. Greenwich), a few score miles from the African coast and on the extreme limit of the ancient world, is sufficient reason why so few records of their state in former times have descended to us. Whether they were really the abodes of the Hesperides; the scene of one of the exploits of Hercules; the garden of Atlas, King of Mauritania, in which grew the golden apple guarded by the dragon; whether the summits of a mountain chain now slowly rising, or the remains of the sunken continent of Atlantis, mentioned elsewhere; or whether the Peak is the Mount Atlas of mythology, which is more than probable, it is impossible that they should have been quite unknown to the Ancients. They are almost visible from Cape Juby in Morocco, and ships could scarcely pass along the coast of Africa without encountering them sooner or later.

Homer (B.C. 9th century) speaks of the discovery and colonisation by Sesostris, King of Egypt (about B.C. 1400), of an island beyond the pillars of Hercules to which the souls of departed heroes were translated, calling it Elysius, whence Elysian (probably derived through the Phœnicians from the Hebrew). Ezekiel says in *chap.* xxvii.; *v.* 7, that the Tyrians were clothed in "blue and purple from the Isles of Elisha" (*mar. ref.*: "purple and scarlet").

Hannon the Carthaginian, who is said to have circumnavigated a great part of Africa about 600-500 B.C., may have visited them, as may the Phœnician expedition which left the Red Sea by order of Necho, King of Egypt, about B.C. 680, and which did undoubtedly sail round the Cape of Good Hope, returning by the Pillars of Hercules or Straits of Gibraltar (*see* Herodotus).

Herodotus, in his description of the lands beyond Libya, says that "the world ends where the sea is no longer navigable, in that place where are the gardens of the Hesperides, where Atlas supports the sky on a mountain as conical as a cylinder." Hesiod states that "Jupiter sent dead heroes to the end of the world, to the Fortunate Islands, which are in the middle of the ocean."

Being re-discovered by the Romans shortly before Christ, they were without much question dubbed "Insulæ Fortunatæ," a name which has clung to them ever since. Juba II., King of Mauritania (about 50 B.C.), sent ships to inspect them, which returned with various curios, including two large dogs from Canaria. In a book, dedicated to Augustus, he must have described them as islands clothed in fire, placed at the extreme limit of the world, as, though his writings are lost, he is freely quoted to that effect by Pliny, Plutarch and others.

King Juba seems to have placed factories for the extraction of the purple dye from the orchilla weed in the islands facing the country of Gœtulia or of the Autoloßes. Many writers have suggested that the place indicated was Madeira, but it seems more likely that Pliny's "Purpuriæ" were Fuerteventura and Lanzarote.

It is true Pliny says that the islands were uninhabited, but elsewhere it is stated that buildings were found. As it is known that the people of Lanzarote were accustomed to hide in the Cueva de los Verdes near where Haria now stands, it may be that the passage from which Pliny obtained his information was corrected after Juba's emissaries had become better acquainted with the country, and that the alteration was not brought to Pliny's notice. Pliny again tells us that the date palm grew with extraordinary fecundity, a little fact which does not apply to Madeira.

The most accurate record of the geographical position of the Fortunate Islands is left us by Ptolemy, A.D. 150, who drew his imaginary meridian line on the extreme west of the known world and through the island of Hierro. This same meridian was afterwards used by the Arabs.

It can scarcely be doubted that the islands were well known to the Phœnicians and probably to the Carthaginians long before Juba's time. Both these peoples, more especially the former, pushed their researches to far greater distances than is generally believed, and endeavoured to hinder others from following them by inventing all sorts of hideous travellers' tales about what took place in far-off countries; tales generally based on much the same description of circumstantial evidence as that of the gold seeking ants in Herodotus.

It is, therefore, strange that no authenticated Phœnician inscriptions have been found, and that all the writings or scratchings discovered as yet have been declared to be disconnected or frivolous marks. These marks, replicas of which have been fully discussed in Paris and elsewhere, do not seem in any instance to resemble the style of decoration fashionable among the aboriginals, as shown by their earthenware stamps (*Pintaderas*), their leather, their pottery, or their painted walls.

There is a tradition that St. Brendan (Spanish Borondon) came to the islands on an evangelising mission during the sixth century, but what foundation there can be for such a belief, if it be not the Brittany romances of the early middle ages, it is difficult to say. These romances, and that of the Almagrurin adventurers, are treated more fully in the history of Madeira.

At the time of the conquest the natives were certainly unable to write, and the Spanish invaders, in the intolerant spirit of their age, took no pains to preserve any records of the language, folk-lore or oral history of the country.

Later on Viana and others did their best to supply the deficiency, but the time for fulness or accuracy was past, and our knowledge of what happened prior to the fourteenth century is exceedingly vague.

Ossuna, quoting the lost writings of the Arabian historian Ebu Fathymah (*see* Dr. Chil, p. 238), says that the Admiral Ben Farroukh, having received information of the existence of land to the west of the African coast, landed at Gando Bay, in Canary, in A.D. 999, finding a people willing to trade and already accustomed to the arrival of visitors. He subsequently visited the other islands, which he designated by corruptions of the names given them by Ptolemy, whose meridian he adopted.

This opportunity is taken of calling the reader's attention to Gando Bay, the principal port of Grand Canary in historic as it probably was in pre-historic times. (*Refer* to Los Letreros near Agüimes and to the M^{ña} de las Cuatro Puertas.)

Edrisi, the Arabian geographer, A.D. 1099-1164, quotes Raccam-el-Avez as authority that, in clear weather, the smoke issuing from the island of the two magician brothers, Cheram and Cherham (note resemblance to Cheyde or E'Cheyde the Guanche name for the Peak) was visible from the African coast, a truth which Humboldt (Cosmos) proves to be mathematically correct. The islands are elsewhere described as "Gezagrel Khalidal" and "Al-jazir-al-Khaledat," translated as the Happy or Fortunate Islands.

It has been argued that the Canaries were visited by 'a Genoese expedition about A.D. 1291, but, as this fleet never returned, the matter is difficult to prove. They are again reported to have been discovered by a French ship about A.D. 1330. It is said that, on hearing of this, King Alphonso IV. of Portugal sent a party to take possession of them in 1334, which was repulsed at Gomera. This expedition was followed up by another from the same quarter in 1341, which seems to have been again without result, although the islands were visited and a considerable amount of information was gathered.

The little knowledge we possess about the Canaries during the early middle ages is accounted for by the turmoil and confusion into which the world was thrown by the fall of the Roman Empire and by the protracted struggles of Christianity against Mahomedanism. If one may judge from the traditions handed down, they must have been a sort of pastoral Arcadia, with the exception, perhaps, of Lanzarote and Fuerteventura, which were more exposed to attack from Africa and from European slave-hunters, and where civil wars seem to have been frequent.

In an evil hour for them, Europe, recovering from the strain of the Crusades and filled with unemployed soldiers, turned its attention their way. In 1344, we find a certain Louis de la Cerda, a French nobleman of royal Spanish extraction, created "King of the Fortunate Islands" by Pope Clement VI., then resident at Avignon, with full power to Christianise them in the best way he could. This decree was much resented by the English Ambassador, who evidently considered the term "Insulæ Fortunatæ" to apply exclusively to Great Britain, which, under Edward III., was then at war with France. Not only in his time, but throughout the middle ages, the name of Albion was generally believed to be derived from the Greek word ὄλβιος, meaning happy or blest. Nothing came of this flourish of trumpets, but, in 1360, missionaries, sent to Grand Canary, converted some of the natives and taught them many useful arts. The majority, however, subsequently suffered martyrdom. In 1393, an expedition from Spain was repulsed off the same island, but met with greater success further west, and Lanzarote was sacked on the way home.

There is no doubt that the Islands must frequently have been visited during the fourteenth century for the purposes of pillage or of trade, but the modern history of the Canaries practically commences in 1402, when Jean de Bethencourt, a Norman gentleman, fitted out a ship with the express purpose of conquering them and settling there.

Lanzarote, in which, according to his own statements, he found the fighting population reduced by constant raids from abroad to some three hundred men, was peaceably occupied. Crossing the Strait, a small fort was built in the North of Fuerteventura, but Bethencourt's forces proved insufficient to bring the island into subjection. Leaving a garrison behind, he returned home in order to procure more means. These he obtained from Henry III. of Castille, who gave men and money, creating Bethencourt lord of four of the group in return for the promise that the archipelago should be conquered in his name.

Fuerteventura, Lanzarote, Gomera, and Hierro, none of which were capable of prolonged resistance, were thus brought under the dominion of the Kings of Castille.

In Gomera the Spaniards seemed to have been treated most affectionately. When Bethencourt left, the people swam for miles by the side of his ship, imploring him not to go away. Many years later the Ghomerythes proved the staunchest of allies, the conquest of the island of La Palma being mainly due to help afforded by them.

In Hierro the newcomers were welcomed with outstretched arms for reasons given a little later on under the head of "Legends." The supplies of the island, however, were small and the guests could not be supported for an indefinite length of time. The secret of a hidden spring being revealed by a native girl to her foreign lover, a quarrel ensued, which led to hostilities, and a number of the Bimbachos were carried away into slavery. For further details, *see* under "Hierro."

Canary, La Palma and Teneriffe proved too powerful for attack by the forces at Bethencourt's disposal, and were not occupied till many years afterwards, the last named island holding out until the close of the century.

Bethencourt, who seems to have been a man of superior character, left in 1406, and died in France in 1425, bequeathing his property in the islands to his nephew, Maciot de Bethencourt.

Under the new owner, affairs seem to have been utterly mismanaged. Prior to his disappearance from the scene, he sold his rights to the Infante Dom Henrique of Portugal. Before this time, however, his tyrannical and grasping behaviour had done much to alienate the goodwill of the natives.

Owing to priestly and other intrigues, the history of the next half century is a chronicle of mean and unsavoury deeds, and the reader desirous of full details must turn to works where more space can be devoted to the subject.

In 1443, a body of Spanish troops under Guillem Peraza attacked La Palma, but Peraza was killed and the invaders were forced to retire.

In 1464, Diego de Herrera, Lord of La Gomera, made an unsuccessful attack upon Canary.

In June of the same year he landed at Santa Cruz in Teneriffe with 500 men, and, without penetrating far into the country, made terms with nine of the Princes, taking possession of the island in the name of the King of Castille and Leon. He obtained a concession from Serdeto, Prince of Anaga, to build a tower, which, later on, was erected by his son and garrisoned with 80 men. The stipulations made were not observed by the Spaniards, and the fort was subsequently attacked by 1,000 Guanches and razed to the ground, the Spaniards being driven away and many of them killed.

After leaving Teneriffe, Diego de Herrera, being reinforced by 800 Portuguese, resolved to attack Canary again. He landed at Gando Bay and marched along the North Coast with a detachment of 500 men.

The Canarios surrounded and drove him into a corner, whereupon Don Diego sent his son-in-law, Diego de Silva, and 200 men by sea to attack the enemy in the rear.

Silva landed near Gáldar, was met by 600 Canarios under Temisor Semidan, and was forced to take refuge in a Tagoror or Place of Council. All escape being cut off, Silva offered to surrender, but quarter was denied.

The state of Silva and his men was absolutely hopeless, when Temisor, advancing as though for a parley, told Silva to seize him as a hostage and then to demand free passage to his ship.

This was done and the request was granted by the Canarios, but the path by which the Spaniards were conducted seemed to them so hazardous that they refused to proceed, imagining that the Canarios meant to take advantage of some precipice and to massacre them all.

To reassure them each Spaniard was allowed to cling to the cloak of one of the natives, so that if one were thrown down the other must go with him.

Arrived at the ship, Silva and his men voluntarily gave up their swords, vowing not to fight against the Canarios again. In spite of the objections of his father-in-law, Silva, and probably many of the rest, kept their word. Some of the men, however, joined Don Diego de Herrera, who renewed the attack.

The Canarios made prisoners of a few of those who had thus broken their promise, and might well have put them to death. They were, however, allowed to remain alive, being condemned to brush away flies, as creatures unworthy even of the honour of execution.

Don Diego met with little success, but, in 1466, made a treaty of commerce, and was allowed to build a tower at Gando Bay, the fly-flappers being set at liberty.

This tower became a source of great annoyance to the Canarios. From it the *Harimaguadas* (vestal virgins) of the temple near Telde seem to have been molested, and it was destroyed on more than one occasion.

The Spaniards, however, had resolved to take the island. Troops were landed near where Las Palmas now stands, and, in 1478, Ferdinand V. of Castille sent Juan Rejon with 600 men to bring the matter to a conclusion.

Rejon commenced by making an intrenched camp, which was attacked by 2,000 Canarios under the Guanarteme of Doramas. The natives were defeated with a loss of 300 men, the victory being principally due to the terror inspired by a small body of cavalry, now used for the first time in the islands, where the horse had hitherto been unknown.

Some Portuguese ships happened to arrive at this juncture. Believing themselves to have strong claims to the sovereignty of Canary, a body of 200 soldiers was sent to the assistance of the Canarios. A second advance was then made, but the Portuguese were drawn into ambush and cut to pieces.

The Spaniards were no sooner established at Las Palmas than intrigues commenced among themselves. Fra Juan Bermudez, Dean of the Cathedral of Rubicon, in Lanzarote, and an official named Algaba, contrived to throw Juan Rejon into prison, and it was with the greatest difficulty that Rejon obtained permission to return to Spain and justify himself.

In the meantime the Dean assumed command and made repeated attacks on the natives, but his successes were dearly bought, and the Spanish losses in engagements at Moya and at Tirajana were considerable.

Rejon then returned, reinstated in his command. The Dean was sent to Lanzarote and Algaba was promptly put to death, but Rejon's severity was disagreeable to the authorities at home and he was replaced by Pedro de Vera.

Vera defeated the Canarios in several encounters. In an attack on Gáldar, made from the sea, he was fortunate enough to capture Temisor Semidan, who was sent to Spain, became a Christian, returned to Canary, and, in 1483, persuaded the miserable remnant of the Canarios to surrender, their number being by this time reduced to some 600 warriors and about 1,500 women and children.

Throughout the hostilities natives of the islands already pacified were brought as auxiliaries for the subjugation of the others. Taking advantage of this fact, Vera persuaded a body of Canarios to help him in an attack on Teneriffe, but, instead of carrying out the agreement, sent them to Spain for sale as slaves. The Canarios, becoming aware of his treachery, forced the sailors to put them on shore at Lanzarote, whence, however, they were never able to return to Canary.

About this time Francisco Maldonado, Governor of Las Palmas, in alliance with Pedro Fernandez de Saavedra, Lord of Fuerteventura, made an attack on Teneriffe, but was repulsed on the slopes above Santa Cruz.

A man now appeared upon the scene who was destined to carry to completion the work begun by Juan de Bethencourt. Don Alonso Fernandez de Lugo, el Conquistador and afterwards Adelantádo (Governor) of the Province of the Canaries, was a Galician nobleman, who had served with distinction against the Moors in the conquest of Granada, and had been presented with the Valley of Agaete (Canary) in return for his services. Whilst there, he conceived the capture of Teneriffe and La Palma, reconnoitring their coasts and acquainting himself with their geographical features.

He then went to Spain and made a report to the Court, which created him Captain-General of the Conquests in the Canaries from Cape Guer to Cape Bojador.

His first attack was made in 1491 on the island of La Palma, which had remained undisturbed by the Spaniards since the original and unsuccessful attempt in 1443. De Lugo took a number of Ghomerythes with him, whose assistance was invaluable. On May 3, 1492, after an arduous campaign of seven months, the island was finally subdued. Further details will be found in the description of La Palma.

On May 1, 1493, de Lugo, accompanied by a force of 1,000 footmen and 150 cavalry, partially composed of Ghomerythes and Canarios, landed at Añaza (Santa Cruz) in Teneriffe. Owing to dissensions amongst the Guanches, he was able to effect an alliance with the Menceyes of Anaga and of Güimar. A tower of refuge was built, and, early in 1494, an expedition was made to the north of the island. This fell into an ambush in the Barranco de Acentejo, at the place now known as La Matanza, or the Place of the Slaughter, and was cut to pieces. The few left, most of whom were wounded, were pursued back to Santa Cruz. The Guanches even attacked the tower of refuge, but were beaten off with heavy loss. It is said that in the fight at Matanza 600 Spaniards and 200 Guanches were killed.

De Lugo was now so closely pressed by the enemy that on June 8, 1494, he evacuated the island.

Reinforced by fresh levies sent by the third Duke of Medina Sidonia, de Lugo landed again in Teneriffe before the close of the year, his force this time consisting of 1,000 foot and 70 cavalry.

The tower of refuge, which the Guanches had destroyed, was first rebuilt, after which an attack was made on the plains of La Laguna, where a large body of natives had assembled. After a hard fight, these were defeated, but were not driven from the district, de Lugo being eventually compelled to fall back upon his base, where, for a considerable time, he lay inactive.

How long it might have taken, under ordinary circumstances, to overcome the resistance of the islanders it is difficult to say. Providence, however, interfered on behalf of the Spaniards.

Dispirited by prophesies of evil predicted by their sages for many years, the majority of the Guanches now lost heart. The Menceyes of Taoro and of Anaga had been killed in fight ; other princes were faithless to the compacts made amongst themselves ; old jealousies led to renewed dissension at this most critical moment, and portions of their forces were withdrawn.

Worse even than this, a peculiar disease, known as the " Modorra," broke out in La Laguna and spread to other parts of the island. The nature of the malady is obscure, but its effects were appalling and ghastly in the extreme.

The Spaniards were spared, but the Guanches were seized with a frightful melancholia, which carried them off by thousands. Whole troops wandered hopelessly into the hills, hid themselves in caves, and crouched down to die. Even at the present day such retreats are occasionally discovered, little heaps of bones or seated skeletons marking the spot where the despairing victims sank to rise no more.

It is said that some Spaniards, reconnoitring on the road to La Laguna, met an old woman seated alone on the Montaña de Taco, who waved them on, bidding them go in and occupy that charnel-house where none were left to offer opposition.

De Lugo, consequently, was able to advance to beyond La Matanza, where he was met by the Mencey of Taoro with about 5,000 followers. These were signally defeated at a place now known as La Victoria, and about 2,000 warriors were killed. In spite of this, the Spaniards were, however, once more compelled to retreat to Santa Cruz.

In the meantime the ravages of the Modorra continued unabated, and at last, in 1496, de Lugo marched into the Valley of Orotava, encamping where Realejo Bajo now stands. At Realejo Alto, separated from the Spaniards by the Barranco de Padronato, lay the last of the Guanches.

The native forces, too reduced to be capable of resistance, surrendered, every man, woman and child being promptly baptized into the bosom of the Church.

Several of the Menceyes were sent on a trip to Europe as an outward and visible sign of the triumph of the Spanish arms, but, after being duly exhibited, most or all of them returned to their own country.

After the conquest many of the horses, on which the cavalry was mounted, were sold and carried to America, which, as the reader will remember, was discovered by Columbus in 1492, the Canaries being used as a port of call both by Columbus and by those following in his wake. From these horses, and from others embarked in Spain at about the same period, the wild American mustang was derived.

The subjugation of Teneriffe was so largely due to the Canario auxiliaries, that de Lugo is said to have been unable to refuse any request of their leader, Fernando Guanarteme de Galdar, usually called King of Canary.

These Canarios were not always subject to the control of their nominal masters, especially when engaged with the enemy.

The following few incidents are of great interest, not only because they bear upon this point and upon the state of the islands immediately after the conquest, but because they show, better than any scientific discussions, statistical tables or anthropological measurements, how the natives gradually intermarried with the new arrivals, and how the present hybrid race, was built up.

The attention of the reader is called to the fact that whereas in Teneriffe the conquered Guanches took two or three Spanish names and often seem to have dropped their old titles entirely, the Canarios continued to be known as of the family of Doramas, Guanarteme, etc., etc.

Imobac Bencomo (Son of Como), Quehevi (King) of Teneriffe, Mencey (Chief) of Taoro, was engaged in the chief of the battles at La Laguna. At the spot on which the chapel of San Roque now stands, finding escape to be impossible, he yielded himself to his pursuers. Unfortunately these proved to be Canarios. One of these, baptised into the Catholic Church under the name of Pedro Martin Buendia, ignoring the protests of the Spaniards near him, killed the Prince with a thrust of his lance. As an example of a noble Guanche the murdered man claims attention. Seven feet high and seventy years old, he was robust, strong, and active. Viana, who describes his points as Shakespeare described those of a war horse, says that his long white beard fell nearly to his waist; that his piercing black eyes were surmounted by heavy eyebrows meeting above the nose; and that beneath his widely opened nostrils a long, twisted moustache scarcely hid "the monstrous row of diamond-like teeth." That he was not alone and singular in his appearance may be gathered from the fact that his body was at first believed to be that of his brother Tinguaro, the two, according to Viana, being twins.

It may be added that though Imobac claimed the title of King of Teneriffe by virtue of his descent from Tinerfe the Great, his legitimacy was not universally recognised. A half-veiled hostility between the North and the South of the Island seems to have been due to this question, the claims of the King of Adeje conflicting with those of his cousin of Taoro.

When the natives joined the Catholic Church they were always baptised under new names. For this reason it is possible, as will be seen, for a family now living in the island to be of pure native blood, though their pedigree, down to the commencement of the 14th or 15th century, shows their ancestors to have borne Spanish surnames.

One illustration is sufficient. It is taken from Teneriffe, the last of the islands to be conquered, but applies equally well elsewhere.

Imobac, Mencey of Taoro, killed in La Laguna, had, by his wife Caseloria, one son and two daughters.

1st.—Ben Tahod (Son of the Valley), who opposed the Spaniards until the peace of Realejo, when he took the name of Cristóbal Hernandez de Taoro, his godfather being the so-called King of Canary. His first wife was called Sañagua and his second wife Inés Hernández Tacoronte, both women of Guanche birth.

By the first he had (a) Derimán (baptised as Cristóbal Hernandez), who married either Guaymina de Güimar or Guacimara de Anaga (baptised Ana Hernandez), (b) Ramagua or Rosalva (baptised Isabel del Castillo), who married Antón Martín of Abona, (c) Collorarpa (baptised María Hernandez), who married the Canary Auxiliary Juan Doramas.

2nd.—Dacil (baptised Mencia Bencomo), first wife of Adxona, Mencey of Abona (baptised Gaspar Hernandez), whose daughter, Catalina Bencomo, married the Captain of Spanish cavalry, Fernan García Izquierdo del Castillo, and had by him four children, all bearing the surname of Izquierdo. For the legend concerning Dacil, the reader will turn to the description of La Laguna.

3rd.—María Bencomo (Guanche name unknown), who married a Guanche of the baptismal name of Cristóbal Gonzalez Verano. Their daughter, Catalina Gonzalez, became the mistress of a Laguna priest, and by him had several daughters. Provided by him with a dowry, she next married Hernando Gonzalez, apparently a Guanche of Buenavista, and their daughter again married a Guanche of the same place. One of the illegitimate daughters of the priest, María González del Castillo, married a Portuguese named Antón Yanes. A second illegitimate daughter married another Portuguese, Juan Fernandez Vasconcellos, settled in Realejo. Both marriages were fruitful.

Ben Tahod's second wife appears to have been a very handsome woman. Hernando Guanarteme de Galdar, apparently nephew of Ben Tahod's godfather, fell in love with her and carried her away by force. The Guanches, under Ben Tahod, rose to arms, and civil war commenced between them and the retainers of the Canario, whose uncle had received large grants of land from D. Alonso Fernandez de Lugo in return for extraordinary services rendered at the time of the invasion of the country.

The position of the Guanartemes was politically very important, and apparently the Spaniards were not in sufficient strength to administer justice with much severity.

According to one account the seducer was banished to Spain; but was allowed to take the woman with him. According to another, Ben Tahod was taken prisoner and kept in confinement by D. Hernando (the Canario), who had been appointed administrator of the district and was responsible for the general peace. The ex-Mencey continued in prison until 1521, in spite of a royal order, dated 1511, declaring that all men born free should be set at liberty. Tradition says that Ben Tahod was set at large, but was eventually assassinated, and that his remaining wife married a Canario named Alonso Ramírez Izquierdo.

The Guanarteme had sons by the woman he stole, who bore the name of Hernández Guanarteme; also one daughter, who married Juan Alonso, son of a Canario named Pedro Mayor.

As years went on, the native names fell out of use, and the writer, although he has been assured by more than one person that they were of pure indigenous blood, does not know any family surname now extant of unquestionable native origin.

Since the conquest the sovereignty of Spain has never been seriously disputed, though both Portugal and Morocco have laid claim to the islands.

The Moors, in fact, made several attacks, landing even in places so remote from the African coast as Gomera and the western side of Teneriffe.

Jarife, King of Fez, occupied Lanzarote in 1569 and again in 1586, claiming possession in virtue of his descent from Atlas of Mauritania. He was, however, forced to retire, carrying with him a number of prisoners. The last Moorish attack took place in 1749.

In 1595, a large English fleet, under Sir Francis Drake and Sir John Hawkins, was repulsed off Las Palmas and met with little success at Gomera. A Dutch fleet, which followed in 1599, did considerable damage to the first place, but was eventually driven away, and was unable to land in the latter.

During Cromwell's Protectorate, in 1656, Admiral Sir Robert Blake, with 36 vessels, attacked Santa Cruz, Teneriffe, and worked great havoc amongst the forts and shipping, sinking 16 great galleons laden with treasure then lying in the harbour. In 1706, Admiral Jennings paid a visit without, however, opening fire. In 1743, Admiral Charles Winton made some unsuccessful attempts on La Palma, Gomera and Grand Canary. In addition to attacks such as those named, the islanders about this time seem to have been frequently molested by privateers.

In July, 1797, Santa Cruz was formally attacked by Admiral Nelson. Though unsuccessful, this combat has aroused an interest to which it does not seem altogether entitled. This is, perhaps, due to the fact that it was Nelson's one defeat; that our popular naval hero lost an arm on the occasion; that the centenary of the event has recently been celebrated in the islands; and that two of Nelson's flags are still to be seen in one of the churches of Santa Cruz. Other trophies captured by the Spaniards were one cannon, two drums, some swords, rifles, etc., and a scaling ladder, which is preserved in the Museo Nacional de Artilleria. The history of the attack is the following:—

Vice-Admiral Nelson, who, under Admiral Jervis, was assisting in the blockade of Cadiz, was ordered to proceed to Teneriffe and take possession of a large treasure just landed there from the Spanish galleon *El Principe de Asturias*.

His force consisted of four ships of war, three frigates, one cutter, one mortar and one gunboat, carrying altogether 393 guns and about 1,500 men. The Spanish forts mounted some 90 guns.

Land was sighted on July 20th. On the same day, the delivery of the treasure was demanded from the Spanish authorities, who refused to give it up.

On the 21st, an attempt was made to occupy the heights above the town, but a strong Levante prevented the ships from supporting the landing party, and on the following day these had to be re-embarked.

On the evening of the 24th, the ships were anchored off the Valle del Bufadero, about two miles to the N.E. of the town, and a feint was made in order to draw the garrison away from the forts.

At midnight, about 700 men in boats were directed against the mole, arriving within half a gun-shot before their discovery by the enemy. About 40 guns at once opened fire. The cutter, containing about 200 men, and several boats were sunk, many of the remainder being dashed to pieces by the surf as the men jumped ashore.

Nelson's arm was shattered by a cannon ball as he stepped on to the jetty, and he was carried back to his ship by the men. Though in great pain and weak from loss of blood, he refused help when climbing the side of the vessel, bidding the crew row back to the assistance of their comrades.

In the meantime those on the mole drove their opponents back, spiked their guns, and, led by Captain Bowen and First Lieut. Mr. Thorpe, endeavoured to win their way into the town. The fire opened upon them from the Fort of San Cristóbal was, however, too fierce. Nearly all the officers were killed or wounded; the scaling ladders had been lost in the surf, and the party on the mole were obliged to retreat, which they did in good order, after holding their position for the best part of the night.

The boats commanded by Captains Trowbridge, Miller and Hood, with some 340 men, having missed the mole, which they could not regain owing to the surf, were run ashore at the south of the town. The pickets were driven in, and possession was taken of the Dominican Monastery, then standing on the site now occupied by the theatre and market, of the Plaza de la Iglesia in the lower part of the town, and of the area now known as the Plaza de la Constitucion. Not being able to meet with Nelson's command, which they imagined to be in possession of the mole, they sent a sergeant to demand the surrender of the fort. No reply was returned, the sergeant being either shot or taken prisoner.

When morning came, Trowbridge retreated to the monastery. Finding victory impossible, he demanded permission to leave the town with all arms, in which case he promised that the squadron should not again attack any part of the Canaries. In the event of refusal he threatened to sack and burn the town.

His terms were granted; he was allowed to purchase provisions, and withdrew without molestation.

The British loss was heavy, namely, 44 killed, 201 drowned, and 123 wounded, as compared with 32 killed and 42 wounded on the Spanish side.

However rudely they may have handled one another during the fighting, the behaviour of both parties after the event was marked by an almost fraternal kindness. The volleys of compliments exchanged between Nelson and Don Antonio Gutierrez, the Comandante-General of the Canaries at the time, though they may seem to us very high-flown, did not lack a certain element of sincerity. Presents of beer, cheese and wine were exchanged between the two commanders. No Englishman can remember, without a glow of gratitude, the solicitude with which our wounded were treated, and the genuine hospitality which caused the Spaniards to present each of Trowbridge's men with a loaf of bread and a bottle of wine on which to break his fast before leaving the mole.

For the defence made on this occasion, Santa Cruz was granted the title of " Leal, Noble é Invicta."

In 1821, the Canaries were created a Province of Spain, with Santa Cruz, Teneriffe, as the capital and chief seat of government. Local jealousy has held the islands apart, and has prevented much of the progress which might otherwise have been realised.

Of late years the ports, however, have been declared free; submarine cables have brought the archipelago into close connection with the rest of the world; coaling stations have been created, and commerce generally has taken great strides. For particulars on these subjects, the reader will turn to the information given locally, or to the pages of the Commercial Section.

In 1839, monasteries were declared illegal, but nuns are still allowed to take the veil on condition of depositing with the Government a small sum, about £150, to guarantee the means of livelihood. The ecclesiastical properties, which were numerous, were at the same time taken possession of by the Government, in return for salaries to be paid to the bishops and priests on a scale agreed upon with the Pope.

However interesting the later history of the Canaries may be as a harbour for Spanish galleons; as a point of departure for Columbus on his way to the discovery of a new world; as the site of the only direct repulse which our greatest of admirals ever suffered, or as a group of islands which, under the somewhat lax rule of Spain, has yet developed into one of the most important coaling stations of to-day; such records, although far the most complete, precise and trustworthy, can scarcely arrest the attention of the most prosaic mind so completely as must the many social and ethnographical problems presented by the earlier traditions, so rudely handed down by mediæval visitors or conquerors, and enshrined in a halo of romance by the fanaticism or vivid imagination of the monkish writers by whom they were preserved.

The ancient names of the islands are given in this work under the description of each island. The accuracy of their application is, in some instances, open to question. An effort has been made to place them as correctly as possible; but neither Ptolemy nor the Arabian writers were very precise as to the particular places referred to. The generic term of "Canaria" is probably derived from "Gannaria," a name used by Ptolemy for that part of the African coast lying near Cape Blanco.

The populations, as estimated by Bethencourt and other visitors of the 15th century, were as follows:—Lanzarote, 300 fighting men; Fuerteventura, 4,000; Canary, which obtained its name of Grand Canary from the stubborn defence it made, from 9,000 to 14,000 warriors, and a population of 90,000, or much the same as to-day; Teneriffe, about 15,000 warriors, and La Palma, 1,200 inhabitants, with some 20,000 animals, both probably greatly under-estimated. These are the only records the writer has met with. In Hierro, where war was unknown, there were no fighting men.

For the sake of convenience of reference, many of the facts known about the indigenous inhabitants, gathered by the writer from a number of historians, are placed under separate headings. Those wishing to study them *in extenso* will refer to the list of books given in the Bibliography.

Origin of the Natives.—Anthropological measurements of many hundreds of skulls show the natives to have been a *dolicocephalic* race of Iberians, those in the Western Islands, which were the least exposed to the introduction of negro blood from the African coast, being closely allied to the Basques and the Kelts of Western Europe.

Tradition and local feuds point to the occasional immigration of foreign settlers, some of whom were perhaps driven on shore and wrecked.

A colony of immigrants has been referred to as having perhaps come from Egypt about 1400 B.C. The reference comes from Homer, but the fact is not altogether dependent upon this somewhat questionable evidence. According to Ossuna, some of the natives carried to Rome about the commencement of the Christian Era expressed the greatest horror at the idea of dying abroad and of being placed in the earth without being previously embalmed. Their fear that decomposition of the body would affect the immortality of the soul, may have been derived from an Egyptian source, as may their skill in the mummification of the dead, a matter discussed at length a little later on. If the islands were uninhabited in the times of Sesostris, the source from which the islanders originally came may well have been the banks of the Nile. On the other hand, their inability to write, and their methods of worship, do not tend to support this view.

Whatever their starting point may have been, it is only natural that a people without literature or ships would soon differ greatly in their language and in their customs.

The occasional advent of strangers, or their exposure to invasion from the coast, would also accelerate the inevitable changes brought about by time.

In Teneriffe it is said that sandals were used similar to those common in Valencia, which were copied from the Moors. One writer says that some of the natives were acquainted with the decimal system, which might indicate some connection with the Arabs.

Language, Inscriptions, etc.—The roots of the various dialects had a common origin, and the earliest visitors were able to make themselves partially understood in one island by means of interpreters from the others.

A number of words and names of places in all the islands were almost identical with Berber words and names, as were also the names of the tribes inhabiting Hierro, Gomera and La Palma, viz., Ben-Bachir, Ghomerythes and Haouarythes.

Certain words were in general use; for instance, *Aemon* meant water in Lanzarote and Hierro, and probably elsewhere; *Aho,* was milk in Lanzarote, Canary and Teneriffe; *Chivato*, meant kid in all the islands, and *Cigueno,* was the name for a goat in Lanzarote and La Palma.

"The Language of Teneriffe" was very ably discussed by the late Marquis of Bute in a pamphlet of that name. The author calls attention to the difficulty of deciding the island from which the words he quotes have been derived, the collections handed down to us being very vague on this point. He proves the use of a definite article, which shows at once that the language had no connection with any of the American dialects. Professor Max Müller, discussing the Marquis of Bute's paper, stated that he "felt inclined to link it with a Semitic origin, or with a Babel language."

A small list of words will be given, spelt according to the Spanish alphabet, which, for the sake of uniformity, the writer has ·adopted in similar cases throughout this book. The pronunciation can be ascertained by referring to the remarks preceding the vocabulary.

T, to, at, atch, ash, as or *ach* = the. *Mencey* = lord. *Achemencey* = one of secondary rank. *Achacuca* = the masses. *Quehevi* = king. *Sigoñes* = gentlemen. *Tibicenas* = demoniacal apparitions. *Efiquen* = temple. *Tabonas* = obsidian knives. *Gañigo* = an earthen vessel. *Xercas* = shoes. *Magado* = a pole about eight feet long, with heavy ends. *Chacerquen* = vegetable honey. *Yoya* = sap. *Mozan* = seed. *Banotes* = javelins. *Xacos* = mummies. *Cairomo* = a goatskin knapsack. *Vaco guare* = I want to die. *Guanarteme* = chief. *Guayre* = one of secondary rank. (The last two are undoubtedly Canario.)

Names of places :—

Guayonje, Ubaque, Izogue, Guamasa, Tijóco, Tejina, Adeje, Taoro, Chirindaque, Anambro, Anaga, Añaza, Guañáka, Asgua, Visogue, Vegeril, Marrajo (all Guanche), *Telde, Tirma, Moya, Gáldar, Mogan, Taidia* (Canario).

Tribal or family names :

Chimber, Korosma, Cherinda, Laravicho, Vigogia, Tajana, Afono, Chinobre, Icono, Vegio.

The common call to a goat, still used in Teneriffe, is *jua-jay*, a fearfully guttural sound, which in English might perhaps be written *hououa haüyı*.

The inscriptions found on rocks in La Palma and in Hierro have been submitted to experts in Paris, and have been declared to be mere arbitrary scratches, without connection, and of different epochs. They do not appear to have been engraved by the inhabitants found at the time of the conquest.

Form of Government, Laws, Marriage Laws, etc.—At some indetermined date, the King or Quehevi of Teneriffe resided at Adeje. Tinerfe the Great divided his kingdom amongst nine sons, of whom the Mencey of Taoro was nominally the head. These matters are treated earlier in this history, and under the description of Teneriffe.

The Mencey possessed rights of seigneurie over all his subjects; the nobles were subservient to him, but enjoyed similar privileges over the serfs. There was a great distinction between the classes, which dressed differently, were forbidden to intermarry, and were buried separately, a convenient belief being maintained that the Creator first made the nobles, and, finding the world would hold more, then peopled it with the common herd to wait upon them. A man of noble descent who sullied his hands by menial work or was discourteous to his inferiors, was not received on coming of age as a member of the upper classes. All, however, worked in the fields, or rallied during war at the points previously fixed, such as the great palm in Villa Orotava. A child born of a noble father by a peasant mother was *ipse facto* noble, but a woman lost caste by marrying beneath her. The daughters of the nobles were sometimes brought up apart (*see* "Religious Customs"), and their marriage required the sanction of the King. As a rule, only one wife seems to have been allowed, but she might be repudiated if barren. One writer states that a man might have as many as he pleased, and that consent alone was sufficient to constitute marriage. The reader will have noticed a few pages back that both the Mencey of Taoro and the Guanarteme of Gáldar had more than one wife. The latter, in fact, seems to have had three, and one, who was barren, was not repudiated, but became the devoted nurse of the children born to her husband by the woman stolen from Ben Tahod.

The sign of authority was the *humerus* or bone of the arm of one of the deceased kings, or, according to Viana the poet, a skull. This was sworn upon at the coronation by both King and nobles, and was used as a sceptre at the council. Justice was ad ministered and laws made in councils, called together at some well-known point, such a council being known as a *taoro* or *tagoror*. The place of meeting might be simply a large cave, round which a rough seat would be cut in the rock, or an open space on which an army might be assembled. In most of the Menceyatos one or two such places can be pointed out, and many still bear a name associating them with their former use.

Nuñez de la Peña says that capital punishment was not inflicted in Teneriffe. In this statement he may be wrong, as the records gathered by him, and indeed by all writers on the early history of the Canaries, are based upon somewhat untrustworthy evidence.

According to other writers a child was put to death for insulting its parents; adulterers were buried alive; and robbery where the door was closed, if only by a wooden latch, was nearly always a capital offence. Homicide was revenged by the relatives, but there were a few places of refuge similar to those recorded in the Semitic writings. The culprit, if brought to justice, seems to have forfeited his property, and to have been banished from his own district for life. It is, however, probable that a distinction was made between homicide and murder. Death was also inflicted on those approaching too near to the spot used as a bathing-place by the Consecrated Virgins or *Harimaguadas*, as they were called in Canary.

In some of the islands, the fear of over-population was so great, that a man was liable to be put to death for merely joining or speaking to a strange woman on the public road. So very severe a law cannot have been always enforced; but that some such restriction on intercourse did exist is proved by the double pathways still to be seen in some of the mountains of Teneriffe and Grand Canary. There is no question whatever that these were constructed for the separation of the sexes, probably with a view to prevent the necessity of child murder, a legal crime which had to be enforced at times in most of the islands. It seems, however, that the firstborn was always spared.

Execution was inflicted by means of crushing the breast with a heavy stone, beating with sticks, throwing from a rock or into the sea, or, in cases of treason, by burning, stoning or burying alive. In Lanzarote there was a pit into which the condemned was lowered, the choice being offered of either food or water. This pit was done away with because one prisoner, more artful than her predecessors, chose milk, remaining alive so long that this form of punishment had to be abolished. (*See* under Lanzarote.)

A most admirable form of nationalisation of the land, and one most suitable to a small and isolated country, was that all the property belonged to the Crown, to which it returned on the death of the head of the house, being at once re-distributed. This prevented any of the nobles from growing too powerful.

The title of a king or prince was hereditary in Teneriffe, from father to son.

It is rather difficult to locate all the above laws as belonging actually or entirely to Teneriffe. The conclusion the writer has drawn from what he has read is that similar necessities in all the islands has caused the fundamental laws of each to bear a great resemblance. Besides this, the inhabitants must have started on a more or less common basis, or at least with ideas bequeathed to them by a common race of predecessors, however remote. As they could only pass the laws on from one generation to another by word of mouth, it is reasonable to conclude that this was done by means of the priests, as was the case with the early Jews, and that the custodians of the law or scribes, if one may call them so, were forced to learn them by heart, possibly in a sort of rhythmic chant. This chant would be difficult to alter suddenly, but it might gradually change by the addition of new matter, and by the deletion of old. As the priests were all chosen from amongst the nobles, any change of this description would not be likely to be in favour of the peasant.

The government in Grand Canary seems to have passed through the stage to which Teneriffe had recently arrived. The island had been divided amongst fourteen chieftains, who endeavoured to take away the territory of the Princess of Gáldar, Andamana, a woman, from all accounts, remarkable for courage, beauty, intellect and power of intrigue. Coquetting first with one chieftain, and then with another, she gradually organised her forces, then, choosing the bravest of her warriors as a husband, eventually subdued the whole island. It was owing to this fact that the Spaniards found Canary so hard to conquer. Had

Teneriffe been equally united, it is difficult, even after making allowance for the *modorra*, to imagine how they could have taken possession of it at all.

Some writers state that both in Canary and Gomera it was customary for a host to present his wife to a guest, or to change wives during the stay of the latter, a refusal being regarded as a deadly insult. For this reason property descended to the brothers, or, failing them, to the sisters or to their descendants. It is not unlikely that this was a custom in several of the islands, not merely from a feeling of hospitality, but because, in a restricted sphere, the introduction of fresh blood becomes a matter of primary importance. An example of this is to be seen in Lapland in the present day, where any traveller sleeping at one of the isolated settlements scattered about this frost-stricken country, is expected to conform to what is nothing more or less than a law of race preservation.

In Lanzarote and Fuerteventura, which, as has already been pointed out, were much more subject to Arab or African influence, the women were jealously guarded, and the royal descent was from male to male.

In Lanzarote one writer mentions a most curious custom, namely, that a woman was allowed three husbands. The husband was free for one month, was obliged to work about the house or on the land for another month, and was master of the house on the third. In Hierro it seems to have been a very usual thing for the brother and sister to intermarry, and the distinction of class, which elsewhere forbade intermarriage between the noble and the serf, seems to have been absent.

Character, Social Customs, Habits, Appearance.—Except in Hierro, where there was a small population under one king and where fighting was unknown, the clans were extremely warlike. This is proved not only by history but by the positions they chose for their habitations, of which the best examples are to be found in Grand Canary and in La Palma. Although in the first-named island they knew how to build houses, of which indeed examples are to be found even now, and though they are said to have been in the habit of squaring and smoothing stones, the bulk of the population no doubt lived in caves. Many of these are in the most inaccessible positions and must have been difficult to enter, even before the narrow approaches leading to them were worn away by the weather. Their colonies were also frequently situated in the centre of a most sterile district, neither the best for cultivation nor for the feeding of stock; in such places, for instance, as the Barrancos of Fatarga or of Tirajana in Grand Canary. One may incidentally remark that they must have been an extremely dirty people, as a good water supply seems to have been a matter quite outside of their consideration. In Lanzarote and Fuerteventura, where they generally lived in houses, the entrance was always small, and the building was surrounded by a wall into which the goats were driven at night. As a further security against attack the owner was allowed to kill anyone found inside this wall after dark, as is the case to-day in a native kraal in Central South Africa.

The warlike habits of the people made the task of conquest heavy. La Palma was only subdued by the help of the people of Gomera, both parties being, it is said, brave to rashness and indifferent to death or suffering. For further details, *see* under La Palma. The history of the reduction of Canary and Teneriffe has already been given.

Children were trained as warriors by teaching them to throw mud and blunted javelins at one another, which they were made to catch and return if possible. Marvellous tales, not worth repeating, are told of their prowess when grown up.

Their agility in throwing, catching, and avoiding stones was considered almost miraculous by the Spaniards, who, however, are not very good judges, as very few Spaniards can catch a thing thrown to them. Admiral Sir John Hawkins himself was an astonished spectator of their skill, strength and intrepidity in jumping, lifting weights and climbing.

Games of skill were indulged in at stated times, during which, if at war, a truce was held. Much emulation was shown, though probably most of the records are absurdly exaggerated.

Their athletic competitions were sometimes carried to the bitter end, as was the case when two rivals committed suicide from the cliffs at La Paz in the Valley of Orotava, because neither would be outdone by the other.

They also met for the purpose of dancing. The dance known as the "Canario," now a favourite in Cuba, is said to have been learnt from the Bimbachos (Hierro). They were fond of declaiming poetry, which was declared by Viana to have been very sweet. It described the achievements of the dead or of the living in a rude chaunt somewhat resembling the Saga of the Scandinavians.

The principal feast of the Guanches was known as the Beñesmen, and took place at midsummer, just after harvest.

By nature, the people were truthful and generous. Their conduct towards the Spaniards showed an abhorrence of treachery among themselves, which, if thrown away upon the greedy generals of the time, is as much admired by the Canary Islanders of to-day as the want of it is reprobated in their own forefathers. Had the Church of that day not demanded their conversion or extermination, and had the greed of slave-hunters been less violent, it is probable that ordinary trade relations could have been established and the islands gradually won to civilisation without any rupture of the peace.

Prisoners of war were generally condemned to menial work, *i.e.*, such work as butchery, the preparing or cooking of meals, the cleaning of cattle sheds, etc., and probably any employment other than the tilling of land, the care of cattle or the pursuit of war.

Generally they seem to have been tall and well-made. In the western islands they may have been fair, but nearer Africa they were dark and thick-lipped. The women are reported to have been beautiful, but it must be remembered that the sailors describing them had been on board ship for some time, and that allowance must always be made for travellers' tales and for distance, which would lend enchantment to the recollection. The standard of beauty in many parts of the Canaries to-day has a great deal to do with the distance round the body or limbs. In Canary at that time it was customary to fatten a girl up for thirty days before marriage, as the Moors do at present. It is also recorded that the people were very sensible, only taking as wives those women who, by their girth and their make about the hips, were most likely to have healthy children. One writer says that females were incapable of suckling from the breast, but did so from the lower lip, which reminds one of the men whose heads did "grow beneath their shoulders."

In spite of the tales of their immense strength, it is unlikely that a race left to itself for so long could develop that tremendous muscular energy attributed to them by the early writers. They were not all killed, and the wives, mistresses and even husbands of the Conquistàdores and their relations have left plenty of descendants now living. Even in those parts of the islands where the native race is known to have remained at its purest, the people do not come up to the ordinary English standard by any means, though naturally there are exceptional cases here and there where gigantic stature may be due to native ancestry.

The history of this people and of their supernatural prowess is in danger of becoming a sort of epic, handing down facts to posterity in a garbled and exaggerated form, in order to add lustre to the deeds of those by whom they were subdued.

Religion, Priests, Vestal Virgins, Forms of Prayer, Legends, etc.—The religion or religions were generally founded on the worship of an invisible god. In Teneriffe this was certainly the case. The summits of mountains were, as is usual, held as fitting places for worship. In Teneriffe the Peak, which was called *Teide* or *E'Cheyde*, probably meaning the seat of fire or hell, seems to have been regarded as the abode of the deity, who, however, there is no reason to suppose to have been a maleficent creation.

The inhabitants called their island *Tehinerfe* (*Tehin*—white and *erfe*—mountain), and themselves Guanches (possibly Vanches), supposed to mean "the sons of *che*," short for *E'Cheyde*. Other names were "Achmech" and "Chinechi," but whether these meant the whole or only a portion of the population is not clear. Their most solemn oath was by "E'Cheyde and Magec," or by "Hell and the Sun," a sufficiently expressive formula.

The names of the deities were—in Teneriffe, "Achaman," meaning God Almighty; "Menceyato," corresponding to our own Lord; "Achuchacanam," highest; "Achuherahan," trebly great; "Achguayaxerax," preserver of all, and others describing Him in his various attributes. It is also said that "Acoran" and "Alcorac," names commonly used in Canary, were employed in Teneriffe, but this is doubtful. The Supreme Being in Canary was known as "Atirtisma." In La Palma "Abora" was the "God of all things," and in Hierro "Eraoranhan" was the "God of Men," and "Moreyba" the "God of Women," a fact which made the Bimbachos accept the Catholic ideas of Christianity much more readily than was the case elsewhere. In Teneriffe the devil, who lived deep down in the Peak, was called *Guayota*; in Canary he was *Gabio*, and in La Palma *Yrueñe*.

In Canary the two most sacred mountains were Umiaya, near Telde, probably that now known as the M$^{ña.}$ de las Cuatro Puertas (*see* Index), and Tirma near Artenara. It was probably in these that the only images known to have been made by the aboriginals were found. One of these was of stone and represented a naked youth carrying a globe. The other, which was of wood, portrayed a naked and fully developed woman, before whom were a male and female goat, the propagation of species being evidently the object of worship. In front of the last it was customary to pour libations of goats' milk, the Spaniards describing the temple as being very filthy and malodorous. André Bernaldez, writing about A.D. 1500, speaks of Teneriffe, Canary and La Palma as the three idolatrous islands. As regards Teneriffe he must have had the image of the Virgen de Candelaria (*see* Index) in his mind, but there seems to be no reason for his having included La Palma. The place of worship in the last was inside the great crater and at the base of a monolithic rock called Idafe, which fell down about the time of the conquest. One writer says that the Haouarythes had no conception of immortality, but such statements cannot be accepted without full corroboration.

The clergy were chosen entirely from amongst the nobles. In Canary they were called *faycayg* or *faycan*, a word bearing some resemblance to the Indian "fakir." Besides conducting the religious ceremonies, the priests assisted in council, had the monopoly of prophesying, and were entrusted with the storage of the tithes, of which the surplus was preserved against times of scarcity. It was by them that the dead were embalmed, as was the case in Egypt, and, by their knowledge of antiseptics, they were probably physicians as well. Historians do not say whether they were allowed to marry or not.

They lived apart from the people in communities of their own. Some of these were seminaries in which novices were instructed and in which the daughters of the nobles received their education until they were married. Such seminaries or convents were jealously secluded. Access to the girls was made as difficult as possible, and they were guarded by very strict laws when away from home, unchastity on their part being punished by the death of both parties. They were clothed in white like the Vestal Virgins of Rome, and were taught to assist in the ordinary household duties of the convent, in the sewing of the skins in which mummies were wrapped, etc.

There is reason to believe that the priests were assisted by male and female communities, whose lives were devoted to the service of the deity.

The best example in the islands of what was undoubtedly a combination of temple and retreat, shared, perhaps, by male and female devotees, is that of the Montaña de las Cuatro Puertas in Grand Canary. (*See* Index.)

Prayer was sometimes accompanied by a sort of frenzied dance, but the ceremonials of which the most accurate record has been preserved are those held at times of great drought. In Teneriffe, in La Palma, and probably elsewhere, when ordinary prayer failed it was customary to assemble a multitude of goats on one side of a ravine and to place their kids upon the other. Their cries and lamentations were supposed to invoke the pity of the angry gods. In Hierro there was a resource beyond this, namely, a little pig kept in the cave of Astcheyta, in the district of Tacuetunta, which was regarded as of the most peculiar sanctity. When all other means failed the pig was released from its home and allowed to run about the island, a curious form of ritual of which it would be interesting to ascertain the origin.

In Teneriffe a ceremony existed greatly resembling our own baptism, namely, that the woman who first washed the head of a new-born child was afterwards looked upon as what we should call its god-mother. In La Palma, any one incapacitated for work by reason of age or illness could demand death, a request which the relations were not allowed to refuse. The moribund was placed in a remote cave with a little food by his side and allowed to die alone.

A few of the native legends have been preserved. It is said that a prophet of Taoro foretold the consummation of an old tradition and the conquest of the island by a people from beyond the sea. For this he was put to death by Bencomo the Good. In Canary they said that "in the beginning God made a number of men from earth and water. The first to be made were specially endowed, but, when God found that they were not enough, he made another race, condemned to perpetual servitude. To the first he gave all the flocks, to the second nothing." Another legend of Canary was that "God placed us in this island and then forgot us, but from the east a light shall come which shall re-awaken us." The same legend was current in Hierro, but was more circumstantial. It was said that when the bones of a king called Yore, who answered to our own King Arthur, should be turned to dust, "white houses shall come from over the sea and shall be the salvation of the people." When Bethencourt's ships were seen to be approaching the island, the head priest went to this cave and found that the bones were dust, so that the arrival of the strangers was considered a matter for rejoicing.

In La Palma it was said that when the island was to be conquered the rock Idafe would fall. The form of prayer in consequence seems to have been a constant repetition of "Idafe, spare us." When the Spaniards attacked the interior of the Great Caldera from Tazacorte and Prince Tanaúsu, with a few followers alone remained, they changed their prayer to "Idafe, fall." Idafe fell and is still said to serve as a sepulchre for the last heroic defenders of their country. At the risk of destroying another pretty romance it must, however, be added that a more trustworthy account declares that Tanaúsu was captured alive and sent to Spain, but that he starved himself to death on the way.

Burial Customs, Mummies and Medicines.—Both in Teneriffe and in Canary the bodies of kings and nobles were mummified. Even those of the lower classes were sometimes subjected to a sort of astringent process, consisting in the abstraction of the stomach and the insertion of certain berries.

Both in Teneriffe and in Canary the dead were placed in caves, though the custom was not so universal in the latter as it was in the former. The spots chosen for the burial of kings were usually most inaccessible, and the people were not allowed to witness the actual interment. This precaution may have been due to fear that the ghosts of the departed might be summoned up to do injury to the living. A parallel case may be cited from South Africa. In Monomotapa (Rhodesia) chiefs were buried in the ruined Arab strongholds, places believed to be enchanted, in which few natives would dare to enter.

Thomas Nicols, writing about A.D. 1526, mentions a cave which he was allowed to visit near Güimar, and states that he was told of the existence of many others in which hundreds of mummies were to be seen, but says that he was compelled to secrecy, the favour being shown him in return for medical services rendered. The Guanche Kings were usually placed upright, their wives being seated by their side. The common people seem sometimes to have been placed one above the other. Caves still exist in which large quantities of bones are to be found.

A king remained unburied until the death of his successor. This was done in order that there might always be two kings, one living and one dead, though whether the mummy assisted in council or was treated as a sort of Delphic oracle is not known.

In Canary the graves were frequently hollowed out from the *scoriæ* near the sea, as, for instance, in the cemeteries on the Isleta near Las Palmas, at Agaete and at Arguineguin. If one may judge from the care with which they were embalmed, the most important people were laid north and south and their inferiors east and west.

The preparation of a first-class mummy was elaborate. The entrails, etc., were first cleaned out by the butcher and the body handed over to the priests. These dried it in the sun and treated it with various astringent vegetable extracts, preserved in resinous lumps and in a form greatly resembling modern hardbake. In Teneriffe the sap and bark of the dragon-tree were employed. A mummy, which took some fourteen days to prepare, was sewn in from one to six goat-skins, excellently tanned and sometimes joined together by needlework of the most delicate description (*see* Museum in Las Palmas). The arms of male mummies were strapped down to the side, but those of females were crossed over the stomach. It is probable that the entrails were burnt and the ashes mixed up with the astringents left inside the body. In Teneriffe, food, such as jars of butter and milk, was placed in the caves by the side of the mummies. In Canary dried figs have been found.

Butchers and those engaged in cleansing the dead previous to embalming were regarded with loathing, and, as was the case in Egypt, were compelled to live apart.

It may be interesting to recall the fact that pieces of Guanche mummies, or of the dragon-tree, were highly prized as medicaments in the Middle Ages, and that both were indispensable ingredients of the philosopher's stone. Later on the dye obtained from the bark of the dragon-tree was used to give that colour to the wood so much prized by the collectors of old violins.

Probably the medical men were acquainted with more vegetable drugs than those used in the preparation of mummies. Viana says that a present was made by the Mencey of Anaga to Bencomo of Taoro of the portrait of a daughter of the former (Dacil), painted in charcoal, coloured ochres, vegetable juices and the sap of the wild fig-tree. The tree meant was probably one of the Euphorbias, as the fig proper was not known in Teneriffe.

One of the chief medicaments was butter, buried and preserved for a great length of time, the longer the better. It is likely that, in a country where surgery or bone-setting were both unknown arts, more benefit would be derived from the massage attending the application of an unguent than from any other course of treatment.

Implements, Industries, Decoration, Clothing, Food, Agriculture, etc.—Iron was unknown, and implements were made of obsidian, other hard stones, wood, and bone, both fish and animal. Fish bones were used for sewing and for fishing; cloth was made from vegetable fibres; leather was tanned as soft as any in Morocco, and considerable skill was shown in the manufacture of pottery. This was shaped by a rounded stone and without the use of a potter's wheel, as is the case to-day in Atalaya (Grand Canary), where the method of manufacture has been handed down directly from the Canarios, and where no change is likely to take place until the crack of doom, unless foreign influence finds it worth while to take an interest in the matter. Handmills were used and were made of basalt hollowed out, probably by means of obsidian.

In warfare, slings, stones, spears, javelins, and clubs were employed. In Canary a light shield was also customary, but in Teneriffe this was replaced by a mantle wound round the left arm. The points of the spears and javelins were either hardened by fire, or, as in La Palma, tipped with horn.

The musical instruments were confined to the drum and to a small reed pipe, but the people are said to have been very fond of music.

An earthenware implement, usually known under the Spanish name of *Pintadera*, was common. It was probably used as a stamp for printing leather, cloth, or, perhaps, the human skin. Various form of beads made of burnt clay and other materials have also been found.

Those who could afford it, or who were allowed to indulge themselves, were probably fond of ornament. Some even decorated their caves by means of coloured geometrical patterns (*see* Gáldar). There were, however, sumptuary laws, such as that in Canary, which compelled the lower classes to wear the hair short. It is also probable that a restriction was placed on the use of the *Pintadera*, as though some writers say that tattooing was general in Canary and that it was customary to stain the skin permanently, others maintain that this was only done during war.

Clothing must have varied very greatly. Kings are represented in monkish missals as naked with golden crowns on their heads

This was no doubt only a conventional way of depicting them as savages, and it is far more probable that they wore at least skins in all the islands. In Lanzarote and Fuerteventura the kings wore a mitre of leather set with sea-shells. Cloth, as well as skins, was used as a covering. It seems that in Lanzarote and Fuerteventura females were concealed almost from head to foot, as is the custom amongst the Arabs. In some of the other islands they were undoubtedly left entirely naked when young, and possibly, in one or two, remained so even after marriage. In Teneriffe the men wore a *tamarca* or sleeveless shirt of goat-skin coming to the knees. Women were clothed down to the ankles. Stockings (*huirmas*) were a mark of nobility.

The principal article of food amongst the islanders was and is *gofio* or *ahorén*, a preparation made of toasted grain, mixed with salt and ground in a mill. The result is highly nutritious. It can be made at little trouble or expense and from any sort of grain, and it is unfortunate that it should not replace bad bread made from bolted and adulterated flour in other places than in the country districts of the Canaries. *Gofio* is used in a few other parts of the world, for instance in India. In times of scarcity the seed of the ice plant (*barrilla*) or the root of the male fern are occasionally made into *gofio*.

From the position chosen to live in agriculture must have been comparatively neglected. In Hierro it was unknown, but in other islands very good wheat was found by the Spaniards on their arrival, as well as barley, beans, peas, yams and dates. Figs had also found their way at least as far as Canary but not to Teneriffe. Land was neither irrigated nor manured, the fields being tilled for a short time until the soil was exhausted, when the surface was broken in some other place. Here again the islanders resembled the negroes of Africa, who migrate at times for the same reason.

Their chief wealth lay in their flocks, the animals known being sheep, goats, pigs, dogs and rabbits. All of these were used as food, castrated puppies being considered a great delicacy in Canary, where it is said, by the bye, that the sheep had no wool. Fish and, in Hierro, a large lizard were also eaten. Food was cooked, fire being obtained by means of friction.

The most important of their animals was the goat, which they had bred to great perfection. The progeny now to be found in the islands is a most prolific yielder of milk.

The shepherds, who included in their number both king and peasant, invented a method of whistling to one another across the ravines. Even to-day two men will carry on quite a long conversation in Gomera, though the art has not survived so well elsewhere. Dr. Sprat, Bishop of Rochester, a man of a very easy conscience, when writing to the Royal Society of London about

1650, says that he met an Englishman in Teneriffe, who, having persuaded a Guanche to whistle into his ear, was rendered deaf for fifteen days.

In Canary fish were driven on shore by men swimming out to sea and beating the water to frighten the fish, which were then caught by others with spears, baskets and nets. It has been stated that in Teneriffe the Guanches could not swim and that the people of La Palma did not fish. The first may be true but the latter is not, as it is now known that the Haouarythes eat fish.

Water was usually drunk, but in Hierro, if not elsewhere, a fermented liquor was made from the berry of the laurel (*visnea mocanera*). It is even possible that a spirit was distilled from the same, which perhaps accounts for the Bimbachos being so fond of dancing.

MADEIRA.

Madeira is the largest of a small group of islands belonging to Portugal, situated in latitude 32° 37' to 32° 52' N., and longitude 16° 39' to 17° 17' W., and about 10° N. of the Tropic of Cancer. It is 1,164 sea miles (2,141 kilos.) S.W. of the Lizard, and 520 sea miles (915 kilos.) W.S.W. of Lisbon; is about 38 miles (60 kilos.) long by 15 m. (24 kilos.) broad, and its superficial area is about. 240 sq. m. (574 sq. kilos.). It is divided into 10 concelhos, and contains 151,125 inhabitants.

The form is oval, and the surface mountainous, a number of deep ravines radiating on all sides from the central ridge, of which the highest points are grouped around the water-shed of the Grand Curral (Curral das Freiras). A narrow neck of considerably less elevation connects the before-mentioned mountains with the Paul de Serra, an extensive elevated moorland on the western side of the island. The highest mountain of all is the Pico Ruivo, 6,059 feet.

The loose nature of the soil has led to great loss by denudation. Most of the ravines are more or less precipitous, especially on the north, where the greater power of the sea, and the greater prevalence of rain in the winter, both aided to a certain extent by the geological substratum, have worn away and hollowed out a succession of gorges, whose wooded summits, dripping rocks and bubbling streams are full of grandeur and beauty. Their loveliness is due to that wonderful fecundity seemingly peculiar to a volcanic soil, which is here aided by the mild climate, under which the yam and the sugar-cane at the bottom join hands with the pine-tree, the heather and the laurel at the top. The warm vapours surrounding the island, the almost hothouse-like air which generally prevails in its valleys, and the colder atmosphere of the unprotected mountains, naturally give a great latitude to the vegetation. All sorts of grain known to Northern Europe, and all flowers and fruits not absolutely tropical or arctic, can be grown, whilst the ferns, mosses, lichens and indigenous flora or fauna are a constant attraction to the student of nature. Cultivation is rarely seen above the 3,000 feet level.

The foregoing remarks might lead to the supposition that the valleys on the north are grander and more beautiful than those on the south, which is not altogether the case. Those unable from want of time or unsettled weather to be away from Funchal for more than a day, will find an excursion up the Grand Curral and across the top of the Serra d'Agoa sufficiently impressive.

An abundance of moisture is derived from the clouds, which, during a great part of the year, hang round the mountain tops.

During the summer all the streams on the south are dry, but, on the north, many continue to run.

Only that water is allowed to run away, however, which is not required for irrigation, long aqueducts (*levadas*) catching and carrying streams for immense distances. The most noticeable work of the kind is at the Rabaçal, where the water is taken by means of tunnels to the southern slopes, a praiseworthy undertaking of great importance to the island.

Volcanic energy seems to have slumbered for many centuries. Evidences of it are to be seen all over Madeira; but many ages must have elapsed since it was so violently exerted as has been the case, even recently in the Canary Islands and the Azores. Where cinders or slag are found, they are fast resolving themselves into earth, their sharp edges are usually rounded off, and they are generally hidden beneath a carpet of moss or a mantle of verdure.

Sugar was once the staple product of the island—witness the arms of Funchal, five sugar loaves—but this was later on almost abandoned for the vine. Special and detailed information on this and similar subjects will be found in the Commercial Appendix.

There is only one macadamised carriage road—namely, the New Road, which leads to Camara de Lobos, 6 miles ($9\frac{1}{2}$ kilos.) west of Funchal. Sledges drawn by bullocks (*carros*) are, however, able to penetrate the country for a few miles from the city along certain tracks. Hammocks are largely used, and good horses may be had; but the healthy pedestrian is best off if he does not mind roughing it a little. The natives, in fact, rather than drive mules, prefer carrying goods on their shoulders, and may sometimes be met with in large parties, the leader playing a *machête*, and the rest singing as they walk. Saddle-bags are unknown, and the guide insists on carrying the rider's luggage, which he does not seem to find an incumbrance.

The peasants are extremely economical, and their habits and manner of living simple. Naturally ingenious, they have learnt how to make a number of small articles to sell to visitors or the wealthier classes, such as basket-work, lace, embroidery, rough jewellery, etc.

Some of the country dresses worn on feast days are little altered from those worn a century or more ago. The customs much resemble those of the Spaniards, serenades, admiring leers and whispered conversations at the window being the accepted method of making love by both rich and poor. The people, on the whole, are fairly prosperous, in spite of overcrowding, and the quantity of black broadcloth, and more or less carefully groomed top hats, to be seen on a Sunday or feast day, bespeak a desire for respectability almost English in its intensity.

Our own countrymen have been so long visitors to the island, that they are regarded almost as natives. Many of the Portuguese can make themselves fairly well understood by those ignorant of their language.

Leprosy is found chiefly in the west. It is not present in a virulent form, nor is the disease known in these islands believed to be contagious.

There are no harbours in Madeira, even Funchal being no better than an open roadstead. A little shelter, however, is provided by the Pontinha, a stone causeway connecting the Loo Rock (Ilheo) with the shore, where tugs can lie at anchor and rowing boats can land in wet weather. There is also a short pier with steps, but passengers are sometimes landed on the beach.

Where accommodation cannot be otherwise obtained, it is often possible to find an empty room, and sleep in the hammock, when one is taken.

The following excursion is recommended to those wishing to get a good idea of the island in a short time. From Funchal *viâ* the Poizo and Ribeiro Frio to Santa Anna, one day. From Santa Anna to Boa Ventura, or São Vicente, two days. Back in the first case *viâ* the Torrinhas, or in the second *viâ* the Encumiada, and down the Grand Curral (Curral das Freiras) three days. Horses can be used along all these routes. Outside the limits of Santa Anna and São Vicente on the N., travellers should use hammocks or go on foot, as the roads are very steep. Telegrams regarding accommodation can be sent all round the island except to Seizal. The post goes two or three times a week.

The best trip for those only on shore for two or three hours is up the Caminho do Meio, past the Quinta Reid, to the Curralinho (Curral dos Romeiros; *angli*: Pilgrim's Fold); that is to say, to the point below the Pico do Infante, where the road branches off to the left for Mount Church. This is better than the road taken by the *carros* to Mount Church, where the view is greatly obscured by walls and trees. The return by running cars is equally exciting. Other pleasant drives are past the Convent of Santa Clara to the Peak Fort, whence there is a very fine view, or up the Hortas Road, along the whole length of the Levada, and down the Saltos Road. The ascent to Mount Church by *carro* is only repaid by the rapid manner in which one is brought back.

The journey up by the new railway, the fares for which will be found a few pages further on, is both picturesque and convenient. The railway in fact, utilitarian as it may seem in a place like Madeira, is an undoubted advantage both to visitors and residents, allowing them to reach a higher level easily and at little expense. About $1\frac{1}{2}$ hrs. is quite sufficient for any of these three trips.

Those ascending by the railway will find the Mount Church itself of little attraction. Their time will be better spent in a visit to that most charming and characteristic estate known as the Quinta do Monte, permission to enter which can, however, only be obtained by means of an introduction to the owner. The gardens command an almost unequalled view of Funchal and the neighbourhood, and form in themselves a little paradise, of which those who have never visited the fertile and exquisite island of Madeira can scarcely form a conception. Lovely as it is, the Quinta do Monte is, however, only one of those enchanting residences for which Funchal is justly famous, and which form so constant a delight to all lovers of the beautiful.

Visitors stopping some time in the island will soon exhaust all the excursions immediately round the town. It is unnecessary to enumerate each of these in their order of merit, as they are all given, with the time necessary to make them, in their proper places.

To any wishing to extend the three days' trip spoken of above, attention is called to the fact that the sunny side of the island, both east and west of Funchal, is drier and less beautiful than the north. That is to say, that the neighbourhoods of Santa Cruz, Machico, etc., on the one side, and Calheta, Paul do Mar, etc., on the other, do not repay for the trouble taken in getting there, although the villages themselves, and the methods of cultivation adopted, etc., may be worthy of study.

Instead of going directly to Santa Anna by the Poizo Pass, it can be reached by the Lamaceiros Pass, Porto da Cruz, the Penha d'Aguia and Fayal. By taking this route, the beautiful views of the Ribeiro Frio and R. do Metade are lost, but the valleys of Santa Cruz and Machico are seen. In order to include the country missed out, a one day's excursion to the Pico Arrieiro should be made. A description of this will be found elsewhere.

On the west of the island the coast can be followed to Porto Moniz, and a return made along the south side of the Ribeira da Janella, past the Rabaçal, the Paul da Serra and São Vicente, *or* São Vicente can be left out, and a descent be made to Ponta do Sol, *or* the road home from São Vicente be joined at the Encumiada. In the last two cases it would be more convenient to sleep at the House of Refuge at the Tanquinhas, or to take a tent.

If there is no wish to see the south of the island, by turning to the left before reaching Porto Moniz, and by keeping to the north bank along the Fanal, the distance is considerably shortened. In either case at least five days are necessary, and, in order that a little rest may be enjoyed and places of interest visited, it is much better to allow a week or more.

Any one who has made the above excursions will have a very fair idea of what Madeira is like.

FUNCHAL, with 44,049 inhabitants, contained in nine parishes, is the capital of Madeira, the seat of a bishopric, and the only port where ocean-going steamers call.

Landing Charges.—Passengers are landed in boats on the open beach, or on the steps of the little stone jetty, except in very rough weather, when they are disembarked on the Pontinha under the shelter of the Loo Rock.

All ships are met by the hotel agents. Some of the lines of steamers land the passengers free of expense; but where this is not the case, the port charges are:—passengers, without luggage, one shilling each way, or, when an ordinary amount of luggage is taken, 800 reis each. Customs House officers, for superintending boats loaded with luggage or goods, 265 reis each, and 50 reis for stamps. For leaving a package in bond, and reclaiming same, 610 reis. Worn linen, clothes, etc., for personal use enter duty free. Passengers landing at night cannot obtain their heavy baggage till next morning. They should therefore carry necessaries in a hand bag.

The Customs House officers are most obliging to visitors, and special orders have been given to treat foreigners on very lenient terms.

Coupons.—Those on shore for a few hours can purchase coupons on board, which include boat, railway, lunch, etc.

Custom Duties.—All goods for use in the island pay duty according to a fixed scale. Such duties are exceedingly high, and are according to the law passed in February, 1892. The duties are remitted on furniture, plate or any other household requisite showing signs of wear (Law of Jan., 1898). Such goods must be accompanied by the owner, or must absolutely be landed within thirty days of his arrival, without grace. Carriages, etc., may remain for eighteen months under bond. After this they pay duty. Household requisites include furniture, linen, crockery, pianos, carpets, etc., etc. It is not advisable to carry more than a small quantity of tobacco, and on no account should visitors run the risk of trying to smuggle anything. (200 grammes, *i.e.*, about 6 ozs. of tobacco pass free, and duty may be paid up to 5 kilogrammes, but not over.)

Passports, Cedulas (Police Tickets), etc., are no longer necessary. Visitors enter and leave tax free.

Hotels.—The New Hotel, and two annexes, in a commanding position on the cliff to the W. of the town; the Santa Clara towards the back of the town, and some height above the sea; the Carmo (Miles') Hotel to the E. of the Cathedral; all belonging to Messrs. W. & A. Reid; Jones' Hotel, "Bella Vista," well situated near the New Road; Cornell's English Hotel, on the New

Road, a little beyond the Casino. Charges at all these hotels are from 8s. to 12s. a day, or so much a month. International Hotel, Carreira, centre of town near Public Gardens, 6s. a day upwards. At the Upper Terminus of the Mount Railway, the Hotel Bello Monte, 6s. a day upwards; Reid's Mount Park Hotel, 8s. a day.

Portuguese Hotels.—The Central, 1$500; the Universal, more moderate, both inside the town, and one or two others.

Boarding Houses. — Residents occasionally take paying guests.

Newspapers.—Diario de Noticias :—Diario do Commercio :— Diario Popular.

(*For Advertisements relating to Funchal, see under Funchal at the end of the book.*)

Public Buildings.—The **Town Hall** or Camara Municipal, in which the Courts of Justice are held, and the Concelho holds its meetings, is situated near the Collegio Church, and is of little interest; the **Prison**, just below the Cathedral; the **Governor's Palace**, or Palace of São Lourenço, a peculiarly constructed building, with a somewhat Chinese appearance, in which the Meteorological Observatory is situated, and below which are the **Fontes de João Diniz**, from which many of those living in the city fetch their drinking water; the general **Hospital**, facing the Praça da Constituição, where medical classes are held; the **Leper Hospital** of São Lazaro; the **Empress's Hospital** (Hospicio), on the way to the New Road, built at a great expense by the late Dowager Empress of Brazil, in memory of her only child, the Princess Amelia, who died of consumption in Madeira in 1853; adjoining this is an orphanage where the inmates are trained to become domestic servants; the **Asylo da Mendicidade** or Poor House, where the indigent poor receive relief, and to which all visitors should make a donation according to their means, so that they may afterwards conscientiously refuse to give alms to the impudent and importunate beggars in the streets; the **Peak Fort** or Castello do Pico, built early in the 17th century, overlooking the town, and worthy of a visit on account of the view it commands; the Fort on the **Loo Rock**, now connected with the shore; the Custom House, **Alfandega**, which was commenced very early in the 16th century, and was formerly an ecclesiastical building; the **Fish and Vegetable Markets** below the Alfandega, which are worthy of a visit in the early morning; the **Opera House**, a fine new building with a handsome interior, where a company is generally engaged for the winter.

Besides the public buildings proper, there is a small but very interesting Museum in the Seminario, just below the Carmo Church, to which visitors may gain admission at certain hours by sending in their cards. The contents are well arranged and intelligibly displayed, one room being specially devoted to Madeira objects. The Seamen's Hospital, near the Pontinha, owes its origin to the English residents. A nominal charge of 500 reis a day is made to those able to afford it.

The walls of the city were commenced in 1572, and practically completed in 1637, though the Varadouros gateway, leading up from the beach to the centre of the town, bears an inscription stating that they were absolutely finished in 1689. Their demolition began about 1700. The Fort of San Thiago on the east of the town, now used as a barracks, was built in 1614.

Churches.—The Cathedral or Sé (1485 to 1514) is of little architectural merit. The interior is gaudily decorated. The fretted ceilings at the chancel end are indifferent examples of the style of decoration almost peculiar to Madeira, the Canaries and certain parts of the Spanish Peninsula; a style which is said to have first appeared in Seville about the period of the expulsion of the Moors. A large silver crucifix of the early part of the 16th century, which can only be seen on application, is of considerable merit. The Igreja do Collegio (built by the Jesuits) has a handsome façade, and the interior is decorated in an effective and imposing manner. The adjoining monastery is now used as a barrack—S. Pedro—Carmo—N.S. do Socorro, the oldest church in the city (the last three are of no special interest). In the Socorro, however, is the shrine of San Thiago Menor (St. James the Less), the patron saint of the city, to which there is a procession of notables every year on the 1st of May. The procession commemorates the cessation of a plague in 1538, immediately after the despairing authorities had handed over the wand of office to the keeping of the saint. There are also several chapels, both public and private.

Besides the churches there are several Convents, some with chapels, and some still used as retreats for novices and as places of worship. First among these is the Santa Clara, founded in 1492, for centuries famous for sweetmeats, feather-flowers, etc., which may still be purchased through intermediaries, or directly from the inmates by means of the turnstile. The chapel is well worth a visit for itself, besides which it contains the tomb of Zargo, the discoverer of the island. The Conventos da Encarnaçáo das Merces—do bom Jesus—de Santa Izabel.

Foreign Churches.—English Church, Rua de Bella Vista, built somewhat on the model of the Pantheon at Rome, because of a law which then forbade any building not destined for a Roman Catholic place of worship to resemble a church. The **Scotch Church**, Rua do Conselheiro, facing the Gardens. The **Methodist Episcopal Church of America**, Mission Hall, a little below the Scotch Church.

Clubs.—The **English Rooms**, between the jetty and the Customs House, with billiard, card, reading rooms, etc., and a library of over 6,000 volumes, admit temporary members. The **Sports Club**, recently formed, where strangers can also be introduced. **Commercial Rooms**, facing the mole, subscribers admitted. **Club Restauração** (proprietary), Praça da Constituição. **Cricket Club**, with ground at S. Martin, about 40 min. on foot from the town, subscription, 4$000 per annum. **Sailors' Rest**, facing the Public Gardens.

In addition to the above, a **Casino and Strangers' Club** was opened in 1895, which was provided with properly administered gaming tables, similar to those at Monte Carlo. The establishment was temporarily closed in 1900.

The situation of the building, and the great superiority of the Madeira climate over that of the south of France, made the Casino a very popular resort. It stands in one of the finest villas of Funchal, the well-known Quinta Vigia, formerly the residence of the Empress of Austria, the Prince of Oldenbourg, etc. The beautiful gardens, which every visitor to Madeira makes a point of seeing, are one of the features of the city. On the seaside they abut on a walled precipice, from which, or from the summer houses built by the edge, there is a most wonderful bird's-eye view of the town and harbour. Altogether, gambling apart, the Casino added greatly to the attractions of Funchal, and served as a pleasant social centre and promenade, very handy for those addicted to afternoon tea and so on.

Squares, etc.—The broad **Entrada da Cidade** leads up from the beach to the **Praça da Constituição**. The latter occupies the space between the Cathedral and the Governor's Palace. Both are planted with trees, and are much frequented. Adjoining the Praça are the **New Public Gardens**, on the site of an old Franciscan monastery. The band plays here twice a week. The **Praça Academica**, to the east of the Custom House. The **Stone Jetty**, provided with seats, communicates by a level carriage road or esplanade with the Pontinha. It is proposed to connect the esplanade with the New Road. From the Pontinha, the Loo Rock may be visited on foot by those obtaining permission to do so.

Railway.—The railway running to just below Mount Church is a great convenience. Particulars regarding fares, etc., will be found on page 146, and amongst the advertisements. The tramway connecting the jetty with the lower terminus was not working in June, 1901.

Funchal is a picturesque town, beautifully situated in a species of vast amphitheatre, the summits covered with verdure, and the sides with villas, gardens and orchards. The houses gradually approach one another, form themselves into streets, and descend to the sea-level, where the dark Loo Rock, the Governor's Palace, the line of houses, the signal tower, the custom house and the black beach form a fine contrast to the deep blue of the arena or sea. The gladiators are replaced by some half-dozen ships, and by an infinity of little boats, hurrying out to meet some newly-arrived steamer; or speeding away the parting guest by endeavouring to sell him a basket deck-chair, or some other knick-knack. These floating bazaars are accompanied by still smaller boats, each containing two little boys, shouting and gesticulating for money to be thrown into the water, for them to dive and fetch up.

The many charming residences scattered about the slopes; the gardens gorgeous with colour; the terraces covered with flowers; here and there a wall crimson with one creeper, or orange with another; the sound of the church bells as a relief from the monotonous four bells or eight bells on board ship, all invite the passer-by to spend at least some hours on *terra firma*. Those who have not time for more, generally ascend to the Mount Church, and return by running *carro*.

The climate is referred to elsewhere; and it need only be said that passengers landing at all times of the year will find it warm on shore, and should, in consequence, wear light clothing. As the cobble-stones, with which the streets are paved, are very slippery, they are also advised to use their india-rubber deck shoes.

Curiosity being generally awakened by the tower on the beach where people are landed, it may be mentioned that it was built in 1796 to facilitate the discharge of cargo. Since then the beach has extended itself a good deal, thus rendering it useless for the purpose. It is now a signal station.

Water Supply.—Complaints having been made in the newspapers about the source of the drinking water, it may be mentioned that it was customary to fetch it from the fountains below the Governor's Palace, to which, indeed, many of the people still go. Whether the outbreaks of typhoid fever, about which one heard so much in 1896, were due to foul water or not, is open to question. Since that time greater precautions have been taken, and the writer has been informed that cases of typhoid have been almost or quite unknown. Water is now brought to some of the public fountains in 3-inch iron pipes from the Corujeira, a point not far from Mount Church, and well above all houses.

Another particularly pure supply of water has been secured, and a scheme for an efficient supply and a good system of drainage has been submitted to the Government.

Lighting.—Since the beginning of 1898, the town has been most excellently lighted by electricity. The enterprise is due to an English company.

Walks, Rides and Drives near Funchal.

(*For cost of horses, boats, hammocks, etc., refer to the end of Madeira.*)

Times are given for riders without allowing for stoppages.

Those taking hammocks must add to the time in about the proportion of five to four.

A. **To the East of Funchal.**—The direct road, or that *viâ* the Lazaretto, both lead to **Palheiro** (1,700ft. ; $3\frac{3}{4}$ m. = 6 kil.) in about an hour. An order must be obtained to enter the Quinta, of which the park-like grounds command good views. A return may be made by the road which leaves the main track a little on the Funchal side of the Quinta gates, and crosses the face of the hills, after which descend the **Caminho do Meio** in running *carro*, altogether about two hours out and home.

Or the ride may be prolonged to **Camacha** (2,203ft. ; 6m. = $9\frac{1}{2}$kil.), the chief summer resort of residents, in $1\frac{3}{4}$ hours, and back by the **Pico da Silva** and the Caminho do Meio, altogether $3\frac{1}{2}$ hours, *or* home from Camacha *viâ* **Caniço** (less attractive) in the same time.

Or instead of returning from the Pico da Silva, the **Poizo Road** may be followed to the summit, some very good scenery being enjoyed, and the road past the Mount Church taken on the way home ; time, five hours. Various excursions can be made by those living in Camacha, for which *see* under Santa Cruz. From Camacha to the church of **S. Antonio da Serra** takes about two hours each way.

B. **Behind the Town.**—To the **Mount Church**, the prettiest route to which lies along the **Saltos Road**. In the morning numbers of peasants will be met on this, as on other roads to the mountains, running down to the town, their sledges piled high with fuel, vegetables, etc. (For hotels, *see* page 126, for railway, *see* page 146, also advertisements.) A description of the Quinta do Monte has already been given.

The church (Nossa Senhora do Monte) was built about 1470, and is 1,965 feet above the sea. (Distance from the city, one hour by *carro* ; $2\frac{1}{2}$ m. = 4 kil.) The façade, which is approached by a long flight of steps, is flanked by two towers, and has a somewhat imposing appearance. The interior is roughly decorated with indifferent paintings. The image of the Virgin on the high altar is much venerated on account of the miracles she is said to have performed. Tradition relates that she appeared, about the year 1700, at the fountain situated some one hundred and twenty yards down the path, to the N.W. of the façade. A shrine and a money-box will be found at the spot whence the water issues. In the road, and opposite the church, is a little wine-shop, whence the running *carros* start on their downward course by the direct Monte Road. If a return be made at once by one of these, the whole journey occupies about 1¼ hours; *or* it is possible to return by the Curralinho, the wildest piece of scenery near Funchal, and descend the Caminho do Meio, also by *carro*. This is a very fine excursion. Time, rather over 2½ hours' total. A view of the Curralinho can be obtained from a point about ten minutes from the church. The above times can be shortened by using the railway.

At a point in the Torrinhas Road, some one-third up to the Mount Church, there is the chapel of N. S. da Consolação. Here the **Levada** of Funchal crosses the track, and may be followed on either side for some distance amidst pleasant views, etc.

A much longer ride past the Mount Church is to the **Pico Arrieiro** (5,893 feet), eight hours there and back. An early start should be made, and guides should be taken. The summit, which shows evident traces of volcanic action, abuts on the Grand Curral, of which, as well as of the central group of mountains, splendid views are obtained. Amongst the latter are the Pico Ruivo, As Torres, Cidrão, etc., and a beautiful bird's-eye view of the Metade and adjacent ravine. Near the summit are some holes (*poços*) in which snow and ice are stored during the winter for use in the summer months. The Portuguese Government have built a house on a large plateau not far from the summit, and about 5,300 feet above the sea. The building is intended for use as an elevated sanatorium and meteorological observatory.

C. **To the North-west.**—The road *viâ* Santa Clara and the **Peak Fort** leads near **Beckford's Fort**, a reminiscence of the English occupation of 1807-10, when the position was chosen as one that effectually commanded the town. It then passes **S. Roque Church**, built in 1579 (1,129 feet), and ascends to the little chapel of the **Alegria**, which stands in a picturesque situation. The double journey occupies about 2¼ hours. To vary this walk, the bed of the **Ribeiro de S. João** can be crossed, and the **Church of S. Antonio** (951 feet) visited. Time necessary, a little under three hours.

Another ride is across the bridge of S. João, past the Maravilhas to **S. Antonio**, returning *viâ* **S. Amaro** and **S. Martinho** (764 feet) in 1¾ hours, *or* as far as the **Trapiche** or the valley of **Vasco Gil**, in 2¼ and 2¾ hours respectively, *or* descend to the left beyond the Church of S. Amaro, which dates from 1460, and home by the **New Road** in about the same time. The last-mentioned rides command some fairly good views of the Grand Curral, especially if the hills are ascended.

Some of the most recent signs of volcanic action are to be seen in this part of the island. In the Pico da Cruz, which is close to the city, the breaking away of the crater-wall, and the stream of lava issuing towards the sea, are vivid and plain to the eye without the trouble of leaving the road.

The upper part of the village of **Camara de Lobos** is reached by the road past S. Martinho. This is the route followed when going to S. Vicente. (*See* Expedition No. 5.)

D. **To the West.**—A pleasant ride or drive, for carriages can pass all the way, is along the **New Road**, which is fairly level, and the greater part of which is macadamised. **Camara de Lobos,** where it terminates, is a quaint little fishing village (population of district 17,250), no inn, about 5½ miles or 9 kil. from the city. Trees have been planted for some distance along this Rotten Row of Madeira, as it is proudly described. Certainly, this tardy acknowledgment on the part of the Portuguese Government of the benefits of civilisation has already greatly improved Funchal, giving an outlet and a means of transport to those anxious to live in the healthy, breezy atmosphere to be found on the cliffs. In the cliff near Gorgulho is an opening called the Cano de Folle, or Blacksmith's Forge, through which the sea is visible, and whence, in rough weather, a good-sized water-spout is often ejected. The R. dos Socorridos, crossed by a three-arched bridge, was a flowing river when the island was first visited. It derives its name from the rescue of two of Zargo's men, who were nearly drowned whilst crossing it. In the cuttings along the road many beds of fresh cinders and volcanic mud will be observed. Time of ride, out and back, 2½ hours. Camara de Lobos is of little interest.

Passing through the village, a steep ascent leads to the summit of Cabo Girão, a magnificent headland, 1,920 feet high. Those wishing to visit the brink of the precipice must go a little to the left. Time, both ways, six hours from Funchal. A little over an hour from here is the **Achada do Campanario,** 8½ miles = 13½ kil., where there is a hollow chestnut tree over thirty-five feet in girth, said to be the oldest and largest in the island. The interior is used as a summer-house, and has been fitted with a door. This spot commands a good view of the western mountains, Paul da Serra, etc. A descent can be made to the beach by a pathway cut in the cliff. Beyond this point, *see* Expedition No. 6.

Expeditions from Funchal.

Parties of more than three should send a telegram, say two or three days beforehand, to acquaint hotels with their arrival.

No. 1.—To the East. (Santa Cruz, Machico, Caniçal, the Fossil Beds, etc., with excursions from the same places in small print, including the Portella and Lamaceiros Passes to Porto da Cruz and Fayal.)

The road passes the Fort of S. Thiago, the Church of N. S. do Socorro, and the Lazaretto (1 m. = 1½ kils.), crosses the R. Gonzalo Ayres, runs past the chapel of N. S. das Neves, ascends to a height of 1,245 feet, and so over the **Cabo Garajão** (Brazen Head), which is not visible from the land side, to **Caniço** (4¾ m. = 7½ kil.), **Porto Novo, Gaula,** the chapel of **S. Pedro** and **Santa Cruz** (three hours; 11 m. = 18 kil.). The scenery is uninteresting.

Santa Cruz. A small town largely devoted to the fishing interest, population, 16,274. Good Portuguese hotel, well situated, charge about 2,000 reis per day. Church of S. Salvador with tombs.

Excursions from Santa Cruz.—To **Madre d'Agoa** (1,411 feet), three hours both ways. Horses cannot go quite up. The point aimed at lies on the E. side of the R., where the **levada** leaves the bed. A pretty spot, a short distance above which there is a good waterfall.

To the Lagôa, the Church of S. Antonio da Serra, and through the Portella to Porto da Cruz and Fayal.—Ascend to the left a little beyond Santa Cruz to the **Lagôa** (about 1¼ hours). This is an unbroken crater, where a pool of water will be found in the winter. It commands a good view of the Lameira, or marsh, and the surrounding country. A quarter of an hour further on is the Church of S. Antonio, 2,059 feet, scarcely worth visiting.

From the paths which join near here, the following selection of routes can be made:—To Machico, *see* Machico, *or* to the **Lamaceiros Pass**, *see* next paragraph, *or* to the **Pico de Suna**, 3,416 feet, 1¾ hours, whence there are good views as far as Santa Anna, Pico Ruivo, etc., *or* past the **P. d'Aboboras,** 4,769 feet, to the **Poizo House,** in 1¾ hours, and so on to Funchal or Santa Anna. (*See* Expedition No. 3.)

The track leads on to the **Portella Pass** (1,800 feet, 2¼ hours), whence there are good views, though less extensive than those from the Lamaceiros Pass; passes through the narrow little cutting, and descends to **Porto da Cruz** in 3¾ hours from the start (distance, 10 m. = 16 kil.). No inn. A rough road leads on the South of the **Penha d'Aguia,** a remarkably bold mass of rock, 1,915 feet high, commanding good views (*see* Excursions from Santa Anna, Expedition No. 3) to **Fayal** in 1½ hours (6 m. = 9½ kil.). From Fayal to Santa Anna, 1½ hours, *see* Expedition No. 3.

To Fayal *viâ* **the Lamaceiros Pass.**—The same road is followed as far as S. Antonio da Serra. From here, branch off to the **Lamaceiros,** the summit of which (2,180 feet) commands a magnificent view, infinitely finer than that from the Portella. The Penha d'Aguia is especially prominent from here.

Time up from Santa Cruz, about 2¼ hours. From here descend to **Porto da Cruz**, total four hours. For Fayal, *see* above, *or* a shorter way to Santa Anna may be taken, which does not touch Porto da Cruz.

Camacha can be visited from Santa Cruz in from one hour and a half to two hours.

To the Poizo House.—A direct road leads from Santa Cruz to the **Poizo** in about three hours. For the Poizo, *see* Expedition No. 3.

Leaving Santa Cruz, a barren country is passed through to **Machico** (four hours; 15m. = 24kil. from Funchal). Pop., 11,918.

Machico is a fishing village in which accommodation can be obtained for a limited number. The Chapel of S. Izabel is said to be built on the spot where Machin and his wife, referred to in the history of Madeira, were buried. A cave, the largest yet found on the island, which is known as the Furna, can be visited.

Excursions from Machico.—**To the Portella Pass.**—A direct road leads to the summit in two hours. Rather over half-way up, a turning to the left leads to S. Antonio da Serra. For further information, refer under Santa Cruz.

To Caniçal.—A footway, where horses cannot pass, leads along the coast in about an hour. There is no object in coming here.

To the Fossil Beds.—These should be visited by boat. (*See* Boat I.) Time from Machico, about an hour. There is a small ascent to make from the beach on the east side.

A great deal of discussion has taken place about the origin and date of this curious sandy stretch, with its apparently fossilised trees. The most generally accepted theory is that the stone branches are casts or stalactites formed in the sand by the gradual action of rain water, which has dissolved the calcareous matter, and caused it to harden into the peculiar shapes found. Similar beds are to be seen in many places. The sand is supposed to have been blown to its present position from a beach formerly existing on the north of the island.

The spot is a pleasant one for a picnic, and the north coast, as far as S. Jorge, may be seen from the neighbouring rocks.

To the Curral do Mar.—A picturesque ravine to the east of Porto da Cruz. Time necessary, three hours each way.

No. 2.—To the N.E. From Funchal to Porto da Cruz and Fayal, *viâ* the Portella (*a*) and Lamaceiros (*b*) Passes.

Neither of these routes is recommended from Funchal, and both will be found sufficiently described under Santa Cruz and Machico. To those who wish to take them, however, the following instructions are given:—

(*a*) To Camacha, 1¾ hours; S. Antonio da Serra, 3¾ hours (*see* Ride A); to the Portella, 4½ hours; Porto da Cruz, 6¼ hours; Fayal, 7¾ hours; and Santa Anna, 9¼ hours (*see* Expedition 1, Excursions from Santa Cruz); *or*, up to the Poizo House (2¼ hours), and past the Pico d'Aboboras to S. Antonio da Serra, 4 hours (*see* Expedition 3), and so on as above.

(*b*) The Camacha route can be taken as before, but the road is left before arriving at S. Antonio. Time to the top of the Lamaceiros, 4¼ hours (refer to Expedition 1, Excursions from Santa Cruz); *or, viâ* the Poizo House, and along the ridge to the Lamaceiros Pass, about 4¼ hours, after which refer as above to Excursions from Santa Cruz: *Viâ* the Lamaceiros Pass is a trifle shorter than *viâ* the Portella Pass.

Mention may here be made of the fact that a path along the top of the hills connects the Poizo with the Lamaceiros, and eventually with the Portella Pass.

No. 3.—From Funchal *viâ* the Poizo and Ribeiro Frio to Santa Anna, with the Coast Roads from Santa Anna to Fayal on the E., and Boa Ventura on the W., and Excursions from Santa Anna. The best road in the island.

Quit Funchal by the straight road to the Mount Church, ¾ hour (if by the Saltos road, one hour. For description, *see* Ride B), and, leaving the church behind, pass over the **Pico Arrebentão**, whence a good view of the Curralinho, the Pico da Silva, Pico do Infante, the Desertas, etc. At 1½ hours a gate is passed through, and the sheep-grazing district or downs are entered. The pine trees are left behind, and bilberries, etc., take their place, the road being only paved where the streams render it necessary. At 2¼ hours (6¼ m. = 10 kil.), the **House of Refuge on the Poizo** is passed.

Free accommodation is provided on the ground floor. On the upper storey there are two bedrooms, 200 reis the night being asked. Those wishing to stop here pay 1,000 reis per diem.

The path which turns to the right a little above the house leads to the Lamaceiros and Portella Passes, S. Antonio da Serra, Machico, Santa Cruz, etc. (*See* Expedition No. 2.)

A few hundred yards above the house, the summit (4,553 feet) is gained, and the north coast appears, with the **Penha d'Aguia** below, and Porto Santo in the distance. On the left, the mountains of As Torres and the Pico Ruivo. The road, which is here well paved, now descends sharply, first laurel and later other woods are entered, and at three hours the bridge over the **Ribeiro Frio** is crossed, a most charming spot.

On passing the second bridge, climb up to the **Levada do Furado** (close by), follow the watercourse through two cuttings, and one of the most magnificent views in the world is below, around and above the enchanted traveller. In the depths beneath, the stream of the Metade valley winds in and out like a silver thread; poised above are the Picos Arrieiro, Ruivo and As Torres, and on all sides the most luxuriant vegetation, availing itself of every crevice and cleft which the precipice affords. Those who are not afraid can follow the **Levada** to its source in the Pico Arrieiro.

Continuing the road, scenery is passed through only inferior to that on the Levada. At $3\frac{3}{4}$ hours, the Cruzinhas is reached, and the road divides. That to the right leads to Fayal in two hours; that to the left descends sharply, and several ravines are crossed. The quaint little houses, with their ridged thatch and universal yam gardens, lend a character of their own to the valleys, whilst the woods higher up are often scarcely to be distinguished from those of our own country, only the blast of the horn and the sight of the hounds sweeping full cry across some hollow being necessary to transport us back to our own homes. The sticky country lane, however, is unknown, though at times, and in wet weather, the slippery surface of the Madeira pathway is scarcely an improvement. At $6\frac{3}{4}$ hours, the Cortado ridge is crossed, with a fine view of the Penha d'Aguia, after which a gradual descent brings us once more to hydrangea hedges and cultivation. The paved upper road to São Jorge is passed, leading away to the left, and at $7\frac{3}{4}$ hours the hotel at Santa Anna is reached (1,090 feet).

Santa Anna, pop. 9,348, is a scattered village, of which the chief charm lies in the number of walks around it, and the excursions which can be most conveniently made from it. Santa Anna Hotel, 2,500 reis a day (wire previously), is a favourite resort during fine weather, or in the summer months.

Excursions from Santa Anna.—To the E.—The coast road, which is fairly good, leads to Fayal in $1\frac{1}{2}$ hours. From Fayal to Porto da Cruz, $1\frac{1}{2}$ hours, *see* Expedition No. 1, Excursions from Santa Cruz.

To the W.—The coast road to Boa Ventura starts immediately below the Hotel, crosses the valley, and descends sharply to Po S. Jorge in half-an-hour, ascends the other side to S. Jorge Church, after which the paving suddenly becomes worse. At $1\frac{3}{4}$ hours it falls abruptly, crosses a fertile valley, and at $2\frac{3}{4}$ hours passes round a precipice at about 600 feet above the sea. Again the road leads down, and at three hours the Ponta de Boa Ventura is crossed, after which another headland is rounded, a sharp turn is taken up to the left, the path dives round the church, and at $3\frac{1}{2}$ hours Boa Ventura and the hotel are entered ($12\frac{1}{2}$ m. = 20 kil.). For description, etc., *see* Expedition No. 4. The scenery along this route is wild and beautiful, and the proximity of the sea most agreeable. The lignite beds of S. Jorge, formerly visible in the R. do Meio, three hours from Santa Anna, have been buried by a landslip.

To the Penha d'Aguia.—Time, six hours there and back. Follow the coast road through Fayal, and towards Porto da Cruz, as far as the Terra de Batista ridge. Here branch off to the left, and ascend by a steep path this wonderful isolated cliff. From the top are seen the Arrieiro, Torres and Ruivo Peaks, the whole of the coast from S. Lourenço, and the lesser mountains as far as the Pico do Arco de S. Jorge on the W.

To the Levada dos Vinhaticos.—This lovely Levada starts from high up in the R. Secco. From Santa Anna it takes rather over two hours to reach the point from which the walk along the aqueduct commences. After another forty minutes a long tunnel is passed through. The course can be followed up as far as desired by those accustomed to precipices. The views are most striking, and the excursion well repays any trouble taken.

To the Pico Ruivo.—This, the highest point in the island, is best ascended from Santa Anna. An experienced mountaineer can reach it with much labour, however, either from the Curral, or across from the Torrinhas mountains. Time required from Santa Anna, 3½ hours up, and three hours down. Hammocks can go to the summit, but horses must stop a little below.' On the way, the Homem-em-Pé (man on foot) is encountered, a basaltic column bearing witness to the great loss by denudation even at this height. The road passes the base of the Encumiada Alta, which may be ascended, if desired (5,893 feet), crosses the neck, and commences to climb the **Pico Ruivo** itself. From the top (6,059 feet) there is a marvellous panorama. On the S. a thin wall of rock connects the Ruivo with the Torres Peaks (highest point, Pico del Gato, about 6,000 feet). Further eastward appear the mountains and ridges through which the Poizo, Lamaceiros and Portella Passes are conducted, with the Serra de S. Antonio and valley of Machico beyond. To the E. lies the ravine of the R. Secco. To the N. the deeply seamed slopes and mountains between Fayal and Boa Ventura. To the W. are the Canario (5,449 feet) and Torrinhas (5,980 feet) Peaks, beyond which again the high moorland of the Paul da Serra (4,611 feet)—*see* Expeditions 5 and 7—with its own Pico Ruivo, some 730 feet higher than the moor itself. Continuing our panorama, we encounter the Pico Grande (5,390 feet), and, lastly, the Pico Cidrão (5,500 feet), after which come the Torres again.

The Curral is only partly visible.

To Bocca das Voltas.—Five hours both ways. A beautiful excursion to a point some 2,500 feet high, whence a descent can be made into the valley of Boa Ventura. The ridge crossed is that of the Torrinhas, which connects the Pico do Arco with the P. Canario. The summit commands a very fine view.

To the Pico Canario.—Four hours up. The road to this mountain lies past the Church of S. Jorge. The view from the summit (5,449 feet) is perhaps the finest to be obtained of the Grand Curral, but towards the S.E. is not very extensive.

No. 4.—To the N.N.W. From Funchal past S. Antonio over the Serrado, along the E. side of the Gran Curral and across the Torrinhas (Turrets) Pass to Boa Ventura and Ponta Delgada, with excursions from Boa Ventura, including the Coast Road to S. Vicente. For Coast Road to Santa Anna, *see* under Excursions from Santa Anna, Expedition 3.

Leaving Funchal the Church of S. Antonio is reached in ¾ hour, and at two hours a point on the Serrado, 3,365 feet high, whence a good view into the Curral Ravine, one of the grandest sights in the island. This is the most convenient spot for visitors from Funchal, who have but little time to spare and who wish to see the Gran Curral.

A descent is now made to the Church of N. S. do Livramento (three hours; 11 m. = 17½ kil.), after which the climbing recommences. Good views are obtained, and the outline of the mountain-tops, which represent a sleeping woman's head, should be noticed. The following panorama is visible: Commencing at the Pico Ruivo (6,059 feet) we find the Pico Canario (5,449 feet) immediately on its left. Next the Pico da Trincka, then the Torrinhas (5,986 feet), then the Pico de Jorge, Pico da Empenha, Pico Grande (5,390 feet), Pico dos

Bodes (3,725 feet), Pico Serrado, Pico de S. Antonio (5,706 feet), Pico do Cidrão (5,500 feet), Pico Arrieiro (5,895 feet), Pico As Torres (6,000 feet), and again the Pico Ruivo. At five hours the summit of the pass (5,042 feet, 16 m. — 25½ kil.), where the Curral is lost sight of, and the descent, *viâ* the narrow Ribeiro do Porco, commences.

From the top, as stated in Expedition 3, Excursion from Santa Anna, the Pico Ruivo can be ascended.

The path downwards leads through a succession of rugged rocks and gorgeous vegetation. If clouds have gathered, the surroundings may be half hidden by a rainbow. Another day they stand out clear and sharp against the sky. Further down the ravine widens, and at eight hours the little inn of Boa Ventura is entered immediately above the church (26¼m. = 42 kil.).

Boa Ventura is a scattered little hamlet. The inn, which is some 1,400 feet above the sea, is beautifully situated and commands extensive views. Fair accommodation, five beds, 2,000 reis a day.

Excursions from Boa Ventura.—The Arco de S. Jorge to the E., can be ascended in a little over an hour and commands good views.

The Pico de Moranha on the W. can be ascended in about ¾ hr., and from here the Torrinhas Peaks, etc., are visible.

To the W.—The coast road to S. Vicente. Descend sharply from the hotel, and in ten minutes cross the little bridge on the left, from which times are reckoned for the convenience of those going through from Santa Anna to S. Vicente.

The track passes round the cliff at a giddy height above the sea, which is seen beating immediately beneath. The W. portion of the N. coast first comes into view. In the extreme distance is P° Moniz with its island in front, and nearer in Seizal. S. Vicente, not yet visible, is round a bend and **Ponta Delgada** just below. This pretty village is presently passed through, half-an-hour (no inn, but a private house is sometimes let; enquire at Funchal). After this the road, which is rough and wet, alternately leads round cliffs, or descends to the beach. At 1½ hours, Porto S. Vicente, a wine-shop with two or three houses around it, then a sudden turn to the left, where the path leads through a couple of tunnels, and across a large stone bridge into S. Vicente proper (two hours; 8½m. = 13⅜kils.). For description, etc., of S. Vicente, *see* Expedition No. 5. The hotel is half-an-hour above the town.

No. 5.—To the N.W. From Funchal past Jardim da Serra, up the west side of the Gran Curral, across the Serra d'Agoa and the Encumiada to S. Vicente, with excursions from the last-named place to the Pico Ruivo do Paul, etc., along the coast road to Porto Moniz, etc. For the coast road to Boa Ventura, *see* paragraph just above.

Take the bridle road past S. Martinho Church, ¾ hr.; cross the R. dos Socorridos by the upper bridge, and bear to the right past the Estreito Church (2 hrs., 1,617 ft.), ascend through the chestnut woods past the Jardim da Serra (2,532 ft., 9¼m. = 15kil.), to the Cova da Cevada (3½ hrs., 4,300 ft.), with a beautiful view of the Curral. At 3¾ hrs. the thin ridge separating the Curral from the Serra d'Agoa is crossed and the latter is first seen. At 4¼ hrs. the summit of the comb, **Bocca dos Corregos** (4,420 ft.), is gained.

From here the prospect on either side is magnificent and the eye wanders from crag to precipice and mountain to hollow in bewildered ecstasy. This is also the best point from which to ascend the Pico Grande (5,390 feet).

By those wishing to explore the Curral a descent can be made and a few nights spent in **Fajãa Escura**, a small collection of cottages three-quarters of an hour down a steep path from the Bocca dos Corregos. The view from Fajãa Escura itself is particularly fine, and the following is the panorama:— Prominently in front stands the Pico do Cidrão (5,500 feet); next on the left comes the Pico do Canario, 5,500 feet, the Pico da Trincka, the Torrinhas (5,986 feet), the Pico do Jorge, the Pico da Empenha, the Pico Grande, and finally the Pico do Meio.

Leaving the Bocca behind, the road winds across and around precipices, amidst the remains of an ancient forest, descends, and at 6½ hours strikes the junction whence the left-hand road leads down to **Ribeira Brava** (*see* Expedition No. 6), on the west side of the Serra d'Agoa in 2¼ hours. Following that to the right, the Encumiada is soon reached (3,338 feet, 21½m. = 34½kil.), where the best views are obtained by walking for a short distance along the footpath leading to Paul da Serra on the W. The two glens almost seem to divide the island, and the mountain scenery on both sides is extremely fine. Going down towards S. Vicente, the giant heather disappears at 7¼ hours. At eight hours the village of **Rosario** is passed through, and at 8½ hours (28m. = 45kil.) the hotel is reached (seven beds, 2,000 reis per day, pleasantly situated some six hundred feet above the sea). This is a most enjoyable place to stay at, and a capital centre for explorers.

São Vicente itself is on the sea level, and is a village with shops, population 8,139. As the hotel is half-an-hour from the town, excursions will be timed from thence and not from the town itself. There are many pleasant walks along the bed of the stream in the immediate neighbourhood.

Excursions from S. Vicente.—**To the W. The coast road to Seizal and Porto Moniz.** This path leads round the face of the cliff, across several beautiful glens, and should only be followed on foot. Seizal is reached in two hours. The town stands on a small promontory of somewhat recent lava. There is no inn, but accommodation may be had.

(There are a few excursions from Seizal and paths lead upwards (1) to the House of Refuge on the Paul (*see* Expedition 7) past the base of the Pico Ruivo do Paul in 3½ hours, and (2) to the Pass over the **Fanal** from the House of Refuge to **Porto Moniz** (*see* Expedition 7), which is entered at a point known as the Cruzinhas in 2½ hours. Both these paths are rough and steep.)

Leaving Seizal the track still winds above the sea. At 3¼ hours (from S. Vicente) **Ribeira da Janella** (no accommodation), where the Fanal route touches the coast, and at 3¾ hours **Porto Moniz**. No inn, but accommodation can be had.

(From Moniz the **Lagôa de Fanal** can be visited, an extinct crater in which water is found during a great part of the year. From Moniz to the S. of the island, see Expedition 7.)

In the Valley.—Opposite the hotel and distant about three-quarters of an hour is the limestone quarry (**Mina da Cal**), the only one known in the island, and as such of great interest to geologists. There is also a lava tunnel to be seen. Lights are required. Besides these the waterfalls, with which the stream abounds, offer many nooks and corners as attractive to the photographer as to the artist.

To the House of Refuge at the Tanquinhas, with the ascent of the Pico Ruivo do Paul.—A long ascent of $2\frac{1}{2}$ hours leads to the spring at the Tanquinhas. Close by is the House. (See Expedition 7.)

The summit of the Pico Ruivo do Paul (5,336 feet), which can be surmounted on horseback, is reached from here in quarter hour. Eastward the view extends as far as the Pico Ruivo de Santa Anna, and includes nearly the whole of the Central Group of mountains. On the N. the cliffs and gullies, even the sea itself, seem to lie at one's feet. To the W. are the grand Ribeira da Janella with the ridges which bound it, and to the S. the deep solitude of the Paul or Marsh. (See Exp. 7 for description of the Paul or for prolongation of excursion to the Rabaçal.)

No. 6.—To the E. From Funchal along the S. coast as far as Calheta.

From Funchal to **Achada do Campanario**, $4\frac{1}{4}$ hours, see Ride D. Half an hour further on is the village of **Ribeira Brava** (16m. = $25\frac{1}{2}$ kil.). No inn.

From here a path leads up the W. side of the Serra d'Agoa to S. Vicente in five hours. (See Exp. 5.)

At $5\frac{3}{4}$ hours, **Ponta do Sol** ($20\frac{1}{2}$m. = 32 kil.), pop. 19,044, where there is some accommodation to be had and near which there is a richly-decorated little Church. Presently Calheta is sighted; Magdalena is left behind, and the road, which is very uninteresting, enters **Calheta** in $8\frac{1}{4}$ hours (30m. = 48 kil.), pop. 18,237. There is no accommodation, but one or two persons can find sleeping room.

No. 7.—From Calheta viâ the Rabaçal to the Tanquinhas House of Refuge on the Paul da Serra; over the Fanal to Porto Moniz, and round the coast back to Calheta. From the Tanquinhas down to S. Vicente, see Expedition 5 (Excursions from S. Vicente).

Leaving Calheta the slopes are ascended and a tunnel is passed through into the R. da Janella, 3 hours. From here to the two principal fountains ($9\frac{1}{4}$m. = 15 kil.) is another half-hour. Some time may be spent in this place admiring the beautiful scene down the valley and the dripping fern-clothed rocks. The rainbows formed by the spray hanging round the waterfalls may be advantageously viewed from various points.

Attractive as the natural loveliness of the spot may be, the visitor will also examine with interest the manner in which the water is caught and carried away for the benefit of the S.W. district. The higher *levada* was commenced in 1836 and finished in 1860. The men, who were suspended by ropes from 700 feet above, worked under the dripping water. The cutting is 300 feet from the base of the cliff, but, in spite of the danger, it is stated that only one life was lost. The lower *levada*, commenced in 1863 and opened in 1884, receives the water from the Fontes do Cedro and the Vinte Cinco Fontes. Each *levada* has its own tunnel through to the S. The upper passes through the ridge at an altitude of 3,430 feet, the lower at 2,975 feet, and they are 1,400 and 2,575 feet long respectively.

Leaving the Rabaçal behind, cross the head of the R. da Janella and enter upon the Paul, literally "marsh," a large elevated moor, similar to no other part of the island. Here and there it is bare, but generally there is an undergrowth of heather, etc. The silence of the Shades reigns over this desolate region which is often enveloped in mist, rendering a guide who knows the country well extremely necessary. It is mentioned in the article on "Geology." At 6 hours, the House of Refuge (4,840 feet) is reached, and, unless the traveller descends to S. Vicente (Expedition 5), the night must be spent here or at the Caramujo, about half-way between the Tanquinhas and S. Vicente, which is the best halting place for those visiting the Levada do Inferno, a very fine excursion. For the road to Seizal, three hours, *see* Expedition 5.

Permission to enter either house must be obtained at the Obras Publicas in Funchal. At such an altitude the nights are cold, and wraps, candles, food, wine, etc., must all be brought up.

Leaving the Tanquinhas behind, the ridge to the N.E. of the Janella valley is followed. At $7\frac{1}{2}$ hours from Calheta, the Cruzinhas road to Seizal (*see* Expedition 5) is passed, and the route continues through a wooded country, known as the Fanal, to Riberia da Janella, $10\frac{1}{2}$ hours, and P° Moniz, 11 hours (pop. 4,475). The scenery is splendid, and the valley is equal in its way to anything in Madeira.

From P. Moniz the road crosses the N.W. spur of the island to the Church of S. Magdalena (1,709 feet, $11\frac{3}{4}$ hours); dips into the R. do Tristão; leaves the Achada da Cruz high up on the left, and, after many an ascent and descent, which are thought little of after those encountered elsewhere, arrives in $14\frac{1}{2}$ hours at the Church of Ponta do Pargo, 1,510 feet. Accommodation may be obtained but not for a large party.

A road down the cliff leads to the Port.

Continuing about midway between the cliffs and the mountains through pretty country, at 16½ hours, the road to **Paul do Mar** branches off on the right.

<small>The descent to the Port occupies a little over an hour. The Church of Fajãa d'Ovelha is passed and a zig-zag path soon leads to the coast, which is here particularly bold and beautiful.</small>

The main road continues *via* **Prazeres** (1,750 feet, 17½ hours), where accommodation may be had; crosses a deep ravine, and descends past the Church of N.S. da Graça to **Calheta**, eighteen hours. From Calheta to Funchal, *see* Expedition 6.

No. 8.—From Porto Moniz over the hills to the S.W. of the R. da Janella, to Paul do Mar, Prazeres or Calheta.

Leaving P. Moniz, keep S. Magdalena well on the right, and bear along the W. side of the ridge. For **Paul do Mar**, 5½ hours, descend shortly before arriving at the P. dos Bodes (4,271 feet); *see* Expedition 7. For **Prazeres**, 5½ hours, descend about ¾ hour further on. For **Calheta**, seven hours, continue to keep for rather over ½ hour along the heights. From Calheta to Funchal, *see* Expedition 6.

EXPEDITIONS BY BOAT.

BOAT I.—To the East. Past Santa Cruz and Machico to the Fossil Bed.

Time occupied, about two hours to Santa Cruz, 2¾ hours to Machico, and four hours to the Fossil Bed. The coast scenery is not particularly fine, but the men will row close in if desired, and the view up some of the valleys is very pleasing. For further information, *see* Expedition 1.

BOAT II.—To the West. Past Ponta do Sol, Calheta and Paul do Mar, to Porto Pargo.

Shortly after leaving Funchal remember to look out for the Cano da Folle, especially if the weather be rough. At ¾ hour, **Camara de Lobos** is passed. The coast now becomes very bold and the gigantic **Cabo Girão** (1,920 feet) arrests the eye. Next in order is **Ribeira Brava**, which is decidedly seen to the greatest advantage from the water. At a little over two hours **Ponta do Sol**, where the first view is obtained of Calheta. The cliffs here are very lofty. At three hours **Magdalena (do Mar)**, and at four hours **Calheta**. (For the Rabaçal, *see* Expedition 7.) It may interest some to know that the magnificent headlands under which the boat pursues its way are the seaward boundary of the Sercial (wine) district. At five hours **Paul do Mar**, and at six hours **Porto Pargo**. For further information, *see* Expeditions 6, 7, and 8.

BOAT III.—To Porto Santo. The journey will, of course, be made in the steam-tug, which carries the mails twice a month.

Porto Santo, lat. 33° 3′, long. 16° 20′, 23 miles N.E. of Madeira, pop. 2,301. The highest point of the island is the Pico da Facho, 1,665 feet. The air is dry and affords, when desired, a pleasant change to that of Funchal. The accommodation is almost *nil*. Unless a tent is taken, it is advisable to obtain introductions before going. It is said that dragon-trees were once plentiful, but now there is little verdure. Vines and corn are chiefly grown, a certain amount of wine being sent to Madeira. The peasants live in huts. The Villa, a town on the south of the island, where most of the people live, has suffered frequently from English and French privateers. Christopher Columbus lived here for some time previous to his residence in Funchal. Most of the lime used in Madeira is taken from quarries on the Ilha do Baixo, one of the satellites of Porto Santo.

BOAT IV.—The Desertas. These islands may be visited by boat, or in the steam-tug, which must be hired for the purpose. Tents, provisions, etc., must be taken. There are a good many rabbits and some wild goats, but the shooting belongs to the proprietors.

The Desertas, eleven miles S.E. of Madeira, are three uninhabited islands, of which the largest, the Deserta Grande, is 1,610 feet high and $6\frac{1}{2}$ miles long by about one mile in width. The next in size is called Bugio, 1,350 feet, and the smallest Ilheo Chão, 340 feet. There are a few pine trees and a number of goats and rabbits. The Sail Rock, noticed by everyone arriving in Madeira from the north, is situated off the last-named island and is 160 feet high.

The Salvages are a group of three small islands, half way between Madeira and the Canaries, latitude 30° and longitude 15° 54′ W. The two larger are called the Great and Little Piton. They belong to Portugal, but are quite uncultivated. They are of little value, being only visited in search of a species of lichen called the Orchilla, and of an aquatic bird known as the Sheerwater, with which they abound.

Prices of Horses, Carros, etc. These, of course, are only approximate, and it rests with every traveller to make his own terms.

Horses.—400 reis an hour inside Funchal and at the same rate for any part of any other hour. Tips in proportion are expected. ¹ For the day, 2$000 to 3$000, according to the places visited; for the week, 8$000 to 12$000; for the month about 36$000. Expeditions, 2$500 to 3$000 the horse and 500 reis the man per day. To Mount Church, 800 single, 1$500 return; Palheiro, 1$000 and 1$800. To S. Martinho; S. Antonio; or S. Roque and back, 1$000. To Camara de Lobos or the Curralinho and back, 1$500. To the Alegría and back, 2$000. To Camacha, 1$500 single, 2$400 return. To the Poizo, 2$000 single, 2$500 return. To the Grand Curral (east side), 2$500; or Cabo Girão and back, 3$000. To the Pico Arrieiro and back, 3$000. To Santa Cruz, 2$500 single, 3$500 return. To Ribeiro Frio and back, 3$000. To Machico, 3$000 single, 4$000 return. To Santa Anna, 4$500 single, 6$000—7$000 return (2 days). To the Gran Curral viá Jardim da Serra and back, 3$000.

Mules.—These are only used for carrying cargo on expeditions, and about 2$500 reis per day is a fair price, including the man, of course, as with the horses.

Hammocks.—500 reis per hour, etc., or about 2$500 to 3$000 per diem inside the town. For expeditions, from 2$500 to 6$000, and 500 reis each man. Per month about 30 dollars, and more when on expeditions. On the N. side men can be found for less.

Carros (two oxen). Per hour in town, 400 reis, etc., and as with hammocks; per month, about 60$000. To S. Martinho and back, 1$500. S. Antonio, or S. Roque and back, 2$000. Camara do Lobos and back, 4$000. On the steeper journeys, it is always better and cheaper to take basket cars than a carro with four oxen.

Basket Cars with two oxen (up to three persons). Per hour, 400 reis. To Mount Church, Caminho do Meio (Curralinho), Palheiro and Alegría (single), 1$500. To Camara de Lobos and back, 3$000. To Camacha, 3$000, return, 4$000. To the Grand Curral and back, 5$000.

Carriages to Camara de Lobos and back, 4$000.

Running Sledges.—Down from the Mount Church about 400 reis each person; from the Pico do Infante down the Caminho do Meio, 500 to 600 reis. Sledges will hold two persons and may be engaged to meet parties returning from excursions to the mountains or from the N. of the island, who can thus save themselves a good deal of time and a long tedious ride down the slippery roads. Arrangements must be made beforehand.

Boats.—With two rowers, about 500 reis an hour. With four rowers, about 800 reis. To the Fossil Bed on the E., about 3$000 to 5$000. To Calheta on the W., about the same, and for longer or shorter journeys in proportion, and according to the weather, or number of passengers.

The writer has been asked to say that visitors will oblige the hotel proprietors and do better for themselves by making their own bargains in all cases, whether for horses, carros, etc., or boats. A very considerable reduction on the above prices may sometimes be obtained, but those starting on an expedition must commence bargaining some days before they leave.

Steamers.—Blandy Bros.' steam tugs run several times a week to Machico, and nearly daily to Calheta. Once a fortnight the mails are carried to Porto Santo. The steamer may be hired to go round the island for about £15. Further particulars as to time and fares, etc., may be obtained at the agency on the beach. Passengers are landed free of charge by the ship's boat.

The Railway (*Caminho de Ferro do Monte*) starts from the Pombal, which is some ten minutes from the beach, and is reached by ascending the Rua das Difficuldades. *Fares:* Up to the Levada, 80 reis; Livramento, 130 reis; Flamengo, 170 reis; Monte, 250 reis. Return (whole distance), 320 reis.

There are several trains a day, and the time occupied from the Pombal to the Monte is about 20 minutes. Special trains may be hired at any time on short notice for not less than 25 fares (6$000).

A Tramway is laid from the Jetty to the bottom terminus of the Railway, but is not working (June, 1901). It is proposed to drive it by electricity.

It is intended to carry the tramway on to Camara de Lobos, and perhaps the railway will be continued to the Poizo and the Pico Arrieiro.

The railway may be advantageously used by those starting on or returning from excursions, and for those visiting Mount Church. The scenery from the railway is superior to that from the road, and the new means of conveyance has already revolutionised Funchal by opening up a number of lovely walks at various levels, formerly almost inaccessible.

Omnibus.—A public carriage runs at intervals from the Entrada da Cicade to a little beyond the New Hotel on the new road; fare, 100 reis. Another carriage runs eastward to the end of the Estrada Nova do Campo da Barca; fare, 100 reis.

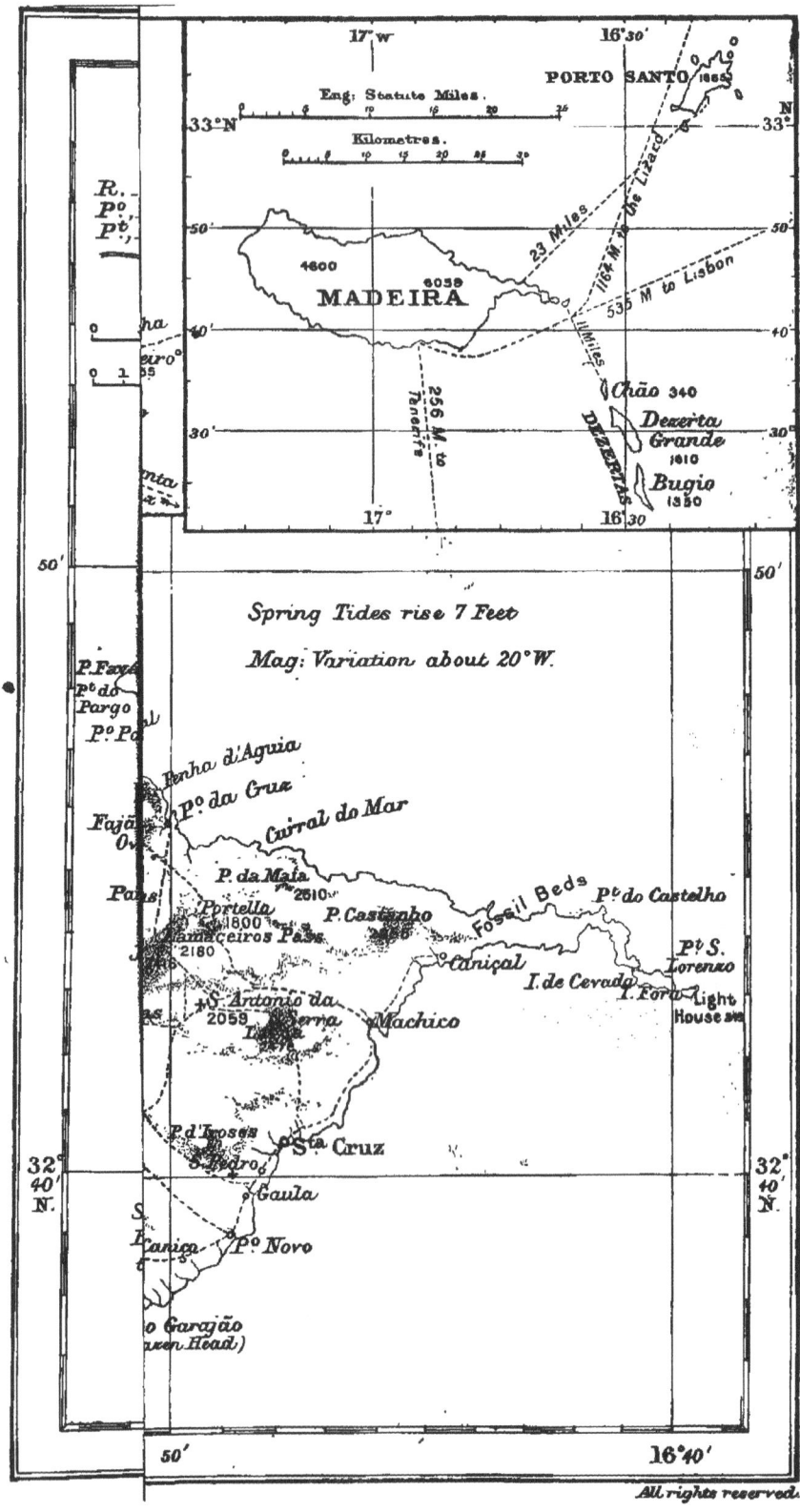

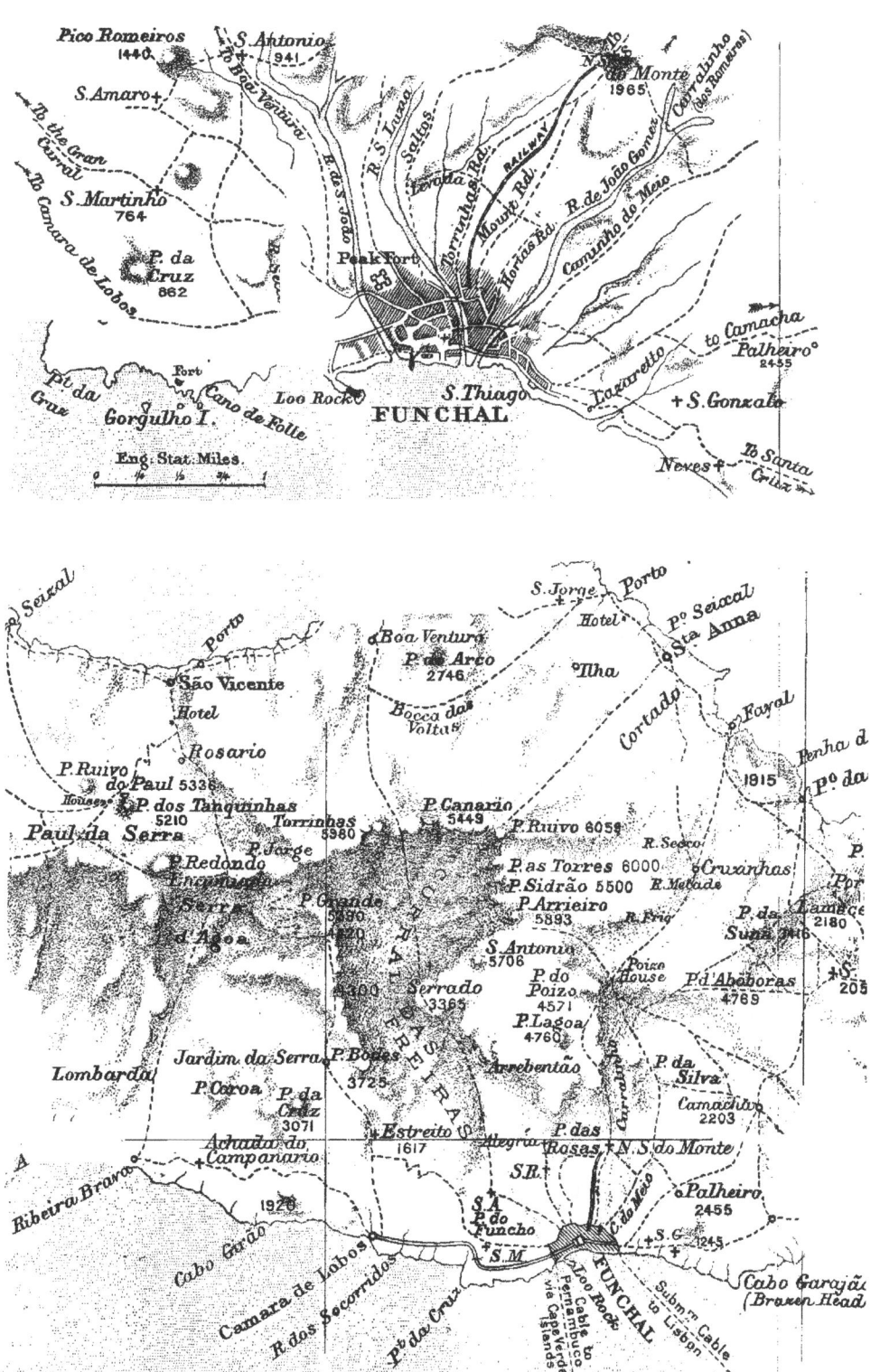

THE AZORES OR WESTERN ISLANDS.

Shipping Facilities.—Travellers from Europe, from the Canaries or from Madeira, can reach the Azores best from Lisbon or Madeira by the boats of the "Empreza Insulana de Navegação." For fares and details, *see* Table of Steamships. The same Company runs a boat monthly to and from New York, 1st class fare, $50. (N.Y. Agents, G. Amsinck & Co., 6, Hanover Street.)

The "Prince Line" boats (Head-quarters, Newcastle, England; N.Y. Agents, C. B. Richards & Co., 61, Broadway, fare $55 to $70), run regularly between New York and Genoa, touching at St. Michael's on the way, and the "Anderson Line" (N.Y. Agents, Hagemeyer & Brunn, 9, Stone Street, Produce Exchange Annex, fare $50), also touch at St. Michael's on their journeys between the United States and the Mediterranean.

Besides this a great number of boats come to the islands for coal, provisions or repairs, but these cannot be relied upon as a means of locomotion.

Communication between the islands depends almost entirely on the steamers of the "Empreza Insulana."

Customs Duties, etc.—These are the same as in Madeira, the islands being regarded politically and judicially as a part of Portugal. Ecclesiastically they are ruled by a bishop, whose residence is at Angra, in Terceira.

Islands as Pleasure Resorts.—Tourists staying for some time in the Azores will find St. Michael's the largest and most attractive island in the archipelago. Next in order is Fayal, from which Pico is easily visited. Angra do Heroismo, in Terceira, is decidedly the most picturesque and interesting town. The Lisbon-Madeira boat, in making its round, usually stays here the whole day, both going and returning, and thus gives sufficient time for ordinary exploration. For further information, refer to the separate description of the islands, of which there are nine in all, namely Sta Maria, S. Miguel, Terceira, Graciosa, S. Jorge, Pico, Fayal, Flores and Corvo.

Accommodation.—This is poor everywhere. The Portuguese hotels are generally run upon the same lines, the chief meals being at 9 or 10 a.m. and 3 or 4 p.m., with coffee or tea at 7 a.m., and a light repast at night, wine free; terms from 1$000 to 1$500 reis *fracos* per diem. Bedding is generally clean, and the main cause of complaint lies, as in most native hotels, both in

Madeira and in the Canaries, in the defective sanitary arrangements. At Ponta Delgada, St. Michael's, there is an English hotel, homely and very simple, but excellent as far as it goes. To make the islands thoroughly comfortable for tourists more and better hotels are wanted.

Expenditure.—As is the case in Madeira and the Canary Islands, prices of commodities, though still low, have practically doubled during the last few years. Rent, however, is cheap, the demand for houses being small.

Tourists will find it advisable to bargain a good deal. Tariffs are rarely official, and there is a general disposition to get as much as possible out of all visitors.

Amusements.—Visitors are thrown very much on their own resources. In all the principal islands there are roads along which carriages can pass, and in many instances long drives can be made from place to place along a surface which leaves nothing to be desired. Those riding into the interior generally employ donkeys, but horses can be obtained. Bicycles are much more useful in the Azores than in Madeira or in the Canaries.

The English communities are too small to allow games or sports to be organised on a large scale, but in St. Michael's, and especially in Fayal, where large staffs are employed both on the English and German cables, matters are better than elsewhere. Several of the Portuguese gentry have constructed tennis courts, but the damp, enervating climate is not in favour of brisk outdoor exercise.

Shooting is better than in the Canaries or Madeira, and there is good deep sea fishing to be had in Fayal Channel, etc., and a little fresh water fishing in some of the volcanic lakes in St. Michael's.

The climate is very favourable to plant life. Lovers of horticulture will find some of the gardens, especially at Ponta Delgada, most wonderful examples of cultivated beauty and botanical interest, whilst the indigenous flora is very varied and extensive.

Money.—This is similar in denomination to that used in Madeira, but the value of the Azorean mil reis is as 8 to 10 as compared with the Lisbon mil reis. For instance, 1$000 reis *fraco* (Azores) = 800 reis *forte* (Lisbon), and 1$000 reis *forte* = 1$250 *fraco*. To turn *forte* into *fraco*, multiply by 8 and divide by 10, and *vice versâ* to turn *fraco* into *forte*. *Fraco* notes and *fraco* copper money are issued, available only in the Azores. No *fraco* silver exists. All payments are made in *fraco* unless otherwise stipulated, and quotations in this Guide for carriages, etc., are in *fraco*.

Postal Rates are similar to those in Madeira. Separate stamps are issued in each of the three political divisions, *i.e.*,

Ponta Delgada, which includes São Miguel and Santa Maria.

Angra, which includes Terceira, Graciosa and São Jorge.

Horta, which includes Pico, Fayal, Flores and Corvo.

Direct Telegraphic Communication exists between the Azores and Lisbon, Hamburg, New York and Halifax, except as regards Santa Maria, Flores and Corvo, to which no cables have yet been laid.

Population.—The total population is 256,000, all of whom are of white origin and speak Portuguese.

Social Customs.—The people are quiet, honest and industrious. In common with their compatriots of Portugal they are very staid and respectable, and do their best to give the lie to that very erroneous proverb, " Les Portugais sont toujours gais." Nothing is more surprising to the passing stranger than to see a group of gentlemen step on board the boat at some remote and insignificant harbour, completely dressed in shiny silk hats, frock coats, varnished boots, and tightly-rolled umbrellas, apparently carefully got up for a stroll in Hyde Park.

On shore contradiction follows on contradiction. An iron crane of modern construction lifts goods into a cart, apparently similar to those used by the Romans. A small heavy platform, generally round in front and square behind, runs on solid disc wheels, united by a wooden axle, which turns along its whole length in wooden bearings. The weighty pole rests on a yoke, lashed to the horns of two oxen. The sides of the cart are sometimes made of strong woven basket work, spreading out at the top. When such a vehicle is full of some heavy material, the noise it makes on its laborious passage closely resembles that made by a pack of hounds in kennel as feeding time approaches. When going down hill a pair of oxen is often tied on behind and taught to serve as a break.

Passing under the gateway of a battlemented wall, dating probably from the 16th or 17th century, when its erection was necessitated by the constant attacks of foreign rovers, one encounters a group of women dressed in the " Capote e Capello," a falling cloak which completely conceals the figure, and which is surmounted by a monstrous hood, fashioned on rigorous and definite lines, as is usually the case with any local costume, and puffed out by strips of whalebone in such a way that the face of the wearer is scarcely visible to the passer-by. This apparently uncomfortable dress, said to be of remote Flemish or Algarve origin, is jealously retained by what may be described as the

Azorean middle class. In Terceira, where the shape is rather different, it is known as the "Manto," and is of black stuff. Elsewhere it is dark blue. The most extravagantly large hoods are worn in Fayal.

The "Carapuça," a male head dress protecting the head and neck, is only worn by the peasants in São Miguel, and is dying out even there.

In Terceira, where there is a peculiarly savage race of cattle, said to be of Spanish origin, bulls are sometimes baited in the public streets. A long rope is attached to the animal's horns, and it is the duty of the lookers-on to hinder the movements of the bull, whilst some enterprising amateur parades in front of it and evades its furious charges. Fatal accidents occasionally occur.

Feast days are frequent, when there are usually religious processions. A curious ceremony is that known as the "Imperio do Espirito Santo," which takes place at Whitsuntide or Trinity Sunday, an emperor and sometimes an empress with their proper retinue being elected for the occasion.

The standard of politeness amongst the Portuguese is a very high one, and though in certain ways they may be less refined than a well-bred Englishman, their general courtesy is far greater than that common amongst ourselves. Visitors should remember that it is their duty to conform to the habits of the place they are in, and that others suffer if they inadvertently or carelessly leave a bad impression behind them.

Except in Terceira the style of architecture adopted is somewhat commonplace, although the façades of the churches are sometimes extravagantly ornate. In Terceira and the islands further west, the curious pyramidal form of the chimneys is worthy of notice.

Knicknacks, etc.—In São Miguel small articles in terra-cotta can be purchased. In Fayal a number of things are made:—Drawn linen (crivo work), straw lace, feather flowers, straw hats, wicker work, etc., etc.

Climatic Conditions.—The temperature is a little lower than that of Madeira or the Canary Islands, rain and cloud being much more prevalent. The mean minimum on the coast during the winter is about 48° F. and the mean maximum during the summer about 74° F., the conditions in the different islands varying but little. The rainfall is considerable and some of the islands are very damp during the winter, ferns, echeveria and lichens growing freely on the walls and roofs even near the coast. The best months for explorers are from June to September, this being the time of year when visitors from Lisbon, Madeira and the United States come to the islands to avoid the excessive heat commonly experienced in their own countries. The mean daily variation is about 10½° F. The weather during the winter is too wet and tempestuous to allow the islands to be regarded as a winter resort for those suffering from chest complaints, but the summer months are delightful, and the good effects of the climate can be aided by drinking or bathing in the mineral waters, which exist in great variety. The Island of Pico is said to be that best suited to consumptive invalids, who should inhabit the intermediate slopes. The higher parts of all the islands are apt to be covered with cloud, especially from October to May. Snow is rare and only lies for any length of time on the top of Pico.

Mineral Waters.—The chief centre for these is at Furnas, in São Miguel. No one should use them without taking proper medical advice. They are both hot and cold and offer a large choice. For further details, *see* under Furnas.

Water Supply.—This is generally but not always as good as it should be, and care should be taken to make enquiries in each locality.

Geological Features.—The writer's acquaintance with the islands only allows him to treat of these very briefly.

The archipelago consists of the visible summits of a chain of submarine volcanoes, all of which, with the exception of Santa Maria, have been disturbed by eruptions or earthquakes within historical times. A list of dates when these occurred is given in the descriptions of the separate islands.

Superficially, the results of geologically recent discharges of cinders and volcanic grit are much more apparent than is the case in Madeira or the Canaries. Records exist of the creation of beds of ash many feet in thickness. Though these are generally cultivated at present, and though the damp atmosphere favours the rapid growth of vegetation on everything but the hardest or most precipitous of rocks, those viewing the islands will aid the eye by remembering that many of the green slopes spread before them have been deposited almost within the memory of those now living.

Cup-shaped craters with unbroken rings are numerous, and many of these contain pools or lakes of fresh water, sometimes, as at Sete Cidades, of considerable extent. Many similar craters lying on the coast, which, in Madeira or in the Canaries, would long since have been destroyed by the rain or by the sea, are here displayed in segment, the successive layers of cinders and the neck through which they were forced, being laid bare. In the centre there is frequently a cavern into which one can penetrate on foot or in a boat, caves both on the beach and in the interior being far more common than in the other archipelagos. Sometimes these are of colossal dimensions, and the various methods by which they have been formed, a subject too lengthy to deal with here, are geologically of the greatest interest. Those making the round trip will pass close to some good examples of bisected *fumaroles* immediately to the west of Villa das Vellas in São Jorge, and can visit a splendid cave and divided crater in a boat from Horta. (*See* Horta.)

One of the most beautiful excursions in the islands, and one which fortunately lies near to Ponta Delgada, and is therefore easily accessible, is that to Sete Cidades. A description is given elsewhere, and it suffices to say that in addition to the delight to be derived from the lovely views, is the interest attached to the knowledge that one is gazing on a scene with a definite birthday, and that wooded heights and glistening lakes are cloaks covering what became a centre of chaos, havoc and desolation within a few months of the first introduction of settlers to the island.

Although many parts of the Azores are precipitous and the views extremely grand, the most recent volcanic deposits are generally of a more friable nature than those to be seen in the Canaries, and the outlines as seen from the sea are usually more undulating, especially when comparison is made with Teneriffe or with La Palma. The culminating point of the Azores, known as Pico, 7460 feet, 2274 metres, rises, however, more abruptly from the sea than the Peak of Teneriffe, and has a slope on the north and east of over 40°, the earlier deposits on this side having been destroyed and torn away by subsequent disturbances. It has therefore an extreme visible horizon of 112 miles, and should theoretically be visible from the summit of São Miguel, 3569 feet, 1088 metres, which itself has a horizon of 79 miles.

Reference has already been made to one of the most distinctive features of the Azores, namely, the mineral waters of Furnas, in São Miguel, where there are a great number of springs and geysers, some of which issue from the ground at the temperature of boiling water.

It has also been mentioned that seismic disturbances have been frequent within the last few centuries, and, in connection with this, considerable interest attaches to the appearance and disappearance of volcanic islands. One of these, Sabrina, rose in 1811 about a mile off Ponta Ferraría, to the west of São Miguel, attained a height of 410 feet, and disappeared by erosion after an existence of 119 days (18th June to 15th Oct.). Its birth, life and extinction were witnessed and carefully noted by Captain Tillard, of H.M.S. "Sabrina," who happened to arrive in the Azores at the moment. (*See* "Philosophical Transactions," of 1812.)

Strangely enough, in the island of Santa Maria, though so near to São Miguel, no record exists of any perceptible earthquakes. For this reason the island seems to lie outside of the more active sphere above which the others are placed. That this is so is also suggested by the fact that on it are found calcareous deposits some twenty feet in thickness, containing great quantities of fossilised marine mollusca, some of extinct, some of living, and some of hitherto unknown species.

History.—Space will not allow of the discussion of ancient maps and problematical voyages, one of which is mentioned in the History of Madeira.

The islands were discovered by the Portuguese between 1431 (Formigas Rocks) and 1452 (Flores). From the abundance of kites (*buteo vulgaris*) found there, they were christened "Os Açores" (*Port.* : *Hawks*) an ornithological error, the Portuguese for kite being "milhafre." With the exception of birds, there were no vertebrate animals of any kind in the archipelago. The country was covered by dense woods, gigantic cedar trees, now extinct, being predominant.

The abundance of timber helped greatly in the work of settlement, and in spite of eruptions, earthquakes, piratical raids, and wars, both civil and national, the islands have steadily progressed until an abundant population has reclaimed and brought into cultivation almost every available yard of ground.

The fortifications and walls by which many of the larger towns are dominated or surrounded were very necessary for the protection of the people against the constant raids of English, French and Moorish rovers, who attacked most of them at various times, acting in many cases with all the wanton cruelty of the later middle ages. It was, however, in the wars between Portugal and Spain, by means of which the islands fell under Spanish dominion from 1580 till 1640, and the struggle for the Portuguese throne between the partisans of Dona Maria II. and D. Miguel (1826-1834), that the people suffered most.

On July 14-20, 1582, São Miguel, then in the hands of Spain, was attacked and ravaged by D. Antonio, of Portugal, with a large force, chiefly recruited in France, and a few days later (July 26-31), D. Antonio was defeated by a body of Spaniards under the Marques de Santa Cruz, who again overran the island, and barbarously punished the unfortunate people who had espoused the cause of D. Antonio.

On June 23, 1583, the Marques de Santa Cruz attacked Terceira, which fell into his hands and was given over to the mercy of the invaders during three days.

Queen Elizabeth then espoused the cause of D. Antonio, and sent her admirals to harass and ravage the Azores, now belonging to Spain under Philip II. It was during one of these expeditions that Sir Richard Grenville made his famous fight in the "Revenge" off Flores, " the one and the fifty-three," though actually he did not engage the whole but only fifteen ships of the Spanish fleet.

Shortly after the engagement, the entire Spanish argosy met at the spot prior to its departure for Europe, when a fearful storm occurred and sank 107 ships out of 140, the "Revenge" also going to the bottom.

On September 17, 1597, Fayal was seized by Sir Walter Raleigh, but a subsequent attack by the whole fleet, commanded by Robert Devereux, Earl of Essex, on the island of São Miguel, was less successful, Villa Franca alone being sacked.

In 1826, severe fighting took place in Terceira between the "Liberals," as the friends of Dona Maria II. called themselves, and the Miguelistas, resulting in favour of the former.

On August 11, 1830, a Miguelista fleet, which endeavoured to force a landing at Praia in Terceira, was repulsed with a loss of 1,000 men, and in July-August, 1831, the Miguelistas were finally defeated in São Miguel, the last of the Azores to remain faithful to the cause of absolutism and its attendant priesthood.

It was largely owing to the aid of auxiliaries from the islands, that the adherents of D. Miguel were finally driven out of Portugal, and the present Royal Family seated on the throne.

The agricultural history of the country has shown the usual vicissitudes common to lands where the climate will admit of the cultivation of almost any product of the temperate or torrid zones. Advantage has been taken from time to time of fiscal regulations to introduce industries more economically conducted elsewhere, of which the most conspicuous instance is sugar, now rarely or never to be seen. The manufacture of alcohol from the sweet potato (*convolvulus batata*), and the growing of pine-apples under glass, now furnish the basis of a large export. Oranges, of which in 1859 no less than 261,700 boxes of 800 each were sent to England, are still grown, but the lower prices now obtainable make their cultivation unprofitable. The old vineyards, which formerly yielded some 20,000 pipes per annum, were nearly destroyed by the *oïdium tuckeri*. Disease-resisting stock has been introduced, and, in spite of the arrival of *phylloxera*, the yield is again of some importance. This is especially the case at Pico, where, however, the wine pressed from the *Isabella* grape has a peculiar, and to many, an unpalatable, flavour.

Tobacco, flax (*phormium tenax*), coffee and tea, almost exhaust the list of what may be described as exotic crops. The last-named shrub is now largely grown in the island of São Miguel, and is there prepared for the market, the export being already considerable.

Many varieties of fruit are to be found, but in none of the islands does the quality seem specially good, whilst in some it is notorious that none of it will keep for long after plucking. This is probably due to excess of damp in the air.

All vegetables can be grown well, and all cereals, some of the land yielding three and even four crops a year without irrigation. Beans are planted very largely, and shipped chiefly to Lisbon, whither a number of cattle, and quantities of cheese and butter, are conveyed.

Woad, which was grown largely during the 17th century, ceased to be planted after the introduction of indigo, and has now entirely disappeared.

The forests, formerly of great value, have been practically destroyed.

With the exception of the cereals and crops specially adapted to the islands, nearly all imported plants have been attacked at some time or another by insect pests or disease, by which, if they have not actually been destroyed, they have sometimes been brought to the verge of extinction. Similar misfortunes have occurred elsewhere ; but in colder latitudes, farmers are aided in their efforts to control them by the frost in winter, and in such a climate as the Canaries, exposure of the dry land to the summer sun by constant ploughing is of material help. In the Azores, where we may say that there is neither winter nor summer, eradication of any insect pest or fungoid growth is more difficult.

The nature of the climate has led to a curious method of storing maize, which is left in the cob and hung to a pyramidal structure of laths, such an erection being found in the yard of nearly every cottage passed along the road.

Commerce has been materially assisted by the erection of efficient harbours of refuge at Ponta Delgada (S. Miguel) and Horta (Fayal) where ships can coal, provision or repair, whilst all the smaller islands have landing stages provided with cranes. For internal communication some hundreds of miles of carriage roads have been constructed, and it is proposed to build a railway from Ponta Delgada to Furnas in S. Miguel.

The whale fishery, of which Fayal is the chief centre, still employs a number of hands, and the visitor may be fortunate enough to witness a capture. Capellas in São Miguel is another centre of what was once a most important industry.

SANTA MARIA, 11 miles (17½ kils.) long by 5 miles (8 kils.) broad, contains 6500 inhabitants, and an area of 42 square miles. It is 480 miles from Madeira and 53 miles from São Miguel. Lisbon boats call twice a month and usually remain from two to three hours.

Villa do Porto, the chief town, lat. 36° 56′ N. by long. 25° 8′ W., has been built, for the purposes of defence, on the crest of a hill. Formerly the forts were provided with some 30 guns. The ship lies in an open roadstead and passengers are landed on a small mole. Accommodation and meals can be had and carriages can be hired.

Columbus stopped at the island in 1493 on his return from the discovery of the West Indies, and the church can be seen at Anjos, 1½ hours on foot, where part of his crew returned thanks in a semi-nude condition in fulfilment of a vow made during a heavy storm.

The geological formation, though volcanic, is much less recent than that of the islands further west, and there are none of the lake-bearing craters so common in other parts of the archipelago.

There is every reason to suppose that Santa Maria has gradually risen to its present level. In several places, and especially at Santa Anna and at Figueiral, ¾ and ½ hour respectively from Porto, there are some most interesting calcareous deposits, mentioned in the article on Geology. Again in the Ilheu do Romeiro, to the N. of the island, there is a cave of which the roof and floor are coated with calcareous stalactites and stalagmites.

The climate is drier than that of the rest of the Azores, and the crops sometimes suffer from drought, but in ordinary seasons the land is fruitful, and both cereals and cattle are exported.

A red volcanic clay found in the island is used in the manufacture of hydraulic cement, and a small industry is carried on in pottery and in the export of potter's clay. The dialect spoken resembles that of mediæval Portugal, and is softer than that used in the other islands.

The highest point is the Pico Alto, 1870 feet, 570 metres.

The **Formigas Rocks,** or Ants, lie some 20 miles N.E. of Santa Maria and were the first part of the Azores to be discovered (Cabral, 1431). They are 800 yards long by 150 broad, and calcareous deposits, similar to those in Santa Maria, are to be found in them. The dangerous shoal known as the Dollabarets lies about 3¼ miles S.E. of the Ants.

SAO MIGUEL (*St. Michael's*), 41 miles (66 kils.) long by 9¼ miles (15 kils.) broad, is the largest and richest of the islands. It contains 119,000 inhabitants, and has a superficial area of 269 square miles (688 square kils.). It is 53 miles from Santa Maria; 98 miles from Terceira; 830 miles from Lisbon; 1,147 miles from the Lizard; and 2,228 miles from New York.

It was discovered by Gonçalo Velho Cabral in 1439, but no colonists seem to have been landed until 1444. The first settlers left, most of whom were negro slaves, narrowly escaped destruction in the frightful volcanic eruption of 1445, which destroyed the high mountains in the W. of the island and left the open crater now known as Sete Cidades. The population rapidly increased, and, in 1522, Villa Franca, then the capital, contained some 5000 people. On 22nd October of that year, this town was overwhelmed by a great earthquake, a hill some 450 yards from the beach, sliding down upon the city, the rush of earth being followed by tumultuous streams of water, and the work of destruction being completed by a tidal wave. The new town was rebuilt above the ruins of the old one. In 1531, the negro population became a menace to the whites, and all the males were massacred.

In 1538, an island rose from the sea three miles from Ponta da Ferraría, but soon afterwards was washed away. In 1563, a series of earthquakes and eruptions lasted throughout the whole of July and great quantities of cinders were ejected, but there was little loss of life. In 1591, and again in 1630, Villa Franca and other towns suffered greatly from earthquakes, part of the island being buried during the latter eruption under from five to seventeen feet of volcanic dust. Dust also fell in Terceira, and was noted, it is said, even in Portugal.

Other eruptions or earthquakes occurred in 1638*, 1652, 1682, 1713, 1719*, 1720*, 1755, 1773, 1810, 1811*, 1849, 1852, 1853, 1862, 1882, and 1884, those marked with a * being submarine and attended in more than one instance by the temporary elevation of islands, and, in at least one case, with flames rising from the water.

The highest mountain in the island is the Pico da Vara, 3,569 feet, 1,088 metres.

In the 16th and early 17th century, alum factories were established at Caldeiras (Ribeira Grande) and, on a small scale, at Furnas, but the industry has long since disappeared.

Ponta Delgada, the capital and chief port, situated in lat. 37° 44′ N. by long. 25° 39′ W. of Greenwich, has a population of 22,000, and ranks third amongst the cities of Portugal.

Lisbon steamers stop twice a month, and usually remain one day both outwards and homewards.

Landing Charges.—About 200 to 250 reis each way, but more if the ship moors outside the harbour, or if at night or if the weather is bad. No official tariff.

Hotels.—Brown's Hotel, Pinheiros, back of town, 2$500 reis a day; Hotel Açoriano, near the landing stage, about 1$250 reis.

Clubs.—Michaelense. Strangers temporarily admitted on introduction.

Newspapers.—*Diario dos Açores; Açoriano Oriental.*

The work of which the inhabitants of Ponta Delgada are justly proud, is the breakwater, by which an open and sometimes dangerous roadstead has been converted into a safe harbour of refuge. When completed, the mole will have a length of 1,400 yards, and will have consumed twice as much stone as Plymouth breakwater.

The landing place is singularly picturesque as compared with the rest of the town, which is uninteresting and conventional. There are three parish churches and several minor churches, none worthy of a visit except the Igreja do Collegio, where there is some good carving. The image of the Christo dos Milagres, in the Igreja da Esperança, is only remarkable for the extraordinary number of gems with which it is decorated (Festival, Rogation Sunday). The public buildings call for no special remark, excepting perhaps the Prison, which is an enormous pile of masonry overlooking the sea, and the Hospital, where paupers are received free, and sick sailors, etc., at a moderate daily charge. There is also a **Theatre**, a **Museum**, and a **Library**, the two latter in an old Monastery, now a Lyceum, known as the Graça. The Museum is well stocked with objects of natural history collected in the islands.

Permission can be obtained to enter the Distillery of Santa Clara, or the Tobacco Factory "Michaelense."

Behind the town matters improve, and there are some imposing palaces belonging to rich members of the nobility. The gardens attached to some of these are very fine. The best worth visiting is that of the late S.r José do Canto, which contains a collection of several thousand different species of trees, and is most admirably laid out. That of the Conde Jacome Corrêa is next door, and is well worth seeing, some of the palms having attained colossal dimensions. The garden of S.r Antonio Borges, below Brown's Hotel, is chiefly remarkable for a most lovely arrangement of rockeries and tree ferns, and a visit should not be omitted. Permission to enter these gardens, the volcanic cave in the Rua Formosa, or any of the numerous pine-houses in the neighbourhood is usually accorded.

The band plays in the Campo de São Francisco, where trees have been planted and seats provided. The town is lighted by gas, and there is a good water supply.

The best short drive is by the Arrifes and Grotinha Road to the **Pico do Salomão**, or to the **Charco dos Limos**, from both of which there are good views. Times, 1 hour and 2 hours return, respectively. As is the case with many of the drives in the Azores, travelling is somewhat tedious, owing to the height of the walls bordering the roads.

Carriages.—Inside town : per course, two persons, 250 reis ; 4 persons, 375 reis, or per hour, 750 and 1,000 reis.

Omnibuses run daily to Lagoa, Villa Franca and Ribeira Grande.

Excursions.—To Sete Cidades. No visitor to the island should omit this. A tedious drive of 2 hours (fare, 3,750 reis return) leads to **Lomba da Cruz**, whence a bridle path leads in ¾ hour to the summit of the crater wall. Donkeys (625 reis, each to top and 750 to Lake and back) are usually hired in Feteiras, 1½ hours, but the ascent is easy on foot. Prior to the eruption of 1445, there was a high mountain on this spot, but now the loftiest part of the wall has an altitude of no more than 1,880 feet. The level of the water below is 866 feet above the sea, and the diameter of the crater about three miles. Accommodation can be obtained in the little village at the bottom by those in search of plants or who wish to thoroughly explore the various craters.

The lakes are known as the Lagoa de Carvão and the Lagoa Empadada, the latter being of a dull, muddy emerald green, and the former of a bright deep blue. Though separated, when the lakes are full, by a mere causeway, through which there is an opening, the colouring of each, due in the first instance probably to mineral springs or deposits, remains clearly defined, even in the neighbourhood of the junction. The slope of the crater walls is somewhat uniform, a fact due to the generally friable nature of the surrounding rock. The scene is beautiful and interesting to a degree. A great variety of ferns can be found, and boats can be had by those descending to the lake (about ¾ hour down).

By following the Arrife Road from Ponta Delgada, it is possible to drive right down into the crater, but the time occupied is much longer and the drive tiresome. Fare about 6$000 return.

To Furnas.—The celebrated Valley of Furnas lies at an altitude of 600 feet above the sea, and 27 miles (43 kils.) from Ponta Delgada. It can be reached either by the North or South road. Fare from 5$500 to 8$250 reis single. It is also possible to go by launch to Ribeira Quente or to Povoação on the South coast (about 30s.), whence the ascent to Furnas, on donkeys or in a carriage, can be made in 1½ to 2 hours. It is proposed to make a railway.

The Northern road is the most picturesque. It passes by **Ribeira Grande**, 10 miles, 16 kils., population 8,500; runs *viâ* the coast to Maia, crosses the island and descends past Pedras do Gallegó, whence the view is very fine, into the Valley of Furnas.

The Southern road passes **Alagoa**, 6½ miles, 10½ kils., population 7,659, where there is a large distillery, some pottery works, and a number of pine-houses, which are scattered all along this part of the coast. At 15 miles, 24 kils., **Villa Franca do Campo**, capital of the island until 1522. Population 8,100.

This pretty little town has more than once suffered severely from earthquakes, and has been invaded and raided on several occasions. Sugar, which at one time was extensively cultivated, has disappeared, and oranges, of which large crops were grown, are no longer a source of revenue, but the inhabitants have turned to new industries and are again prospering.

The road now leaves the coast and climbs to the beautiful Furnas Lake, 865 feet above the sea, whence it descends 1½ miles further on to the Furnas Valley, a fertile and picturesque spot, 600 feet above the sea, and some 4 miles in length by 3 in breadth, surrounded by the lofty walls of the crater in whose bed it lies. Population 2,100.

Hotel :—Jeronymo's, 1$000 to 1$500 per diem.

During the summer many visitors from Ponta Delgada and Portugal come to the valley, partly because of the cooler air, lovely excursions and agreeable surroundings, and partly because of the numerous mineral springs to be found. These issue in many parts of the valley at various temperatures, cold and boiling water being ejected in close proximity, sometimes gently and sometimes in the form of a geyser, of which the most conspicuous instance is that known as the Caldeira de Pedro Botelho. This vent vomits turbid water and blue mud, which are thrown up at intervals and again recede. The action is accompanied by a throbbing, rumbling noise, which has caused the vent to be regarded as one of the channels connecting us with the infernal regions. There are well-fitted bathing establishments, where good attention can be had and where the charges are low. For an analysis of several of the springs of which the characteristics differ greatly, the reader is referred to "The Azores or Western Islands," by W. F. Walker, F.R.G.S., etc. (Trübner & Co.)

Waters are found which are beneficial in cases of rheumatism, rheumatic palsy, chorea, psoriasis, skin and throat affections, asthma, and chronic diseases of the mucous membrane.

There are a number of beautiful gardens and parks to be seen in and near Furnas, and some very fine collections of trees and shrubs, the best being perhaps that in the park of the late Sr. José do Canto. The little Gothic Chapel, on the shore of the lake, was designed by M. Berton, of Paris. There are numberless walks and excursions, the points commanding the best views being the **Pico do Canario, Salto do Cavallo, Pico do Gafanhoto** (2,300 feet), and the **Pico do Ferro.**

On September 2, 1630, a furious eruption broke out near Furnas and large quantities of ashes were ejected, many houses being buried and cinders falling as far away as in Santa Maria and Terceira.

To the Caldeiras da Ribeira Grande and Lombadas.—A drive of three hours from Ponta Delgada leads to the Caldeiras, a valley where there are some thermal springs and a small bathing establishment (fare about 3$000 reis). From here a good path leads in about an hour through picturesque scenery to Lombadas, where there is an establishment for bottling the water of that name.

To the Lagoa de Fogo.—This can be reached on foot from the carriage road by those making a circular drive to Villa Franca and Ribeira Grande. The lake, one mile long by half-a-mile wide, lies in an extinct crater formed in 1563, and is surrounded by lofty peaks, with an altitude in one case of over 3,000 feet.

Other drives are to **Capellas**, 9 miles (fare 2$000 to 3$000 reis), the head-quarters of the whale fishery of São Miguel; the **Pico do Fogo**, 1,023 feet (fare 1$750); **Mosteiros**, *viâ* Feteiras or *viâ* Capellas and Bretanha (fare, either way, about 6$500 reis).

Between Ribeira Grande and the solitary lakes known as Fogo and Congro, round Furnas and in the neighbourhood of the Pico de Vara, 3,570 feet, there are numerous walks and excursions, in many of which it is advisable to take a guide in case of the sudden appearance of fogs.

TERCEIRA.—19 miles (30 kils.) long by 9 miles (14½ kils.) broad, contains 46,637 inhabitants. It is 98 miles from São Miguel and 45 miles from Graciosa.

Whenever fighting has been going on, Terceira has taken a prominent position amongst its sister islands.

When Philip II. of Spain caused Terceira to be attacked in 1581, his troops were routed and driven away by the peasants of S. Sebastião, who massed a number of the savage breed of cattle reared in the island, kept them out of sight until the Spaniards were all on the beach, and then drove them headlong at the enemy, following up the charge themselves, killing nearly all the invaders and capturing several guns. In 1583, however, a Spanish force of 13,000 men returned to the attack, and the island fell temporarily into the hands of Spain. For other facts, see History.

Observers declare that Terceira is slowly rising. Earthquakes or disturbances are recorded in the years 1614, 1761, 1800, 1801, and 1841. In 1867, a volcano rose from the sea 12 miles (21½ kils.) N.W. of the island, but became inactive and was soon swept away by the sea. The highest point of the island is 3,435 feet, 1,047 metres.

The land is fertile and the cattle particularly fine, cheese and butter being exported in considerable quantities.

Angra do Heroismo, pop. 32,100, the headquarters of the Bishopric of the Azores, and, until 1832, the capital of the archipelago, lies in lat. 38° 38′ N. by long. 27° 16′ W. The Lisbon steamers touch twice a month, and usually stay all day going and returning. Passengers are landed on the mole. Charges about 125 reis each way.

Carriages.—Two hours' drive, about 800 reis ; whole day, about 3$000 reis.

Hotels.—The Michaelense ; the Central. About 1$250 reis a day.

Public Buildings, etc.—The **Casa da Camara** has a fine hall where sessions are held. The **Memoria de D. Pedro IV.**, a pyramid overlooking the town and commanding a fine view, was erected in memory of the King whose name it bears, and is best approached through the **Public Gardens**, which are small but prettily laid out. The old Castle of S. João Batista, built by the Spaniards in the 17th century, is picturesque and worthy of a visit. The walk should be extended to the extinct crater of the Monte Bresil, as the hill commanding the harbour is called. A round form of volcanic bomb to be picked up there is said to be almost peculiar to this volcano. Those acquainted with Rame Head, near Plymouth, will note the strong resemblance between the mediæval Spanish and the ancient British or Danish lines of fortification.

Churches.—The Igreja da Sé (Cathedral) is uninteresting, but possesses some curious vestments. Misericordia ; S. Francisco with Seminario, and others, call for no remark.

Without any question Angra is the most picturesque and interesting town in the Azores. The impregnable nature of its fortifications long rendered it the chief and safest rendezvous for the ships of Portugal or Spain. Though it now lies at the mercy of any passing gunboat, the afterglow of old-world military romance hovering about it is apparent to the dullest eye. Its bright and orderly streets and decorated house fronts, shaded by their over-hanging eaves of brightest vermilion, glaring blue and emerald green ; the fortified slopes by which it is surrounded ; the winding ways wandering above the sea front and leading insensibly to the gates and pitted moat of the old castle, still smack of times gone by. Down the main thoroughfares the spurred commanders of the Spanish galleons clanked noisily. In the side streets the motley crews of the crowded vessels in the harbour lounged and loved, swore and fought, or, leaning over the low walls, apparently built on the cliffs for their special convenience, discussed the merits of the high-pooped craft below.

Drives.—The best short drive and the prettiest is along the Rua de Baixo to S. Carlos, thence round the back of the town at an altitude of about 500 feet. (Fare about 1$200 reis.)

Those wishing to take a long drive of about five or six hours should leave the town on the N.E. and cross the Paul, a long, flat, green moor, to Praia, about $12\frac{1}{2}$ miles (20 kilos.) The air is invigorating and the scenery, before descending into Praia, is good. The drive along the coast homewards from Praia is wearisome. (Fare 3$000.)

It is possible to drive round the island in about ten hours, but much of the scenery is uninteresting.

GRACIOSA, 8½ miles (13½ kils.) long by 5 miles (8 kils.) broad, contains 8,440 inhabitants. It is 45 miles from Terceira and 35 miles from São Jorge.

Santa Cruz, the chief port, 39° 6′ N. by 28° W., is a pretty little town to the N. of the island facing the open sea. Praia, where the Madeira boats touch, faces east. The Lisbon service calls fortnightly, staying about three hours.

The chief sight in the island, and one of the most interesting in the Azores, is the Furna do Enxofre, an enormous volcanic cave, situated inside the Caldeira about 1½ hrs. from Praia.

SAO JORGE, 36 miles (57½ kils.) long by 4½ miles (7 kils.) broad, population, 17,065, is 35 miles from Graciosa, 11 from Caes do Pico, and 24 from Horta (Fayal). Steamers fortnightly. Stay about three hours.

Villa das Vellas, 38° 41′ N. by 28° 14′ W., is the chief port to a somewhat uninteresting island, population, 8,944. Passengers going on shore can visit the craters (fumaroles) passed by the steamer immediately to the westward of the town, of which the sections are so beautifully exposed on the seaward side.

PICO, 30 miles (48 kils.) long by 10 miles (16 kils.) broad, contains 25,411 inhabitants.

Caes do Pico, where the Lisbon steamers call once a month (stay about three hours), is 11 miles from S. Jorge and 15 miles from Horta (Fayal), and lies in lat. 38° 32′ N. by long. 28° 22′ W. It is connected by a carriage road with Magdalena.

There are several small coast towns where passengers or goods can be landed in fine weather, but much of the trade of the island is carried on by way of Fayal, which is separated from Pico by a channel scarcely four miles (six kils.) in width. A considerable amount of wine is produced in the island, of which the climate is considered particularly good. On the N. it is well wooded, but on the S. a great part of the surface is covered by streams of lava.

Those visiting Pico for the sake of climbing the mountain generally cross from Fayal, landing at Area Larga or Magdalena. The ascent is usually made from the S.W., the night being spent at Serra, about half-way. For a short distance beyond Serra donkeys can be used, after which a stiff climb on foot, especially up the little Peak at the top, which is very steep, leads to the summit, 7,460 feet, 2,274 metres. As is the case at Teneriffe, hot air still issues from the crevices in the little crater. The view is very fine. The sea, washing the very base of the cone on two of its sides, seems to lie almost vertically beneath one's feet. A tent must be taken, which can be borrowed of the Obras Publicas at Fayal. Cost of expedition for one or two persons, including boat, donkeys, guides, etc., about 5$000 to 6$000 reis.

FAYAL, 14 miles (22½ kils.) long by 9½ miles (15 kils.) broad, population, 23,630, lies 4 miles west of Pico, and is visited by the Lisbon boats twice a month, which usually remain all day. It forms the terminus for the boat touching at Madeira. The climate is damper than that of Pico.

Horta, the chief town and port, 38° 33' N. by 28° 38' W., is a pleasant little town, with a disproportionate number of enormous churches and ecclesiastical buildings, many now disused and none of any special interest to the visitor. The Hospital, with church attached, was formerly a monastery. Pauper patients are treated free; sick sailors at a moderate charge.

Fayal is now a great telegraph station, with cables running to New York, Halifax, Hamburg, Lisbon, and (indirectly) S. Miguel (Azores).

Hotel.—Fayal, 1$500 a day, accommodates a limited number.

Clubs.—Amor da Patria; Sociedade Luz e Caridade.

Landing Charges: About 200 reis, according to distance, etc.

Nature was kind in giving to Fayal one of the best sites for a harbour in the whole Atlantic. The shore at Horta is exposed to the ocean on the S. E. only, and to make it a complete harbour of refuge, a breakwater has been erected 800 yards in length, which has created a perfect haven of refuge. On a fine day, the view from the slopes above the town, with the placid channel of Fayal in front; the imposing mass of the Pico in the near distance, and the neighbouring coast lines of S. Jorge and Graciosa on the horizon, is pleasing in the extreme. Should the isthmus of Panama ever be pierced by an effective water way, the future of this land-locked sea, beautiful as an Italian lake, and the sunny slopes by which it is surrounded, cannot fail to be brilliant, if it be only as a station for coaling and provisioning ships. Whaling was formerly an important industry. Though temporarily checked by the export duties imposed, it is still carried on, and the harbour is generally full of the graceful little boats from which the quarry is harpooned.

Boats can be hired for a row round the Monte da Guia, 488 feet, as the crater is called which protects the harbour from the west. At ½-hour the Furna is a fine example of a cave hollowed out by the action of water. A little further on, the boat can be rowed into the heart of the crater itself (Caldeira do Inferno), and by continuing the journey, the passengers can be landed at Porto Pim, close to the town (one hour), or they can return with the boat to the harbour.

The best drive (two hours, 1,500 reis), is up the Lomba on the way to the Caldeira, which forms the centre of the island. There are fine views of the Valley of the Flamengos, originally peopled by Flemish emigrants, of the Valley of Praia and of the city of Horta. The hydrangea (*hortesa*) hedges lining the road are particularly fine. From the end of the road donkeys can be ridden to the Caldeira, about four hours total, from the walls of which (3,350 feet, 1,021 metres) views of the whole island can be obtained. To walk round the Caldeira, which has a diameter of nearly a mile, takes about two hours; to descend to the bottom, 1,300 feet, and return, a steep climb of about two hours.

Another drive is to Ribeirinha, about 2½ hours return, fare about 2$000 reis.

FLORES, 12 miles (19 kils.) long by 9 miles (14½ kils.) broad, is the most westerly of the Azores, and lies only 1,680 miles from Newfoundland. It is visited by the Lisbon boat once a month. Population, 8,838. The chief town is **Santa Cruz,** which lies in lat. 38° 38′ N., by long. 31° 8′ W. The highest point is 3,087 feet, 941 metres. There is but little to attract visitors.

CORVO, 12 miles to the N. of Flores, population, 806, is little more than a rock whose centre is a great crater. It is 4½ miles (7½ kils.) long by 3 miles (5 kils.) broad, and is visited by the Lisbon boat once in three months.

Those intending to visit the Azores will do well to provide themselves with Admiralty Charts before leaving home. The following are issued:—

Azores (whole archipelago on a small scale), 1/6; Corvo and Flores, 1/6; Terceira and Graciosa, 1/6; Fayal, Pico and S. Jorge, 1/6; St. Michael's, 1/6; Santa Maria, 1/6; Fayal Channel, 1/6.

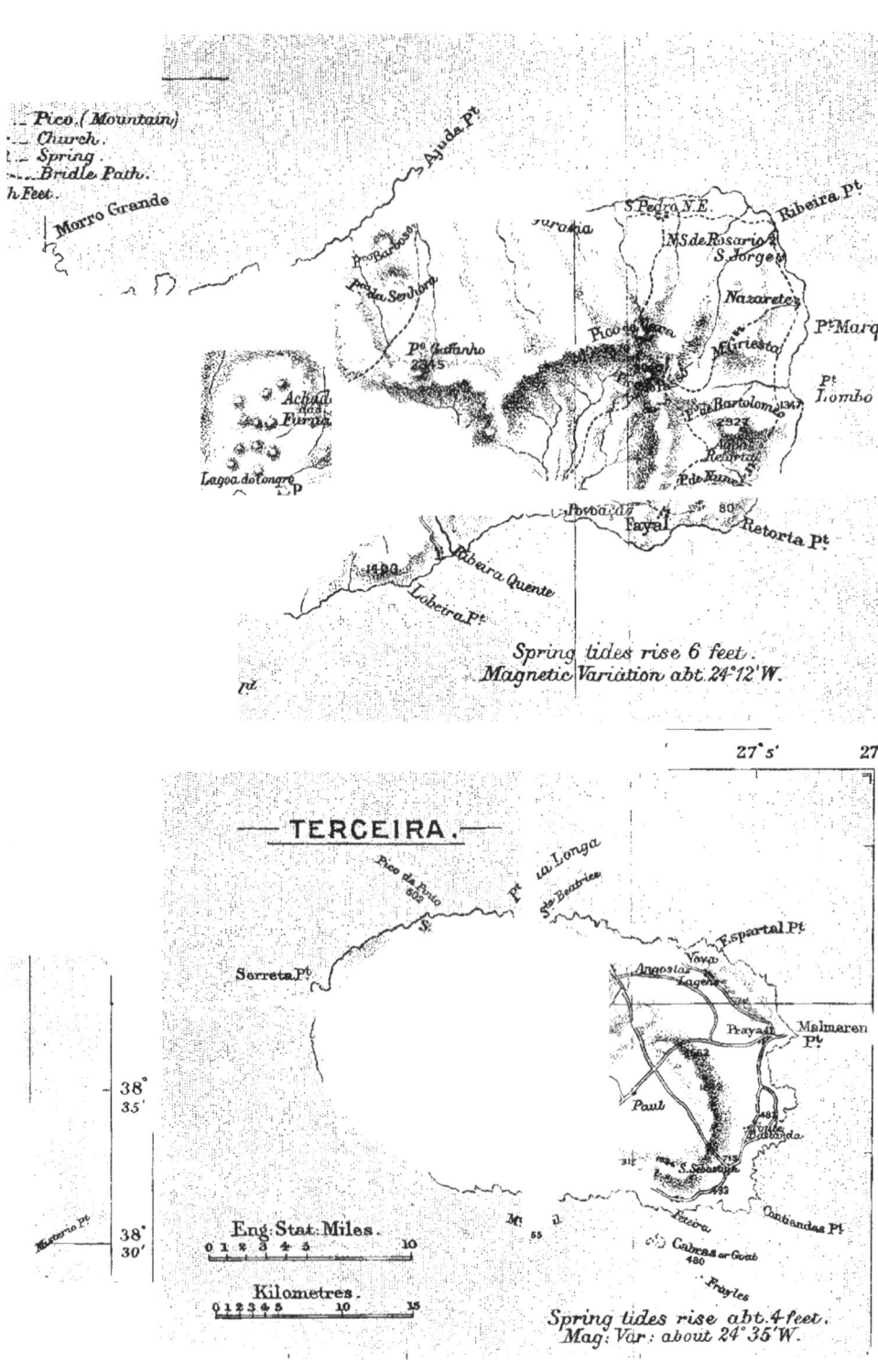

LA PALMA.

The island was formerly known as *Junonia Mayor* or, according to Ben Farroukh, as *Aproposito*. The inhabitants at the time of the conquest called themselves *Haouarythes*. It contains 41,997 inhabitants in one city, one town, and sixty-nine villages or hamlets; is divided into thirteen districts; is 29 miles (46½ kil.) long, 17¼ miles (27½ kil.) broad, 318 square miles (814 square kil.) in superficial area; is situated to the N.W. of Teneriffe and Gomera and to the N. of Hierro; is the furthest west of all the Canary Group with the exception of Hierro, and lies between lat. 28° 26′ to 28° 51′ N., and long. 17° 43′ to 18° W. of Greenwich.

Commercially the third in importance of the Canary Archipelago, this island is by many considered the first in point of beauty. Probably the western slopes facing the Atlantic would, if provided with proper accommodation at different levels, be ultimately selected as the most advantageous to the general run of invalids, both as a summer and winter resort. The atmosphere is certainly no damper than that of the N. of Teneriffe, and, whilst the wind lacks the dryness of that in Grand Canary, it seems more beneficial in cases of irritation of the throat. The high wooded mountains do not attract the clouds nearly so much as those of Madeira, and the air is pleasantly soft without being relaxing. If a hotel could be built high up among the pines, the wonderful scent of the native tree could not fail to exercise a very healing influence in cases of lung disease, for which this particular cure is adapted.

The general aspect of the island would lead those who had not thoroughly explored it to expect it to be watered by a number of small streams. This is unfortunately prevented by its size and formation and by the proximity of the watershed to the sea. The shape can be almost exactly imitated by cutting a pear in half lengthwise and laying it, flat side downwards, on a table. The round end of the pear should be laid to the north, the stalk to the south. A large hole must be scooped out where the core would be to represent the Crater or Gran Caldera, and a deep trench should be cut from this to the sea on the west. Now tear out the stalk and the small hole left is the Crater of Fuencaliente.

The bottom of the Gran Caldera is less than 1,000 feet above the sea. The highest part of the surrounding walls is the Roque de los Muchachos, 7,768 feet, which overlooks the Crater from the north. The broadest part of the pear is only 17¼ miles, of which the Crater accounts for about 4½. This leaves only some 6½ miles on each side to serve as a catchment for the water, that is to say, a declivity with an average gradient of one in $3\frac{7}{8}$, from which the rain naturally soon runs off. In addition to this the deep ravines furrowing and draining the slopes and the porous nature of a volcanic soil must be taken into account. As a matter of fact, by far the greater part of the island relies upon rain water for drinking purposes, a matter which must be remembered by those thinking of camping out. The best place for this is the interior of the Crater, whence some good springs are carried by stone water-courses (atarjéas) to Los Llanos, Argual, etc. The surplus water, when there is any, runs away down the bed of the Barranco de las Angustias. There are also springs outside the Crater on the E. and N.E. slopes, which supply Santa Cruz, Los Sauces and San Andres, and there are a few dripping rocks here and there.

In spite of all hindrances, the great extent of forest does collect a fair quantity of moisture which is always to be found in sandy places by kicking up the surface. A great deal of this filters through into the sea at short distances from the coast line.

There are also mineral springs, of which the most notable is El Charco Verde below Las Manchas. A famous mineral spring in the S., at Fuencaliente, disappeared, in 1646, in consequence of a volcanic eruption. Another, called the Fuente Santa, vanished, in 1677, from a similar cause.

The highest mountains are those grouped round the Gran Caldera. The upper part of the inside of the circle is principally composed of precipices of from two to three thousand feet in height. The outside is simply a slope of which the upper half is by far the steepest part. This slope has been worn into a succession of water-courses, which make the coast roads most laborious and of which the depth often exceeds 1,000 feet. The sides, as a rule, are thickly clothed with heather, laurels or pines.

The Cordillera connecting the Caldera with the S.-of the island is steep and narrow, and runs down to the sea at a great angle. The western side is covered with rough lava for many miles. In fact in the whole Canarian group there is no island where volcanic fury has been more extravagant or where its effects are more apparent than in La Palma.

The chief object of interest is the Gran Caldera, a cauldron so vast and of such colossal proportions, that it is often able to enjoy a weather of its own, without reference to what is taking place in the island of which it forms a part. The Haouarythes used to say that the Peak of Teneriffe, which they saw standing white and fair on the unknown horizon, was thrown from the Caldera during some unusually energetic outburst.

It is over four miles across, between 6,500 and 7,000 feet deep, and circular in shape, except where broken by a great outlet towards Argual. It was the last part of the island to submit to the Spaniards and was vigorously defended by its Prince Tanaúsu. The sacred rock Idafe was situated near the centre.

After the Caldera, which is believed by some to be the remains of two or more craters whose individuality has been lost by denudation, the Time (a black precipice facing Argual), and the wide stretch of lava commencing to the S. of Las Manchas and terminating near the crater of Fuencaliente, are the most startling examples of plutonic force. No disturbances, however, have taken place since 1677. In 1585, the lava ran down into the sea and killed all the fish for three miles around the coast, the noise being so great that the people in Teneriffe are said to have been frightened by it.

There is a good carriage road ascending from Santa Cruz at a very low gradient and leading *viâ* Mazo to Fuencaliente, whence it turns up the Western Coast and is rapidly approaching Los Llanos.

The people have retained the old Canary costumes once worn in some of the other islands. The Breña Baja dress and cap (*gorra*) are now quite unique. In Garafía the *gorro* is replaced by the *mantera*, a sort of sou'wester made of cloth woven in the district from the wool of the native black sheep. The cap is turned up in front like that of Breña Baja, but fits closely to the head. The flap hanging down behind is lined with red flannel, and, when not required to protect the shoulders, is brought forward by means of buttoning the two corners over the peak in front. A better headgear was never invented. The cap worn by the women has no flap and is most unbecoming. The apron is even more *de rigueur* on gala days in Garafía than it is in Breña Baja. It will be noted with interest that the people living in the north are of an entirely different stamp from those of the south, and are evidently descended from other ancestors. The little round hats made from the pith of the palm tree, so common among the latter, are never seen to the North of the Gran Caldera.

On the whole the island is prosperous and the population industrious. There are a number of large shops in the capital, which seem to do a good trade, though what those living in the north of the island import beyond soap and red flannel for lining their caps, it is difficult to say. It is the last of the Canaries to cultivate silk, which, as well as flax, is spun and woven into cloth. Tinned fruits and almonds are exported.

A constant intercourse is kept up with Cuba, to which a number of the inhabitants emigrate. Many of the schooners run as far as New York. La Palma has thus become a depôt for most of the mineral oil consumed in the Canaries. In many particulars the island rather resembles Madeira than the remainder of the group to which it belongs, and in nothing more than in the dexterity of the people, who manufacture a number of pretty little articles, which can be bought as mementoes, such as brushes, baskets, miniature barrels and furniture, the above-mentioned hats, knives, lace-work, embroidery, etc.

Those who merely land at Santa Cruz should go to the Barranco del Rio on mules or on foot. This is a most beautiful excursion occupying from one-and-a-half to three hours. Description further on. Those who do not care to ride or walk should drive to El Mazo and back, visiting Buena Vista, the summit of the Crater (la Caldereta) overlooking Santa Cruz. From the chapel, a few minutes to the left of the road, is a very fine view.

Those stopping in the island for three days, the time occupied by the inter-insular boats in visiting Gomera and Hierro, will naturally wish to see the Gran Caldera. This can be done by visiting the Pico del Cedro or the Roque de los Muchachos, and a return be made the same day. The crater is thus seen from above. Those who wish to see it from the Cumbrecita should go to El Paso and sleep, visit the crater in the early morning, and, if strong enough, return the same day. If the crater is to be entered, it is best to go to Los Llanos, spend the whole of the next day in the crater, and return on the next. The aspect of the crater when viewed from the interior is infinitely more picturesque than when seen from above.

As it is strongly urged that those visiting La Palma should stay ten and not three days, many will be able to make the above and several more excursions. There is a beautiful drive through El Mazo to Fuencaliente, where the small crater should be visited, and whence the journey can be continued in the direction of Los Llanos. El Mazo can also be reached on foot by way of the beach and along the paths below the *carretera*, or by crossing the Cumbre Vieja from Los Llanos and dropping down into the Mazo road.

Other excursions are from Santa Cruz to Garafia over the Roque de Los Muchachos and back through Los Llanos or round the N. of the island. The last route is of no great interest, and the constant succession of ravines is most tiring. Travelling is more toilsome than in any other part of the Canaries. It is only in El Paso and Los Llanos that accommodation can be relied upon. Elsewhere a tent should be taken, or not more than two should travel together. All the excursions given above are properly detailed later on.

Santa Cruz de La Palma, 7,037 inhabitants. East side of island. 103 miles (165 kilometres) from Santa Cruz de Tenerife
Passengers landed in boats at the mole, which is being improved. Charges: One peseta each person; half a peseta each package.

Hotels.—Hotel Aridane, 5 pes. to 5s. a day; Fonda Marina; Fonda Verbena, both about four or five pes. a day. There is a Spanish Club (Casino).

Public Buildings.—The **Town Hall**, a fine building faced with arches, finished in 1563. When the French corsair Sombreuil (Jambe de Bois) attacked the town with 700 men in 1553, the Town Hall and Archives were burnt before the invaders could be driven away.—The **Circo de Marta** is a circular building in the centre of the town used for cock-fights.

Churches: **San Salvador**, facing the town hall, with a good tower and doorway. In the interior there is a handsome ceiling, a richly gilded pulpit, some fairly carved woodwork, and a praiseworthy picture above the high altar. **Santo Domingo**, with a picturesque tower and an old convent. **San Francisco**, with a convent now used as a barracks. **San Francisco Jabier.—Iglesia de la Luz.—San Sebastian.—Santa Catalina.—De la Encarnacion**, with good view towards the hills. **La Virgen de las Nieves** (¾ hour) above the town; interesting.

There is also a small but very well arranged **Museum** a short distance above San Salvador Church. It is most carefully arranged and will be found of great interest, especially to those who desire information on the geology of the island.

Santa Cruz is a cheerful and most artistically built little town, situated in a valley facing the sea and immediately to the north of a large extinct crater, of which the crest, known as Buena Vista, dominates and protects the town from the south. The position much resembles that of Funchal, Madeira, but egress from the town is much easier. The country around is very fertile and large quantities of water are obtained by means of covered-in aqueducts and iron pipes. Part of the principal street is called O'Daly, many Irish seeming to have emigrated here as well as to Teneriffe. There is generally a pleasant breeze from the N.E. There is one public garden, or Alameda, which is little used. Owing to the beautiful vegetation and barrancos in the neighbourhood there are numerous walks and excursions. The town was the first in the Canaries to be provided with the electric light.

The peasants in speaking of Santa Cruz always call it **la Ciudad**.

Walks.—Towards the Alameda, a turning to the left, called los Molinos, leads into the **Barranco de la Madera**. Follow the left-hand side of the same until crossed by a wooden aqueduct, when cross and bear to the right. The bridle road is met with just below a church, which is close above and slightly to the left ($\frac{3}{4}$ hour, 630 feet). The church (sixteenth century) is prettily situated, and the interior worth visiting; good gallery. The **Virgen de las Nieves** (to whom it is dedicated) is represented by an ancient and much venerated image, which is carried in procession down to the town every fifth April, beginning at the decade, when Spaniards congregate from all parts of the world. A ship made of stone, to be seen at the bottom of the barranco, is then rigged, general rejoicings taking place for two months, when the image goes back. A return can be made along the paved road, bearing a little to the left, past the Iglesia de la Encarnacion, or by a short cut from the same road down into the barranco to the back of the town, past the hospital. Either way about fifty minutes.

From above the church (Virgen de las Nieves) a path through a garden climbs the slope at the back and leads in half-an-hour to the entrance of the **Barranco del Rio**. Here the aqueduct can be followed up the gorge as far as desired through most beautiful rocks and precipices, clothed with innumerable plants and ferns, this being one of the most lovely places in the islands. Only persons with strong nerves must go, as the path is at times dangerous. The **Barranco del Rio** can also be explored by bearing up to the left by the wooden aqueduct and following the bed of the ravine. This is the way taken by mules and all danger is avoided, but the views looking down from the aqueduct are lost. If the Church is included on the way up it is necessary to return again to the bottom of the barranco.

Those descending the **Bco. del Rio** by the aqueduct need not return to the church on their way home, but may follow the continuation of the aqueduct round the mouth of the next barranco on the N. side. They can then pass through the *finca de* **Miraflores** and return past the Iglesia de la Encarnacion.

A path leads to the south, one hundred yards above the Iglesia de las Nieves, across several barrancos to the carriage road above **Buena Vista** (one hour), whence a return can be made by the old road to Santa Cruz in forty minutes, or by the carretera in one hour, or the walk may be prolonged to **San Pedro** ($1\frac{1}{2}$ hours from las Nieves) and a descent made by a rough bridle path down the **Bco. de Agua Censia**, on the S. side of the Caldereta to the sea ($2\frac{1}{4}$ hours from Nieves), whence home *via* the **Playa** (beach) and round the bottom of the Caldereta, impassable at high tide, to Santa Cruz ($3\frac{1}{4}$ hours or four hours altogether). At Buena Vista there is a venta where wine and biscuits can be had.

Another walk is to leave Santa Cruz by the *carretera* or by the old paved road to Buena Vista, one hour. A turning to the left leads from the *carretera* to the Iglesia de la Concepcion, 970 feet, in about three or four minutes. The view from the church, which is visible from below, is extremely fine. The *carretera* can then be followed to San Pedro half-an-hour further on, and a return be made round the Playa as before. Total time about 3¼ hours.

Towards the N. a road leads straight through the town along the shore to the Bco. del Carmen (twenty minutes) and so up the barranco past the little Church to Miraflores (1¾ hrs.) and back by some other way, in all 2¾ hours. There are *fêtes* here in July.

Immediately behind the town the pretty Bco. de los Dolores may be ascended to the Ermita de S. Vicente in three-quarters of an hour. By bearing to the right a return can then be made by N.S. de las Nieves or, by bearing to the left, by Buena Vista, etc.

A somewhat longer walk is to the Mña. de Tagóje, 3,150 feet, best reached by passing the Iglesia de la Encarnacion. The scenery becomes very beautiful towards the end of the walk, which takes at least three hours both ways. This route is recommended to be taken on the return from the Pico del Cedro on the R. de los Muchachos.

Excursions.

Round the N. of the Island to Los Llanos.—An interminable succession of deep barrancos may be avoided by taking a boat, the best scenery being after passing los Gallegos. A landing can be made at S. Andrés, Barlovento and, in calm weather, at the Bco. del Poleo below Los Franceses (bargains must be made) *or* the direct rough mountain track, possible for mules, past the Roque de los Muchachos (*see* elsewhere) entails a climb but is much shorter and easier. Round the coast, unless on foot, the Camino Real in all its detours must be followed. A guide in most parts is indispensable.

Bridle Road along the N. Coast.—Follow the beach to the Bco. del Carmen, twenty minutes, and ascend and descend to the Bco. Seco, one hour and twenty minutes (half-an-hour may be saved on foot by clambering under the cliff at low tide, very rough work). At two hours, the Cruz de Tenagua, 990 feet, venta. Soon the bed of the Bco. de Sta. Lucia, 2¼ hours, after which, at three hours, the entrance to the village of Punta Llana.

Here the bridle path bears to the left, passes through the village and ascends past the chapel of S. Bartolomé, below rocky wooded views to los Sauces in about seven hours. (If the laborious footpath is taken, wild bare country is traversed, **S. Andres**, 100 feet, six hours, fair church and altar is passed, and los Sauces reached in 6½ hours).

Los Sauces, 800 feet, is pleasantly situated and possesses a church and pretty plaza. Water is here obtained from springs in a barranco about two hours above the town, and the **Roque de los Muchachos** may be visited in about 4½ hours up. There is no regular inn, but accommodation is provided.

The next place reached is **Barlovento**, 1,700 feet, church, beds possible, 1½ hours (the lighthouse may be visited in about 1½ hrs.). Next **las Toscas de Barlovento**, 1,530 feet, 1¾ hours, thickly planted with dragon trees (no beds); then the bed of the Bco. Gallegos with a long descent of 1,200 feet is crossed, and at 3½ hours the venta of **los Gallegos**, 900 feet, beds possible. After this the scenery improves, especially by the footpath.

<small>Those following the bridle road must bear down to the right, the following being the *approximate* times:—**Los Franceses**, beds possible, 1½ hours; **Santo Domingo de Garafía**, beds, 6½ hours; **Punta Gorda**, beds, twelve hours; **Tijarafe (Candelaria)**, beds, 15½ hours. This road which is monotonously precipitous will probably be taken by very few.</small>

The shorter footpath from **los Gallegos** to **Tijarafe** is as follows:—Bearing to the left the gigantic and beautiful Bco. del Poleo is crossed. An ascent of 1,350 feet from the bed leads to the Cruz Preñada, 2,400 feet, 1½ hours, where the Camino Real, coming up from los Franceses, is rejoined and followed through enchanting woods of heather, laurels, pines, etc., past the Cruz del Castillo, 3,130 feet, 2¼ hours, until at 3¼ hours the footpath again branches off to the left. At 3½ hours, **Machin**, 3,850 feet, where rough shelter may be obtained and whence the Roque de los Muchachos may be reached in about two hours, or a descent made to Santo Domingo in about the same time. At 4¼ hours, the undergrowth ceases and water becomes scarcer than ever. At 5¼ hours, El Revolcadero, 3,650 feet, a few houses, whence a path to Santo Domingo. At 7 hours, los Redondos (water), 4,200 feet, where a path leads down to Punta Gorda in about three hours, or up to the Roque de los Muchachos in about the same time, many paths both down and up being in fact crossed on the way, only the principal of which mentioned. Passing through pines, at 7¾ hours, the top of the Lomo de la Castellana, 3,400 feet, whence a steep descent leads to **Tijarafe**, 2,000 feet, nine hours, the Camino Real being joined close to the village.

Candelaria de Tijarafe (beds) has a small church with a fair altarpiece, A.D., 1588. Following the Camino Real the **Bco. Agujerado**, with curious natural basaltic archways, is crossed, and the Ermíta del Buen Jesus passed (half-an-hour). At two hours, the edge of the precipice of the Time, 1,760 feet, a most remarkable volcanic eccentricity with an extensive view of the Caldera and the W. side of the island.

A long descent follows to the bed of the Bco. de las Angustias, 3¼ hours, 200 feet, the outlet from the Great Caldera. At the bottom there is a chapel containing the famous image of N.S. de las Angustias, said to be the first before which High Mass was held in La Palma. The opposite slope is now climbed, and at 3¾ hours Argual, 900 feet, followed at four hours by Los Llanos, 1,000 feet.

Over the N. of the island to Tijarafe, etc., passing the summit of the Caldera at the Roque de los Muchachos.—A steep bridle road, where guides are necessary, leads up past Miraflores, 850 feet, ¾ hour, to the top of the Asomada Alta, 2,540 feet, 1¾ hours; el Llanito de la Barrera, ordinary resting place, 3,850 ft., 2½ hours; the Fuente Nueva, water generally, 2¾ hours; the Llanos de Olen, 5,350 feet, 3½ hours; and the Roque de los Muchachos, 7,768 feet, in about seven hours. The path leads a little inside of the Roque and descends to Tijarafe, Garafía, etc., in about another four or five hours. All points on the N. of the island are accessible from here. There is a grand bird's-eye view of the Caldera, which is, however, far less picturesque from above than from below.

To the Pico del Cedro and back in one day, with bird's-eye view of the Caldera.—Follow the path as given above as far as the Llanos de Olen, when bear to the left past the Pozos de la Nieve, 6,330 feet, some pits where snow is stored for summer use, and on to the Pico del Cedro, 7,470 feet, so called because of the stump of a dead cedar tree close to the summit, 4¾ hours from the city. The view is rather better than that from the Muchachos.

The survey height given is 7,680 feet. The writer, using a new aneroid, made it 7,280 feet, and Dr. Simony's careful measurements declare it 2,150 metres (7,465 ft.). A return, slightly farther, should be made by bearing a little to the N., past the Mña. de Tagóje, 3,150 feet, where the views are very fine. Mules can be of assistance on this journey, but a considerable part must be done on foot.

It must be understood that in islands so mountainous as the N. of Palma, it is nearly always easier to ascend to the hills, or even to the extreme summit, and then drop down on to the point aimed at, than it is to try and travel along or near the coast. On the Camino Real between Garafía and Barlovento, for instance, there are scarcely a hundred yards of level ground throughout the whole distance, and it is much easier to climb some 5,000 feet or more at once and have done with it, than to pile up an enormous total by 500 or 1,000 feet at a time.

Although the expedition to the N. of La Palma is not recommended, it is in some ways full of interest. The people are handsome and well made; the men lithe, active and tall, and there can be few places in the world where there is less dependence upon outside help for the ordinary necessaries of life. How so much physical excellence is maintained by a people who must intermarry so much and who are so very abstemious by force of circumstances is a matter worthy of study. Rye is one of the chief articles of food, and the peasants seem to contemplate the alternative of being reduced at times to living on the roots of the bracken, as though such a contingency were by no means infrequent.

To the Gran Caldera and back *via* El Paso, two days, or Los Llanos, three days.—Follow the *carretera* or the old road past Buena Vista and go up the lane at the back of the wine shop, 1,000 feet. Soon heather, laurel and the chestnut make their appearance, the Barranco de los Mimbres is crossed, in which a small wine shop, the last till El Paso, is passed on the left. The road winds through the most enchanting woods until the laurel gradually disappears and the giant heather alone is left. Soon the top, or Cumbre Nueva (4,750 feet), is reached (2$\frac{3}{4}$ hours). From here there is a most magnificent view embracing the whole country from the Montaña de Mirca to Mazo, with Santa Cruz sparkling at the foot of the plain, and Teneriffe and Gomera in the distance. To the S. is the Cumbre Vieja, from a mountain in which, the Volcan de Tacande, a stream of lava issued in 1585. The last flow of lava is upheld by another stream, overgrown with vegetation, which must have flowed down at some very remote epoch, from the same crater. Beyond the black stream is Las Manchas; on the horizon is Hierro, and due W. are the group of villages above Tazacorte. Beyond them is the mountain range of Time, a black and forbidding precipice bounding the Barranco de las Angustias on the N.W. Beyond this Tijarafe and Garafía lie, and, further to the right, a break in the mountains, called the Cumbrecita, discloses a view of the interior of the Gran Caldera.

On the W. slopes pines soon commence and increase in size until the Pino de la Virgen is reached—a giant measuring rather over twenty-five feet round. A little shrine is placed at its foot and numerous offerings are to be seen. A money-box for the support of the shrine is placed in the trunk. The splendid avenue passed through belongs to the Government. No trees may be felled until dead, which is, however, the time when the wood is worth most. The road now becomes level (2,900 feet), and the Barranco de las Cuevas de los Llanos is entered with some old native caves up a small barranco to the right ($3\frac{3}{4}$ hours).

From here a path leads up to the **Cumbrecita** (3,800 feet) whence there is a fine view of the Crater. Two hours there and back. Visitors unable to bear any great amount of exertion can see the Caldera most easily from this spot. The watercourse which passes near the Cumbrecita can be followed for some little distance.

There is water a little lower down, the first good drink to be had. Bearing to the left **El Paso**, $4\frac{3}{4}$ hours, 4,033 inhabitants, is reached.

Fonda Ingles, $\frac{1}{4}$ hr. below the village, 4s. to 6s. a day.

El Paso is a pleasantly situated little village where those who can only devote two days to seeing the Gran Caldera will do well to stop. The village is a good centre for the purchase of knives, pipes, native silks, miniature drinking barrels and various articles in mulberry wood.

For track from El Paso to Las Manchas and Fuencaliente reverse **Santa Cruz to Los Llanos** *vià* **Mazo and Fuencaliente.**

(A return from El Paso to Santa Cruz can be made over the arid summit of the **Cumbre Vieja** by a path which joins the Mazo *carretera* near the Bco. Aduares, $6\frac{3}{4}$ m. = $10\frac{1}{2}$ kil. from the city. This route is rather further but not so steep as the Cumbre Nueva. The pretty Bco. Aduares with its springs (about 1 hr. above the road) forms in itself a pleasant excursion from Santa Cruz. In coming from Los Llanos, Mazo might be used as a stage on the way to Fuencaliente.)

Below the straggling little town turn sharp to the right, and cross the barranco near a stone aqueduct. The straight road leads to **Tazacorte** ($1\frac{1}{2}$ hours). From here to Los Llanos the traveller passes through a succession of gardens and orange groves, almond, quince, and other fruit trees, the beauty of which must be seen to be appreciated.

At $5\frac{1}{2}$ hours, **Los Llanos**, 1,000 feet, 6,660 inhabitants, a pleasant little village where the night should be spent by those who intend to explore the interior of the Gran Caldera. There is a small inn with about five beds (charges, 3s. and 4s. a day).

By 1903-4 the *carretera* leading round the south of the island from Santa Cruz will probably be available as far as Los Llanos. On its completion it is proposed to make a *carretera* to Argual, 1 m. ($1\frac{1}{2}$ kils.), and Tazacorte, 3 m. (5 kils.).

Argual, 900 feet, is a small village twenty minutes further down. The Mña. Redonda, some ten minutes from the road, commands a good view, and is a good hunting ground for visitors who wish to carry home mementos in the shape of small volcanic bombs. There is no inn.

Tazacorte is another village half-an-hour below Argual. No inn. The harbour where the Spaniards, under D. Alonzo Fernandez de Lugo, landed in 1490, is half-an-hour away from Tazacorte and at the mouth of the Bco. de las

Angustias. A boat can be taken from here to the **Cueva de Candelaria**, a basalt cave in the cliff, both ends of which communicate with the sea. Time necessary about three hours.

The path to the Gran Caldera leaves Los Llanos a little below the Fonda and then passes the cemetery on the way to Tijarafe *viâ* the Time.

The zig-zag path on the opposite side of the Bco. de las Angustias (¾ hour) can be seen ascending the black and precipitous slope of the Time, 1,760 feet, two hours. For the road and times round the N. of the island, reverse the Excursions from Santa Cruz headed "**Round the N. of the island to Los Llanos, etc.**"

At 150 yards beyond the cemetery turn up the small Barranco de los Barros on the right, follow the bed for some distance and, emerging to the left, cross the plains, keep along the S. edge of the Bco. de las Angustias, and descend sharply to the stream in its bed (670 feet, one hour).

From here the bottom of the Caldera (950 feet) can be reached by climbing and wading up the stream, and active mountaineers can emerge by the Cumbrecita. Ropes and guides should be taken for this and all the neighbouring mountains.

The mule track crosses the stream, then ascends on the left. At last the Caldera is entered at a point below the caves of the former Kings of Taguriente, now inaccessible. At four hours a point called **Tenero** is reached (3,650 feet), with fine views of the crater, and here lunch may be had. Twenty minutes further is the little farm of Taguriente. The return occupies rather less time than the ascent.

The interior of the great crater is in every way most interesting. The dimensions have been roughly given as from four to five miles across and the depth as from 6,500 to 7,000 feet. Whether the basin is the site of a single cauldron or of more is difficult to determine with exactitude. There is, however, strong reason to suppose that the Barranco de las Angustias and the structure of the S.W. wall between that Barranco and the Cumbrecita, are at least partially due to a second series of eruptions, subsequent to those stupendous disturbances which gave birth to the remainder of the basin.

The outer walls are basaltic, but in the interior, throughout a vertical distance of 1,200 feet, there are deposits of hypersthenite, a rock that is far from common in the Canaries, and seldom seen in Madeira.

In the Museum at Santa Cruz are a number of geological specimens collected inside the crater, which include some of the older formations found in such districts as Scotland, in curious juxtaposition with recent plutonic rock. Amongst minerals copper ore and pure copper globules have been discovered.

The present depth of the crater is chiefly due to denudation. The lava flowing from the Caldera was probably diverted by the Time along the present course of the Bco. de las Angustias and was subsequently undermined and carried away by water. As the bed of the stream became deeper, the quantity of material taken from the crater would progressively augment and the precipitous walls would gradually increase in depth, as they have done since the days of the Haouarythes, whose caves, now inaccessible, may be seen some distance above the mounds of detritus piled against the bases of the cliffs.

When standing on the slopes of Tijarafe and gazing from the summit of the Time over the *vega* (plain) of Los Llanos, it seems hard to believe that the two districts were not once united, and that the Time itself is not a great fault cutting them asunder.

As might be expected the ravines in the bottom of the crater are often very deep. Many of these are covered with great pine woods, which shed their needles in a thick slippery carpet and render passage amongst the rocks difficult or even dangerous. Although, from above, the trees seem far apart and look no larger than pins, they offer many delightful and shady spots to those below, and are of great service to those bringing a tent and camping out. As a camping ground, in fact, the Caldera is particularly well suited. It has never been thoroughly investigated, and it is quite possible that payable copper ore might be found, though the Canaries generally do not offer a very promising field to the prospector. In pitching a tent it is as well to keep away from the bed of what may suddenly become a stream. Near the exit towards Tazacorte there is a mineral spring.

A return can be made from Los Llanos to la Ciudad *via* the Cumbre Vieja, *see* El Paso, or Fuencaliente can be reached *via* las Manchas by reversing the next route.

From Santa Cruz to Los Llanos *via* Mazo and Fuencaliente.

—The *carretera* to Mazo, 11¼ miles, 18 kilos, forms a delightful drive: On foot or on mule the distance at the start may be shortened by following the old road. Ascending the hill behind the town the back of the Caldereta (Buena Vista) is passed in about one hour. The district of the Breña is now entered and numerous tracks are crossed, those to the right leading up to the Cumbres, those to the left to the villages on the coast. Presently the church of S. Pedro, 5¾ miles (9 kil.), a little beyond and below which the village of S. José. At 6¾ miles, 10½ kil., the Bco. Aduares (mentioned under El Paso), after which several extinct volcanoes are passed, and Mazo is entered, 1,400 feet, beds possible. (Pop. 4,082.)

From here Los Llanos may be reached *via* the Cumbre Vieja in about 5½ hours from la Ciudad, *see* El Paso.

A return to town can also be made on foot or mule by leaving the *carretera* just beyond the windmill and keeping along the old lower road amidst a labyrinth of walls and gardens. The church of San José is passed in 1¼ hours, a sharp descent is made for a time, the road turns to the left past some dragon trees and reaches the beach just beyond the fort, two hours, whence home *via* the Playa, round the rock, etc., 2¾ hours. The Playa is only passable at low tide.

The *carretera* passes the Mña de los Rios (1 m., 1¾ kil. beyond Mazo). At about 20 kilos., a path to the right leads to the Fuente del Roque de Niquihomo, about fifty minutes above. At about 21 kilos., 1,900 feet, a path to the left leads to the famous cave of Belmaco, 1¼ hours below, residence of the former Kings of Tedote, in which are two stones engraved with what may be writing, supposed to be of great antiquity and as yet undeciphered.

As stated in the history a *facsimile* of the characters have been examined at Paris and have been declared to have had no meaning. The larger stone is 132 inches long by 99 broad and the smaller 58 long by 41 broad.

There are several more caves in the neighbourhood, some with deposits of goat guano.

The country continues to be green and agreeable, although there are no springs. At 15 miles, 23½ kilos., 2,100 feet, a path to the left leads down to Tigalate. There is a *venta* here. Shortly afterwards, at 2,300 feet, the lava or *mal pais* commences. Soon a beautiful pine forest with grassy glades and occasional vineyards. At about 30 kilos., the Pino de la Virgen with shrine, where a bridle path to the left leads down to Las Caletas. Keeping to the right the land becomes gradually more cultivated and vines increase. At 20½ miles, 33 kilos., the church of S. Antonio, beautifully situated as in a gentleman's park, 2,150 feet, is passed. On the left is los Canarios (beds), one of the four divisions (*pagos*) of Fuencaliente, the district in which the best wine of the island is said to be produced.

At a quarter of an hour below the church is the volcano of 1677 which buried the Fuente Santa, the position of which is still indicated by a piece of the old wall. The cindery sulphur-streaked cup of the volcano, which so far has scarcely given a foothold for vegetation, is very perfect and about 250 feet deep. The scenery in the neighbourhood is somewhat plutonic, but the views from the summit, 1,900 feet, are extensive and reach to Mazo on the E. and Punta Gorda on the W. coasts. It is well worth visiting.

Leaving Fuencaliente the road ascends past the church and enters the forest. The highest point of the pass is 2,850 feet and the scenery good. Lava streams covered with pines are now continuous. The forest is left behind, and the road crosses a dreadful succession of naked grey lava streams, which ran apparently with great fury. At 26 miles, 42 kilos., is the junction whence a *carretera*, 3 miles, 5 kilos. long, is to be made to the Charco Verde, a medicinal spring (purgative) much visited by local invalids in the summer. The mineral water runs away below the rocks at low tide.

The water has been analysed by Dr. Adam, of Liverpool, who states that it closely resembles that of Carlsbad, and is of use in case of gout, rheumatism, diabetes, and liver and kidney complaints.

The main road is being made to Las Manchas, 31 miles, 50 kilos., the country now being better cultivated and more agreeable. The total distance to Los Llanos by the *carretera* will be about 55 kilos., which it is proposed to complete by about 1903-4. Between Las Manchas and Los Llanos a track to the right leads to El Paso. The west of the island from Fuencaliente to Los Llanos is only worth visiting for scientific purposes.

Approximate Prices of Carriages in Santa Cruz.

Carriages.—(5 persons) to la Concepcion, Buena Vista, 10 pesetas; Mña de la Breña, 12½ pes.; El Mazo, 15 pes.; Tigalate, 17½ pes.; Fuencaliente, 25 pes.; Las Manchas (when *carretera* finished), 30 pes.

Mules.—For short rides, 3 pes. 75 c.; per day, 5 to 6 pes.; to El Paso, 6 pes. 25 c.; to Los Llanos, 7½ pes.; los Sauces, 10 pes.; Fuencaliente, 10 pes.

Los Llanos into the Caldera and back, 5 to 7½ pesetas.

The above prices include the keep of man and beast, and are more than should be asked in country places outside Santa Cruz.

HIERRO.

This island is further to the W. than any of the Canaries. The imaginary meridian line conceived by Ptolemy about A.D. 150 would have intersected it at Punta Dehesa. Reckoning from Greenwich, it lies between long. 18° 10′ to 17° 53′ W. and lat. 27° 37′ to 27° 51′ N., *i.e.*,S. by W. of La Palma and S.W. of Gomera and Teneriffe.

Its ancient name was Ombrios, or, according to Ben Farroukh, Hero. The natives called themselves Ben-Bachir, corrupted to Bimbachos by the Spaniards. It is $18\frac{1}{4}$ m. ($29\frac{1}{4}$ kils.) long by 13 m. ($20\frac{3}{4}$ kils.) broad, and its superficial area is 122 sq. m. (312 sq. kils.). There are 6,519 inhabitants, contained in one town and eleven hamlets, the whole island constituting one district.

The coast is so steep and uninviting that, before the present service of inter-insular steamers, it was almost impossible for visitors to land, all the anchorages being mere open roadsteads. The cliffs rise so suddenly from the sea that there is no room for houses on the coast and consequently no seaport town to find the means of building a mole.

The interior is a sort of table land along which most of the paths are conducted. The mountains, of which the Alto del Malpaso (4,990 feet) is the highest, are only partially wooded, and there is far less sylvan scenery than is to be found in the other islands of the western group, although in some places, and more particularly in the neighbourhood of El Golfo, there are a fair number of trees.

There are practically no springs and the people depend for water on the rain, which is preserved in tanks. The air which passes, however, is sufficiently laden with moisture. Were the question properly studied and plantations made in judicious positions, it is probable that a good supply could be obtained.

On the arrival of the Spaniards there appears to have been a tree near Valverde called *El Garoe*, which, according to legend, distilled enough water from its leaves to supply all the people with what they required. Although the Bimbachos were friendly, they covered this tree with dried grass so that the Spaniards should know nothing about it, and, thinking the island barren and dry, should sail away and leave them in peace. However, a Bimbacho young lady fell in love with a caballero and revealed the secret. This led to a quarrel. The result was that a number of Bimbachos were carried away as slaves. On the departure of her lover the young woman was condemned to death, the only instance of capital punishment in Hierro of which there is any record.

If the above tale be true the tree could not have been very large. It has now disappeared, but, if the exact site could be ascertained and a few laurels or pines planted, it is not unlikely that the new trees would distil water in the same way that the other did. Indeed it has been stated, and with apparent truth, that it was nothing more than a laurel or group of laurels standing at the head of a ravine up which the moist sea-breeze generally blew.

Fr. Juan de Abreu Galindo gives a most circumstantial account of it, but his ignorance of natural laws led him to look upon the tree as being something quite special, or even as a miraculous favour granted to the people because of their form of worship, which, as remarked in the history, bore some external resemblance to that of the Roman Catholic Church.

The products of the island are the same as those to be seen in the others, but all parts are not cultivable and the land can only support a limited number. The chief export is figs, which are of delicious flavour, and which are planted, as in Fuerteventura, in the bottoms of the barrancos and in the crevices of sheltering rocks.

There is a very famous mineral spring at Sabinosa, which is said to be most useful in cases of skin and other malignant diseases. It resembles that of the Charco Verde in La Palma, in that it is close to the sea and that it rises and falls with the tide. This does not necessarily imply that the rise is due to the infiltration of sea water, as the barrier presented by high water outside would tend to prevent the escape of that yielded by the spring.

The customs of the inhabitants call for no special remark. Occasionally a parti-coloured cricket cap is worn, otherwise they dress as elsewhere. Before the discovery of America this island was regarded as the end of the world, and from Punta Dehesa, in the W., the longitude of most countries was reckoned. Louis XIII. of France even passed a law to this effect in 1634, and Cardinal Richelieu called a conference on the subject in the same year.

War being unknown in the island before the arrival of Europeans, the inhabitants were an easy prey to the freebooters and in a few years were nearly all killed or carried away.

They seem to have been a happy, careless folk, fond of dancing and ignorant of agriculture. Some method was probably adopted for keeping the population within limits so that the island might support those imprisoned in it. The cave of the pig mentioned in the history under " Forms of Prayer" was situated by the rocks now known as los Santillos de los Antiguos de Bentayga, which were supposed to be the seats of the male and female deities already mentioned. The people were altogether pastoral. They used to dry goats' flesh in the sun and make biltong, which they called *jocinte*, a custom and a name retained by the present race until quite recent years.

Valverde.—From the landing-place, which is a tiny cove protected by some masses of fallen rock, a steep pathway leads in two hours on foot, or one and a quarter on mule, to the little capital of Valverde (1,750 feet). A mole is to be built.

The *Cura* is usually kind enough to provide a meal, and some ten beds might be had in the village; one dollar a day. Feeding fair. Mules up 2½ pesetas, or a dollar both ways. Those on foot should follow the bridle track all the way, as the short cut to the left, which may be pointed out, is most laborious, saves very little in the distance, and does not lead across any pretty or interesting tract of country. The whole walk is in fact very dull, and Valverde itself is not worth a visit for its own sake.

There are no roads, but the bridle paths along the elevated plateau, which averages about 2,000 feet in height, are fair and present few difficulties. It is possible to see the best part of the island in from two to three days, but accommodation is not easy to obtain and a tent should be taken by those spending any length of time.

To the south a path leads upwards past Tinor and across a plain to San Andres (two hours), near which is a spring, the Fuente de Asofa. At 3,500 feet, heather commences, and shortly after thin pine woods. A precipice here overlooking Las Playas commands a fine sea view. At five hours the village of El Pinar (2,600 feet), with view of the Puerto de Naos, is reached. The descent to the Port takes about 1½ hours.

To the S.W. of the village of El Pinar and about two miles from the coast is a place called *los Letreros*, so named because of some characters engraved on the rocks, of which a copy was forwarded to Paris at the same time as the copy of the characters scratched on the stones found in the cave of Belmaco in La Palma. The marks, which are effaced by time, were declared to be merely idle scratches. They are near what was apparently at one time a *tagoror* or ancient place of assembly and are very difficult to find. The site is reached by passing the Pinos de Julan.

Proceeding westwards from El Pinar the path again ascends and leads through gradually thickening forests, past **Los Reyes**, to the summit of the **Alto del Malpaso** (4,990 feet), whence there is a fine view of El Golfo. Cinders and lava here take the place of the trees for a short time, but, descending the W. side to **El Golfo**, giant heather and laurel are found growing luxuriantly here and there, interspersed with patches of Monte Verde. At 9 hrs., **Sabinosa** is entered, or from the Alto del Malpaso a path leads *via* the Ermita de los Reyes to the **Puerto de los Reyes** on the extreme W. of the island in $3\frac{1}{2}$ hrs. A return may be made from here to Sabinosa in about 2 hrs. Twenty minutes below the village is the mineral spring previously mentioned.

The return road follows the lower part of El Golfo, a huge crescent facing N.W., partially wooded and fairly fertile. At 2 hrs., Los Llanillos is passed, and at 3 hrs. Tigadaye (750 feet). Belgara is left on the right, unless the pass up the cliff to Valverde *viâ* Tinor is taken ($4\frac{1}{2}$ hrs. from Tigadaye).

The path up the precipitous ascent leading to Tinor has been greatly improved. It passes through beautiful woodland scenery and commands very fine views. The vegetation found is of great interest to botanists.

The coast road passes Los Palos and Güimar, and ascends the cliffs on the N.W. corner of El Golfo by an extremely steep and rather narrow path. The Virgen de la Peña (2,200 feet), on the summit, is passed at $5\frac{1}{4}$ hrs. The path now leads along the plateau, past S. Pedro and Mocanal, and descends to Valverde in $7\frac{1}{2}$ hrs. through fair but not very interesting scenery.

A shorter excursion is from Valverde to Alto del Malpaso direct. About 6 hrs. must be allowed for this each way.

GOMERA.

Gomera lies between lat. 28° 1' to 28° 13' N. and long. 17° 5' to 17° 22' W. of Greenwich; is S.E. of La Palma, N.E. of Hierro and W.S.W. of Teneriffe, from which it is divided by less than 20 miles of sea.

It was formerly known as Junonia Menor and its inhabitants called themselves Ghomerythes.

It is 15¾ m. (25¼ kils.) long by 13 m. (20¾ kils.) broad, and covers 172 sq. m. (440 sq. kils.). The population is 15,025 spread over one town and 36 villages or hamlets, divided into six districts.

The shape of the island is almost circular and the coast generally is extremely precipitous, especially towards the west. Villages are scattered here and there on the slopes, generally at a considerable height above the sea. The summit of the island undulates and the surface is mostly composed of a rich, fine earth. There is an abundance of verdure and every available space is cultivated. The highest point is 4,400 feet, and the country in the Cumbres is often thickly covered with splendid woods, the heather growing to a height almost unknown in the other islands.

Accommodation is poor, which is unfortunate, as the climate is good.

Water is plentiful, and the land is fertile, silk being cultivated, as well as cereals, cochineal and the ordinary crops seen in Grand Canary and Teneriffe. Dates ripen in the neighbourhood of San Sebastian, and palm trees are found up to 3,000 feet.

There are no carriage roads, communication being carried on by mules and horses and by means of bridle paths, which are very slippery in wet weather.

A custom of the former inhabitants still survives, namely, talking by means of whistling. Not only can a peasant make himself heard at a distance of three or four miles, but a sufficiently rich language has been developed to enable conversation to be carried on.

The town people can rarely do this, but in the country, and especially in the neighbourhood of the Montaña de Chipude, where the best whistlers are said to reside, all messages are sent in this way.

For instance, a landed proprietor from San Sebastian, with farms in the south, secretly took lessons. The next time he visited his tenants he heard his approach heralded from hill to hill, instructions being given to hide a cow here or a pig there and so on, in order that he should not claim his "*medias*" or share in the same.

The same gentleman, when entertaining a foreign tourist in another part of the island, whistled across to his *medianero* to get them a partridge, these birds being so plentiful as to be almost looked upon as vermin. Some little time after, the tourist objected that it was out of season, and that, in any case, only a cock should be shot. The next whistle found the *medianero* stealthily creeping towards his prey, but he understood what was said and picked out a male bird.

Other messages that can be vouched for are, " There is a Caballero here who wants to send a letter to San Sebastian. Tell Fulano to take this place on his way and fetch it." This was understood at once and acted on. Another message : " Come here at sunrise to-morrow and take the Caballero's bag, who is staying with me, down to the beach (*playa*)." The answer came to repeat, which was done, when the usual reply of " Aye, Aye," was given. It appeared that the recipient was not sure the first time whether the last word was " playa " or " valle."

The best whistlers do not use the fingers at all, and convey their meaning apparently by intonations and variations of intensity on two or three notes. It is said that there is a tribe in the Atlas Mountains which talks in the same way.

San Sebastian.—3,187 inhabitants ; E. coast ; 42 m. (67 kil.) from Santa Cruz, La Palma, and 39 m. (62½ kil.) from Hierro.

A village situated at the mouth of a large green barranco. Passengers are landed in boats and carried on shore. Charges (nominally), one peseta each person ; packages extra ; inn, with nine beds, four pesetas a day. There is a quaint old church, with painting of the repulse of the Dutch fleet from the harbour in 1599. The few walks round the town are of no interest. Horses are difficult to procure, and bargains should be made.

When Columbus started on his voyage for the discovery of the Indies he took in water and provisions at San Sebastian and attended Mass in the church. An old house is still pointed out as having been occupied by him during his stay. He left Gomera on September 7, 1492.

The point to which excursions are generally directed is Valle-Hermoso. This can be reached in several ways, the most direct from San Sebastian taking about 10 hrs.

Leaving San Sebastian the barranco is crossed. Bear to the left up the ascent to Mona, 2 hrs. (water), then on to the *Ermita de las Nieves*, 3½ hrs. (water). After this there is less climbing. At 4¼ hrs. thick woods are entered, and the track leads round the S.W. base of Alto Garajonay (4,400 ft.).

In fine weather the forest scenery in the Cumbres is unsurpassed in the Canaries, and the Alto Garajonay, or the Montaña de Chipude, 3,947 ft., are well worth visiting. The latter is situated about an hour to the W. of the route to Valle-Hermoso. To thoroughly enjoy an excursion of this sort the visitor is advised to camp out during the fine weather towards the end of the summer and to take a gun. Partridges are more plentiful in Gomera than is the case elsewhere in the Archipelago.

The woods are now left behind for a time and at about 7 hrs. the **Laguna Grande** is passed. Keeping to the right, a descent is made through other beautiful woods below which a spring (**La Fuente Santa**) is situated, near a chestnut tree (2,200 ft.), then along a ridge, through the little village of **Puestelagua**, down the **Barranco del Ingenio** and into the village of **Valle-Hermoso** (500 ft.), 10 hrs. Accommodation may be had here (3s. a day), but is not to be relied on.

Below the village a road leads towards the sea, and from here, if a boat can be procured, the peculiar basaltic rocks, known as Los Organos (the organ pipes), may be visited in about 2 hours. An excursion can also be made to the summit of the Montaña de Chipude and back in 8 hrs. The peculiarly bold character given to the scenery by the alternate rock and soft earth so prevalent in the island, the one remaining harsh and erect where the other has gradually melted away, cannot fail to delight and surprise the tourist who sees them for the first time.

From Valle-Hermoso a return may be made, in even less time than is necessary for the route given above, by means of a path which is impracticable for horses. Guides must be taken.

A more pleasant way is *via* Hermigua. The old track ascends the Barranco de las Rosas, leaving the Roque del Valle, one of the upstanding rocks mentioned above, on the left, and ascends very steeply to a point called Buena Vista, subsequently passing **La Cruz Eterna**, a cross about 2,300 ft. above the sea, the road being good and well shaded. The **Roquillo Pass** is surmounted, and a deep descent made to **Agulo**, a well-cultivated district about 550 ft. above the sea, with a village and church.

An easier, better and rather shorter path of recent construction connects Valle-Hermoso with Agulo. The descent into Agulo, however, is still bad.

A little further on is **Hermigua** (5 hrs.). Accommodation may be had, but there is no inn.

From here a path ascends the mountains, which are crossed at an altitude of rather over 2,700 ft., and San Sebastian is reached in about 6½ hrs. The scenery is very good, though not quite so fine as that around the Valle-Hermoso.

Those able to choose their own landing place and not compelled to leave the ship at San Sebastian as a starting point, can go on shore at the following places :—For Hermigua and Agulo at Peñon or at San Lorenzo (in all weathers); for Agulo at Piedra de la Rosa (in good weather); for Valle-Hermoso at El Palito or at Guindaste; for Valle Gran Rey at Vuelta.

At Punta de San Cristobal a lighthouse, below which there is a landing stage, has been erected. It is proposed to make a small port at San Sebastian.

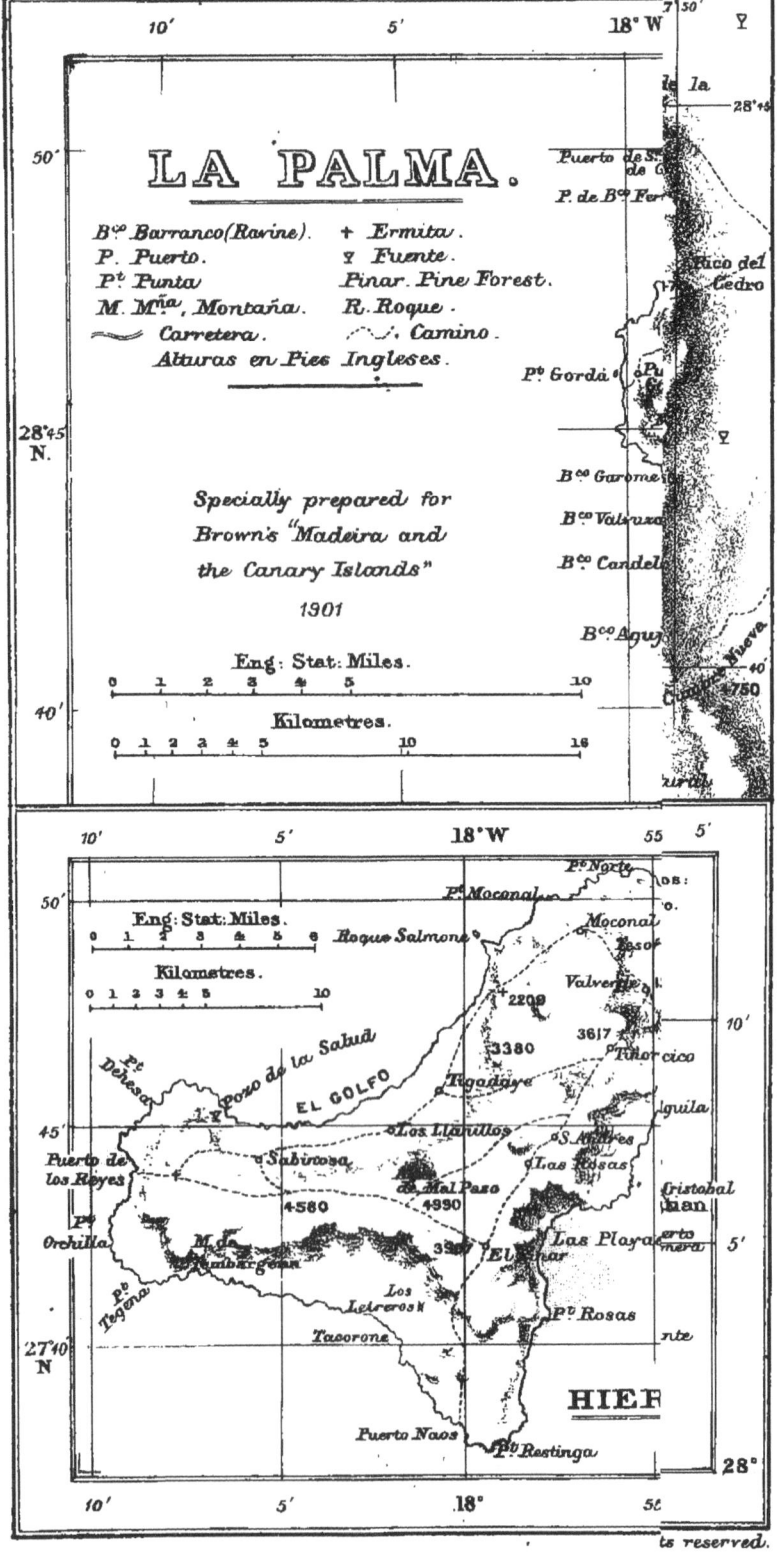

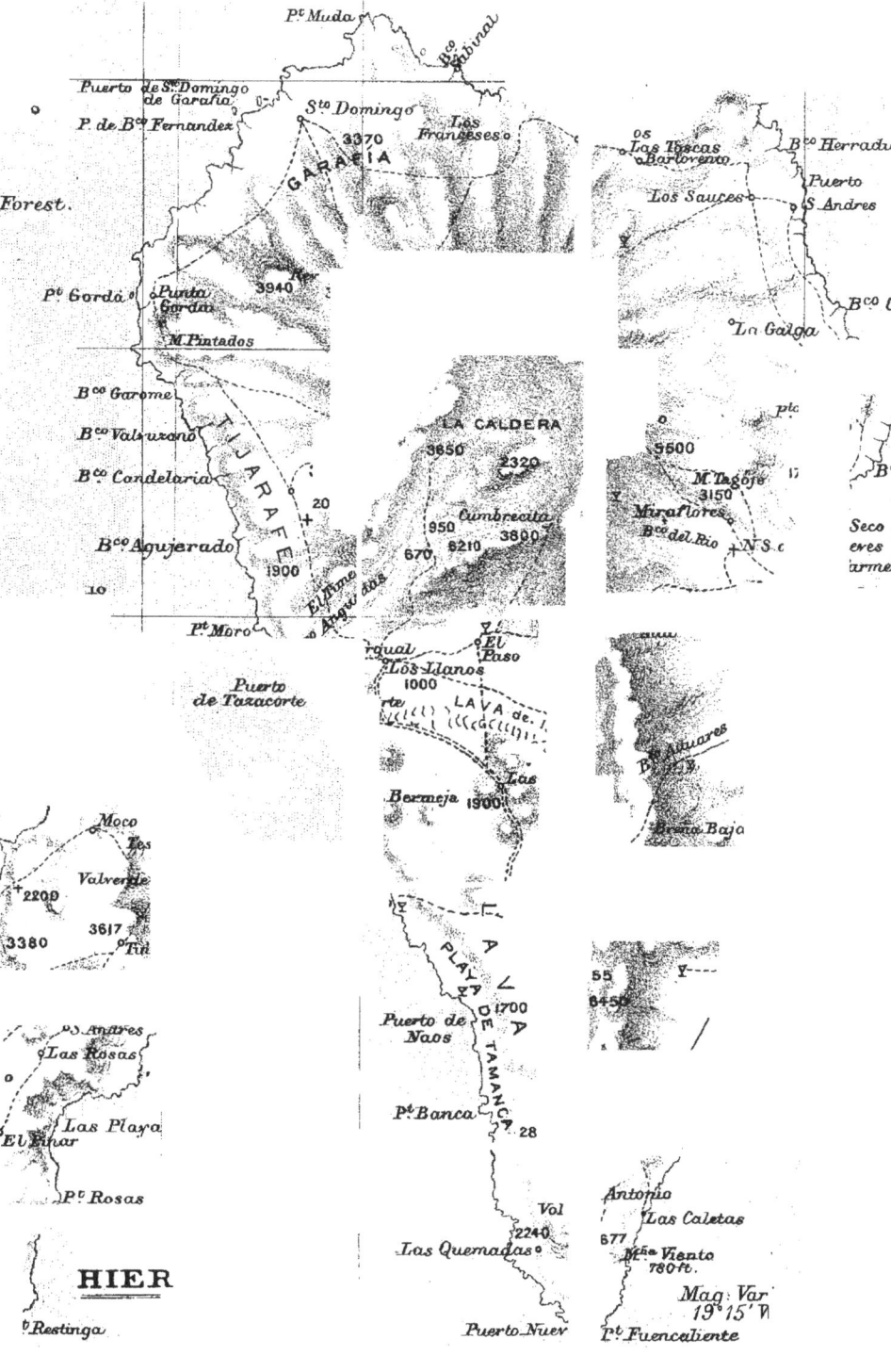

TENERIFFE.

This island is shaped like a shoulder of mutton, of which the broad end faces S.W., and the thin end points N.E. The Peak rises in the centre of the broadest part.
It lies between lat. 28° to 28° 37′ N., and long. 16° 7′ to 16° 56′ W. of Greenwich; is 52¼ m. (83½ kils.) long by 31¼ m. (50 kils.) broad; has an area of 919 sq. m. (2,352 sq. kils.), and contains 136,273 inhabitants, spread over 2 cities, 4 towns, and 152 villages or hamlets, divided into 33 districts.

Leaving the above inhabitants to discuss the question of commercial and political supremacy with those of Grand Canary, Teneriffe is, by virtue of its height, the meteorological centre of this part of the world. The term "Satellite," applied in a climatic sense, cannot be justly resented by the most enthusiastic advocate of Las Palmas *versus* Santa Cruz.

The celebrated Peak, whose majestic summit may well be said to support the sky, generally thrusts its snow-clad cone far above the clouds into the glittering sunlight, there to serve as a beacon and a guide to the wandering sailor. When the atmosphere is clear, its apex can be seen from an enormous distance, though, because of the clouds hanging round the island, it is often invisible to ships when close under the land. Humboldt calculated that it was mathematically visible from the M^ñas Negras on the African coast, and that it must have often been seen by the Mauritanians when in eruption. The writer has seen the last 3,000 feet of the cone, outlined against the setting sun, from the deck of the ship off Morro Jable Point in the S. of Fuerteventura, 125 sea miles (230 kils.) away, long after all but the highest points of Grand Canary had sunk below the horizon, and has no doubt that it would be visible under the same circumstances from the hills in Lanzarote.

It is still active, but the more recent volcanic disturbances have found a vent much below the sulphurous little crater, 12,192 ft. above the sea, whence puffs of steam occasionally float away as evidence of its fiery origin. The island was formerly called Tehinerfe, Nivaria and the "Isla del Infierno." The early Spanish settlers evidently imagined that there was some connection with the infernal regions. "E'cheyde" or "Teide," meaning Hell, was the name given by the Guanches to the Peak. Curiously enough, this people chose the mountain as the seat of the Deity. One must presume that "Achaman" (God Almighty) sat on the sunny crest, and prevented "Guayota" (the Devil) from leaving the bowels of the mountain, to which he had been condemned.

Some of the ancient maps adopted the Peak as a meridian. A conference was even summoned by Cardinal Richelieu with the view of inducing the various European nations to recognise it as such by common accord.

The indigenous inhabitants have been fully discussed in the history. It is only necessary to add that the nine kings who succeeded Tinerfe the Great reigned in the following districts:— Taoro, Güimar, las Lanzadas, Anaga, Abona, Tacoronte, Tegueste, Icod and Daute. Of these, the King of Taoro (Orotava) was the chief. There was also an illegitimate Prince who lived beyond Tejina, in the part still known as the Punta del Hidalgo. In Guanche, his title was "*Archimencey*," which is equal to "Hidalgo pobre" in Spanish, or "Poor Knight" in English.

Returning to our shoulder of mutton, it must be understood that the whole island is little more than a long mountain ridge, with steeply sloping sides. Commencing with the narrow end at Anaga point, where the ridge is sharpest, there is a depression, and a broad saddle-back, or rather plain, at La Laguna. This is followed by a narrow and constantly rising *cordillera*, running S.W., and breaking about Pedro Gil into two walls, which form the boundaries of the Cañadas, the name given to the undulating floor of a crater, eight miles broad, on which the Peak itself is built. The island then slopes away on the W. towards a large group of volcanoes, and a more or less wooded tract of mountainous country, terminating in the cliffs of Teno Pt. and the fertile little plain of Buena Vista. Towards the S. there are more mountains and volcanoes, the valleys and barrancos here being particularly precipitous and deep.

A great part of the island is able to obtain a never-failing source of water from the huge basin of the Cañadas and the melting snows of the Peak. Little of this is allowed to go to waste, being conducted to the land by means of open channels, often running along the tops of the walls. To the N.E. of La Laguna, and in the extreme W. near Teno, most of the land is uncultivated. The mountains in these districts are extraordinarily razor-backed. These tracts are composed of the earlier lavas. Fuller details are given in the Geological Section. It will be noticed that the candle-shaped Euphorbia (*E. Canariensis*) is most common and most prolific where the surface is composed of basic lava.

La Laguna itself is the most fertile spot in the island, because of the abundant moisture; but, were a better system of forestry, and a more comprehensive means of storing water, adopted, a great deal of land might be reclaimed which is now practically worthless. This applies particularly to the S. of the island; but, even on the N., there are most extensive tracts of country entirely dependent on rain.

In addition to a few isolated forests, there is a belt of pine trees stretching almost continuously from La Esperanza round the top of the slopes overlooking the S. of the island, past Guia and los Partidos on the W., to Agua García on the N. The belt is very thin in some places, and in others quite swept away, besides which, up till quite recently, the peasants have been allowed to take away the pine needles for manure. However, in addition to the pines, there are laurels and heather, which must collect a great deal of water; but the slope is so steep, and the barrancos so short, that nearly all of it runs into the sea at once.

All climates are to be found, and most plants can be cultivated, for which reason the Spanish Government has granted a small subsidy for the maintenance of a botanical garden near Orotava, originally intended as a sort of half-way house for the acclimatisation of tropical fruits, etc.

Agriculture has only recently recovered from the widespread ruin consequent upon the discovery of aniline dyes, the resultant collapse of cochineal, and the blow given to the wine trade by the disease which attacked the vineyards in 1852. The growth of the fruit trade, to which the present prosperity of the islands is due, is discussed in the Commercial Section.

The most picturesque buildings in the Canaries are to be found in Teneriffe and in Santa Cruz de la Palma. Wood was largely used in their construction, and the balconies, windows, patios (courtyards) and galleries are often most attractive.

The most peculiar dress is that of the peasants near La Laguna, whose leggings, coloured waistcoats, white knickerbockers and black woollen saddle protectors look effective and manly. The *manta*, an English blanket doubled and gathered into a leather collar, is the common overcoat of the peasant, as the *capa*, a circular piece of black cloth, faced with some bright colour, is of the well-to-do Spaniard.

Amongst knick-knacks to be purchased, the imitation flowers made of fishes' scales and drawn linen are the favourites. Very good cigars can be obtained at most moderate prices. Few people who have tried them return home without carrying back as many as they think they can smuggle through the customs.

The dragon-tree (*dracæna draco*) is a plant, native to the Canaries, of which the dead branches serve as a support for the tufts or crowns, the roots of which encircle and conceal the original stem, which gradually rots away inside. Those roots which fail to grasp the stem, or rather to attach themselves to the bark of the stem, may be seen hanging withered in the upper tree. Owing to this peculiar method of growth, the inside of the trunk is hollow. That of the old tree in the Villo was open, and made a very spacious chamber. Dragon's blood is an article of commerce, and was used as an ingredient by the Guanches for preserving their mummies, etc. (*See* History.)

It is supposed that dragon-trees, which are to be found in various parts of Africa, were once more common on that continent, and that those left represent a species of African flora, abundant about the time of the Ice Age, when the climate was much colder, but since gradually replaced by more tropical plants.

The famous dragon-tree of Villa Orotava, estimated by Humboldt, perhaps erroneously, as being at least 6,000 years old, was finally destroyed by fire in 1867. A cutting is still growing in one of the conservatories at Kew. Many dragon-trees are to be seen in the island, notably at Icod and at La Laguna.

The first recorded ascent of the Peak was made by some members of the Royal Society of London at the instigation of King Charles II. and the Duke of York, for the purpose of weighing the air, and taking other observations. The conduct of the Spanish Ambassador on the occasion became a European joke. He treated the deputation calling to ask his permission as a couple of madmen, then hastened to the King and related the matter with shouts of laughter.

There are several ports, but all the mail steamers touch at Santa Cruz. A few steamers touch at Orotava, but even the inter-insular boats do not run there regularly, the recognised means of approach being to disembark at Santa Cruz and cross the island.

A good road, commenced in 1852, leads from Santa Cruz past La Laguna, Orotava and San Juan de la Rambla to Garachico. This will eventually be completed to Buena Vista. A branch, commenced in 1864, leaves this road on the way to La Laguna, and runs through Güimar to Escobonal. It is proposed to carry this round the island, and connect it with the Orotava road, *viâ* Santiago and Palmar. A road also leaves Santa Cruz for San Andres, and is to go on to Taganana. There is a road from La Laguna to Tegueste and Tejina, where it connects with a road from Tejina to Tacoronte, and a small branch from the main *carretera* leads to Realejo Alto.

Much inconvenience can be avoided where there is no high road by using the boats engaged in the fruit trade if practicable.

There are so many excursions to be made in Teneriffe, that it is difficult to place any one as first in order of merit.

Those who have but a short time will do best by hiring a carriage in Santa Cruz, for two, three or four days. A carriage for two persons, with one horse, should cost about 15 pes. a day; two horses about 20 pes. A carriage for four, with three horses, should cost from 25 to 30 pes. a day. Carriages kept waiting usually charge about 10 pes. a day. General prices will be found further on. Only a little luggage can be taken.

The best short drives for those who can only afford three or four hours, whilst the steamers are coaling, are to La Laguna, $3\frac{1}{2}$ hrs. return, *or* to San Andres, $2\frac{1}{2}$ hrs. return. The La Laguna drive can be extended to Las Mercedes, 6 or 7 hrs. return. The return journey to La Laguna by electric tramway occupies about $1\frac{3}{4}$ hours. Details elsewhere.

A two days' drive is to Orotava and back the next day, or, if this has already been taken, to Güimar and back the next day.

A three days' drive is to Orotava and sleep; to Icod and back the next day, and back to Santa Cruz on the third.

A five days' drive can be made by returning to La Laguna to sleep, and on to Güimar the next day to sleep. It is possible to drive to Güimar and back in a day, either from Santa Cruz or La Laguna, but it is really too much for pleasure and for the horses.

The places which ought to be seen if possible *en route* are :—

From La Laguna: the forest of Las Mercedes as far as the Cruz de Taganana, a most lovely ride or walk.

From Tacoronte: the woods of Agua García, which are most beautiful.

From Orotava: the Peak (2 days), the Cañades (1 day), the woods and rocks near Agua Manza. The valley itself can be seen in a day's drive, whether the Villa, the Grand Hotel or the Puerto be taken as a centre. The carriage can be abandoned in Realejo Bajo, and the two Realejos visited on foot, or the new road taken to Realejo Alto, and the carriage rejoined below Realejo Bajo. The beautiful drive to San Juan de la Rambla can be extended to Icod if desired. The mule track to Icod *viâ* Icod-el-Alto is very beautiful. The footpath between the same places, which leaves Realejo Alto, climbs to the La Corona, and, keeping, on the 3,000 feet level, descends through the Pine Forests to Icod, is one of the most lovely excursions imaginable. It is best taken from Icod home. The pass over Pedro Gil, or by the Pilgrim's track to Güimar is magnificent.

From Icod de los Vinos: Garachico; La Culata; the Pine Forests; Valle Santiago; the Crater of Chahorra (desperately rough).

From Güimar: The Bco. Badajoz; the Bco. del Rio; the pass over Pedro Gil, etc., to Orotava.

The passes to Vilaflor, Adeje, etc., will all be found in their proper places, as will the detailed description of all the above excursions. The scenery below Vilaflor, between Güimar and Adeje, is not attractive.

Telegrams can be sent, booking accommodation to any station between Santa Cruz and Garachico. No wire has yet been laid along the south coast.

Santa Cruz de Santiago.—Capital of the Canaries since 1821, and a city by decree since 1859; 37,496 inhabitants; N.E. corner of Teneriffe; 256 m. (409 kil.) from Madeira, and 53 m. (85 kil.) from Las Palmas; formerly called Añaza by the Guanches (Ang., see *Ships*).

The city has been the chief military centre of the Province since A.D. 1700, and is also seat of the Diputacion Provincial.

Passengers are landed in boats on the unfinished mole, which is to be extensively lengthened. All ships are met by the hotel agents. Charges for boats (official) from vessels inside the port, each passenger, 1 peseta each way, unless more than three in boat, when 75 c.; children under 10, half price. By night, double. Boxes, etc., 1 peseta, 75 c., or half a peseta, according to size. If the vessel lies "within the roadstead," the charges are 1.50 pes. each up to three persons, and 1 pes. each when more than three. There are no customs duties on passengers' luggage, but cases are sometimes opened at the *fielato* on the mole. Since 1852, Santa Cruz has been declared a free port.

It is better to leave the carriage of luggage to the hotel in the hands of the representative. The official charges are far higher than those commonly accepted.

Hotels.—Camacho's, central position, established several years, 8s. to 12s. a day; Pino de Oro, above and behind town, good view and garden, about the same charges; Salamanca, similar position to Pino de Oro, large grounds, about 3 guineas a week; Olsen's English Hotel, open situation, facing the Plaza Weyler, top of town, from 6s. a day; Victoria Hotel, facing the Square (Plaza de la Constitucion, No. 7), 8 pes. a day upwards; El Tenerife, 86, top of the Calle del Castillo, 4s. a day upwards; Fonda Panasco—La Peninsular—El Teide—Antonio Abreu.

Newspapers.—*El Diario de Tenerife; Cronista de Tenerife; La Opinion.*

(*For advertisements, see under Santa Cruz, Teneriffe, at the end of the book.*)

Public Buildings.—**The Town Hall**, a part of the old Franciscan monastery. **The Gobierno Civil**, on the Plaza de la Constitucion. The *patio* is one of the best designed courtyards in the island. **The Captain-General's Palace,** facing the Plaza de Weyler at the top of the town, and commenced by the General after whom the plaza is named. **The Civil Hospital,** a large building on the south of the town, admirably managed, and open when free to foreigners. The charge for a private room and medical attendance is from 6s. a day, according to means. **The Military Hospital,** a little to the West of the Plaza de Weyler. **The Lunatic Asylum,** in the open country to the N.W. of the city. **The Custom House** (*Delegacion de Hacienda*), a little to the south of the mole. **Courts of Justice,** near the Custom House. The new building in the Barrio de Ensanche is approaching completion. When finished, the pictures and sculpture, now located in the hall used by the Diputacion Provincial, and the Library and Museum mentioned below, will be placed here. Near the new Palacio de Justicia are the **Public Elementary Schools** (both sexes). **Municipal Court,** in the old Franciscan monastery. **The Theatre** and **Market Place** (*Recoba*), close together on the site of the old Dominican monastery. The Theatre will hold 764 people. **Bull Ring** (*Plaza de Toros*), a large stone circular building at the top of the town (Salamanca). **Cock-pit,** in the Calle de Santa Clara. **Library** and **Museum,** in the old Franciscan monastery. There are several forts commanding the bay and protecting the town, which may be visited by those obtaining permission to do so.

Churches.—**Iglesia de la Concepcion** (often called the Cathedral), is a rambling building with five naves and a square tower 166 feet in height. Commenced early in the 16th century, *i.e.,* just after the conquest, it gradually increased in size as the town grew. In 1652, it was burnt down. There has never been any attempt to improve it architecturally, and its only charm lies in the interior, where there is some excellent carved woodwork, both on some of the altars and in the unfinished Capilla de Carta. Amongst the sacred relics are two of Nelson's flags, taken in 1797. They are enclosed in a glazed case, which hangs in the central chapel on the north side. There is also a piece of the true cross, which may be seen and kissed on May 3rd; part of the thighbone of Pope Clement, and the cross planted by the Conquistadores on their arrival in the island. The vestments and plate are worth seeing. **The Iglesia de San Francisco,** founded in 1680, tower in 1777, about which time the whole building was restored, is of pleasing appearance, and has a good frontage. The interior, which is paved with marble, has three naves. The monastery adjoining is now used as a prison, a court of justice, a school, a town hall, etc., etc. The marble Virgin and Child, formerly standing on the handsome tower, was unfortunately blown down in 1892. It is proposed to utilise this site for the erection of large Municipal Buildings, the Church to stand inside the quadrangle or to be moved a little to one side. **The Capilla de Dolores** faces the Calle del Tigre, and adjoins the Church just described. **Del Pilar,** A.D. 1774, a church with a very well-designed roof. **Ermita de San Telmo—de N.S. de Regla—de S. Sebastian.** The foundation stone of an English church has been laid in the upper part of the town. Subscriptions are received by Messrs. Hamilton and Co. At present, services are held during the winter only.

Cemeteries.—Both to the south-west of the town. The Spanish cemetery dates from 1811. It took 12 years to bring the necessary depth of earth. The Protestant cemetery dates from 1837.

The Lazareto lies away beyond the cemeteries near the sea.

Clubs.—**The Casino Principal** (Spanish), facing the Plaza de la Constitucion. Monthly members admitted. A number of dances are given during the winter. **The English Club**, at the top of the same square. Weekly members admitted. **Circulo de Amistad. Lawn Tennis Club,** with courts at the back of the town. Temporary members admitted.

Squares and Gardens.—**Plaza de la Constitucion,** paved with stone, and the favourite promenade of an evening. The marble group at the lower end is supposed to represent the lost image of the Virgen de Candelaria (*see* Candelaria), supported by the four Guanche Kings first converted to Christianity. The old fort of San Cristóbal, just below the Plaza, is that in which George Glas was imprisoned in 1776. There is some talk of knocking it down and leaving the Plaza open to the sea. **Alameda del Principe de Asturias** (or de la Libertad), behind the Iglesia de San Francisco, a shady square planted with Indian laurels. The band plays in this square, and in the Plaza de la Constitucion.

Alameda de Ravenet or **de la Marina,** adjoining the mole; **El Muelle** (the mole), which might be a pleasant resort at sundown after a hot day. It was commenced soon after the arrival of the Spaniards, and was repaired in 1585; but, until the present century, was only a few yards in length. It now measures something over 2,000 feet, and is to be extended to a length of 4,850 feet, making a closed basin for the shelter of vessels. The work will take many years and it seems as though the ships used by that time may have some difficulty in getting in. It is to be hoped that the authorities will see their way to clear away the concrete blocks encumbering the commencement of the road to San Andres, and to make the part facing the harbour a little more worthy of the town. More stringent regulations should also be adopted on the mole. **The Plaza de Weyler,** in the upper part of the town, is rapidly improving as the trees grow, and already makes a pleasant place to sit in. It is adorned with a handsome marble fountain.

Water Supply, Lighting, etc.—Measures to increase the water supply, the deficiency in which hinders the growth of the town, are in progress.

Santa Cruz is provided with a good system of telephones, which connect with La Laguna.

Since the end of 1897, the town has been lighted by electricity from the dynamo works, near the Iglesia de la Concepcion. The installation gives a brilliant result, and is at the disposal of residents.

Electric Tramway.—This starts from the bottom of the town and runs to La Laguna, 11 kils. (7 miles). Single journey, 45 min. Cars up and down each hour from 6 a.m. to 10 p.m. 1st class, 1.50 pes.; 2nd class, 1.05 pes., to which a transit tax is added. Intermediate fares are posted up in the cars.

The power-works, to view which apply at the office, are situated half-way up, at the Cuesta. The installation is very elaborate and up to date. Two engines (direct action) drive the dynamos (Dulait system), which work up to 200 kilo-watts. Galloway boilers. Green economisers. Tudor accumulators. The condensing water is cooled by a tubular refrigerator (Koerting system). On account of the steepness of the inclines, the cars are each provided with two motors of 50 horse-power. Apart from the actual beauty of the journey, the ride is most interesting as an example of modern electrical engineering.

Cabs for Hire.—Generally to be found at the top of the Plaza de la Constitucion. Fares about town, 50 to 75 centimos.

Santa Cruz is a picturesque and pleasing town, full of handsome balconies, cool shady patios and quaint nooks and corners. The "miradores" or "view-towers" placed on the roofs prevent any idea of uniformity, whilst the projecting eaves of inverted gutter-pipes and long wooden gargoyles help to lend shade, effect and depth to the sunny streets and lanes.

There is a gradual rise towards the back of the city, where a pleasant avenue of pepper-trees and geraniums commands a good view of the town, with the two church towers conspicuous and Grand Canary dimly visible on the horizon. A soft breeze generally makes itself felt, and the air on the mole of an evening is most delicious, even in the hottest part of the summer.

During late years a number of new buildings have been erected behind the town in what is known as the Barrio de Ensanche or Toscal, which bids fair to join hands with Salamanca, and where the surroundings are pleasant and salubrious. The best and healthiest positions fronting the sea, however, have been somewhat overlooked.

On the N. and N.W. lies the arid ridges of Anaga Promontory. On the W. and S. the land rises in a great slope towards La Laguna and the mountains round the Peak, the latter being scarcely visible from the city. The Spanish society is the most lively to be found in the islands, and assembles in considerable force on Sundays and holidays to hear the band play. The public gardens are shady, and the view of the harbour from the town animated and picturesque. Visitors wishing to gain an idea of the town and neighbourhood without much trouble are recommended to ascend the tower of the Concepcion Church.

The climate is very good, but, for various reasons, Santa Cruz has not received the attention it deserves. The inside of the town is very hot in the summer. The heat rarely approaches that commonly experienced in London or Paris during the dog days, but extends over so long a period that it becomes trying. There is, however, no reason whatever why people should not live there all the year round.

In the winter the few additional degrees of warmth and the very large average of bright sunshine are, to many, a great advantage. Illnesses complicated by rheumatic or asthmatic symptoms will probably find Santa Cruz particularly adapted to their cases. The percentage of clear sky and the consequent radiation of heat into space are reflected in the daily range of the thermometer as given in the Meteorological Tables.

Although less frequented than Las Palmas, Santa Cruz is an important coaling station.

Walks and Excursions from Santa Cruz.—The Laguna road is described later on.

The **water course** (*atarjéa*) which crosses the hills behind and above the town can be followed in either direction. It is reached by keeping up the road past the **Pino de Oro Hotel** at the back of the town. At about 10 min. to the right, keep on through a deep cutting and some short tunnels. The masonry affords a level and most charming walk, overlooking the Barranco de Ameida and eventually leading to the **Aguirre springs** in about 3 hrs. It is possible to reach **La Laguna** by bearing off to the left at the top in about 5 hrs., or **Taganana,** by bearing to the right in about 6 hrs. total.

The **level carriage road leading to San Andres** is a beautiful drive. At 2½ m. (4 kils.) is the **Valle del Bufadero,** the spot where the Spaniards first landed and which has more than once been used as a base of operations against the city. A fort is being built here.

The hill on the city side of the barranco, 1,500 ft., 1 hr. from the road, commands a magnificent view of the Peak, etc., and is well worth climbing. The path ascends from the telegraph hut. Donkeys can get up.

The path leading up the valley divides at about twenty minutes from the road. **To the left** is a pretty walk by a stream. Crossing this at about 1 hr.

up, an easy ascent leads to the summit of the ridge, 2,680 ft., in about 2½ hrs. To the right a steeper but more direct path leads to the top in about 2¼ hrs. (After passing through about half-a-mile of laurels, a narrow and insignificant track which turns to the right through some rushes is that which must be taken for the Lighthouse.)

Keeping straight on a slight ascent leads to 3,300 ft. (whence a fine view of the Peak), and the path descends to the Cruz de Taganana, 2,800 ft., 2¾ hrs., *see* under La Laguna. The path along the ridge connecting La Laguna with the Lighthouse is more fully given under excursions from La Laguna.

The above are the prettiest ways from Santa Cruz to Taganana. That on the left is more or less practicable for horses and donkeys. The right hand valley is, perhaps, to be preferred by those on foot. Times are given as from the *carretera*.

San Andres, 5 m. (8 kils.) is a dirty, uninteresting fishing village where nothing beyond wine and biscuits can be procured. There is an old martello tower by the beach, which partially fell down in 1895.

From San Andres a path leads up the valley to the central ridge, 2,680 ft., in 2½ hrs. Owing to the small crystals into which the basalt in this ravine solidified, the scenery is tame. The descent to **Taganana** is much finer. Time 3½ hrs. This is the route generally taken by those riding from Santa Cruz to **Taganana**. A track to the right half-way up joins the central path along the ridge, and leads to the village of **Anaga**. No inn, no food. San Andres to Anaga about 3½ hrs.

Beyond San Andres a path, best on foot, leads to **Igueste** in 1 hr. No inn. After this the coast must be left and the track up the barranco taken to the central path, 2 hrs., and **Anaga**, 2,000 ft., 2½ hrs. (from Igueste). For the descent to the Lighthouse and **Taganana**, *see* excursions from La Laguna.

The scenery along the ridge is some of the finest in the archipelago, and the Barrancos del Bufadero, de Igueste, and de Chamorga (between Anaga and the Lighthouse) are all beautiful. Many of the paths are bad and slippery after rain, and a guide is advisable in the hills.

The Semaphore, visible from Santa Cruz, stands 730 ft. above the sea.

A *précis* of times on foot is:—Bufadero, ¾ hr.; San Andres, 1¾ hrs.; Igueste, 2¾ hrs.; Anaga, 5¼ hrs.; Lighthouse, 6½ hrs.; Taganana, 9½ hrs.; (Anaga to Taganana direct, 3 hrs.); up the Vueltas to the Cruz de Taganana, 11 hrs.; Laguna, 14¼ hrs. (or from the Cruz de Taganana *viâ* the Valle del Bufadero to Santa Cruz, 14 hrs.) total. From Santa Cruz to the Bufadero, ¾ hr.; to the Cruz de Taganana, 3½ hrs.; to Taganana, 4½ hrs. total.

It is proposed to continue the *carretera* from San Andres to Taganana, *i.e.*, to add another 10½ miles (16½ kils.). At the 14 kil. post, a branch, 2½ kils. long, would be carried to Igueste.

The population of all the villages between Santa Cruz and the Lighthouse, are included in the figures of Santa Cruz.

To the South of the Island.

(*For Public Coaches, see Table at the end of the description of Teneriffe*)

Santa Cruz to Candelaria, Güimar, Vilaflor, Adeje, Valle Santiago, and round to Icod de los Vinos.

Take the Laguna road up the **Cuesta**, where the electric tramway works are, 40 minutes driving, 960 feet, 3¾ miles, 6 kils., or by electric tram, 20 minutes, fare 75 centimos. For further details along the way, *see* road to La Laguna. From the venta bear round to the south along the Güimar road.

The country passed through is dry and not particularly interesting. The woods on the right (La Esperanza) are best reached from La Laguna itself. At 8 miles (13 kils.) San Isidro is passed, and at 11 miles (17 kils.) the half-way house, 875 feet.

At 2¾ hrs. the village of **Barranco Hondo** (1,312 ft.) is seen well up on the right, followed shortly after by the romantically situated village of **Igueste de Candelaria**, 13 miles (21 kils.).

A bridle path leads from the *carretera* to Igueste in about ½ hr.; to the Cumbres in about 2 hrs., and down to Tacoronte in about 3½ hrs. total. The views from the top are very fine. Described more fully under Tacoronte.

The broad valley of Güimar is now fully exposed. At 16¼ miles, 282 feet (26 kils.) a path leads down to **Candelaria** and the sea (½ hr.). Beds possible. Candelaria is to be connected with the high road by a *carretera* 3 kils. long.

On the Playa (beach) de Chimisay (Socorro) the famous image of the Virgin and Child, found in possession of the Guanches, is said to have appeared in 1393 to two Guanche goatherds, who suffered from trying to drive it away. Certain miracles having convinced the Guanches of its sanctity, it was held in great reverence. Sancho de Herrera stole it in 1464, and carried it to Fuerteventura, but, plague breaking out, was forced to bring it back again. In 1826, it was lost in a flood which broke from the mountains and carried the image and part of the monastery into the sea. The image was probably the figure-head of some ship. At the feast of the Candelaria (August 15), and again on February 2, large numbers of pilgrims visit the village, in which there are an old church and Dominican monastery. The monastery was founded in the 16th century, and contained cells for some 30 friars. It was never completed. The cave of San Blas (Guanche *achbinico*) in which the Guanches kept the image, may still be seen. The pictures are interesting. Mass is occasionally held there. A few of the villagers are employed in making pottery.

A little further on the main road crosses a stream of lava, and at 17 miles (27 kils.) passes the carriage road leading up to **Arafo**, a large village some two miles above the *carretera*, 1,570 ft. above the sea, and situated on the so-called Pilgrims' Route between Candelaria and the neighbourhood of Orotava. There is no inn, but beds may be had with difficulty. Pop. 1,602.

Above Arafo a path leads in 35 minutes to the **Bco. Cambuesa** where a tunnel has been sunk for about 500 yds. in search of water, but without result. Keep to the right through grand precipitous rocks up the **Bco. Añavingo** to the tunnelling works ($1\frac{1}{4}$ hrs.) where water has been struck. There are many other tunnels both in this neighbourhood and near Güimar, but this is the only one which has so far been successful.

From Arafo a pass leads over **Pedro Gil**, 6,800 ft., $3\frac{1}{4}$ hrs., to Villa **Orotava**, 6 hrs., joining the Güimar route just below the Volcan de Arafo, *see* Güimar.

Another pass known as the **Pilgrims' Route** leads over the Cumbres, 5,650 ft., to **Victoria** in about 6 hrs. It is not so beautiful as that over Pedro Gil, but there is less climbing. A descent from the summit can be made to Villa **Orotava** *via* la Cuesta de Bacalao and Florida, $6\frac{1}{2}$ hrs., or the *carretera* can be joined at **Sta. Ursula, Victoria, Matanza, etc.**, in about 6 hrs. There is a path along the saddle back to the N.E. leading to **Tacoronte, La Esperanza, La Laguna, etc.**, which is easy enough when fine, but dangerous in foggy weather. Those losing their way in a fog should choose some well marked track and bear N. not S., because the barrancos to the S. absolutely prevent further progress.

Leaving the Arafo road behind, a more recent stream of lava (A.D. 1705) is crossed, a remarkable example whose hollowness in parts admits of entrance. At 20 m. (32 kils.),

Güimar, 985 ft., a scattered village of 5,120 inhabitants, is reached.

Hotels.—El Buen Retiro, a villa with pretty garden, 8s. to 10s. a day; Güimar Hospital, specially built for the open air cure (Nordrach system); fine, commanding position near the hotel, terms 5 guineas a week; small Spanish inn, 3s. a day.

(*For advertisements, see under Güimar at the end of the book.*)

The climate of Güimar is sunny, dry and of the gently stimulating order. It has proved of great service in several cases of pulmonary affection.

From the hotel in Güimar, 1,200 ft., there is a very fine view of the valley, and the course of the two lava streams emanating from the Volcan de Arafo is easily traced. With the exception of these streams and a few distinctly recent deposits, the grit beds forming the surface of the valley and of the neighbouring slopes to a height of at least 5,000 feet, would seem to have been laid in their present position at a time when the country was covered by water, perhaps by the sea. The thin, impervious, calcareous layers covering each stratum of grit, appear to have settled slowly into their present position, and to have followed the heavier matter, which sank to the bottom first. In entering the Barranco del Rio, shortly before arriving at the woods (about 2,550 feet), attention is called to a mass of hard mud, burrowed in all directions by what was apparently an aquatic worm.

Excursions from Güimar.—**To Arafo**, 40 minutes on a mule.—To the wild and precipitous **Bco. Badajoz** (1½ hrs.), inside which the Cueva del Cañizo of the Guanches is to be seen far up on the left. The original beams are plainly visible, but access is now very difficult. The Madre del Agua (source) is about 2,500 feet above the sea. This is a very fine walk.—To the **Bco. del Rio** (1½ hrs.), a beautiful ravine from which most of the Güimar water is derived, and in which there are several springs and fern-clad rocks to be seen. Both these barrancos are mere chasms worn by water.

The atarjea connecting the waters of the two barrancos crosses the Lomo at a height of 2,370 feet. It can be followed from one ravine to another in about ½ hr., or a rather longer but less dangerous path, coming from the bed of the Barranco Badajoz, can be taken.

To Villa Orotava, etc., *viâ* **Pedro Gil.**—A steep climb leads through the Monte Verde and to the junction with the path leading up from Arafo, 2¼ hrs., 4,950 ft. A wide expanse of black sand is crossed and the remarkable gorge known as the **Valle** is entered, one of the most stupendous efforts of eruptive force to be seen in the world. A sketch and a description of this will be found in the "Geological" article. (*See* Garganta de Güimar.)

The gap appears to have been absolutely thrown into space. Attention is called to the direction of the strata exposed on each side, as well as to the want of similarity between the two surfaces. The N. side of the gate is strangely intersected by a perfect network of dykes.

The interest does not diminish on the way up to the summit of **Pedro Gil**, 6,800 ft., 3¼ hrs., whence there is a good view of the Peak and Cañadas.

Turning to the left, a descent amidst barren rocks leaves **Agua Mansa**, 3,930 ft., 4¾ hrs., about a mile to the right, and enters the Villa at the extreme top. Time, 6 hrs., total.

Instead of descending into the Valley of Orotava, a path to the left leads from Pedro Gil into the Cañadas in about 2 hrs. and so on to Vilaflor, *see* elsewhere. It is also possible to reach La Laguna, etc., by turning to the right, *see* Pilgrims' Route.

To Villa Orotava, etc., *viâ* **Arafo and the Pilgrims' Route.**—To Arafo, 40 minutes. For further details, *see* Arafo.

To Mña. Grande, Socorro, and Candelaria.—Some ½ hr. below Güimar, to the right of the path to Socorro, is the cup-shaped fumarole known as the Mña. Grande, 960 feet, 1 hr., easy of ascent. The unbroken crater is about 200 feet deep and 1,025 yards in circumference. Volcanic bombs are scattered plentifully round the edge. The bird's eye view of the valley is very fine.

About 1 hr. from Güimar is Socorro (Guanche, *Chimisay*), where there is a deposit of the fine tufa from which the celebrated drip-stone filters are made. The famous Virgen de Candelaria was found here, and was first conveyed to the Cueva de Chinguaro, in a barranco, ¾ hr. from Socorro, and near the old *camino real* from Güimar to Candelaria. The Cueva was then the residence of the Mencey of Güimar, and is now an Ermita with a tiled roof. The most prominent object near it is a round tower-like building.

Leaving Socorro the path crosses dry, barren slopes, where there is a small fossil bed. Calcareous casts of plants are numerous, and the method by which they are produced can be observed in its several stages. The peculiar poisonous plant known as the Verolillo, very rare in the island, grows abundantly here.

At about 2¼ hrs. Candelaria is entered.

Beyond Güimar the road crosses a wide stony barranco and ascends the **Ladera de Güimar**, a steep volcanic wall bounding the south of the valley, of which latter there is a very fine view at the bend (2½ m., 4 kils.).

The country from here to Adeje is dreary and arid to a degree, a thin fringe of forest land above being a very inadequate reservoir for the dry tufa plains below, which are generally of the second period of formation. Botanists will find the vegetation of interest, but the travelling is hard and the scenery *nil*. The few points worth seeing will be noticed in their proper places. The productions are a quantity of white wine, potatoes, tomatoes, grain, and formerly cochineal. The easiest way to reach any given point is to go by boat to the respective port, generally 1 to 2 hours below the village, or to come over the Cañadas. The "Golden Eagle" touches at Abona, Medano and Abrigos, on its way to and from Gomera.

At 28 m. (45 kils.), 2 hrs. on foot from Güimar, the *carretera* ends at the entrance to **Escobonal** (1,530 ft.), the next section to Fasnia, 50 kils., not being open to the public yet.

According to the proposed route of the *carretera* to be carried round the south of the island, the approximate distances to the principal places passed through will be as follows:—

Icor, 35 m. (56 kils.). Arico Junction, 38 m. (60½ kils.), whence to village 2½ kils. Lomo Junction, 39¾ m. (63½ kils.), whence to village 4 kils. Rio, 41 m. (66 kils). Granadilla, about 47½ m. (76 kils.). San Miguel, about 52½ m. (84 kils.). Valle de S. Lorenzo, about 55 m. (88 kils.). Arona, about 57½ m (92 kils.). Adeje, about 64 m. (102 kils.). Guia, about 75 m. (120 kils.).

It is proposed to carry a road from Guia to Villa de Santiago, 20 kils.; El Tangue, 25 kils., and Icod de los Vinos, 31 kils., where it will effect a junction with the *carretera* now serving the north of the island. Should this project ever be completed, there would be a drive round the slopes of Teneriffe of 132 m. (211 kils.), which would carry visitors past a strange diversity of scenery, varying from the sterile deserts below Arico, to the verdant garden of the Valley of Orotava, and from the orange groves of Granadilla or pine forests of Guia, to the leafy shades of the laurel and heath trees at Agua Garcia and beyond Las Mercedes.

Those going on beyond Escobonal must now accept the times given in this book as being **on foot from Güimar.**

Passing below Escobonal the deep **Barranco Herques,** 3 hrs., is crossed by a bridge (water is generally to be found by digging a hole in the sand at the bottom). At 3½ hrs., **Fasnia,** 31 m. (50 kils.) (wine shop), after which the path descends through an absolute desert to the sandy beach, 4¾ hrs., where the bathing is excellent.

The desert is not without its interest, and the gnarled and twisted plants of the *tabaiba dulce,* whose age is often apparently far greater than that of the oldest dragon trees, are a conspicuous feature. The calcareous deposit accumulated on the surface of the various strata of the tufa, which was perhaps deposited in its present position whilst this part of the island was covered by the sea, cannot fail to attract attention. It is always impervious to moisture, and in some places so hard that the traffic of centuries has failed to break through half an inch of it. Water will be seen oozing from above it in the roadside cuttings, and it must be an important factor in preventing the escape of water into the sea by means of subterranean filtration.

At 6½ hrs., Arico, 1,188 ft. (beds, very dirty) and at 7¼ hrs. Lomo de Arico, 1,765 ft. (beds), a few houses with a church. A *carretera* is being made between Arico to the Puerto de Abona, 4 m., 6½ kils., and a lighthouse is to be built on Pta. Abona.

At 8¼ hrs. Rio, 1,419 ft. (venta) and at 10¼ hrs. the pretty village of

Granadilla, 2,026 ft., pop. 3,381. Fair inn with several beds, 3s. a day. The village is prettily situated on fertile soil, where the best oranges in Teneriffe are grown. It has the advantage of being large enough to kill a beast occasionally, and is the first decent place stopped at after leaving Güimar. A *carretera* is being made between Granadilla and the Puerto de Medano, 6½ m., 10½ kils.

Excursions.—To the Coast where the Cable Hut stands.— A 2 hrs. walk leads to **Tejita**, which is not at all a bad summer camping ground. The people living on the S. side do not go up the hills during the summer as is generally supposed, but down to the beach, where the eddy, caused by the deflection of the trade wind round the sides of the island, blows in cool from the sea. Higher up it is heated again by passing over the land. The fishing and bathing is also an inducement. There is a fresh-water spring near the beach.

To Vilaflor, Orotava and Icod.—A climb of about 2 hrs., foot or mule, leads to **Vilaflor**, 4,335 ft., the highest village in the Canaries, and destined, according to what some say, to become their chief summer resort. At present there is little accommodation and access is difficult. There is a large church in the village, in which the marble statue of St. Peter is a good work. To the N.E. of the town are two mineral springs, of which the water is said to be a good tonic. The name Vilaflor is modern, and has replaced that of Chasna, by which the village was formerly known.

A mountain called the **Sombrerito**, commanding a magnificent view of the Peak and Cañadas, can be reached in about 1½ hrs. from Vilaflor. There are also many romantic walks along the mountain sides and through the pine woods.

For ascent to the Cañadas, etc., 3½ hrs., from Vilaflor and routes to Orotava (10½ hrs.) or Icod de los Vinos (9½ hrs.), *see* under Orotava, Icod, etc. The distances from Vilaflor to such points as Santiago or Santa Cruz are also less by the Cañadas or Cumbres than they are by the lower road.

Bridle paths descend from Vilaflor to **San Miguel** and **Arona**, as well as to Granadilla, in about 2 hrs.

It is possible to reach Arico *via* the Pinar and the Bco. del Rio in about 3 hrs., or Adeje direct from Vilaflor in about 3 hours by paths crossing the upper slopes.

Plans have been made for a *carretera* to connect Vilaflor with Orotava by way of the Cañadas. The necessary zig-zags would make this road about 60 kils. in length.

Leaving Granadilla the land passed through becomes more productive.

San Miguel, 1,950 ft., 11½ hrs., a substantially built village with an inn; 3s. a day. A quantity of square paving stones (*losas*) are produced here for export to Cuba and America and for use in the islands generally. Pop. 1,784.

A path leads up to Vilaflor in about 2 hrs., and down to the coast in about 1½ hours.

TENERIFFE (ROUND THE SOUTH OF THE ISLAND). 188

Passing below **El Roque** and by the Ermita de S. Lorenzo, $12\frac{1}{4}$ hrs., the path crosses the fruitful volcanic valley **de los Hijaderos**, and enters

Arona, 2,085 ft., $13\frac{1}{4}$ hrs. (beds). Pop. 1,971.

Path up to Vilaflor about 2 hrs. Down to the Port, about $1\frac{1}{2}$ hrs.

On leaving the village the **Roque del Conde** is left on the right, and the path becomes very bad as far as Adeje.

Adeje, 990 ft., $15\frac{1}{4}$ hrs. Comfortable, clean inn with five beds; 3s. a day. Distance from the sea, 1 hr. Pop. 1,712.

This village was formerly the residence of the Guanche King Tinerfe the Great. To-day nearly all the houses and the surrounding country belong to the family descended from the former Counts of Gomera, who were also at one time supreme lords of Gomera. They lived in the so-called **Casa Fuerte**, now used as a store-house. Visitors are allowed to enter, and it is well worth seeing. There is a handsomely decorated oratory, a few pieces of cannon, weapons, etc. Some of the utensils formerly used by the black slaves who worked in the sugar factory, still remain in the rooms where they lived. The owners were possessed of rights of *horca y cuchillo*, *i.e.*, summary judgment and execution. An old rule mentioned in their archives states that all strangers must be granted hospitality for three days, after which they were to be shown where the door lay.

The church, built by the above-named family, contains a good altar and some handsome old tapestry, badly cared for and quite thrown away on the villagers. Unfortunately it is entailed. There are some curious old wall-paintings and some very old images, one of which, N.S. de la Candelaria, dates from the Conquest.

Excursions from Adeje.—To **Vilaflor** *viâ* **Arona**, about 4 hrs. This route can be followed to Santa Cruz or to La Laguna.

To the **Boca de los Tauces (Cañadas)** *viâ* **Tedesma**, about 3 hrs., a road which is rarely used.

Up the **Bco. Infierno** to the waterfalls, 1,848 ft., $1\frac{1}{4}$ hrs., a grand walk through one of the most stupendous and remarkable chasms in the island. The left-hand waterfall, at the top, filters through a soft white rock, of which the solution deposits itself in the form of stalactites and as a horny pink or yellow covering on the stones. Enquiries did not result in showing that the water is injurious to those who drink it, though this may be the case.

Leaving Adeje, the Finca de la Hoya Grande, a large farm, is passed at $16\frac{3}{4}$ hrs. At 17 hrs. **Tijore**, after which a wearisome succession of barrancos. At 18 hrs. the church of **Tejina** and, at $19\frac{1}{4}$ hours,

Guia, 1,800 ft., a large village with a church and an inn (3s. a day) about 2 hrs. above the sea. Pop. 3,322.

From here a path leads to the Cañadas, which are entered a little to the N. of the **Fuente del Cedro** in about $2\frac{1}{2}$ hrs.

Beyond Guia there are a number of lava streams to be crossed. At 20 hrs. **Chio**, 2,227 ft., is left a little to the right, and a long ascent commences. The fringe of the pine forest is entered and the views of the western extremity of the island, with Gomera in the distance, become more and more imposing.

The traveller can, if he wishes, take paths from the neighbourhood of Guia or of Chio, which ascend at once and leave Arguayo to the left, entering the Valley of Santiago nearer to Chajorra, or bearing across the base of this mountain more directly to Icod. It is advisable to engage a local guide.

At **Arguayo**, 3,006 ft., 21 hrs., the Peak at last comes fairly into sight.

A path to the left, just below Arguayo, leads to the lower part of the Valle de Santiago, whence **Masca**, **Carrisal**, **Palmar** and **Buena Vista** can be reached.

Climbing to the base of the **Risco de Arguayo**, 3,729 ft., the mountain is encircled by a path commanding a wide and magnificent view. A rapid descent follows, the upper part of the valley is crossed, and at 22 hrs. is the village of the

Valle de Santiago, 3,000 ft., 1,432 inhabitants. No inn, but beds can be had. Lying as it does in a broad, windy gully the place offers few attractions, and the lack of accommodation does not invite travellers to stay long. It is, however, one of the best centres from which to explore this part of the island.

Palmar, 1,650 ft., lies two hours to the N.W. and the track over the pass, as well as that leading to **Masca**, 2,070 ft., and **Carrisal**, 2,115 ft., command splendid views. For **Palmar**, **Icod de los Vinos**, 3¾ hrs. and neighbourhood, *see* under Buena Vista.

It is advisable to ta Vilaflor to San Miguhills, but they are not wanted in the *camino* hrs.

a Arico *viâ* the Pinar and ct from Vilaflor in about 3 h.

een made for a *carretera* to Cañadas. The necessary zig-zag length.

Leaving Granadilla the land productive.

San Miguel, 1,950 ft., 1 an inn; 3s. a day. A qu are produced here for expor in the islands generally. Pop.

A path leads up to Vilaflor in a. about 1½ hours.

N.W. road from Santa Cruz to La Laguna, Tacoronte, Orotava, Icod, Garachico and Buena Vista, with subsidiary excursions, etc., etc.

(*For Public Coaches, see Table. For Tramway, see page 180. Private carriages for Orotava should not start later than 10 a.m. Lunch can be had at La Laguna, Tacoronte or La Matanza.*)

The road leaves the back of the town and winds up the slope through terraces planted with cereals and the cochineal plant.

On leaving the town the bull ring of Salamanca is seen on the right. By bearing to the right either just by or just above the **fielato**, a pretty walk can be taken past a succession of water-dams and up the barranco as far as may be thought convenient. The country to the left of the *carretera* is not interesting.

A little further on, the old paved road, along which horse and foot passengers travel, leaves the *carretera*.

At 500 ft. and close to the *carretera* are some caves which may be entered and followed for some distance. Lights required.

Half-way to La Laguna (40 min. driving, 20 min. by tram), the Café de la Cuesta, 960 ft., 3¾ miles (6 kils.), is reached, where the horses are generally rested. The main road to Güimar branches off here. Close by are the electric tramway generating works.

A little higher than the Cuesta a path on the right leads to the Valle de Jimenez, an isolated glen bounded by a precipice on the S. and separated from the vale of La Laguna by a range of bare basaltic hills on the N.

Still a little higher a second path leads to the Valle de Tabarez, a valley which is almost equally isolated, but which is broader, is provided with a small church and has a rather larger population.

At 4½ m. (7 kils.) an old house on the left, known as Macary is passed, in which Captain Cook slept when on his voyage round the world in 1772.

A little above this is the church of Sta. Maria de Gracia, the oldest in the island, founded by D. Alonso Fernandez de Lugo, the Conquistador. This is the spot where the Mencey of Anaga was killed in 1495. The Ermita de S. Roque, higher up in the hills to the right, is the place where Imobac Bencomo, King of Taoro, lost his life. (*See* "History.")

Gradually the air becomes colder and the eye turns from Santa Cruz, glittering in the sun with its white houses in strong contrast to the deep blue sea, and encounters the sombre towers of San Cristóbal de la Laguna. The keen air and grass-topped walls show how greatly the climate differs from that of the coast, and the invalid should be well provided with wraps. The district was once the bed of a lake or marsh, and, although there is now no standing water, a great amount passes below the surface. The land is extremely rich and free from stones, crops of all sorts growing most luxuriantly. On account of the low temperature the city is much frequented in the summer. During the winter the air is fresh and invigorating.

La Laguna, $5\frac{1}{2}$ m. (9 kil.), 1,804 ft., 13,080 inhabitants. Seat of Bishopric of Teneriffe and Western Canaries since 1819.

Hotels.—Agüere and Continental, with good patio and views, near the Cathedral, about 8s. to 10s. a day; Hotel Tenerife, near the Aguere, from 6s.; Fonda Parilla, 5 pes.

(For advertisements, see under La Laguna at the end of the book.)

La Laguna is connected with Santa Cruz by telephone.

Public Buildings.—The **Town Hall**, with some curious old paintings on the staircase, representing scenes from the Conquest. In the hall above is the standard of the Conquest, embroidered by Isabel the Catholic. The original embroidery has been transferred to a new piece of crimson damask.—The **Instituto** (formerly Convento de San Agustin) and **Universidad de San Fernando**. The interior of the large church is plain. The convent is the present official centre of instruction, and contains, among other things, a **Public Library** of nearly 20,000 volumes; open from 10 a.m. till 4 p.m. A curious manuscript (Dutch) of the fifteenth century, in good preservation, and some early printed works of the sixteenth century, may be seen. The **Bishop's Palace** (No. 28), a little further down the street, is a handsome building with decorative stone façade. In the interior there is a staircase with well designed hip-roof. The beautiful iron gate at the entrance of the patio is a piece of local work.

At No. 20 Calle Anchieta there is a small private museum, open from 12 to 4 (gratuity expected). In the Plaza de la Concepcion there is also a good collection of butterflies and birds (private).

Churches.—The **Cathedral** (commenced in 1513):—The interior, which is on the whole plain, boasts some good altars, carved and gilded, also the tomb of Don Alonso Fernandez de Lugo, the conqueror of the island, who died in 1525, and whose remains rested until 1860 in the Convento de San Francisco. There is a highly valued marble pulpit, brought from Genoa, which is fairly good.—The **Iglesia de la Concepcion**, with high tower. The oldest church in the city (commenced in 1511). There is some handsome carved wood-work, especially about the pulpit. In the altar to the north of the chancel is a small picture of St. John the Evangelist, greatly prized owing to the face having been covered with what appeared to be human sweat during a period of forty days. This miracle happened in May, 1648. In the Baptistry is the " Piedra de los Guanches," a green glazed basin erroneously stated by some authors to have been made by the aboriginals.—The **Convento de las Monjas**, still inhabited, contains in the public church some good altars and a few curious old pictures. One end of the church is composed of a heavy iron grille, separating it from the chapel of the nuns, who remain invisible. A portion of the grille is arranged as a confessional box, and a small hole serves for administering the Eucharist to the inmates.—The **Convento de San Francisco**, now the Barracks. The church contains a curious altar in silver with a famous crucifix.—**Iglesia de Santo Domingo** and the **Ecclesiastical Seminary**, with an old *dragon tree* in the garden of which the age is unknown, but which was large enough at the time of the Conquest to cause the land on which it stood to be described as the *finca del drago*.

Squares.—The **Plazo del Adelantado**, well planted and ornamented with a large marble fountain. It is here that the band plays in the summer. There is a Club (Spanish) in the Calle de la Carrera.

Upheld by many as a winter resort for the first stages of pulmonary disease, La Laguna is unquestionably a pleasant residence in the summer, although probably too cold for the majority of invalids from January to April. When the weather becomes warm, the wealthier classes assemble here in great numbers. To the inhabitants of Santa Cruz it is a godsend during the hot weather, being comparatively close to their doors. All the high officials migrate upwards, bringing with them the military band, etc., the quietude of the winter being replaced by what must almost seem dissipation by comparison. There is more level country about than is the case anywhere else in the island, and many rides and drives may be taken, the first not being confined to those stated below, as branch roads permit of many a canter when desired. Those who are not absolutely invalids will find La Laguna a most agreeable centre for a time, some of the spots to be visited from here being of most extraordinary beauty.

La Laguna, the Gaunche paradise and the point whence the first and chief defensive operations were directed against the Spanish invaders, was the scene of many of the early legends and tales of the Conquest.

Some of these are mentioned in the historical section, but space cannot be given in this work for a tithe of the romances so ably treated by the poet Viana and others.

The chief and most sentimental is that of Dacil, daughter of Bencomo of Taoro. Tradition says the damsel lay hid in the boughs of a laurel tree overhanging the spring at Las Mercedes, when the Spanish knight, Fernan Garcia Izquierdo de Castillo, who had come to spy out the land, drank from the pool, saw her beautiful face and form reflected in the water, and loved her at first sight. It had been prophesied that, after the country was ruined, she should marry a man from over the seas.

The girl, whose choice may have been influenced by the prediction, does not seem to have been unduly coy. The poet says that she saw him coming and waited with bright, expectant eyes. He also adds that she had a string of beads round her neck, and that, as with the young lady in the song, "her golden hair was hanging down her back."

Subsequently the poem says that they were married and lived happily ever after, the knight probably squatting on Dacil's land.

It is a pity to disturb so pretty a picture, but readers of the historic section will have noticed that the lady the knight really married was Dacil's daughter.

Possibly the story of the love-making is not an invention, and the gentleman, after making love to the mother, married one of the next generation. Such things have been done. The son of our own good King George III. by his marriage with Hannah Lightfoot, bought a black slave in Cape Town, lived with her for several years at the Knysna, then turned her adrift and lived with her daughter, whose father, a white man, formerly owned the mother.

Excursions from La Laguna.—**To Tegueste and Tejina.**—A good carriage road shaded by eucalyptus, cork and other trees leaves the town on the east, and skirts the fruitful basin of La Laguna, which is left on the right. On the left the mountains, such as the Mesa Mota, can easily be ascended. A short distance from the town a bridle road bears to the right and leads to Las Mercedes in about ¾ hr. At 3 kils. (2 miles), 1,890 feet, the road turns to the left and passes through a deep cutting. From near this point paths lead away into the hills, where there are a number of delightful walks, or points in the forest, such as that known as **La Mina**, where there is a large spring, can easily be reached.

Beyond the cutting, the road enters the upper ramifications of a broad and picturesque valley, which only needs a torrent in the bed of the ravine to closely resemble many of the glens on the Italian side of the Alps. At 6½ kils. (4 miles), 1,270 feet, **Tegueste** is passed, a small village with a large church and a population of 1,859 people. The road continues to descend and at 10 kils. (6¼ miles), 490 feet, reaches the little church of Tejina. No beds.

From Tejina the coast can be reached in about ¾ hr., and a carriage road, 3 kils. in length, is being made to the rocks. Beyond this road, and 1¼ hrs. from Tejina, is the little fishing village of the Punta del Hidalgo.

From just above Tejina a carriage road has been made to the Valle de Guerra, 2½ m., 4 kilos., and Tacoronte, 7 m., 11 kilos. This crosses the barranco to the west of the town and continues to the Ermita del Rosario in the Valle de Guerra, 1¼ hrs. on foot, 690 feet, whence to Tacoronte in another 1½ hrs. on foot (*see* Tacoronte), or any of the paths to the left can be followed and a return to La Laguna may be made in from 1¾ to 2⅓ hrs., according to the road selected. If desired, the Mña. de Guerra or the Mña. de la Atalaya, both of which command good views, may be climbed on the way to Tacoronte. (For details, *see* under Tacoronte.) Those returning to La Laguna by the Ermita del Socorro and the Mña. del Pulpito, can leave the bridle path and climb the Caldera at the foot of the Mesa Mota.

To the Mesa Mota, etc.—This is the name of the chief of a group of mountains bounded by the plains of La Laguna and of Guamasa on the South, and by the slopes of Tegueste, Tejina, and the Val de Guerra on the North. Its eastern boundary is the cutting through which the *carretera* passes on the way from La Laguna to Tejina, and its western, a bridle path connecting the main *carretera* at a point near the Mña. del Pulpito with the Ermita del Socorro in the Valle de Tegueste. The mountains, 2,493 feet, command magnificent views, and the precipices to the north are covered with hanging woods, which afford some slight protection from the wind. At the foot of the group is a mountain known as the Caldera, an extinct *fumarole* or blow-hole, of which the crater has remained quite perfect. The geological characteristics of the group and of the Mña. de Guerra to the west, belong to the north-eastern or older portion of the island, and not to the more recent formation supporting the Peak.

To Las Mercedes and the Forest of La Mina.—Las Mercedes can be reached by following the *carretera* to Tejina from the Cathedral and by turning to the right into the fields at the second branch road, or by passing through the Plaza de San Francisco and by following the straight track. The distance by either way is about 2½ miles, and the latter road is quite practicable for carriages during dry weather, when, indeed, it is possible to ride right up to Las Mercedes, 2,010 feet, on a bicycle.

On leaving the village of Las Mercedes, follow the aqueduct to where the path forks close to a small bed of rushes (*jonquillos*), climb up the path to the left from here and enter the forest. At 25 min. from Las Mercedes, 2,455 feet, is the **Casa del Agua**, where a round stone table and seat have been provided for those wishing to picnic. The names of visitors will be found adorning the table and the grove of laurel and chestnut trees in the midst of which the table stands. A little above the table, 2,505 feet, the spring itself issues from the clefts of a basaltic rock, which probably lies upon a bed of more or less impervious tufa, and has been shifted or crushed by some movement of the surrounding rocks subsequent to crystallisation and cooling down. The gallery sunk in the neighbouring tufa has not been successful. It is curious to see how the original gallery, excavated probably by the Guanches, has been stopped at a point where the tufa seems to sink below the level of the floor.

There are several other smaller springs in the forest which are carried to the main aqueduct, and any little boy will show the way to these for a penny or so.

To Las Mercedes, Cruz de Afur, Taganana, the Lighthouse, Anaga, Igueste, San Andres, the Valle del Bufadero and Santa Cruz.
—The same as above, but on leaving Las Mercedes bear up to the right. At 1½ hrs. the Ermita de Sta. Maria del Carmen, after which the scenery becomes most magnificent, and, when seen in a good light between drifting clouds, is best described as a cross between a Dante's Inferno, a Doré's Heaven, and a very first-class transformation scene at a theatre.

At 2¼ hrs. the Cruz de Afur, 3,230 ft., whence it is possible to descend to Afur. A little further on is one of the ways (2,680 ft.) up from the Bufadero, which is, however, very difficult to hit off. The path runs as near as convenient to the top of the ridge, and at 3¼ hrs. passes the Cruz de Taganana, 2,800 ft., which may be known by the small round cave under the cross.

(From here to the Bufadero and Santa Cruz refer Bufadero. The same reference will also show which is the path to the Lighthouse. Times to the Lighthouse are—⅜ hr. from the Cruz de Taganana to the Cruz de San Andres, 2,680 ft., where the ascent from San Andres crosses the summit ; 3 hrs. to the point where the path leads down to Igueste ; 3½ to Anaga, 2,000 ft., no inn, no food ; and down the beautiful Bco. de Chamorga to the Lighthouse, 4¾ hrs., or a total of 8 hrs. from La Laguna. For further information turn to Exc. from Santa Cruz.)

The road from La Laguna to Taganana leaves the Cruz on the right. The first turn to the left leads to Afur, the second to the Vuelta de Taganana, a steep picturesque zig-zag, 1 hr. down, 1½ hrs. up. It is not worth descending unless Taganana is to be taken *en route* for further on.

Taganana, 700 ft., 4¼ hrs., is divided into two groups of houses. Inn with a few beds, 4s. a day. The neighbourhood is uninteresting, but there is a church, A.D. 1530, with an old altar-piece and Virgin, and there is a fine old dragon tree in a garden a little above it. It is proposed to connect Taganana with San Andres by a *carretera*, 10½ miles (16½ kils.) long.

A descent to the sea leads round the steep Roque de las Animas to Armásiga, Venta, 4¾ hrs. from La Laguna, and so to the sandy shore, where the breakers are sometimes very fine.

(At 1 hr. a path to the right leads through very fine scenery and wooded cliffs to Anaga, 3 hrs. total.)

Further along the path another ascent to the right goes round the coast to the Lighthouse (*el Faro*), 810 ft., 7¼ hrs. total. The closer in of the Anaga Rocks can be visited at low water.

From the Lighthouse to Anaga, 1½ hrs., and for further details, *see* Excursions from Santa Cruz.

Beyond the Cruz de Taganana a guide is advisable, but no one visiting Teneriffe should omit to make the excursion as far as this. Dry weather should be chosen as the paths are sometimes very slippery.

Excursions to the S.W. of La Laguna.—A bridle path reaches La Esperanza, 3,280 ft., in 1¼ hrs., and may be continued along the Cumbre or ridge as far as the Cañadas and so on to Vilaflor, etc. Distances, Cañadas about 8 hrs., or by turning down to the left, Arafo, 6 hrs., and Güimar, 7 hrs. If the ridge is descended on the other side, La Matanza can be reached in about 5 hrs., or less if desired, and Villa Orotava in about 7 hrs. The climb from La Laguna is fairly gradual, and the scenery, when clear, most beautiful. The saddle back itself nearly always affords capital travelling. Guides are advisable in case of clouds, as the precipices which terminate many of the mountain spurs on the S. are impassable even with ropes, and the pine needles render the descents very slippery. The highest point of the path is about 7,000 feet.

To Agua Garcia, Tacoronte, Matanza, Victoria, etc.—The old *camino real* leaves the *carretera* at the 14 kils. milestone on the N. side of La Laguna, and passes the fountain below the woods of Agua Garcia,

1¾ hrs., 2,350 ft. (*see* Tacoronte), and gradually descends to the *carretera* again, which it joins near **Victoria**, about 3½ hours. Numerous paths connect the bridle road with the *carretera* between La Laguna and Victoria. **La Matanza** can be reached in a little less time by bearing to the right, or a lovely walk, terminating at the same place, can be taken by climbing up through the woods of **Agua García** to 3,200 ft., and bearing off to the right along that level. About 5 or 6 hrs.

To **Güimar, Arafo**, etc., by the *carretera*.—See *S. of the island from Santa Cruz.*

About a mile to the N.E. of La Laguna is the Convento de San Diego de Monte, probably the oldest monastery in the island. This formerly stood in the forest, on the border of the lake, across which the friars used to pass in boats.

Main Road.—Leaving La Laguna behind, a long avenue of eucalyptus trees are passed, and the summit of the pass, 2,030 ft., is reached. Directly after this there is a pleasant glimpse of the Valley of Tegueste and the sea beyond, the road swings round to the left, and the long descent to Orotava is commenced.

Just by the turn is a mill standing a little to the west of a mountain called the Pulpito, because of the cross to be seen drawn on the hill in the part know as the Altar. The path leading down past the Pulpito leads to the Ermita del Socorro, Tegueste, Tejina, etc. (*See* excursions under La Laguna.)

The pine-clad hill a little beyond the mill is known as the Montaña de Cifra. It is 2,075 feet high, commands magnificent views and is a favourite spot for a picnic (permission required). The subsoil is a volcanic tuff, and affords good building material.

The slope to the west of the Mña. de Cifra is known as **Guamasa**, 1,855 feet. Many of those living in this picturesque little village are well-to-do people.

The volcanic cinder-heaps now passed on the right, are described in the excursions from Tacoronte.

As the road descends, the plants become more varied, and a delightful succession of green terraces and orchards, houses and flower gardens are passed, whilst there is a magnificent view of the Peak in clear weather.

At 12½ m. (20 kil.) **Tacoronte**, 4,205 inhabitants, a pretty village a little below the road.

Hotel.—The Tacoronte (Camacho's), a large building with a fine view just above the *carretera*, 8s. to 12s. a day. (Connected by telephone with La Laguna.)

(*For advertisement, see under Santa Cruz at the end of the book.*)

The hotel, 1,695 feet, is one of the best centres for excursions in Teneriffe and the climate is usually bracing enough to make walking or riding a pleasure. The air is not quite so keen as in La Laguna, but contains less moisture. Invalids needing a change from lower levels will find Tacoronte suitable to most cases. A meteorological table is given.

Walks, Excursions, etc.—The village of Tacoronte can easily be reached in a few minutes from the hotel. To the right is the Church of the **Convento de San Agustin**, founded A.D. 1662, with a stone façade bearing the arms of the Castro family in marble. The interior is plain, with the exception of the chancel, which has a handsome roof. Behind the altar is the famous wooden Christ of Tacoronte, made in Genoa, probably during the 17th century, and to which a great number of miracles are attributed. Once a year it is carried round the neighbourhood, which is then crowded with sightseers and worshippers. In the sacristy is a curious portrait of the Virgen de la Candelaria. (*See* Candelaria.) The church is well paved with black and white marble, and the Plaza in front is a pleasant place to sit in. Height above the sea, 1,540 ft. A small branch of the *carretera* is being made from the Plaza to the Calvario.

The Parish Church (**Iglesia de Santa Catalina**) is about 10 minutes from the hotel and more on the left. It is a good specimen of a country church and well worth visiting. The roofs at the chancel end, though not in the purest style, are attractive, and combine with the altars to lend an air of great richness to the interior. This is not inappropriate, as the church has one of the largest collections of gold and silver plate in the province of the Canaries. Especially noteworthy are the silver candelabra before the altar, which weighs 80 lbs.; the front of the altar itself, which is entirely covered with beaten silver; a large number of solid silver candlesticks, cups, beakers, etc., etc.; a chalice of solid gold; and especially a magnificent repoussé silver lectern, generally locked up in the sacristy. Some of the silver is very old, the largest part dating back to the Spanish conquest of Mexico. Much of it no doubt was beaten out in that country. The statue of St. Catherine behind the altar came from Italy in the 17th century and is well executed. The two holy water basins near the *coro* are of antique design, but the stone appears to be local. The picture of San Jeronimo to the S. of the *coro* was brought to the island by the Conquistadores in the 15th century.

The picturesque village of Tacoronte is intersected by a labyrinth of winding lanes, sometimes bordered by houses, sometimes by sloping fields and orchards. The architecture is simple but pleasing. Many of the cottages are kept gay by flowers, the rose, carnation, fuschia, etc., reaching considerable perfection. The three fountains, from which the whole population fetches its scanty supply of water, are centres of life and chatter from morning till night; and lastly a good glass of wine can be obtained from almost any of the *ventas*. In fact the people of Tacoronte pride themselves on growing the best red wine in Teneriffe, and the best cabbages in the whole universe, as far as they know it.

The new carriage road to Tejina is described further on.

Barranco de las Higueras.—This picturesque ravine is reached by following the path immediately to the W. of the hotel for about ¾ mile. The walk is recommended.

Excursions from Tacoronte.

To the Sea.—This can be reached in about 1½ hrs. by almost any of the roads leading downwards from the village. Those on foot can find paths through many of the fields, but most of the paths and bridle roads below the village are very bad. The cliffs, which closely resemble those to the north of Camborne in Cornwall, are some 700 to 800 feet high. The shore is provided with a number of natural breakwaters, consisting of streams of lava, the little harbours between which are occasionally used. The sheltered caves and holes in the beds of lava, afford some good bathing-places. One of the largest and deepest coves, the Puerto de San Fernandez, can be reached in the saddle. In one or two places there are springs of fresh water, that known as Guayónja retaining, no doubt, the original Guanche name. The caves in the cliffs were inhabited by this people at one time, and a steep path leading down to the rocks is still known as the Callejón de los Guanches.

An easy path can be followed along the edge of the cliffs from below Tacoronte into the village of Sauzal in about one hour. In places the rocks are very precipitous, and at one point, known as La Garañona, a stone can be lobbed from a height of 935 feet into the water below. The place is easily identified, as a large colony of vultures builds its nests between the edge and the sea, and numbers of the birds are usually to be seen. Some of the vistas down the gullies are very beautiful, especially where advantage has been taken of some little terrace or spring to cultivate the soil. These little hanging gardens where the vine, the cane (*arundo donax*), the yam, etc., form a little oasis amongst the surrounding euphorbias or other indigenous scrub, are common in the mountainous parts of the Canaries, and always add greatly to the charm of the view.

To the Group of Mountains to the North East.—Follow the new *carretera* past the Convent Church, to the foot of the **Mña. del Picon** or **de la Atalaya**, as it is called, 1,580 ft., ¾ hr. Go straight up to the wood, then bear to the left and presently climb up a steep path on the north side of the hill. The summit, 1,875 feet, commands a good view of the north coast from Punta del Hidalgo to beyond Buena Vista. Villa Orotava is not visible, but there is an extensive view of the Cumbres from the Rodeos de la Laguna to the Peak. The hill is really an extinct blow hole, and the crater at the top, which has a diameter of 180 yards, is quite perfect. Heather grows round the rim; shade can be obtained under the trees, and altogether the spot is a good one for a picnic. Animals can go to the top.

The small round hill due south, the **Mña. de las Palmas**, 1,965 feet, can easily be ascended by beasts from near the Ermita de la Caridad on the north side. The crater at the top is small but quite perfect. The view is not quite so good as from the Picon, but the terraces of vines so noticeable from the main *carretera*, are interesting as an example of enterprise and industry.

The broken crater between the Mña. de las Palmas and the hotel, is called the **Mña. de las Retamas**, because of the broom growing on its slopes. It can easily be ascended by beasts during dry weather, and is a happy hunting ground for mushrooms about October or November. The best view of Tacoronte is from near the palm tree on the western slope, but both the summits command extensive views. The heights are:—West summit (25 minutes from the Hotel) 1,985 feet; Eastern or Crater summit (5 minutes further away by easy path) 2,100 feet.

The mountain further to the N.E. is called the **Mña. de Guerra**. Those visiting the Mña. del. Picon, can descend from the top to the path crossing the north slope of the same, and ride directly across the fields. The ascent of the Montaña de Guerra must then be made on foot. The pleasantest and shortest way to reach it from the hotel, is to follow the *carretera* to the bridge whence the footpath crosses the fields to the Ermita de la Caridad (next to the large white house), whence pretty bridle paths lead between the two hills to the western slope of the Mña. de Guerra, ¾ hr. Thence on foot to the top, 2,085 feet, about 1 hr. total. Of all the short walks round Tacoronte this is the best. By driving towards La Laguna and turning in at the *fielato*, a road, passable for carriages, leads past the quarry known as the **Cantería de la Huerta Trobisca**, whence there is a path to the top along which horses can pass. Total time to the top a little over one hour. The view far surpasses that from any of the other hills, nearly the whole valley of Tegueste being visible, and the plain between the mountain and the coast lying apparently under one's feet. The crescent-shaped precipices on the north, which are geologically very distinct from the rounded slopes of the *fumaroles* described above, are covered with vegetation. From their exposure to the trade wind, the trees, etc., are all bent in one direction, and the various lichens, leeks and mosses, assume most gorgeous tints as the dryness of summer begins to be felt. Picnic parties can always obtain shelter from the wind, but there is no shade. A few yards to the east of the pinnacle rock, and on the edge of the precipice, is a cave, easily entered, where a numerous party could take refuge in case of rain.

The slopes, precipices and hanging woods beyond the Mña. de Guerra afford countless climbs and rambles. The passes through them are usually provided with paths, leading from the Valle de Guerra, etc., to La Laguna or to some point in the Rodeos, but such paths can be left at any time, and the walk can be extended in accordance with the climbing capabilities of the walker.

The large group of hills beyond Guamasa, chief amongst which is the Mesa Mota, are given amongst the excursions from La Laguna, but can be reached easily from Tacoronte.

To the Valle de Guerra, Tejina and La Laguna.—Pass the Convent Church, and follow the new *carretera*. At $\frac{3}{4}$ hr. on foot, 1,580 feet, pass the base of the Mña. del Picon, leaving same on the right. At $1\frac{1}{2}$ hr., is the Ermita del Rosario in the Valle de Guerra, 690 feet. From here it is possible to reach La Laguna by bearing to the right and passing through Guamasa. Tejina, 490 feet, is 7 miles (11 kils.) from Tacoronte. From here to La Laguna there is a *carretera*, 10 kils. ($6\frac{1}{4}$ miles) in length. (*See* under La Laguna.) Another *carretera* leads to Bajamar on the coast, 3 miles (5 kils.).

To Sauzal.—Pass the Parish Church, and bear to the left along a rough road where animals can pass to Sauzal, $\frac{3}{4}$ hr., 1,000 feet, a small village with a plain church (A.D. 1514), with dome and tower. Just below the houses is a spring, known as Los Lavaderos, and almost immediately under the village is a small natural harbour sometimes used by schooners. A return can be made by a path running along the upper edge of the valley and commanding good views. The *carretera* is reached in $\frac{1}{2}$ hr. at the Finca de Don Siste, about $22\frac{1}{2}$ kilos from Santa Cruz. The walk along the edge of the cliffs is given elsewhere.

To Agua García, the Cumbre and beyond.—A good bridle path leaves the *carretera* about 100 yards east of the hotel and ascends by a fairly easy gradient to the **Fuente de Agua García**, 2,350 feet, in $\frac{1}{2}$ hr. on foot. From here to the spring or *madre*, 2,600 feet, another $\frac{3}{4}$ hr. (follow the water-course). Before and after entering the wood a most remarkable diversity of trees is met with, including the willow, laurel (*viñatico*), cork, broom (*codeso*), wild orange, sweet orange, pear, mulberry, walnut, chestnut, palm and others, the giant heath, which finds its counterpart in Eastern Africa on the slopes of Kilima n'jaro, being most abundant at the commencement of the forest. Some of the heath trees are over five feet in girth and as much as fifty feet high, but these are utterly dwarfed by the immense laurel trees around them.

The tall heather commonly met with in the island, and which sometimes attains a height of 20 feet or more, is mingled with the blackberry, the bracken and a variety of ferns. Altogether the walk along the water-course is most beautiful, and the little triangular forest will be found fairly extensive by those exploring its ends and depths.

By leaving the woods of Agua Garcia on the right, and by keeping the Mña. de Cerro also on the right, paths leads to La Esperanza, 3,280 feet, in about 2 hours from the hotel, *or*, by bearing more to the left, La Laguna can be reached *via* Los Ortigales in about 3 hrs., *or* by bearing to the right above the Mña. de Cerro any part of the Cumbres can be ascended.

By turning sharp to the right below Agua Garcia, and by keeping more or less along that level, La Matanza can be reached in about $1\frac{1}{2}$ hours. The groups of thatched cottages passed on the way are very characteristic. About $\frac{3}{4}$ hr. from Agua Garcia there is a small spring issuing from below a grove of giant heath and chestnut trees (Barranco de las Higueras). Fortunately the water makes the grove sacred or the heath trees would long since have disappeared.

The most direct route to the top of the island, and one that is quite practicable for animals, leaves the woods of Agua Garcia on the left and climbs across the Monte Verde to a stone beacon, 3,200 feet, in 1 hr. from the hotel. From here there is a most magnificent view of the peak and of the wooded slopes above La Matanza, etc., this being a good spot for a picnic. From the beacon a path leads in 1¼ hrs. to the Ermita de la Esperanza on the left, and down to La Matanza, 1½ hrs., on the right.

Following the direct path, the Monte del Gobierno is entered, and a gradual climb through scented laurels, etc., which bears slightly to the left, leads to the foot of the pine forest, 1¾ hrs. from the hotel, 4,000 feet, when turn to the left up a small barranco and climb up a steep path through the pines, leaving the red mountain (Mña. de la Fuente Fria) to the left, and so to the **Fuente Fria**, a constant spring of water, 4,400 feet, 2 hrs. total. A further climb of 15 minutes now leads to the broad, stony plain of **Las Lagunetas**, 4,600 feet.

The plain is crossed by numerous paths leading from La Laguna, La Esperanza, etc., to La Matanza, etc. By bearing to the left round the Cabeza del Toro and the Mña. de Cerro, a return to the hotel can be made in about 2¼ hrs., *or* by travelling due south the top of the Barranco Hondo (South Side) is crossed, the little spring known as the Fuentiña is passed, and **Igueste de Candelaria** is entered in about 3 hrs. from the hotel. The path runs through a great pine forest and commands good views of Santa Cruz, etc. A few minutes below Igueste is the *carretera* connecting Santa Cruz with Güimar.

Those travelling to **Güimar**, etc., should keep more to the right, crossing the plain of Las Lagunetas and climbing straight through the pine-clad hills in front. An uninterrupted ascent leads, in 3¼ hrs. total, to the little spring on the N. side of the **Mña. de los Chupaderos**, 5,270 ft. Leave the path and climb for 5 minutes straight up to the summit of the Montaña, 5,400 feet, the remains of a vigorous blow-hole, still covered with slag and volcanic bombs and almost destitute of vegetation. From here there is an extensive view embracing both coasts from Candelaria to the Lighthouse at Anaga Point on the south, and from the Lighthouse to Punta de Teno on the north. Orotava Valley and the Puerto lie far below, but the Villa is hidden by the Cuesta de Bacalao.

The path now crosses a curious ridge of white tufa, and at 3½ hrs. ascends to the higher Cumbres, leading to **Pedro Gil** in about another 1½ hrs., whence paths lead down to Arafo, Güimar, Villa Orotava or to the Cañadas, for which refer elsewhere. In case of losing the way in this part of the island, bear to the north, as all but a few descents towards the south are dangerous.

From where the white tufa ends, a descent can be made on foot only by the ridge to the right. Visitors will not fail to notice the terraced barranco at this point, and those acquainted with South Africa will be struck with its resemblance to Bushman's Kop between Molteno and Queenstown, the *codeso* with which the slopes are covered being scarcely distinguishable at a short distance from the South African mimosa. Artists in search of effect will be delighted with the extraordinary and gorgeous colouring of the surrounding rocks. The surface water runs into the Barranco Hondo (North Side), crossed by the *carretera* between Victoria and Santa Ursula.

A descent of 1,000 feet leads to the bed of the barranco, whence Victoria or La Matanza can easily be reached, or paths through the forest lead past the aqueduct above Victoria, 4,000 feet, 1 hr. from the top, to Tacoronte (hotel) in about 3 hrs. It is well to have a compass here, as the paths are too numerous to give in detail.

Main Road.—A little beyond the hotel the new road, mentioned in the excursions, branches off for Tejina.

At 14½ m. (22½ kil.) a path leads in 20 min. down to **Sauzal.** At 15⅓ m. (24½ kil.) **La Matanza**, 1,420 feet, is reached. Two inns: Fonda de Maria, one dollar per diem; Fonda de José Manuel, 4 pesetas. Population 2,030.

La Matanza, 1,920 inhabitants, with a good view of the Peak, is a pleasant spot to spend a few days at in fine weather. It is here that the Spaniards, after driving the Guanches from La Laguna, were repulsed and had to retreat to Santa Cruz. (*See* History.) The village itself is some 200 ft. above the *carretera*.

At **San Antonio**, a small village ¾ hr. up the hills, a curious *fête* is held in January, when all the beasts in the neighbourhood are brought round to be blessed.

Victoria, pop. 2,789, 1,350 ft., is 1½ m. further along the main road, 17¼ m. (27½ kils.) from Santa Cruz.

The church lies prettily embowered in trees a little above the road and near the spot where the Spaniards, on their return to the north of the island, revenged their losses at La Matanza.

Pilgrim's Pass.—A badly-kept bridle path leads from here to Arafo in about 6 hrs. *See* Arafo for further on, or for diversion along the central cordillera.

At 19 m. (30¼ kil.) the old *carretera* dips into the deep **Barranco Hondo**, descends to the bridge, which lies some 800 feet above the sea, and ascends to a grove of palms, immediately after which (20 m. = 32 kil.) **Santa Ursula**, 920 feet, with square and church. Population 2,119.

The new *carretera*, which branches off at the 29 kil. post, will avoid the descent by taking a circuit, the distance by either way being about the same.

Below the village is a large villa commanding a very fine view of the Orotava Valley, which is considered by many to be the remains of an immense crater, corresponding to the valley or crater of Güimar on the S. An avenue a little on the Santa Cruz side of Sta. Ursula, leads to the villa, close to which is a 9-hole golf links, belonging to the Grand Hotel, Orotava, and laid out by John Dunn. A substantial stone dressing-house has been built on the Links.

A little further on, the main road turns to the left, and the same valley is seen from what is generally called by foreigners "Humboldt's Corner," as it was near here, on the old road, that the great traveller threw himself on the ground, and saluted the sight as the finest in the world.

From near this spot, *i.e.*, at about 33 kils. from Santa Cruz, it is proposed to make a new *carretera* to cross the Barranco de Llarena and the top of the Villa at a level or at an easy gradient, and thence to carry it through La Perdoma and La Cruz Santa, to the church at Realejo Alto. Here it will meet another new section, 4 kilos. in length, allowing of a return at a lower level, to the *carretera* of Icod at a point just below the Mña. de Chaves, 41¾ kils. from Santa Cruz.

It is also proposed to make a road from Realejo Alto across the Barranco del Padronato to Realejo Bajo, and thence to the existing *carretera* below the last-named town at 44 kilos. from Sta. Cruz. The completion of this section will make the new upper road through the Villa part of a high level through route from Santa Cruz to Icod.

A slight description of the panorama, seen from Humboldt's corner, may be of service. Close below, on the left, some 4 m. from the sea, are the spires and domes of Villa Orotava. On the same level the eye can trace, by a broken line of houses, a road leading across the upper valley through La Cruz Santa to the two Realejos, which are only partially visible. Beyond these and on the heights is the little village of Icod el Alto (1,720 ft.). In the far distance are the white houses and the rock of Garachico. Returning along the coast, San Juan de la Rambla is seen, rather beyond the extreme W. of the valley or crater, and about 9 m. away. There are scattered groups of houses everywhere, the local names for which are of little importance; and lastly the Puerto itself on a little surf-encircled promontory. Above the Puerto is a crater or cinder heap (the Mña. de las Arenas), behind which is another, the M. de Chaves, and, in a straight line, yet another much smaller one, the M. de los Frailes. The opposite wall of the valley rises to the Cañadas, which are immediately beyond the Fortaleza, so called from its resemblance to a military glacis. The back is composed of the central ridge of the island. The mountains on the left are thickly wooded, and numerous fires may usually be seen where the charcoal burners are at work. This part of the valley is very rough riding, but some beautiful excursions may be made.

Beyond the Fortaleza is the Peak, which, although more hidden here than in La Matanza or Tacoronte, stills forms a majestic pyramid of colossal dimensions.

The angles of the incline of the Valley of Orotava are :—In the lower part, 5° to 10°; at about 1,600 feet the slope increases to 20° and over, but at 3,000 feet again falls to about 10°. The steep mountain slopes of the Cumbres commence at about 5,500 to 6,000 feet, but these are not inclined at so great an angle as the walls to the west and to the east of the Valley, where the angle in some parts is from 30° to 40° or even 50°.

The road now descends and crosses the **Bco. del Pino** and the **Bco. de Llarena**, which may be explored both up and down, as well for the sake of the scenery as for the numerous ferns, etc., to be found. At 23 m. (37 kils.) the *Empalme* or Junction, 900 feet, where the roads to the Villa and the Puerto separate.

The **Villa**, 24 m. ($38\frac{1}{2}$ kils.), is a little higher on the left, and the **Puerto**, 27 m. (43 kils.), is reached by a winding road which passes to the W. of the **Mña. de las Arenas**, separating there from the road to Icod (Junction 500 feet above the sea, $24\frac{1}{2}$ m. = $39\frac{1}{3}$ kils.), skirts the **Bco. de las Cabezas**, and bearing to the left, where the private drive leads to the Grand Hotel, enters the town. The pavement has been improved of late years, and all the hotels can now be reached in the carriage.

From a point somewhere near the Mña. de las Arenas a new carriage road is projected, leading eastwards to the Botanical Gardens, and descending probably by La Paz and the Barranco Martianez to the Puerto.

Passengers in the *public coach* must go to the Villa or must change for the Puerto at the Empalme. The same remark applies on the return.

Puerto de la Cruz, Orotava, 5,553 inhabitants, N. side of Teneriffe, is 27 m. (43 kils.) from Santa Cruz; 4¾ m. (7½ kils.) by the *carretera*, and 3½ m. (5½ kils.) by bridle road from the Villa, and 15¾m. (25 kils.) from Icod. (Letters must be addressed Puerto Orotava; telegrams—Puerto-cruz.)

Passengers by sea are landed by boats on the mole. One peseta each person. Packages, half a peseta each; double at night. There are no customs duties on luggage, but cases may be opened at the fielato.

Coaches to and from the Villa twice a day, changing at the Empalme for Santa Cruz or Icod. (*See* Time Table.)

Hotels.—The Grand Hotel, about 350 ft. above the sea. Airy situation, fine views, and extensive grounds, 10s. to 20s. a day; Hotel Martianez (old Grand), good position and large gardens near Bco. Martianez, about 10s.; Hotel Marquesa, facing the Plaza de la Iglesia, from 6 pesetas.

Boarding Houses.—The Misses Nicol (private), 32, Calle Perez Zamora, centrally and pleasantly situated, about £10 a month.

A few residents in the valley accept guests according to private arrangements.

There is a good circulating library (English). The town is to be lighted by electricity, this light being already supplied to many of the private houses.

(*For advertisements, see under Orotava at the end of the book.*)

If enough passengers require them, waggonettes leave the Grand Hotel for the golf links at Santa Ursula, fare 2s. each.

Public Buildings and Churches.—The **Convento de las Monjas**, an old convent now used as a school in which the cockfights are held on Sundays. **Iglesia (Church) de N. S. de la Peña de Francia.** Fair interior; the tower was completed in 1897. **Convento de S. Francisco**, now shut up.

The **English Church** with parsonage adjoining is in the grounds above the Grand Hotel, and is well worth a visit as a curious example of what British enthusiasm can accomplish in a foreign valley, which, half-a-dozen years before the foundation stone was laid, was almost unknown to the general public. Its completion was largely owing to the munificence of the late Mr. Walter Long-Boreham, but other visitors and residents were extraordinarily liberal. The stained glass windows are really excellent modern productions; there is a good organ and a great part of the church is well paved with encaustic tiles. The chaplain is resident all the year round.

Squares.—**The Plaza de la Iglesia**, recently much improved. **The Plaza de la Constitucion**, near the mole, well shaded.

Puerto Orotava, the most widely-advertised health-resort in the Canary Islands, has already been so much written about that it is almost impossible to venture an opinion without contradicting some one. Having spent one whole winter there, and other winters, or portions of them, in various parts of the Canaries and Madeira, the writer begs to relate his own experiences, which he hopes may be of service.

In normal weather clouds form around the Peak shortly after sunrise and descend more or less into the valley in accordance with the temperature. In mid-winter the shadow should not reach the Puerto in fine weather. It may thus be raining in the Villa whilst the sun is shining over the mile or so of land next the coast. In the evening the Peak should again be clear. It is repeated that this is normal weather, such as lasts at times for weeks. There are seasons when, for days at a stretch, no clouds at all are formed. In the Puerto the warmest temperature is found. If the invalid ceases to benefit from it and becomes lax, or is attacked by diarrhœa, a move further up should be made.

In a good winter there is but little cold weather, but what cold there may be is felt, as it is accompanied by damp. From the middle of January to the end of February is the worst time, and, in a bad year, may be disagreeable, the sky being overcast day after day and the sun being obscured by the thick mantle of clouds which will then envelope the island. Such winters are, however, the exception. In cases of widespread disturbance the influence of the Peak is overcome and the wind bloweth from whither it listeth, but both here and elsewhere in the islands a day when there is no sunshine, or when one cannot be out of doors for at least three or four hours is almost unknown.

Such statements are scarcely more than a repetition of what has already been said in the chapter for "Invalids," to which the reader will turn for further details. The writer wishes to point out that Orotava has many friends and enemies, some damaging it unwillingly by describing it as an impossible earthly paradise, others vilifying it because they really were not happy there, or because of jealous motives. Orotava, like Funchal, Santa Cruz, Las Palmas, etc., is only one of the units out of which an efficient oceanic sanatorium is being gradually evolved.

Mention must here be made of the new carriage roads projected in the upper part of the valley. When completed they will be of inestimable value from a medical point of view, as the invalid will be able to enjoy a daily drive in a bracing atmosphere and thus to shake off the feeling of depression and inertia which a long sojourn in a somewhat relaxing situation frequently entails. Nor will the bracing air be the only advantage. Change is almost as necessary mentally as physically, and the contrast between the geological contours and laboured vegetation of the lower valley, and the expansive slopes, precipitous ravines and superabundant verdure of the higher levels, must be a daily delight to any man with eyes to see, and especially so to the sufferer fresh from home, or newly emerged from some sick room with its rows of bottles and general flavour of sour milk and faded flowers.

The town itself is rather pretty, especially near the mole, where the groups of old houses and balconies offer some capital opportunities to the artist. One of the most lovely views of the valley is to be had from the smaller jetty. Permission would readily be given to any one wishing to sketch from some particular roof or *mirador*. The rocks at low tide are full of interest to visitors, and bathing may be indulged in in places, in spite of the magnificent breakers constantly rolling in. It is to be hoped that the authorities will shortly see their way to provide proper accommodation for bathers of both sexes.

At one time the Puerto was a very prosperous place, and, in 1812 to 1815, was at the height of its commercial prosperity. When steamers replaced sailing vessels, the ports to the south of the islands soon took the place of the old ones to the north, although the neighbourhood of the latter is usually the most productive. On the day of S. Juan (June 23), there is a great fiesta in the Puerto.

The centre of the valley has been opened up by the construction of the Grand Hotel, by its gardens and by a group of English villas. These crown a bluff where formerly there was an inaccessible and useless stream of lava.

In the grounds of the hotel is a private course where *corridas de sortija* are organised by the Grand Hotel during the season. (The public *corridas* are held in the bed of the Barranco Martianez.)

Walks and Excursions inside the Valley.—On the E. of the town is the Bco. Martianez, and, immediately beyond, the cliffs of La Paz, once a rendezvous where games of skill were held by the Guanches and where it is said that the articles of peace between the natives and the Spanish invaders were formally ratified.

The path which crosses the Bco. near the sea leads up the cliff by a steep path below an old Guanche burying-cave, where the bones may still be seen sticking out. It then passes the Fuente Martianez ($\frac{1}{4}$ hr.), a very good spring whence all drinking-water should be brought, and follows the face of the cliff by a small path (perfectly safe to careful walkers) below and above the most extraordinary volcanic rocks and air chambers in the lava, now exposed owing to the inroads of the sea. There is also a deposit of red ochre, and many wild flowers and maiden-hair ferns can be picked. Altogether this is a most interesting walk, and may be prolonged indefinitely towards Sauzal, crossing the mouths of the barrancos, many of which are exceedingly deep, or ascending the bed of any of the same to the *carretera*, whence a return home may be made.

If the bed of the Bco. Martianez itself is ascended from the Puerto, the cinder heap (Mña. de las Arenas) is skirted and the *carretera* gained just above and to the E. of the same, $\frac{3}{4}$ hr., grand basaltic rocks; *or* a path crosses the same Bco. and ascends by bridle road in $\frac{1}{2}$ hr. to the **Botanical Gardens**, about 500 feet above the sea. One-third up the last, a road to the left leads to La Paz, and may be followed along the top of the cliff. Less interesting than the lower path.

The Botanical Gardens, founded in 1795, are a most agreeable resort. All the plants of the Archipelago suitable to a garden may be seen here, and a few pleasant hours be spent under the shade of a cosmopolitan group of trees and a collection of flowers and creepers, scarcely to be found elsewhere. The original object of the gardens, namely, to provide a place where tropical plants might be acclimatised on their way to Europe, seems at present to have been almost lost sight of. A list of the plants still growing in it in 1893, was published by Dr. Morris, of Kew, in "Plants and Gardens of the Canary Islands," 1895. (The nearest way from the Grand Hotel to the Gardens passes partly through the grounds of a private villa.)

Passing the Gardens the road from below bears to the right, then to the left, the *carretera* is crossed, and the Villa is reached in a short hour from the start.

On emerging from the Barranco Martianez and gaining the *carretera*, by bearing to the right the **Mña. de las Arenas** is passed. On the west side of this a private carriage road leads to the summit, 850 feet, whence there is a good view. Permission to ascend this can be obtained from the owner.

To Realejo on foot.—Towards the W. a long street leads from the Puerto and along the coast, passing the Chapel of San Telmo, below which is the mineral spring discovered in 1895. Walking easily the **Cemetery** and an old fort are reached in 10 min.; the Lazareto and Punta Brava in 20 min. (Punta Brava is a garden and farm which has been prettily laid out and can be visited by those obtaining permission). A little further on are some handsome clumps of *euphorbia canariensis*. At 30 min., the path turns up to the left, but it is possible to walk for a considerable distance round the cliff or to descend to the fine, bold rocks. At 45 min., the old road is entered, by which a return can be made direct to the Puerto in ½ hr. *or* the walk continued to the right through **El Toscal de la Gorvorana** and across the **Bco. del Patronato** to the *carretera* below **Realejo Bajo** in 1½ hrs. total. Just below the junction of the roads but above the *carretera* is a very handsome young dragon tree.

Realejo can also be reached by leaving the *carretera* just beyond the **Cabezas** (the houses immediately above the Puerto), crossing the **Bco. de las Cabezas**, and keeping along the old road for 35 min., when turn to the left and rejoin the *carretera*, 1¼ m. from Realejo. Time on foot, 1½ hrs.

The bridle path leading up the Bco. de las Cabezas to **La Cruz Santa**, ¾ hr. (and eventually to the Cañadas) can be followed to the right to Realejo, 1¼ hrs., or to the left to the Villa, 1¼ hrs. The Barranco changes its name above the Puerto to the Bco. de la Vera, and afterwards to the Bco. de la Cruz Santa.

The **drive to Realejo** along the main road occupies about ¾ hr. and is 5 m. (8 kil.). *See* further on.

Any of the cinder heaps in the valley can be climbed, and all command extensive views.

Besides the above there are several walks amongst the farms, where those can go who are not afraid of dogs. As all these walks are on other people's land, visitors chancing to meet the proprietor should adopt the Spanish standard of courtesy, which is far more formal than our own.

Excursions to the Peak, Cañadas, Agua Manza, etc., follow the description of the Villa. To la Corona, Icod el Alto, etc., follow Realejo. For drives on the main road, *see* the large print.

Villa Orotava, 9,188 inhab., 1,100 ft. Formerly Arautápala, the capital of the Menceyato of Taoro, 24 m. (38½ kil.) from Santa Cruz, 4½ m. (7 kil.) by the *carretera*, and 3¼ m. (5½ kil.) by bridle path from the Puerto, and 15½ m. (25 kil.) from Icod.

Fondas.—Hotel del Pico, near the Public Gardens. 1$ per day.

The Villa has been lighted by electricity since 1894.

Coaches to and from the Puerto twice a day, changing at the Empalme. (*See* time table.)

Public Buildings.—For the convenience of visitors from the Puerto, these are arranged in the best order in which to take them when ascending the Calle del Agua, *i.e.*, the bridle road.

On the left the old Convent and Church de Santo Domingo. Pretty patio, and interior of Church handsome. A few houses higher up is the **Spanish Club**. Ascend and bear to the left to the Plaza de la Constitucion, whence there is a fine view of town and valley. At the end of the Plaza is the **Church and Convent of San Francisco.**

Walk on a little further, turn down to the left, and return across the town by a lower street to below the Church. Here is the house of the Sauzal family, in whose garden may be seen the tallest palm in the islands, 110 ft. high. Four hundred years ago it was much the same height as it is to-day, and was a famous Gaunche landmark. Near this was the old dragon-tree previously mentioned, the hollow trunk of which, after having served the aboriginals as a temple for ages, was put to the same use by the Spanish conquerors, who held Mass there. According to Mrs. Murray it measured in 1843,—girth, near the ground, 52 ft.; height to lowest branches, $16\frac{1}{2}$ ft.; to the top, $65\frac{1}{2}$ ft. According to other writers it was from 75 to 95 ft. in height. In the house of the Cologan family, immediately above, is a chestnut tree planted by the Spaniards in 1496, which measures $27\frac{1}{2}$ ft. round. Opposite is the **Convent and Church de las Monjas**, now closed. A few paces higher is the **Iglesia de la Concepcion**, a fine building with a good interior and a fair marble pulpit. Some of the silver plate in this church formerly belonged to old St. Paul's Cathedral in London. It appears to have been sold in the time of Oliver Cromwell.

This is the fashionable part of the town. At the back, a little higher than the Church, are a group of large buildings with admirable balconies, more particularly that of the last on the left, which is painted, and which, as well as the interior of the house, is modelled after the far-famed Casa de Toledo. Now descend again to the left, pass the **New Town Hall and Gardens**, and turn up the hill to the right. At two-thirds up the **Church of San Juan**, with good roof to nave and worthy of a visit, and at the top a most picturesque conjunction of aqueducts.

From the aqueducts turn down to the right, and, descending a steep street, pass the hospital with beautiful vista of three arches in the entrance, formerly a convent. The projected *carretera* to Realejo would leave the Villa from a spot near here.

A return to the Puerto can now be made past the Church, or, by turning to the right and passing the prettily laid-out Public Gardens at the entrance of the town, the *carretera* can be taken if desired.

There is a large tomb of coloured marbles to be seen in a garden belonging to the Marquesa de la Quinta, with an inscription resenting the conduct of a local priest to her deceased son, a Freemason. Visitors are permitted to enter here and elsewhere by sending in their cards or procuring introductions, but the gardens in the Villa are small and admission must not be looked upon as a right.

No one can enter the Villa without being struck by its quiet exclusive character. Many visitors stop here on account of the climate, which is much fresher than that of the port.

Every year, on the eighth day after Corpus Christi, a religious *fête* is held in the Villa, when the streets are carpeted with flowers, elaborate designs being carried out in a most curious and remarkable manner.

The new carriage road which is to connect the top of the Villa with the *carretera* near Santa Ursula, and with the Church at Realejo Alto, *viâ* La Perdoma and La Cruz Santa, will be a great convenience to residents and visitors.

The proposed *carretera* to lead across the summit of the island to Vilaflor, a distance of about 60 kilos., though apparently an extravagance would really be of great benefit to the island.

Walks and Excursions.—*Viâ* **La Perdoma and La Cruz Santa to Realejo.**—A bridle path, which is level for some distance, leaves the Villa just above the Hospital and leads across the valley to **La Perdoma** (¾ hr.), **La Cruz Santa** (1 hr.), **Realejo Alto** (1½ hrs.), and across the Bco. Patronato to **Realejo Bajo** and the *carretera* in 1¾ hours. This road communicates at more than one point with both the upper and lower parts of the valley.

Another bridle path, parallel to the above, leaves the Villa below the Church and crosses just above the Mña. de Chaves, through pleasant country to Realejo Alto in 1½ hrs.

To La Florída, Sta. Ursula, Victoria, etc.—Passing the aqueducts at the top of the town and bearing to the left **La Florída** is passed in ¾ hr.; the **Bco. de Llarena** and the base of the **Cuesta de Bacalao** are crossed, and the *carretera* is entered when desired in about 2 to 3 hrs. or less.

To Arafo, etc., *viâ* **the Pilgrim's Pass.**—Follow the same path and join the pass above Victoria in about 3 hrs. and to Arafo in 6½ hrs. (*See* Arafo.)

To Arafo or Güimar *viâ* **Pedro Gil.**—Ascend straight up the Villa leaving Agua Manza, 3,930 ft., 1¾ hrs., where permission to pass the night in the farmhouse can be obtained, about a mile to the left, and so on to Güimar, 7 hrs. (*See* **Güimar.**) One of the very finest excursions in the Archipelago.

To the Pinar.—The **Pinar** above La Florida and the Villa, bounded on the W. by Agua Manza and on the S.E. by the Mña. Blanca (not that adjoining the Peak) is full of romantic beauty and affords numberless climbs and walks. The paths are steep and easily lost in foggy weather. A guide should be taken as this part of the island, at the height where the forest is found, is very subject to the sudden formation of clouds. The paths in this direction communicate with those described under Tacoronte.

To the Cañadas and the Peak.—From the Puerto.—Since the paths have been repaired by the English visitors, the best way, especially in wet weather, is to drive to Realejo and mount the mules there. Both the Realejos are passed through, and the path taken to the **Palo Blanco**, $1\frac{1}{2}$ hrs. from the Puerto, 2,200 ft., where water can be obtained. This is at the foot of the **Monte Verde**. At $2\frac{1}{2}$ hrs., the top of the **Monte Verde** is reached, the slope so far being at about 12°. The road now becomes more even and passes among rough hillocks where the heather has given place to the codeso, pumice-stone being occasionally seen. At $3\frac{1}{3}$ hrs. the codeso ceases and the retama begins. Passing through the **Portillo** (7,150 ft., $4\frac{1}{4}$ hrs.), the **Cañadas** appear as a glaring desert with ranges of mountains in the distance, and the Peak standing grim and solitary in the centre. The path now leads to the S.E. side of the **Montaña Blanca**, a round trachytic hump, 8,985 ft. high, adjoining the E. base of the Peak, and thickly covered with small pieces of pumice, of which a certain quantity is extracted and shipped home to Europe.

The foot of the **Lomo Tieso** or cone, which rises at an angle of 28°, is reached in $7\frac{1}{2}$ hrs., time being given for lunch. A well-marked path climbs the E. face of this, over lava blocks and loose cinders, to the **Estancia de los Ingleses**, 9,710 ft. ($8\frac{3}{4}$ hrs.). If there is time before sunset, after which it becomes suddenly cold, a short rest may now be taken, then on to the **Alta Vista**, 10,702 ft. ($9\frac{1}{2}$ hrs.), a small space below a bifurcation of lava on which a stone hut has been built.

This hut is the result of the philanthropy of Mr. G. Graham-Toler. It has three rooms with bedsteads, bedding and washing conveniences, stoves and other necessaries, and stabling for about ten beasts. Its construction has conferred a great benefit on those ascending the Peak. A small charge is made for the use of the hut. Visitors are advised that there is still a heavy debt on the building which should, in all fairness, be gradually liquidated. Hon. Treasurer, Mr. Thomas Reid.

As Alta Vista faces the E., it is not necessary to climb to the top before sunrise. In this matter travellers will of course please themselves, but the cold is often severe, more so than at sundown when the rocks continue to shed a little warmth. As the sun rises it is seen reflected in the sea as a round ball; the waves are invisible from so far away, and any clouds there may be seem rather to rest upon the water than to be three or four thousand feet in the air. At sunset the shadow of the Peak is thrown like a great pyramid to an immense distance. When the track is in order, mules can be used for a short way above Alta Vista, except when there is deep snow, when they must often stop much lower down.

Leaving the camp, tell the guides to keep to the right on the large blocks of lava. At $1\frac{1}{2}$ hrs., the **Rambleta** (11,700 ft.) is reached. This is the crater from which the Pilon or Sugar Loaf rose. It is now only distinguishable by the temporary decrease in the steepness of ascent, by the change of colour and by the fact that no lava streams are to be found issuing from higher up. The stones and dust rolling down the Sugar Loaf gradually widened its base till it covered the parent crater. One hundred feet below this side of the Rambleta, which, by the way, is considerably lower on the W., is the **Nariz**, the first blow-hole encountered. The angle of the Pilon itself is from 33° to 38° and the **summit** (12,192 ft.), which is of a whitish colour and which is believed to contain a large percentage of sulphur, is reached in about 2 hrs., or $11\frac{1}{2}$ hrs. altogether. For the purposes of comparison it may be mentioned that the angle of the cone of Vesuvius is from 40° to 45°.

The little crater at the top is about 80 ft. deep and 300 ft. in diameter. The centre is smooth and in colour white and bright yellow, tinged with red here and there. Many of the blow-holes, which are about two or three inches across, emit a sulphurous vapour of such heat that it is impossible to bear the hand near them. Any one may safely walk about the inside, but care must be taken or the chemical deposits will spoil the clothes. Birds, bees, flies and spiders are found congregated here for the warmth.

As regards the view, those who cannot ascend the mountain would probably greatly help their imagination by looking at a lunar crater through a telescope. The surroundings are the essence of desolation and ruin. On one side the rounded summit of the Montaña Blanca, on the other the threatening crater of **Chahorra**, sometimes called the **Pico Viejo**, $\frac{3}{4}$ of a mile in diameter, 10,500 ft. high, once a boiling cauldron and even now ready to burst into furious life at any moment. Below the once circular basin of the Cañadas, seamed with streams of lava and surrounded by its jagged and many-coloured walls. Around a number of volcanoes standing, as Piazzi Smyth says, like fish on their tails with widely gaping mouths. Below the pine forest and the sea, with the "Six Satellites" floating in the distance, the enormous horizon giving the impression that the looker-on is in a sort of well rather than on a height which, taken in relation to its surroundings, is second to none in the world. The sun rises 12' 55" earlier on the top of the Peak than it does on the coast immediately below.

A descent is made over large lava blocks to the N.E., and the **Ice Cave** (11,040 ft.) is visited. An entrance can be made from above by means of ladders. The cavern is divided into three long passages, snow and ice remaining unmelted inside all through the summer. The natives believe that it is connected with the interior of the mountain and the Guanche burial cave below Icod. Alta Vista is reached again in about 1 hr. from the summit.

Other roads from the Puerto to the Peak are :—By the bed of the Bco. de las Cabezas through **La Cruz Santa**, 1,450 ft., $\frac{3}{4}$ hr., to the **Palo Blanco**, $1\frac{1}{2}$ hrs., and through the **Portillo** as before, *or* drive to Realejo Bajo and ride up to **Icod el Alto**, 1,720 ft., $1\frac{3}{4}$ hrs. from the Puerto, across the **Corona** and pass the **Fuente Pedro**, a spring marked by two trees, $2\frac{3}{4}$ hrs., up the **Monte Verde**, and over the **Fortaleza**, 5 hrs., into the Cañadas, the tracks followed by those coming *via* the Portillo being joined at about $5\frac{1}{2}$ hrs. This route is rather longer than the others and is best taken on the return journey, but should not be used in rainy weather.

The best road from the Villa is to take the **Perdoma** Road above the Hospital, turn up through a gate sharp to the left at $\frac{3}{4}$ hr. and make for the **Fuente de la Cruz**, 3,350 ft. The path from the Palo Blanco to the Portillo is then joined. Time a little less than the first route given. This track should also be avoided in wet weather, when the start should be made, as before stated, from Realejo. There are other paths known to the guides which need not be described.

Hints to those Climbing the Peak or the Cañadas :—It is possible for a very active man to walk up the Peak and back at a stretch. To do this a moonlight night should be chosen and the walk so timed that the summit is gained as near sunrise as possible. The usual time of departure is in the forenoon so that there is time to make things comfortable in the hut before nightfall.

The ordinary plan is to take a mule and a man to each traveller, with extra beasts and men to look after the wraps, water, and other necessaries. Plenty of clothing is wanted during the night which is sometimes very cold. Care should be taken that the men do not drink all the water.

A firm hand is necessary with the guides, who cannot be trusted in any but the finest weather. When snow is on the ground they are of very little use. Any attempt to shirk their duties should be stopped at once. Matters cannot be left in their hands as is customary in Switzerland. Taking it as a general rule, only very strong and experienced climbers should attempt the Peak in mid-winter.

The observations given regarding the ordinary height of the trade-wind clouds, etc., in the article on "Permanent Currents of the Atlantic," should be read by those wishing to explore the upper part of the island.

According to Piazzi Smyth, the dust haze exists up to 9,000 feet. Beyond this point the shadows are very dark and distance is very difficult to estimate, whilst photographers will find details faithfully reproduced from very far off. Fires can easily be made from the dead retama, a broom which is only found on the Cañadas, and which is very odoriferous. The native palm-tree bee-hives are often taken up in the summer in order that their inmates may extract the honey from the flower.

Von Buch suggested that the Cañadas are the floor of a crater of elevation formed under the sea, and Piazzi Smyth thought that he found evidence of the action of waves on the outside of the S.W. wall at about 7,000 ft., leading him to believe in a slow and unequal rise of the whole island. Signs of great heat are visible at times in the basaltic side walls of the crater, which vary in height from 1,900 ft. at Guajara on the S.E. to seven or eight hundred feet at other places, the N. wall being lower than the S. From the Fortaleza on the N., to where they recommence on the S.W., the Cañadas and their walls have been destroyed and carried away by successive floods of lava. In addition to this large gap, the gateway or Portillo above Orotava would allow easy egress to any stream of lava or flood of water coming in this direction. In fact the whole remaining basin of the Cañadas slopes towards it. It is probably owing to this fact that the disastrous rush of water, which so enlarged the Bco. de las Cabezas, burst upon the unsuspecting valley on the 6th November, 1826. (*See* under "Storms.")

The Cañadas or crater itself, about 7,200 ft. high, is an undulating plain partially overspread by yellow pumice-stone, which, in conjunction with the hard blue shadow, has, from a distance and in certain lights, a green appearance almost like grass. This fact has led to some very erroneous statements about the vegetation by others besides Père Feuillée. Lava streams intersect or cover the greater part of its surface. Progress is made between these, where the crevices are filled up with soft rubble, or by skirting the outside wall. Other remarks will be found in the "Geological" article.

Obsidian is common but is generally very friable. Almost the only plant that grows is the retama, which is found from about 6,000 to about 10,000 ft. and of which the bushes are sometimes very large. An interesting evidence of the rate of descent of the hills of rapilli may be seen in the distances separating the withered branches of the dead retama from the parent root, the state of the branches showing how regular is the progress. An indigenous Violet (*Viola Teydensis*) is to be found. Lavender, grass and a few other plants slightly relieve the monotony of the desert, and in one or two instances a pine-tree just shows its head over the top of the wall.

From the Valley of Orotava to Vilaflor, etc.—Take the road to the Peak a short distance beyond the Portillo, then bear to the left. (At 4½ hrs. a path climbs the hills on the left in the direction of La Laguna.) At about 5 hrs. is a cave, to which a door has been fixed, in which shelter can be found for several men and animals.

At about 6¼ hrs. is the **Fuente de la Grieta**, a perpetual spring of excellent water. This is a good p ace to camp out during the summer.

At 7 hrs. the spring below **Guajara** is reached, another convenient spot for camping.

In fine weather any one can sleep out in the open, but it is advisable to keep a good fire going all night. The guide will soon find a sheltered corner in amongst the lava. Wraps of course must be taken, and insect powder is advisable.

The character of the Cañadas is here different to what it is nearer Orotava. The pumice-stone desert interspersed with lava has become a desert of lava with a fringe of pumice, along which it is alone possible to make headway. The surrounding walls are very high. Up these the path is carried to Vilaflor, passing only a short distance below Piazzi Smyth's astronomical station. From here the road descends through a constant succession of cinder heaps, dolomite rocks, pumice stone, etc. At $8\frac{3}{4}$ hrs. the **Fuente de Ucanca**, after which the pines above **Vilaflor** are seen, and the town is entered ($10\frac{1}{2}$ hrs.). (From here to Icod or for the S. of the island, *see* the journey from Santa Cruz round the S. of the island.)

As there is not much inducement to descend to Vilaflor for one night, those on the way to **Guia, Santiago,** or **Icod,** can continue along the path inside the Cañadas past **Los Azulejos** and the **Peñones de Garcia,** to the **Boca. de los Tauces,** where the pass from Vilaflor to Icod is joined in about $1\frac{1}{2}$ hrs. and a saving of over 4 hrs. is effected.

Those camping out on this side can easily ascend the Peak. The path from the south is believed to be better during the winter than that usually chosen by the guides.

Main Road.—Leaving Orotava for the west, at $25\frac{3}{4}$ m. ($41\frac{1}{3}$ kils.) from Santa Cruz, and 2 kils. from the point where the Puerto and the Icod roads divide, a branch *carretera* to the left leads to Realejo Alto, $2\frac{1}{2}$ m (4 kils.) from the junction. It keeps the Mña. de Chaves a little on the right, and, if the road from the Villa through Realejo Alto should ever be made, will form part of a very pleasant circular drive through La Cruz Santa, etc.

Realejo Bajo, 780 ft., 2,962 inhabitants, is $27\frac{1}{2}$ m. (44 kils.) from Santa Cruz, and about 5 m. (8 kils.) by road, either from the Villa or from the Puerto, the drive occupying something under the hour.

Realejo Alto, 1,110 feet, 4,077 inhabitants, now best visited *viâ* the new *carretera*, is divided from its sister town by the deep Barranco del Patronato. Both towns suffered severely from a flood in 1820.

Entering from the old *carretera* at the bottom of Realejo Bajo, the Church of **S. Augustin** with good carved ceiling and the adjacent **Convento de las Monjas** are encountered. Keep to the right below these, and ascend to the **Parish Church,** a large plain building of which the north door is noticeable. Without fixing a date to this, it may be mentioned that some of the ecclesiastical work in the Realejos was executed in the early days of the Spanish occupation, and that the gothic decorative stone work round the north doorway of both parish churches, is probably due to the same hand. The writer cannot recall any similar examples in the Canaries.

A steep climb now leads to the **dragon-tree,** 1,010 feet, a younger but at least as fine a specimen as that in Icod, measuring 15 ft. 8 in. in girth at 4 ft. from the ground, although less than 200 years old. There is a good view of the valley.

Below the Corona it will be noticed that there is an enormous fault in the rock, the wooded hump above Realejo having slipped down several hundreds of feet. The fault which extends for some distance up, is mentioned in the "Geological" article.

The Barranco del Patronato is crossed and the **Church of Santiago**, 1,110 ft., in **Realejo Alto** is arrived at. The part of this building next the spire is said to be one of the oldest churches in the island. The whole of the interior is quaint and well worth visiting. The ceilings and fretted beams are particularly good and should be of interest to architects, or to those concerned in the construction of churches.

The old altar with curious statues of St. James and St. Isidro is most interesting, as are two recumbent *repoussé* tombs to the left of the chancel, both dating from the 17th century, one of bronze and the other of wood. The candelabra in front of the altar is of solid silver. Artists fond of painting interiors are recommended to visit this church.

A return is now made by direct descent to the *carretera*. There is no inn or accommodation worth mentioning, nor can lunch be procured. It may be of interest to state that the Guanches were finally subdued in this neighbourhood, and that the last kings were baptised on the site of the old church.

Excursions from Realejo.—From the parish church in Realejo Bajo a paved road leads in 1 hr. to **Icod el Alto**, 1,720 feet, and the **Bco. de Castro**. This beautiful excursion can be continued through La Guancha to Icod. (*See* Icod.)

To the Corona, etc.—When crossing the Bco. Patronato between the two villages, a turning to the right ascends the cliffs known as the **Mña. de Tigaiga** and leads to the top of the **Corona**, 2,800 ft., in about 1½ hrs. from the *carretera*. This magnificent walk can be continued along fairly level paths at the 3,000 ft. level to **Icod de los Vinos** which is reached through the pine woods and past the Ermita Sta. Barbara. Time about 6 hrs. total.

To the Villa.—There are two paths, both more or less level, one leading through La Cruz Santa and La Perdoma, and the other below the new *carretera* and above the Mña. de Chaves. Time either way about 1½ hrs.

The paths up to the Peak and the Cañadas are mentioned below the description of Villa Orotava.

Main Road.—Leaving the Realejos the road rapidly descends to the bottom of a high cliff, though it still remains at some height above the sea. This part of the drive is very beautiful, and does not suffer at all by comparison with the very best parts of the Corniche Road on the Riviera. The distances marked on the mile-stones are those from the junction where the Puerto and the Icod *carreteras* separate. Those given in this book are as from Santa Cruz.

After passing the Barranco Espinosa, up which a track leads to Icod el Alto in about 2 hrs., the road passes the **Barranco Ruiz**, 31½ m. (50½ kils.), where there is a fine stone bridge. The barranco itself is very beautiful and a good place for picnics, though apt to be wet under foot. The ordinary visitor will not get very far up, but it is possible to reach Icod el Alto by a somewhat dangerous path in about 1½ hrs.

San Juan de la Rambla, 32½ m. (52 kils.), is a small town lying just above the sea at the western extremity of the Orotava valley. Pop. 2,024.

Fonda, 3s. a day. The old church has a quaint, picturesque interior. Notice the curious old clock. The lattice-work balcony over the door of No. 2 is by far the best specimen of its class still existing in the Canaries, and, being made of *téa*, it is trusted that it may continue to stand for a good many years to come.

The road now leads through dry volcanic valleys and ravines. Presently the Peak is sighted, a splendid view being obtained at Buen Paso.

When entering the outskirts of Icod, the *carretera* to Garachico will be seen descending on the right.

Icod de los Vinos, 700 ft., 37½ m. (60 kils.); 6,177 inhabitants.

Hotels.—Ingles, 10 pes.; Federico, 5 pes.

Churches.—**San Marcos**, a building of little interest. Attention is called to the handsome silver cross to be seen in the Capilla de la Cruz; **San Francisco**, formerly a convent. The chapel, now used for cock-fights, has a good ceiling. The cells are occupied by the police.—**San Agustin** and convent.

The chief attractions of Icod itself are the views of the Peak, which are magnificent, the best being obtained from the roofs of the houses around the plaza; the dragon tree near the church, the largest in the island and said to be 3,000 years old; and the Guanche burying cave below the town.

The great stream of lava which overwhelmed Garachico, as well as that town itself, can be easily visited. Icod is prettily situated, being built on a great slope, intersected by many streams of lava, now covered with earth and vegetation.

Silk is made in the town on a small scale, also straw hats.

The water supply is excellent.

On the coast below there is a small harbour known as the **Puerto de S. Marco.** At a point on the *carretera* to Garachico, 3 kils. from Icod, a branch *carretera*, 2 kils. in length, is to connect the port with its hinterland. Carros only can pass at present.

A *carretera* is proposed from Icod to El Tanque, 6 kils.; Villa de Santiago, 11 kils.; and Guia, 31 kils., where it will join the projected *carretera* round the south of the island from Santa Cruz. (*See* below Güimar.)

Excursions from Icod.

To Garachico, Los Silos, Buena Vista, Palmar and Santiago.—Those driving must return to the entrance of the town and take the new *carretera*. At 40 m. (63 kils.) is the branch for the Puerto de S. Marco; at 41½ m. (66 kils.) Garachico; at 45 m. (72 kils.) Los Silos; at 47½ m. (76 kils.) Buena Vista. Carriages cannot pass beyond Garachico, but a road to Buena Vista is being constructed.

Those riding or walking may take the old road down the Calle Hercules, past the church, and join the *carretera* thus.

Those wishing to visit the **Guanche Burial Cave** must go the same way but must bear away to the right. It takes about 20 minutes to get there, and it is best to take someone to show the way. Visitors are not allowed to enter without permission from the owner. Torches should be taken.

The walking inside is rough but the cave may be followed to a hole in the cliff overlooking the sea. A few little bits of bone are still mixed with the earth near the end, but the rest have been carried away. The cave is supposed to communicate with the Peak, but can only be followed upwards for about 400 yards.

The *carretera* below Icod is much more picturesque than the old road, and is more direct.

Garachico, 41½ m. (66 kils.); 2,930 inhabitants. No inn, but beds can be had (with difficulty). Formerly the chief port of the island but now unimportant. The black streams of lava to be seen descending the cliff behind it, rushed upon the town in 1706, destroying a great number of houses and a quantity of property, in addition to filling up the harbour and finally ruining the town. This had already suffered severely, in 1645, by a flood of water, which carried away eighty houses and upwards of a hundred people, and again by a fire in 1697, when the Convento de S. Agustin and 109 houses were burned down.

Public Buildings.—**Church of Santa Ana**, with handsome interior and roof.—**Church and Convent of San Francisco**, now the school. The double church is poor, but the pair of patios with old picture are well worth visiting as good specimens of their class. A cross over the church door is made of old Delft tiles.—**Church and Convent of Santo Domingo**; Church now used for burials, and convent as a hospital. A "torno," or turnstile, for foundling infants, may still be seen.—**Convento de Monjas de la Concepcion**, still contains a few nuns; Church, without interest; closed from 12 to 3.—**Convento de San Agustin**; burnt down and façade only left.—**Castillo de San Miguel**, with five heraldic shields over the door.

From the long list of convents and churches still remaining some idea may be gained of the former importance of the place. It is easy to trace the descent of the lava, but not to divine all the damage done until gazing through the so-called Puerta de Tierra, a small *cul de sac* passage, just to the right of the running fountain in the Plaza de la Fuente. This passage formerly led down to the sea, but now abuts on to a confused mass of lava piled high in the air. The houses above crown a bluff on which was once a large iron hook to which vessels could be made fast, the harbour being at the mouth of a barranco of which no trace remains. The wine trade has fallen away so much that the necessity for a port near Icod, formerly a great centre for wine, is not so great, but nevertheless the Puerto de S. Marco has been constructed. Doubtless Garachico could be made into a fair harbour by connecting the rock in front with the shore.

The bridle road from Garachico traverses the lava slope and proceeds across a fruitful plain, where a quantity of sugar is grown for the large factory at Daute.

Los Silos, 1,452 inhab., no inn, 1 hr., lies beneath a gigantic cliff. The coast road continues fairly level, passes to the south of the Mña. de Taco, and crosses a sterile tract of country, chiefly composed of volcanic detritus, to

Buena Vista, 47½ m. (76 kils.), 2,113 inhab., 1¾ hrs. from Garachico on mule. Accommodation very poor, 1 dollar.

Buena Vista is an unattractive village where a quantity of good wine is still grown.

From here to **Palmar** (1,650 ft.), a steep climb by bridle path of 1¼ hrs. No inn, but a bed may be had. Palmar is a pretty valley, from which the **Pico de Barracan**, a mountain to the W., about 6,000 ft. high, can be ascended in 1½ hrs. A fine view is obtained of the Peak and the group of volcanoes to the N.W. of the same. Excursions can also be made towards **Punta de Teno, Carrisal**, etc. This part of the country belongs to the same formation as the Punta de Anaga, and the scenery of both is somewhat similar.

The track then ascends the valley, and the scenery becomes more volcanic, **Santiago** (3,000 ft.) being reached in about 4 hrs. from Buena Vista or a total of 7¼ from Icod. Refer elsewhere for details or continuation of journey to **Guia, Vilaflor, Güimar**, etc.

Buena Vista can be omitted, and a more direct road followed from **Los Silos** to **Palmar** over the Cumbre de Volico in 2 hrs.

From Icod to Valle de Santiago *via* **La Culata.**—Leaving Icod cross the Bco. de la Haceña, go through the tunnel, and keep along the top of the cliff to **La Culata** (1,625 ft.), a small village, 1 hr. on mule. The cliff can be descended to **Garachico** on foot from La Culata or from the Fielato, ½ hr. from Icod.

Immediately after the village the stream of lava which overwhelmed Garachico is encountered. This frightful exhibition of volcanic fury takes twenty minutes to cross. It is a succession of ravines, where the hot lava in the centre has ploughed great furrows in the partially cooled mass which preceded it. It is only after seeing this that the country as far back as San Juan de la Rambla can be properly appreciated by those unaccustomed to a volcanic country. It will now be recognised that the whole distance is covered by a succession of similar outbreaks, now more or less disintegrated or overgrown, but nevertheless destructive in their time, although no doubt necessary as buttresses to the mountain side. The lava of 1706 is only commencing to decompose, and it would seem that much of the igneous rock ejected during the third period is of a less friable character than that which immediately preceded it. It is difficult therefore to estimate the antiquity of that which passes through Buen Paso or the town of Icod itself by comparing it with this newer example.

The path now bears slightly to the left and at 2 hrs. **El Tanque** is passed. At 2½ hrs. **Rigomaz**, and ¼ hr. further **Las Tronqueras**. A few minutes further **Los Dornajos de Erjos**, where there are several springs, and at 3 hrs. the **Summit or Cumbre del Valle** which commands a good view. Passing the Iglesia Vieja the village of **Santiago**, 3,000 ft., is entered, 3¾ hrs. total. For further details refer under journey round the S. of the island.

This part of the island is greener than usual and the land is fertile. There is a certain amount of sport to be found, as well as a succession of mountains and valleys which can only be explored properly by those taking a tent.

A lighthouse has been built at the Punta de Teno.

From Icod to Santiago *viâ* la Vega.—A rough and somewhat longer road leaves the top of Icod, passes the Ermita San Antonio, ¼ hr., the Ermita del Amparo, ½ hr., crosses the **Bco. de la Vega**, 1 hr., on mule, passes through some houses to the **Cruz del Almorzadero**, 1¾ hrs., situated just below the **Mña. de Serrogordo**, and so *viâ* **Los Partidos** to Santiago in about 4 hrs. Guide necessary.

From Icod over the Cañadas to Adeje, Vilaflor, etc.—Ascend past the Ermita San Antonio, pass the turning to the right and keep on up to the **Fuente de la Vega** where there are a few heath trees (1½ hrs. mule). The **Mña. de Serrogordo** is kept on the right.

The Monte Verde is now entered, and heath, jara, laurels and pines gradually succeed one another. At 3 hrs. **El Llano de los Hermanos**, near which seven travelling friars were once frozen to death. Close by is a mountain (La Caldera) from which there is a fine view of the N.W. group of eleven volcanoes. Soon the road climbs an old lava stream, and at 4½ hrs., about 4,500 ft., the lava stream, coming from the base of Chahorra and flowing towards Garachico, is crossed. From near here **Chahorra** can be ascended. It is a hard rough climb and takes about 8 hrs. from Icod. The crater is ¾ mile wide and about 150 ft. deep.

At 4¾ hrs. the **Cruz de Téa**, 7,612 feet, a half-way mark is met with. The stones only remain, however, as the cross has disappeared. Close to this are the **Hornillas del Teide**, two holes in the lava, apparently very deep and supposed, of course, to communicate with Hell. The travelling on this part of the journey is very bad.

At 5 hrs. the lava stream which runs towards Guia is crossed, the last eruptions of lava in Teneriffe having taken place up here in 1796 and 1798. (Those going to **Adeje** will here descend to Guia unless they prefer to take Adeje *via* Vilaflor. For times, *see* Guia.)

There is a good view here and there of the coast and the lower volcanoes with Palma and Gomera in the distance, the Peak, which is at first quite close, being gradually hidden by Chahorra. At 5½ hrs. the Peak again becomes visible, the slag and clinkers at length give way to the smooth pumice floor of the **Cañadas**, and the S.W. extremity of the walls of the same commence. Here and there, however, lava is again crossed, and at last, at 6½ hrs., the path leads through the **Boca de los Tauces**, 6,680 ft., to the outside slope.

It is a very bad road from here, along coarse pumice and rocks, to the **Bco. del Dornajito**, where good water may sometimes be found a little to the left of the path (7¼ hrs.). From 2 minutes beyond the spring the path descends all the way to Vilaflor, 4,335 ft., passing the Ermita San Roque immediately before arriving. Total time, 9½ hours, not allowing for stoppages.

(For Vilaflor and excursions or for the other side of the Cañadas *via* los Azulejos, *see* elsewhere.)

A return from Vilaflor to **Icod** can be made *via* **Guajara Pass**, 7,700 ft., 4 hrs. to the spring, across the **Cañadas**, and under the **Fortaleza**, 7½ hrs.; down through the pine forest over rough rolling lava, pass the **Fuente Pedro**, 9½ hrs., where the water is caught up and carried into Icod by an iron pipe, and so through the Monte Verde and amidst a number of intricate paths to Icod in about 14 hrs. The night must be passed on the Cañadas and the journey is a most villainous one, though there are some good views on the descent.

(For the best way to reach Icod from the Fortaleza, *see* the next excursion.)

From Icod to the Fortaleza *via* **La Guancha.**—Leave Icod by the Orotava end and ascend to the **Ermita Santa Barbara**, ¾ hr., to **La Guancha**, 1,950 ft., 1,697 inhabitants, no inn, 2 hrs. Keep to the right by little frequented paths up to the **Fortaleza**, 7,300 ft., in about 5½ hrs. It is not necessary to go through La Guancha. The way is difficult to find and a guide is required. A return can be made to **Orotava** by **La Corona** and **Realejo**.

The side of the **Fortaleza** exposed to the Cañadas is very fine. This is the only part of the wall from the Portillo on the N.E. to the Mña. de Chabao on the S.W. that has fought the fight and survived. Its many coloured scars and fire-eaten front are a standing record of the high temperatures of which they have borne the brunt.

From Icod to La Corona, Realejo and Orotava.—Pass the Ermita Santa Barbara and work straight up to the pine-woods. Keep along the 3,000 ft. level to La Corona, from which there is one of the most astonishing views in the world. Then drop down to Realejo and on to Orotava. This journey is best done on foot without guides, is extremely lovely and occupies some $7\frac{1}{2}$ hrs. No guides would take the paths referred to.

From Icod to La Guancha, Icod el Alto and Orotava.—To La Guancha, as above, 2 hrs., whence cross the top of the lovely Bco. Ruiz, $3\frac{1}{4}$ hrs., to the Church of Icod el Alto, 1,720 ft., $3\frac{1}{2}$ hrs. A few minutes later the spring in the Bco. de Castro is passed and at $3\frac{3}{4}$ hrs. the splendid view over the valley is reached. Descend to Realejo Bajo, $4\frac{1}{2}$ hrs., and on to Orotava, $5\frac{3}{4}$ hrs. This is a regular mule track. The distance is about $17\frac{1}{2}$ miles, and it has been walked in $4\frac{1}{2}$ hours.

Approximate Prices of Horses and Carriages.

(In Santa Cruz).	Carriage to hold Four (with hand-bags) (Three Horses).	Carriage to hold Two (Two Horses). No Luggage.	Riding Horses.
For about 1 hr.	5 pes. Return	5 pes. Return	3/-
La Laguna	10 ,, ,,	$7\frac{1}{2}$,, ,,	4/-
Las Mercedes	20 ,, ,,	15 ,, ,,	6/-
Tegueste	$17\frac{1}{2}$,, ,,	15 ,, ,,	6/-
Tejina	20 ,, ,,	15 ,, ,,	6/-
Tacoronte	15 ,, Single.	$12\frac{1}{2}$,, Single.	6/-
Matanza	20 ,, ,,	15 ,, ,,	6/-
Villa Orotava	30 ,, ,,	25 ,, ,,	8/-
Puerto Orotava	30 ,, ,,	25 ,, ,,	10/-
Realejo Bajo	35 ,, ,,	30 ,, ,,	12/-
S. Juan de la Rambla	40 ,, ,,	35 ,, ,,	—
Icod	60 ,, ,,	50 ,, ,,	—
Garachico	70 ,, ,,	60 ,, ,,	—
Arafo (end of *carretera*)	30 ,, ,,	25 ,, ,,	8/-
Güimar	30 ,, ,,	25 ,, ,,	8/-

Where "single" is written above, those wishing to return the next day must add 10 pes. to the prices given, or, in the case of Garachico, 20 pes.

There are no riding horses to be had in Santa Cruz at present, but the prices given are those formerly asked, and a fair basis should a new livery stable be started.

Donkeys, 1·25 pes. an hr. or 5 pes. a day. Pack animals from the Mole to any part of the town, 0·25 to 0·75 pes.

Special carts with luggage to Orotava, 15 to 20 pes.

Horses and mules for expeditions should be hired further in the country. They differ in price in different localities and in accordance to the work to be done. A fair price is 5 pes. a day, the man to find everything, including his own bed and food. For steep mountain paths as much as $7\frac{1}{2}$ pes. must often be paid and for a single day even more.

Carts carry luggage by the piece and charge according to size. These carriers are constantly coming and going where the *carretera* runs, or mules can be engaged elsewhere, but the special days from Santa Cruz to Orotava are Tuesday and Friday and back again on Monday and Thursday. Private carriages will take as much as possible and the omnibus will carry handbags and so on.

When carriages or horses are kept waiting for an unreasonable time an extra charge is made.

Prices in La Laguna.—Horses can be had for a short ride of not over two hours for 3 pesetas; over two hours, 4 pes.

Named rides: La Esperanza, Tejina, Valle de Guerra, Santa Cruz, all 1$; Agua Garcia, Cruz de Afur, $1\frac{1}{2}$$; Cruz de Taganana, 2$; Taganana and back, 3$; Arafo and Güimar, single, $2\frac{1}{2}$$; returning next day, 4$; Lighthouse and back, 2 days, 5$.

Carriages with three horses: To Tegueste, 10 pes.; Tejina, 10 pes.; Las Mercedes, from 10 pes.; Santa Cruz, 10 pes.; Güimar, 25 pes. (return, 30 pes.); Tacoronte, 10 pes.; Matanza, $12\frac{1}{2}$ pes.; Villa Orotava, 20 pes. (return, 25 pes.); Puerto Orotava, 25 pes. (return, 30 pes.); Icod (single or return), 50 pes.; Garachico, same, 60 pes.

Carriage with two horses for moderate distances at about three-quarters the above prices.

Prices in Tacoronte.—Carriages to La Laguna, 10 pes.; Santa Cruz, 15 pes. (single); Golf Links and back, or Puerto Orotava (single), 20 pes.; (return), 30 pes.; Villa and back, 20 pes.

Horses.—To Agua García, 3 pes.; to the Cumbres (Mña. del Chupadero), $7\frac{1}{2}$ pes.; to La Esperanza, 5 pes.; to Igueste de Candelaria, 10 pes.; to Güimar (single) 15 pes.; short rides, 3 to 5 pes.

Prices in Puerto Orotava.—Hammocks, 2 pesetas an hour, or extra if taken into the hills. From the Puerto to the Villa, 1$.

Horses.—Short rides of about 2 hrs., 5 pes.; short day inside valley, 6—8 pes.; per wk., for half the day, 20—25 pes.; per wk., whole day, 35—40 pes.; per mnth., 30 to 40$. Expeditions, including man and horse, per day, 2½$, or for a mule, 2$. For the Sortija, 3$; for practice for same, 2$.

Named rides.—Sta. Ursula (Golf Links), 7½ pes.; San Juan de la Rambla, 10 pes.; Florida, 7 pes.; Matanza, Fuente de la Cruz, Agua Manza, 10 pes.; Agua García, Icod de los Vinos, 15 pes.; returning from Icod next day *viâ* Icod el Alto, 20 pes.; Icod el Alto and La Corona, 9 pes.; La Laguna, Santa Cruz, Pedro Gil, Mña. Blanca, Las Cañadas, 15 pes; Güimar (single), 17½ pes.; The Peak, Vilaflor, or Güimar and back next day, 25 pes.

Horses hired by the month are at the responsibility of the hirer unless otherwise arranged. Owners expect 1½$ extra when their horses are used in the Sortija, and 1$ when used in practice for same.

Donkeys.—Up to 2 hrs., 2 pes.; over 2 hrs., 2½ pes.; whole day, 4 pes.; by the week, 24 pes.; by the month, 75 pes.

Mules.—About two-thirds the price of a horse.

Guides.—Special guides are only necessary when climbing the Peak. In other cases the mule drivers are all that is required. Although guides in Orotava now ask fairly high prices, they can in no way be compared to Swiss guides, and cannot always be depended upon even to show the way.

Carriages to hold 4 persons: To the Villa or Realejo Bajo, 7½ pes.; Realejo Alto, Rambla de Castro, 2$; Barranco Ruiz, 2½$; San Juan de la Rambla, 3$; Icod, 5$ (return next day, 6$); Garachico, 7$; Sta. Ursula, 2$; Golf Links, 3$; Victoria, 2½$; Matanza, 3$; Tacoronte, 4$; La Laguna, 5$; Santa Cruz, 6$.

Prices of horses or mules in Icod.—To Garachico, to the lava stream beyond La Culata and similar districts, 3 pes.; to the Pinar or pine-forest, or Buena Vista, 1$; La Guancha, 6½ pes.; the Fortaleza, 10 pes.; per day for excursions, from 5 to 7½ pes., according to roads and time taken, etc.

Of carriages: To Buen Paso, 6½ pes.; S. Juan de la Rambla, 10 pes.; Realejo, 12½ pes.; Puerto or Villa Orotava, 20 pes.

Prices in Güimar.—Mules, 2 to 3 hrs., ½$; 4 to 6 hrs., 1$; to Orotava, 2$. Carriage to Fasnia (end of *carretera*), 15 pes.

For Public Coaches, *see* next page.

PRICES AND APPROXIMATE TIMES OF THE PUBLIC COACHES.

Kilos.	Miles.		A.M.	P.M.	Prices. In-side. pes. c.	Prices. Out-side. pes. c.		A.M.	P.M.	
		Santa ᛚ, Plaza Weyler Lur Town	6.30	2.15			Puerto Orotava	6.0	1.15	⎫ These times are from 1st October to 31st March. During the Summer they are about ½ hr. earlier. The hours are in any case thr unreliable, as is the ase with every fixed time in this my. Only one st of prices is given. Fuller details are Me at the ff.
9	5½	Ditto.	8.30	2.30			Villa do.	6.45	2.0	
19	12	La Laguna	9.30	4.30	1.25	1.0	Empalme	7.0	2.45	
23	14½	Tacoronte	9.45	5.45	2.25	2.25	Sta. Ursula	7.30	3.45	
24½	15½	Sauzal	10.15	6 15	2.50	2.50	Victoria	8.15	4.15	
28	17½	Matanza	10.15	6.45	2.75	2.75	Matanza	9.0	5.0	
32	20	Victoria	11.10	7.15	3.0	3.0	Sauzal ...	9.30	5.30	
		Sta. Ursula...	11.10	8.5	3.50	3.50	Tacoronte	9.45	6.30	
37	23	n or Empalme	11.40	8.30			La Laguna	11.0		
38½	24	Villa Orotava	12.15	8.40	4.50	3.0	Sta. ᛚ, Plaza de W ydr	12.0	8.0	
42	26	Puerto do. ...	12.30	9.0	5.25	3.50				
			P.M	P.M.	Prices			A.M.	A.M.	⎫ This part of the journey has been purposely separated from the st. Though the Coaches ought to meet those ascending and descending from the Villa to the Puerto, no reliance can be placed on their doing so. The Coach leaving Icod at 4 a.m., and Orotava for Icod at 8 p.m. only carries the mails and five passengers.
37	23	Empalme, or Junction of the Villa	12.30	8 0			Icod	4.0	9.0	
45½	28½	Realejo	1.45	9.15	1.0		S. Juan de la Rambla	5.0	10.15	
53	33	S. Juan de la Ma	2.45	10.15	2.0		Realejo	5.45	11.15	
63	39½	Icod...	4.0	11.30	3.25		Empalme	6.30	12.30	
			A.M.	P.M.				A.M.	P.M.	
		Puerto Orotava	6 0	1.15			Empalme de la Villa	11.45	8.30	⎫ Of little use to visitors.
5½	3½	Empalme de la Villa	7.0	2 15	1.0		Puerto Orotava	12.45	9.0	
			A.M.	P.M.				A.M.	A.M.	⎫ In addition to the through Coaches, there are special Coaches in the Summer.
		Santa Cruz ...	9.0	3.0			La Laguna	9.0	11.0	
		La Laguna ...	11.0	5.0	1.25		Sta. Cruz	10.0	12.0	
			A.M.	P.M.				A.M.	P.M.	⎫ The Coach leaving Santa ₢z at 7 a.m. and ₢ at 2.30 p.m. charges a little more than the 1 ail coach.
		Sta. ᛚ, Plaza de Weyler	7.0	3.15			Arafo	5.0	2.30	
		San Isidro ...	8.15	4.45	1.25		Candelaria	5.30	3.0	
		Igueste ...	9.15	6 0	1.75		Igueste...	6.0	3.30	
		Candelaria ...	9.45	6.30	2.00		San Isidro	7.0	4.15	
		Arafo	10.15	7.15	2.25		Sta. Cruz, Plaza de	8.30	5.45	
		ᛚar	10.45	7.45	2.50		ᛚ	9.30	7.30	

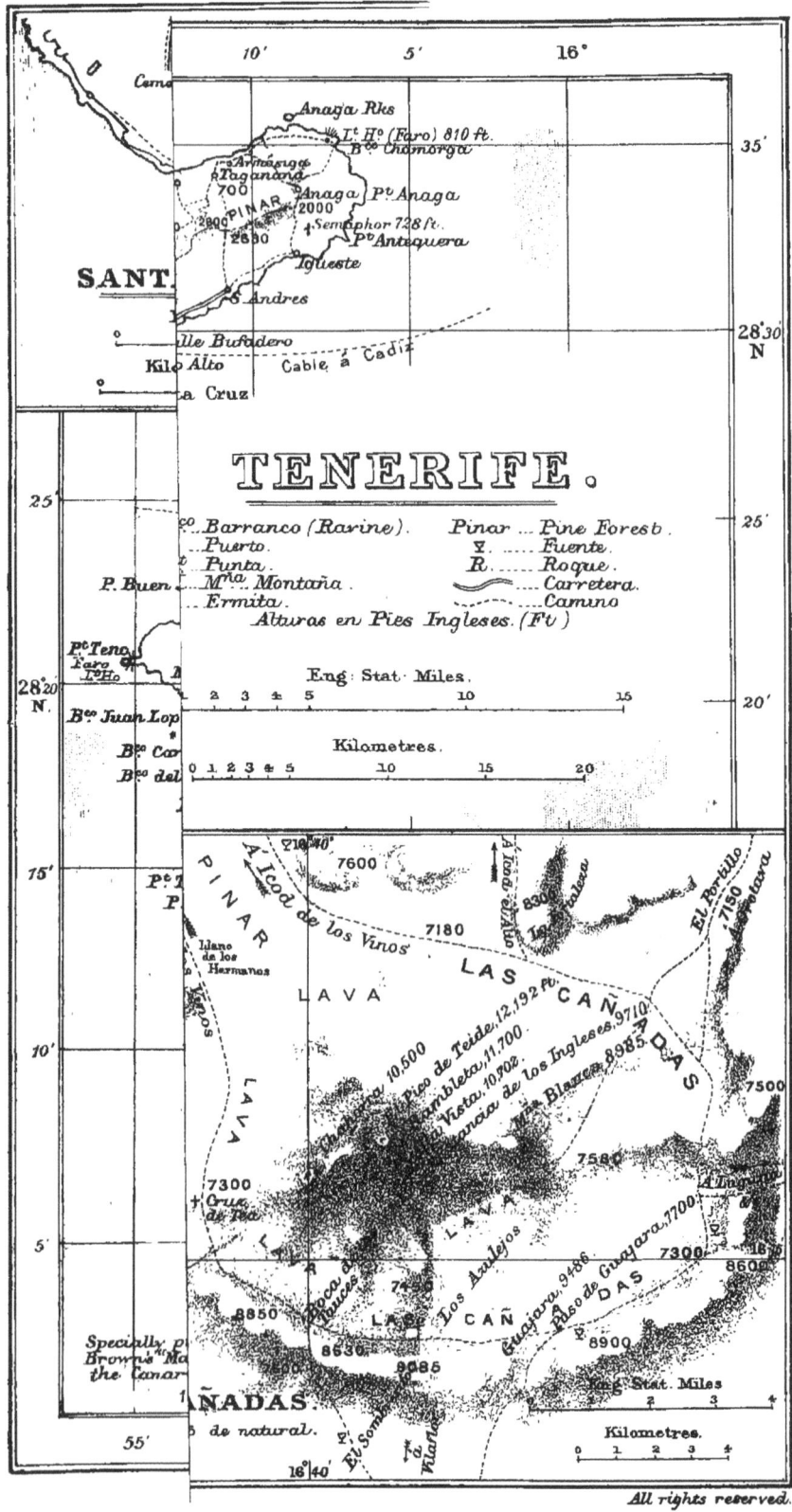

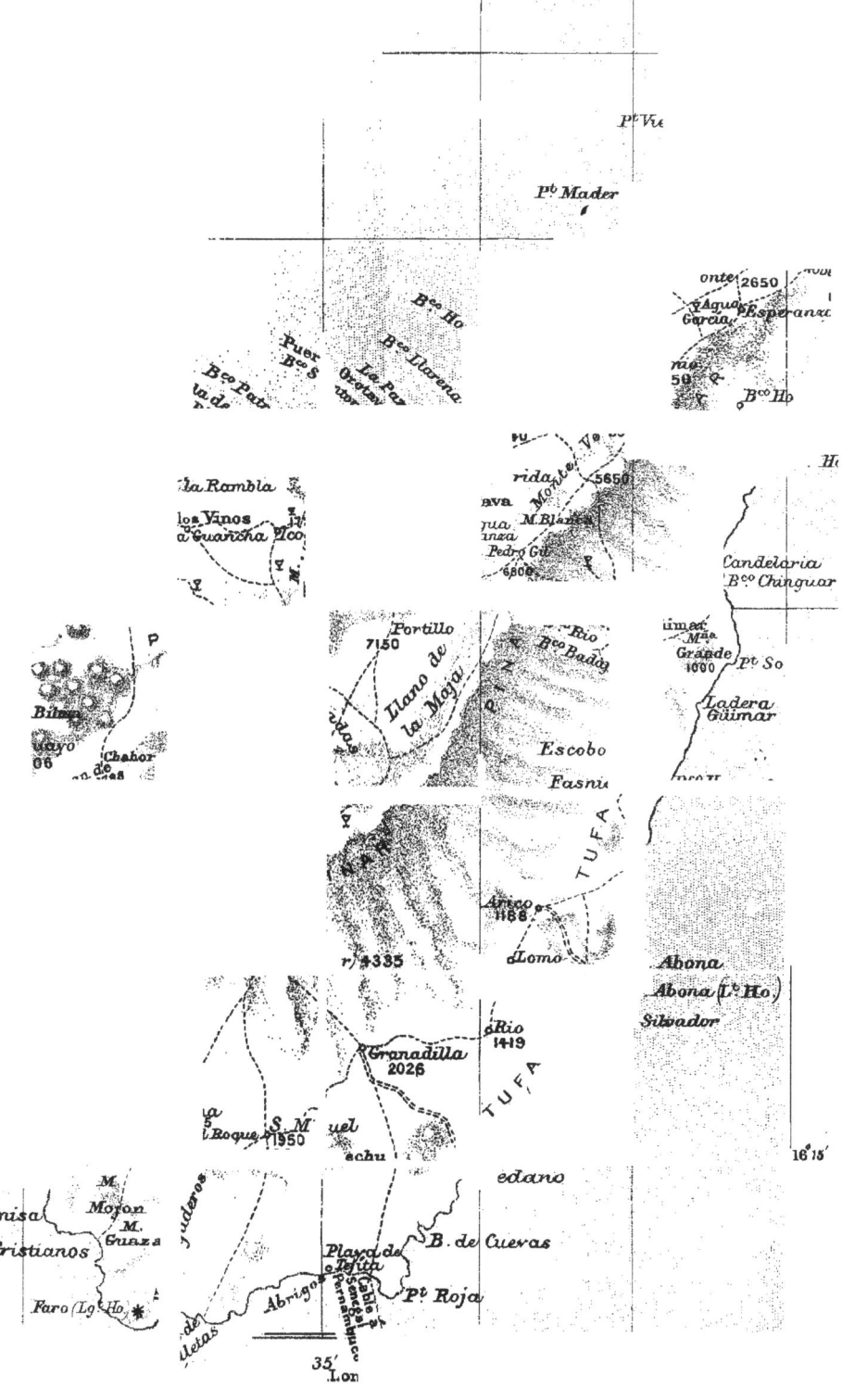

GRAND CANARY.

THE island was formerly known as Canaria, and obtained its present name of Gran Canaria because of the heroic defence made by the aboriginals, who called themselves Canarios. Some connection has been inferred between this name and a supposed breed of large dogs, of which a pair are referred to by Pliny as having been presented to King Juba II., of Mauritania. Ptolemy speaks of a part of the neighbouring African coast under the name of Gannaria.

The island is situated between lat. $27°\ 44'$ to $28°\ 12'$ N. and long. $15°\ 21'$ to $15°\ 50'$ W. of Greenwich, is $34\frac{1}{2}$ m. (55 kils.) long by $29\frac{1}{2}$ m. (47 kils.) broad, and covers an area of 634 sq. m. (1623 sq. kils.). There are 123,200 inhabitants spread over 3 cities, 3 towns and 178 villages or hamlets, which are divided into 22 districts, and its geographical position is E.S.E. of Teneriffe and W.S.W. of Fuerteventura.

The form of the island is nearly circular, and greatly resembles a saucer-full of mud turned upside down, with the sides eaten into long and deep ravines by the overflow from the little basin at the top, of which the highest point is a swelling upland known as the Pico del Pozo de las Nieves, 6,400 ft.

Of the ravines, the Bco. de Tejeda is the greatest. It is indeed so large that, as seen from Granadilla in Teneriffe, it seems to split the island in two. Other large Barrancos are those known as the Bco. de Tirajana, de Fatarga, de la Virgen, etc.

The ravines and watercourses of all the islands greatly resemble one another. Whether they commenced their existence as volcanic fissures, or are entirely due to denudation, is a question of minor interest. On the S.E. coast of Grand Canary there is an exceptionally wide plain, stretching from below Agüimes to Arguineguin, and consisting of the *débris* washed down from the hills, which terminate abruptly at some distance from the sea. The formation is so different to that found elsewhere, and the cleavage of the rocks so marked and so widespread, that the curiosity of all who pass cannot fail to be excited. As far as the writer's very cursory examination indicated, the centre of disturbance would probably be found in the Bco. de Tirajana, but there are outcrops of cinders, etc., in other places which are not immediately noticeable, as they have been reduced to the level of their surroundings, perhaps by the action of the sea.

There are many places where the crust of the island has been penetrated by volcanoes. Amongst these, that known as the Caldera de Bandama, near Tafira, can be easily visited. The rim of the crater was never broken by the lava, and is now a great

R

cup, of which the bottom has subsided to a level floor, leaving the walls exposed to sight.

That part of the island known as the Isleta is thought to be of more recent creation than the mainland. The isthmus by which the two are connected is formed of sand, drifted across from the African coast by the action of the wind and tide. A similar growth of sand is to be seen at Maspalomas.

The length of the Barrancos is much greater than is the case in Teneriffe, and a great part of the water, which gradually filters from the Cumbres, is caught up and carried on to the land. The quantity of water available might be largely increased by the planting of forests. The island, however, is better off as regards water than either Teneriffe or La Palma, although the climate is undoubtedly drier. A good deal of energy has been shown in the construction of tanks, without which cultivation during the summer months would often be impossible.

There are several mineral springs, notably those at Firgas, Agaete and Santa Catalina.

Beyond the Pinar between Tejeda and Tirajana, and the woods in the upper part of the Bco. de la Virgen there are few trees. In fact, the destruction of forest land has been so reckless, that there is nothing left from which charcoal can be made, and all that is used has to be imported. The pine, the laurel and the heather will grow as well as elsewhere, but, unfortunately, only the eucalyptus is planted, if one excepts the *escobón*, a species of broom from which faggots can be cut about five years after the seeds are put into the ground. The various euphorbias, etc., are, of course, well represented, and the chestnut, fig, olive, almond, vine and orange thrive luxuriantly.

Cochineal is still cultivated to a certain extent, but the tomato, banana, potato, sugar-cane, maize and other cereals are now the principal crops. The oranges are particularly fine.

The history of the island prior to the arrival of the Spaniards has been sufficiently entered into elsewhere. It only remains to add that the most perfect examples of ancient caves and dwelling places are to be found in Grand Canary.

The modern history is chiefly commercial. As a coaling station, and as a business centre, Las Palmas has made enormous strides during the last few years.

The customs of the Canarios of to-day call for no special remark. The only peculiarities in their dress are the white shawls worn by the women, which have a somewhat Moorish appearance, and the *mantas* worn by the men. The latter, instead of being made of English blankets, as is the case in Teneriffe and La Palma, are woven by the women from wool grown in the island. The black stripe is the natural colour of the wool.

The villages and towns are very plainly built, and are far from picturesque. There are, however, some handsome houses in Las Palmas built of blue stone (lava basalt). Of this stone there are several quarries, notably one at Atalaya, and the art of stone cutting is far more advanced in Canary than elsewhere in the archipelago.

The special local industries are embroidery, native tanned goat-skins, rough red pottery, drip-stone filters, coarsely woven cloths, and very handsome knives with ornamented handles.

Palm leaves are used for making a number of articles, for instance, the *seron*, in which manure, etc., is placed when carried on horse-back.

A speciality of Grand Canary is a cheese known as Flor de Canaria. The milk is curdled by means of the flower of the *cardo*, a wild artichoke with a handsome thistle-like blue flower, of which the leaves can be scraped and eaten like a vegetable.

The chief port is the Puerto de la Luz, $3\frac{1}{2}$ m. ($5\frac{1}{2}$ kils.) from Las Palmas, with which it is connected by a steam tramway. The port at Agaete is only used by schooners, and that at Punta de Gando has been sacrificed to the Lazareto.

There are several good roads which radiate from Las Palmas as a centre, and connect it with Telde and Agüimes on the South; San Mateo on the S.W., and Arucas, Guia and Agaete on the W. The last road has a branch to Teror and another branch is being made to Moya, with a subsidiary branch leading to Firgas. It is intended to continue the S. road from Agüimes to Tirajana, and probably further later on. A direct road is also to be made from the Puerto de la Luz to Tamaraceite, San Lorenzo, and Tafira. Within a few years it is probable that these roads will form a very useful and complete system of electric tramways, connected here and there by subsidiary carriage roads.

Those stopping at Grand Canary for a few hours will do best by driving to the **Monte**, 10 m. (16 kils.), about 3 hrs. there and back (fare, 12s. to 14s. for a carriage with five people), *or* to the **Gran Caldera**, 12 m. (19 kils.), about 5 hrs. including an hour to visit the Caldera and Atalaya, fare, 14s. to 16s.; *or* on to **San Mateo**, 17 m. ($26\frac{1}{2}$ kils.), about $6\frac{1}{2}$ hrs., fare, 18s. to 20s.; *or* by the S. road to **Telde**, 12 m. (19 kils.), about 4 hours, fare, 12s. to 14s.; *or* past Tamaraceite to **Teror**, 13 m. ($20\frac{1}{2}$ kils.), about 5 hrs., fare, 18s. to 20s.

All the above fares and times are return from the Puerto de la Luz **not** from Las Palmas. For fares from Las Palmas itself and for sights in the city, *see* elsewhere.

By those stopping longer, the above drives can be extended. Full details are given in the proper places.

Owing to the want of good accommodation in most parts of Grand Canary, it is more difficult to explore the island than it should be. There are, however, two English hotels in the Monte, and some of the native inns are fairly good; but a little more enterprise is wanted before the latter can hope to secure a very large custom.

The two strategic points from which a good idea of the island can be quickly secured are the summit of the Pico de los Osorios, near Teror, and of the Pico de Bandama in the Monte.

The prettiest road is that leading up to San Mateo. Taking the **Monte** as a centre, the best excursions from here are:—To the **Gran Caldera** and **Atalaya,** or across country through **Teror, Firgas,** and **Moya** to Guia. On the last journey the best halting-place is Firgas.

Taking **San Mateo** as a centre, where an hotel is badly wanted, the best excursions are:—To the **Cumbres** on a clear day, taking care not to omit the view of the **Bco. de Tejeda** from above, one of the most magnificent sights in the islands; to **Tirajana** *viâ* the Cumbres, and back to Las Palmas *viâ* **Aguimes** (no inn), *or viâ* **Tejeda** (beds); or to **Agaete** or **Guia** (inns) across the upper part of the **Bco. de la Virgen.**

It is also possible to make a centre of **Firgas,** in the neighbourhood of which there is some very fine scenery, or of **Agaete,** if one is not too particular. **Teror** also offers many attractions, but an inn is wanted. **Gáldar** and **Guia** are rather climatic resorts than centres for exploring the country.

It is not impossible that at some future time Agaete will be the leading health resort of Grand Canary. The country between it and Tejeda or San Mateo is often charming, but very mountainous, which is the case with that lying between Tejeda and Mogan.

The **Bco. de Fatarga** and the upper part of the **Bco. de Tirajana** are both beautiful, but the accommodation is either *nil* or is villainous. The villages on the S. swarm with fleas and flies to such an extent that life is only endurable under canvas.

For a short run over the island the following is recommended. Drive to San Mateo, and back to the Monte. See the Gran Caldera and Atalaya in the afternoon, and sleep at the Monte (1 day). Engage mules, and ride to Firgas, taking Teror and the top of the Mña. de los Osorios on the way (2 days). Ride past Moya and Los Tilos to Gáldar or Guia (3 days). Rest and drive over to Agaete and back (4 days). Return by coach or

GRAND CANARY (LAS PALMAS).

carriage to Las Palmas (5 days). Drive to Telde and the Mña. de las Cuatro Puertas (6 days). If desired, an early start can be made from the Monte, and the Cumbres be visited from San Mateo, returning to the Monte in the evening, this adding one day to the tour, or it can be reduced to 5 days by omitting Agaete.

Accommodation can be booked by telegram as far as Telde or Agaete. Wires are not laid elsewhere, but there is a telephone to Santa Brigida.

The Puerto de la Luz is a harbour formed by the Isleta on the N., the Isthmus of Guanarteme on the W., and two moles, commenced in 1883. The eastern or principal of these measures over 1,200 metres. Passengers are usually landed on the smaller (Santa Catalina), mole. There is a slip capable of taking vessels up to 2,000 tons, and some large engineering sheds, allowing of extensive repairs being executed.

Houses are rapidly rising in the neighbourhood of the harbour, which bids fair to cover the whole of the isthmus, and eventually to effect a junction with Las Palmas.

Landing Charges : All passengers are landed on the mole, and all ships are met by the hotel agents.

The **port charges** are, each passenger each way, by day with two handbags, one peseta. Each trunk, up to 50 kilos., 50 centimos ; over 50 kilos., one peseta. A private boat to and from ship, 4 pesetas ; if detained over 1 hr., one peseta per hour extra. Boats by time : first hour, 4 pesetas ; subsequent hours, 1½ pesetas. By night add 50 % to all above charges.

There are no **custom duties** on passengers' luggage, but cases are opened at the **fielato** on the mole. When the quantity is large, a declaration must be made, and a ticket taken at the same place. Otherwise the guardian at the fielato, opposite the Santa Catalina Hotel, may refuse to let the carro pass.

Conveyances to Las Palmas are : Carriages, from a stand, to hold five persons, one dollar ;—**Tartanas** (two-wheeled dog carts), to hold up to four, 4 pesetas, and 2 pesetas an hour if kept waiting over one hour. For this fare the tartana must carry passengers from either mole to any point within two kilometres of Las Palmas, wait one hour and bring them back. For single or short journeys an arrangement must invariably be made. Usual fare, Mole to Las Palmas, 2 pesetas. From 8 p.m. to 4 a.m., 50 % extra ;—**Steam tramway** running about every hour. Fares from 15 c. third to 35 c. first class.

The distance from the harbour to the city is about 3½ m. (5½ kils.).

Conveyances inside Las Palmas (Coches de calle). Up to 3 persons, 1½ pesetas ; if more, ½ peseta each. Time :—4 Wheels, up to 4 persons, 2½ pesetas per hour. Tartanas, 2 pesetas an hour. At night 50 % extra. Fares should be arranged before starting.

Note.—For other coaching fares, *see* pages 249 to 251.

LAS PALMAS, 40,636 inhabitants, capital of Grand Canary and the seat of a bishopric since 1485, is situated on the N.E. of Grand Canary, 53 m. (85 kils.) by sea from Santa Cruz de Teneriffe.

Hotels.—On the road between the Port and the City.—The Santa Catalina Hotel, built by an English company, stands in its own grounds with a fine sea view, from 10s. 6d. a day upwards; the Metropole, also newly built, well situated on the sea shore, with gardens and a good glazed patio, from 8s. upwards. Inside the Town.—Quiney's English and Continental Hotel, old-established, with garden, and facing open square, 6s. to 8s. a day; Hotel "La Union," central position near the Theatre, from 6s.; the Cuatro Naciones, facing the Alameda, 5s. to 6s.; La Montañesa, 101, Triana, 5 pesetas; Elephant and Castle, 14, Constantino, 5 pesetas; Catalan and others.

Boarding Houses.—Sea View House, near the Port, facing the Western Bay, with fine view, from 30s. a week.

For hotels in the Monte (pages 236-7), etc., *see* under the description of the district.

Restaurants.—La Union, Plaza de Democracia, near the Stone Bridge.

Newspapers.—*El Diario de las Palmas; El Diario de Avisos; La Telegrama; El Telégrafo; La Patria; España.*

(*For advertisements, see under Grand Canary at the end of the book, and on page H.*)

A good telephonic system exists throughout the city, and as far as the Monte. The town is well lighted by electricity.

Public Buildings.—The Town Hall (Municipio), at the top of the Plaza Sta. Ana, and facing the Cathedral; erected in 1842.

On the first floor is the **Public Library**, open every day from 11 till 3, with some 5,000 vols., and a good collection of historical works, including some in MSS. by the director, D. Pablo Padilla.

On the second floor is the **Museum**, the largest in the islands, and rich in remains of the aboriginals, with a fair collection of objects of natural history. Nominally open on Thursdays and Sundays from 11.30 till 3. If closed, the key can be obtained of the porter at the Municipio (fee expected). The contents are not catalogued, and are imperfectly arranged.

Some help is afforded by the colour of the labels affixed to the specimens. Objects marked with a Green ticket come from Grand Canary; Red from Teneriffe; Blue, La Palma; Yellow, Fuerteventura; Cream, Lanzarote; Rose, Hierro; Violet, Gomera; White, foreign to the islands. This arrangement is only partially carried out, and the colour has faded out of a good many labels.

Room No. 1.—The cases are mostly occupied by a collection of Geological specimens, which are not very well grouped, and are badly sorted.

Rooms Nos. 2, 3 and 4.—Rooms 2 and 3 contain objects collected in the Archipelago; Room 4, objects from elsewhere. Amongst a considerable collection of pottery should be noted the "*Pintaderas*," or earthen dyes, which were used for stamping patterns on the skin, on leather, etc. The ornaments, tools and implements made from bone, shells, stone, etc., will also be remarked.

Room No. 5.—The insects and Crustaceans are well arranged, and the land and sea shells are classified on an MS. catalogue. The fish would repay more attention. The "*manta*," or devil-fish, which is said to embrace its victims and carry them away under water, is not uncommon round the Canaries.

Room No. 6.—The Anthropological Department is by far the richest and best arranged, and contains the best collection of Canary Island mummies in the world. Printed measurements of the skulls, etc., will be found hanging on the walls. Amongst the specimens of leather work are some wonderful examples of sewing.

The **Gobierno Militar**, completed in 1894, a substantial stone building facing El Parque, and occupied by the Military Governor.

The **Law Courts**, in the disused Convent of San Agustin (with plain chapel adjoining). **Hospital de S. Martin**, above the Santo Espiritu, where a torno or receptacle for foundlings is still used. Children placed by their parents into this turn-stile are brought up by the town, and are trained as servants. Even married women sometimes dispose of their offspring in this manner. **Leper Hospital**, in the old monastery of Santo Domingo. This disease, as present in the Canaries, does not seem to be catching. **Prison**. **Market Buildings**, at the end of the Calle de la Triana, and across the lower bridge. Both the fish and fruit markets should be visited. **Opera House**, a large building, well designed, and with a good interior, capable of holding 1,400 spectators. **Queen Victoria's Hospital for Seamen**, at the Port, where sick sailors and a few private patients are received at very moderate rates. **International Red Cross Hospital**, facing Western Bay. Installed on most modern lines for free and paying patients. Terms moderate. **Sailors' Institute**, at the Puerto de la Luz.

Churches.—The **Cathedral de S. Cristóbal**, a large heavy building with an imposing façade, commenced in 1497, but pulled down and rebuilt in 1781. The interior and main part of the structure, including the handsome groined roof, were designed and executed by Canon Edwards, a Teneriffe priest of English descent. The façade is by a Canary architect named Lojan Perez. The building is still unfinished, partly in order to avoid the contribution to Rome, for which all completed cathedrals are liable. The interior is high, but sombre and far from pleasing. A *porta-paz* in silver gilt by Benvenuto Cellini, may be seen by special order to be obtained from the President of the Cathedral. There are the usual vestments and church plate, which are shown in return for a small fee. Some of these once belonged to Old St. Paul's Cathedral in London, and were sold about the time of Oliver Cromwell. The lectern is said to have come from the same place; **Iglesia de San Francisco**, in the Alameda, 1689, an old church with a curious and irregular interior; **del Seminario**, built by the Jesuits in 1756, with some curious masked galleries. The south altar-piece is supported by four columns, which are very fine pieces of wood-carving indeed; **San Telmo**, a quaint old church, most frequented by sailors and by fishermen, whose votive offerings in the shape of model ships, etc., may be seen hanging in various places. The interior is richly decorated, and the effect at night, when the lights are reflected by the heavily gilded wood-work, is striking; **Santo Domingo**, at the west end of the town, possesses some very good specimens of carved wood; **San Antonio**; **San José**, by the same architect as the Cathedral; **San Antonio Abad**, where Columbus attended Mass in August, 1492, before setting out for America. The present edifice dates from 1756. The building previously occupying the site was the first church erected in Grand Canary; **San Agustin**; **del Padronito**, both near the Port Road. There are also a number of Ermitas or Chapels, few of which are of any special interest.

The English Church is a substantial and well-designed stone building, about 1½ m. along the Port Road.

Clubs.—The **Casino** (Spanish), in the Alameda, with a small theatre, admits monthly members. **Circulo Mercantil**, Plaza de la Democracia, a most admirable example of decoration in blue basalt. **The Golf Club**, with links above and behind the Santa Catalina Hotel. The links are 2 miles round, with 13 holes, and are kept in very fair order. There are two championship cups, a monthly medal and other prizes. Subscription, 15 pesetas. **The Cricket Club**, with ground and pavilion near the Metropole Hotel. Subscription, 25 pesetas. **Lawn Tennis Club**, with several concrete courts. Subscription, 20 pesetas. The game is also played at most of the hotels. The Alfred Jones Championship Cup is open to all comers.

It may here be mentioned that the place of an English Club is filled to a certain extent by the hotels themselves, which have maintained for many years the admirable custom of inviting guests at other hotels when dances or entertainments are given. In 1901, a mixed committee was formed for the purpose of providing fortnightly *al fresco* entertainments, a result of the very successful battle of flowers and open-air *fête* which took place in the spring of that year.

Squares and Promenades.—**Plaza de Santa Ana**, between the Cathedral and the Municipio;—the **Alameda de Colon**, where the band plays, well planted with trees, and ornamented with a bust of Columbus. It occupies the site formerly belonging to the Convento de Santa Clara. In the garden below the Alameda, and in front of the Casino, is a bust of Bartolomé Cairasco de Figueroa, a native poet, 1540–1610. This is the favourite rendezvous of an evening;—**el Parque**, a garden near the Mole. **Plaza de la Feria**, where the electric lighting works are built. The large building near the sea is the **Commandancia de Marina**;— the **Mole** itself, which was to have been greatly extended, but failed to stand against the sea. It is proposed to build a promenade on the sea front between the Mole and the Theatre.

Cemeteries.—The Roman Catholic Cemetery is near the sea on the Telde side of the town. The Protestant Cemetery lies in the same direction, but above the road.

Las Palmas is a town of flat roofs and low houses, from which the Cathedral and the new Theatre rise conspicuously, and in a manner somewhat opposed to its generally oriental appearance. It is slightly above the level of the sea, faces east, and mosquito curtains should be used all the year round. On the west it is protected by hills, but the heat is always tempered by a breeze from the N.E., to which the stretch of sand connecting the town with Puerto de la Luz and the Isleta offers no obstacle. The country in the immediate neighbourhood is dry, but an ample supply of water is obtained from the mountains by means of small stone channels. Drinking water is laid on in the city and down to the Port by iron pipes, communicating with the Fuente Morales, a spring some distance above the town, in such a manner that contamination is prevented. A supply is laid on to the hotels and larger houses directly from the main.

The principal street is the Triana, a continuation of the road from the Port, where the largest shops are situated. The fashionable part of the town is the Santo Espiritu, where some of the houses are handsomely designed and constructed.

The temperature on the sea level during the autumn is sometimes high, but visitors do remain at times all through the hot months, although the season for invalids does not really commence until October or November. The climate in the hills, however, is most delightful, and it is to be hoped that suitable accommodation in several places, as well as in the Monte, will soon be supplied.

The public gardens and squares are provided with seats where a pleasant hour or two may be passed occasionally. A walk on the mole during the middle of the day is also enjoyable on account of the refreshing breeze. Since the American war the town has been fortified, and visitors should not approach the batteries without permission.

The arid slopes behind the town give a very misleading idea of the interior of the island, many parts of which are green and well watered.

Drives, Walks, and Excursions near the town.—Several drives have been mentioned under Puerto de la Luz with the view of allowing those with little time to make their plans without unnecessary trouble. All the short drives round Las Palmas are there named. The prices of carriages from the town or from the hotels outside it are given with the other prices at the end of the section referring to Grand Canary. If it is desired to go further afield, reference should be made to the pages devoted to the particular road selected. A time table of the public coaches and their fares is given.

There are a few walks at the back of the town which can be taken by following any turning out of one of the *carreteras*.

To the Puerto de la Luz, Confital Bay, the Isleta and the Lighthouse.—The methods of reaching the Puerto have been detailed under the space allotted to the Puerto itself.

The road is too full of traffic to form a favourite promenade, but the sands between the town and Santa Catalina are very agreeable.

About a mile out of the town, the Santa Catalina and Metropole Hotels and the English Church are passed. A few paces further on is the **Santa Catalina bathing establishment** with 10 baths, charge 1 peseta. The spring is situated between the road and the sea, and the temperature of the water is some 10° warmer than the latter. The analysis shows that one kilogramme of water contains

Chloride of Sodium	grammes	6·049
,, ,, Potassium	,,	0·108
,, ,, Calcium	,,	0·281
Bicarb. ,, Lime ...	,,	0·147
,, ,, Magnesia	,,	1·157
Sulphate ,, ,,	,,	0·870
Silicate	,,	0·108
Free Carbonic Acid	,,	1·004

A direct road is to be made connecting the Puerto with Tamaraceite, 4½ m., 7 kils., and consequently with Arucas, Tafira, etc.

Until recently, the dismantled remains of a **Canario burial-ground** were to be seen not far from the base of the long Mole.

The Isleta appears to have been regarded by the natives as a spot of peculiar sanctity, in somewhat the same way as was the case formerly with our own Isle of Anglesea.

By bearing to the left at the entrance of the Isleta, **Confital Bay** is reached in a little over a mile. The rocks are a favourite hunting ground for shells and sea-weeds, and are a pleasant spot for a picnic. A little beyond are the saltpans.

A road along which carriages can pass leads across the Isleta to the **Lighthouse (Faro)** in about 2 hrs. The lanterns can be seen, and the summit commands a very fine view of the N. of the island. Paths lead out of the road to the signal stations.

Main Road, North Side of the Island. — Tamaraceite (Teror), Arucas (Firgas, Moya), Bañadero, Guia, Gáldar and Agaete, with excursions from the same. (For Public Coaches, *see* page 251.)

The road leaves the Mole and ascends the barranco, leaving the fort on the left. At 1 m., Mr. Thomas Miller's farmstead is passed on the left. The country is dry, but there are several tanks, and a great part of it is under cultivation. Mounting the hills to the right, 650 ft., a descent is made to **Tamaraceite**, 580 ft., $4\frac{1}{2}$ m. ($7\frac{1}{2}$ kils.), where a small sugar mill (*trapiche*) is to be seen.

From here a path leads in about $1\frac{1}{2}$ hrs. by **San Lorenzo**, the Vega de Abajo and the Bco. del Dragonal to **Tafira** and the **Monte**. The direct *carretera* from the Puerto de la Luz to Tamaraceite, $4\frac{1}{2}$ m., 7 kils., is to be continued to San Lorenzo, $2\frac{1}{2}$ m., 4 kils., and Tafira, 5 m., 8 kils.

A little further on a branch of the *carretera* to the left leads to **Teror**, 13 m. ($20\frac{1}{2}$ kils.), 1,750 ft., 4,795 inhab. Small inn, 3s. a day. Teror is a large village situated in the midst of an attractive valley. In the Barranco de la Fuente Agria, a few minutes below the houses, are some mineral springs dedicated to Our Lady of Lourdes, where there is a bathing establishment with 4 baths. Charge 25 centimos.

The **Church** (N.S. del Pino), A.D. 1740, is the chief object of interest in the village. The *exterior* is good of its kind. The tower to the left is a part of the old church, now pulled down, and almost the only good example of Gothic renaissance in the whole island. The church is dedicated to the Virgen del Pino, who is said to have appeared in the branches of a pine tree which once stood in the square in front of the church, on the spot now marked by a cross. The pine tree close by is said to be a direct descendant of the original pine. Formerly there was a holy spring on the spot of which the waters are said to have been very efficacious. It was, however, proposed that it should be sold, and it is said that it dried up in consequence. The *interior* of the church is handsome and the group of five altars at the chancel end cannot fail to attract attention. The church was very wealthy before the confiscation of ecclesiastical property by the State, and the robes and jewels, many of which are very valuable, are well worth seeing. The image of the Holy Virgin is upstairs above the chancel and stands in a large shrine of beaten silver. The picture of St. Joseph and Child opposite the shrine is above the ordinary standard of art to be seen in the Canaries.

The **Bishop's Palace**, formerly a convent, stands behind the church and is of no particular interest.

The **Convent**, some $\frac{1}{4}$ mile on the way to Firgas, is occupied by about 25 to 30 nuns. The church is plain and without merit.

Walks and Excursions from Teror.—A most beautiful walk is to the woods of **Los Osorios**, 2,480 ft., $\frac{1}{2}$ hr., where there is a spring. This is a good spot for a picnic, and from it the **Pico de los Osorios**, 3,250 ft., can be ascended in about $\frac{3}{4}$ hr., and the walk can be continued to **Firgas**, $1\frac{3}{4}$ hrs. (*See* Firgas.) The Pico commands a marvellous view, which stretches from the Mña. de Galdar on the N.W. to the Pico de Bandama on the S.E.

To Santa Brigida and the Monte *via* **the Vega del Centro**, $2\frac{1}{4}$ hrs. (*See* Excursion from the Monte.)

GRAND CANARY (NORTH ROAD: TEROR, ETC.). 232

To Valleseco, 3,150 ft., 1 hr., and the Cumbres (Cruz de Tejeda), 4½ hrs., is a pretty excursion. Valleseco is an uninteresting group of houses where a large church is being built. No inn but beds possible. For continuation to Tejeda, Tirajana, etc., *see* elsewhere.

To Firgas, 1¾ hrs., Moya, 3 hrs., Mña. de Doramas, los Tilos, 4 hrs., and Guia, 6¼ hrs. (*See* Guia.)

To Artenara *viâ* Valleseco, etc., about 4 hrs., whence on to Tejeda, about 5½ hrs., or down to Agaete, about 8 hrs. total. All fine but tiring excursions.

To San Mateo *viâ* the Vega de Arriba, about 3½ hrs. Not so fine as to Sta. Brigida *viâ* the Vega del Centro.

To Tafira *viâ* the *carretera* to Tamaraceite and through San Lorenzo, about 2 hrs. The easiest road to the Monte, but only picturesque when the Bco. del Dragonal below Tafira is reached. This is known as the route by the Vega de Abajo.

To Arucas, about 2½ hrs. (Mules in Teror from 4 to 5 pes. a day).

Main Road.—After passing the junction for Teror the *carretera* is carried through a tunnel, 6¼ m. (10 kils.), passes the little village of Tenoya and descends into the picturesque barranco of the same name. This is perhaps the most beautiful part of the whole of the N. road. A long climb then leads to

Arucas, 770 ft., 9,016 inhab., 10½ m. (17 kils.). Two Spanish inns, charges about a dollar a day.

Arucas is a fairly large town with a market place and is the chief centre of the cochineal and sugar industry. There are two sugar mills which may be seen and several large quarries. The mountain, ¾ hr. to the N. of the town, commands a good view

Excursions from Arucas.—To Teror by the bridle path, 2½ hrs. The country passed through is pleasant and the scenery improves towards the end. (*See* Teror.) A return can be made *viâ* Firgas or the Mña. de los Osorios can be ascended. Mules for the round in Arucas should cost from 3 to 4 pesetas.

Branch carretera to Firgas and Moya.—An unfinished carriage road leaves the main road at Arucas and bears to the left. At 14¾ m. (23 kils.) a subsidiary road, 1½ m. (2½ kils.) long, will lead to Firgas when completed. At present this part must be passed on mules or on foot. The main Moya branch descends from the junction into the bed of the Barranco Azuaje, 15½ m. (24½ kils.) some two or three hundred yards below the bathing establishment. From here it will be carried on to Moya, 18½ m. (29½ kils.).

Firgas, 1,625 ft., is a prettily situated village and a good centre for excursions or for a summer residence. Population, 2,088.

Inns.—Fonda Azuaje; Fonda de Firgas; charges, one dollar a day.

The village is best known as the site of a mineral spring which affords a wholesome and palatable drinking water. The spring, however, is really some half-hour up the barranco.

Analysis shows that a gallon of water contains
    Calcium Carbonate 12·6 grains
    Magnesium ,, ... 11·2 ,,
    Sodium ,, ... 1·5 ,,
    ,, Sulphate ... 1·2 ,,
    ,, Chloride ... 5·0 ,,

In the same barranco but immediately below the town is the warm spring known as the Fuente de Guadalupe. A steep path leads to the bathing establishment, 760 ft., in ½ hr., 2 baths; Charge : Morning, 1 peseta ; afternoon, 75 c. Temperature, 85° F. An analysis shows that 1 kilogramme of water contains

Chloride of Sodium	0·116	grammes
Bicarb. ,, Soda	0·797	,,
,, ,, Potash	0·020	,,
,, ,, Lime ...	0·422	,,
,, ,, Magnesia ...	0·265	,,
Sulphate ,, ,,	0·107	
Silicate	0·118	
Free Carbonic Acid	1·058	,,

Excursions from Firgas.—To los Osorios, Teror, the Monte, etc. —Teror can be reached by a path which leads below the Pico de los Osorios, crossing below the Pico at a height of 2,220 feet, but the usual route and by far the most attractive one is that which strikes almost due S. This leads in one steady climb to the Pico de la Laguna, as the southern spur of the Pico de los Osorios is called. The cumbre of this, 2,800 ft., is reached in 1¼ hrs., and commands fine views. Visitors, however, should make time to go to the top of the **Pico de los Osorios** itself, 3,250 ft., twenty minutes away from the path, whence there is a magnificent bird's-eye view of nearly the whole of the N. of the island. The Mña. de Doramas is best seen from here, and the Cumbres seem to lie close at hand ; Teror is just below, with Valleseco a short distance above it, and the Mña. de Galdar and the Pico de Bandama form landmarks on either horizon.

A return can be made to the path and a descent made directly into **Teror**, 1¾ hrs. from Firgas, not allowing for the above digression, or Teror can be reached from the Pico *via* the avenue of pine trees and the **chestnut woods of los Osorios** be taken on the way. The difference in time is not great.

From Teror to the **Monte** 2¼ hrs., *see* Monte. For excursions from Teror, etc., *see* Teror. Most of the paths in this district are very muddy in wet weather.

To Moya for Los Tilos, Guia, etc.—The same path that leads to the bathing establishment crosses the bed of the Bco. Azuaje, ½ hr., 760 ft., and ascends to **Moya**, 1¼ hrs., to **Los Tilos**, 2¼ hrs., **Guia**, 4½ hrs. (*See* Guia.)

Besides the above excursions there are a number of beautiful walks in the Bco. de la Virgen as the upper part of the Bco. Azuaje is called.

Mules in Firgas cost from 3 to 5 pesetas a day.

Moya, 1,530 ft., no inn, is a small village on the precipitous edge of the barranco. It is neither so pleasant nor so good a centre for walks as Firgas.

A descent can be made from Moya to **Pagador** near Bañadero by bridle road in ¾ hr.

Firgas can be reached in 1¼ hrs., **Teror** in 3 hrs., and the **Monte** in 5½, or **los Tilos** in 1 hr., and **Guia** in 3¼ hrs. Refer elsewhere. When the road to Moya is finished it will be the nearest spot from which **los Tilos** or the **Mña. de Doramas** can be visited.

The Mña. de Doramas is a wooded mountain covering an extensive tract of country and affording many spots suitable for picnics. The path up from Moya to **San Fernando** 1 hr., and the **Finca Corvo** 1½ hrs., is easy to find.

From Arucas the main road winds down to the coast, and passes the seaside villages of Bañadero (14 m. = 22½ kils.) and Pagador a mile further on, both uninteresting and dirty. Keeping close to the sea for a mile or two, a long ascent is commenced amidst wild and rocky surroundings. At 20 m. (32 kils.) there is a deep cutting called the Roque del Moro, immediately below some caves formerly occupied by the Canarios. The side of the mountain is known as the Cuesta de Silba. It was near here that Diego de Silba was surrounded by the Canarios, for which story refer to the history. The caves may be easily reached from the road and are well worthy of a visit. A guide should be procured and torches and candles taken.

The number of caves is said to be 364 and to correspond with the number of days in the year. This may be a coincidence or an untruth, as the writer has never counted them.

Shortly after passing the caves, the top of the hill (750 ft.) is reached and the wide slopes of Guia and Gáldar lie stretched in front. To the right is the great mountain of Gáldar, a monstrous mass of volcanic mud, of which, indeed, with the exception of the mountain to the west of Gáldar, the whole of the surface rocks of this corner of the island are composed.

Guia, 580 ft. (22 m. = 36 kils.), 5,237 inhabitants. Fonda Francisco Artiles, fairly good, rooms large; 5 to 8 pesetas.

Guia presents little of interest. The soil is fertile and well irrigated. Sugar is now largely cultivated, and one of the best mills in the island is situated half-way between the town and Gáldar.

Excursions from Guia.—To Agaete.—A tiresome ride leads across the slope and joins the main road a little before Agaete, 1½ hrs.

To Los Tilos, Mña. de Doramas, Moya, Firgas, etc.—The bridle path leaves the *carretera* a little on the Las Palmas side of Guia and passes the Ermita de San Juan, ½ hr. At the second water-mill, 1,600 ft., 1 hr., take the path to the left and cross the Bco. Calaboso. At 1¼ hrs., 1,950 ft., another path goes off to the right (either of these paths can be followed to Artenara, Tejeda, the Cumbres, etc.).

Keeping to the left the track leads amongst heather, laurels (til), chestnuts, etc. At 1¾ hrs. Santa Cristina, a few houses, 1,920 ft. A descent is now made into the precipitous Bco. de los Tilos and a shady spot at the bottom, 1,450 ft., 2¼ hrs., forms a good halting place. (If the Bco. is ascended a scattered wood is entered, the Ermita de S. Bartolomé is passed and eventually the Cumbres, etc., are reached.)

Ascending the other side of the Bco. the path to the right leads up the Mña. de Doramas (*see* Moya), that to the left turns down to Moya, 3¼ hrs., 1,530 ft.

From Moya to Pagador, ¾ hr., or to Firgas, 1¼ hrs., Teror, 3 hrs., etc., *refer* under Moya.

Coaches run from Guia to Agaete and back twice a day. Fare 1 peseta.

The main road turns to the right at Guia and leads across a fertile plain to

Gáldar, 500 ft. 25 m. (40 kils.), 5,280 inhab. Accommodation may be had.

Gáldar is a small town of very Eastern appearance, and possesses a large church of little interest which is said to occupy the site of the former palace of the Guanarteme, once the headquarters of the Princess Andamana. Close by is a small cave, the entrance to which was accidentally discovered in 1881. Owing to the air and light having been excluded, the interior is well preserved, and the greater part of the wall is still decorated by a geometrical pattern worked out in red and white ochre and charcoal. Many of the drip-stone filters used in the Canaries and the West Indies are made in the vicinity. In the patio of the Casino is a small dragon-tree. A *carretera* leads from Gáldar to the Puerto de Sardina, $3\frac{3}{4}$ m. (6 kils.).

The **Montaña de Gáldar,** 1,533 ft., the mud mountain previously mentioned, which commands a good view, can be ascended in about an hour. A number of caves in its sides were once used by the Canarios. In some the beams, placed by the natives, were to be seen until comparatively recently.

The *carretera* is continued through arid scenery to **Agaete,** $30\frac{1}{2}$ m. ($48\frac{1}{2}$ kils.), 2,837 inhabitants. Small inn, 3s. a day.

Agaete is prettily situated a short distance from the sea. There is a small harbour and a mole 1 m. ($1\frac{1}{2}$ kils.) from the town, which can be reached by the main road, of which the jetty is the terminus. On the beach is a Canario burial ground, in which many scores of graves yet remain unopened.

The church at Agaete seems very large for the village, but it is possible that at some time the place may grow up to it. A trade is carried on with Teneriffe by means of schooners, considerable quantities of butter and oranges, which grow very well here, being shipped across. Great damage was done by a flood which swept down the barranco in February, 1896. There are two houses in Agaete, said to have been built by the Canarios. (*See* Webb and Berthelot.)

Excursions from Agaete.—To the Mineral Springs, Artenara, etc. —A climb up the fertile, mountainous ravine at the back of the town leads to the spring, 1,650 ft., in about 2 hrs. There is a small bathing establishment, 2 baths. Charge $\frac{1}{2}$ peseta. The water is highly charged with mineral matter, and is said to be of great use in skin diseases.

GRAND CANARY (NORTH ROAD: AGAETE, ETC.). 235A

The water issues at a temperature of 77°F., and is strongly charged with carbonic acid gas. The following analysis has been made :—

	Grains per Gallon.
Silica	8·0
Ferrous Carbonate	10·0
Calcium ,,	3·0
Magnesium ,,	33·5
Sodium Sulphate	2·5
,, Chloride	4·5
Total Salts	61·5

It is said to resemble the Lower Soda Spring (No. 1) at Salem, Or., U.S.A., and to be adapted for those suffering from anæmia.

Following up the barranco, **Artenara**, where a bed may be found, can be reached in about 6 hrs., the **Cumbres** in about 7, or **Valleseco, San Mateo**, etc., can be reached in a little more. Guide required. There is a remarkable basaltic wall, or exposed dyke, to be seen in the Valle de Peñones. Several detours can be made from the barranco by those stopping in Agaete, and a number of very fine excursions can be made. The barranco itself is very beautiful.

To Aldea de San Nicolas, Tejeda or Mogan.—A path leads along the cliffs to Aldea in about 5 hrs. The rocks passed through are very fine, and at one time a height of 2,300 ft. is gained. It is from this path that the Mña. de **Tirma** is visited, one of the two most sacred mountains of the Canarios. A guide must be taken, and care must be exercised that he knows what mountain he is to go to, as very few indeed are acquainted with the place.

There is no inn, but beds can be procured in **Aldea**. From here a path leads to **Tejeda** (beds possible) in about 6½ hrs., or another path along the coast leads to **Mogan** (beds possible) in 5 or 6 hrs. Refer elsewhere.

Aldea de S. Nicolas can be reached more conveniently in a boat from Agaete in about 1½ hrs. Fare about 4$.

Central Main Road from Las Palmas to Tafira, the Monte, Santa Brigida and San Mateo, with side excursions and routes from San Mateo to the Cumbres, to the S. of the island, etc. (Public Coaches, page 251.)

The road crosses the stone bridge over the Bco. de Guiniguada and turns up to the right. Passing through a beautiful grove of palms, past some banana gardens, and under some quarries from which the white tufa is taken out of which the best part of the city is built, a long climb leads up to the Pico del Viento, 820 ft., a spot a little on the right of the road, which commands a view of San Lorenzo, etc., and allows an idea to be formed of the lie of the land.

A little further on the left a turning leads to **Jinamar** in about 1½ and **Telde** in about 2½ hrs. The journey is best made on foot or horseback. The path is rather intricate and it is frequently necessary to ask the way. It is possible to climb the **Gran Caldera** or to ascend to **Atalaya**. The Telde *carretera* is joined at a point 6½ m. (10½ kils.) from Las Palmas.

Above the turning amongst a row of houses is a venta known as the **Half-way House**, 4 m. (6 kil.), 950 ft., where wine, etc., can be obtained.

The barranco on the right is here called the Bco. del Dragonal, lower down the Bco. de la Ciudad and at its mouth the Bco. Guiniguada. Higher up the name changes successively to the Bco. Angostura, Bco. de Alonso, and ultimately Bco. de Utiaca. This succession of names in a long barranco is of common occurrence. It is in the Bco. de la Ciudad that the Fuente de Morales, which supplies the town and ships with drinking water, is situated.

At 5 m. (8 kils.) the village and church of **Tafira**, 1,080 ft. Inn :—Fonda Esperanza, from 5s. a day. *(See advertisement.)*

The village is of no interest and need only be mentioned as the starting point for the path which descends into the **Bco. del Dragonal**, and leads *viâ* **San Lorenzo** and the **Vega de Abajo** to **Tamaraceite**, about 1 hr., and so on to **Teror**, etc. A *carretera* is to be made from Tafira to San Lorenzo, 2½ m. 4 kils.; Tamaraceite, 5 m. 8 kils., and the Puerto de la Luz, 9½ m. 15 kils.

On leaving Tafira the view down into the Bco. del Dragonal is very striking, the air becomes cooler, the vine-clad hills greener, and the eucalyptus trees by the side of the road straighter and more stately.

This part of the island is known as the Monte or Ex-Monte de Lentiscal, because the cindery expanse, now covered with vines, was, until the beginning of the nineteenth century, given up to euphorbia and the native scrub. It is now the chief and best source of the canary wine (red).

At 6 m. (9½ kils.), 1,320 ft., Quiney's Bella Vista Hotel, 7/6 a day, pleasantly situated and a good centre for excursions. At 7 miles (10½ kils.) the Hotel Santa Brigida, 1,360 feet, newly erected in a commanding position, charges from 10s. Both hotels have good gardens.

(For advertisements, see under Grand Canary at the end of the book.)

The Monte is not only the chief summer resort of the residents in Grand Canary, but is regarded by competent authorities as a very favourable position for those suffering from pulmonary and other complaints. Dr. Brian Melland in his work "Climatic Treatment in Grand Canary," speaks loudly in its praise. This gentleman has not only lived in the Monte himself, but has practised in the island for many years and has had opportunities of studying the progress of his patients. As a possible alternative to Las Palmas, the bracing, pure atmosphere of this semi-mountainous resort is an advantage to invalids visiting the islands, who may choose between the sea-board, the intermediate station of Gáldar, and the place under discussion. The opening up of isolated country sanatoria in Grand Canary is a distinctly progressive step in the right direction.

Walks, Rides and Excursions from the Monte.—Along the Bco. Angostura to Santa Brigida.—From either hotel paths lead down to the Bco. which is here some 300 ft. below the road, in about 20 min. In starting from the Bella Vista Hotel the turning to the left is taken at the bottom and is followed past the **Finca de los Laureles** to **Sta. Brigida** in about 1¼ hrs. total, whence return by the *carretera*, 2½ m. (4 kils.).

Down the Bco. to Tafira or to the Bco. del Dragonal, etc.—Turning to the right at the bottom of the Bco. the gorge known as the Angostura is passed through. Presently the caves and cottages of **Los Frailes** and then **La Calzada**, whence a path to the right leads to **Tafira**, total 1 hr., or following the Bco. a wooden bridge is passed and El Dragonal is entered. Lower down at 1½ hrs. is a farm where there are two shrivelled old dragon trees. From here the path leading from Tafira to San Lorenzo (*see* Tafira) can be taken and Tafira regained in a total of two hours. From Tafira to the Bella Vista Hotel is about 1 m., and to the Santa Brigida about 2 m.

To San Francisco, Telde, etc.—Another walk is to **San Francisco**, ¼ hr. on the Telde side of Tafira. This can be reached by taking any of the turnings to the right as the *carretera* is descended from the hotels. It is possible to reach Telde by the same path, which leaves the *carretera* below the Half-Way House, or a return may be made by the road leading to the Gran Caldera. Donkeys or mules can be used if desired.

To the Gran Caldera, Atalaya, Valsequillo, etc.—At 6½ m. (10 kils.) from Las Palmas, and between the two hotels, a rough carriage road descends to the left and leads to the foot of the **Gran Caldera de Bandama**.

Turning to the right, ascend to a group of cottages, pass through these and bear to the left a few yards along the path leading down into the crater, ½ hr., 1,350 ft.

The crater is one of the most perfect known. There is no outlet; the width is over a mile, and the bottom, which has gradually subsided, is nearly 1,000 ft. below the crest of the walls. The layers of cinders around the lip and the vivid colours of some of the rocks sufficiently attest its origin. The bottom is cultivated, and a descent can be made on mules, ¾ hr. down and up. A glass of the wine made from vines grown inside the crater can be obtained in one of the neigbouring cottages.

From the cottages a path (safe for animals) leads to the top of the **Peak**, 1,840 ft. in ¼ hr. This is well worth climbing, not merely for the view of the crater but for that of the surrounding country, forming as it does the complement to that visible from the Pico de los Osorios above Teror.

On the N.E. is the Isleto, floating in the sea like a separate island, and the houses of the Puerto. Nearer in, part of Las Palmas and the villages of San Lorenzo and Tafira, with innumerable groups of houses scattered about. To the E. is the valley of Jinamar, and to the S.E. Telde, Los Llanos, the Mña. de las Cuatro Puertas and the Lazareto at Gando Point. The crater is close below, then follows a somewhat dreary stretch, until a few of the houses of Valsequillo are seen to the S.W. Running the eye along the Cumbres, Atalaya is the only inhabited place visible. The Pico de los Osorios is prominent on the W. horizon; part of Arucas is seen to the N.W. and the circle is completed at San Lorenzo. The best time to photograph the Gran Caldera is about 2.30 p.m.

From the cottages another path leads along the ridge of the hill and up a deep, hilly lane to **Atalaya**, 1,720 ft., in ½ hr. The most important quarry in the island is passed just before arriving at the village.

Atalaya (Watch Tower) is the most perfect collection of troglodyte dwellings in the Archipelago. It overlooks the picturesque Bco. de las Goteras and was formerly a native stronghold. The present inhabitants manufacture pottery out of clay found in the neighbourhood, fashioning it with a round stone and without a wheel, in precisely the same manner as the Canarios themselves. For some reason the people are unfavourably regarded by their neighbours, who rarely intermarry with them. Whether this aversion is a legacy left from before the conquest or not is difficult to ascertain.

Those who have driven from Las Palmas can send their carriage from the Caldera to a point a little below Santa Brigida and rejoin it there from Atalaya (a short half hour) or a return can be made by turning to the left out of the path leading back to the Caldera and rejoining the carriage by a little wine-shop at the foot of the hill.

From Atalaya a path leads to **Valsequillo** in 2 hrs., **Telde**, 4 hrs., or up to the Cumbres from Valsequillo.

To La Gloria and beyond.—La Gloria is a pleasant, shady picnic resort. Near it are a fine waterfall, some 70 feet high, and a large tank, supposed to have formerly served as a Canario temple. Leaving the *carretera* a little beyond Santa Brigida, pass La Gloria (½ hr. from hotel), bear to the left and ascend to a water-course on a high ridge. Cross a valley and climb again to another ridge, 2½ hrs. total, whence there are magnificent views of the island from Agüimes to Gáldar. Thence to San Mateo, ¾ hr. and home *viâ* the *carretera*. A good walk.

To Teror, Firgas, Guia, etc.—The most attractive route to Teror is by the **Vega del Centro.** Ascend the *carretera* to **Santa Brigida**, 1,580 ft., whence on foot or mules. Times from Santa Brigida.

Descend into and cross the **Bco. de la Vega** and as due N.W. as possible. A rock with some beautiful specimens of basaltic crystals, some 45 ft. long, will be noticed. Near it a few caves and a large dragon tree. At ¼ hr. the bed of the **Bco. de Alonso**, 1,410 ft., which is impassable during heavy rains. An ascent is made and then the **Bco. del Pino Santo** is crossed, 1,820 ft., ½ hr.

[Instead of descending to this barranco, a path to the left can be followed which leads through the beautiful chestnut woods of San Isidro, 2½ hrs., interesting old church (private property), whence return or bear to the right down to Teror, 3½ hrs. total. A very fine excursion.]

A long climb follows to just below the **Caldera de la Vega**, 2,450 ft., 1¼ hrs., a small, unbroken crater invisible from but close to the path. On the upper side are a small group of trees and a spring, which in fine weather would form a capital camping ground.

A short distance further on is the **Cruz de Lobrelar**, 2,430 ft., whence there is a very fine view of the upper part of the amphitheatre of **Teror**, etc. (Those who are staying at the Monte should return from here). A steep descent now leads into **Teror**; total time, 2¼ hrs. For further on, refer to Teror, etc. Firgas is the best place to sleep. **Other routes from the Monte to Teror** are *viâ* San Lorenzo and Tamaraceite (*see* Teror, etc.), about 2 hrs., *or* by San Mateo and the Vega de Arriba in about 3½ hrs. (*See* San Mateo.) The Vega del Centro is the most picturesque.

For Artenara, the Cumbres and S. of the island, *see* San Mateo.

The **Main Road** leaves the Monte and ascends to 7¼ m. (11½ kils.), whence a road is being made to Atalaya, 2 m. (3 kils.); the Barranco de las Goteras, and later, *viâ* the Barranco de las Higueras to Telde, 9½ m. (15 kils.) total. At 8 m. (13 kils.) a path to the left leads to Atalaya, ½ hr., Valsequillo, 2½ hrs., etc. (*See* Atalaya.)

At 8½ m. (13⅓ kils.) **Santa Brigida,** 1,580 ft., pop. 4,920, a village built on the edge of the barranco. The church is not of much interest. There are one or two fondas, 4 to 5 pesetas a day. Accommodation poor. The excursions from here are given under the Monte. There is a pretty walk to the left just above the town.

At **Los Pasitos,** 11 m. (19 kils.) there is a grove of trees with one enormous chestnut standing close to the road, said to be the largest in the island. It is not very high but measures 25 ft. 7 in. round.

At 13 m. (21 kils.) **San Mateo,** 2,680 ft., 4,170 inhab. Small fonda, 2 rooms. Indifferent. Arrangements might be made to secure beds elsewhere.

The town is beautifully situated. In the neighbourhood are groves of walnuts, chestnuts, pines, &c. The place offers great attraction as a mountain climatic resort and as a centre for a number of excursions. It is also the best point of departure for the Cumbres and for the S. of the island generally. The village itself, where the *carretera* ends, is of no interest.

Excursions from San Mateo.—To los Chorros.—A path up the Bco. between the town and the **Mña. de Cabreja** leads in 20 min. to the springs. A little higher up is a waterfall some 120 ft. high. The bed of the stream is followed and crossed and the walk is altogether a very pretty one. The Mña. de Cabreja can be climbed if desired, about 1 hr. of rather rough work.

To El Charco de la Higuera, Valsequillo, etc.—Turning to the left at the top of the village, a good path leads in 25 min. to El Charco de la Higuera, a waterfall 60 ft. high, prettily situated. The slopes beyond command a fine view of the plains of **Valsequillo**, which can be reached on foot or mule in about 1½ hrs.

To Teror.—A path to the W. leads under the Mña. de Cabreja, across the **Vega de Arriba** and down to **Teror** in about 3½ hrs.

To Tejeda direct.—The direct road is taken past the **Cruz de Tejeda**, 5,740 ft., about 2½ hrs. and down the Bco. de la Culata to **Tejeda**, 3,160 ft., about 4 hrs. Poor accommodation, 1 dollar.

The view of the Barranco de la Culata from the Cruz de Tejeda with the isolated Roque Nublo, 6,110 ft., boldly defined on the left; the vast succession of precipitous ravines in front and on the right, in strong contrast to the startling verdure of the cultivated patches below; the blue sea in the distance, and the lofty mountains and majestic Peak of Teneriffe towering above and crowning the whole, form a picture never to be forgotten and second to none in Switzerland or the Alps.

The Peak is visible almost all the way down to Tejeda. Its great height is never so well appreciated as when it soars higher and higher over the adjacent cliffs, which appear to shrink away as the traveller descends, as though reluctant to hide it from sight.

About a mile below Tejeda is an isolated rock known as the **Roque de Bentaguaya** near which are some Canario caves.

Excursions from Tejeda.—To **Artenara** in about 1½ hrs. and thence to **Agaete** in about 6 hrs. Fine scenery.

To **Aldea de S. Nicolas** in about 6½ hrs. whence boat to **Agaete**, 1½ hrs., or by the cliffs in about 6 hrs. (*see* Agaete), *or* to **Mogan** in 5 or 6 hrs. along the coast. Very rough work.

To **Mogan direct** in 6 or 7 hrs. An arduous journey.

To **Tirajana.**—Ascend the Bco. de la Culata, leave the Roque Nublo on the right, cross the Cumbres and descend the Paso de la Plata to **Tunte**, 5 hrs. (*See* Tunte.)

From San Mateo to Agaete, Artenara, etc.—Pass below the Mña. de Cabreja, descend into and cross the **Bcos. de Utiaca**, 40 min., **Ariñes** and **San Isidro**, in the last of which a fiesta is held once a year, to just below the **Caldereta de Valleseco**, where turn to the right for **Valleseco**, about 3 hrs.; to the left for **Artenara**, about 4 hrs., or the **Cruz de Tejeda**, about 4 hrs.; or continue to **Agaete**, about 7 hrs., etc. (*See* Map). These roads are practicable for animals, but a guide is absolutely necessary.

From San Mateo to the Cumbres.—The path up to the **Cruz de Tejeda**, 5,740 ft., 2½ hrs., has already been mentioned.

The most direct and most frequented track is that known as the **Paso de la Cueva Grande**, which leaves the top of the village and ascends the ridge dividing the Bco. de los Chorros from the Bco. de la Lechucilla. At about ¾ hr. there is a good view of San Mateo and of the whole country between it and Las Palmas. Eventually a projecting wall of basalt is passed through, where a cross marks the spot on which a man was frozen to death, and the Cumbres are reached in a little over 2 hrs.

The most picturesque route is to bear to the left at the top of the village. The Barranco de la Lechucilla is then followed one-third up. The stream is crossed, and a zigzag path leads directly to the summit of the ridge, dividing this barranco from that called "del Rodeo." Fine view. Pedestrians may now keep up the ridge, and skirt the cinder mountain on the left side, pass between the summit and the **Roque de los Saucillos**, and the Cumbres lie in front, 2½ hrs. That surmounted by a cross, the **Montaña de la Cruz Santa**, 6,068 ft., may be climbed, but the highest point, 6,400 ft., is near the "**Pozos**," further to the right. The "Pozos" are a depository of snow and ice, which can be descended by a wooden ladder. They are sometimes locked up.

Those on mules must cross the head of the Barranco del Rodeo (fine view as far as Telde and the sea), and ascend the mountain side, leaving the Roque de los Saucillos on the right. The two parties can meet at the place of the fiesta, at the W. foot of the Holy Cross, where twice a year there is a religious gathering and a small fair (Saint days of St. Peter and St. John).

From here the **Pico de los Pozos** is crossed and the Paso de la Cueva Grande is met at a point marked by a cross.

Those ascending the Cumbres will understand that on arriving at the summit there is no difficulty in moving about. The summit of the island is a shallow undulating basin with an inclination towards the Bco. de Tejeda. Here and there the surface is broken by such projections as the Mña. de la Cruz Santa, the Roque Nublo (a most remarkable stone pillar easily visible from Teneriffe and some 370 ft. in height), and by basaltic walls or dykes exposed by denudation, but the general impression left on the mind is that of a great shadowless waste, covered with loose stones and silent as Hades.

The magnificent view from near the Cruz de Tejeda has already been mentioned. Whether the ascent be made by the Cueva Grande or by the Roque de los Saucillos route, it is suggested that a return be made which shall embrace this view.

A fair price for mules in San Mateo is from 3·75 to 5 pes. a day, though more may be asked. Times may be calculated as $2\frac{1}{2}$ hrs. up, 1 hr. to cross the Cumbres and 2 hrs. down.

South of the Island from San Mateo.—The route *viâ* Tejeda to San Nicolas and Mogan has already been given.

To Tirajana (Tunte), Mogan, etc.—Ascend by the Paso de la Cueva Grande, $2\frac{1}{2}$ hrs., cross the **Cumbres**, $3\frac{1}{2}$ hrs., and descend the paved **Paso de la Plata** to the cross, $4\frac{1}{2}$ hrs.

From here to **Mogan** about 6 hrs. and Aldea about 12 hrs. A wild rough road.

From the cross, the path descends through the Pinar, as a number of scattered pine-trees are called, passes the Cemetery and enters **Tunte (S. Bartolomé de Tirajana)**, 2,660 ft., beds possible, in $5\frac{1}{2}$ hrs. (*See* Tunte.)

To Santa Lucía, etc.: Leave San Mateo by the Roque de los Saucillos route, $2\frac{1}{2}$ hrs., cross the **Cumbres**, $3\frac{1}{2}$ hrs., descend by the **Vueltas de Taidía** past **Taidia**, where the circular Canario house once stood (refer Taidía), to the bottom of the **Barranco de Tirajana**, 1,850 ft., $5\frac{3}{4}$ hrs., and turn to the left to **Santa Lucia**, $6\frac{1}{4}$ hrs., 2,056 ft., bad accommodation, *see* elsewhere, *or* cross the bed of the barranco and ascend to **Tunte**, $7\frac{1}{2}$ hrs.

Both the above routes command very fine views, but the first is the best for travelling. On the second the road down the Vueltas is difficult to find, but the bird's-eye view into the Bco. de Tirajana, described elsewhere, is magnificent.

Agüimes can be reached from Santa Lucía in $3\frac{1}{4}$ hrs. or from Tunte in $4\frac{1}{4}$ hrs. and **Maspalomas** can be reached from the latter in 5 hrs. Refer elsewhere for details.

Main Road to the South of the Island.

From Las Palmas to Telde, Ingenio, Agüimes, Santa Lucia, San Bartolomé (Tunte) with continuation to San Mateo, Tejeda, etc. (Public Coaches, page 251.)

The high-road leaves the stone bridge, turns up by the Municipio and bears to the left into the Telde *carretera*, leaving the Protestant Cemetery on the right and skirting the coast by the side of a number of banana gardens.

At 4 m. (6 kilos.) a tunnel is passed through, and at 5¾ m. (9 kils.) is the village of **Jinamar**, 210 ft., a scattered group of houses spread over a valley lying below the Gran. Caldera, bounded on one side by a wide stream of lava, and on the other by a black cinder wall. In spite of its volcanic surroundings, good limestone is found close to the village.

A number of paths lead inland from here, and **Tafira** can be reached in about 1½ hrs. or **Atalaya** in about the same time. Refer elsewhere.

A walk of about ½ hr. from the road leads to **La Cisma de Gallego**, a volcanic hole or perpendicular lava cave supposed to be unfathomable. The hole is dangerous.

At 6½ m. (10½ kils.) a stream of lava crosses the road and allows those driving to Telde to examine the *Euphorbia Canariensis*, an indigenous euphorbia peculiar to the Canaries from which a strong caustic exudes in the shape of milk. Care must be taken not to get it on the hands or in the eyes. In case of accident a fleshy-leaved plant, which frequently grows near or inside the euphorbia bush, supplies a remedy. This euphorbia is seldom found in positions where the roots are not in actual contact with basic lava. The milk is sometimes used by the fishermen to stupefy fish.

A path leaves the road at the foot of the hill from which the lava flows and leads to **Tafira** in about 2½ hrs. (*see* Tafira) or, by bearing to the left, the **Bco. de la Higuera de Canaria** can be reached, a little higher up than the orange groves mentioned under Telde.

Very soon Telde comes into view, the groves of palm trees, Moorish dome of Los Llanos, and groups of white houses seeming rather to realise one's ideal of an old Syrian city than that of a town in the Canaries. The barranco is next crossed by a handsome stone bridge, on the right of which are a number of old Canario caves, and the town is entered.

Telde, 390 ft., 8¼ m. (13 kils.), 8,894 inhabitants. No fonda, but beds can be had.

With better accommodation Telde might form a good centre for visitors. The rainfall is scanty and the climate good, added to which there is generally a refreshing breeze. The scenery in the neighbourhood is far less attractive than that to be found on the N. of the Island.

There are two churches, San Juan and San Pedro, neither of much interest. A good supply of water is obtained from the hills, and there are several well cultivated farms in the neighbourhood. There is also a sugar-mill, and a certain quantity of cane is grown.

A pleasant walk is to follow the bed of the Barranco de la Higuera de Canaria, to the W. of the town, for about $2\frac{1}{2}$ m., to the far-famed orange groves, where the best fruit of the Archipelago is produced. Little care is taken of the trees. The soil is a sandy loam, and all the trees are planted on the N. slope.

A *carretera* is to be made leaving Telde by the Barranco de la Higuera, and ascending to near Santa Brigida, $9\frac{1}{2}$ m. (15 kils.), by way of the Barranco de las Goteras and Atalaya. The upper part is in course of construction.

Leaving the main street of Telde by the Calle de Cubas, and turning to the right at the bridge, some 300 yds. up, the adjacent village of **Los Llanos** is reached, about $\frac{1}{2}$ m. from Telde proper. It is here that the best country knives are made, but it is rarely that the makers have any in stock. The Church is large but of no interest.

A tiresome bridle path leads from here to **Valsequillo**, 2 hrs., an uninteresting village, where a quantity of almonds are grown (no accommodation), to **Atalaya** or **San Mateo**, about 4 hrs.

By the Church, a turning to the left leads into the main road to Agüimes. The drive is very dull and barren, but the land gives large crops of wheat in rainy years.

At $12\frac{1}{2}$ m. ($19\frac{1}{2}$ kils.), the **Montaña de las Cuatro Puertas** (four doors) is passed on the left. It is within ten minutes of the road, and is the most perfect example left of what was undoubtedly an aboriginal place of worship ; probably that known to the Canarios by the name of **Humiaya**. (Read pages 113 to 118.)

On the N. side of the summit is a large and carefully excavated cave, with a square platform in front, both facing directly towards the Isleta, where the most sacred burial ground of the Canarios was situated. Owing to the protected position, and the fact that this is one of the driest parts of the island, everything has remained nearly intact.

The four entrances, which give the mountain its name, are only separated by columns, thus allowing free entrance to the wind. As this part of the island is nearly always windy, this alone is sufficient to prove that the place was never intended as a shelter. The socket holes in the platform were probably used for erecting some timber structure to support the body during the funeral ceremonies, before the procession set out for the burial ground.

Keeping the top of the hill on the right, and proceeding to the sheltered side, a well cut path in the rock leads to a succession of caves. Acting on the supposition that this was a residence of priests (*faycans*) and consecrated virgins (*harimaguadas*), these can be explained as follows.

The path is superior to that usually leading to Canario caves, and such as might be made in a case where a heavy body had to be carried carefully.

The small caves on the right probably belonged to the sentries who guarded the entrance.

The first large cave on the right, with the three trenches pointing towards a common centre, was probably used for drying the bodies in the sun after they had been cleaned and prepared, the bodies being placed in the trenches so that they could easily be covered up in case of rain. The space behind would suffice for the chief mourners, who would accompany the body round to the temple, and the small caves in the side may have served for litters, etc.

The small cave below, on the other side of the path, was probably devoted to the preparation of the dead body, the three receptacles in the wall being used to hold the various medicaments required.

The passage leading from the drying trenches to the caves inside must be presumed to have been closed by a door, so as to allow of communication between the inmates and the outside world, without actual contact. It will be noticed that there are no steps descending into the interior.

The large cave which this passage overlooks, and the three small chambers in its walls, across one of which the sockets for the beams are to be seen, was no doubt partly used as a store chamber. The dry position it occupies would make it very suitable. It should be remembered that it was one of the duties of the priestly order to store what remained over from their tithes against times of scarcity. Grain was usually kept in pots or in holes in the ground.

In the next cave the beams were evidently carried right across, and it seems likely, from the shape of the western buttress, that this was the kitchen. The men of the establishment would have slept on the beams, as it would have been dangerous to place stores so close to the fire.

The next cave is small, and the beams must have been so near the roof that they could only have served as an ornament. This indicates that it was occupied by some dignitary, such as the chief priest, who would thus sleep between the men and the rest of the colony. If this supposition be correct, the passage above would generally be closed.

Following the path to the barrier of stones, doubtless placed there to shut in the goats at night, a large semi-circular cave in the background, which is too low to allow of a man standing upright, appears to have been the shelter for the goats. The small cave on the right, into which a goat could easily be driven, would serve as a milking shed and for making butter and cheese. It is perhaps well to remind the reader that butter, kept for several years in a pot, was one of the chief medicines used by the natives.

The goats would be milked and the leather for covering the mummies would be sewn by the *Harimaguadas*. The window in the goats' cave and the look-out above, would both afford some little recreation to a number of young girls, kept for years secluded from all intercourse with the outside world.

One cave remains to which access is more difficult than to the rest. This may well have been the sleeping place of the maidens. It is the most remote of all. The sockets in the walls point to the erection of several beams, on which a sufficient number would find room to lie down. Finally, the curved socket-holes in the window, from which the beams could be immediately lifted, indicate a last means of escape in case of imminent danger. The window was timbered, but the Canarios knew little about carpentry, and space enough would have been left to spring through. Springing through meant falling down a precipice, but, as a last means of escape, this sacrifice would probably be expected of an *Harimaguada*.

Returning along the path, a low natural wall must be surmounted, and another small group of caves is found. One of these is much blackened by fire, and it is not unreasonable to suppose that this discolouration dates, at least partially, to some period prior to the conquest. It is again called to the attention of the reader that butchers, as in Egypt, were outcasts. To them belonged the duty of first cleaning the body of the dead, and burning the entrails preparatory to putting the ashes back into the corpse. That this was not the kitchen to the other caves is apparent. From its careful construction in comparison to the adjoining caves, it seems much too good for the butcher, whilst smooth walls and a small aperture into the open air, such as those to be seen, were absolutely necessary if the ashes were to be properly gathered up.

Those who have studied the subject more deeply may differ from the writer's conclusions, but, apart from the question of what state of civilisation the Canarios lived in before the arrival of Europeans, the mountain is worth ascending. It is 923 ft. high, and commands a view which includes Ingenio, Carrisal, the Lazareto, Telde, Las Palmas, Puerto de la Luz, the Pico de Bandama and the Cumbres. The sheltered caves are also a capital spot for a picnic.

Further along the **Main Road,**

At $13\frac{1}{4}$ m. ($21\frac{1}{4}$ kils.) a track to the left leads away to Maspalomas, etc. *See* next excursion.

At **Agua Tona** there are a few palm trees, and the country looks a little greener. Between here and Ingenio a road to the left, along which carriages can pass, leads to **Punta de Gando** and the buildings of the **Lazareto,** which can be seen below.

Travellers by ships coming from infected ports can perform quarantine here. The authorities might have been more generous with the space allotted. Gando Bay was the point at which the Spaniards were allowed to trade prior to the conquest. The natives permitted D. Diego de Herrera to build a fort here in 1466, which was eventually destroyed owing to excesses on the part of the Spaniards. (*See* History, page 97.)

At $16\frac{1}{2}$ m. ($26\frac{1}{2}$ kils.) a path leads up on the right to **Ingenio,** 860 ft., 3,487 inhab. ; no inn, $\frac{1}{2}$ m. from the road.

Ingenio was the name given to a place where sugar used to be cultivated. An ancient sugar-factory existed in the village, and some of the houses are very old. The foundations on which one or two of them rest are attributed to the Canarios, but are much more likely to have been made by the early Spanish settlers.

A little further on the deep Barranco de Guayadeque is crossed, and the road terminates at

Agüimes, 18 m. ($28\frac{1}{2}$ kils), 810 ft., 2,888 inhabitants. No inn, accommodation miserable.

The village is of no interest and has a destitute, poverty-stricken appearance. In the Bco., about $1\frac{1}{2}$ hrs. above the town, are a number of caves where the Canarios lived, in some of which bones and mummies have been found. There are also a few caves in the Bco. below the town. Agüimes can never become a favourite resort, as it is almost constantly swept by a high wind.

Leaving the village past the three crosses, the bridle path traverses a bare windy plain. The village of **La Pileta** is left to the right, and at 1 hr. **La Mina** (water-tunnel) in the entrance of the Bco. **Angostura** is passed, 440 ft.

The Bco. is crossed in a slanting direction. At 100 yards from the point where the path leaves the bed is a rock, rising from the middle of the Bco. known as **Los Letreros**.

On the side of this rock which faces up the Barranco a number of names are written. Of these the earliest bears date 1854, and is some 3½ ft. above the bed of the Barranco. Others are higher up, more lower down, and by scratching away the soil, still more can be found The reason of this is that the rocks in the surrounding country are very much broken up by cleavage and are constantly carried down by the rain, whilst the rock under discussion has, for some reason, remained intact, so that it remains *in situ* and is gradually being buried.

The name **Los Letreros** has belonged to this rock for centuries. There is a tradition that a Bishop, in making the round of his diocese, stopped here and made his mark some other Pagan writing, in order to show that Paganism had been succeeded by Christianity. In process of time the Pagan mark would first be buried, then the Christian, and lastly those now visible, which, worthless in themselves, serve to show more or less the rate of the growth of the bed of the Barranco.

Amongst these modern marks is a peculiar hieroglyphic formed by an equilateral triangle standing on its apex, and surmounted by a perpendicular line crossed by two horizontal lines, of which the upper one is the shorter. At first sight it appears to be a rough way of drawing a ship, but enquiry shows that it bears a resemblance to some of the early mediæval trade marks, of which specimens stamped on pottery may be seen in the British Museum. Whether this sign was repeated in recent years on different parts of the rock by idlers copying marks unknown to them, which they saw disappearing by degrees, or whether it was a species of advertisement cut in several places by the early traders, with the object of attracting the attention of the natives and inducing them to deal only in goods protected by that particular trade mark, history fails to say.

The point marked by the rock was the best central meeting place for the traders using Gando Bay, as all traders seem to have done up till the conquest. The country about the caves in Tirajana and in the Bco. de Fatarga was well populated. It was a miking place where strangers would be allowed to enter the native settlements, and remind the reader a good half-way mark easily discernible from the coast.

It is possible that by scraping the gravel away some inscriptions might be found which have been preserved from the effects of the weather. If any visitor to the Letreros would be sufficiently curious to stop on the spot and dig, it is to be hoped that he will have wax and all that is necessary with him, so that if the sailors who passed round the Cape by the order of Necho, King of Egypt, ever landed here and wrote the fact on stone, the world may obtain an undoubted replica of what they had to say.

Following the path up the **Cuesta de los Cuchillos**, past a point where a track to the left leads away to **Sardina** in ½ hr., the plateau known as **Las Mesas de la Burra** is crossed, and a gradual ascent is made to 1,980 ft., when, by bearing to the left, a descent is made to the edge of the **Barranco de Tirajana**.

At 2¾ hrs. a path leads away to **Juan Grande** in about 1¼ hrs., crossing the Barranco and passing **Los Gallegos**, where there is a settlement of negroes, probably descended from slaves imported in the early sugar days, and whose blood has been largely introduced into the surrounding peasantry.

At 3¼ hrs. **Santa Lucia**, 2,056 ft., no inn, bad accommodation, is prettily situated, and is surrounded by cultivated land and groves of trees, but the village is dirty and swarms with fleas, etc.

At 3¾ hrs. the bottom of the **Vueltas de Taidía** leading to San Mateo, etc., is passed.

> There was once a large circular native house at Taidía, said to have been built of squared stones, and so strongly supported on solid timber that the roof was used for centuries as a threshing floor. This was unfortunately destroyed some years ago, and the proprietress built another house partly out of the stones of the old one. The new house is plastered over. In front of the site is a mountain of which the side is honeycombed with caves, now inaccessible.

Crossing the bed of the Barranco, 1,850 ft., a pretty ascent, through almond and pear trees, leads to (4¼ hrs.) **Tunte (S. Bartolomé de Tirajana)**, 2,660 ft., beds possible. Pop. 4,642.

The village is beautifully situated in the midst of delightful scenery, and would make a good centre for excursions if accommodation were provided.

The enormous valley in which it is placed has been called a crater. It probably was so originally, and seems to have been the centre of disturbance mentioned in the next route under Juan Grande. At present all prominent signs of the crater itself have been swept away or buried.

The church is of little interest, but contains an image of Santiago, said to have appeared miraculously where the Ermita now stands on the other side of the Paso de la Plata.

At the top of the village there is a circular hut which there is every reason to believe to be of Canario origin. It is still inhabited, and is in perfect repair. The form is circular, and the foundation is of very large stones, the diameter of the interior being about 20 ft. None of the stones were shaped, and earth was used as mortar, as it often is to-day by the Spaniards. The lintel of the door and of the two chambers built in the wall are of large mis-shapen pines, as is the span roof, and nearly the whole of the last two or three feet of the building. The style of architecture is most primitive. The roof is covered with mud, as has probably always been the case. The number of fleas inside is stupendous. Anyone who has studied the old British circular dwellings still intact on the Bodmin Moors in Cornwall will at once notice the resemblance. There are said to be five more of these round huts in Tunte.

Excursions from Tirajana.—**To the Cumbres, San Mateo, etc., by the Paso de la Plata.**—Leave the top of Tunte and pass the cemetery, then climb through the Pinar, amongst scattered pines, to the cross on the **Paso de la Plata**, 1 hr. On the opposite hills is the **Ermita de Santiago**, where the miraculous image mentioned above is said to have first appeared.

(From here a path to the left leads to **Mogan** in about 6 hrs., which can be continued to **Aldea de S. Nicolas** in another 5 or 6 hrs. A most fatiguing journey.)

Bearing up to the right the road proceeds by zig-zags, and the pavement leaves off at the entrance to a shallow barranco where water can generally be procured. This is followed until the basin of the Cumbres is reached in about 2 hrs. (*See* elsewhere.)

Times.—2 hrs. to the **Cumbres**, 1 hr. across them and about 2½ hrs. down to **San Mateo** or **Tejeda**. Total 5½ hrs.

To the Cumbres and San Mateo by the Vueltas de Taidía.—Descend from Tunte into the Barranco and cross same, leaving Santa Lucia on the right. Refer under San Mateo. Time 3 hrs. to Cumbres, 1 hr. across same. 1½ hrs. down. Total 5½ hrs.

To Maspalomas by the Bco. de Fatarga.—Leave the top of Tunte and swing round to the left just below the cemetery. Top of ridge with very fine view, 2,758 ft., ½ hr.; **Fatarga**, 1 hr.; **Maspalomas**, 5 hrs. A rough road, refer to Maspalomas for details.

From Las Palmas *viâ* Telde to Carrisal, Juan Grande, Maspalomas, Arguineguin, Mogan and Aldea de San Nicolas or Tejeda, or from Maspalomas *viâ* the Bco. de Fatarga to Tirajana.

Leaving the Agüimes *carretera* at 13¼ m. (21¼ kils.), a road to the left leads in 1 hr. to **Carrisal**, 340 ft., a little village where there is a spring in the Bco. de Guayadeque below Agüimes. There are several Canario caves in the neighbourhood, but nothing of any particular interest except the out-crops of sandstone along the track.

A long straight road leads to the S. The country is very flat, and is built of the *debris* washed down from the hills on the right. **Areynaga** with its salt pans is passed on the left, and **Sardina** is left on the right. In the neighbourhood there is workable lime.

A path leads past Sardina, ½ hr., to Santa Lucía, about 3 hrs.

At 1¾ hrs. the bed of the **Bco. de Tirajana** is crossed (times taken from the *carretera*), and at 2¼ hrs., **Juan Grande**, 100 ft., is reached, a miserable cluster of houses with no accommodation.

A path from here leads *viâ* los Gallegos up to Santa Lucía in about 3½ hrs. (*See* elsewhere.)

The road again continues over flat, dull country where little more than euphorbia and balo are met with.

The interest of this part of the journey is confined to the geological formation of the surrounding country. Owing to some great pressure brought to bear, the rocks are laminated almost like slate, and are rapidly crumbling away. The ground is strewn with stones which have been but little worn, as though the eruptive force had made itself felt when this part of the land was too much below the surface of the sea for the action of the waves to have any effect, and had then been raised quickly above them. In one place the schistose rock is interrupted by a large patch of cinders, probably the remains of a blow-hole, but the direction of the principal line of force seems to have been from near Tunte. Were it not for the caps of lava protecting the mountain spurs, all the country, from the coast to the Cumbres, would probably be a great swelling plain. It is not unlikely that most of the land could be rendered fertile by the aid of wells and windmills.

At 3¼ hrs. a small spring is passed, the road is gradually covered with sand blown up by the southerly winds, and at 4¼ hrs. **Maspalomas**, 100 ft., is reached. No inn. A bed or two can be had. Letters of introduction should be taken.

A certain amount of interest attaches itself to the sandy plain and to the **Lighthouse**, ½ hr. from the village. The country also affords a happy hunting ground to the naturalist. Carriages can be driven as far as this, but the jolting is tremendous, and the foot or saddle are to be preferred.

Carts can be driven round the coast to **Arguineguin**, 6¼ hrs., accommodation the same as in Maspalomas. Near the village is an old Canario burial-ground on the beach, but the tombs have been rifled. Arguineguin or Alguin Arguin is said to have been the name of some Canarian chief, who came, at some very remote period, from the opposite African coast. There is a factory here for tinning tunny.

From Arguineguin it is best to take a boat to the Bco. de Mogan, 1$ to 1½$, whence **Mogan**, 2 hrs., is easily reached.

The land journey takes about 6 hrs., and the road is very bad. The route from Mogan *viâ* **Veneguera** and **Tasártico** to **Aldea de San Nicolas** takes another 5 or 6 hrs.

Mogan, 1,300 ft., pop. 768, is a very small village in the mountains where beds may be procured but with difficulty. There is an old burial cave near the village. Tunny fishing gives good sport here. Fish run up to over 500 lbs.

Maspalomas to Tirajana.—A path leaves Maspalomas to the N., and descends into the rocky and magnificent **Bco. de Fatarga**. Keeping the *acéquias* on the right, a number of Canario caves are passed on both sides, many, without doubt, unexplored. Progress is very difficult in wet weather, but, when fine, it would be easy to camp here and hunt for mummies. There is good water, and plenty of pigeons to be had for the shooting. The *acéquia* ends at 1½ hrs., 450 ft.

At 2 hrs., just after passing a small farm, a path leads up out of the barranco, and, at 2½ hrs., 900 ft., another farm, nestling in palm trees, is passed. At 4 hrs., **Fatarga**, 1,785 ft., a village most picturesquely placed on a hill, and situated in a fruitful valley full of almonds and olives.

The ascent now becomes rapid, and at 4½ hrs., 2,758 ft., the summit of the ridge dividing the Bco. de Fatarga from the Bco. de Tirajana is reached. The view is magnificent. Santa Lucía is seen a little on the right, part of Tunte on the left, the houses of Taidia in between, and the Paso de la Plata on the left.

Bearing to the left, and swinging sharply round to the right below the cemetery, the path enters **Tunte** (**S. Bartolomé de Tirajana**), 2,660 ft., 5 hrs. (*See* elsewhere.)

Approximate Prices of Carriages, Horses, etc.

(For carriages from the Puerto de la Luz, *see* the commencement of the description of Grand Canary.)

In Las Palmas: Carriages to hold up to 4 or 5 persons—To the North: Puerto de la Luz, 7½ pes.; the Lighthouse, 3$; Tamaraceite, 2$; Teror, 4$; Arucas, 3$; Firgas, 4½$, and 1s. each for a mule up to the village; Bañadero, 4$; Cuesta de Silba, 5$; Guia, 6$; Gáldar, 6$; Agaete, 8$ (return next day, 12$); on the central road: Tafira, 2$; the Monte, 2½$; the Gran Caldera, 3$; landaus, 4$; Santa Brigida, 3$; San Mateo, 4$; landaus, 5$; on the South road: Jinamar, 1½$; Telde, 3$; Mña. de las Cuatro Puertas, 4$; Agüimes, 4½$. An additional charge is made for landaus.

Saddle-horses (with English saddlery): Puerto de la Luz, 3s.; Lighthouse, 5s.; Tamaraceite, 1$; Teror, 2$; Arucas, 1½$; Firgas, 2$; Bañadero, 2$; Cuesta de Silba, 2½$; Guia, 3$; Gáldar, 3$; Agaete, 4$ (single); Tafira, 1$; the Monte, 5s.; Gran Caldera, 1½$; Santa Brigida, 1½$; San Mateo, 2$; Jinamar, 1$; Telde, 5s.; Mña. de las Cuatro Puertas, 1½$; Agüimes, 2$.

All the above prices are for return journeys on the same day, with the exception of Agaete. Those taking such long journeys as Guia and back in a day (44 miles), will of course take care to allow so much time that their horses need not travel more than 6 m. an hour not including stoppages.

The Official tariffs may be inspected at the Inspeccion de Vigilancia, Perez Galdós, No. 1.

By Time:—Horses, per ½ day, 1$; per ¾ day, 1½$; whole day, 2$. Donkeys, 2s. to 3s. a day. All these prices may be reduced by bargaining, and mules, etc., can be obtained for less, either in Las Palmas or in the country town driven to.

In Guia.—Horses, or mules (approximate): Half a day, 3 pesetas; a whole day, 1$, or for long expeditions on bad roads, 5s. per day. Named rides—To Agaete, 1$.; to the spring above Agaete, 1½$; to the Finca Corvo, in the Mña. de Doramas or top of the Bco. de los Tilos, 1½$ (all these are return). Single journey *viâ* Doramas, Moya and Firgas to *carretera* 2$, or on to Teror 2½$.

Carriages: To Gáldar, 5s.; Agaete, 3$; Las Palmas, 6$ to 7$.

Donkeys: 3 pesetas a day.

PRICES AND APPROXIMATE TIMES OF THE PUBLIC COACHES.

Kilos.	Miles.		A.M.	P.M.	Prices.		A.M.	P.M.	
7½	4½	Las Palmas	7	2.30	1 pes	Agaete	2	10 a.m.	
17	10½	Tamaraceite	8	3.30	1.50	Gáldar	4	12	
22½	14	Arucas	9½	5	1.50	Guia	4.30	12.30	
36	22	Bañadero	10½	6	2 pes	Bañadero	6.15	2.15	
40	25	Guia	12.0	8.0	2 pes	Arucas	7	3	
48½	30½	Gáldar	1.0	8.30	2½ pes	Tamaraceite	8	4	
		Agaete	3.0	10.30		Las Palmas	9	5	
7½	4½	Las Palmas	7	2.30	1 pes	Teror	6.30	3	
20½	13	Tamaraceite	8	3.30	2 pes	Tamaraceite	8.30	5	
		Teror	10	5.30		Las Palmas	9.30	6	
8	5	Las Palmas	7	3.0	1 p. 10	San Mateo	6	3	The Coach leaving Las Palmas in the afternoon and San Mateo in the morning is irregular and has no fixed time or tariff.
9½	6	Tafira	8	4.0	1.35	Santa Brigida	7	4	
13½	8½	Monte	8.15	4.15	1.35	Monte	7.45	4.30	
13½	8½	Santa Brigida	9	5.0	2.00	Tafira	8	4.45	
21	13	San Mateo	10	6.0		Las Palmas	9	5.30	
13	8¼	Las Palmas	8	2.30 / 3.30	1 pes.	Agüimes	6	4	Coaches to Telde of an afternoon leave at different hours, but start homewards at the same time.
28½	18	Telde	9.15	4.0 / 4.30	2 pes.	Telde	7.45	5.15	
		Agüimes		6.0		Las Palmas	9.15		

NOTE.—On Sundays and Holidays extra coaches are often put on, and the regular coaches frequently start ½ an hour earlier.

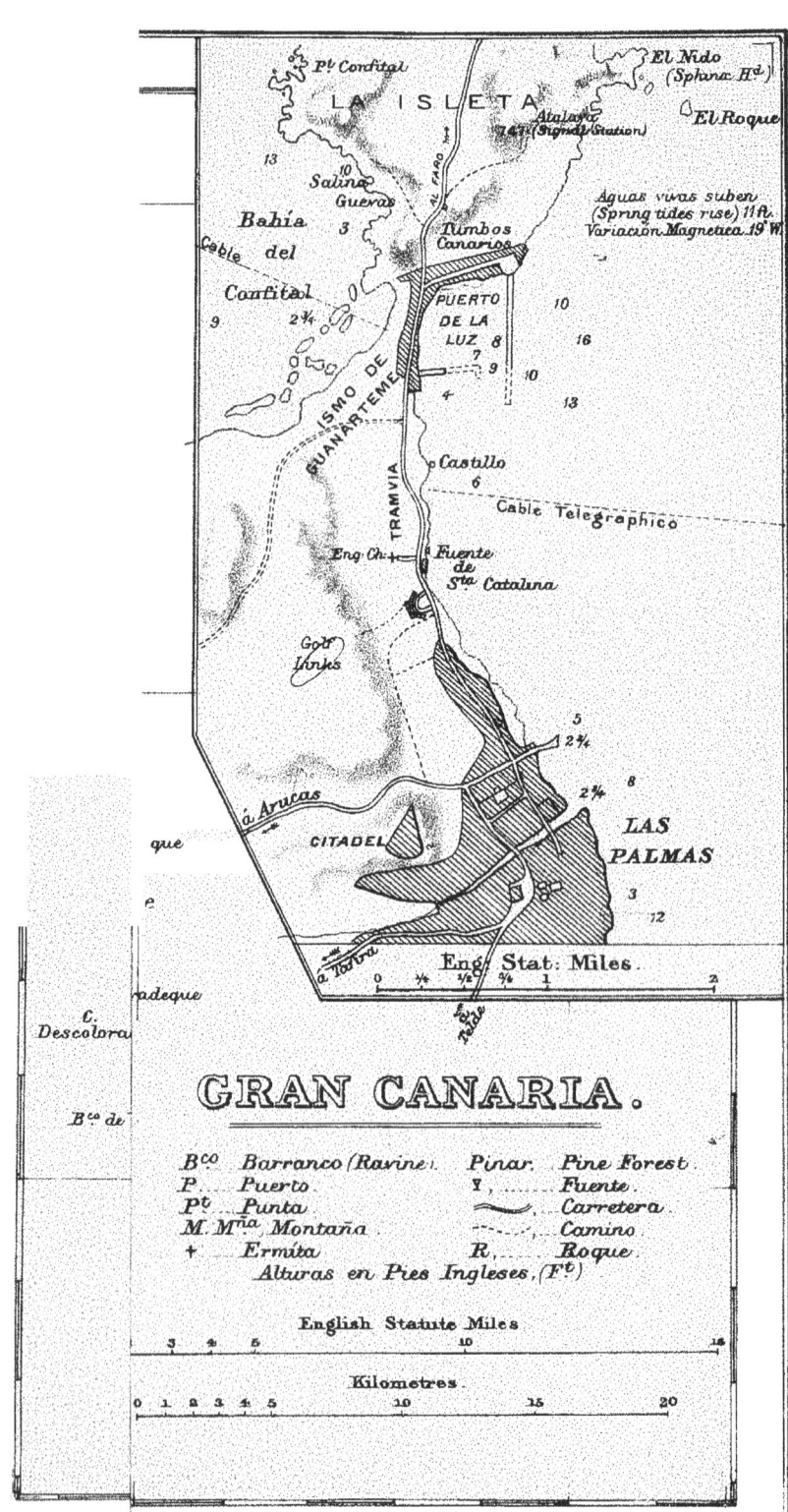

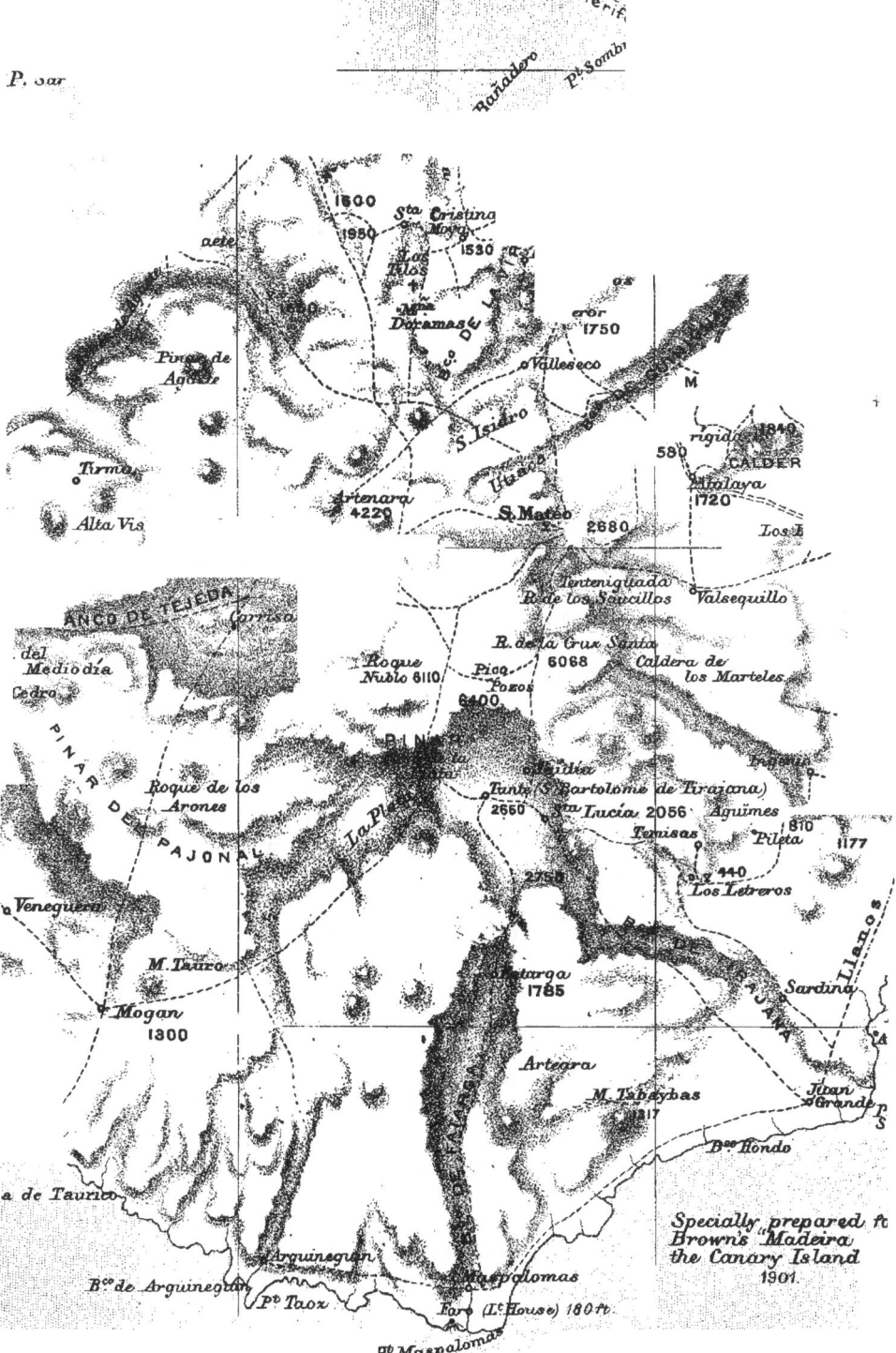

FUERTEVENTURA.

This island lies between lat. 28° 1' by 28° 43' N. and long. 13° 49' by 14° 32' W. of Greenwich; to the E.N.E. of Grand Canary; to the S.W. of Lanzarote, and 2 degrees to the E. of Teneriffe. It was formerly called Herbania or Planaria, or Majorata, and the people were known as Majos, a name supposed to be derived from a tribe of African invaders. It is also supposed that Ben Farroukh, in describing the Island of Capraria, referred to Fuerteventura. It is 156 sea miles (287 kils.) from Santa Cruz de Teneriffe, and 103 sea miles (190 kils.) from Las Palmas. It is 61¾ m. (99 kils.) long by 18¾ m. (30 kils.) broad; covers 797 sq. m. (2,040 sq. kils.) and contains 11,676 inhabitants, spread over one town and 13 villages or hamlets, and is divided into 8 districts.

The form is long and narrow, especially at the S. end, which terminates in a sandy peninsula, on which are situated the Ass's Ears (Orejas de Asno), 2,770 ft., the highest point in the island, the general plan of which is a sandy, rocky, barren plain, intersected by two lines of extinct volcanoes running north and south.

There is less water and consequently less verdure than in any of the seven islands. What vegetation there is, is exceedingly varied and of the greatest interest to the botanist, having been described as a miniature reproduction of certain parts of Northern Desert Africa, the coast of that continent being distant only 68 sea miles (125 kils.) from point to point, and Cape Juby being at times visible. There are no forests and very few trees, cultivation depending entirely on rain water and being confined to cereals, cochineal, etc. In spite of the want of fresh-water springs, this island grows more wheat in a wet year than all the others put together, but, although the population is so scanty, emigration alone enables the inhabitants to survive in a succession of bad seasons. The climate is very dry, and, were accommodation available, might be of advantage to some invalids. Cultivation might be greatly extended were advantage taken of the limestone beds running through the island, where undoubtedly water could be found by sinking wells and erecting windmills. Where water is present the soil is fertile enough, and produces good crops of bananas, tomatoes, etc.

As yet there are few roads and communication is carried on by rough, uncared-for paths, well adapted to the camel or the donkey, the former being always used for long distances.

On the arrival of the Franco-Spanish filibustering expedition in 1402, there seems to have been thick groves of palms and other trees and much more water. The country was divided by a wall, the inhabitants on either side of which were hostile and warlike in the extreme. Bethencourt estimated the number of warriors as about 4,000.

Puerto Cabras.—506 inhabitants. East coast; 103 sea miles (190 kils.) from Las Palmas.

An insignificant village situated in an open bay, where passengers are landed in boats. Port charges, one peseta each person; packages extra. A mole is being built, but at present passengers are carried ashore. There is a fairly comfortable inn, with four beds; charges, 3s. a day, including wine.

The aspect of the island is uninviting in the extreme. Vegetation is in many instances almost microscopic. Water is scarce, nasty and must often be paid for. The natives live largely on *gofio*, sometimes made from the seed of the barrilla (ice-plant) which is gathered when ripe and baked.

Camels cost from 4s. to 6s. a day.

The chief villages are La Antigua (the old capital), Sta. Maria de Betancuria, with old church, in which the standard borne at the time of the Spanish Conquest is still preserved, and La Oliva, the last being situated in the most fertile, or rather least barren, part of the island. As this is one of the largest of the group, distances from point to point are often very great, but travelling is easy. There are several copious salt-water springs.

A few of the times are: From Puerto Cabras to Oliva, about $3\frac{1}{2}$ hrs.; from Puerto Cabras to La Antigua, about 4 hrs.; from La Antigua to Betancuria, $1\frac{1}{2}$ hrs.; from Betancuria to Pájara, on which route there is some rough, wild scenery, about 2 hrs.; from Betancuria to Casillas del Angel, about 5 hrs.; from Puerto Tarrajol to Tuineje, about $2\frac{1}{2}$ hrs.

A *carretera* has been made from Puerto Cabras to Tejüate, $6\frac{1}{4}$ m. (10 kils.), and is being constructed *via* Casillas del Angel to la Antigua, 14 m. (22 kils.), whence it will later on be carried to Tuineje, $19\frac{3}{4}$ m. ($31\frac{1}{2}$ kils.).

LANZAROTE.

This island lies between lat. 28° 50′ by 29° 15′ N. and 13° 26′ by 13° 53′ W. of Greenwich; is N.E. of Fuerteventura, and 2½° W.N.W. of Teneriffe, being 197 sea miles (362 kils.) from Santa Cruz (Teneriffe) and 144 sea miles (283 kils.) from Las Palmas. It is 36½ m. (58½ kils.) long by 13¼ m. (21¼ kils.) broad, with an area of 380 sq. m. (973 sq. kils.) and contains 17,545 inhabitants in one town and 63 villages or hamlets. It is divided into 8 districts.

The name Lanzarote is derived from that of Lanzarote (Lancelot) de Malvoisel, a Genoese captain who constructed the tower found in the island on the arrival of Bethencourt. In the middle ages the island was marked on the map with the Genoese coat-of-arms as a token that it belonged to that municipality. Ben Farroukh seems to have alluded to it under the name of Pluitana.

The surface is less mountainous than that of the Western Islands and there are broad sandy or stony plains, quite as fertile in wet years as those of Fuerteventura. A curious phenomenon, frequently to be observed, are the moving sandbanks, which emerge from the sea, march across a tract of country in the shape of a demi-line and finally disappear in the W.

There are many extinct volcanoes. One group, called the Montañas del Fuego, which were active in 1733, are still so heated that wood will burn in some of the crevices. There were violent seismic disturbances about this time in many parts of the island. The forests are extinct and even the euphorbia is scarcely seen, the nature of the indigenous plants being not unlike that of those found in the Desert of Sahara.

The southern part of the island is barren and cultivation is almost confined to wheat, barley and the cochineal plant, which depend entirely upon rain for the necessary moisture. In the north, where a quantity of tomatoes are planted, there are a few springs, but none of sufficient size to be used for irrigating purposes at any distance. Owing to the paucity of water the barrancos are of no depth or beauty. The highest mountain is the Risco de Tamara, 2,244 ft., near N.S. de las Nieves. Good white wine is grown, and from 800 to 900 pipes are exported every year. A capital road connects Yaiza on the south with Arrecife on the east and is continued on the N. as far as Haría.

On the N. are the little islands of Alegranza, Montaña Clara and Graciosa and on the S. that of Lobos. None of these are inhabited, but all are used by the fishermen at certain times of the year. On Graciosa are some extensive sheds erected for the purpose of drying and curing fish, and on Alegranza and Lobos there are lighthouses.

The towns are uninteresting and dirty, and communication is almost entirely carried on by camels, which are also used for agricultural purposes. Charges from 4s. to 6s. a day. Donkeys may sometimes be hired at about one-third the price of camels.

According to some of the old writers the island was formerly divided into two kingdoms by a wall running N. and S. It is, however, questionable whether this statement is correct.

It was the first to be victimised to European influence in 1393, when one king alone ruled. So great were the barbarities of the earliest visitors that, when Bethencourt arrived in 1402, only 300 warriors were left.

The people lived principally in circular houses built of stone and surrounded by a wall. These were described as very evil-smelling, even by the sailors of the time, accustomed as they were to all the filthy customs introduced and encouraged by the bigoted monks of the middle ages. Glas, writing of the island in 1764, says that most or all of the inhabitants of his day suffered from the itch.

The reigning king when Bethencourt arrived was Guadarfia, son of Yeo, daughter of King Nuazama, in whose house Martin Ruiz de Avendano lived whilst in Lanzarote. He was driven to the island, in 1377, by a storm when in command of a fleet despatched by Don Juan I. of Castille against the King of Portugal, who was supporting the Duke of Lancaster in his claim to the throne of Castille by virtue of his marriage with the eldest daughter of King Pedro.

Nuazama's wife gave birth to a daughter, Yeo, whose hair was suspiciously fair. Guadarfia, son of this daughter, was consequently not allowed to ascend the throne after his grandfather's death until his legitimacy had been proved. Yeo was tried by ordeal. She was placed in a house with three other women and a fire was lighted. All were suffocated but her, her escape being due, it is said, to the use of a wet sponge with which she covered her nostrils. However this may be, her purity was acknowledged and her son became king.

In 1824, a volcano burst through the middle of a maize field near Teguise, but soon quieted down again.

S. Berthelot, about 1825, published a sketch of a piece of wall near Zonzamas, which he believed to have been built by the aboriginals or the Phœnicians.

Arrecife, 3,081 inhabitants, east coast, 31 miles from Puerto Cabras.

Passengers are landed in boats on the quay, which is well protected by a broken range of rocks extending some miles up the coast and serving as a natural breakwater to the numerous ramifications of the harbour. Port charges : Each person, 1 peseta ; packages extra.

There is a fairly good fonda with eight beds ; charge, 3s. a day, including wine.

The appearance of the town is eastern and the greater part is extremely dirty and badly built, the houses rarely exceeding one storey in height. The Church is uninteresting, and the market, where the cock-fights are also held, is poorly supplied with a few vegetables and tomatoes, neither oranges nor bananas being usually procurable.

The visitor is first struck by the number of camels lying or standing about and by the old fort on the right, still connected with the town by a wooden drawbridge. If his time is limited, an excursion can be made by camel to the old capital of San Miguel de Teguise, $6\frac{1}{2}$ m. ($10\frac{1}{2}$ kils.) on the N. road (1 dollar). A good 4 hrs. must be allowed.

At $1\frac{1}{2}$ m. from Arrecife, the road crosses a startlingly fresh stream of lava running some distance into the island. In the interstices fig and other fruit trees are planted, the moisture beneath the lava being thus utilised, whilst walls are built above the lava as an additional protection from the sun. Numerous villages are dotted on the surrounding slopes. In the neighbouring volcanoes large holes may be seen, from which cinders have been extracted and spread about the land for agricultural purposes.

For a long time the road is level, this part of the country being sometimes 5 ft. or 6 ft. under water when the rain is heavy.

Further on a hill is climbed and the old castle of Guanapay is seen on the right. Presently the neglected little town of **San Miguel de Teguise**, 2 hrs., is entered. The Church is quaint and the roof of the sacristy good. There is also a fair picture on the N. side of the choir. The old Convent of Santo Domingo contains an image of the Virgin which is said to have stopped the flow of lava in 1824. There are also some tanks on which a large tract of country depends for water during the summer months.

Further along the N. road is another much revered image called the Virgen de las Niéves which is said to have left the church during the night to save the crew of a shipwrecked schooner which had implored her aid. She was found in the morning, her robes dripping with sea-water and the doors still locked. The same tale is related of many images, both in the Canary Islands and Madeira.

Still further to the N., at 17¼ m. (27½ kils.) from Arrecife, is a village called Haría, situated in a more or less fertile valley (no inn), whence (about 2 hrs. to the N.E.) the celebrated Cueva de los Verdes may be visited, the stronghold to which the ancient inhabitants retreated in cases of invasion. This is said to be the largest lava grotto known. The writer has been told that there is a subterranean deposit of water somewhere in this neighbourhood in which there is a race of fish without eyes. So far he has not been able to verify the fact. About 1½ hrs. to the N. of Haría is a cliff known as El Risco, 1,523 ft., where there is a fine view of the Islands of Graciosa, Alegranza, etc. The extinct crater, known as La Corona, near Haría, is 1,940 ft. high.

It is proposed to make a *carretera* from Haría to the Puerto de Arriete, 4 m. (6 kils.).

Should the visitors' time admit of it, an excursion across country may be made to the W. of the island to the Montañas del Fuego, already mentioned. Time required, from 5 to 6 hrs. each way. A guide advisable. Rough sleeping-quarters may be procured in the vicinity.

The same excursion may be made by the road to Yaiza where there is a small fonda, 14 m. (22 kils.). The volcanoes are distant from the village about 1¼ hrs. About 2½ hours from Yaiza in the same direction is a curious lava grotto, known as the Cueva del Mojon.

A few miles S. of the same village is the Torre del Aguila, a tower built by Bethencourt, near where he landed in 1402.

The Strait known as El Rio, separating Lanzarote from Graciosa, would make by far the best harbour in the Canaries and might easily be fortified. It suffers, however, from want of fresh water and could never be more than a naval station, as the country in the vicinity produces and consumes too little to afford any freight to merchant vessels.

A *carretera* is being made from Arrecife to Mozaga, 6 m. (9½ kils.), which later on is to be continued to San Bartolomé, Tao and Tinajo, 11½ m. (18½ kils.).

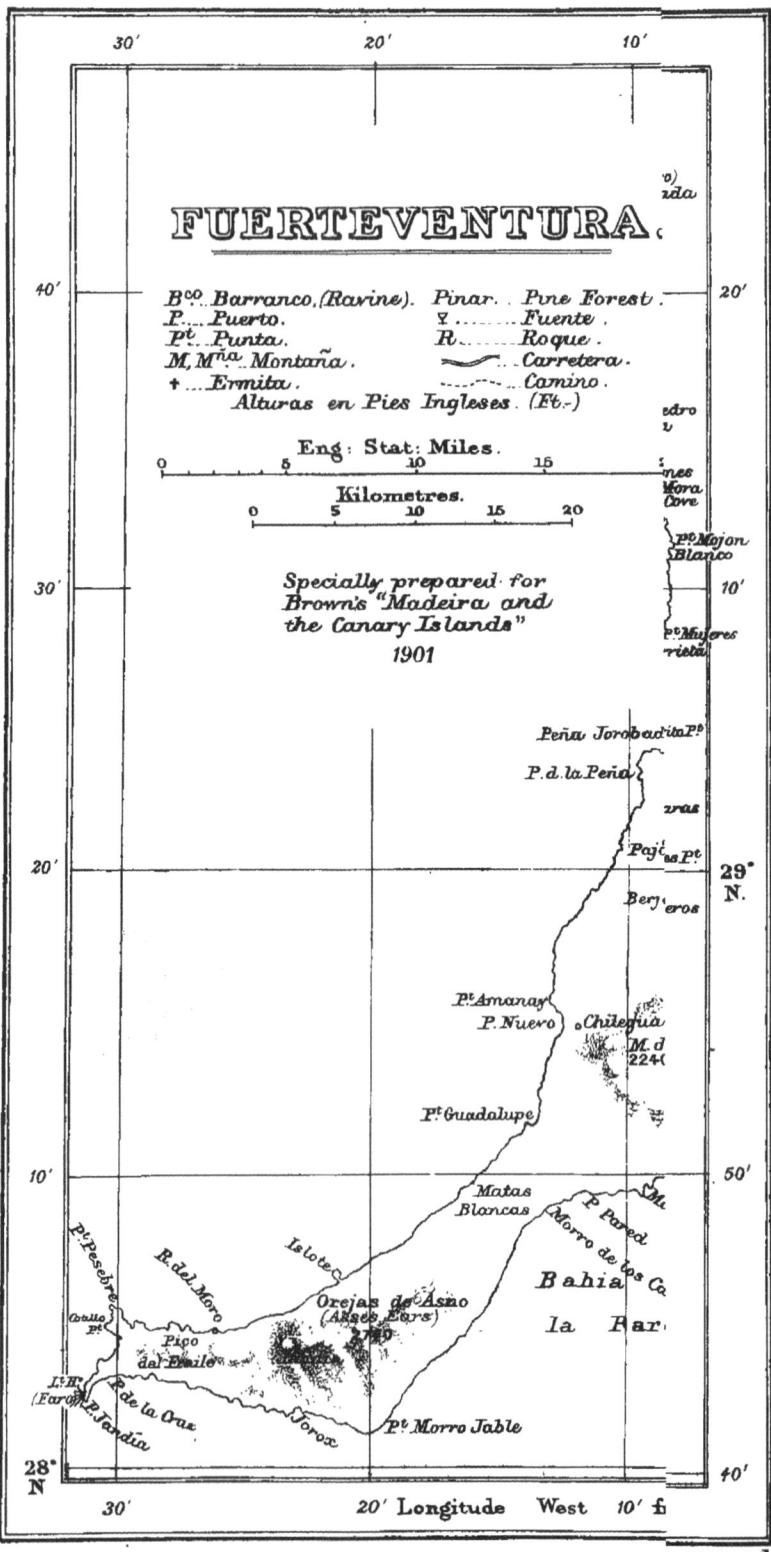

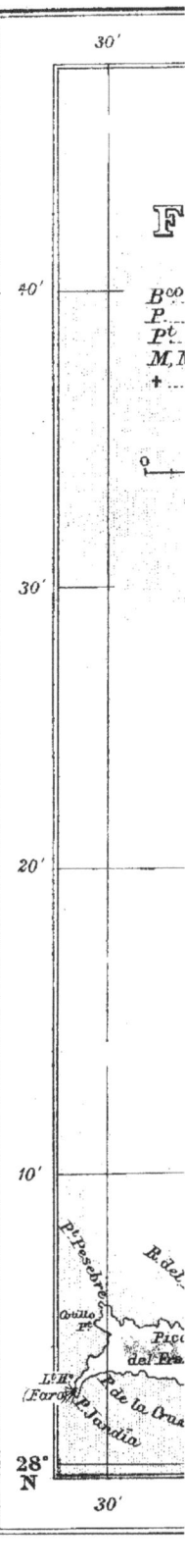

COMMERCIAL SECTION.

Report on the Condition of Labour and Social and Economical Condition of Madeira and of the Canary Islands, together with Statistics and other Observations compiled for the aid of Traders or Intending Settlers.

ABSTRACT OF CONTENTS.

	PAGES
Introduction	259
Pumice stone ; sulphur	260
Tables of shipping movements	261–264
Tables of Imports and Exports, etc.	264–268
Agriculture, its past and present.	268–291

    Sugar ; the Vine ; the ice-plant ; cochineal ; tobacco ; spirits ; the tomato ; the potato ; the banana ; the orange ; methods of shipping fruit ; freight ; experimental remittances ; vegetables ; citrons ; figs, etc. ; the walnut ; the osier ; the wattle ; marram grass ; the carob tree ; the tagasaste ; the sweet potato ; india rubber ; castor-oil ; the aloe ; pickles and jams ; silk ; tinned fruits ; the manufacture of perfumes ; cultivation of bulbs, etc.

Some indications of the capabilities and value of land in different positions   291–298

    Incline of the hills ; maize as a basis of valuation ; quantity of water required for irrigation ; seasons and harvests ; cereals ; cost of land ; rent of land ; mortgages ; land as an investment ; responsibility of landlord ; waste land tax free ; climate.

Zones of vegetation, forestry, pasture and live stock   298–301

    The Zones and the plants growing in each ; forest land ; the planting of pines in Madeira ; care of forests ; pasture ; live stock.

Method of agriculture and of conveying and storing water, with statistics concerning irrigation...   302–306

    Implements ; manure ; the Medianero and Bemfeitoria systems ; best watered islands ; cost of tanks, etc. ; pipes ; open watercourses ; searching for water.

The actual condition of the islands and possible effects of novel circumstances on the future of agriculture   306–312

    Abrogation of entail ; increase in shipping and coaling ; birth of the trade in perishable fruit ; high roads ; harbours ; telegraphs ; the peasantry ; foreigners engaging in agriculture ; fluctuations in the rate of exchange.

NOTE.—In this portion of the Guide the Azores are not included.

	PAGES
Results and reasons of the influx of visitors, with hints regarding the building of villas, etc.	312-315
Enterprise induced by visitors; storing of food a necessity; cost of building materials, etc.	
The fisheries	315-320
The Selvage islands; the tunny fishery; the great African fishery; results of the researches of George Glas; number of ships and men employed; figures of catch; method of curing; names of the fish.	
Statistics of population, emigration and education	320-323
Tables of population; movement towards towns; emigration; education; percentage of illiterate, etc.	
Methods of taxation, national and municipal	323-326
Taxation; justice; charity; thrift; hospitals, etc.; begging; wants of the poor.	
Position of labour	327-331
Factory laws; wages; payment of wages in kind; lodging of labourers; food of labourers; unions; strikes; prices of commodities.	
Market prices of certain commodities ...	331

Commercial Section.

The following is an amended and enlarged version of the author's report on the "Social and Economical Condition of the Canary Islands," presented to the Foreign Office and published by the British Government in 1892. (Miscellaneous Series, No. 246. Reports on Subjects of General and Commercial Interest. Spain.)

Madeira has now been included and the whole corrected and revised.

At a time when the labour question is so acute and when there is a wide-spread opinion that human beings will soon elbow one another into space, it is no loss of time to pass in review the methods of existence adopted by a people who have been crowded out for centuries. By working on the same system, countries, with a similar climate, could support an equally large proportionate population. If the Government were more consistent and more enterprising, and were not afraid to pledge the public credit for the creation of fresh resources, the islands under discussion and places resembling them could provide labour and food for a still larger number to the square mile. A certain amount of space has been devoted to this subject, where the writer has tried to point out a few neglected industries which might be undertaken, to indicate means of increasing the supply of water, and so on.

The necessary figures are specially arranged with a view to the furtherance of British mercantile interest. Incomplete as they undoubtedly are, they will serve as a local basis to measure its future progress or decay, even if they do not fulfil the writer's desire by accelerating the former.

Since the landing of Bethencourt in Lanzarote in 1402, the discovery of Madeira in 1419, and the final subjugation of Teneriffe in 1496, the history of Madeira and of the Canary Islands has been chiefly interesting as a record of agricultural success or failure. The condition of all classes has been so dependent upon the productive power of the land, that it can scarcely be ascertained without first entering into a critical examination of the value of the soil itself, prior to and since the extraordinary changes of the last few years.

Minerals.

Amongst the successive layers of comparatively recent volcanic deposit of which the islands are almost wholly constructed, no mineral deposits have as yet been found which would pay for working.

A company is quarrying **pumice stone** from the base of the Peak of Teneriffe, and is said to be turning out a good material at more moderate prices than those quoted elsewhere.

On the summit of the same mountain there is a large deposit of pure **sulphur** which might easily be extracted. A concession has been granted to a company to work 900,000 cubic metres. Three samples, assayed by Mr. Frederic Claudet, of London, showed 45·9 %, 98·0 % and 93·1 % respectively. It has been stated that the deposit is even richer than that of Sicily.

As hitherto the industry of mining has played no part in the history of the islands, the following remarks will principally deal with the innate capabilities of the land itself and the various fiscal or municipal burdens which hinder its cultivation directly, or which, by preventing the establishment of manufactories, tend to impede a proper freedom of development. It is hoped that this part of the work will be of service to settlers in some of the British Colonies where climatic and other conditions are more or less similar to those of the islands under discussion.

The fishing industry, which is considerable, the state of labour in the coaling ports, and the changes brought about by the recent influx of invalids and visitors will receive due attention.

NUMBER and Tonnage of **Steam Vessels** entering the **Port of Funchal, Madeira,** with a statement of the quantity of Coal supplied to them:—

Year.	British.		Percentage of British.		All Nations.		Coal Supplied.
	No. of Vessels.	Tons.	No. of Vessels.	Tons.	No. of Vessels.	Tons.	Tons.
			Per Cent.	*PerCent*			
1886	...	...	...	...	618	887,497	...
1887	360	528,992	60	64	596	827,674	57,078
1888	371	499,264	57	56	653	888,660	59,410‡
1889	405	598,587	59	60	693	1,002,770	80,335
1890	390	606,683	60	60	645	1,023,708	67,574
1897	506	1,238,293	68	72	796	1,725,503	93,525
1898	504	about 1,690,000	63	69	800	about 2,480,000	98,598
1899	509	about 1,384,000	69	64	734	about 2,154,000	115,175

‡ Tonnage and anchorage dues taken off for a term of five years.—Loo Rock connected with the shore by the Pontinha breakwater.

TABLE showing Percentage of **Steamers** entering Madeira.

Year.	Portuguese.		French.		German.		Belgian.	
	No. of Vessels.	Tons.	No. of Vessels.	Tons.	No. of Vessels.	Tons.	No. of Vessels.	Tons.
	Per Cent.	*PerCent.*	*Per Cent.*	*PerCent.*	*Per Cent.*	*PerCent.*	*Per Cent.*	*PerC'nt*
1887	11	11	...	...	19	18	6	6
1888	11	10	...	...	...	...	6	7
1889	9	9	...	...	20	19	7	7
1890	11	15	...	...	16	14	7	7
1897	10	10	2	3	11	13	¼	...
1899	9	...	3·7	...	12	...	0	...

NUMBER and Tonnage of Steam Vessels entering the Ports of **Santa Cruz (Teneriffe)** and **Las Palmas (Grand Canary)**, with a statement of the Quantity of Coal supplied to them :—

Teneriffe.

Year.	Coasting Trade.		British.		Percentage of British.		All Nations.	
	No. of Vessels	Tons.	No. of Vessels.	Tons.	No of Vessels.	Tons.	No. of Vessels.	Tons.
					Per Cent.	PerCent		
1884	...	...	195*	263,700*	45	58	429	457,000*
1885	...	...	206	278,560	44	55	465	501,382
1886	...	...	246	317,669	43	51	553	620,229
1887	...	...	250*	395,000*	46	48	542	843,440
1888	51	12,904	310	444,238	47	47	666	948,802
1889	158	41,696	349	549,375	48	49	733	1,118,652
1890	178	40,432	350	575,000	46	48	766	1,204,036
1895	165	111,375	452	828,600	45	55	1,006	1,495,292
1898	...	...	529	822,362	43	51	1,224	1,602,067

Grand Canary.

Year.	Coasting Trade.		British.		Percentage of British.		All Nations.	
	No. of Vessels.	Tons.	No. of Vessels.	Tons.	No. of Vessels.	Tons.	No. of Vessels.	Tons.
					PerCent.	PerCent		
1884	...	...	160*	264,000*	68	52	238	505,000*
1885	...	...	220	263,000	66	50	336	725,000*
1886	...	...	369	600,500*	72	63	506	950,000*
1887	...	...	414	680,000*	63	61	660	1,103,700*
1888	51*	12,904*	539	890,977	59	59	912	1,505,089*
1889	158*	41,696*	601	1,360,000*	59	56	1,022	2,432,000*
1890	178*	40,432*	718	1,635,000*	57	56	1,263	2,918,570*
1895	165	111,375.	1,074	2,465,077	54	77	1,983	3,192,939
1898	...	...	1,073	2,403,129	59	63	1,816	3,827,495

Total for the Canaries.

Year	Total of both Groups. Steamers only. No. of Vessels.	Tons.	Coal Supplied. T'n'riffe Tons.	Grand Canary. Tons.	Total. Tons.	Remarks.
1884	667	962,000	28,924	6,700	35,624	Telegraph cable laid to Cadiz early in 1884, and extended to Senegal in December, 1884. Cholera in France.
1885	801	1,226,382	33,963	18,390	52,353	Prolongation of Santa Cruz mole commenced.
1886	1,059	1,570,229	38,046	38,827	76,873	Harbour works, Grand Canary, rapidly advancing.
1887	1,202	1,938,140	53,277	73,070	126,347	
1888	1,578	2,453,891	76,913	136,188	213,101	The inter-insular service of steamers commenced running in September.
1889	1,755	3,550,652	101,432	166,341	267,773	
1890	2,029	4,122,606	107,519	226,400	333,919	
1895	2,989	4,688,231	133,896	260,000*	393,896*	
1898	3,040	5,429,562	133,480	213,000	346,480	

NOTE.—The figures marked with a * could not be obtained, but are probably nearly correct.

TABLE showing Percentage of **Steamers** entering the Undermentioned Ports.

Ports.	Spanish. No. of Vessels.	Tons.	French. No. of Vessels.	Tons.	German. No. of Vessels.	Tons.	Remarks.
	Per Cent	Per Cent	Per Cent	Per Cent	Per Cent	Per Cent	
Teneriffe, 1885	15	9	19	28	5	6	The movement of sailing vessels, most of which are coasters, calls for no remark. Entries in 1885, 1,939. In 1898, 1,913.
Teneriffe, 1890	14	11	20	19	17	17	
Teneriffe, 1895	11	8	10	12	11	16	
Teneriffe, 1898	31	17	11	11	10	15	
Grand Canary, 1885	...	...	1	1	1	1	
Grand Canary, 1895	14	8	4	5	6	9	
Grand Canary, 1897	13	7	6	6	12	13	
Grand Canary, 1898	16	7	4	5	9	10	

In 1850, the last year of the wine trade, the number of vessels calling at Teneriffe (only) were 15 steamers and 262 sailing vessels, with a tonnage of 32,697 tons.

In 1852, 79 steamers (50 English and 13 French) and 195 sailing vessels with a tonnage of 40,725, whilst 1,738 tons of coal were supplied.

In 1869, 86 steamers (72 English, 55,655 tons; and 12 French, 4,307 tons) and 142 sailing vessels (50 English, 10,147 tons; 20 French, 5,383 tons; and 5 German, 1,019 tons), and a delivery of coal of 4,837 tons.

The figures in the tables do not include sailing vessels, most of which are engaged in the local trade.

The vessels touching at Teneriffe during the year 1900, carried 118,051 passengers. Those at Grand Canary, during 1899, carried 117,609.

A Comparative Synopsis of the Progress of Trade in Madeira.

(Values expressed in £1 sterling at 4$500.)

Year.	IMPORTS (not including coal).					EXPORTS.				
	England.	America.	Germany.	Dry Goods	TOTAL.	Wine.	Vegetables	Fruit	Fancy Work.	TOTAL.
	£	£	£	£	£	£	£	£	£	£
1883	...	...	...	...	134,736	108,143	1,260	1,992	2,820	152,052*
1886	39,372	26,188	6,393	19,592	116,701	160,410	2,600	2,646	4,707	176,142
1887	71,550	21,149	4,244	15,631	122,458	156,439	3,070	2,598	4,243	204,273†
1888	72,769	17,685	6,658	27,832	131,993	168,630	4,873	3,835	5,232	188,047‡
1889	65,864	18,194	6,937	25,410	130,977	151,250	3,514	4,245	6,103	169,985
1890	58,794	25,936	10,155	26,640	175,894	154,249	2,291	5,523	5,978	171,393§
1891	34,297	38,761	14,091	29,118	146,104	174,493	2,821	4,399	2,177	188,453‖
1892	20,083	28,782	5,807	17,230	114,227	146,009	560	4,637	2,332	163,001∷
1895	68,782	49,723	13,186	21,973	184,524	167,948	8,201		9,311	205,940
1897	75,879	65,573	20,779	30,565	183,648	184,061	13,049		32,747	272,222
1898	84,091	76,833	26,340	37,077	225,503	179,477	17,522		39,676	307,597**

REMARKS.

* Sugar, £34,107.   † All the sugar-cane killed by disease.
‡ New cane from Demerara and the Canaries looking healthy.

§ Consul Keene reports that dry goods chiefly imported from Germany and little from England. Also says that export of fruit and vegetables is very much understated.

|| Consul reports entire cessation of dry goods from England owing to excessive import duties. Says increase in export of wine due to large shipments with object of evading new French protective tariff coming into force at end of 1891.

No wine sent to France.

** Trade and shipping between Madeira and Portugal were much interrupted by the outbreak of cholera in Portugal.

NOTES.— The imports from France for six years (1887-1892) amount to less than £32,000. In 1897 their value was £2,838.

The export of bananas from Madeira is said to be some 30,000 bunches a year, but this is simply an estimate. The consumption of coal in the island (estufas, sugar-mills, etc.) is about 2,000 tons a year.

Amongst the exports of fancy work, which includes embroidery, wicker-work, and inlaid wood, the sales to passengers on board steamers and the very large amounts sent away without being declared, are not included. The great growth of this export in 1897 is largely due to the German demand for Madeira embroidery.

The apparent increased value in imports and exports is partly due to the decrease in the international value of the local currency. The official rate of exchange of 4,500 reis to the £ is adopted throughout, although the average rate has long been much higher.

In the Madeira returns the stability of the exports is the most healthy sign. Wine forms a very large proportion of the whole and provides employment to a number of men in the making of casks, etc., as well as in the actual cultivation. The result is a considerable import of American oak, and of cereals from the United States.

Resumé.—As regards what is wanted, Imports consist of almost all necessary articles, such as soft goods, iron, timber and groceries. Food is also largely imported.

During the six years 1886-91 the average yearly import of Maize was £29,015; of Wheat £15,551; of Rice £4,333; of Molasses £8,271, or a total annual outlay on these four articles of £57,170. In 1890, Maize and Wheat alone rose to £53,617. The Cereals grown in the island are supposed to yield sufficient for 3 or 4 months per annum; the sugar sufficient for about 10 months.

A Comparative Synopsis of the **Progress of Trade** in the **Canary Islands.**

(Values expressed in £1 sterling at 25 pesetas).

IMPORTS.					
Year.	England.	France.	Germany.	Spain.	TOTAL.
	£	£	£	£	£
1865 ...	179,914	51,004	11,669	47,866	391,492
1869 ...	215,781	127,979	11,298	162,690	719,544
1874 ...	206,714	84,771	8,435	66,000	486,239
Total ...	...	...	...	...	1,597,275
1884 ...	163,398	38,785	26,923	70,035	335,820
1885 ...	210,464	59,574	31,590	75,036	419,944
1886 ...	207,380	70,280	49,115	45,966	447,568
1887 ...	224,996	51,675	49,922	48,920	438,340
1888 ...	273,449	57,306	56,873	50,875	476,793
1889 ...	286,296	48,642	61,024	42,116	517,918
1890 ...	315,259	70,133	85,954	39,465	591,136
Total ...	...	...	...	...	3,227,519
1892 ...	307,160	55,826	84,141	33,876	575,018
1895 ...	343,695	123,442	112,423	114,006	816,320

EXPORTS.					
Year.	Cochineal.	Wine.	Spirits.	Tobacco.	TOTAL.
	£	£	£	£	£
1865 ...	295,208	11,007	4,630	Wanting.	404,055
1869 ...	789,993	5,470	Wanting.	,,	845,390
1874 ...	429,931	Wanting.	,,		566,432
Total ...	...	...	...	...	1,815,877
1884 ...	100,844	6,740	5,530	10,380	224,418
1885 ...	127,028	4,855	6,358	10,454	351,097
1886 ...	151,486	10,009	10,570	50,937	341,720
1887 ...	117,819	10,957	8,027	25,458	248,774
1888 ...	97,050	21,126	5,456	21,107	281,180
1889 ...	82,923	18,264		32,557	302,175
1890 ...	60,940	23,963	9,648	30,064	319,577
Total ...	...	...	...	...	2,068,941
1892 ...	50,877	20,785	5,761	—	438,941
1895 ...	109,234	56,055		29,980	893,112

NOTE.—Of recent years the authorities have only published the volume and not the value of Imports and Exports. Comparative figures therefore cannot be given.

REMARKS.

1865.—Woven goods imported, £119,313, chiefly from England. Silk figures among exports for £12,615.

1869.—The largest sum realised by the export of cochineal was in this year; price 3s. to 3s. 6d. per lb. in London.

1874.—Panic in cochineal; price 1s. 6d. to 2s. per lb. A commission was appointed by the Spanish Government for fomenting the growth of tobacco, but the results were disappointing.

1884.—Company formed to start Grand Hotel in Orotava.

1885.—About 45,000 bunches of bananas exported. Woven goods imported, £112,215. The Government agreed to take tobacco of a fixed quality at a fixed price, and much land was planted in consequence.

1886.—About 300 visitors to Orotava. About 50,000 bunches of bananas exported.

1887.—Tomatoes first exported. Bananas, tomatoes and potatoes exported from Grand Canary to England roughly valued by the Consul at £16,000. Owing to sale of tobacco monopoly to a company, Canary crop largely refused as below sample.

1888.—Export of silk, £608; sugar, £8,500. English church commenced in Orotava. Company formed for building Sta. Catalina Hotel in Las Palmas, and other objects.

1889.—The Vice-Consul at Orotava speaks hopefully about the increase in export of tomatoes and potatoes. Tobacco largely imported in the raw and exported as cigars.

1890.—Completion of steam tramway in Las Palmas (Belgian material).

1892.—It is impossible to rely upon the figures being exact, but the following are those obtainable. Exports of fruit:—Almonds, £7,361; Bananas, 63,601 tons, valued at £60,697 (59,508 tons to England); Vegetables, 96,842 tons, valued at £130,652 (59,124 tons to England and 27,970 tons to the West Indies). There is nothing to show which are tomatoes, potatoes or onions; Dried vegetables, 13,804 tons, valued at £19,380 (319 tons to England and 11,735 tons to the West Indies). The exports return does not state which is Grand Canary and which Teneriffe, but it may be taken for granted that most bananas come from Canary and most tomatoes and potatoes from Teneriffe.

1894.—Export of fruit from Grand Canary only. Tomatoes, £16,800; Potatoes, £9,389; Bananas, £33,785; Onions, £12,254; Oranges, £150; Vegetables, dried fruits, etc., £26,638; Almonds, £8,410; Sugar, £51,528.

1895.—Exports of fruit from Grand Canary.—Tomatoes, £35,817; Potatoes, £6,182; Bananas, £42,125; Onions, £10,823; Oranges, £681; Vegetables, dried fruits, etc., £32,622; Almonds, £2,733; Sugar, £43,254. Same from Teneriffe.—Tomatoes, £74,850; Potatoes, £57,422; Bananas, £39,804; Onions, £10,164; Chick peas, dried vegetables and fruit, £12,478; Almonds, £837; Tinned tunny, £17,006. Imports, which, according to the Consular Report, are for Teneriffe only.—Soft goods, £20,712. The Consul says that Great Britain held a monopoly in carpets, oil-cloth, waterproof stuffs, iron bedsteads, sheet iron, bars and chains, salt fish and dyes. Of sawdust or peat for packing tomatoes 243 tons were imported. The figures for Grand Canary given alone are extracted from two Consular Reports which do not agree. The Vice-Consul in Grand Canary estimated the shipments of tomatoes from that island at 3,000 tons and of bananas from 8,000 to 10,000 tons. The imports from France, which are for Teneriffe only, include £55,592 for flour, most of which now (1898) comes from Liverpool.

1896.—350,000 bunches of Bananas exported from Grand Canary.

1897.—Exports from Teneriffe — Tomatoes, £70,000 (7,955 tons); Bananas, £6,350 (85,444 bunches).

1898.—Exports from Teneriffe—Tomatoes, £67,350 (7,660 tons); Bananas, £10,500 (104,865 bunches). The Consular Report gives a summary of Imports and the Nations whence derived, which is too long for insertion in this work. Exports from Grand Canary—Tomatoes, £13,195 (3,047 tons); Bananas, £161,736 (534,580 bunches); Potatoes, £3,675 (997 tons); Cochineal, £36,957 (317 tons); Wine, £3,300; Sugar, about £30,000 worth. The total Imports into Grand Canary were valued at £438,412.

1899.—During 1897-98, the spending power of the community decreased greatly owing to the effects of a long drought, but in 1899 the Imports rose considerably. Exports from Teneriffe—Tomatoes, £55,320 (6,230 tons); Bananas, £14,950 (149,519 bunches).

The statistics available are far from exact, and are not made up every year. They are, however, the best obtainable.

Resumé.—A glance at the table of imports will show that England holds the ground as the chief provider. On the other side it is not necessary to dissect the returns, as there can be no question whatever that at least eighty per cent. of the exports leave for Great Britain.

Taking it on the whole, whether by true or false economy, the average Spaniard will buy the lowest priced article without paying much regard to its merit, and English traders must make allowance for this propensity.

AGRICULTURE, ITS PAST AND ITS PRESENT.

Sugar.—In Madeira sugar was at one time by far the most important industry. It is stated that in 1552 it gave employment to no less than 2,700 slaves. In 1772, Captain Cook said that he found a prodigious number of negroes and mulattos, some slaves and some free, showing that there was a tendency to intermixture between the whites and the blacks. In 1775, when the wine trade took the first place, slavery was abolished. Thus sugar and slavery were closely connected with one another in Madeira as, curiously enough, they always seem to have been elsewhere.

The cane is said to have been introduced from Sicily in 1425. In 1453 the first mill was erected. By the end of the century there were some 120 mills in different parts of the island. About the year 1500, some 35,000 cwt. of sugar seems to have been produced. Although sugar as a crop afterwards practically disappeared, the nunneries of Madeira have remained famous for their sweatmeats until the present day.

The replanting of sugar, which commenced after the vine disease of 1852, is encouraged by the fact that the produce is admitted into Portugal duty free. At present there are three steam mills at work. The best figures obtainable show that during the eleven years, from 1875—1885 inclusive, there was a total production of cane of 212,727 tons, of which 116,247 tons were made into sugar, molasses and rectified spirit, and 96,480 tons into brut spirit.

The averages were (per annum) 19,339 tons of cane, producing 939 tons of white and brown sugar, and 364 tons of molasses which last was distilled into 130,964 litres of rectified spirit, and in addition 844,273 litres of brut spirit made from the cane direct. The annual value of the above is stated to be :—Sugar, 186,654$ (at 4,500 reis to £1,= £41,478); rectified spirit, used in the manufacture of wine, 30,909$ (£6,868); and rough or brut spirit, consumed by the peasantry, 161,455$ (£35,879), or a total per annum of 379,018$ (£84,225), or 12s. 11d. per head of the population.

The greatest production was 27,800 tons in 1878, with a total value of 550,400$ (£122,311).

An average taken over the whole period shows that 100 kilos of cane, manufactured into sugar, etc., produced 2,058 reis, and that the same amount distilled into brut spirit produced 1,840 reis.

In 1897-99 the annual production was about 20,000 tons, of which half was turned into sugar and half into spirits. The sugar weighed about 700 tons, and supplied the demand of Madeira for about 10 months, the deficiency being imported.

The cultivation of the sugar-cane shows a tendency to increase. The disease (*nonagri sacchari*) which practically annihilated the cane between 1885 and 1890, does not attack the Canary or Mauritius stock, which remain strong and healthy. The new canes only show a density of 8° to 9° Beaumé as against 11° to 13° in the old Bourbon plant. It is thought, however, that they are gradually improving. The yield of the cane in Madeira is about 7%, as against 6½% in the West Indies, but the process of extraction is much more thorough.

The cutting of the cane lasts from March till May, and two arrobas (64 lbs.) of cane, of which the market price in 1898 was about 450 reis, are supposed to produce 17 litres of juice (*garapa*) equalling approximately 1¼ kilos of white sugar (not loaf), ½ kilo of 2nd or 3rd quality sugar, and ½ kilo of molasses, from which ·179 of a litre of rectified spirit is distilled. Four gallons (18 litres) of cane juice which is entirely distilled should produce 2½ litres of spirit 26° Cartier.

The cane is planted by putting one or two joints of the top of the stem into the ground and watering it. It is ready for cutting in two years and will last some seven years before being replaced. The leaves are given to the cattle.

In 1891-92, the growers of cane induced the Government to raise the import duty on foreign molasses from 23 to 60 reis per kilo with the object of retailing their cane at a higher price. The owners of mills, however, who had formerly kept themselves employed by distilling imported molasses throughout the year, finding their work stopped for some eight or ten months at a stretch and the ground cut from under their feet by spirit from the Azores, were obliged, in order to make a living, to combine to give only a certain price for cane. The duty on molasses was lowered in 1897 to 30 reis, importers of molasses agreeing to take all cane offered at a certain minimum price to be fixed by the Government. The injurious effects of both these forms of legislation on other industries of the island will be apparent to all.

The industrial tax on sugar factories was estimated at 200 dollars per annum in 1898, which practically covers everything. This 200 dollars being multiplied by the number of factories, the owners meet and divide it equitably amongst them according to the importance of the factory. For instance, the mill owned by Messrs. W. Hinton and Sons in Funchal paid some ¾ of the whole of the amount demanded by the Government from the entire island. As in the case of sugar factories, so the industrial taxes are distributed on all trades.

Owing to the price paid for sugar-cane in Madeira, its cultivation is probably quite as remunerative as that of the vine, to which it is said to form a good alternative when rotation is thought necessary. On irrigable land it is sometimes planted underneath the trellises on which the vines are trained, side by side with vegetables, maize or even pumpkins.

Sugar (in the Canaries).—But few records are obtainable of the earlier times, but it appears that about 1490 **the Canaries** were at least partly planted with sugar and had entered into competition with Madeira, then the principal producer. During the 16th century the large landowners, who were the immediate result of the conquest, employed negro labour, and seem to have made large profits. Lord Verulam (Francis Bacon), writing about 1600, says that being first in an invention "doth sometimes cause a wonderful overgrowth of riches, as it was with the first sugar man in the Canaries."

No figures are now obtainable to show what these exports were, but there is no doubt that the profits, if not the production, decreased early in the 16th century, the islands being unable to compete with the West Indies.

Afterwards, with the exception of a temporary activity due to the vine disease in 1850-52, sugar fell more or less into abeyance. During the last few years a fresh start has been made, and a considerable amount of English and other capital has been ventured.

Sugar-making has lately become the most important industry in **Grand Canary.** Several steam factories have been built there; one **in Teneriffe,** and one in **La Palma.**

The manufacturers are able to find a good market for a large proportion of their output locally. Over and above the tax on farming profits, charged to the land-owner, the factories must pay the industrial duty, which varies in proportion to the population of the district.

As sugar-cane taken from the Canaries has successfully replaced the diseased sugar-cane in Madeira, there is every reason to hope that it may remain healthy and that the large amount of capital laid out in plant of late years, much of which is English, may secure the remuneration it deserves.

The yield of cane is estimated to be from 600—1,200 quintales per fanegada, which is sold under contract to the mills. Cane is supposed to produce from 6% to 9% of sugar, but the figures given for Madeira apply almost equally well to the Canaries. One hundred kilos of first-class sugar fetch about 90 pesetas, the price being high owing to the heavy import duty imposed by the Government on foreign sugars.

The increase in this duty over what was formerly paid is a heavy tax on the public. Whilst it protects an industry not natural to the islands, the only ones to really benefit by it are the owners of the land. The best that can be said in favour of sugar growing is that an estate employs about five times as many hands as say a banana plantation.

Sugar is generally planted in March, and cutting commences in the following March. Labour costs little, and the manure wanted is about 20 cwt. per fanegada, *i.e.*, twelve sacks, costing about £1 a sack.

The Vine.—In Madeira.—Before the close of the fifteenth century the vine was introduced into Madeira and from thence into the Canaries. The original plants were obtained by Prince Henry of Portugal from the already famous vineyards of Malmsey or Malavesi in Crete.

Up till 1850, this grape continued to grow and fruit freely, but was then attacked and nearly exterminated by the ravages of a fungus known as the *Oïdium Tuckeri*, a disease which first appeared in Kent in 1845, and spread thence to the Continent, the Mediterranean, etc. Unfortunately it has since been found impossible to grow it on its own root, and it has been replaced in the Canaries by American and other vines. In Madeira it is still grown budded on to an American stock.

The history of the vine in Madeira is even more important than that of sugar. The soil and climate of the island are so favourable to the growth of the grape, that, in face of the large returns now to be gained by forwarding market-garden produce to London, wine still accounts for some 70 per cent. of the total exports.

It formed a part of the stipend of the parish priests as early as 1485, but the first mention of shipments was in 1566, when a pipe was officially valued at 3$200. In 1646, some 2,000 pipes seem to have been exported. In 1774, 7,073 pipes; in 1790, 13,713 pipes; in 1800, 16,981 pipes; in 1824, 10,980 pipes; in 1851, 7,301 pipes; (this was the year when the vines were attacked by the *Oïdium Tuckeri*); in 1855, 1,776 pipes; in 1865, 536 pipes; in 1873, 2,154 pipes; in 1881, 3,447 pipes; in 1888, 5,870 pipes; and in 1896-99, a mean of 6,174 pipes of 92 imp. galls.

In 1873, the phylloxera appeared and caused immense damage until 1883, when the growers began to obtain the mastery over it. That its effects, however, were of little importance compared to the ravages of the fungus pest of 1852 may be gathered from a few simple figures. The total exports for the ten years previous to the fungus (1843-52 inclusive) show an average export of 6,885 pipes; the average for the ten years following the fungus (1853-62 inclusive) was 1,779 pipes, whilst in the next ten years (1863-72), when old wine was becoming very scarce, (see prices down below), the export fell to an average of 991 pipes, the lowest year being 1865 with 536 pipes. Although in the next ten years the phylloxera bug spread everywhere, the average export (1873-82 inclusive) rose to 3,793 pipes, and in 1883-92 inclusive to 4,071 pipes.

Again the expense of combating the fungus is continuous, as much as 32 lbs. of sulphur an acre being sometimes necessary. The phylloxera, on the other hand, seems to be most easily combated by the use of resistant stock, such as the American vine, on to which the special grapes used in Madeira are grafted.

The actual produce of the island is difficult to estimate. Jeaffreson, in 1676, computed it at 25,000 pipes, and it is stated to have reached as much as 30,000, though probably the highest during the present century was about 22,000. At present it is estimated at about 9,000 and is expected to increase. Porto Santo, which never suffered from the phylloxera, produces from 800—1,000 pipes.

The fluctuations in price, taking "London Particular" as a standard, have been as follows:—In 1778, £27 per pipe; in 1798, £40; in 1816, £77; in 1826, £46, at which price it remained until 1852. A great rise followed the destruction of the vintage, the year of highest price, viz., £75, being reached in 1865, which was also the year of least exportation. It then gradually fell, until, in 1885, it was £38, at about which price it is still quoted.

The most approved method of cultivation is to plant cuttings from American Stock some four feet deep, the soil having previously been turned over to the same depth. Fruit may be expected on the third year, but is delayed one year by grafting. Some of the poorer peasantry, unable to wait another year, do not graft, a little fact which bears more or less upon the question of small holdings.

The vines used for grafting are Verdelho, Tinta, Bûal, Sercial, Malvazia Candida, Moscatel and Bastardo, which are named in the order of their importance.

The vines are trained on trellises on the south, or allowed to straggle on the ground on the north of the island. In the latter case the fruit is lifted by means of small stakes, and in the former vegetables, pumpkins, etc., are planted in between the vines. Pruning takes place just before the swelling of the bud and is generally slight, probably too slight. Flowers appear in April and May and the grapes are gathered from the end of August up to October according to the zone.

The average produce of a vineyard is from 3—4 pipes of *must* per acre (a pipe of *must* equals 528 litres and is supposed, after making all allowances for after treatment, to give a pipe of wine of 92 Imperial gallons). In cases, however, of high and scientific cultivation, as in Messrs. Leacock and Co.'s vineyard at São João it sometimes reaches 7 pipes. Vineyards are said to require replanting every 20 years, but if well treated may last up to 50.

A hundredweight of grapes should produce about a *barril* (44 litres) of *must*, which can be sold to the wine merchants at from 8s. to 14s. per *barril*.

When thought desirable fermentation is checked by the addition of from 5% to 10% of spirit, and the wine is matured by submitting it to a temperature of from 90°—140° Fahr. for from 3—6 months, a process which reduces it by from 5% to 14%. The finer the wine the lesser the heat to which it is exposed and the longer the time. The buildings used for this purpose are called "Estufas" and are sometimes of very great size, necessitating the employment of a large amount of capital. They are supposed to take the place of the hold of the ship, where the heat and the constant movement used to give the value to a wine best expressed perhaps by quoting such initials as "V. O. W. I." Madeira, meaning Very Old West India Madeira, or wine which had taken a voyage for the benefit of its health. Where the merchant does not use the "Estufa" the wine is often exposed under a glass roof to the heat of the sun, the change in temperature between day and night being supposed to add to the aroma.

The cost of a wooden cask is some £2, and this, together with the export duty (50 reis per decalitre) and the labour involved in shipment, causes an expenditure of about £5 a pipe, free on board. The evaporation of the cask represents some 5% per annum.

Madeira is shipped at an average strength of 32° Sykes of proof spirit, and the fact that the shilling duty limit is fixed at 30° seems a great injustice to the island, where by far the largest amount of business is in the hands of our own countrymen, a fact which is not so much the case on the continent.

The Wine trade in Madeira is probably the best illustration that can be given of the openings for foreigners in this part of the world. As is pointed out on page 281, it is a source of "steady and sure" profits and it must be some satisfaction to an Englishman to know that the chief industry of the flourishing little island of Madeira is due largely, or even mainly, to the exertions of his own countrymen. What has been done before can be done again. Though it may take many years to thoroughly establish a business, it is well for the invalid to reflect that there are still chances even in this minute island, and that there are many places with similar climates where a sick man can live a healthy life and be of assistance to the commonwealth by developing the resources of the country he adopts.

Among the many English and Portuguese shippers of Madeira wines, let us take one instance in order to show that expatriation, whether on account of illness or otherwise, is not always a misfortune.

In 1745, a young gentleman, named Francis Newton, left England for Madeira and started in the wine trade. At that time the total export of the island was about 3,000 pipes, the price of a pipe of good wine being about £20. Mr. Newton, who died in 1805, lived to see a total export of some 17,000 pipes, with a gradually increasing value. The price of a pipe of "London Particular" at the time of his death was about £45, and the highest price on record, viz., £77, was touched eleven years later.

It is a well-known fact that Mr. Newton and the partners who afterwards joined him were largely instrumental in this all-round improvement. The wine was produced in enormous quantities a century before Mr. Newton's arrival, but it needed the energy and knowledge of the foreign element and years of hard labour to force the islanders to turn the juice of their grapes into that famous, golden drink which, for a time, swept every other wine out of the market.

The wonderful quality of the wine produced under these new conditions soon attracted the attention of the English officers on the way to and from the East and West Indies, who presently carried the fashion of drinking Madeira into England, and afterwards to every English-speaking community. A long period of prosperity for Madeira was the result, and the islanders gradually became accustomed to depend solely upon their vineyards, so that when the vine was attacked by the *oïdium tuckeri* in 1850-52, some of the makers, thrown absolutely on their beam-ends, shipped inferior wine in order to make a living, thereby disgusting their customers and seriously damaging the English market for the time being. Fortunately for themselves, Mr. Newton's firm, then known as Newton, Gordon, Cossart and Co., preferred to lie low for a few years, with the consequence that Messrs. Cossart, Gordon and Co., as the house is now called, have to a large extent retained the goodwill of the old business.

Here, then, we have an instance of an Englishman coming to a foreign country under what must have been disadvantageous circumstances. He could not speak the language; was a heretic, and therefore had little or no legal status. Yet this man was able to become a benefactor to the whole population and to found a business, which is a well-known and flourishing concern at the end of 150 years.

Though traders in similar countries to Madeira may not become rich in the London or Parisian sense of the word, there is no doubt that the position of such a firm as that selected is one that may well be envied; indeed, from the vast amount of labour employed, directly and indirectly, it is locally of considerable importance. Scarcely a stranger comes to the island who does not visit their Wine "Armazems," which are certainly one of the most interesting sights in Funchal, upwards of a hundred men being constantly at work in the various stores. The firm or some of its members also own some of the most charming villas in that most charming valley of Funchal, and probably other assets of which the writer knows nothing.

In any case, a business which can maintain partners both in the Island and in London, and which can profitably occupy a large space in so crowded a town as the capital of Madeira, must necessarily be more or less successful, and the writer sees no reason why Messrs. Cossart, Gordon and Co.'s business should differ materially, except perhaps in magnitude, from that of a number of other firms trading in Madeira or in the Canaries, most of which no doubt reap a fair and proper profit in proportion to their turn-over.

Messrs. Cossart, Gordon and Co.'s house, though one of the most prominent, is by no means the only case in point that could be given, even in the wine trade alone. Historically, the career of the firm is perhaps the most striking, but it appears to the writer that the future of many of the present generation occupied in opening up the export of fresh fruit, or in establishing general commercial relations between Madeira or the Canaries and Europe, may lead to equally interesting results, and that the names of some of the gentlemen so engaged, possibly some of our own names, as far as that goes, may be cited a century hence as Mr. Newton's name has been cited here, and that their memory may also be held up to honour for the same or for very similar reasons.

The Vine in the Canaries.—The date of the introduction of the vine into the Canaries has already been given. The frequent references by Shakespeare to Canary Sack prove that the wine was commonly drunk in England in his time.

In consequence of the disease of 1850, the export from the Canaries, which, in 1804, amounted to 48,000 pipes and had gradually fallen in 1845-50 to about 22,000 pipes per annum, almost disappeared. Glas stated, in 1764, that at that time 15,000 pipes of wine and brandy were exported from Teneriffe alone, chiefly to British North America, and that the trade was in the hands of Irish Roman Catholics.

During the time when it was most in request, Teneriffe white wine (Malmsey probably), rose to 75 and 80 silver ducats the pipe, a ducat being worth about 9 shillings.

Owing to the enterprise of a few merchants the trade is again reviving. The export, which was valued at £6,740 in 1884, and at £4,855 in 1885, has now advanced to some £25,000 a year.

Vines in the Canaries are planted on unirrigated slopes and find a congenial home amongst volcanic cinders or slag. They have been and will probably again become the most important of all products of the country.

The grapes grown are the *tentillo* and the *negra molle*, both black; the *moscatel*, black and white, and the *verdelho*, *Pedro Jimenez*, *forastero* and *vija-riega*, all white.

A fanegada of vines produces more or less according to the situation. For instance below La Matanza in Teneriffe the yield is said to be from 3 to 6 pipes of *must*, and above from 2 to 4 pipes. In the Monte (Grand Canary) it is estimated at from $1\frac{1}{2}$ to 3 pipes, though, exceptionally, it may be much greater. The *must* produced in the lower and consequently warmer vineyards is more valuable and may fetch as much as £5 10s. a pipe in a good season. Higher up it might not fetch more than half as much, and in the Monte (Canary) is worth from £3 15s. to £5 10s. a pipe.

A country pipe (480 litres : $106\frac{1}{2}$ gallons) of common new wine sells at from 150 to 175 pesetas and an average price would be about 250 pesetas. A matured pipe for export (450 litres : 100 gallons) is worth much more.

The expenses may be reckoned at about 33% and consist of pruning, hoeing, sulphuring, lifting the bunches on to small stakes, pressing, fermenting, etc. More sulphur is required in vineyards higher up than in those lower down. It must always be used when the grapes appear, but need not necessarily be repeated in favourable positions, though in unfavourable it may have to be dusted on as many as three or even four times.

Besides the *oïdium tuckeri* there is a parasitic disease in the Canaries known as *Midlen*, which appeared about 1878 and is treated by an application of quick-lime and sulphate of copper. It principally attacks and dries up the leaves and prevents the proper ripening of the fruit. Vineyards in the hills suffer more from both of these diseases than those lower down, so that the expenses for labour with an inferior vineyard are often actually greater than is the case with superior land. In all cases, however, the above diseases can be successfully treated, and the produce of the vines is now as good and as abundant as ever it was, whilst a bad vintage in the best vineyards is very rare. The ordinary method of manuring is to plant lupine between the vines in the winter and dig it in in the spring. The leaf falls in the commencement of January and pushes again in the latter half of March. The phylloxera never reached the Canaries.

The vine is planted by taking a cutting some 3 feet in length, tying it into a knot and placing it rather deeply into the earth. Little can be gathered before the third year, but a tenant, planting vines, cannot be ejected unless compensation is made.

The wine contains from 16 to 21% of alcohol (Salleron) and about 8% of spirits is added after fermentation, or, in the case of superior qualities, a small quantity of sweet wine known as *gloria*. Red Canary, in order to enter England under the 1s. duty, cannot be fortified with more than 5% of spirits.

Wine matures in the wood in about 8 years but improves up to 25. By placing the vine under glass roofs in the sun it matures more quickly, but heated *estufas* are not used as they are in Madeira.

Pipes, which are made in the islands, cost about £2 each. The chief consumers are France and Germany, but the Canary wine trade has suffered severely by the recent rise in the duties on spirits and because of the refusal of the Spanish Government to allow merchants to prepare it for export by means of bonded spirits.

The quality of wine produced by the best houses both in Madeira and in the Canaries, has, for some years, been equal to any made in the palmiest days. Stocks have accumulated largely, and it is questionable whether as sound a glass of wine can be procured anywhere else for the same prices as those quoted at present in both archipelagos.

The sugar cane and the vine have always been and still continue the main sources from which the people of Madeira derive their revenue. In the Canaries, however, special crops have been culivated at various times, prominent among these being the ice-plant, the cochineal cactus, and latterly the tomato and the banana. The last named is also grown to a certain extent in Madeira. From both of the groups, potatoes, onions and sweet potatoes have been exported in large quantities to the West Indies and to other tropical countries, long before the shipment of more perishable fruit to Europe became possible.

The Ice Plant.—In 1742, a cura of Lanzarote (D. José García Duran) was captured by the Moors. Whilst in slavery he learned the art of extracting soda from the ashes of the mesembryanthemum.

Returning to Lanzarote, he showed his fellow-countrymen how to do this, with the result that a consignment was sold shortly afterwards to a Venetian Captain (Sanqui) at the price of four reales (about two pesetas) the quintal (100 lbs.). The buyer must have made a large profit, for, in 1810, 150,000 quintales were sold at ninety reales the quintal.

The plants from which the soda was extracted were suitable to the very dry climate of the eastern part of the archipelago, and were extensively cultivated there.

According to Viera y Clavijo, those principally grown were the Mesembryanthemum noctiflorum (*yerba de vidrio* or *cofe cofe*), M. crystallinum (*escarchosa*) and the Aizoon Canariense (*patilla*). In 1815, Leopold von Buch found only the second in cultivation, and that principally in Lanzarote.

The first blow to the industry was the discovery that soda could be extracted from sea-water, and the second was the dishonesty of the shippers, who mixed stones with their remittances and thus helped to destroy the trade.

Cochineal.—In the Canaries the next in importance to the vine was cochineal, which was originally brought to the islands in 1826. At first it met with great opposition from those who were afraid that this new and loathsome form of blight would spoil their prickly pears; in fact in the previous century it was forbidden to land cochineal at all. Prejudice was overcome, and it was found that the cochineal cactus (*nopalea coccinellifera*; locally, *tunera*), which grows freely in the islands, was the best adapted to the insect's wants; also that the cheapness and abundance of labour and the climatic conditions allowed it to be produced more plentifully and of better quality than elsewhere. Elsewhere had previously been Mexico, Honduras, and Guatemala. In 1814, 176,259 lbs. were sold in London at about £1 16s. per lb.; in 1820, 158,840 lbs. at about £1 5s. 6d. per lb.; in 1830, 297,985 lbs. at about 10s. 6d. per lb.

The first shipment from the Canaries was in 1831, and consisted of 8 lbs., which in 10 years had increased to 100,566 lbs.; in 1850, to 782,670 lbs.; in 1860, when fuchsine was first chemically known, to 2,500,000 lbs.; and, in 1869, to the highest total of 6,076,869 lbs., with a value of £789,993, the medium price for that year in the market at Grand Canary being 3·25 pesetas per lb.

The population at this period was about 270,000, so that cochineal alone produced a revenue of about £3 5s. to every man, woman, and child in the place.

All the aniline dyes were discovered by this time, but were not commercially manufactured to such an extent as to seriously interfere with cochineal. The islanders, however, became somewhat alarmed at the low price and began to talk about overproduction and the means of preventing it.

In 1874, the crisis had reached a more acute stage, and the price in the London market went down to from 1s. 6d. per lb. to 2s. per lb.—The export in this year was from—

	lbs.
Teneriffe	2,270,138
Grand Canary	2,531,176
La Palma	198,895
Lanzarote	88,536
Total	5,088,745

In order to combat the fall a company was formed in Orotava with a capital of £12,000 (Union Agricola de Tenerife) with the avowed object of placing the cochineal on the market by degrees. Its methods were immediately denounced as commercially unsound by an Englishman, Mr. George C. Bruce, almost the only man who seems to have kept his head. The company in their turn denounced Mr. Bruce, and, in May, 1874, heroically defied all the machinations of the market wire pullers and the competition of any other dye as a rival to cochineal. Mr. Bruce's answer was a journey to Belgium, followed by statistics of the production of aniline at the date, namely about 95,000 cwts. a year, at the price of 2 fr. 50 c. per kilo.

The result was, of course, a foregone conclusion. The company was unable to fight the rest of the world. In spite of defiance, the price and production gradually diminished, until, in 1882, the latter was 4,840,262 lbs., and, in 1886, 2,330,947 lbs.

In 1879, the manufacture of aniline dyes received a sudden impulse owing to the tropical rains which gave rise to rumours of a short cochineal crop, and caused the price to jump from 2·45 pesetas to 3·62 pesetas, and even more.

The damage was exaggerated, but the evil was done. The merchants, who congratulated themselves upon the ready sale of their old stock at enhanced prices, were astounded and in most cases ultimately ruined by the fall which ensued, the best qualities of dried insect going as low as 10d. and 11d. per lb.

Some recovery has taken place now that it is known that cochineal is after all the only red dye which satisfactorily resists hard wear and heavy rain, but the output for 1895 was only valued at £109,234.

Cochineal still remains one of the principal exports, because it is easy to cultivate and because the cactus grows in situations unsuitable for other plants.

Effects of the boom in cochineal.—The economical results of the cochineal culture are yet widely felt in the islands, and have still so great an influence that it is impossible to pass them over in a review of general progress.

Immediately after the collapse of the wine trade the owners of land found themselves face to face with an unsuspected mine of wealth which enriched them almost without an effort on their own part. Everyone shared in the golden shower. The peasant was able to gain as much as 2 pesetas a day, and his wife and children to find constant employment at equally remunerative rates. The merchant and the shipper benefited by a state of affairs where the commonest coin was the gold ounce (£3 4s.), and the expenditure of all classes rose by leaps and bounds.

The price at first was about 10 pesetas per lb., but, fast as the export grew, the market widened. It is true that the quotation gradually sank to 5·12 pesetas in 1849, and 3·25 pesetas in 1869, but the producers were justified in thinking that a fair but remunerative limit would at length be permanently reached. The gross profits were larger than ever, and it appeared as though the gold mine was inexhaustible.

Land was unpurchaseable and everyone wanted to buy. Old streams of lava were broken up and built into walls in order to expose the ancient soil below; hills were terraced where terraces could be made; property was gladly mortgaged at any percentage in order to build new fields, with the certainty that the loan would soon be wiped off. What the cost of all this was can never be known. The labour in many instances was enormous in proportion to the superficial results. It is questionable whether any other country can show farms which, foot for foot, have entailed so much wear and tear of sinew and muscle.

Crowds of dealers were only too glad to buy the cochineal and to employ their capital or credit by storing it. The landed gentry ordered expensive furniture, silver-mounted saddlery and other costly goods from Europe, or spent their time in general dissipation.

Retribution was swift, sudden, and universal. Aniline dyes took the public taste and left merchants loaded with stocks which never ceased to fall; money lenders with heavy mortgages on comparatively worthless property; resident land owners insolvent, and a peasant population temporarily demoralised by high wages and easy living.

The English have been reproached as being the only gainers by cochineal in the end. How this can be is not apparent. It is true that the dye was sold chiefly in London, but it has long since disappeared. On the other hand, some of the furniture and saddlery still exist, though a little out of repair; and the fields, which were constructed to a large extent on English capital, have not vanished. After all, it was not the fault of Great Britain if extravagance and waste left nothing but a memory of better things, instead of a number of fat kine to tide over the somewhat dismal period to follow.

Below a certain altitude cactus was planted in every corner, grain and most necessaries being constantly imported. Now the bewildered farmer found he must either root the cactus up or starve.

Attempt to replace cochineal by *Tobacco*.

—What little had been saved was wasted in building sheds for the drying of tobacco, which it was hoped would take the place of cochineal. A commission was appointed to the islands by the home Government with the object of fomenting the new industry, but the encouragement it gave proved to be a misfortune. The monopoly was sold to a company, which refused to take the tobacco sent in, declaring that it was not up to sample. A little tobacco is, however, still grown in Teneriffe, but the industry is a small one.

Utter ruin caused by cochineal.

—That riches should lead to poverty seems absurd and paradoxical. However, to give one instance. In 1885, a gentleman from the West Indies built a sugar factory in one of the most productive parts of Teneriffe, and not only planted sugar himself, but induced all his neighbours to do so as well. Before any work could be done, he came to the end of his resources and left without paying his rent. The owner of the property was a large land owner in this and other parts of the island; sugar can only be planted on irrigated land, which is naturally the best, and those who had planted were therefore by necessity the principal men of the neighbourhood. The factory was practically completed and little outlay beyond coal was needed to set it going. Yet the machinery was allowed to rust, and the sugar, which was just coming into bearing, was grubbed up, because the pecuniary position of the planters would not allow them to speculate by growing a crop of which the return might be temporarily delayed, or of which the ultimate result was in the least problematical.

That such a pitiful condition was mainly caused by the excessive profits derived from cochineal is scarcely to be doubted. The steady and sure gains in the wine trade gave no room for extravagance. Though each has benefited the islands, it has been in quite a different way.

Development of land caused by cochineal.

—The cochineal, growing as it did near the coast, caused a great area to be brought under cultivation which was formerly worthless, for instance, the slopes above Santa Cruz in Teneriffe. The land so reclaimed, however, was not paid for when the collapse came, and left a load of debt which greatly impeded development for years to come.

The fairest monuments of the wine trade, on the other hand, are those cool, spacious old houses, whose roomy balconies and broad staircases look down into a shady "patio" or yard, and which stand in reproachful contrast to the buildings run up at a time when everyone was anxious to be rich. There are a few exceptions to the rule, but, taking it all in all, the modern village or small country town is little more than a collection of mud huts, daubed with lime. The degradation of art in the Canaries is largely to be attributed to the utilitarian style of architecture adopted in the cochineal times by choice and continued by habit or by necessity afterwards.

Cultivation of cochineal.—It is useless to give a very extended series of facts and figures regarding the best method of cultivating cochineal. It is nearly impossible to make any profit by it in the Canaries, where it is best grown, and no one is likely to try it anywhere else. In case, however, that the experiment should be made, the leaves from which the plants are grown should be planted a yard apart, in alleys 2 yards wide, and in earth from 2 ft. to 3 ft. in depth. At the end of 18 months or 2 years they are ready to receive the insect, which is either dusted on to the leaf in the embryo state during the rainless season, or allowed to attach itself to a piece of muslin in the spring, the muslin being laid for a few minutes on to a box full of "madres" (mothers) in a room kept at a temperature of $85°$. The muslin is then fastened on to the leaf by means of thorns taken from the wild prickly pear cactus (*Opuntia Dillenii*).

The female is wingless and is characterised by the tarsus, which terminates by a peculiar hook. The body is round and fat like a currant, and terminates in two small hooks. When once attached to the leaf she cannot move any more.

The ordinary expenses are stated to be about £30 an acre per annum, and the yield from 8,000 to 10,000 lbs. of fresh, or 2,000 lbs. to 2,500 lbs. of dry cochineal per acre in the summer harvest. It is said that certain very good land has produced as much as 6,000 lbs. in the summer crop.

Guano is the best manure, as it makes the skin of the cactus tender. The allowance is about 1,000 lbs. to the acre of ordinary cochineal bug, or 2,000 lbs. an acre for "madres."

White cochineal is killed by being smoked with sulphur, and black cochineal by being shaken in sacks. The colour is due to the process employed in preparing the insect for the market.

The land in the Canaries which owes its existence to cochineal is now largely planted with tomatoes, etc. If it has now risen to the value of its original cost, it is because of the fruit and vegetable trade, started and fostered by Englishmen, and maintained entirely by the English demand.

In Madeira conditions have been somewhat different. The climate is not dry enough for cochineal, and wine has, roughly speaking, always been the chief article of export. As already stated, the cultivation of the vine has little of the speculative element in it. Land laid down as vineyards does not yield a sudden profit and give rise to unduly extravagant habits. Reclamation of land in Madeira was therefore originally undertaken on a more stable basis.

Spirits.—In Madeira the manufacture of spirits has always had a certain importance. That made from grapes or molasses is free, but all other kinds are taxed.

In the Canaries there has been a small tax on spirit made from the grape since July, 1892, and a much heavier tax on all other kinds of spirit. This law was made in order to enable some of the heavy stocks of wine lying in the bodegas of Spain to be disposed of in the form of brandy. As is usually the case, this interference with the free course of trade has been unfavourable to all concerned, and has ultimately prejudiced the very industry it was intended to foment.

Tomatoes, which are most largely cultivated in the Canaries, are considered one of the most profitable crops, but are looked upon as possibly temporary, and are more subject to disease than cereals.

Seeds imported from England are planted in August and September, and the plant pricked out on irrigable land when from 6 in. to 8 in. high. Calculations differ very much, but a crop of 10,000 lbs. of selected fruit per fanegada in the Canaries may be looked upon as a good average result, though it is possible to gather as much as 20,000 lbs. One estimate is that, by pricking the plants out 2 ft. apart, and in rows 3 ft. from one another, about 9,300 plants go into a fanegada (79 yards each way), and each plant yields from 1 lb. to $1\frac{1}{4}$ lb. of selected fruit, that is to say, 9,300 lbs. to 11,627 lbs. as an average crop. Other growers reckon 10 to 15 lbs. of fruit gross on each plant, and 5 to 6 lbs. of selected.

The fruit is large and of splendid flavour, and the earliest ripens by about November.

Taking 10,000 lbs. (100 quintales) as a standard yield, selling at from 2$ to 3$ a quintal, the return would be from 200$ to

300$ a fanegada. Such a price would be on contract, but growers preferring to take the risk of the market might get any price from half-a-dollar to six dollars a quintal. Large allowances must be made for disease when no fruit at all is sold.

This disease is probably greatly owing to the ignorance in the islands on the subject of the rotation of crops. Tomatoes are planted year after year on the same land and are followed by potatoes, until at last the soil is so impoverished and the plants so weakened, that they become quite incapable of resisting disease. Manuring is not always successful. It often produces too rapid a growth of wood, the best results being sometimes obtained without manure. It is found that land on the south side of the island, where water can be procured, not only gives better crops, but is less affected by disease. Perhaps if the fields were well ploughed several times during the summer and the soil thoroughly exposed to the rays of the sun, the disease germs might be destroyed.

From the returns given above must be deducted the cost of labour and any manure that is used. Labour, if the fruit is properly lifted, may be calculated at an average of three women and half as many men per fanegada constantly from start to finish. If water has to be purchased, it is of course in this as in other cases a further more or less onerous outlay. Note will be taken of the fact that the fanegada is reckoned as all land, and no allowance is made for walls. (For labourers' wages, *see* elsewhere.)

Potatoes.—On low-lying lands potatoes must be planted on irrigable soil even in the winter. Ground, however, at a slight elevation, if it is largely mixed with tufa or rotten pumice-stone, can do without watering. The earliest shipments commence about the end of January, and the magnum bonum is the favourite. Seed potatoes are shipped from England as soon as they can be procured in September or October, and should be planted whole at a good depth.

Stable and chemical manure are generally used, but, if the castor oil plant were planted, as it should be, and the berries crushed in the island, the cake or refuse would prove of great service if used in proper proportions.

The English potato produces from 3 to 5 fold, and, exceptionally, up to 8 fold. A fair contract selling price is 6·25 pes. per quintal for shipment. It has been found that if the same potato is replanted for several years it degenerates in quality but becomes more robust, and yields from 7 to 15 fold. It has almost replaced the potatoes formerly in favour.

The potato disease appeared in October, 1843, near La Laguna, and, by 1845, had spread to all the islands. At the time it committed great ravages. Unfortunately it again shows a tendency to become malignant. This is very likely because tomatoes and potatoes are planted in succession, or even at one and the same time. The Palmera plant is rarely attacked. It has been found that a breezy situation is most favourable, though planting in exposed positions leads to great loss in case of storms.

Neither tomatoes nor potatoes are shipped very largely from Madeira, but the peasants at a certain level obtain three crops of potatoes off the same land every year.

Bananas.—Bananas only grow on irrigable land up to an altitude of about 800 feet. They are shipped more especially from Grand Canary. Land planted with bananas takes about eighteen months to come into bearing, but potatoes, etc., may be planted between the rows while they are maturing. The roots should be planted about 3 yards apart in rows about 5 yards apart. This gives about 400 plants to the acre, or about 430 to the Canary fanegada. New land planted with old trunks will give fruit at from 4 to 6 months earlier than similar land planted with suckers.

The first harvest consists of one bunch to the plant, which is then cut down. In the meantime several suckers spring up. These should be reduced to not more than three. An acre of land may thus, under favourable circumstances, produce 1,200 bunches a year. Bunches with less than eight hands, or say 180 fingers, are not usually shipped. Such bunches sell in the Canaries for about 1·75 to 3·75 pesetas. In Madeira the buyers cut them from the trees, and pay from 800 to 1,200 reis each.

The age of a plantation is probably limited to nine years, after which the fruit deteriorates. Out of the nine, only seven years are fruitful. The annual result when in bearing is therefore rather larger than the actual mean yield. When fairly started, a banana plantation gives little trouble, but the plant is rather difficult to kill when it is necessary to clear the ground for other crops.

The manure used is generally chemical. The leaves used as litter rot slowly, but form a good manure, or they are used for packing. The stems serve as fodder for cows.

Certain varieties, notably the *musa textilis*, yield from $1\frac{1}{2}$ to 2 per cent. of a fibre closely resembling manila hemp. There are some 57 varieties of the banana in the Philippine Islands and the Indian Archipelago alone. The original home of the plant is believed to be Southern Asia, but it is known to have flourished in America for the last four centuries. The banana most common in Madeira and the Canaries is the Chinese banana (*musa chinensis*). The botanists of ancient Greece, who accompanied Alexander the Great into the Punjaub, classed the banana as a cross between the maize and the sugar cane. It is said that drawings of the banana and maize have been found on some of the ruined temples of Yucatan in Central America.

It will grow in nearly every soil except those composed almost entirely of sand or calcareous matter, and is said to produce 133 times as much as wheat, and 14 times as much as potatoes. When cooked or dried bananas are very digestible, and a large fortune awaits the man who can place a palatable, white banana flour on the market, if only as a food for infants and invalids. By fermentation, a refreshing but somewhat intoxicating beverage can be produced.

Oranges.—As a rule, oranges grow best on the south side of the Canaries. The finest are to be found at Telde in Grand Canary and at Granadilla in Teneriffe. Those in Grand Canary weigh sometimes as much as 10 ounces, and are very thin skinned. The largest are rather dear, costing as much as 1d. each, and the smaller ones, fit for shipment, about 3 pesetas per 100.

Oranges first ripen in November and could be shipped in considerable quantities were they carefully picked and packed without bruising. No great extension of the trade can, however, be expected unless plantations are started by experienced foreign growers. The Spanish farmers rarely or never bud or graft, and never prune with a view to shape, the consequence being that, when the branches of the trees are swung by the wind, much of the fruit is pricked by the thorns. Such fruit will not stand a voyage.

Again, the residents will grow nothing on a large scale unless it gives an immediate return. Overplanting of oranges in the Canaries is practically impossible. Only certain parts are suitable, but, if half the archipelago could be turned into an orange grove, the superior quality of the fruit would secure a good market at the best current prices.

The trees of all the islands suffer from a slow consumptive disease believed to have been hatched in America, and due to an insect which attacks the root. Dr. Morris, of Kew, says that this and other maladies, such as scale, can easily be combated.

Method of shipping.—Tomatoes, potatoes, and oranges are shipped in substantial boxes for which the wood is imported ready sawn. Bananas are packed in wooden crates. Dry, sifted German peat, mixed with sawdust, is usually placed round the tomatoes, experience showing this to be the coolest material available for the purpose.

Freight.—The cost of freight to London or Liverpool, is 15s., plus 10 per cent. primage per ton measurement, and in the case of bananas 2s. a bunch to London, and 1s. 6d. a bunch to Liverpool. In the latter case, if the crate measures over 6 cubic ft., it comes under the 15s. a ton category.

Experimental remittances.—Beyond the above four fruits practically none are as yet shipped to England unless in very small quantities or by way of an experiment. **Peas** and **French beans** have, however, been sent from Madeira during the last few years, and what may be done if fast ships are ever properly equipped or built for the trade it is difficult to say. In the meantime there is no doubt that **cauliflowers** are superior to those grown in England; that **peas** can be grown quite as well; that **onions** are mild and of good flavour, and that **French beans** are excellent. All these vegetables and half-a-hundred more can be obtained in relays all through the winter.

Citrons could be shipped in moderate quantities, but the packing costs about £2 a pipe and the freight £1, the selling price in London varying between £2 and £7, so that there is practically no profit.

Figs, grapes, etc.—Among the more delicate fruits, such as the grape, mango, custard apple, apricot, etc., is the fig. This grows in great variety, and is especially good in the Island of Hierro. During the season the fig is extremely cheap, and there is no reason why it should not compete with the Greek fig if properly dried and packed, although it is never likely to be shipped fresh.

The **Walnut** is kiln dried and sent away to a small extent. The tree grows well in suitable situations in all the islands. The absence of all risk to the shipper should lead to a more extensive development of the industry.

The **Osier** will grow well wherever it can be planted on the bank of a stream or of a tank. Stripped osiers from Madeira (*salix viminalis*) are said to fetch the highest price in the London market, namely, from £10 to £15 a ton. No use has so far been made of the bark. The plant is believed to be indigenous, is easy to propagate, and grows freely.

Neglected Industries.—The **Black Wattle** grows luxuriantly in all the islands and might be used to replace mountain scrub or even be planted on land now devoted to lupine. So far it has not been planted commercially in the islands and a few figures may be of use.

The seed, which must be of the *acacia pycnantha mollissima*, is either baked or thrown into boiling water. It is then planted on furrowed land along the top of the mound. When once fairly started the plantation is thinned out by pulling up the young shoots, after which the trees are kept straight by lopping. At 5 to 7 years they are cut down and the bark, which should contain from 35% to 40% of tannin, stripped off. The result should be at least 5 and possibly 20 tons of bark to the acre. Taking 5 as an ordinary result and presuming it to be properly stripped and dried, it is torn into small shreds by machinery, packed in bags and sent to London, where it fetches an average price of about £8 15s. a ton or £43 15s. to the acre gross. Avenues of oaks should be planted between the wattles in case of fire. The timber makes good firewood or can be turned into pick handles, etc.

The **Silver Wattle,** which does not contain more than 12% of tannin or thereabouts, fetches a lower price, but grows best on sandy flats, and could therefore be employed beneficially near Las Palmas.

It might be used for reclaiming sandy wastes both in Grand Canary and in the Eastern Islands. Where it would not thrive, marram grass might serve the same purpose.

Marram Grass has been used with great benefit in the colony of Victoria (Australia). It grows well in shifting sand. Plants are raised from the seed and pricked out in holes from 9 to 15 in. deep, according to the stability of the sand. The holes are made 2 ft. apart and in rows 6 ft. wide, *i.e.*, 3,630 plants to the acre. Plants are sold in Australia at about 25s. a ton (2,800 to the ton). Cattle must not be allowed to graze until the grass is well established, but they are then beneficial, as they prevent it from becoming rank. It will grow to a height of 4 ft. and is much relished by oxen, etc.

The Carob Tree.—Some attention has been directed to this plant as a means of reclaiming dry hill-sides and producing fodder for cattle. In certain parts of Italy, even horses are fed on nothing else but the pod of the bean mixed with bran.

It will grow in dry, stony situations, bears fruit very freely and is a great ornament to the landscape. Specimens may be seen both in Madeira and in the Canaries, but the extraordinary conservatism of at least the Canary peasant, prevents the fruit being utilised as an article of food. The writer has seen the ground covered with pods left to rot within twenty yards of a poor man's pig-sty. When remonstrated with, the man merely shrugged his shoulders and said that no one thought of picking them up. Though urged to do so, he would not gather a few for his pigs, even by way of an experiment.

The plant must be sown *in situ* or grown in pots. When in pots the tap root must not be allowed to enter the ground. If this happens the *carobaster* is difficult to move. The seed is soaked for three or four days before being put into the earth. At three or four years of age the tree must be grafted or budded with good varieties, which are best obtained from Italy. Twenty-five per cent. of unbudded male trees must be left in each grove, or the fruit will not hang on the female trees, which alone are prolific. They should be planted from 12 to 15 yards apart in situations where the top root cannot penetrate to water laden sub-soil. The tree arrives at maturity in from four to eight years. The best report issued on the subject is Italy, No. 431, 1897 (Foreign Office).

The Tagasaste *(Cytisus Proliferus Varietas)*, is a plant, indigenous to La Palma in the Canaries and but little cultivated even in the islands themselves. It deserves mention from the importance it may ultimately acquire in countries where the pasturage is liable to suffer from long droughts.

It may be planted on mountain sides inaccessible to the plough, gives a great number of tender young branches, may be cut 3 or 4 times in the year and sprouts again very rapidly. It has very long roots, which allow it to grow during rainless seasons when other plants would die. By cutting it early it is prevented from becoming too fibrous.

The leaves are trifoliate and the seed pod much resembles that of the vetch. It is sown from the seed and should be pricked out early. It is much relished by the animals, may be dried in the same way as hay in Europe, and has the additional advantage of forming a complete food, or at least does so in hot climates.

Attention was first called to it by the late Dr. Victor Perez, of Orotava, who experimented on it for years. The result of his labours may be obtained in pamphlet form ("Le Tagasaste, etc.," Kirkland Cope & Co., London).

The Sweet Potato *(Ipomœa Batatis)*, of which the Demerara variety is chiefly cultivated, is a tuber of the convolvulus family. It grows freely at most altitudes, giving up to 3 crops a year. The leaves are given to the cattle. Large quantities of spirits are extracted from it in the Azores.

India-Rubber.—No attempt has so far been made to grow this or even to extract the sap from the native plants for commercial purposes. Yet it cannot be doubted that the milk of the Euphorbia Canariensis *(cardon)*, which is a strong caustic and a poison, sometimes used by the fishermen for stupefying fish, must have a value. The E. Balsamifera *(tabaiba dulce)* is neither hot nor poisonous. The sap of this plant could also be obtained in considerable quantities.

Amongst the recognised India-rubber trees there seems no reason why the Ceara rubber *(Manihot Glaziovii*, S. America), the *Kicksia Africana* (West Africa), and probably others should not do well at a suitable elevation. Neither of these plants requires much moisture. A bulbous plant also grows in the dry districts of Southern Madagascar which might be introduced to advantage.

Castor Oil.—Besides the yield of the bean of the castor oil plant as an oil producer, it has already been stated that the refuse, after pressing, is a valuable manure to a country where such plants as the potato and the tomato are cultivated to any extent. The plant grows wild in the most arid situations and could no doubt be made to fill up a great part of the waste unirrigated lands on the south side. An additional profit might be drawn by the cultivation of the silk worm known as the *Bombyx Atlas*, which feeds on the castor oil plant and produces one of the largest cocoons known.

The silk is of the "*Tusseh*" or unreelable varieties and is of considerable commercial value. This value would increase enormously if the parechyma or glutinous matter, binding the thread together, could be dissolved, not an unlikely discovery to be made in these days of chemical progress.

The Aloe.—Like the castor oil and the prickly pear this will thrive almost anywhere and seems to require no moisture. That in the islands has not hitherto been cultivated commercially, although samples of sisal hemp made from it have proved to be of the very finest quality. The variety grown in the Bahamas the *Agave Sisilana of Perrine* or *Bahama Pita*, does well in all the islands, and might be cultivated with advantage.

This is propagated from small plants taken from the pole when in flower or from suckers, matures in the Bahamas in 4 years, and yields leaves as much as 5 ft. long which have no teeth. It thrives in the driest situations. If planted 12 ft. by 6 ft. or 605 to the acre, it should yield about $\frac{1}{2}$ ton of fibre annually to the acre. The leaves are cut monthly as they arrive at maturity. With wages at from 50% to 120% higher than in Madeira, etc., a plantation is estimated to yield an annual profit of between £5 and £6 an acre in the Bahamas.

Miscellaneous plants.—A number of plants, such as esparto grass, camphor, etc., would ultimately give profits if suitable situations could be obtained at reasonable prices. Pickles or jams might be made or fruits dried if the natives would encourage the introduction of foreign capital or if the Governments should cease to impose the present high duties on sugar, etc.

Silk and Tinned Fruit.—Silk was once a considerable export, and continues to be grown and woven on a small scale in La Palma. There is a small manufactory of tinned fruits in the same island.

The Manufacture of Perfumes, Culture of Bulbs, etc.—

This is an industry which has as yet received no attention, yet one for which Madeira and the Canary Islands are singularly well adapted, not only by virtue of the climate, which allows of so wide a range of culture, but also because both archipelagos are directly connected by passing steamers with so many parts of the world. The women engaged in embroidery in Madeira or in the making of drawn linen, etc., in Teneriffe, are the very class which might be expected to adapt itself more easily to the manufacture of scented fats by the *enfleurage* process. Accustomed to keeping their fingers scrupulously clean, they might be relied upon not to impart disagreeable scents to the fat and thus to spoil it for the European market.

Of all places in the islands, Realejo in Teneriffe should be that first inspected for the purpose. Lying one thousand feet above the sea and in a situation where the sun rises late, the flowers might be gathered in the morning with all their perfume latent in the petals.

To form some idea of the magnitude to which such an enterprise might attain, it is sufficient to quote a few figures from the South of France.

In Cannes, Nice and Antibes the perfume factories used in the year 1895, 3,332,000 kilogrammes of flowers for pomades, and 1,666,000 for scented oils, to which must be added millions of kilogrammes of scented plants distilled for essences. The culture of bulbs is conducted on a colossal scale. In Hyères alone some 5,000,000 white hyacinth bulbs, 400,000 narcissus bulbs, and 100,000 lily bulbs are produced annually. A single perfume factory on the Riviera uses every day in May some 40,000 lbs. of orange flowers, 20,000 to 30,000 lbs. of rose leaves, and 4,500 lbs. of jasmine flowers. The same factory consumes during the season some 1,100,000 lbs. of mint; 220,000 lbs. of peppermint; and 22,000,000 of lavender. To all this must be added an enormous seed culture, and an immense export of cut flowers, a trade which is hardly likely to pay in Madeira or the Canaries. In Grasse some 80,000 kilogrammes of violets are grown every year, and, on the top of all this, comes the manufacture of crystallised fruits and high-class bonbons. Altogether on the Riviera there are over 1,000 hectares of land devoted to the cultivation of flowers.

Some Indications of the Capabilities and Value of Land in Different Positions.

Those desiring to emigrate must determine whether the very great price of land in Madeira and the Canaries, as compared with that in many of our own colonies, is compensated for by the products which the present or future propinquity of the base of operations to the great European markets allow or will allow to be grown at a profit; by the cheapness of labour, consequent upon the large population, and by the gain in the exchange of English money into the currency by means of which debts for land or labour are discharged.

The writer takes this opportunity of emphasizing the fact that though this Guide refers particularly to Madeira and the Canaries, many of the points discussed apply equally well to other parts of the world, such as South Africa and Australia, where the climate and conditions are so similar as to allow of the same methods of tilling the soil. Many of those visiting Madeira or the Canaries will do well to examine the country closely and to study the methods of tillage and irrigation thoroughly, with a view to availing themselves of the knowledge gained should they afterwards decide to live in one of the British Colonies named above. In his "Guide to South Africa," the author repeatedly refers to these little islands of the Atlantic, especially when treating of such subjects as market gardening.

Incline of the hills.—Owing to the rapid incline, often 16 per cent., at which the cultivated coast lands rise towards the hills, narrow zones or belts are formed, each of which is more adapted to one culture than another. These zones may be said to be divided by irregular isothermal lines which approach or separate in accordance to the steepness of the incline or the atmospheric conditions induced by the contour of the immediate neighbourhood. Under equal conditions the fall in temperature is about 1° Fahrenheit to every 300 ft., and the fall in the barometer 1 inch for every 1,000 ft.

On the nature of the product of any particular zone the value of land within it greatly depends. Other considerations are: firstly, whether it is irrigable or dependent upon rains, and, in the former case, what is the quantity of water obtainable and what the size and cost of the tanks and means of storage or distribution in proportion to the area cultivated; secondly, what is the nature of the soil itself; and thirdly, what are the means of communication with the outside world. The question of taxation is dealt with elsewhere.

On irrigable land in the Canaries the planting of tomatoes in a good year no doubt gives the best return, but it is too speculative and too uncertain of continuance to have formed a secure basis for valuation. Bananas are also remunerative, but the best standard to adopt is that of maize, which in a few remote parts of the islands still forms the currency by which small payments are made. If land does not show a profit on two crops of maize a year it is probably best to leave it alone.

Value of land as shown on the basis of maize.—The following figures were supplied by a farmer in the Canaries, but are applicable to Madeira or to any country with a similar climate.

On first class irrigated land two crops of maize would be planted, the first in March (gathered in July), the second in August (gathered in November). These should give an average of 50 fanegas and 33 fanegas respectively per fanegada. In amongst the maize, black beans (*Judías*) would be planted. When gathering these from the second crop, about the end of October, they would be replaced by broad beans. The two crops of Judías should give 9 fanegas to the fanegada, and the broad beans would be eaten down by the cattle. A fanegada of land could fatten about 1½ head of cattle if one fanegada to every six fanegadas were planted with lucern in order to help out the *pasto* (maize straw) given to the beasts. A few pumpkins might be cultivated, and the weeds and refuse maize would fatten a pig. Taking the price of maize at 10s. a fanega (3 pesos and 1 toston) delivered, and the Judías at 18s. (6 pesos) and the exchange at 25 pesetas to £1 the result would be as follows:—

1st class land. Sale of 83 fanegas of maize, £42 10s. Sale of 9 fanegas of Judías, £8 2s. Fattening 1½ beasts twice a year at a profit of £3 each beast, £9. Sale of pumpkins and of stripped corn cobs (the latter for fuel), say £1. Profit on one pig, say £2 5s. Total £61 17s. Spanish.

2nd class land. Sale of 67 fanegas (40 + 27) of maize and 7 fanegas of Judías, otherwise the same. Total £52 1s. Spanish.

Expenses in either case. Share of the land planted with lucern say at a rent of £15 per fanegada, £2 10s.; insurance of beasts costing say £4 10s. and selling at say £7 10s., say 10s.; extra stable manure required, say 200 *serons* or mule loads at 3d. a seron, £2; fetching the manure and putting it on the land from say 1½ miles (2 men and 2 mules and 10 journeys a day) £2; 6 sacks of chemical manure, £6; opening up soil, watering same, planting and making furrows (*surcos*); irrigating 12 times a year; putting on guano and hoeing; collecting, and carrying crops; separating, winnowing and storing all crops; cost of selling and cartage; attendance on 1½ cattle and carrying of stable manure; wear and tear of implements, rope for oxen, etc., Total £23 10s. Spanish.

The above calculations have been made from a practical farmer's notes and on the basis of a man's wage being 1s. a day, a woman 6d. and a man and two mules, 3s. If the wages are heavier, if water has to be purchased, or if the land is of such a nature that it soon dries after irrigation, an allowance must be made. If there is no water as much as £20 may have to be paid in some parts for sufficient water per fanegada per annum.

In the case of first class land, without allowing for rent, there appears to be a margin of £38 7s. Spanish, and on 2nd class land of £28 11s. Spanish. The latter, however, might not be able to support as much as 1½ head of cattle.

In some places £25 and even £30 rent per fanegada is paid by the natives, but they generally have some other work to do, they manure insufficiently, they provide all the labour themselves, live on gofio and get up at three every morning, and, lastly, they never keep books and really don't know whether they are making a profit or not.

It must be remembered that the above crops leave the land free between November and March, giving time for an intermediate crop of potatoes or tomatoes, the profits of which must be added to the above. From some land even four crops can be obtained in one year.

The returns to be obtained from the vine, the sugar-cane, the tomato, etc., etc., have already been discussed.

Quantity of water required for irrigation.—There is naturally a great difference between the value of land into which water can be carried and that where reliance must be placed upon the rains. The emigrant may choose to invest in the latter, and to employ his capital in the storage or carriage of the water necessary for irrigation.

In the islands most distant from Africa, including Grand Canary, droughts are unusual and rarely serious, but in the Eastern Canaries, and especially in Fuerteventura, great distress is sometimes felt for want of rain, although in a wet year it is here and in Lanzarote that the greatest quantity of grain is produced.

The seasons are fairly well fixed. Rain may be expected to fall on the coast lands early in October, and to cease early in May.

Sir J. B. Lawes and Dr. Gilbert's observations show that wheat, oats or hay, in a climate like that of England, can mature into average crops with an allowance of 700 tons of water per acre, provided that the moisture be distributed at the proper time. One inch of rain equals about 100 tons per acre. In England there is an average of 25 inches. It has been shown in the meteorological statistics that, even on the sea shore at Grand Canary there is more than the seven inches absolutely necessary. Granted that in a drier climate, where the water must be run into the fields, double the quantity named, *i.e.*, 14 inches is required, it is obvious that, except in Grand Canary and the S.E. side of Teneriffe, the requisite amount falls even on the coast.

But water is best stored on the hills, where, as has just been said, the greatest rainfall is to be found. To this rain could be added the moisture which fringes of trees, judiciously planted, would extract from the mountain mists, more common be it remembered in the summer, when a renewal of the supply is most wanted, than in the winter. So copious is the quantity sometimes extracted by trees, that anyone standing to the leeward of a small pine whilst the warm mid-day mist is passing would be wet through in five minutes, though the ground outside of the radius of the tree would be perfectly dry.

Seasons and harvests.—The gathering of vegetables or the harvest of cereals depends, to some extent, on the zone in which they are grown and the time of planting. On irrigable lands a wide latitude is enjoyed as regards nearly everything. On land which is watered by the rain the winter is of course the season of growth and the summer of rest.

Cereals.—On unirrigable land the staple crops are cereals and beans, only one crop of wheat or barley being usually obtainable per annum as compared with two, three, or even four of potatoes, maize, tomatoes, etc., where water is available. However, where the rainfall is sufficient, the question of purchasing water does not affect calculations, and, at the usual altitude at which wheat, etc., is grown, every crop is a certainty. The price of wheat may average about £2 5s. (86 pesetas) per quarter of 480 lbs. The yield is probably always under-estimated in order to escape taxation, but the worst arid land should produce from twelvefold to twentyfold, and good land (high up) fiftyfold or more. It is said that in a good year in Lanzarote and Fuerteventura as much as two hundred and forty fold has been gathered. The price of cereals, reckoned in sterling, does not fluctuate so much as was formerly the case, the attention of importers having been attracted of late to the foreign markets.

Wheat land is generally situated at from 1,600 ft. to 2,300 ft. above the sea, the irrigated lands below being planted with crops which mature more quickly. At its best it might cost 500 to 1,000 pesetas per fanegada, worked into sterling at the exchange of the day.

Cost of unirrigated land.—To quote an instance. Good unirrigated land around and below Tacoronte in Teneriffe gives up to 20 fanegas of wheat per fanegada. Above Tacoronte and nearer to the Monte Verde, from 6 fanegas upwards is a fair estimate. On good land as much as 3 fanegas is required as seed.

Land around Tacoronte is approximately worth: 1st class, 750 to 1,150 pesetas the fanegada; 2nd class, 450 to 825 pesetas; third class, 375 to 550 pesetas. More would be paid if the position were specially good. Unirrigated land below Tacoronte can be made to give 3 crops in one year if the rains are fairly plentiful.

In Madeira, wheat rarely gives more than 12 bushels to the acre, rye less, and bearded wheat only eightfold or ninefold. For this reason it has been found advantageous to plant pines on many of the hills. This subject is referred to under " Forestry."

The prospective buyer will find the holder somewhat reluctant to recognise the loss of land due to the presence of walls or of heaps of stones, erected at the time that the farm was cleared for cultivation.

In Madeira, indeed, owing to the *bemfeitoria* system, it is almost impossible to buy or hire land, so that it is difficult to give any basis for prices. The government valuation, however, at which properties are confiscated for expropriation is :—for corn land 100 reis per sq. metre ; market gardens, 180 reis ; vineyards, 240 reis ; forest land, 40 reis ; first class pasture, 60 reis ; inferior pasture, down to 8 reis. A proprietor may appeal against this valuation if he wishes.

Cost of vineyards.—This differs very much according to position and yield.

Near Orotava vineyards are said to be worth :—1st class, from 3,500 to 4,500 pesetas a fanegada ; 2nd class, from 2,500 to 2,250 ; 3rd class, 1,750 to 2,500, and for inferior sites very much less. These prices were taken with the exchange at about 50% in favour of sterling.

In Grand Canary the Consular Report for 1898 (No. 451) gave certain valuations for land in Grand Canary which do not agree with the writer's information.

Cost of irrigated land.—Irrigated land with water in such a situation as the valley of Orotava, Teneriffe, might sell at the following prices :—1st class, 3,750 to 5,000 pesetas per fanegada ; 2nd class, 2,500 to 3,000, and very much lower for indifferent or unirrigated soil. Including water rights, which must be separately mentioned in the deed of conveyance, the prices might be even higher. In such a locality as Telde, in Grand Canary, where there is a sugar-mill, good irrigated land with plenty of water might fetch from 500 to 750 pesetas a fanegada per annum rent.

No owner of waste land is inclined to sell to foreigners at spot prices. This is because of the idea that, by their greater knowledge, they will turn it to some good account, the holder preferring that a neighbour should be the seller and allow him to copy the methods of the astute stranger and make the gains himself.

This timorous feeling is a great bar to the progress of the islands, as it prevents the acquisition on reasonable terms of tracts of country or of forest land, capable of yielding some small return, but remaining useless because the owner clings to them and yet is unable to derive any benefit from them personally.

Rent of land.—As regards rent the limits are naturally wide, and the price varies greatly. It will be seen from the taxation returns that the contribution to Government (land and house tax) in the Canaries should amount to from 19% to 25% and in Madeira to from 9% to 10% of the yearly value.

It is a fair estimate to add to the amount of the taxes from 2½% to 5% interest on the value of the farm. In the case of tomato land, however, position would be a paramount consideration.

Mortgages.—Loans on land should return from 6% to 10%, not more than 50% of the face value being lent.

Popularity of land as an investment.—One reason for the dearness of land is that those who have saved money in the islands, or who have emigrated and been fortunate, know of no other investment than houses and land. The few wealthy people have no idea of distributing their money in various countries, or of undertaking works of public utility on a large scale where a certain amount of risk is encountered. Unfortunately they do not even care to plant timber as a source of future wealth, but prefer to hold land giving hand to mouth crops and perhaps only returning them a very low rate of interest, or to lend money on mortgage, which is, after all, only another way of buying real estate.

This reluctance to look a few years ahead is the real chance of the foreigner. Anyone who can buy suitable land at a fair price and plant oranges, coffee, or some other crop of slow development, or who can acquire some large tract in the mountains and lay it out for wattle bark, etc., might look after his health while the trees were growing, pay his way by raising tomatoes and vegetables between the young plants, and eventually step into a good property giving a large annual income without an undue amount of labour.

Responsibility of landlord.—The custom in the Canaries regarding tenants is that the landlord shall be responsible for the exterior dilapidations of all buildings, for the repairs of all watercourses and walls, and for the loss of buildings by fire.

The custom of working a farm on the part profit system will be found fully detailed under "methods of cultivation."

In Madeira the landlord is responsible in the case of villas but not in that of farms.

Waste land tax free.—In the Canaries absolutely waste land, brought under cultivation, may obtain a concession to be considered as a "colonia agricola," and the farm and those resident upon it obtain the privilege of exemption from both territorial and municipal taxes during a period of about 20 years.

Climate.—Some indications have now been given of the price of land and the crops to which it is adapted, and the next consideration is the climate. But little need be said about this in connection with agriculture, except that it is notably as perfect as can be found, and that on irrigated land, barring disease, one year's crop is as good as another.

The matter has been fully entered into in another part of this volume where figures of temperature, rainfall, etc., will be found.

The statistics given, however, only refer to the towns, and by no means indicate the actual amount of moisture available in the islands. The rainfall and the vapour collected on the mountains, especially when covered with wood, exceeds by many times that to be measured below the Monte Verde.

Zones of Vegetation, Forestry, Pasture and Live Stock.

The value of land in the islands depends greatly upon its altitude, firstly, because of the crops cultivable ; secondly, because of the methods of irrigation available, and, thirdly, because of the facilities of carriage.

Firstly, as regards the various plants which flourish in the various zones, where conditions as regards water and soil are favourable.

Climatic Zones.—Zone I.—*From the sea-level to about 500 ft.*—Pineapples (indifferently), tobacco, and among fruit trees, date palms (in protected situations) and mangoes. Tomatoes as a winter crop on the North side of the Canaries. (*Limit of coffee in Madeira*).

Zone II.—*From the sea-level to about 1,000 ft.*—Bananas, sweet potatoes, gourds, arrowroot (little planted), cochineal, cactus, castor oil, sugar, bamboo, cape-gooseberry, and among fruit trees, alligator pears and custard apples. Potatoes as a winter crop. Tomatoes as a winter crop on the South side of the Canaries. (*Limit of figs in Madeira.*)

Zone III.—*From the sea-level to about 2,000 ft.*—Tomatoes, potatoes, yams, onions, beans, lentils, peas, lucern, sweet peppers, flax, garbanzos, lupine, tagasaste, and *cereals*, wheat, bearded wheat, barley, maize, rye and oats (little planted). All vegetables grown in England, such as Jerusalem artichokes, parsley, lettuce, carrots, turnips, cabbages, cauliflowers, spinach, vegetable marrows, etc. Celery is not first rate, and asparagus is rather bitter. Among fruits, the vine, orange, lemon, citron, almond, olive, fig, prickly pear, mulberry, pomegranate, peach, apricot, custard apple, guava, coffee, Japanese loquat, melon, strawberry, granadilla. (*This applies to both Madeira and the Canaries except for coffee and figs.*)

Also the osier and the *arundo donax*, a cane largely used in making trellises and tying up tomatoes.

Zone IV.—*From 1,000 ft. to 4,000 ft.*—The limit of cultivation very rarely exceeds 4,000 ft., and is generally reached at 3,500 ft. or thereabouts.

Many of the plants of Zone III. can be cultivated at the higher level, but the most general crop is cereals, followed by beans or lupine, the last of which is eaten down by the oxen for the sake of manure, as turnips are eaten in England, helping to prepare the land for the next year's harvest.

The chief crop at a great altitude is the Spanish chestnut, but many of the hardy fruit trees do very well, and there seems no reason why some of the large expanses of cinder and pulverised lava in the hills should not be planted with vines brought directly from Germany or other cold countries. The local vine is killed by the snow in the winter, and cannot be acclimatised.

Zone V.—*Forest Land.*—In the Canaries heather, laurel, bracken and scrub sometimes commence as low down as 1,200 ft., but the usual commencement of what is known as the "Monte Verde," or green mountain side, is at 2,500 ft. to 3,200 ft.

The forest itself has been cut down so much, that it is rare to find pine trees growing below 2,500 ft., and many of the *pinares*, or pine forests, only commence at about 4,000 ft.

The greatest height at which any shrub or tree is found is that of the Cañadas of Teneriffe, where the broom, known as the *retama* (*cytisus fragrans*) grows from 5,600 ft. to nearly 11,000 ft. The *pinus Canariensis* (*téa*) lives at a height of nearly 8,000 ft., and the native cedar (*juniperus oxycedrus*), now nearly extinct, is found at about the same level.

The principal forest trees are the pines, of which the *pinus Canariensis* is peculiar to the islands, and a slow-growing but most valuable timber; the *viñatico* (*persea indica*) or native mahogany; the *palo blanco* (*picconia excelsa*), a hard white wood; the *barbusano* (*phoebe barbusana*), a dark wood of great strength and endurance, used for making the beams of wine presses; the *til* (*oreodaphne foetens*), also a hard dark wood; the *laurus Canariensis* and several species of heather, one of which (*Erica arborea*) grows upwards of 40 ft. in height, and measures sometimes over 5 ft. round the stem.

On Mount Ruenzori, west of Lake Victoria Nyanza, trunks of this heath are to be found indicating a height of about 80 ft., the base of the same mountain being clothed with laurels resembling those found in the Canaries. These two trees would appear therefore to share with the dragon tree, and perhaps with a few other plants, the honour of representing the class of vegetation commonly found on the African continent in the period intervening between the Ice Age and the Tropical Epoch of to-day. The subject has been referred to when describing the dragon tree in the introduction to Teneriffe.

There are many more trees, including the cork, the elm, the oak, the eucalyptus, the plane, the beech, the cypress, the coral tree, the stone or umbrella pine (*pinus pinea*), the camphor, india-rubber, wattle, pepper, acacia, araucaria, rose apple, etc., etc. In fact, it is evident that in a climate where the orange and the fir, the mango and the blackberry find a congenial home, it is difficult to name any tree which cannot be cultivated with more or less success.

Doubtless, under a far-seeing Government, the islands might not only grow all the timber necessary for the repair of ships which call at their ports, but might even see the produce of their forests become a valuable export and a means of employing some of the vacant space in the colliers leaving for home.

In Madeira the conditions are much the same, except that the mountain scrub commences as low as from 1,000 to 1,500 ft., and that the *pinus Canariensis*, so widespread in the Canaries, is wanting. Owing to the discovery, however, that a pine forest pays better than bad wheat land, a great many hills are clothed with verdure which would otherwise be bare and brown.

The tree usually planted is the *pinus pinaster*. The method of planting adopted is for the owner of the land to allow some neighbouring peasant to sow the pines, together with a crop of barley, and to take the barley for his trouble. Where the land has been long under cultivation, it is sometimes difficult to get the pines to start growing. Two or 3 years may be wasted in this way, but, when once started, they continue to do well and to renew themselves. In from 3 to 4 years the trees are large enough to make trellises for the vines; in 4 or 5 years they are large enough to make supports for the same. In good positions, they can be chopped up for firewood in about 7 years, though sometimes they take from 10 to 12. To get a plank a foot wide the tree must remain over 20 years. It does not pay to let them go beyond the firewood stage, and woods are then generally sold by auction. A sledge load of firewood is worth from 9 to 10 dollars.

Care of Forests.—There is but little natural forest land left in Madeira, and even in the Canaries most of the woods have been burnt or destroyed. At present their chief value lies in the charcoal made from the heather and laurel, and from the sale of cattle finding food within their limits. The Spanish Government, however, has commenced to recognise the value of planting trees. If orders are properly carried out, the goats kept away from young plantations, and the peasants prevented from carrying away pine needles to make manure, the importance of wooded hills as a means of storing water can be indefinitely increased, and the mountains, which are now too often bare, can be covered with a more wonderful and more varied verdure than was ever the case before.

The malignant neglect of centuries has been mercifully rendered almost harmless by the shortness of watercourses and by the adamantine nature of the rocky spurs, whose millions of pockets still hold the earth, which only requires a minimum of expenditure to become a source of revenue in more ways than one.

Pasture.—In certain parts of the Canaries extensive open pasture land is found, but most of the feeding ground is actually in or about the Monte Verde. The proportional value of pasture, as compared with arable land, appears from the taxation returns.

Probably the most economical method of fattening cattle for the ships or for export is by means of planting land with beans, lupine, etc., and allowing them to eat it off.

Those animals put out to graze are generally goats, although of course both sheep and oxen are seen feeding on the hills.

In Madeira the centre of the island is almost entirely surrounded by a stone wall, the pasture land inside belonging as a rule to the adjacent municipality in the same way as common land does in England.

Live Stock.—A certain amount of cattle is bred for the use of ships and for export. Sheep are worth little and are small. Goats are of a good breed for milk, but the flesh is not much relished. Fowls, etc., do well but fatten badly.

In the Canaries horses are bred small but wiry, and are willing workers, but mules and oxen are more usually employed for heavy work. The oxen, which do all the work in Madeira, are handsome animals, and sometimes of enormous size, but the bone is very large in proportion to the meat, and they rarely cut up well. A pair of oxen trained to the plough may be worth from £17 to £25. Jersey cattle have been imported, and seem to do well. Camels and donkeys are chiefly bred in Fuerteventura and Lanzarote, and are of a good strain.

Method of Agriculture and of Conveying and Storing Water, with Statistics concerning Irrigation.

The *implements* used in agriculture differ but little in the two archipelagos. The plough is simply a beam with an iron point, usually drawn by oxen, or in the eastern islands by camels. The greater part of the work is done with a heavy hoe, single and narrow in districts where the ground is hard, broad and partly forked where it is soft. It is customary for an overseer to sit by and watch the men working, even if they are very few in number. All threshing is done by oxen on paved floors, and the broken straw is used as fodder. Half the straw is considered fair payment for the work of threshing.

In the Canaries the oxen are harnessed to a sledge, of which the bottom is studded with sharp pieces of hard basalt (*piedra viva*). Such a sledge is to be seen hanging up in the British Museum as one of the few existing examples of the stone implement age. Maize is separated from the cob by hand machines imported from America. Owing to the hilly and stony nature of most of the land, it is questionable whether the introduction of heavy machinery would be advantageous.

Manure is poor in quality owing to the way horses and cattle are fed. Less is given to the ground than is customary in England, great reliance being placed on the recuperating power of the sun during the summer rest.

The Medianero system in the Canaries.

—The overseer is often also the "medianero"—that is to say, a species of tenant or bailiff receiving a share of the profits. The terms between the owner and the "medianero" naturally vary, but the following may be said to be a fair sample agreement.

The proprietor provides a house for the "medianero" and his family.

When cereals, potatoes, vegetables or fruit are the crops, the proprietor pays for half the seed, but none of the labour. The results are divided equally. When tomatoes, onions or bananas are the crop, the proprietor pays half the expense of preparing the land and planting, and half of the gathering and sending into market, but none of the intermediate labour.

When cochineal is grown, the proprietor pays half the seed (or rather insects), and half of the subsequent labour.

* All manure raised on the farm is used on the farm unless otherwise arranged. When any is bought the proprietor pays half.

When water has to be bought half is paid by the proprietor; but all the labour of watering is provided by the "medianero."

The proprietor buys the live stock, and replaces that which dies, and pays the half of any food which has to be bought. The proceeds, such as milk, eggs and young are divided.

Repairs are paid for by the proprietor.

Taxes are generally two-thirds proprietor and one-third "medianero." Any losses are halved.

When land is let, the tenant can claim for improvements.

The Bemfeitoria system in Madeira.—In Madeira it is customary for the land to belong to two parties, the *senhorio*, who owns the soil and the water brought to irrigate it, and the tenant (*colono*) who is called *caseira* or *meyro*, according to whether he has a house upon the property or not.

The *colono* owns all the property which is the work of man. With the exception of houses he may construct what he likes, and cannot be ejected without full compensation, the amount being fixed by official arbitrators (*avaliadores*).

The produce of the land is halved or divided according to arrangement. Partly for this reason the hiring of land is generally most difficult. The system has one advantage, viz., that it causes the tenant to add improvements in order to secure his tenure, and, therefore, leads to the ground being brought up to its full bearing capacity.

The tenant tills, plants, manures and threshes, or, in the case of grapes, presses out the juice. He generally tries to grow as many vegetables as possible, as it is difficult for the landlord to keep them under supervision and to claim his half share.

The system of *bemfeitorias* is not altogether popular with landlords, who sometimes find it very difficult to get their land back if they wish to cultivate it themselves. The tenant has to keep all work in repair.

Irrigation statistics.—The next important consideration is water. Speaking generally, at over 1,500 feet, irrigation is rendered unnecessary by reason of the rainfall.

It may be taken as correct, that, in proportion to their size, the quantity of water available for irrigation is as follows:—

First, Madeira; second, Grand Canary; third, Teneriffe; fourth, La Palma and Gomera; and fifth, Lanzarote.

The last has very few springs; Fuerteventura and Hierro have none.

Fuerteventura and Lanzarote depend on the rain which occasionally does not fall in the winter, both the islands being comparatively low and bare of trees. Lanzarote is essentially volcanic. In Fuerteventura there are considerable deposits of limestone which retain the moisture, with the result that water can generally be found by digging wells.

Hierro, owing to its position and to its being more directly in the course of the Gulf stream, is less dependent upon springs.

The same remark applies to both Gomera and La Palma, in the latter of which, owing to the steep descent of the coast, water in any quantity issues from no more than four principal springs, all situated on the walls of its famous and gigantic crater.

Teneriffe, from its formation and the height of its mountains, should apparently be best supplied, and, as a matter of fact, parts of it are well watered; but if ten times as much water were available it could be profitably used.

Efforts, so far unsuccessful, are being made to find water and bring it to Santa Cruz, Teneriffe, where it is much wanted. There is no doubt that a fortune is awaiting the first man who perambulates the province with a properly inspired hazel-twig. Curiously enough no one seems to have thought of sinking wells in the great plain of the Cañadas round the Peak, although there are good indications of the presence of large underground springs.

Grand Canary is to be congratulated on the possession of many springs, especially of one near Tejeda, estimated to yield a supply of 2,500 cubic metres per diem (88,289 cubic feet), a part of which is carried to Las Palmas by means of an aqueduct many miles in length. Grand Canary is better supplied with tanks for storing water than Teneriffe.

In Madeira some of the levadas are very long. That known as the Levada do Furado will measure 50 miles when complete. Municipal water is put up for auction every year. The holder has the first right to it at the price he was last paying, but no one may buy it for the purpose of re-selling. A fair sample of the cost of water at Funchal is that given by the Levada Piornaes near S. Martinho, one of the largest levadas, where 8 to 9 dollars a year is paid for a fourth part of the stream for one hour every fortnight.

The same quantity of water in the Canaries would scarcely be obtainable. A mere dribble will sometimes cost a dollar or more for one single hour. At Telde in Grand Canary sufficient water for 1 fanegada of land once in 15 days, was sold recently for £24 per annum.

Cost of tanks and watercourses.—Tanks in the Canaries are often constructed of stone and locally burnt lime, and lined inside with hydraulic cement. The estimated cost is 1 dol. a pipe—that is to say, roughly speaking, a tank 40 ft. long by 40 ft. broad by 10 ft. deep, would hold 1,000 pipes, and costs about

£200 less exchange. No estimate can be made of the cost of the stone watercourses, because this depends so much upon the nature of the course, etc. Over a long distance it might average from 3s. to 4s. a yard.

In Grand Canary and elsewhere, when the earth is suitable, tanks are also made by means of embankments. A clay-like soil is required which will not allow of the least percolation, a matter which must be reported on by an expert.

With a large tank of this description as much as 15 pipes of water, or even more, may be stored at the cost of one dollar. The relation of the width of the base to the height of the embankment must be as four to one, and the angle of elevation must not exceed 40 to 45 degrees. Nothing but grass must be planted on the sides. Trees and plants with long roots may break up and destroy the embankment. The area occupied by an earthen as compared with a stone tank is necessarily much greater in proportion to the water each will hold.

In Madeira the government levadas completed before the commencement of the Levada do Furado measured 110 miles, and cost 500,000,000 reis or about £100,000, and the private levadas 130 miles at a cost of 230,000,000 reis or say £46,000. The government levadas include compensation, and are usually those built in the most inaccessible positions.

Pipes in every way would be better and more economical because of the loss by evaporation, by leakage and by robbery from the stone channels.

Those desirous of investing capital in watercourses may find the following figures of service:—

On September 1, 1889, the water was measured at the Aguirre springs, about 5 miles away from Santa Cruz, Teneriffe. Result at the spring, 37,690 litres an hour, reduced on arrival in the town to 32,729 litres, or a loss of about 13 per cent.

On July 14, 1891, the same measurement gave 35,703 litres and 26,706 litres respectively, or a loss of about 25 per cent.

On September 6, 1891, the same measurement resulted as 30,538 litres and 25,210 litres, or a loss of about 16 per cent.

It is evident that had pipes been in use, nearly as much water would have arrived in Santa Cruz on September 6, 1891, as on September 1, 1889. Now 1891 was a year of drought, as practically no rain fell after March 4. The result was that water in Santa Cruz was almost unobtainable in the autumn of 1891, and irrigation was partially suspended, the water being even taken away from those who had a right to it by ancient privilege. All had to give way to the necessities of the town, and at least the orange crop was in consequence lost.

It will therefore be seen that during July, August and September, the springs which supply Santa Cruz run at the rate of about

35,000 litres an hour, and probably at least at an average rate of 40,000 litres during the whole period of 8 months (April—November), during which water is most valuable; also that the average loss between the spring and the town is about 17 per cent., or say one-sixth. It is an easy calculation to show the total loss which ensues, which is equal to about 9,000,000 gallons more or less.

Santa Cruz is only one instance out of many. It is probable that if the disposal of the water generally were under the hands of an honest and energetic man or board, working in connection with the Department of Forests, it might not only pay its way, but show a gradually increasing surplus applicable to the building of storage tanks, the augmentation of supply, and the replanting of the hills, with a result that in a few years or decades of years might be of the greatest advantage to the islands. By the use of pipes pollution is also rendered impossible, the yearly charge is less, and those living in the neighbourhood cannot steal water on its way.

Small iron pipes for private use landed in the Canaries cost:—2 inches, inside measurement, about 2s. per foot; 1½ inches, about 1s. 6d. per foot.

The judicial authorities can compel any landed proprietor to allow the passage of water through his territory, on consideration that he is indemnified beforehand.

In cases where wells or horizontal tunnels are made for the sake of finding springs, the jurisdiction or parish in which the works are situated are able to demand that, in case of injury to their own springs, they shall continue to receive from any new supply which may be found the same quantity of water as before, and that, if the works result in an increase in the total flow, 25% of this increase shall be retained for their use.

Water having been brought to the land is distributed by means of furrows which are successively filled. For household purposes it is stored underground in cemented tanks. Drinking water is usually fetched in barrels from the public fountain.

Actual Condition of the Islands and Possible Effects of Novel Circumstances on the Future of Agriculture.

Having passed in review the gains and losses of former years a fair general idea may be formed of the capabilities of the islands had circumstances remained unchanged.

Two factors, however, have now to be reckoned with. One is that the soil has been distributed amongst a great many hands by the abrogation of the law of entail and by the dispossession of the clergy.

For readers to draw a just conclusion as to the effect of these acts it would be necessary to study the emigration returns and the statistics of taxation. No comparison can be made with what might happen in England, as, whatever may be the case at home, the large landowners in the islands never seem to have seriously endeavoured to improve either the agricultural implements or the breed of live stock, whilst the lodging and clothing of the poorer classes were and are a matter of entire indifference to them. Too much has always been left to the Government, and the duties of rank and station have never been properly recognised by the upper classes.

The second factor, and from an English point of view by far the most important, is the extraordinary growth of late years in the means of communication with other countries.

To fully appreciate this the accompanying table of shipping movements should be studied, from which it will be seen that in Teneriffe and Grand Canary together 373 steamers called in 1895 where 100 called in 1885, and that the deliveries of coal had increased by nearly 800 per cent. That Madeira should have failed to keep pace with the above figures does not affect the present question, as steamers calling at the Canaries for fruit, etc., are only too glad to call at Madeira as well if freight can be given them. Besides this the ships which do call in Madeira are both quicker and larger than they were a few years ago and offer all the facilities required.

Apart from the matter of freight, the statistics give valuable evidence of the popularity and fitness of the islands as great Atlantic coaling stations and as a half-way house between the old and the new world; for coal, and coal alone, is the reason why most of the ships call at all.

Both **the Canary ports** have been declared by the Spanish Government as of first importance. It is true that Grand Canary has progressed faster than Teneriffe, but it is equally certain that both are sure to advance in the future to a point hitherto undreamed of, unless coal should be replaced by some less bulky fuel.

The competition of a number of coaling stores and the confidence in a constant and unlimited supply continue to attract fresh lines of steamers on their way from Europe to the West Indies, South America, the Cape and Australasia. As the population and requirements of these countries augment, so must the need of these and other coaling harbours increase.

It is a well-known axiom that trade will follow the flag. Consequently it is not to be wondered at that England holds the first place among both imports and exports. German shipping and German trade have increased of late years, but the full figures of imports and exports for the various periods not being obtainable, a critical analysis of the reasons can only be made at some future date by means of the careful preservation of returns yet to be issued.

The British flag being that most commonly seen in these waters, it is found that the wealthiest and most enterprising commercial houses are British too, and that the coasting steamers are largely employed in gathering together produce which goes to the British market.

Fruit.—It is entirely owing to this growth of rapid communication that the trade in perishable fruit has been brought into existence. What the progress of this trade may be depends largely upon the facilities of storage, etc., which the shipping companies may be induced to offer it. It is worthy of remark that the ships specially fitted up for the new export of fruit from South Africa necessarily take coal either in the Canaries or at Madeira. At present, under somewhat adverse circumstances, its growth has been both rapid and considerable. From its influence on the value of land and the condition of labour, its future forms an interesting subject for speculative thought.

Hitherto it has been found most advantageous to ship fruit to Liverpool and London, a comparatively small quantity going to Spain or Portugal. The French trade is prevented by the want of energy on the part of steamship companies running thither, by the duties, and by the heavy railway and market charges. The demand for Germany is small, and limited practically to potatoes.

A small amount of fresh vegetables goes to the West African Coast and there is, of course, a constant demand for the ships. Potatoes and onions have been largely shipped to the West Indies by sailing vessels almost as long as the potato has been known, and a temporary trade in early potatoes was carried on in the same manner with England many years ago.

It is, however, only recently that Madeira and the Canaries have become an early market garden for Northern Europe, earlier by several weeks than either Malta or the Channel Islands. The remarks upon communication may be aptly supplemented by a list of the various European ports with which the islands are in direct homeward touch.

	Canaries. Days.	Madeira. Days.
Liverpool	7	6
Plymouth	5	3
Southampton	6	3
London	6	5
Havre	6	—
Bordeaux	5	—
Cadiz	3	—
Marseilles	6	—
Barcelona	5	—
Gibraltar	3	—
Hamburg	7	6
Lisbon	—	2

and, subject to delays at the above-mentioned ports, with Glasgow, Rotterdam, Antwerp, Flushing, Genoa, Valencia, Malaga, Oran, and Tangier. A line of steamers also runs directly from the Canaries to the Morocco Coast.

Apart from the fruit trade, commerce generally is facilitated by the fact that either steam or sailing vessels place the islands in constant and intimate relationship with Australia and New Zealand, the eastern ports of South and North America, the West Indies, the whole African Coast from Mozambique to Oran, and nearly all the European ports from Genoa to Christiania and Stockholm.

It is not unreasonable to suppose that as the population of the remote parts of the earth increases so will the number of ships increase which call at these islands.

In any case the distance in point of time between them and Europe is constantly diminishing. Every day gained is of vital importance to the fruit trade.

High Roads, etc.—As regards the Canaries a third, but less important, factor is that during the last 50 years some 250 miles of excellent high road have been constructed, and that plans for the extension of the same have been approved by the Government. It is needless to say that the facilities for sending fruit quickly to Europe must necessarily be seconded by the means of placing that fruit in an undamaged state on board of the steamers, a result which is scarcely possible when it must be carried hurriedly for long distances on the backs of men or animals and along rough bridle roads.

In Madeira there is only one macadamised road, which is of no commercial value. Fruit is therefore chiefly grown in the neighbourhood of Funchal.

In all the islands small steamers now ply from port to port, a fact which will no doubt largely add to the area of the land devoted to the foreign fruit trade.

Harbours.—The improvement in the harbours has also contributed towards the same end. Steamers up to 1,500 tons can be warped alongside the mole, both in Teneriffe and Grand Canary.

The prolongation of the mole in Santa Cruz practically commenced in 1885. In June, 1898, it had attained a length of over 2,000 feet with a depth alongside in places of about 60 ft. The harbour works of Puerto de la Luz in Grand Canary were commenced somewhat earlier, are nearer completion, and when finished will have a superficial area of 286 acres, with a depth of about 45 ft. near the mole, which has a length of about 1,200 metres. In Madeira the Pontinha breakwater allows boats to be loaded in rough weather without wetting the fruit.

Railways. — In Madeira there is a railway up to Mount Church, 3,000 metres long, with a gradient of $20\frac{8}{10}\%$. The material was procured from Belgium and the rolling stock from Germany.

No railways have been built in the Canaries, but a steam tramway runs from Las Palmas to the Puerto de la Luz ($3\frac{1}{2}$ m.), and an electric tramway connects Santa Cruz and La Laguna, Teneriffe, between which towns the road rises 1,804 ft. in 6 m.

It is proposed to continue the electric tramway to Orotava, distant 42 kils. (27 m.) from Santa Cruz. Some of the gradients must necessarily be steep.

Submarine Cables. — By inducing the stoppage of vessels to coal, the telegraphic facilities have been to some extent the cause of all the modern innovations. A submarine cable was laid from Cadiz to Teneriffe in 1883-84 by an English Company (the Spanish National Submarine Telegraph Company). The same company laid a cable from Teneriffe to Senegal in December, 1884, and another from Senegal to Pernambuco in 1892, thus making the Canaries an important half-way station.

Cables are laid from Teneriffe to Grand Canary and Lanzarote on the east and to La Palma on the west. The inland communication requires extension.

Madeira was connected in 1874 with Lisbon, the Cape de Verde Islands and Brazil. The Lisbon and Cape de Verde cables have since been duplicated, and a submarine cable has recently been laid to the Azores.

Resumé. — In conclusion and in order to give an accurate idea of the present position the following deductions may be drawn. The soil in the Canaries remains as it was at the time of the collapse of cochineal, and the small amount which has gone out of culture, such, for instance, as some of the unirrigated southern slopes, could soon be reclaimed at far less cost than before. Were the re-afforesting of the islands and the distribution of the water carried out on broad and liberal lines, there is no doubt that not only this waste land would become of value, but that places now planted with comparatively worthless crops, might be made to yield a good return from the vine, the olive, the almond, the carob bean, or other plants which do not require much moisture.

The prickly pear, the eradication of which in Australia is an expense to the State, is easily kept in subjection. The labour expended upon the soil can only be compared to the care bestowed upon market gardens in England.

This close and productive manner of tilling the ground is the result of the subdivision of the land, of the density of the population, and of the admirable characteristics of the working class.

It is, of course, an important adjunct in the cultivation of tomatoes and other vegetables for so critical a market as that of London.

The peasant class supports itself and the gentry. Both men and women are temperate and industrious when working on their own account. Owing to the marked social distinction maintained between them and the bourgeois and titled families, they have not, as a rule, sufficient sympathy with their masters to continue labouring without the constant supervision of an employer or overseer. They are also careless and ignorant in the extreme, and their want of foresight is a great hindrance to the full development of such industries as the wine, fruit, or dairy trade. However, such as they are they are an admirable instrument in the hands of those capable of utilising them, though the attention they demand prevents the conduct of operations on so large a scale under one head as would otherwise be possible.

The same remarks apply more or less to Madeira, but, as might be imagined from what has previously been said, unless one includes poor wheat land now planted with pines, little or no land has gone out of cultivation in this island. The Madeira peasant is a more careful, a more long-headed and consequently a more permanently industrious man than his cousin in the Canaries. He is also much more thrifty and more easily kept in order.

Foreigners engaging in Agriculture, etc.—Strangers farming in the Canaries will find themselves regarded in the light of competitors by the gentry, who have unfortunately imbibed the very erroneous idea that in order for one man to make money some one else must lose it. He will also find himself at a disadvantage as compared with them when buying or hiring land. Labourers will work, as a rule, better under the eye of one they have been born and bred to respect and look up to, than under that of a foreigner, whose new-fangled ways and improvements they quietly oppose or fail to understand, and whom they are taught to regard as an interloper to be exploited for the benefit of the islands. In Madeira the *bemfeitoria* system and the distribution of property into minute areas, practically prevent the foreigner from farming at all.

As merchants the English are the most successful in all ways. Their quiet and steady persistence has earned for them a good deal of admiration, and possibly some concealed dislike from those who seem less fortunate, or at least cannot achieve the same results.

A tribute should, however, be paid to the graceful courtesy and flattering consideration with which they and foreigners generally are invariably treated.

If the foreigner is at some slight disadvantage on this side, he is better able to gauge the requirements on the other, and is more capable of availing himself intelligently of the means of communication which have sprung up.

He should possess a certain amount of capital; must learn to speak the language, which can be done in three or four months; and should know something about business, book-keeping and shipping.

Fluctuations in the Rate of Exchange.—Owing to the outbreak of war in 1898 between Spain and America, these were so violent in the early part of that year that business was almost brought to a standstill.

Up till 1890, a £ sterling was worth 25 pesetas or a little over. In 1891, the exchange rose to about 27 pesetas; in 1892, to about 28½ pesetas; in 1893, to about 30 pesetas. In 1894, it fell to about 29½ pesetas; and, in 1895, to about 29 pesetas. In 1896, it rose again to 30 pesetas, and by the end of 1897 to about 33 pesetas. In April, 1898, a sovereign was worth 45½ pesetas. In 1901, 34 pesetas.

In Madeira the £ sterling passed current until 1890 as 4,500 reis. From that date the exchange gradually went against the rei, until in June, 1898, as many as 8,700 reis were obtainable for an English sovereign. In 1901, the rate was about 6,300.

Results and reasons of the Influx of Invalids and Casual Visitors, with Hints regarding the Building of Villas, etc.

In the Canaries, where industrial occupations, with the exception of the manufacture of sugar and the building of a few coal lighters and schooners, are confined to the making of a little linen and woollen cloth for household use, of a few casks for the vine growers, of the plaiting of straw, rolling of cigars and baking of a certain quantity of tiles and unglazed jars, a new and lucrative source of employment has been created by the wants of an army of foreigners which invades the islands regularly every winter, and has increased in number from some hundreds in 1885 to several thousands in 1901.

That most of these are English might be expected. To the benefit of all, the islands have become a station where English ships are coaled, a garden where vegetables are grown for English tables, and a recreation ground or sanatorium where Englishmen can spend their holidays or recruit their health.

The change in the last few years is marvellous. At Las Palmas beautiful hotels with extensive lawns and flower gardens have sprung up from what was a sandy desert, and a Protestant church has been built. In Orotava an inaccessible and useless lava stream is crowned by a spacious and handsome building in whose gaily planted grounds are an English church and parsonage, the former being even provided with stained glass windows and encaustic tiles. Many of the largest and best houses in the towns have been metamorphosed into hotels, whilst the village must indeed be small which does not boast its inn or fonda, all bent on turning a certain quota of the golden shower in their own direction.

In the livery stables there are ten carriages where there used to be one, a fact probably recognised with gratitude by those merchants whose duty it is to gain a livelihood by exporting worn-out cabs or landaus, for which the Canary Islands seem to be a sort of dust heap.

Does a horse trot along the road there is an Englishman on its back. By one of this same energetic race, who, curiously enough, were the first to ascend the Peak in historic times, a stone hut has actually been built for the accommodation of climbers at a height of 10,700 ft. above the sea.

The above remarks apply less to Madeira, because it preceded the Canaries by several years and the change lately has not been so rapid. Even here, however, fresh hotels have lately been built, or older ones enlarged to meet the constantly growing demand.

What amount of money is actually left by visitors to the two archipelagos is open to argument, but it is probably not less than £100,000 per annum. A part of this is expended on articles brought from England, such as bacon, butter, cheese, etc., but up till now far more English capital has been sunk in new enterprises than has been taken out.

Many of the wealthier Spanish residents hold shares in the hotel companies, but it is doubtful whether their class has profited by the movement, as the price of meat, eggs, fowls, vegetables, etc., has naturally risen. The working classes, however, have been directly benefited by the same cause.

The Canary islander is slow to receive an impression and still slower to risk any money by acting on an idea, but measures are being taken by the peasantry to meet this new demand and doubtless all classes will be gainers by it sooner or later.

Besides the profits derived from what is consumed, many of the visitors come to stay, invest money in land or in building houses, and take part in trade, or, by spreading a knowledge of the islands and their products, are an important help in the extension of markets.

Good shops and stores have been started to provide for the wants of visitors, and merchants generally have increased their stocks. Establishments have also sprung up for the manufacture of ice and soda water, dairy produce, etc., but the bulk of the supplies of all kinds are derived from a native source. In all the islands, but especially in the Canaries, there is room for improvement.

As regards food for invalids there is much to be done. Game is far from plentiful, fowls are thin and dry, and the excellent frozen mutton, etc., which passes through the harbours is unobtainable. Cellars or cool chambers where these can be stored are required and would pay as an enterprise if properly worked in agreement with the hotels, which would probably be glad to offer some sort of guarantee. Such an establishment would be materially aided in the Canaries could a refrigerator be placed on the inter-insular steamer running to the western islands, which would permit partridges to be brought from Gomera, etc., and allow all the hotels to be supplied from one centre. In Madeira there is but little game to be had.

Though many things may be wanting as regards feeding there is also much to be thankful for. Fruit and vegetables are always plentiful, and a good native cook will make delicate dishes out of more unpromising materials than those found in English markets. Fish is also in some instances delicious, and the climate is a very good sauce which compensates for many shortcomings.

Building.—In case visitors should determine to build or that speculators should feel inclined to erect villas in the Canaries, the following data may be of service in calculating the cost.

Lime is brought from Fuerteventura and, when burnt, slaked and sifted, sells in the ports at from 1·25 pesetas to 1·50 pesetas per fanega of 80 lbs. The quality is very good. Unburnt limestone costs from 0·30 pesetas to 0·50 pesetas per quintal. Unsifted quick-lime is sold at double the price of the prepared article. If sifted, one of quick should equal three of slaked.

The proportions adopted are as follows: For building walls, 8 of earth; 4 of sand and 3 of lime; for plastering, 3 of sand and 2 of lime.

Cement.—This is all imported and is very dear. A barrel weighing 180 kilos is sold for about $12\frac{1}{2}$ pesetas. Hydraulic lime is rather cheaper. Ceilings are usually made by plastering *yeso* on to split woven canes, the second coat being 5 of plaster (*yeso*) and 2 of lime to give whiteness. Cement floors, 2 of rubble to 1 of cement. None of the volcanic muds have so far been used for making cement.

The ordinary price charged for strong lime-built walls such as those placed along a *barranco* for the purpose of protecting land, is from 12 to 15 pesetas the cubic metre.

Local **architects** require close supervision when a house is being built for the accommodation of Englishmen. They know little about drainage or ventilation, and are so accustomed to the expensive method of enclosing a "patio," or yard, that they seem to find it impossible to dispose of a staircase inside the building.

The local **carpenters** are very good, but have never been required to make windows or doors which can both open and exclude draughts. Wood shrinks and swells so much in accordance with the season, that a close fit is sometimes apt to stick fast.

All large **cast-iron work** must be imported.

Country Bricks are soft and rough and cost 12 dol. per 1,000. They measure 3 × 6 × 12 inches. **Imported perforated bricks** (*ladrillos tubulares*), 5 centimetres deep, about 10$ per mil.; 7 centimetres deep, about 16$ per mil.

Country Tiles are always of the gutter-pipe shape and cost about 9$ per mil. They require a slope of 1 in 5 and run about 30 to the square yard, necessitating a heavy timber roof. **French Tiles** (exchange as above) about 38$ per mil., running $14\frac{1}{2}$ to the square metre. Hips for apex of roof, 40$ per mil. Roofs are very often flat, being made of lime and sand rubbed down with a smooth stone and washed over with hydraulic lime.

White Deal sells at about 50$ per 1,000 ft. superficial by 1 inch thick, and **pitch pine** at about the same. **Spruce** is about 6$ below white deal.

Cut **stone work** is cheaper in Canary than elsewhere. The cheapest stuff for square corner work is "tosca," a very friable red or white stone, of which well-shaped blocks (20 in. by 11 in. by 6 in.) cost from $2\frac{1}{2}$d. to $4\frac{1}{2}$d. according to the distance from the quarry. Rough blocks cost less.

The cheapest and commonest method of building is to use the boulders and stones found on the spot and make a shell some 20 in. through, the interior being filled with puddled earth, which sets in this country almost like mortar. If means are taken to prevent the damp from rising, such a wall is as good a one as can be built for a low house and costs very little.

Summer is the best time for building, owing to the fact that the hours of labour are from sunrise to sunset.

For labourers' wages, *see* elsewhere.

The Fisheries.

On the warm and shallow banks along almost the whole of the **West African Coast,** fish of several species are to be found in great numbers, and the deep water stretching from Cape Noun on the north to Cape Blanco on the south, and bounded by the

Canary Islands on the west, affords a fishing ground which has been stated by competent authorities to be perhaps the best in the world.

There are other less important fisheries, notably that of the Selvage Islands, half-way between the Canaries and Madeira, where a number of fishing boats are engaged during August.

There is also a company engaged in catching and tinning tunny and sardines off Gomera, which was originally established in 1884 to work at Gando Bay in Grand Canary, but has removed the seat of operations.

It is with the first fishery that this report must deal. It is by far the most important, and by virtue of its situation with the sands of Africa on the one side and the shores of Lanzarote and Fuerteventura on the other, the best adapted to any extensive operations in which the scientific drying and salting of fish or extraction of oil might be carried on at a profit.

So far but little has been done to develop it, partly because of the apathy of the islanders, and partly because of the caution or jealousy of the Spanish Government.

As far as the Moors themselves are concerned they have no boats, and the population near the coast is extremely scanty, but there is no doubt that if Cape Juby or the neighbourhood ever becomes practical for the purposes of trade, there is a good opportunity for those with enterprise and capital.

Certainly one of the greatest authorities on the subject was George Glas, the Herodotus of the Canary Islands, who actually started drying fish at Mar Pequeña in 1765 or 1766.

What he might have done cannot be said, as he was seized and imprisoned by the Spaniards, but, in his " History of the Canary Islands," published in 1764, he gives the following particulars. His remarks apply almost as much to the present time as they did to his.

That the cherne, a sort of cod, caught there is "much better tasted than the cod of Newfoundland or those of the North Sea," and that " another fish of a yet more excellent taste is caught here, called mero " (the mero is the tunny). That about 30 ships of an average of from 15 tons to 50 tons were engaged, the smallest carrying 15 men and the largest 30 men. That during the spring the fish congregate to the north, but gradually go southward, where they are found in the autumn and winter.

The fish are very voracious, and bait may readily be caught near the shore by trailing at the rate of about 4 miles an hour, or horse mackerel can be taken with the rod and line and a piece of red flannel or other lure.

In fine weather a bark, if well manned, can often load up in 4 days, the sama and cherne being taken in from 15 fathoms to 60 fathoms of water.

The fish are gutted and washed and stacked to drain; then salted and stored in the hold; but Glas says: "They do not, like the French on the banks of Newfoundland, wash their fish a second time and resalt them, so that they will not keep above 6 weeks or two months."

Glas was a practical sailor, and goes on to describe the kind of ships necessary, which, he states, must hold a good wind on account of having to beat up against the north-north-east breezes. These blow almost constantly on these coasts except close to Africa, where the wind blows off shore in the morning and landward in the afternoon. For this reason, he says it is customary for barks to run out early in the day and fish till the afternoon, when they sail back under the shelter of some promontory and cure the fish they have caught. Needless to say this morning and evening breeze would be of particular service to curers on the African beach.

It must, however, be stated that Glas found, after setting up his establishment at Mar Pequeña, that the boat he had brought was of no use. It was while seeking another in the Canaries that he disappeared into prison at Teneriffe.

He says these barks make 8 or 9 voyages a year from Grand Canary, but stop at home for repairs from the middle of February to the middle of April, when the fish are only found to the northward and in a place where the coast is much exposed to the north-west wind common at that time.

Glas sailed round both Fuerteventura and Lanzarote, noted the prevailing winds and tides, made charts of the harbours, passed along and explored all the Barbary coast, and personally visited places which would even now remain practically unknown were it not for the praiseworthy exertions of the British Admiralty; experimentally fished in the waters he wrote about, and eventually determined to gain his livelihood, or perhaps his fortune (for Glas was not a poor man), by their help. It is only fair that any conclusions he came to should receive the most careful consideration and be treated with the greatest respect.

Glas says:—"It is strange that the Spaniards should want to share the Newfoundland fisheries with the English when they have one much better at their own doors—I say better, for the weather here and everything else concur to make it the best fishery in the universe. What can be a stronger proof of this than the Moors on the Continent drying and curing all their fish without salt or by any other process than by exposing them to the sunbeams, etc."

He afterwards says, "That the English have no reason to be apprehensive of the Spaniards ever being able to bring it to any degree of perfection so as to rival them in the Spanish and Italian markets," from which it will be seen that Glas in his way was a prophet.

Poor Glas was imprisoned in the Fort of San Cristóbal, next the mole at Santa Cruz, Teneriffe. At the end of eighteen months he made his position known by writing messages on crusts of bread, which he threw over the wall. Someone picked one of these up, and eventually the British Ambassador obtained his release. On regaining his liberty, Glas found that his wife and daughter had fled from Morocco on the sack of the factory (Port Hillsborough) which he had established there. With them he took sail for England in the "Earl of Sandwich," but a mutiny broke out during the voyage, all the officers and passengers being murdered and the ship scuttled. So ended the most deliberate attempt yet made to open up these valuable waters.

Number of ships employed.—Instead of the 30 ships employed in Glas's time, various estimates place them now at from 50 to 80, employing from 1,000 to 1,500 men, some of which are capable of carrying as much as 300 quintales of dried fish.

Most of the boats belong to Canary and most of the fish is landed at Canary, Teneriffe, or La Palma *en route* for its destination, a large proportion being actually consumed in the islands. It is difficult to obtain any reliable figures as to the total catch.

Those received state that the cherne (? cod) fishery gave in 1868, 2,738 tons; in 1871, 1,885 tons; in 1881, 1,000 tons; and, in 1888, 284 tons, which seems to show an unaccountable falling off. The total annual fishery of the islands was calculated about this time at 7,360 tons.

Whatever the figures are is of little moment. The fishery never has been properly worked. What the production might be with well-arranged drying and salting sheds both on the islands and on the mainland, so that ships could run easily on shore on any wind, remains to be proved.

As in the time of Glas, the fish is badly cured, and will not keep long. Besides this, though habit may have endeared its somewhat high flavour and smell to the Canary Islanders, both at home and in the West Indies, the world generally prefers something rather milder. It sells in the market at from 0·94 to 1·25 pesetas per $\frac{1}{4}$ roba (6$\frac{1}{4}$ lbs.). Its emaciated appearance when discharged from the boats is almost revolting.

On the Island of Graciosa, north of Lanzarote, are spacious sheds, erected for the drying and curing of fish. Because the position was too far north for ships to run readily home, or for some other reason, the work was abandoned, and the buildings are standing idle.

In 1884, an American was engaged in negotiations with the Spanish Government with the object of obtaining a concession to build curing sheds in the south of Lanzarote. For years he had been passed from one official to another without result, and, in 1885, was unfortunately drowned off the Lanzarote coast.

There is no such fishery near Madeira, but the market is usually plentifully supplied, more especially with tunny, which forms one of the chief supplies of the poorer classes and of which three species are caught.

Salt fish is consumed in much smaller quantities than in the Canaries and comes principally from Canada, being of much better quality than the *pescado salado* mentioned above.

Pilchards are caught off all the islands, but not in sufficient quantities to make a paying oil industry, though this might be possible were methods employed to capture them on a larger scale.

Ships entering at night will often notice the water covered by a multitude of lights. These come from the fishing boats which burn a fire in the bows for the purpose of attracting the fish. The anchors used are composed of wooden prongs to which a heavy stone is fastened. These, as is the case with the sledges used for threshing, are a relic of the stone age.

Laws have been passed against the use of dynamite, but this destructive method of catching fish is far too commonly practised.

List of the Edible Fish, commonly caught off Teneriffe, as given by D. Felipe M. Poggi y Borsotto in his "Guia de Santa Cruz de Teneriffe," 1881.

(Those fish marked with a * are most appreciated.)

* Abadejo, abad (cod fish). Gadus Pollachius.
Aguja (needle fish). Esox Belone.
Albacora (var. mackerel). Scomber Albacares.
Almeja (mussel).
Atun (tunny). Scomber Thynnus.
Bésugo (var. sea bream). Sparus Pagrus.
Boga (var. herring). Sparus Boops.
Bonito (var. tunny). Scomber Pelamis.
Bosinegro. Sparus Pagrus Rubescens.
* Breca (bleak). Sparus Erythrinus Minor.
* Brota. Gadus.
Búcio (sea snail). Buccinum.
Burgao (periwinkle). Nerita.

* Caballa (horse mackerel). Scomber Hippos.
* Cabrilla. Perca Cabrilla.
Calamar (var. cuttle fish). Loligo.
* Camarón (shrimp). Cancer Squila.
Cangrejo (crab). Cancer.
Cantarera. Scorpœna Scropha.
Catalineta. Sparus Lurta.
Catalufa. Priacanthus Boops.
Cazón (tope). Squalus Galeus.
* Cerruda. Sparus Spinus.
* Cherne (ruffle). Sparus Orphus Cernua.
* Chicharro. Scomber Trachurus.
Choco (var. cuttle fish). Jibia.
* Chopa (var. sea bream). Sparus Melanurus.
* Conejo del Mar. Scomber Pelagicus.

COMMERCIAL SECTION (POPULATION STATISTICS). 320

Congrio (conger eel). Murœna Conger.
Cornudo. Squalus Zigœnea.
* Curvina (var. hake). Merlus.
* Dorado (gilt-poll). Sparus Aurata.
* Escolar. Rovetus Pretiosus
Fula.
* Galana. Sparus Mœna.
* Goraz. Sparus Synagris.
* Guelde. Blennius Webbii.
* Herrera. Sparus Morminis.
Jurel. Scomber Glaucus.
Langosta (var. lobster). Locusta Marina.
Lapa (limpet). Patella.
Lenguado or Tapaculo (sole). Pleuronectes Linguala.
* Lisa (large grey mullet). Múgil Cephalus.
* Logobante (var. lobster). Astacus Gammarus.
* Longorón (var. anchovy). Clupea Encracicolus.
Mero (pollock). Gadus Monopterigius Cirratus.
* Morena (var. lamprey). Morœna Nigricans Unicolor.
* Morion, the male of the Morena.
* Palometa (var. mackerel). Scomber Glaucus.

* Pampano (gold-line). Perca Labraj.
* Pargo. Sparus Annularis.
Peje-perro. Labrus Rubescens.
* Peje-rey. Scomber Amia.
Peje-tamboril. Tetrasdon Honckenii.
* Peje-Verde. Laurus Viridis.
* Picuda. Esox Sphyrana.
Pulpo, or Capullo (octopus). Polipus.
Raya, or Chucho (var. skate). Ralae.
* Rascacio. Scorpœna Porcus.
Roncador (in Spain). Perca Striata.
Roncador (in Canaries). Trigla Güinardus.
* Rubio (red gurnard). Trigla Thirundo.
* Saifía. Sparus Variegatus.
Salema, or Pachonas. Sparus Cantharus.
* Salmonete (surmullet). Mullus Surmuletus.
* Sama (sea bream). Abràmis Marinus.
* Sardina (pilchard). Clupea spratus.
Sargo (sea-roach). Sparus sargo.
Trompetero. Centriscus.
* Vieja. Labrus Psitta Corostratus.

Fresh Water :—

* Anguila (fresh water eel). Murœna Anguila.

Population, Emigration, and Education.

RETURN showing the population of the Canary Islands according to the last returns published.

Islands.	1834.	1867.	1877.	1887.	1900.	Area in Square Miles.	Pop. to Sq. Mile in 1900.
Teneriffe	71,000	93,709	105,366	109,993	136,273	919	148
Grand Canary	57,615	68,970	90,154	95,415	123,200	634	194
La Palma	28,700	31,308	38,872	39,605	41,969	318	132
Gomera	9,497	11,360	12,024	14,140	15,025	172	88
Hierro	4,336	5,026	5,422	5,897	6,519	122	53
Fuerteventura	11,860	10,996	11,609	10,130	11,676	797	15
Lanzarote	16,176	15,837	17,517	16,409	17,545	380	46
Total	199,194	237,206	280,964	291,589	352,207	3,342	104
Increase on preceding census		19%	18%	4%	21%	...	...
Males	...	...	...	130,745	167,347	...	...
Females	...	...	...	160,844	188,730	...	...
Population to sq. mile	...	59	71	84	87	104	...	...

George Glas stated in 1764 that the population of Teneriffe was 96,000; of La Palma, 30,000; of Hierro, 1,000; and estimated that of Canary at 40,000; of Fuerteventura at 10,000; of Lanzarote at 8,000; and of Gomera at 7,000.

Population of the Principal Towns.

	1867. Number.	1877. Number.	1887. Number.	1900. Number.
Las Palmas (Grand Canary)	14,233	17,789	20,756	40,636
Santa Cruz (Teneriffe)	12,952	16,689	19,722	37,496
Total	27,185	34,478	40,478	78,132
Increase on preceding census		27%	17%	93%

Movement towards towns.—It will thus be seen that where the whole population increased from 1867 to 1877 only 18 per cent., the increase in the two coaling stations, which best represent our own English manufacturing towns, was 27 per cent.; and in the 1900 return 21 per cent. in the country generally against 93 per cent. in the towns.

A considerable allowance must be made for the understatement of population both in town and country in order to avoid taxation. Such misstatement being, however, a constant factor tends to equalise itself.

Cultivable land in the Canaries.—An estimate for the year 1869 states that all the cultivated land, including woods, vineyards, and pasturage, amounted to 541,032 acres (845 square miles, or 15.8 per cent. of the whole); and another in 1890, that the total amount of irrigated land in Teneriffe was 5,830 acres (4,495 fanegadas), and in Grand Canary 9,481 acres (6,971 fanegadas).

Return showing the Population of Madeira.

	1768.	1835.	1870.	1890.	1900.	Area in sq. m.	Pop. to sq.m. in 1900.
	63,912	113,436	125,000	134,085	151,125	240	629
Increase on preceding census		77%	10%	7%	12·7%		
Males				47·52%	72,135		
Females				52·48%	78,990		

Funchal, the only large town, contains about 44,049 inhabitants.

Were the natural increase of the people to remain unchecked the islands would soon become hopelessly crowded. As it is they are very full and the proportion to the square mile is in reality misleading, because of the small area of the land capable of being brought under cultivation. This is probably about $\frac{1}{7}$ in the Canaries and about $\frac{2}{7}$ in Madeira.

Emigration.—One check is supplied by emigration which, although rarely permanent and sometimes very temporary, yet often entails the separation of husband and wife during several years. It is customary for the men to leave the women and children behind and to remain away until they can bring back enough money to buy a little piece of land or a house.

Some of the steamship companies canvass actively for emigrant passengers, and the sailing ships carrying wine, onions, filters, paving stones, etc., to the West Indies also take a great many.

As far back as 1750, there was a great trade and a permanent emigration to the same quarter, and a large proportion of Government officials in the West Indies were from the Canaries. These seem to have enjoyed to a certain extent the very unenviable reputation that our own East Indian nabobs did at the same period.

The Canary islanders seem to have benefited so much by the strain of Guanche blood they possess that they are much in request, and are reputed to be the best of all Spanish colonists.

There is a fashion in emigration as in other things, and scarcely a family can be found of which some member is not absent. The people of La Palma nearly all go to Cuba; those of the north of Teneriffe to Cuba and Venezuela, and those of the south to Brazil; those of Lanzarote and Fuerteventura to Montevideo, etc., and those of Canary indifferently to many places, and largely to Buenos Ayres. The war with the United States in 1898 does not seem to have diverted emigration into new channels. During the three years preceding it, the rebellion in Cuba did materially affect the emigration figures.

Emigrants from Madeira formerly went to Demerara and the Sandwich Islands but now go chiefly to Brazil.

Electoral rights.—The right of voting at elections in Spain is given to all men who are Spanish, are 25 years of age, and have been registered residents since two years. In Portugal the age is 21, but the voter must be able to read and write, be a householder or have an income of 100$.

Religious freedom.—There is perfect freedom of religious belief as far as civic and military rights are concerned, but no church which is not Roman Catholic is allowed to advertise its existence by a bell or exterior emblem.

Education.—The attendance of children at school is compulsory in Spain under penalty of a fine. In addition to this no man may hold any Government appointment unless his children do attend. No payment is exacted from the children of the very poor.

In the Canaries public schools are divided into primary and secondary, and primary into complete and incomplete, the latter being the most elementary, and only to be found in country districts, where the interruption to studies admits of little being taught.

The amount expended on education is not very great. Teachers, whether male or female, are paid in accordance with the population of the district. In addition, all are entitled to a house rent free, and a supplement of 25% to their salary to pay for the expenses of stationery, etc. The fees of those able to pay are from 1 peseta to 5 pesetas a month, and are also retained by the teacher. Schools are also maintained by some of the mutual benefit societies for the use of the children of members.

That the result of such a system should be favourable is clearly impossible. Firstly, the salaries paid are insufficient to attract men of superior intellect, or to enable teachers to be sufficiently disinterested in forcing children to come to school and to eat up a part of their slender pittance by demands for pens and paper.

In 1887, from a total population of 291,589, 80·08 per cent., or 233,528, could neither read nor write; 12,948, or 4·45 per cent., only knew how to read; and 45,103, or 15·47 per cent., knew both reading and writing. There is no means of ascertaining the age, sex, or occupation of these, nor the proportion of urbans and rustics; but from the size of the islands, the number of schools, and the small proportion of incomplete primary schools as compared to others, the difficulties of attendance do not appear to be unreasonable, and the result seems lamentably small.

In Madeira all parents are obliged to send their children to school between the ages of 6 and 12.

The statistics for 1878 showed that there were only 7% in Madeira who could both read and write, and another 3% who could read only. Were later figures obtainable there is no doubt that they would show a more favourable result.

Methods of Taxation (National and Municipal).

Taxation seems to be chiefly directed against the poorer classes, and imposed upon articles which are necessary, so that a contribution to the State cannot be avoided, whilst articles of luxury and manufactured goods come in free. For this reason, and because of its effect upon the value of the land and on industry, the condition of the labouring classes is more immediately influenced by taxation than in England.

Classification of Taxation.—Taxation is of two classes—first, national or devoted to the purposes of the Treasury (*tesoro*); second, municipal, or devoted to the expenses of the town and neighbouring roads (*caminos vecinales* and not high roads, which belong to the State).

All taxes are regulated in proportion to the population of the parish, town, or district. On this account it is customary to find the census returns hesitate considerably at the round figures, the passing of which greatly increases the burden to be borne all round. In the case of taxable salaries, the percentage varies according to the amount of the salary.

National Taxation.

Direct Taxes such as—

I. **Farms and Houses.**—Farms are taxed in accordance with their annual value, which is estimated by the authorities of the parish or jurisdiction. Land is valued as first class, second class, and third class, of irrigated or of dry; first class land in one locality may only equal second class land in another, and be taxed accordingly.

Houses are taxed on their estimated rental, which may be higher or lower than the actual, and a deduction of 25 per cent. is allowed for repairs, etc.

The rate on houses is about 22 per cent. in the towns. On farms and farm-houses from 2 per cent. to 3 per cent. less. There is no direct taxation of named crops. It will be seen how the above method prevents any reliable statistics of the productive power of the land.

II. **Industries and Commerce.**—A factory is taxed in accordance to the number of the machines employed, and according to the population of the neighbourhood.

Industries generally are divided into twelve classes, and are taxed in a constantly diminishing scale, which also varies in accordance to the population. For instance, a vendor of drugs comes under Class I., and would pay about five times as much in a city of more than 40,000 inhabitants as he would in one of less than 2,300 inhabitants.

Various Direct Taxes.

Duties on probate and conveyance of property, mines and titles. Income Tax (Impuesto de Utilidades) on a graduated scale.

Cédulas personales, a species of passport which all must hold, and which must be renewed annually. Taxes on travellers' tickets.

Taxes on Government contracts which are taxed in accordance to their importance (deductions are made when paying the contractor).

Indirect taxes, such as duties on tea, coffee, spirits, etc., also on telegraphs and telephones.

The duty known as *fielato* (French, *octroi*), on goods entering towns.

Market and slaughterhouse dues, etc.

Military Service.—Able-bodied men are liable to be called out during 12 years, which must be between the ages of 18 and 33, and all are compelled to serve in the ranks for three years unless they can obtain exemption because of physical inability, or because of their being necessary for the support of a widowed mother, etc. The local militia may be ordered to Spain to serve their term or *vice versâ*. Able-bodied men, exempted from three years' service, must attend drill on one Sunday in each month.

Taxation in Madeira.—The taxation on land is about 10 per cent.; on houses and luxuries such as men-servants, horses, carriages, etc., about 9 per cent.

The industrial taxes are levied on an industry, which is estimated at so much yearly value. The representatives of that industry thus have to meet and apportion the amount fairly among themselves that each should pay towards it. Houses of less than 15$ annual value pay no tax.

Machinery in Madeira is taxed without regard to its position, but shops are taxed according to their trade and their *ordem*, *i.e.*, according to the size of the town they are in. There are 6 *ordems*.

Military Service.—Able-bodied men are liable from 19 to 30. One battalion of foot and a small detachment of artillery are usually kept in the island.

The duties imposed in February, 1892, on goods entering Portugal (and consequently Madeira) are very heavy, but are not levied on goods introduced temporarily. (*See* under Funchal.)

The detailed Sections with statistics referring to Education; Taxation; Local Government, its Resources, Expenditure and Duties; Methods of administering Justice with statistics of crime; Municipal and State-aided Charity; Encouragement of Thrift; Mutual Benefit Societies; Conduct of Hospitals and Public Institutions, etc., will be found in Report (Spain, Miscellaneous Series, No. 246, Foreign Office), which formed the basis of these pages.

The author cuts out the following paragraphs, which, of course, refer more particularly to the Canaries:—

Justice.—Legal proceedings are tedious in the extreme, the results are most uncertain, and no foreigner should indulge in such an expensive and unsatisfactory amusement if he can help it.

Conduct of the Hospitals.—The conduct of the hospitals, which, taking all the circumstances into consideration, is most excellent, is mainly due to the efforts of the local ladies' committees, who are admirably seconded by the sisters of charity. Private rooms may be secured by the payment of a very moderate sum; the public rooms are free.

Begging.—Beggars are by custom allowed to ask alms on Saturdays, and destitute persons can obtain permission from the Alcalde (Justice of the Peace) to beg at any time. Indiscriminate charity of this sort is an institution, and beggars are numerous on every day in the week.

Wants of the Poor.—The wants of the poor are few, and when from old age or other reasons it is impossible to earn a living by work, the neighbours, who are probably more or less related, will never allow a family to starve. If room cannot be found in the houses, there are the caves or lava streams in the neighbourhood where dwellings can be erected rent free. Clothing consists of nothing more than a linen shirt and drawers and a worn-out blanket, and for food a little *gofio* or potatoes will suffice. The standard of comfort is so small that a bed is not a necessity, and to sit all day doing nothing in the sun is only what is customary to everyone during idle moments.

In fact the destitute are nearly as well off as the wealthy, and all the administrative expenses of more highly organised charity are done away with, whilst in country districts it is much more difficult to impose upon one's neighbours than it would be upon an appointed officer foreign to the intricacies of local affairs.

Position of Labour and Prices of Commodities.

In Spain there is an Employers' Liability Act. The employer is also criminally responsible for the result of accidents to his hands when he fails to appoint a qualified manager to look after the conduct of the work ; and the manager is criminally responsible when it can be proved that he has not done his duty. In Portugal there is, as yet, no Employers' Liability Act.

Wages.—Skilled artisans in the Canaries receive from 3·50 pesetas to 5 pesetas per diem in the towns, and from 2·50 to 3·50 pesetas in the country. In Madeira the wages would be 800—1,000 reis in the town, 600—800 reis in the country.

A labourer or carter receives from 1·25 to 2 pesetas a day and in Madeira from 400—550 reis. Labourers on the public roads or in quarries where there is a certain amount of danger receive a trifle more.

For breaking stones on the high road 2 to 3·50 pesetas per cubic metre.

A man and a mule or camel from 2·50 pesetas to 3·75 pesetas per day, with one feed for the animal.

Stone-cutters 1·50 pesetas to 4 pesetas per day in accordance with skill. The Canary stone-cutters are the best and cheapest, and rarely get more than $3\frac{1}{2}$ pesetas per day, labour in Canary being rather cheaper all round than in Teneriffe. In Madeira, 600 to 800 reis.

Women in almost any employment are paid from 0·50 peseta to 1·25 peseta a day. Among the lower classes the woman is very badly treated. That she should work in the fields is only natural, but the husband, brother, or even son is a species of petty tyrant who struts about the yard like a cock on a dung-hill, and ninety-nine times in a hundred, if on his way to the town in company with his wife and his donkey, rides the animal while she carries the burden on her head. A great weight is often so supported. Though a man will carry things when alone, he never does so if a woman is with him. In fact, except during courtship this slave of a slave does not hold a position one iota superior to that of an ordinary Indian squaw.

Women are a little more considered in Madeira, but their wages are no higher.

Domestic Servants are fed in the house, and in the Canaries receive approximately, for a man or cook, 3$ to 6$ a month ; a maid, 2$ 50 c. to 5$. They always drink water, and the cost of their keep may be roughly estimated at about 1 peseta a day each.

In Madeira a man is paid from 9$ to 12$; a cook, 8$ to 10$; a maid, 4$ to 6$. Wages show a tendency to rise. Grooms and gardeners feed out of the house, and receive about 12$ a month both in Madeira and the Canaries.

In the outlying islands, and in places where the male hands have not been excessively reduced by the emigration of able-bodied men, labour is rather lower than here stated.

By piecework in coaling ships as much as, or even more than, 1$ can be gained on a busy day, and more by night.

In a few parts of the Canaries labour is still paid for in kind. The old valuation was that a *peon* should receive one almud of maize or its equivalent. A man with a mule might earn double this or even a little more. A ploughman with a "*junta*" (pair) of oxen would be paid half a fanega of "*chochos*" (lupines) per day or its equivalent. A ladder made of wood cut in the mountains would be estimated as two, three or four days' labour, and would fetch two, three or four almudes of maize in accordance. Even women with eggs or other country products for sale will sometimes ask how much maize you will give in exchange. The custom only exists in the depth of the country, and is rapidly dying out, to the manifest disadvantage of all concerned, as business in 1898 began to suffer severely from the rise and fall of the artificial currency. Were it possible to quote values in so stable a medium as grain, the commerce of the islands would at once be liberated from the injurious effect of the fluctuating tokens commonly employed.

Lodging of the labouring classes.—The expense of lodging depends greatly upon the neighbourhood. Speaking generally, both the richer and poorer classes are content with accommodation far inferior to that common in England. In very few cases is a thought given to either exterior or interior ornamentation or to the creation of shade by the planting of trees. Ventilation or scientific drainage is unknown, and some of the crowded quarters of the towns are dirty to a degree. Thanks, however, to the wonderfully purifying influence of the sun, and to the promixity in all cases of mountain and sea, zymotic diseases are not at all frequent.

In a closely built town, such as Santa Cruz, Teneriffe, a room may cost from 3·75 pesetas to 5·50 pesetas a month, and a small house from 9 pesetas to 15 pesetas, without furniture, water supply, or any conveniences whatever. The cooking is very likely performed on a fire-pan in a dirty little yard, where a few fowls are kept, and the pig, sleeping on the manure heap, acts as scavenger to the house on the principle of nothing be wasted. This is, however, a bad case, and sometimes the poorer classes are particularly clean, but always badly lodged, even when regard is had to the climate.

In a country town such as Puerto Orotava, the accommodation would be better, and the rent about two thirds as much. In a country village a room might cost 2 pesetas and a house 1$ or less.

Some of the people live rent free in caves and holes in the rocks, and the poor are always allowed to build themselves shanties in the lava streams or "mal pais" if they find it to their advantage to do so.

In Funchal, Madeira, the rent of a room would be about 1$, and a small house would rarely be under 3$. In the country, the houses are generally owned by their occupants, and caves are not used. The sanitary conditions are no better, but the Madeira labourer is naturally much nattier and more cleanly than his brethren in the Canaries, who have no idea of anything beyond just living.

Food of the Labouring Classes.—As will be seen from the returns, many of the articles consumed by the poor are heavily taxed.

The staple food in the Canaries is not bread but *gofio*, which is grain prepared by a method known to the Guanches, namely, by toasting and grinding it with the addition of a little salt. The chemical result of heat thus applied is said to greatly add to its value as a nutriment. The best gofio is made from wheat or maize, but any edible seed can be used in times of scarcity. It is mixed with water and eaten in lumps resembling dough. Gofio is eaten in some parts of India.

Bread is more common in the towns, but even there is less eaten than gofio. The price of this and of some other articles is given a page or so further on. In some towns the loaves are called lbs., though really weighing less. When the inspectors of weights and measures are going round, it is customary to announce the fact in the newspaper.

Potatoes are again so important an article of food that the population could not be supported without them.

Sweet potatoes (batatas) and *yams (ñames)* are both rather cheaper than potatoes.

Salt fish forms the greater part of the animal food eaten.

Fresh fish is fairly plentiful. The price depends greatly on the locality. When a very plentiful catch is made, some twenty or more fish, from 8 to 10 inches in length, may occasionally be bought for a penny on the beach.

Goat's milk, cheese, figs, fruit, and sometimes *salt pork* form the remainder of the labourer's diet.

In Madeira gofio is unknown and bread is not largely eaten. The chief articles of food are *yams, potatoes, cabbage, pumpkins, lupine, kidney beans, maize porridge, chestnuts* and *fresh fish* (*tunny, etc.*). The Rev. R. T. Lowe argues that the pumpkin, because of the readiness with which it assimilates itself with fatty substances, and because of the large quantity of saccharine and farinaceous material it contains, forms a most nutritious food, and that a good deal of the muscular power of the peasantry is due to it.

Drink.—Except during fiestas and holidays the labourer in the country rarely drinks anything but water. There is a certain amount of drunkenness at carnival time, but the people, on the whole, are abstemious.

Resumé.—Most of the population being to a greater or lesser extent owners of land or members of a family to which land belongs, it is usual about harvest time to see the public works, quarries, etc., almost deserted.

Beyond the mutual benefit societies there seem to be no co-operative unions of any kind. One reason for this may be that the ordinary profits of a middleman are reduced to a minimum in a country where the producer and the consumer are so constantly brought face to face.

As far as imported goods are concerned the peasant is quite incapable of organising any society which could compete with or alter the prices of the merchants. In fact, by no class is the advantage of joint-stock co-operation appreciated or acted upon to any extent worth mentioning.

Newspapers being few, and the proportion of the illiterate so large, the doings of the labour unions in Europe are ignored. In spite of the want of sympathy between the upper and lower classes, strikes, when not provoked by paid agitators, are almost unknown. Nearly everyone is poor, and everyone knows pretty well what his neighbour's position is, the labourer being well aware that it is useless for him to try to squeeze milk out of a stone.

In such small islands there is also a natural barrier to discontent created either by actual family relationship or by family traditions. The upper classes maintain a certain geniality towards the employed, so that it is probable that the labour question will have gone far towards its solution elsewhere before it becomes very prominent here. Besides this the grinding misery of poverty is unknown. The climate not only makes the wants fewer, but acts with a sedative effect all round.

The hours of labour are generally from daylight to sunset, with an interval of two hours during the day or two intervals of one hour.

1898.

Approximate Prices of some Commodities in the Public Markets.

Articles.		Canaries Value.			Madeira Value.	
			Pesetas	Pesetas	Reis.	Reis.
Bread	Per ½ kilo		0.22 to	0.30	Per kilo	70 to 120
Beef	Per kilo		1.50	3.00	,,	220 280
Mutton	,, ,,		1.00	2.00	,,	260 350
Veal	,, ,,		1.50	3.00	,,	260 350
Pork	,, ,,		1.00	1.50	,,	250 300
Fresh Fish (best)	,, ,,		1.00	2.50	Per piece	— —
,, (common)	,, ,,		0.50	1.00	tunny, per kilo	150 250
Salt Fish	,, ¼ arroba (6¼ lbs.)		0.94	1.25	Per kilo	160 200
Fowls	Each		3.00	5.00	Each	500 700
Potatoes	Per 7 lbs.		0.31	1.00	15 kilos	400 900
Rice	,, ½ kilo		0.25	0.45	Per kilo	120 160
Butter	,, ,,		1.50	3.00	,,	600 800
Cheese	,, ,,		0.47	2.00	,,	500 1100
Milk	,, 1¾ pints		0.25	0.60	Per 1¾ pints	40 80
Eggs	,, 8		0.60	1.25	,, 8	160 280
Sugar	,, ¼ arroba (6¼ lbs.)		2.50	4.50	,, kilo	250 360
Tea	,, 1 ,,		4.00	7.50	,, kilo	2000 3000
Coffee	,, 1 ,,		1.50	2.50	,, ,,	650 900
Petroleum	65-lb. case		11.00	18.00	,, 10 gallons	4200 5400

Prices of fruit, vegetables, eggs, etc., have risen enormously of late years, both in Madeira and the Canary Islands.

Country wine in the Canaries costs from 31 c. to 62 c. the cuartillo (1¾ pints), or from 3 c. to 10 c. a glass. In Madeira it costs from 15 to 40 reis a glass.

It will be noticed in the case of fish, eggs, milk, etc., that there is considerable latitude in prices. This is due to the abundance or scarcity of supply, owing to the season of the year, to the weather, to the increase in demand occasioned by visitors, or, in the case of fish, by the ecclesiastical laws. It also stands to reason that the price in a large town is not the same as in the country.

The writer concludes by tendering his hearty thanks to those gentlemen who have kindly helped him in collecting the various items of information included in the foregoing report, and amongst those more especially Illos. Senhores Francisco de Paula Sarrea Prado; Luiz Alex. Ribeiro de Mendonca, Barão d'Uzel; D. G. von Hafe; Messrs. Wm. Keene (H.B.M. Consul); John F. Healy (U.S. Consul); Cossart, Gordon & Co.; Wm. Hinton and Sons; da Cunha & Co.; Blandy Bros. & Co.; Mr. Leacock and others of Madeira; Señores D. Ramon de Ascanio; D. Juan Ballester y Marti; and D. José Mádan Guezala; Messrs. Hamilton & Co.; Mr. Henry Wolfson, the late Mr. A. H. Bechervaise and others of Teneriffe; Señor D. Francisco Gourié and Messrs. Miller & Co.; Richard Blandy; Harold Withers and others of Grand Canary. Illo. Senhor Francisco Affonso Chaves and Mr. W. W. Nicholls (U.S. Vice-Consul), of Ponta Delgada, St. Michael's, Azores.

FORMS OF ANIMAL AND VEGETABLE LIFE IN MADEIRA AND THE CANARY ISLANDS.

The following remarks are necessarily incomplete and are only intended to serve as a reference for those wishing to have some rough idea of the Fauna and Flora. The writer hopes at some future time to go into the matter more thoroughly. In the meantime he will be very glad to receive corrections or suggestions.

A list of some of the works issued will be found in the Bibliography.

Fauna.

Birds.—Canon Tristram, of Durham, and Father Ernesto Schmitz, of the Seminario, Funchal, have very kindly corrected the author's notes, with the following result.

Madeira.—153 different birds are known, of which 39 breed in the island; 4 birds are common to Madeira and the Canaries but unknown elsewhere; 2 are found in the above islands and in the Azores, and 3 are peculiar to Madeira.

Canary Islands.—At least 164 species of birds have been noted in the Archipelago. Besides the 6 referred to above as being also found in Madeira, 10 others are, so far as is known, peculiar to some one or more of the Canaries.

The most interesting of these are two very large species of pigeon, very distinct from the peculiar pigeon of Madeira, and a large blue chaffinch said to be peculiar to the neighbourhood of the Peak of Teneriffe. Of the birds found in the Canaries 79 species are known to breed there.

The birds of Fuerteventura and Lanzarote are, for the most part, entirely distinct from those of the other five islands, and belong to the desert inhabitants of North Africa. Amongst these are the Houbara bustard, the sandgrouse, and the cream-coloured courser.

Reptiles.—Mr. Yate Johnson says that in Madeira there is only one lizard. The Loggerheaded Turtle is found off the coast. Canon Tristram is again kind enough to help and says:—In the Canaries there are a vast number of species of lizard, but all belong to the Mediterranean or North African fauna with the exception of three, one very common throughout the islands, another in Lanzarote, and a third only found on a rock off Hierro.

Batrachians.—Two species of frogs have been introduced into both Madeira and the Canaries.

APPENDIX (NATURAL HISTORY).

Fishes.—The only fresh water fish in both Madeira and the Canaries is the eel.

Madeira. About 250 different marine fishes have been taken and their species determined. A portion of an illustrated work on the subject was issued by the Rev. R. T. Lowe, and several papers by the same author and by Mr. Yate Johnson, both of whom have described many new genera and species.

The marine fishes of the Canaries have not received so much attention. The most complete work on the subject is probably that of Messrs. Webb and Berthelot, 1839. A list is given in this book under the heading of "Fisheries."

Insects.—Mr. Yate Johnson classifies 1,331 insects found in the Madeiras, and states that his list, which is given below with some very slight alterations, is still very incomplete. Mr. Wollaston in "Insecta Maderensia," a most elaborate work, describes 483 species of beetles and has since extended his researches. The latest and most complete catalogue is that published by M. Albert Fauvel, of Caen, who gives 597 species.

Canon Tristram says that in the Canaries there are several species of diurnal lepidoptera, as well as many South European and North African forms, and not a few introduced from America. The late Mr. Arthur H. Bechervaise has kindly given the number of butterflies, moths and beetles according to the latest computation, and D. Ramon Gomez the Orthoptera and Dermatoptera.

	Species.	
	Madeira.	Canaries.
Diptera (two winged insects, *e.g.*, gnats, house-fly, etc.)...	160	
Hymenoptera (ichneumons, gall-flies, wasps, ants, etc.) ...	217	
Coleoptera (beetles) ...	687	930
Hemiptera { Heteroptera (bugs)...	54	
Hemiptera { Homoptera (aphides, etc.)	14	
Thysanoptera (midges) ...	6	
Lepidoptera Rhopalocera (butterflies) ...	11	23
do. Heterocera (moths) ...	101	36
Orthoptera (grasshoppers, locusts, cockroaches, etc.) ...	19	11
Neuroptera (dragon flies, white ants, etc.)	37	
Trichoptera (caddis-flies, water-moths, etc.) ...	10	
Aphaniptera (fleas) ...	3	
Dermatoptera. Forficulidae (earwigs) ...	4	5
	1,323	
Arachnida (spiders) ... . over	100	
Miriapoda (centipedes)	10	

(It is believed that there are over forty Miriapoda in the Canaries.)

Land and Fresh Water Shells.—The most complete work on this subject is "Testacea Atlantica," by Mr. Wollaston, 1878. In it he gives the mollusca of the Madeiras as 158, of which 6 live in water and 152 on land. Of these 70 are peculiar to Madeira; about 40 to Porto Santo; and only 3 or 4 common to all the Madeiras.

The writer could not obtain any complete or satisfactory information regarding the Canaries.

Marine Mollusca.—Mr. Yate Johnson, who gives the matter in some detail, says that about 300 or 400 species have been taken in the Madeiras. Mr. Robert McAndrew classified some 156 species in 1854, and the Rev. R. B. Watson 382 in 1897. Others have been discovered by the Rev. Canon Norman, but the result of his labours had not been published in June, 1898.

The Marine Mollusca in the Canaries have been only partially collected. The writer believes that some 150 species have been classified.

Cephalopods (Cuttle Fish).—Eleven in Madeira, described by M. A. A. Girard, and at least as many in the Canaries.

Bryozoa or **Polyzoa.**—Mr. Yate Johnson states that he possesses over 100 species found in the Madeiras.

Cirrepedia.—In the Madeiras there are over a dozen.

Crustaceans.—Numerous both in the Madeiras and Canaries, but the number of species wanting.

Worms (Land worms).—Four species are known in the Madeiras, and D. Ramon Gomez states that there are 5 or more in the Canaries.

(Sea worms).—Dr. Langerhans collected upwards of 240 species in the Madeiras. Species in the Canaries not known.

Echinodermata.—In the Madeiras 10 species of sea-urchins and several star-fish are given by Mr. Yate Johnson. In the Canaries 4 sea-urchins and 5 star-fish by D. Ramon Gomez.

Acelaphae.—The Portuguese and the Sallee man-of-war are known in both Madeira and the Canaries.

Zoophytes.—Mr. Yate Johnson mentions 30 corals and 10 sea-anemones in the Madeiras.

Foraminifera.—The same writer says that 60 species have been found in his collection made off the Madeiras.

Sponges.—In the Madeiras about 70.

By dredging and wading Mr. Isaac C. Thompson, F.L.S, F.R.M.S., collected in Grand Canary 5 species of nudibranchs, several axidians, a few species of star-fish, sea-urchins, actiniae, etc. By the tow net in Orotava 65 species of Copepoda (of which 23 are found in British waters). He states that the surface water in Orotava is more prolific than in Grand Canary.

Flora.

Trees and large shrubs.—In Madeira there are some 80 species, of which 11 are peculiar to Madeira and the Canaries; 2 peculiar to Madeira and the Azores; 4 to Madeira, the Canaries and the Azores, and 6 to Madeira alone.

The author has been told that the number of forest trees in the Canaries is about 42.

Flowering plants.—Mr. Yate Johnson's list in Madeira includes 363 genera and 717 species, of which Monoctyledons 70 genera and 128 species, and Dicotyledons 293 genera and 589 species. Some 80—90 are peculiar to Madeira, and about 110 to Madeira and other Atlantic Islands.

Of truly wild plants, flowering or otherwise, Dr. Morris says that the Canaries contain some 800. Dr. Christ says that 414 of these are endemic, and 392 are found on the adjoining African coast, or occasionally in the south of Europe. These, when left alone, show no tendency to disappear.

Ferns.—In Madeira 45 varieties have been classified, of which 3 are peculiar to Madeira and 5 to Madeira and other Atlantic Islands (Macaronesian).

In the Canaries Dr. Morris states that there are 30 varieties, of which 5 are endemic.

Lycopods.—In Madeira 4. In the Canaries 3.

Mosses.—More than 100 mosses and about 50 species of Hepatica have been collected in Madeira by Mr. J. Yate Johnson.

Lichens.—In Madeira about 60 are known.

Fungi.—No collections have been made in any of the Islands.

Marine Algæ.—About 60 species have been collected in the Madeiras and 110 in the Canaries (Dr. Hillebrand).

For the basis of the foregoing remarks the author is chiefly indebted to Mr. J. Yate Johnson's most valuable work, whose publishers, Messrs. Dulau & Co., kindly consented to the publication of a *précis*. Additions obtained from competent authorities have since been included, and it has been endeavoured to give a fairly complete list in the Bibliography of Works of Reference. To make these few pages of real service to the student, it is, however, obvious that the writer must rely upon the goodwill of those more competent than himself.

Bibliography.

A few books treating of Madeira, or of the Canary Islands.

English.

"Madeira: its Climate and Scenery." James Yate Johnson.
"The Climate and Resources of Madeira." Dr. M. Grabham. 1860.
"Madeira: its Scenery and how to see it." Ellen M. Taylor.
"The Island of Madeira." Surgeon-General C. A. Gordon.
"Teneriffe: an Astronomer's Experiment." C. Piazzi Smyth. 1858.
"Tenerife and its Six Satellites." Mrs. Olivia Stone. 1887.
"Rides and Studies in the Canary Islands." Charles Edwardes. 1887.
"History of the Canary Islands." George Glas. 1764.
"The Health Resorts of the Canary Islands." Dr. J. Cleasby Taylor. 1893.
"Orotava as a Health Resort." Dr. George Perez. 1893.
"The Climate of Teneriffe. Orotava as a Health Resort." Dr. Frederick Lishman. 1898.
"Climatic Treatment in Grand Canary." Dr. Brian Melland. 1897.
"Plants and Gardens of the Canary Isles." D. Morris, C.M.G., M.A., Dr. Sc. F.L.S.
"The Principles of Geology, Vol. II., Chapter xli." Sir Charles Lyell. 1868.
"Coleoptera Atlantidum." Wollaston. 1865.
"Testacea Atlantica." Wollaston. 1878.
"Insecta Maderensia." Wollaston.
"On the Geographical Distribution of Testaceous Mollusca, &c." R. M'Andrew. 1854.
"Manual. Flora of Madeira." Rev. R. T. Lowe.
"Baker's Notes on the Lepidoptera of Madeira." Transactions of the Entomological Soc. of London. June, 1891.
"Catalogue of the Moths of the Madeira Islands." Lord Walsingham, LL.D., &c., in the same Publication. Dec., 1894.
"On the Marine Mollusca of Madeira." Rev. R. B. Watson, LL.D., &c., in the Journal of the Linnean Society. Nov. 1897.
Accounts of the birds of the Canary Islands given in a series of papers in the "Ibis" for 1889-90, by Canon Tristram and Mr. Meade Waldo.

French.

"Description Physique des Iles Canaries." L. von Buch. 1836. From the German.
"Voyage aux Régions Equinoxiales." Alex. von Humboldt. From the German.
"Les Iles Fortunées." Pegot-Ogier. 1869.
"Histoire Naturelle des Iles Canaries." Barker Webb and S. Berthelot. 1839. (Perhaps the best general work extant.)
"Ethnographie et Annales de la Conquête." Sabino Berthelot. 1839.
"Madère." Station Medicale Fixe, by Dr. C. A. Mourão Pitta. 1889.
"Madère." Le Marquis degli Albizzi. 1891.
"Les Céphalopodes des Iles Açores et de Madère." Albert A. Girard. 1892.

German.

"Madeira und seine Bedeutung als Heilungsort." Dr. Julius Goldschmidt. 1885.
Funchal auf Madeira und sein Clima." Ferdinand Christmann. 1889.
Ornithologische Forschungsergebnisse." Dr. A. Koenig. 1890.
Geol. Beschreibung der Inseln Madeira, &c." Dr. G. Hartung. 1864.
"Die Insel Tenerife." Dr. Hans Meyer. 1896.
"Vegetation, &c., der Canarischen Inseln." H. Christ in Engler's Jahrbücher. 1885 und 1888.
"Flora von Lanzarote und Fuerteventura." C. Bolle in Engler's Jahrbücher. 1891-2.
"Das Thal von Orotava." Dr. A. Rothpletz in Petermann's Mitteilungen.
"Zur Lepidopterenfauna der Canaren." Dr. H. Rebel and A. Rogenhofer.

Portuguese.

"Catalogo das Phanero-gamicas da Madeira e do Porto Santo." (Supplementary to the Rev. R. T. Lowe.) Carlos A. Menezes. 1894.
"Annaes de Sciencias naturaes." Oporto, 1896. (Contains a number of articles on the Madeira fauna.)

Canarias," by Agustin Millares.
"Los Germanos en las Islas Canarias," by F. von Loeher.
"Cronología Religiosa de las Islas Canarias," by A. Diaz Nuñez 1865.
"Diccionario Estadistico Administrativo de las Islas Canarias," by Pedro de Olive. 1865. (The most complete statistica work extant.)
"Catálogo de los Aves del Archipielago Canario," by A. Cabrera y Diaz.
"História de Santa Cruz de Tenerife," by D. José Desiré Dugour
"Guia de Santa Cruz de Tenerife," by D. Felipe M. Poggi.
"Primeras Nociones sobre las Islas Canarias," by D. José Garcia Ramos.

MAPS.

Madeira. The Admiralty Charts, or Capt. A. T. E. Vidal's Surveys, or Stanford's 10s. Map (J. M. Ziegler), with panoramic outlines.

Canary Islands. The Admiralty Charts. (Unsatisfactory for the interior.)

Imp. Falconer, Paris (gravé chez L. Wuhrer, Gay Lussac, 52) (good.)

Cartas por el Capitan A. T. E. Vidal, Direccion de Hidrografía Madrid.

Islas Canarias, by Francisco Coello. Madrid.

ADVERTISEMENTS.

NOTICE.

Advertisements of Steam Shipping Companies and of Firms domiciled in Europe are usually to be found at the commencement of the book. Those of Houses trading in Madeira or in the Canaries are grouped together after the text in the same order as that followed by the Guide itself, Madeira being first and the Canaries second, each Town being kept separate. The two portions of the book are thus kept in touch with one another. Steamship Companies taking an advertisement are starred.

Readers should refer to the advertisement pages, as they form part of the scheme of the Guide, giving information about ships, hotels, shops, wine, tobacco, medicines, etc. By consulting them Travellers are able to dispense with a large amount of luggage, and Merchants or Shipping Firms are enabled to select the most enterprising Agents.

It can be taken for granted that those who advertise are anxious to secure the patronage of Visitors, and that Visitors are most likely to obtain what they want by dealing with Firms desirous of securing their custom, be they Shipping Companies, Bankers, Hotels or Stores. As nearly all of his Advertisers either trade in the Islands or are closely connected with them, the author feels justified in emphasizing this fact.

All applications for advertisements in this or any companion publication should be made to the author,

A. SAMLER BROWN,
3, Fenchurch Street,
London, E.C.

Letters regarding Picture Blocks or Artistic Reproductions, should be sent to the same address.

CAUTION.

Visitors to both Madeira and the Canaries are advised to visit the shops advertising in this book and not to place themselves into the hands of the so-called guides, known in Madeira as *ciceroni* and in the Canaries as *pláticos*. Readers are warned that, should they do so, the commission due to the guide is added to the price paid for the article purchased, and that this commission is sometimes equal to the original price of the article itself.

MADEIRA.—Mean Winter Temperature, 61 degrees.
„ Annual „ 66 „
ABSOLUTE FREEDOM FROM DUST.

REID'S HOTELS
ESTABLISHED 1850,
BY APPOINTMENT TO H.R.H. THE DUKE OF EDINBURGH.

SANTA CLARA HOTEL. — "Admirably situated, overlooking Funchal, fine view of the Mountains and Sea."—*Vide Rendell's Guide to Madeira.*

REID'S NEW HOTELS AND ANNEXES. — Situated in a garden of several acres on the Cliffs to the West of Funchal, on the New Road, overlooking the Sea, grand view of the Mountains. Sea Bathing and Boating. Bungalow in Hotel Garden.

CARMO HOTEL.—In sheltered central position.

MOUNT PARK HOTEL.—2,000 ft. above the sea at the terminus of the Mount Railway.

Those going ashore can obtain COUPONS on board at 8s. each, which frank the purchaser from and to the ship, include a trip by rail to the Mount Church, toboggan down, and a lunch either in the town or in the country.

These FIRST-CLASS HOTELS afford every comfort for families and travellers. Excellent Cuisine and Choice Wines. Tennis Courts, Large Gardens, Baths, Reading and Smoking Rooms. English and German Newspapers. Billiards. The SANITARY arrangements have been carried out by the Banner Sanitation Co., of London. All Steamers met.

DARK ROOMS FOR PHOTOGRAPHERS.

FIRST-CLASS RETURN TICKETS FROM
LONDON, SOUTHAMPTON, AND LIVERPOOL, FROM £15.

Also, during the Summer Months, Cheap First-Class Excursion Tickets by the Union-Castle Line, with One Week's Hotel Coupons, £18 inclusive.

FREQUENT COMMUNICATION WITH THE CANARY ISLANDS.

Telegraphic Address—**"REID, FUNCHAL."**

Pamphlets free. Apply to F. PASSMORE, 124, Cheapside, London, E.C.; HOTEL TARIFF BUREAU, 96, Regent Street, London, W.; J. and H. LINDSAY, 7, Waterloo Place, Edinburgh; Bolton Mansions Hotel South Kensington, S.W.; or to any of the Steamship Companies.

Proprietor—**WILLIAM REID.**

JONES' HOTEL,
BELLA VISTA.

THIS HOTEL HAS BEEN RECENTLY RENOVATED WITH MODERN IMPROVEMENTS.

Sanitary arrangements perfect. 150 feet above sea level and standing in Three Acres of Gardens. New Balconies 210 ft. long, commanding magnificent Views all round. Tennis Courts, &c. Electric Light throughout Hotel and Grounds.

Healthiest situation in Funchal. Seven minutes' walk from English Club.

EVERY ATTENTION PAID TO INVALIDS. LARGE SUITES OF AIRY ROOMS. SOUTH ASPECT.

Charges Moderate.   Special Terms for a Protracted Stay.

ALL STEAMERS MET BY THE PROPRIETOR, EUGENE E. G. JONES.
A B C CODE USED. *Telegraphic Address:*—"SANSPAREIL, MADEIRA."

Illustrated Pamphlet free from HOTEL TARIFF BUREAU, 96, Regent Street, London; E. G. WOOD, 1 & 2, Queen Street, Cheapside, London; and W. H. HAYWARD, 42, Union Passage, Birmingham.

Mr. E. G. JONES will engage Quintas, Servants, or give any other information to families, on receipt of telegram or letter.

CORNELL'S
ENGLISH HOTEL,
Madeira.

This First Class Hotel is splendidly situated in the best and most bracing part of FUNCHAL, facing and overlooking the sea, within five minutes of the Casino and ten minutes of the Town and Pier, and commands an extensive view of the Sea and Mountains.

LARGE GARDENS AND GRASS TENNIS COURT.

Sea Bathing within two minutes. Bath Rooms, Drawing Room, Smoking Room, and Large Balcony.

ELECTRIC LIGHT THROUGHOUT. EXCELLENT SANITATION.

Charges from 8/- per day upwards, according to Room, including Meals, Lights, Attendance, &c.

All Steamers met on arrival, and Passengers saved all trouble of Customs, Baggage, &c.

TELEGRAMS:—"CORNELL, MADEIRA."

ICI ON PARLE FRANÇAIS.   Proprietor—F. CORNELL.

HOTEL BELMONTE,

Near the Mount Church, 1,900 feet above the sea.

This beautifully situated Hotel with its Fine Gardens forms a most Delightful Resort. The Elevator Railway Terminus is Opposite the Entrance Gates.

BREAKFASTS, LUNCHEONS and DINNERS served in and out of doors at all hours.

Ten large and airy BEDROOMS with every comfort for the reception of guests.

JNO. PAYNE & SON,
Proprietors.

IN CONNECTION WITH THE ABOVE

THE INTERNATIONAL HOTEL

in the Carreira, very centrally situated and close to the Public Gardens.

First class accommodation. Restaurant attached where meals can be obtained at all hours.

For particulars apply to the Manager.

JOHN PAYNE & SON

(Opposite the Custom House). Established 1825.

Wine & Spirit Merchants,
HOUSE & COMMISSION AGENTS.

ALL QUALITIES OF MADEIRA IN CASKS AND CASES.

Shipping supplied. Orders promptly forwarded to all parts of the world on receipt of cash or satisfactory references.

Agents for the Royal London and Royal Cork Yacht Clubs.

HIS MAJESTY'S NAVAL CONTRACTORS.

Telegraphic Address:—"PAYNE, MADEIRA."

BLANDY BROTHERS & CO.,

Madeira, Las Palmas, and London,

BANKING AGENTS AND SHIPPING AGENTS,

AGENTS FOR "LLOYD'S."

Foreign Money Exchanged. Bank-Notes, Bills, and Cheques cashed.
Bills granted on London, Paris, Berlin, Lisbon, &c.

WINE MERCHANTS.

A LARGE STOCK OF MADEIRA WINES DATING BACK TO BEFORE THE 1850 WINE-DISEASE.

LUIS V. DE FREITAS BRANCO

Successor of

FIDELIO DE FREITAS BRANCO & Fo.

Commission Merchant, Importer and Shipping Agent.

Agent for the following Steam Shipping Companies.

A Empresa Insulana de Navegação

A Empresa Nacional de Navegação (to Cape de Verde and the Guinea Coast) and for

The "Companhia de Seguros Fidelidade."

JOÃO DE FREITAS MARTINS,

Funchal, Madeira. Ship Owner, Steamship Agent and Insurance Broker.

Agent for—
Linha de Vapores Portuguezes, de J. H. Andresen Successores (Oporto);
Prince Line of Steamers (Newcastle-on-Tyne);
Austrian Lloyd's Steam Navigation Company (Trieste);
Royal Hungarian Sea Navigation Company "Adria" Limited (Fiume);
Austro-American S. S. Company (Trieste);   Messrs. Burrell and Son (Glasgow);
Messrs. Geo. Booker & Co. (Liverpool);   Deutscher Lloyd (Berlin);
Companhia de Seguros A Commercial (Oporto);
Norwich Union Life Insurance Society (Norwich).

Telegraphic Address—SHIPBROKER. Codes used—WATKINS, A. B. C., SCOTT'S & RIBEIRO.

GENERAL COMMISSION AGENT.

DIARIO DE NOTICIAS
ESTABLISHED IN 1874.

This newspaper has the largest circulation in Madeira, and in consequence is the best medium for advertisers.

It has subscribers in England, France, Brazil, Africa, Demerara, Honolulu, and all over Portugal, with correspondents in most of these places.

DIRECTOR AND PROPRIETOR:
TRISTAO V. T. BETTENCOURT E CAMARA.
(Barão do Jardim do Mar.)

FOR

Lessons in Portuguese, English & German

H. HEMPEL,
QUINTA JASMINEIRO,
FUNCHAL.

Henry P. Miles,

Wine Exporter,

MADEIRA,

POSSESSES A VERY LARGE

Assorted Stock of Fine Wines

From Good Young to Finest Old Reserve, at prices ranging from £20 to £250 per pipe of 92 imperial gallons, f.o.b.

These Wines are shipped, at customers' option, in pipes, hogsheads, quarter-casks, or octaves.

ARAUJO & HENRIQUES

(Successors of HENRIQUES & LAWTON, Established 1852),

Vineyard Proprietors, Wine Makers

AND

Wholesale Wine Merchants,

Own the greatest area of Vineyards of any Wine Merchant in the Island of Madeira, and possess an unequalled and varied assortment of *fine, old, genuine* Madeira Wine.

STORES in FUNCHAL, 37 Rua do Dr. Camara Pestana.

WELSH BROTHERS,
Rua da Carreira.
WINE MERCHANTS, Madeira.
Established 1794.

HAVE A LARGE STOCK OF

WELL MATURED MADEIRA WINES.

OLD WINES IN CASK AND BOTTLE A SPECIALITY.

Orders Carefully executed.

Tel. Address—"WELSH," Madeira.   A.B.C. Code used.

Agents for Baring Bros. & Co., Limited, and Glyn, Mills, Currie & Co.

THE GOLDEN GATE.
ESTABLISHED IN 1841.

6. ENTRADA DA CIDADE 7.
FUNCHAL, MADEIRA.
Viuva J. A. CORREA, Proprietor.

WINES, SPIRITS, BEER (In Bottle and on Draught), LIQUEURS, AERATED WATERS, &c.

WINES.—Madeira, Port, Claret, Champagne, &c., &c.
SPIRITS.—Whiskey, Brandy, Gin, Rum, Hollands, &c.
BEER.—Bass, Guinness, Pilsener, Münchener, &c., &c.
LIQUEURS.—Chartreuse, Benedictine, Kummel, Cherry Cordial, Vermouth, Absinthe, Angostura Bitters, &c.
AERATED WATERS.—Ginger Beer, Lemonade, Soda Water, Gerolstein, &c., &c.

Large Stock of the liquors named always on hand, of the finest quality and best brands. Supplied at shortest notice.

TOBACCO, CIGARS, CIGARETTES, &c., of the most famous Brands. ICES.
ENGLISH AND FRENCH BILLIARD TABLES.

JÕAO MARIA DA CAMARA

26, Praça da Constituição, 28,
FUNCHAL, MADEIRA.
COMMISSION, GENERAL AGENT and DISCOUNT BROKER.

Accepts and executes all classes of Commissions, Sale of Cheques, Clearance of Goods through the Customs, Despatch and Receipt of Wines, Merchandise, &c., &c.

CONFEITARIA ROCHA

26, Praça da Constituição, 28.

An extensive stock of all descriptions of SWEETS, of WINES, LIQUEURS, SPIRITS, and of other articles usually sold in similar establishments.

JOSÉ LUIZ DE NOBREGA,

WHOLESALE and RETAIL DEALER in all MADEIRA WINES.

All wines matured and guaranteed by me.
Wine Cellars at Rua do Castanheiro, No. 57.
Also Exporter of Wines and Wicker Work.

MANOEL D'OLIM PERESTRELLO

PHOTOGRAPHER,
Rua de Julio da Silva Carvalho n.° 18
FUNCHAL, MADEIRA.

Has a large collection of photographs of Madeira and the Canary Islands. Groups, hammocks, carros, etc., taken from 9 a.m. to 4 p.m. Films developed and printed. All steamers are met.

DENTISTRY.

AZEVEDO RAMOS,
FRENCH AND AMERICAN DENTIST.
Bridge-work, Crowns, Inlays, &c., &c

RUA DOS FERREIROS, 76 (1st FLOOR),
FUNCHAL, MADEIRA.

ENGLISH CHEMIST AND DRUGGIST,
BOTICA DOS DOIS AMIGOS.

Established 1805. Prized in the Paris Exhibition, 1878.
2 to 8, Rua da Carreira, FUNCHAL.

Prescriptions and Family Recipes will be dispensed by a qualified Chemist and Assistants under the personal superintendence of the Proprietors, who respectfully solicit the honour of your patronage and recommendation.

Foreign prescriptions CAREFULLY DISPENSED according to their respective PHARMACOPŒIAS.

Orders forwarded by post and Shipping orders receive immediate attention.

N.B.—The PUREST CHEMICALS and FINEST DRUGS are alone used. NIGHT ATTENDANCE.

Managing Proprietor: PAULO PERESTRELLO DE ARAGÃO, Surgeon.

BOOTS AND SHOES

Visitors to MADEIRA will find that the best are to be had from

JOÃO MANUEL BORGES,
43-45. Praça da Constituição. 43-45.
(CLOSE TO THE HOSPITAL).

Boots and Shoes of all sorts to measure. English shapes if desired. Only the best materials used.

REPAIRS CHEAPLY & NEATLY EXECUTED.

Canvas and Soft Leather Shoes for those whose feet suffer from the stones.

MADEIRA EMBROIDERIES.
F. A. FIGUEIRA.

Permanent Exhibition of the finest Embroideries made in the Island. Varied assortment of White Clothing for ladies and children made according to the latest English and French fashions. Prices moderate.
The Proprietor of this establishment begs the favour of a call at.

MADEIRA HOUSE,
Rua dos Capellistas n°. 3 & 5
Close to the Gate of the Custom House.
LONDON DEPOT AT 40, CHEAPSIDE, E.C.

COG-RAILWAY to the MOUNT CHURCH FUNCHAL, MADEIRA.

Several trains a day, and additional trains on Sundays and Holidays.

Fares to the top of the Railway, 1/- single; 1/6 return. Extra trains at any time for a minimum of 25 fares. Time occupied in the ascent 20 minutes.

Those wishing to do so are able to return from the Mount Railway Upper Terminus in running carros in about 10 minutes, or a total of about half-an-hour for the whole trip. The views rom the Railway itself are most magnificent.

A CARRO WITH OXEN, MADEIRA.

RALEIGH C. PAYNE & CO.,
MADEIRA.

WICKERWORK, a speciality; manufactured and exported in large or small quantities, as well as other Madeira produce. Particulars and priced catalogues sent on receipt of 6d. in stamps.

Every effort made to meet Customers' wishes.

LOWTHER ARCADE,
21, RUA DO ALJUBE,

Has a large and assorted stock of Wicker-work, Chairs, Sofas, Tables, Fancy Baskets, also Embroidery, Feather-flowers and Native Worked Jewellery.

Proprietor - - - JORGE P. COSTA.

THE BIT-MAN,
PRAÇA DA CONSTITUIÇÃO,
FUNCHAL, MADEIRA.

A large assortment of Madeira Wicker-work Chairs, Sofas, Tables, and Fancy Baskets, also a big variety of Native Embroidery.
Catalogues to be had on application.

Proprietor - - JOÃO AUGUSTO PEREIRA.

ANTONIO GOMES JARDIM,
COMMISSION AND SHIPPING AGENT,
ENTRADA DA CIDADE.

Large Bazaar of native industries in this City.

Has always a large and assorted stock of Osier-Work Chairs, Sofas, &c., also Fancy Baskets, Embroidery, Feather Flowers, Jewellery, &c.

Goods delivered on board ship at a small extra charge.

EGGS SHIPPED TO ORDER.

BAZAR DO POVO,
LARGO DO CHAFARIZ, FUNCHAL, MADEIRA.

THE above Establishment has a constant and large supply of goods, both of native manufacture and imported :—Stationery and Office Requisites ; Jewellery ; English and French Perfumes ; Violins, Guitars, and Machetes, also Strings for the same Instruments ; Glass, Crockery, Cutlery, and a variety of those articles generally to be found in a Store of this description.

PRINTING. Visiting Cards and other printing orders executed.

PHOTOGRAPHY. Ilford Dry Plates ; Sensitized Paper ; P.O.P. ; Eastman's Films ; Kodaks ; Developing Solutions, and all necessaries.

A large choice of Photographs, Views of Madeira, Native Costumes, Scenery, &c., &c.

CHAPELARIA DA MODA,
35, RUA DO ALJUBE, 35.

A large assortment of Felt, Straw, and Silk HATS for gentlemen; also a great variety of CAPS.

Proprietor - ALFREDO CECILIO DE AGUIAR.

THE COCHINEAL CACTUS OR PRICKLY PEAR.

SANTA CRUZ DE LA PALMA.

JUAN CABRERA MARTIN,
SANTIAGO 2, SANTA CRUZ DE LA PALMA (Canarias).

BANKERS AND GENERAL MERCHANTS.

Large Exporters of Preserved Fruits, and of all the Products of the Island.

Agents for the Interinsular Service of Mail Steamers and for the Compañia Transatlantica (antes A. Lopez & Cia.) de Barcelona.

Société Anonyme des Tramways électriques de Teneriffe.

ELECTRIC TRAMWAY BETWEEN SANTA CRUZ, TENERIFFE, AND LA LAGUNA.

REGULAR AND CONTINUOUS DAILY SERVICE
From 6 a.m. to 10 p.m.

Time from Santa Cruz to the La Laguna terminus or vice versa 45 minutes.
Tickets:—1st Class, 1 peseta 50 centimos; 2nd Class, 1 peseta 5 centimos.

The journey along this Tramway is extremely interesting, and the views which open out one after the other are both exceedingly beautiful and very varied. The length of the line is 11 kilometres (7 miles), and the rise between the two termini is no less than 580 metres (1,804 feet).

The Laguna terminus is the best point from which to make excursions into the interior of the Island, as for instance to the famous forests of Las Mercedes, to Tegueste, to Tacoronte, to Agua Garcia, to Orotava, to the Peak, &c. Those driving to Güimar, leave the Tramway at the Cuesta (half-way) Station, 293 metres (960 feet) above the sea.

CAMACHO'S HOTELS,
TENERIFFE.

SANTA CRUZ.

The oldest, best, and most centrally situated Hotel in Santa Cruz.

Forty large well-ventilated bedrooms; sitting, billiard and smoking rooms, &c.

Bath-room on each floor, and every convenience.

Sanitary arrangements superintended and examined by Dr. Paget Thurstan.

TACORONTE.

Half-way between Santa Cruz and Orotava. 1,700 feet above the sea. The Resort par excellence for those desiring a bracing mountain climate. Extensive views. Grand Excursions, see Brown's Guide, pages 194 to 198. Thirty-six fine airy bedrooms. Dining, drawing and billiard rooms, &c.

Direct Telephonic communication with Santa Cruz. Messages sent at any time of night and carriages provided for those departing by steamers, thereby avoiding all risk of missing same.

All Steamers are met by a representative of the Hotel, and Passengers' Luggage, etc., taken in charge and landed, thus saving much trouble and inconvenience.

Terms: **ROOMS FROM 8s. TO 12s. PER DAY.**

Special arrangements made for Families or Persons staying for a prolonged period.

LOUIS G. CAMACHO, Proprietor.

The English Hotel, "PINO DE ORO."

THIS CHARMING FAMILY RESIDENCE, situated in a well-planted garden of over three acres, about 250 feet above the sea, and half-a-mile from the landing stage, has been much enlarged, with a special view to the accommodation of Visitors. It overlooks the town and harbour and commands wide views of the mountains and of the neighbouring coast. No expense or trouble has been spared to ensure its popularity as a resort for those spending the winter in the Islands.

SPACIOUS AND AIRY BEDROOMS CAPABLE OF ACCOMMODATING SOME FORTY GUESTS.

RECEPTION, BILLIARD, AND SMOKING ROOMS.

A Special Feature of the Hotel is the Magnificent, Lofty and well-ventilated Dining Room,

THE BATH ROOMS, SANITARY ARRANGEMENTS, &c., ARE ON THE MOST APPROVED PRINCIPLES.

The Extensive Grounds abound with Tropical Flowers and Fruits, and with pleasant shady walks and corners.

LAWN TENNIS, CROQUET, AND BADMINTON.

ALL STEAMERS MET BY AN ATTENDANT OF THE HOTEL.

For further particulars apply to the Proprietor and Manager—

H. JAMES.

TELEPHONE NO. 32.   TELEGRAPHIC ADDRESS:—"PINO, TENERIFFE."

Visitors forwarded to Orotava if desired, and every information given.

"SALAMANCA"

Beautifully situated in an extensive garden, a mile out of Santa Cruz.

THE WIDOW OF AN ENGLISH PHYSICIAN RECEIVES A LIMITED NUMBER OF VISITORS.

Telegraphic Address :—" **DOUGLAS, TENERIFFE.**"

VICTORIA HOTEL
7, Plaza de la Constitucion, SANTA CRUZ, TENERIFFE.

LARGE AND COMFORTABLE BEDROOMS.   FIRST CLASS COOKING.

Terms:—ROOMS FROM 8 PESETAS PER DAY, INCLUDING WINE. **Best Wine and Habana Cigars.**

English Spoken.   Man spricht Deutsch.   On parle Français.

OLSEN'S ENGLISH HOTEL & PENSION

Facing the Governor-General's Palace, and the Plaza Weyler (Public Gardens), in the healthiest part of the Town, and commanding splendid views of the Bay, the Mountains and the surrounding Country.

The Electric Trams and Public Coaches pass close to the Hotel, which is most conveniently situated for those wishing to make excursions into the interior.

First Class accommodation for Visitors. Spacious and lofty Drawing, Dining, Billiard and Smoking Rooms. Large and airy Bed Rooms, Bath Room, &c.

SPECIAL TERMS FOR A PROLONGED STAY.

For full information apply to the Proprietor:

H. P. OLSEN.

Transit Passengers can be served with Breakfasts, Luncheons, Dinners and Suppers à la carte at short notice.

Danish, English and German spoken.

CUATRO NACIONES
AT THE TOP OF THE PLAZA DE LA CONSTITUCION,
SANTA CRUZ.
THE BEST BAR AND LUNCHEON ROOM IN THE TOWN.

The choicest selection of Beers and Ales (Lager, Bass, Pilsener, &c.) Spirits and Liqueurs of the first quality. Carefully selected Foreign and Native Wines, Ices, Sherbets, &c.

HAVANA CIGARS OF THE FINEST BRANDS.
THE ONLY DEPOT OF "PARTAGAS" AND "HENRY CLAY" IN SANTA CRUZ.

CUBAN CIGARETTES.

TINERFEÑA
FÁBRICA DE TABACOS
DE
MANUEL HERRERA
CRUZ VERDE, 18
SANTA CRUZ DE TENERIFE,
ISLAS CANARIAS.

LA CORONA,
Tabaquería de Casimiro Fernandez,
CALLE DE SAN JOSÉ, CORNER OF THE MARINA.
CIGARS, CIGARETTES AND TOBACCOS FROM THE BEST FACTORIES IN THE HABANA.

Henry Clay, Pedro Moreda, Gêner, Murias, Flor de Tomas Gutierrez, La Sabrosa, La Luisa, Legitimidad, Colonia de la Palma de Vives. Cigarettes "Brea," "Especiales" and "Pectorales."

Only Habana Tobacco is sold in this Establishment. Connoisseurs will find a choice of the very Best Brands.

A VISIT IS SOLICITED.

HIJOS DE JUAN YANES,
SANTA CRUZ DE TENERIFE AND SANTA CRUZ DE LA PALMA.
Bankers, General Merchants, and Shipping Agents.

Agents for the following Steamship Companies :—La Société Générale de Transports Maritimes; N. Paquet & Cie.; Hijo de J. Jover Serra; Pinillos Isquierdo & Cia.; A. Folch y Cia.; Sociedad de Navigation é Industria.

SPECIALITY IN BUILDING MATERIAL: TIMBER, TILES, CEMENT, &C., &C.
Best quality at the lowest Current Prices.

WHOLESALE DEALERS IN
RUM, SPIRITS, CEREALS, AND ALL CLASSES OF MERCHANDISE.

HARDISSON FRÈRES,
~ ~ Merchants ~ ~
SANTA CRUZ DE TENERIFE, CANARY ISLANDS.
ESTABLISHED 1842.
Telegraphic Address:—"HARDISSON, TENERIFFE."

Agents for the "Assurance Maritimes" of France, Belgium, Germany, etc.
Agents for the "Société des Chargeurs Reunis, Compagnie Française de Navigation de Vapeur," & for the "Compagnie Générale Transatlantique."

CONTRACTORS TO THE FRENCH GOVERNMENT.

Correspondents of the Banque Transatlantique de Paris.

A LARGE STOCK OF TENERIFFE WINES, SEC & MALVOISIE

Four Gold Medals, Bordeaux 1882, Barcelona 1888, Paris 1878 and 1889, and Diploma of Honour in Brussels 1883.

PRICE LIST FREE ON APPLICATION.

Cardiff Coal, Provisions, Fresh Water, &c., supplied.

Accept consignments of ships of all nations and despatch the same with the greatest promptitude and economy possible.

HENRY WOLFSON

= = 1, MARINA = =
(facing the Mole)

Santa Cruz de Tenerife.

Shipping, Commission & Bankers' Agent.

Drafts cashed at the highest current rates of exchange, and general banking facilities granted with England or the Continent.

HAMILTON & CO.
ESTABLISHED 1799·
Steamship, Telegraph, and Forwarding Agents.

Correspondents for all the principal British and Foreign Banks.

Agents for Lloyds; Liverpool Underwriters' Association; New York Underwriters; The Assicurazioni Generali, Trieste; La Compagnia Mutua Camogliense, Camogli; The Rhenania Versicherungs A. G. Köln; The Italia Societa d'Assicurazioni Marittime Fluviali è Terrestri, Genova.

PROPRIETORS OF
STEAM COAL DEPÔT.

Every Facility for Supply and Quick despatch of Steamers day or night throughout the year.

Contracts with nearly all the leading lines of Steamers passing this way.

FREE PORT; NO CUSTOM-HOUSE FORMALITIES.

Central Station for Telegraph Cables to Europe and West Coast of Africa. Visitors for Orotava land here.

WINE MERCHANTS.
OLDEST EXPORTERS OF THE CHOICEST QUALITIES OF TENERIFFE (VIDONIA) WINE.

Telegraphic Address: "HAMILTON, TENERIFFE."

CODES USED: 'SCOTTS,' 'A B C,' 'A 1,' AND 'UNIVERSAL SHIPPING.'

General Agents in LONDON:—
MESSRS. SINCLAIR, HAMILTON & CO.,
17, ST. HELEN'S PLACE, E.C.

THE
TENERIFFE STEAM LAUNDRY
COMPANY,
SANTA CRUZ, TENERIFFE.

This Steam Laundry is fitted with Bradford's Latest Appliances, and is worked by Experienced English Laundry Hands.

It offers great facilities to Steamers, especially on their homeward trips, as in all cases where the Steamship Owners keep a reserve stock in Teneriffe, they can have their soiled linen replaced by clean linen at a few moments' notice.

TERMS MODERATE.

SANTA CRUZ, TENERIFFE.

THE TENERIFFE COALING Co.,
SANTA CRUZ, TENERIFFE.

Central Telegraph station for cables to Europe, West Coast of Africa and the Brazils.

STEAMERS COALED AND PROVISIONED WITH THE UTMOST DESPATCH NIGHT AND DAY THROUGHOUT THE YEAR.

FREE PORT.   LARGE STEAM LAUNDRY.

BEST SOUTH WELSH STEAM COAL ONLY SUPPLIED.

FIRST CLASS BARGES BUILT AT MODERATE PRICES.

Coaling Signal, the "J" flag of International Code. "Scott's," "A 1," and "A B C" Codes used.

Telegraphic Address—**"COALING, TENERIFFE."**

Agents:—LIVERPOOL, Head Office :—34, Castle Street.   LONDON :— 101, Leadenhall St.   GLASGOW :—30, Gordon St.   HAMBURG :— 4, Bei dem Zippelhause.

ALFRED WILLIAMS,

11, San José *(Close by Camacho's Hotel).*

EXCHANGE BUREAU.

Bank Notes and Gold exchanged at favourable rates.
Circular Notes and accredited Cheques cashed.

Telegraphic Address:—"WILLIAMS, TENERIFE."
Codes used—"A B C (4th Edition)," and "Lieber's."
Telephone 200.

"DIARIO DE TENERIFE,"

FOUNDED IN 1886.

Journal of General News, Notices and Advertisements. The largest circulation in the Canary Islands, and consequently the best medium for advertisers.

Subscription per annum, in Europe or America, 32 pesetas. Contains the largest amount of telegraphic information of any Newspaper in the archipelago, also special periodical correspondence from Madrid, Paris, London, New York, Buenos Ayres, Habana, &c.

Director, **P. ESTEVANEZ.** Manager, **J. M. BALLESTER.**

Correspondents in Europe who receive Advertisements:—Messrs. G. Street & Co., Ltd., 30, Cornhill, London, E.C.; John F. Jones and Cie, 31 bis, rue du Faubourg Montmartre, Paris; Sociedad general de Anuncios, Alcalá, 6 and 8, Madrid; Roldós y Ca, 30, Escudillers, Barcelona; also Cebrian & Cia, 18, Puertaferrisa, Barcelona.

THE
LION TRADING COMPANY
(A. GRANT).

AGENT FOR COMMERCIAL UNION ASSURANCE CO. LIMITED.

English Store of all requisites for Ladies' and Gentlemen's Outfits. Specialties in Tenerife Drawn-Thread Work and Embroidery, Spanish Fans, Cigars, (Tenerife and Havana), and Photographs of the Islands.

SANTA CRUZ DE TENERIFE
40 CASTILLO 42.

SANTA CRUZ, TENERIFE.

Top of the Plaza de la Constitucion (corner of the Calle de San Francisco).

ALEXANDRE

WATCHES AND CLOCKS, JEWELLERY, PRECIOUS STONES, SILVER AND ELECTRO PLATED GOODS, OPTICAL INSTRUMENTS.

Objects of Native Industry and Photographic Views.

The chief Depôt in the Island for the Purchase and Sale of ANTIQUE CURIOS, COINS, JEWELLERY, PICTURES, ENGRAVINGS, &c.

MARCOS PERAZA,

Wine Merchants,

Santa Cruz de Tenerife.

Office: Calle de San Francisco No. 69.
Stores: Calle de San Francisco, Nos. 67, 69, 70, & 72.

EXPORTERS OF WINE SINCE 1834.

Nine Medals in Gold, Silver and Bronze, as well as several Diplomas obtained in Paris, Bordeaux, Barcelona, Philadelphia, Vienna, &c.

In Cask or Bottle for Export or Home Consumption.

Orders delivered free on board at Santa Cruz for all parts of the world against cash or satisfactory reference.

CATALOGUES FREE ON APPLICATION.

ASK FOR SAMPLES.

SALÓN NOVEDADES,
51, CASTILLO, 51, SANTA CRUZ DE TENERIFE.

Horlogerie, Réparation de Montres,
Bijouterie, Joaillerie, Orfévrerie, Optique, Objets d'Art, de Fantaisie,
et Meubles de toute espèce.

Dr. V. CABRERA.
(From the MADRID UNIVERSITY.)

Pharmacy and Laboratory of Chemical and Microscopical Analysis.
Prescriptions made up according to the Formulas of the Pharmacopœia Britannica, the Code Français, the Farmacopea Española, and the Universal.
Patent Medicines (Home and Foreign).
Examination of Sputa for Koch's Bacillus.   Analysis of Urine.

Drug Store: 13, SAN FRANCISCO, 13 (next to the Hotel Camacho),
SANTA CRUZ DE TENERIFE.

PEREZ JORGE y Ca.,
CASTILLO, 44 (Next to the Lion Trading Company), SANTA CRUZ DE TENERIFE,
SOMBRERÍA = HATTERS,

Have in Stock Hats and Caps of all sorts from the best English, French, German, Italian, and Spanish Houses.

Hats adapted on the Premises to the taste of the Purchaser.

LA LAGUNA, TENERIFFE.

HOTEL TENERIFE,
Proprietors - PEDRO & ATANASIA PERAZA,

For many years at the Hotel "Buen Retiro," in Güimar, and in the "Aguere," in La Laguna.

Special Accommodation for English Guests at Moderate and Inclusive Prices.

GOOD COOKING AND CLEANLINESS A SPECIALITY.

The Hotel, which is situated in the centre of La Laguna and close to the Tramway, is the favourite
RESTAURANT
for all those visiting La Laguna by the Electric Tram.
Breakfasts, Luncheons, Dinners, Suppers, at all Hours.   Good Wines and Cigars.

Hotel Aguere & Continental,
LAGUNA, TENERIFE.

1,804 FEET ABOVE THE SEA.
OPEN ALL THE YEAR ROUND.

Under the same Management as the
HOTEL MARTIANEZ, PUERTO OROTAVA.

La Laguna is the Teneriffe summer resort *par excellence*, and possesses a most agreeable climate at all seasons, particularly adapted to those requiring a more bracing atmosphere than that of the Coast.

Formerly known as the Paradise of the Guanches, it is recognised as the best centre for Rides, Walks, and Excursions in Teneriffe. The Forests of the Aguere and of Las Mercedes, and the mountains beyond, declared to contain some of the very finest scenery in all the Canaries, lie comparatively close to the door.

This old-established Hotel has recently been entirely renovated under the present Proprietors, who have spared no trouble or expense in endeavouring to meet the wants and wishes of their Visitors.

Large airy Bed and Public Rooms.   Cleanliness and Comfort.
Unexceptionable Water Supply.   First-class Sanitary Arrangements.
Bath Room, &c.   Good Billiard Table by Thurston.

A New Entrance has been made leading into the Calle Herradores, up which the Electric Tram Cars from Santa Cruz pass hourly.

MODERATE CHARGES.   REDUCED TERMS FOR A LENGTHENED STAY.
Apply to the Manager, Hotel Aguere and Continental, La Laguna.

Telegraphic Address:
"AGUERE, TENERIFFE."

TRENKEL & KNÖRNSCHILD,
Proprietors.

OROTAVA, TENERIFFE

HOTEL MARTIANEZ
(LATE GRAND),
PORT OROTAVA, TENERIFFE.
Open October 15th till May 1st.

FINEST WINTER CLIMATE IN THE WORLD.
(In connection with the Hotel Aguere and Continental, La Laguna.)

THIS first-class favourite Hotel is situated just outside the town, commands magnificent views of the sea and coast, and is surrounded by one of the loveliest gardens in Teneriffe. The shady walks and Verandahs afford a most delightful lounge for visitors at all hours.

**LARGE PUBLIC & PRIVATE ROOMS. ELECTRIC LIGHTS.
EXCELLENT COOKING. GOOD WINES.**
The Water used is from the Martianez Springs.
Latest Improved Sanitary Arrangements installed by an English Plumber.
**FIRST-CLASS LOW-CUSHION BILLIARD TABLE BY BURROUGHS & WATTS.
TENNIS COURT.   MODERATE CHARGES.**
Reduction on the Ordinary Tariff for a lengthened stay.
For Terms and Particulars apply to **C. H. TRENKEL,** *Manager.*

Telegraphic Address: MARTIANEZ, PUERTO CRUZ.

Letters from Oct. 15th till May 1st, should be addressed to the *Martianez Hotel, Puerto Orotava,* and during the summer to the *Hotel Aguere and Continental, La Laguna.*

GÜIMAR, TENERIFFE.
EL BUEN RETIRO.

HOTEL EL BUEN RETIRO.

THIS charming little Hotel is situated about 20 miles from Santa Cruz, on the south and sunnier side of the Island, and is 1,200 feet above sea level. It is entirely under English management, and good food and English-cooking are special features.

There are delightful Excursions to be made in the neighbourhood; the beautiful *barrancos*—Badajoz, Rio, and Añavingo—all being within easy distance. The scenery between Güimar and Orotava by way of the Pass of Pedro Gil is magnificent.

"The driest, sunniest, and best climate in the Canary Islands is undoubtedly that of Güimar. For the treatment of chest diseases it is unique.

"The Hotel Buen Retiro . . . . . . has a very lovely shady garden, in which mangoes, oranges, custard apples, bananas, figs, guavas, citrons, loquats, and coffee flourish as they do nowhere on the northern side.

" . . . The water which supplies the town is brought from the charming Ravine de Las Aguas, and is irreproachable."—A. J. WHARRY, M.D.

CROQUET LAWN.   FULL SIZED BILLIARD TABLE.

THERE IS AN ENGLISH PHYSICIAN RESIDENT IN GÜIMAR.

Tariff will be sent free by Mail on application to
THE MANAGER.

GÜIMAR, TENERIFFE.

GÜIMAR HOSPITAL FOR THE PURE AIR TREATMENT OF TUBERCULOSIS
(ON THE NORDRACH SYSTEM).

English Nurse and Manageress. Two English Physicians.
The Hospital stands 1,200 feet above the sea level, and commands an extensive view of mountain and sea.
Full particulars may be obtained from Messrs. SQUIRE & SONS, 413, Oxford Street, W., from whom a "Guide to Güimar," by Dr. Harris, may be purchased, price 6d.
TERMS (which are absolutely inclusive), £5. 5s. per week. N.B.—This is inclusive from the arrival in Güimar, and not, as stated in the "Guide," from arrival in Santa Cruz.
Carriages can be sent from Güimar to meet guests after due notice.
Mean Winter Temperature, 9 a.m., 63°; Summer, 9 a.m., 70°.
Mean Maximum   ,,   Winter, 60°; Summer, 76°.
Mean Minimum   ,,   Winter, 55°; Summer, 59°.

STANFORD HARRIS, *Medical Superintendent.*

DRAGON TREE, LA LAGUNA.

OROTAVA, TENERIFFE.

PEDRO S. REID,
PUERTO OROTAVA,
General Merchant, Commission Agent, &c.

AGENT FOR ENGLISH AND SCOTCH BANKS.

HOUSE AGENT.

CHEQUES, CIRCULAR NOTES, &c., CASHED.

Drapery, Hosiery, Woollen, Silk, and Linen Goods.
SPECIALITY IN DRAWN THREAD WORK.

IRONMONGERY, PROVISIONS, FURNITURE & SADDLERY.

FOREIGN WINES, SPIRITS, AND BEERS.

Native Wines for Sale and Export. Fruits, &c., Exported.

THE ENGLISH GRAND HOTEL,
PORT OROTAVA, TENERIFFE.

The most popular Health and Pleasure Resort in the World.

THE TAORO COMPANY, LIMITED, have much pleasure in announcing that the above building is now finished and furnished throughout, so that all guests are noused under the same roof and are able to avail themselves of the magnificent series of apartments and the many conveniences which the establishment offers them, and to enjoy the fresh air and beautiful scenery which its position commands. Every room is now provided with the electric light, and the grounds are illuminated at night by several powerful arc-lights.

Lawn Tennis, Billiards, Riding and Driving, "Sortija." Extensive Gardens and Grounds. Pure Water, Dry and Bracing Air, finest Climate in the World Absolutely no Winter. No charges for Billiards, &c.

The Hotel is close to the Church, where there is a Resident Chaplain. There are two English Physicians in the town, one being attached to the Hotel. There is also a trained English nurse who lives permanently on the premises.

The Sanitary arrangements were carried out by certificated English plumbers, under the supervision of a trained qualified English Physician. Hot and Cold Baths at all hours.

For terms and particulars address: The Manager, Taoro Hotel Co., Port Orotava, Teneriffe; *or the Company's Agents:* Messrs. Sinclair, Hamilton & Co., 17, St. Helen's Place, London, E.C.

Telegraphic Address: "TAORO, PUERTO, CRUZ."

A private Golf Links has been constructed by the Company at Santa Ursula, within an easy drive of the Hotel. The course was laid out by the well-known professional, John Dunn.

LAS PALMAS, GRAND CANARY.

SANTA CATALINA HOTEL,

Facing the sea, and surrounded by its own beautiful gardens of about 20 acres.

SANITARY ARRANGEMENTS PERFECT.

Private Sitting Rooms and Complete Suites of Apartments.
English Physician and Nurse. Near English Church.
GOLF LINKS ADJOINING THE HOTEL.
Two Tennis and two Croquet Courts inside the Grounds.
BILLIARDS, TWO TABLES.
Reduced Terms during the Summer Months.

Manager, J. R. EDISBURY.

Every information may be obtained and plans seen at the Offices of the

CANARY ISLANDS COMPANY, Limited,
1, Laurence Pountney Hill, London, E.C.

Telegraphic Addresses—"*SANSOFB, LONDON,*" "*SANSOFB, LAS PALMAS.*" *A.B.C. CODE USED.*

LAS PALMAS, GRAND CANARY.
HOTEL METROPOLE.

This Hotel, standing in its own grounds, facing the sea, situated within easy range of, but quite apart from, the City and Harbour, thus enjoying the full advantage of the ozone and sea breezes, occupies an **unrivalled position**, and is the **most comfortable** and Healthiest Hotel in the Canary Islands.

Dining Room to seat 150 visitors. Reception, Billiard and Smoke Rooms, electrically lighted throughout. Drainage perfect, arranged by English Engineers, passed by medical experts.

Resident Trained Nurse and Private Laundry. Tennis Courts, Golf Links, Boating, Fishing, Sea Bathing and Photographic Dark Room are available. Close to English Church and residences of leading Doctors.

TELEGRAPHIC ADDRESS: METROPOLE, LAS PALMAS.
A.B.C. and A1. Codes used.

Address the Manager, or **ELDER, DEMPSTER & CO.,** Agents.

LIVERPOOL .. .. African House, Water Street.
LONDON .. .. Leadenhall Chambers, 4, St. Mary Axe.
MANCHESTER .. .. 8, Commercial Buildings, Cross Street.
BRISTOL .. .. Canada House, Baldwin Street.
CARDIFF .. .. Merchants' Exchange, Bute Docks.
HAMBURG .. .. Luisenhof, Neue Groninger Strasse.
ANTWERP .. .. 7, Quai Plantin.

Under the same Proprietorship, the "Constant Spring Hotel," and the "Myrtle Bank Hotel," at Kingston, Jamaica.

The San Bernardo Hotel.

THE oldest-established English Hotel in the Canary Islands. Recently considerably enlarged.

Situated in the Plaza de San Bernardo, Las Palmas, and within five minutes' walk of the sea, affords first-class accommodation for Visitors. In addition to a fine open frontage, it has a large well-planted Garden and Terraces.

Spacious Dining, Drawing, and Billiard Rooms, Library, &c. The Bedrooms are light, well ventilated, and comfortably furnished.

Cuisine Excellent.

QUINEY'S
ENGLISH AND
CONTINENTAL
HOTEL,
LAS PALMAS.

QUINEY'S
ENGLISH HOTELS,
GRAND CANARY.

Terms 6s. to 8s. a day. Special arrangements for a prolonged stay.

All incoming steamers are boarded by a representative of the Hotel, who attends to the safe landing of Visitors and their luggage.

Telegraphic Address:—"QUINEYS, LASPALMAS."

Full information can be obtained from

THE PROPRIETOR, QUINEY'S HOTELS, LAS PALMAS, GRAND CANARY,
OR FROM
MESSRS. QUINEY BROS., 10 & 11, MINCING LANE, LONDON, E.C.

The Bella Vista Hotel.

THIS WELL-KNOWN HOTEL is situated 1,200 feet above sea-level, and six miles from Las Palmas, in the Monte District, which is recognised as the healthiest and loveliest in the Island, and allows of a delightful change for those requiring bracing mountain air. It is in close proximity to the far-famed Caldera (or Crater), and the Caves of Atalaya, and within easy distance of the picturesque district of San Mateo.

Beautiful walks and drives in every direction. Large Reception, Billiard, Reading, and Ladies' Rooms. 26 spacious Bedrooms.

Lawn Tennis Ground & extensive Gardens.

QUINEY'S
BELLA VISTA
HOTEL,
MONTE.

THE SANITARY ARRANGEMENTS IN BOTH HOTELS ARE EXCELLENT.

Hotel... Santa Brigida.

The only first-class Hotel at The Monte,

GRAND CANARY

ENQUIRIES CAN BE MADE IN LONDON AT
THE HOTEL TARIFF BUREAU,
275 (late 96), Regent Street,
LONDON, W.

HOTEL SANTA BRIGIDA,
MONTE, GRAND CANARY.
THE HÔTEL DE LUXE OF THE CANARY ISLANDS.
Newly erected "English Hotel" at an altitude of 1,450 Feet.

TELEGRAPHIC ADDRESS: "JORGE LASPALMAS." CODES USED: A.B.C. AND A1

$\mathcal{S}$PECIALLY built as a summer and winter residence, amidst the most beautiful sub-tropical scenery of the Canary Islands; enjoying an equable and healthy climate and absolute freedom from dust.

This Hotel faces due south; stands in its own attractive grounds on the finest carriage road in the Islands, at about one hour's drive from Las Palmas; is sheltered from the N.E. wind, has a south aspect, and commands a magnificent panorama of the interior of the Island. The neighbourhood abounds in interesting rides, drives, and walks, shady palm and pine woods, and extensive vineyards.

Fine drawing, dining, smoking and billiard rooms; large entrance hall with lounge galleries; spacious bedrooms all facing south.

Lawn Tennis, Roller Skating, Picnics, and every kind of Outdoor and Indoor Amusement provided for Visitors.

Hot and Cold Baths.   **Improved Sanitary Arrangements.**
         Pure Water.   **Excellent Cuisine.**

Telephonic communication with the Doctors and with Las Palmas generally.

CARRIAGES, RIDING HORSES, etc.   *All Steamers met by the Hotel Agents.*

For terms, which are moderate and inclusive, and all information, apply to

THE PROPRIETORS,
Hotel Santa Brigida, Monte, Grand Canary.

SPECIAL NOTICE TO TRANSIT PASSENGERS.

Travellers whose steamers touch at Canary and who have only a few hours at their disposal, ought not to fail to visit this Hotel, both for the beauty of the drive from Las Palmas and the magnificent scenery amidst which it is situated, and especially its close vicinity to the two most interesting features of Grand Canary The Caldera (the most perfect extinct volcano known) and Atalaya (the cave village of the Aborigines).

For special convenience of transit passengers, parties of four or more will be conducted from the ship to the Hotel and back for 10s. including all charges for boat, carriage, and good luncheon at the Hotel. 3½ hours give ample time for this beautiful excursion.

English, French, German, and Spanish spoken.

HOTEL RESTAURANT,
"LA UNION."
PLAZA DE LA DEMOCRACIA, LAS PALMAS.

Meals à la Carte at all hours. French, English, and Spanish Cooks. High Class Cuisine. Refreshments of all descriptions. Ices, Sherbets, &c. Finest Wines, Liquors, and Cigars.

In connection with the Restaurant, there is an Hotel with accommodation for sixty guests, and a Bathing Establishment with Shower Baths, &c.

SPACIOUS DINING, SITTING, BILLIARD ROOMS, &c.

Moderate Prices, and according to arrangement.

Proprietor: VICTORIANO BARRETO.

SEA VIEW HOUSE,
PUERTO DE LA LUZ.
ENGLISH (PRIVATE) BOARDING ESTABLISHMENT.

The house is very pleasantly situated, close to the sea and facing the Western Bay. It commands most extensive views of the north of the Island, of the Peak of Teneriffe, &c. Though close to the Tramway it lies away from the road. No dust. No noise.
Visitors will find a comfortable English home, liberal table, every attention, and a bracing healthy climate.

PLAIN ENGLISH COOKING.

Further information can be obtained from the Proprietress:
MISS L. HODGSON (formerly of Mildmay Park Institute, London, N.).

HOTEL ESPERANZA, TAFIRA, MONTE.

Situated in the most beautiful part of the Island, 1,080 feet above the level of the sea, in the midst of the vineyards of Monte and within an hour's drive of the Port.

Passengers having only a few hours to remain in the Island should drive to the Monte of Tafira and lunch at the Esperanza. Time for the double journey, including ample time for lunch, 3 hours.

The best centre or excursions to the cave dwellings of Atalaya, the Crater, and the Caves of the Friars.

Terms from 5s. per day, including early morning tea, coffee or chocolate; breakfast, lunch, afternoon tea, dinner and attendance. Wine included at breakfast and dinner.
Modified terms for families and for the fortnight.

Telegraphic Address: "NANSON, ' Las Palmas. *A.B.C. and A1 Codes used.*
Telephone Number 55.

CAFÉ DE MADRID,
PLAZA DE CAIRASCO.

OPEN DAY & NIGHT.
All kinds of Wines, Spirits and Beer.

Lunch.   Coffee.

B.B.B. LOOK OUT FOR THE THREE B's ON THE FRONT.
84 TRIANA 84.
CAFÉ COSMOPOLITAN.
FIXED PRICES.

Spanish and Canary Wines sold in barrels (from 4 to 100 gallons) and cases of 12 bottles.   Whiskies, Beer, &c.

As all Wines, &c., are bought in large quantities the B.B.B. can compete with all.

TRY THE MARK - (B.B.B.) CANARY CLARET.

WHOLESALE AND RETAIL.

DOMINGO ALVARADO.
SANTA CATALINA BAR AND MADEIRA STORES.
On the Main Road to Las Palmas,
between the Hotel Metropole and the Hotel Santa Catalina.

English provisions Tinned and in Bottles of the best qualities only. Tobacco, Cigars and Cigarettes of all kinds. Best Scotch Whiskies, Wines and Liquors. Bass' Ales and Stout, &c., &c.

Madeira Furniture of all kinds. Baskets, Jewellery, Embroidery, Silk Shawls, Cloths, Straw Hats, &c. Boots and Shoes. Madeira and Oporto Wines, Walking Sticks, &c., &c.

THE SAILORS' INSTITUTE,
PUERTO DE LA LUZ, LAS PALMAS.
Founded in 1891.

Open to Sailors of all Nations and Sects. Reading and Sitting Rooms, provided with Books, Papers, Billiard Table, Bagatelle Board, &c. Tea, Coffee, Aerated Waters and Light Refreshments.

This establishment is entirely supported by voluntary contributions. A visit is earnestly solicited.

Superintendent: A. CARR.

MILLER AND CO.

(Late THOMAS MILLER & SONS),

BANKERS & GENERAL MERCHANTS

The Oldest Established English House in the Island.

Exporters of Bananas and all other Produce of the Island.

MANAGERS OF THE

LAS PALMAS COALING CO.

PUERTO DE LA LUZ.

BEST SOUTH WELSH COALS ALWAYS IN STOCK.

Foreign Money Changed. Bank Notes, Bills, and Cheques Cashed. Bills granted on London, Paris, Rome, Madrid, &c.

AGENTS FOR THE FOLLOWING BANKS:

American Exchange in Europe . London	Hong Kong & Shanghai Banking Corporation . . London
American Exchange National Bank . , Chicago	Jacob E. Dybwad . . . Christiania
Banca Alliança . . Porto	John Stewart & Co. . . . Manchester
Bank of Scotland . . London	London and County Banking Company, Limited . . London
Bank of New York . . New York	
Bank of New South Wales . Sydney	London and South Western Bank, Limited . . do.
Bank of Australasia . London	
Banque Russe pour le Commerce Etranger . . St. Pétersbourg	London Chartered Bank of Australia . . do.
Barclay, Bevan, Ransom & Co. London	London Joint Stock Bank, Ltd. do.
British Linen Company Bank . Edinburgh	Lloyds Bank Limited . . do.
Canadian Bank of Commerce . Toronto	Manchester and Liverpool District Banking Company, Ltd. Manchester
Capital and Counties Bank . London	
City Bank, Limited . . do.	National Provincial Bank of England . . . London
Colonial Bank of New Zealand . do.	
Coutts & Co. . . . do.	Merchants' Loan and Trust Co. Chicago
Comptoir National d'Escompte . Paris	London and Westminster Bank, Limited . . London
Commercial Bank of Scotland, Limited . . Edinburgh	
	London and River Plate Bank . do.
Cocks, Biddulph & Co. . London	Northern Banking Company . Belfast
Crédit Lyonnais . . do.	Northern Trust Company . Chicago
Cox & Co. . . . do.	National Bank of Scotland, Ltd. Edinburgh
Child & Co. . . do.	Preston National Bank of Detroit . . . Detroit
Dresdner Bank . . Berlin	
Drummond & Co. . . London	Royal Bank of Scotland . . London
First National Bank . San Francisco, Ca.	Société Générale pour favoriser le dév. du Commerce, etc. . Paris
Glyn, Mills, Currie & Co. . London	
Grindlay, Groom & Co. . Bombay	Thomas Cook & Son . London
Grindlay & Co. . . London	Ulster Bank, Limited . Dublin
Herries, Farquhar & Co. . do.	Union Bank of London . London
Henry S. King & Co. . do.	

THE GRAND CANARY COALING CO.,

LIVERPOOL AND GRAND CANARY,

Steamship, Telegraph, and Forwarding Agents,

Merchants and Bankers.

Cheques, Bank Notes, and Foreign Moneys changed. Telegraphic remittances made.

COAL SIGNAL 'J.'

Contractors to the British Government and 150 of the leading Steamship Lines, British and Foreign.

SUPPLY ONLY THE BEST DESCRIPTION OF WELSH STEAM COAL.

Steamers Bunkered and Provisioned by day or night, with quickest despatch.

AGENTS TO

THE GRAND CANARY ENGINEERING CO.

EXTENSIVE WORKSHOPS UNDER ENGLISH ENGINEERS
With Plant for executing all kinds of repairs to Hull and Machinery.

LARGE STOCKS OF KEROSENE.

"SCOTT'S "A 1," "A B C," "WATKIN'S" and "SLATER'S" CODES USED.

Telegraphic Addresses :—" COALING, LIVERPOOL."
" COALING, LASPALMAS."

BLANDY BROTHERS & CO.
LAS PALMAS, MADEIRA, AND LONDON.

LLOYD'S AGENTS.

Bankers, Shipping Agents & Coal Merchants.

BANK NOTES, CHEQUES, CIRCULAR LETTERS, &c., CASHED.

Agents for a large number of British and Foreign Banks.

DRAFTS ISSUED ON LONDON, PARIS, BERLIN & MADRID.

STEAMERS COALED AND PROVISIONED, NIGHT OR DAY.

EXTENSIVE SHIPBUILDING & ENGINEERING WORKS.

LEONCIO DE LA TORRE

Fire Insurance Agent, and Store for the Sale of Provisions and Groceries.

CANARY, SHERRY & FOREIGN WINES, COGNAC
AND LIQUEURS OF ALL CLASSES.

ENGLISH, FRENCH, AND ITALIAN SPOKEN.

TELEPHONE No. 23. TRIANA, 52, LAS PALMAS, GRAN CANARIA.

The Queen Victoria Hospital for Seamen.

ESTABLISHED IN 1891.

SUPPORTED BY VOLUNTARY CONTRIBUTIONS.

Has large General Ward for Seamen of all Nationalities, also several Private Rooms for paying Patients.

Funds are greatly needed for the purpose of erecting a Hospital in a more suitable position. Subscriptions towards this object received in London, by any of the following:—

Messrs. Blandy Brothers & Co., 16, Mark Lane, E.C.
Messrs. Elder, Dempster & Co., 4, St. Mary Axe, E.C.
Messrs. Swanston & Co., 1, Laurence Pountney Hill, E.C.

CHARLES E. MEDRINGTON
(Of Medrington's, Limited, Liverpool),

Photographic Artist.

HIGH-CLASS PORTRAITURE. GROUPS AND OUTDOOR PHOTOGRAPHY.
VIEWS OF THE ISLANDS, &c.

Studio Metropole, Adjoining the Hotel Metropole Grounds, **LAS PALMAS.**

HORLOGERIE, RÉPARATION DE MONTRES.

BIJOUTERIE, JOAILLERIE, ORFÉVRERIE, OPTIQUE.
Objets d'art et de fantaisie.

Víuda é Hijos de

J. BONNY
LAS PALMAS, GRAN CANARIA.

ANDRÉS GARCIA DÉNELY,
2, ABISPO CODINA, 2.

JEWELLER, WATCHMAKER, AND OPTICIAN.

On the right-hand side after passing the Stone Bridge.

Native Work in Gold and Silver made in my own Factory.
Brooches and Breast Pins in Gold, in form of Canary Knives. A large Stock of Foreign Jewellery.

WATCHES, CLOCKS, BRACELETS, RINGS, BROOCHES, &c.
DIAMONDS MOUNTED.

All classes of Jeweller's Work done. Watches repaired and guaranteed for twelve months. Old Jewellery bought or exchanged for new. Fountain Pens.

IRONMONGERY DEPARTMENT,
13, TRIANA, 13.

All classes of Hardware. Rifles, Guns, Revolvers, Cartridges, &c.
SHEFFIELD PENKNIVES.
CANARY KNIVES IN ALL SIZES AND PRICES, AND MANY OTHER ARTICLES IMPOSSIBLE TO ENUMERATE.

FERNANDO BOJART,
Chemist and Druggist,
Calle de Muro and Plaza de la Democracia, LAS PALMAS.

English and Foreign prescriptions carefully prepared, according to their respective Pharmacopœias and from the purest drugs.

All Prescriptions are registered and numbered, and repeat orders can be made up from the number only.

PATENT MEDICINES.   MINERAL WATERS.   PHOTOGRAPHIC CHEMICALS at Special Prices.

ENGLISH SPOKEN.

PHARMACY DE LAS PALMAS.
B. GABAS,
CHEMIST AND DRUGGIST,
2, GENERAL BRAVO STREET, at the corner of Cairasco.

Only the Purest Drugs used. Modern Medicines, Patent Medicines, Native and Foreign Antiseptic cures.

Sr. GABAS wishes to point out that all prescriptions are registered and numbered and carefully prepared, English and foreign prescriptions being made up according to their respective Pharmacopœias.

"DIARIO DE LAS PALMAS."
The Leading Daily Paper in Grand Canary.

The "Diario de las Palmas" has the largest circulation of any local newspaper, and has subscribers in all parts of Spain and in all the Spanish Colonies. As a medium for advertisement it is unsurpassed, and those wishing to push their business, fruit or otherwise, to hire or let houses, or to effect sales and purchases of any commodity, will find its pages the best for their purpose.

Special attention paid to local news and to Telegraphic intelligence from all parts of the world. Correspondents in the principal towns of Europe and America.

Annual Subscription: 24 pesetas.   Advertisements at a fixed tariff, according to space occupied and number of insertions.

Address:—

The Director, D. Alfredo S. Perez, Calle de Torres, Las Palmas.

BON MARCHÉ,
73, TRIANA, LAS PALMAS.

ENGLISH STORE of high-class drapery. LADIES' and GENTS' clothing of every description. BOOTS and SHOES. TENNIS SHOES. SLAZENGER'S RACKETS and all requisites. DEPOT for the best NATIVE hand-drawn Linen work, and Lace Goods.

Orders per post promptly despatched.

FREDERICK LAWSON, Proprietor.

LORENZO Y FRANCHY
15, GENERAL BRAVO, 15,
LAS PALMAS, GRAN CANARIA.

Ready-made Suits in all sizes kept in stock. A good supply of Gentlemen's Shirts, Collars, Cuffs, Ties, etc., always on hand. Photographic Views, Post Cards, Native goods, and various other articles for presents and other purposes.

Prices and qualities will defy competition.

| ENGLISH SPOKEN. | | ON PARLE FRANÇAIS. |

GRAND BAZAAR
OF
JUAN MIRANDA TALAVERA.

The only complete Exhibition of Native articles. Teneriffe Embroideries. Curiosities of the Islands and Africa. Ladies' and Gents' General Outfits. Haberdashery. Underwear. Hosiery. Boots and Shoes. Perfumery. Spirits. British Stores. General Provisions. Liqueurs. Branch of the Tobacco and Cigars Manufactories "La Reguladora," "La Igualdad," "La Asturiana," &c., with Depots in London and S. Africa. Direct Imports from Havanah.

CHANGE OF MONEY.

95 TRIANA 95
Between Elder Dempster & Co., and Grand Canary Coaling &c. Co.
LAS PALMAS, GRAND CANARY.

LAS PALMAS FROM THE OLD MOLE.

EMPREZA INSULANA DE NAVEGAÇÃO
Caes do Sodre 84, LISBON.

THE fast and beautifully=fitted Steamers of the above-named Company are subsidised by the Portuguese Government for the carriage of mails between Lisbon, Madeira, and the Azores, are fitted with electric light and every modern comfort, and provide first=class accommodation for passengers.

> The *S.S. Funchal* leaves Lisbon on the 20th of each month, touches at Madeira about the 22nd, Santa Maria and S. Miguel about the 25th; Terceira about the 27th; Graciosa, S. Jorge, Pico, and Fayal about the 28th; returning by the same route and arriving at Madeira about the 3rd or 4th of the month, and at Lisbon about the 6th or 7th.

FARES, First Class,
INCLUDING FOOD.

LISBON TO MADEIRA	Single	Rs. 25.500
MADEIRA TO ST. MICHAEL'S	..	21.000
MADEIRA TO FAYAL		23.000

Visitors to the Azores, whether they be invalids in search of the wonderful mineral waters of Furnas, or tourists anxious to make a flying survey of the lovely scenery for which the Islands are so famed, will find it most convenient to ship by this Company's boats, either at Lisbon or at Madeira. Those arriving at Madeira in time to catch the steamer leaving for the Azores on the 22nd can book accommodation beforehand by wire.

Agents in Madeira ... **LUIZ V. DE FREITAS BRANCO.**
Telegraphic Address: "BRANFILHO."

Agents in Lisbon ... ... **GERMANO SERRAO ARNAUD.**
Telegraphic Address: "GERARNAUD."

Union=Castle Line.

ROYAL MAIL SERVICE

FROM

LONDON and SOUTHAMPTON

TO

CAPETOWN, MOSSEL BAY, PORT ELIZABETH, EAST LONDON, NATAL, DELAGOA BAY, BEIRA AND MAURITIUS,

CALLING AT

MADEIRA, LAS PALMAS, TENERIFFE, ST. HELENA, AND ASCENSION.

THE ROYAL MAIL STEAMSHIPS OF THE UNION-CASTLE MAIL STEAMSHIP COMPANY, Limited, under contracts with the English and Colonial Governments, are despatched from Southampton every Saturday for the Cape of Good Hope and Natal, *via* MADEIRA.

In addition, Intermediate Steamships are despatched every week from London, calling at Southampton, for the Cape Colony, Natal, and Delagoa Bay, taking passengers at lower rates than by the Mail Steamers. These Steamers proceed alternately *via* LAS PALMAS (Grand Canary), and TENERIFFE, and call at St. Helena for Ascension once a month.

For information as to Fares, &c., apply to—

DONALD CURRIE & CO., MANAGERS,
3 and 4, FENCHURCH STREET, LONDON, E.C.

And at SOUTHAMPTON, MANCHESTER, LIVERPOOL, AND GLASGOW.

Lightning Source UK Ltd.
Milton Keynes UK
UKOW06f0415040616

275586UK00012B/127/P